*the FLAVOR of SPAIN*

# the Flavor of
# SPAIN

*William H. Emery*

CBI

CBI Publishing Company, Inc.
51 Sleeper Street
Boston, Massachusetts 02210

*Production Editor*/Becky Handler
*Text and Jacket Designer*/Joseph Kredlow
*Compositor*/Modern Graphics
*Illustrator*/Mimi Turner

**Library of Congress Cataloging in Publication Data**

Emery, William H.
  The flavor of Spain.

  Includes index.
  1.  Cookery, Spanish.  I.  Title.
TX723.5.S7E43   1983        641.5946        82–14685
ISBN 0–8436–2254–7

*For Maggie*

# Contents

INTRODUCTION .................................................. ix

THE CULINARY PROFILE OF SPAIN ....................... 1

THE WINES OF SPAIN ..................................... 11

ALL ABOUT POTS, PANS, AND COOKING UTENSILS ....... 41

THE BASICS OF SPANISH CUISINE ........................ 53

*TAPAS* AND *ENTREMESES* ................................ 67

SOUPS ................................................... 85

EGGS, OMELETTES, AND TORTILLAS ..................... 99

SAUCES ................................................. 115

RICE ................................................... 131

FISH AND SHELLFISH .................................... 139

MEATS ................................................. 201

POULTRY AND GAME .................................... 235

FRUITS AND VEGETABLES ............................... 265

DESSERTS ............................................... 313

ENGLISH/SPANISH DICTIONARY OF KITCHEN UTENSILS ..329

GLOSSARY OF COOKING TERMS ......................... 333

INDEX .................................................. 335

# INTRODUCTION

Spain is a country of contrasting landscapes: from the snow-capped mountains of the Sierra Nevada to the sun-baked plains of La Mancha; from the lush, green pastures of Andalucia to the harsh, granite-strewn ground of Galicia. It is indeed a country of many faces.

In character and temperament, too, its people are as different from province to province as are the areas in which they reside. In each province the Spanish language is spoken somewhat differently. Although Castilian is the official language, in many areas the residents still use their own ancient tongues in their day-to-day transactions, to the complete bewilderment of the outsider. Further, in each area, customs and traditions differ as do the general physical characteristics of the residents.

But if one examines the history of Spain, this is not surprising. For in ancient times, long before the discovery of the New World, Spain was the melting pot of the known world. Indeed, from more than twelve centuries before the birth of Christ until the middle of the fourteen century, foreigners came overland from the north and east, and across the sea from Africa to Asia. Some came as traders and settlers: many as invaders. Goths, Celts, Romans, Phoenecians, Greeks, Iberians, Carthaginians, and finally the Moors, lived, fought, and died, leaving their marks on the land and its people.

While these influences were mainly parochial, or at most provincial (for only the Moors left a distinctive national culture), the polyglot effect of these different backgrounds is said to account for the one single trait that is common to *all* Spaniards throughout the country. Each person has a deep and fierce provincial pride which often overrides nationality. Dependent upon birthplace, a person is a Madrileño, a Malagueñan, a Castilian, or a Basque first—a Spaniard second. And this has been the case throughout the centuries.

But this diversity of character and attitude makes for excitement, interest, and culinary adventure. For the dishes that the Spanish prepare are a true reflection of this vital, vibrant, and fascinating land. You will be struck by the differences in provincial cooking styles and area specialties. You will discover that, despite what some people tend to believe, Spanish cooking does not depend on the heavy use of garlic and olive oil, although both ingredients are characteristic of their food. You will find that while most dishes are unpretentious, modern Spanish cuisine provides a wide range of dishes with a high degree of culinary excellence.

I have chosen the recipes for this book from among these varied and delicious dishes. They have been picked to include new and beautiful flavor combinations, different and unexpected texture contrasts, and simple but interesting and colorful methods of presentation.

For readers who have not been to Spain, these dishes will go some way in introducing you to the country and the true "Flavor of Spain." For those who have visited the country, the recipes will help you recreate some of the excellent dishes that you may have had during your stay or, on the other hand, show you what you missed! For others who plan to stay in a villa, house, or apartment, this book can be your guide around the shops and marketplaces. It will not only provide a sound culinary background, but also will introduce the reader to the somewhat different types and varieties of foods available: what they look like, how to determine good quality, how to buy, what to avoid, and how to prepare and serve these good things from Spain.

Of course, one cannot discuss the cuisine of Spain without mentioning its wines, for these are as varied as the provinces from which they originate. Further, each type from each province has a character as distinctive as a fingerprint. Many of these wines are absolutely excellent; a great many are very good indeed. The majority of the rest stand head and shoulders above comparative wines from other countries. Spain is certainly a wine-lovers paradise.

So with your fork in one hand and your glass in the other, I wish you . . . *Bueno Apetito*.

W.H.E., 1982

1

# 1 THE CULINARY PROFILE OF SPAIN

**S**panish cooking is as varied as its people and generally is based on a wide variety of fresh ingredients available in the different areas. If one takes broad characteristics, it may be said that Andalucia specializes in fried foods; the Castilians prefer roasts; and the Levante is the area where rice is a favorite ingredient. In Aragon and Navarre they use many piquant sauces to flavor their foods as do the Basques and Galicians. However, this is only the tip of the gastronomic iceberg. While these generalities may often predominate on regional menus, each province can offer a wide range of foods cooked in a subtle and imaginative manner.

## CATALONIA

Catalonia is the most cosmopolitan of all Spanish provinces and is, without doubt, one of the most independent. Many people native to the area prefer to speak Catalan instead of Spanish; they dance the *sardana* rather than the more flamboyant *flamenco;* and they regard their province as the best place in the whole world in which to be born and to live.

The culinary area of Catalonia stretches some 124 miles (200 kilometers) north of Barcelona to a point well below Tarragona. Perhaps here more than in any other area the restaurants take pride in introducing new items on their menu as the seasons change.

At the beginning of the year, fresh young beans called *habas* (similar to fresh limas) come on the market. This is the first of many culinary delights. When the early lime-green and tiny beans are removed from their silky, silver inner pod, they are plunged into boiling salted water, cooked for just three minutes, and eaten with a drizzle of fresh butter: nothing more. A truly Lucullan feast, if ever there was one.

The province was once united with France, and consequently many of their recipes are influenced by this association. *Habas a la Catalana* (Beans with sausage and bacon) is one example as is *Habas con Callos* (Beans with

3

tripe). This last is a somewhat hearty dish to say the least, but tripe lovers will find it delicious.

The season for fresh habas is quite short and, as they mature, they go particularly well with grilled pork in an onion and tomato sauce.

Young asparagus appear on the market the first week in April. A warm garlic-butter sauce usually accompanies the earliest arrivals or, if served cold, a garlic-flavored mayonnaise. As the stalks grow bigger, they are a delicious accompaniment to chicken, eggs, or veal.* Tender asparagus tips are also blanched in boiling water for three minutes, then drained and dried, wrapped in strips of pastry, and baked in an oven for 25 minutes or so until the pastry is cooked. Once again, a gastronomic treat.

In a restaurant in Tarragona I had a *tapa* (appetizer) that seems to be exclusive to this area. Young scallions (*cebolletas*) are cooked over a charcoal grill for a few moments, then the scorched and blackened outer skins are stripped. The succulent onions are served with an accompanying bowl of lemon mayonnaise.

In May it is the turn of the *tollinas*, the tiny local clams which are cooked in white wine, a little *sofrito* (a tomato and onion paste), and a trickle of olive oil. These delicate morsels are served as a prelunch appetizer or as an ingredient in a major dish, such as *Cerdo con Almejas* (Pork with clams). You really should try this excellent flavor contrast. Local clams may be used readily in this recipe.

Late June is the time for melon: cantaloupe, honeydew, casaba, watermelon in profusion. And the Spanish take full advantage of this bounty. Dependent upon type, one will see them served in slices with a squeeze of lemon; with vanilla ice cream dusted with powdered ginger; melon chopped and sprinkled with the sweet dessert wine from Malaga or, as a distinct contrast, with an oloroso Sherry. Melon may also be a basis for a cold soup or may be mixed with avocado. It is very popular cut into bite-sized pieces and wrapped in Serrano ham or chopped and mixed with salami.

In the height of summer when temperatures hit 30°C (90°F) and above, the appetite tends to fade and fish and shellfish, accompanied by a crisp salad, is the preference. And what a selection of fish there is! In most markets no less than twenty varieties of molluscs, shellfish, and freshwater and saltwater fish are seen. From lobster to shrimp, from sole to salmonettes, from mussels to scallops, the choice is excellent, so there is no excuse for a boring diet.

With the cooler weather in October, the hunting season begins, and this is reflected in the shops and markets where pheasant, partridge, and

---

*You will find recipes for these, and all other dishes mentioned, by referring to the index.*

hare abound. A popular way with pheasant is to roast it and serve it with a sauce of stewed apples, spiced with both clove and nutmeg. Partridge is a favorite when cooked in the style *Felipe Secundo* named after Philip II, perhaps the greatest king ever to sit on the throne of Spain. Rabbit and hare are seen on the menu: the former as a stew often perfumed with oregano, the latter quite often roasted on a bed of fresh wild rosemary.

Toward Christmas, young men scour the fields for the distinctive mushroom called *revellon*, for its deep, pungent flavor is used in meat stews and casseroles. Red wine is always a part of a dish containing revellones, for the two ingredients seem to have more of an affinity than other mushroom varieties have with red wine.

Artichokes too flood the market at this season and are served stewed, fried, boiled, or stuffed. Oddly enough, they are seldom served whole with an oil and vinegar dressing.

So we come again to the New Year when the young habas appear, and the gastronomic year in Catalonia starts afresh.

## VALENCIA AND LEVANTE

This is the area where rice is dominant, for Lake Albufera, just south of Valencia, is the largest rice-growing district in Spain. The important dish of the region is of course the saffron-tinted *Paella Valenciana* which does not seem to have any special recipe, but within certain limits, relies upon the inventiveness of the cook. However, no authentic paella valenciana should contain onion, so I was told, as this conflicts with other acceptable ingredients; neither are red peppers allowed, although they are very often included in paella elsewhere. I was also informed that the purists do not include fish of *any* sort and that, if fish is added, it automatically becomes *Paella Marinhera*. Of course, if the suffix *Valenciana* is not used, then almost anything may go into a paella and frequently does. So it is not unusual to encounter bacon, artichokes, sausage, and any other bits and pieces that the cook may find.

Apart from paella, they cook their rice in a number of different liquids to obtain flavor contrast. You will find rice cooked in orange juice, cider, chicken stock, and tomato juice. Sometimes it is just boiled, then fried in chicken fat, something like Chinese fried rice.

The area is abundantly supplied with seafood and in Murcia, for example, one may try *Lubina a la Sal* (Sea bass baked in rock salt), a treatment that keeps the delicate flavor of the fish intact, without any flavor of salt reaching the flesh. In Castellon, the succulent giant shrimp should not be missed; in Alicante, one finds the home of what is perhaps the most popular sweetmeat in Spain—the *turron*, made from caramel, honey, and hazelnuts.

# ANDALUCIA

This is the picture-book province of Spain where one sees enclosed courtyards with tinkling fountains and beds of flowers in colors to match the rainbow.

The Moorish influence is still prevalent in much of Andalucian cookery, and here, perhaps more than in any other province, a wide range of spices are used. Almonds, another Moorish heritage, and fruits unexpectedly appear in some meat dishes and sauces.

Shrimp is very common in many of the local soups, although oysters are preferred in *Sopa a la Cuarto Hora* (Quarter-hour soup), which incidentally takes considerably longer to prepare than the name implies. Here also, *gazpacho* is a constant favorite because, for one thing, tomatoes are plentiful the year-round. Andalucia is the true home of gazpacho, although many forms of this excellent soup are found elsewhere. In its most simple form it may contain little more than garlic, wine vinegar, bread, water, and a few tomatoes, for it originated as a peasant dish. More sophisticated versions include cucumber, green peppers, onions, and scallion. Some other recipes include egg yolk or almonds.

Malaga is the home of a very special gazpacho called *Ajo Blanco con Uvas* (White garlic with grapes) made from a very modest gazpacho base plus almonds and white grapes.

In general, the specialty of this vast province is deep-fried fish. In Malaga, the "city of salt," so named by the Phoenecians who traded their goods for this precious seasoning, the favorite style is *a la Malagueña*. A *Fritura Malagueña* would contain six or more different types of tiny fish and shellfish including shrimp and squid. The assorted pieces are dipped in seasoned flour and quickly fried.

Further along the coast toward Cádiz, the style is *a la Gaditana*. In this style, more fish is used than shellfish, and your dish may include sole, mullet, and bass, as well as cuttlefish and shrimp. The fish are chopped into bite-sized pieces, dipped in a very light batter, and deep-fried.

In other towns along the coast, one may enjoy squid prepared in a number of ways, pickled tuna or *bonito*, and fresh sardines cooked on a spit. Small, fresh anchovy—no more than two inches long—called *boquerones* are dredged with flour and fried in hot oil. Andalucian cooks present these baby fish in the form of a fan by first filleting them, then pinching four or five together at the tail before dropping them into the hot oil.

Inland we find that Córdoba is famed for its stewed lamb in red wine; Granada is justly proud of a modest dish—*Tortilla del Sacromonte*, an omelette with peppers, zucchini, onions, green beans, and sometimes bone marrow.

One unusual dish found nowhere else in Spain, a favorite in the area around Seville, is a stew which contains both fish *and* lamb, called a *Caldereta de Cordero*, to differentiate it from the more usual *caldereta* which is a true fish stew.

For dessert one may have a problem in choosing from the *Tocinos de Cielo*, a luscious tart filled with caramelized sugar and egg yolk or the fritters made from honey and aniseed called *Pestiños*. Tropical fruits from the Valle de Vélez are often set before you or, failing this, fresh figs, ripe peaches, or a choice of the numerous local fruits in season.

## MADRID AND CASTILE

The high central plateau of Spain of which Madrid is the center, and the arid and harsh countryside around the capital, is the land of roast lamb and roast suckling pig.

To the north of Madrid, around the area of Valladolid, one may eat *lechazo*, a delicious milk-fed lamb, killed much earlier than is usual in the United States or United Kingdom. Often the lamb is cooked on a turning spit or in an old wood-burning oven, but always to the right degree of pink perfection.

*Cochinillo* (suckling pig) is a specialty of Segovia and Madrid, where in a number of restaurants they are cooked in bakers' ovens to such a degree of tenderness that the carcass may be carved literally with the edge of a *plate*. Waiters perform this feat as part of the show.

Less dramatic fare is the *Cocido Castillano*, a rich, thick meat stew designed to keep out the bite of the bitter Castilian winter. This hearty dish is made with beef, chicken, bacon, sausage, and any oddments that are appropriate, stewed together with chickpeas and a variety of vegetables. The liquor from the stew is served as a first course (soup), then the remaining meats and vegetables are presented on another plate as a main course.

The Spanish omelette, made throughout Spain and known all over the world, is of Castilian origin. Nowadays, all sorts of ingredients are added to the beaten eggs, but to the true Castilian, the omelette should include just the beaten eggs, potato, onion, and a flavoring of smoked bacon.

One food that stamps Castilian cooking is the abundant use of *chorizo*, the small, hard, piquant sausage made most often from pork and red pepper. Almost inevitably any savory dish that has the label *Castillana* will contain this ubiquitous sausage.

Turning to the capital, Madrid has given her name to a few favorite dishes, such as *Callos Madrileña* (Tripe cooked with chorizo, Sherry, lemon, and tomatoes), but is too large a city to have a truly parochial cuisine.

Around the area of Cuenca, one may sample pork chops roasted on a bed of vine shoots or *Gazpacho Manchego*—not a soup, but a dish of hare, partridge, chicken, and ham. Game abounds in Castile also, and during the hunting season, one will eat partridge cooked in a pot with cabbage croquettes or served in a sharp sauce with a vinegar base. In Toledo, the birds are stewed in white wine, and in Soria, they are pickled.

Hare too is popular either in a pie with ham and veal moistened with brandy or as a roast with a flavoring of garlic and rosemary.

As with many Spanish desserts, the Moorish-inspired concoctions of honey and almonds often are too sweet for many palates, but for those with a very sweet tooth the dry cakes like *manoletes* and *yemas* are very good indeed.

## THE NORTHERN PROVINCES

The Basques take the business of gastronomy much more seriously than do the natives of other provinces, and their regional dishes are far more inventive than those from other parts of the country.

For here, food (that is good food) is held in such reverence that there are numerous gourmet clubs in the area. But these are clubs with a difference. For, at each meeting, the members purchase the food, prepare it, cook it, serve it, share it with their friends, then wash the dishes. No staff are employed in any capacity.

In these clubs, members prepare such dishes as *Pulpitos a su Tinta* (baby squid cooked and served in their own ink) and *Angulas* (the tiny silver eels cooked whole and served in garlic sauce). Perhaps *Kototas* will be served. These are strips cut from the throat of freshly caught hake and lightly cooked with a little garlic, chopped parsley, and green peas. This part of the fish is considered by connoiseurs to be the most delicate and is cut from the fish before it reaches the market stall. The kototas (pronounced "co-cochas") are sold separately and are always eagerly sought by the gourmet clubs and other discriminating cooks.

Of course, the famous *Bacalao a la Viscayna*, which is the classic method of preparing sun-dried cod, is copied in every part of Spain.

Much of the Basque cooking technique is based upon just one main feature—perfect simmering or *pil-pil*. The technique involves heating olive oil in an earthenware casserole to a temperature just below boiling point before adding the fish and potatoes, or whatever food is being prepared. The ingredients are cooked very slowly and the pot is *shaken* from time to time. The lid is never removed nor the pot stirred. In this way the juices from the fish amalgamate with the oil to produce a thick sauce. On the face of it, the simmering technique does not seem too complicated, but for some reason

Basque food cooked in this manner when eaten elsewhere does not seem to have the distinction it possesses in its native territory.

Two other features set Basque cooking apart. The first is their liberal use of fresh cream; second, the widespread use of lard in their cooking.

In contrast to some other parts of Spain, the northern territories possess large areas of lush, green pastures where cattle graze by the thousands. Milk and cream are produced in vast quantities and the Basques use these products to good effect.

Westward along the coast from Bilbao and San Sebastian lies the province of Asturias, and here, while seafood is always prominent on a menu, their most famous dish is *Fabada*, a type of *cassoulet* made with special white beans slowly stewed together with salt pork, chorizo, and the famous Asturian sausage. The white beans that are used in this dish rarely are obtainable outside the province so the dish is almost exclusive to the area. However a good facsimile can be prepared from dried white lima beans. Here also one finds fish stews are popular, one of the best being *Caldereta Asturiana*.

Still further west along the coast, Galicia is the area where once again gentle stewing has reached a fine art; but here, unlike in Basque cooking, the stewing is in stock rather than oil. Consequently their gastronomic riches lie in the most simple preparations of very fresh foods. In this respect their dishes are similar to those of their neighbors across the border—the Portuguese. For example, the local vegetable soup, *Caldo Gallego*, which includes shredded turnip greens, is similar to the Portuguese *Caldo Verde*, although the latter uses shredded cabbage to supply the color and flavor.

The seafood too offers a few unexpected but delicious surprises. The rock barnacles called *percebes*, which have the grotesque appearance of a black, withered hand, are a specialty. So are spider crabs, the *centollas*. Another dish high on the list of local delights is *Lacon con Grelos* (Cured ham with turnip greens), a hard-hitting dish if ever there was one.

Finally, the Galicians make excellent use of their outstanding vegetables, not only as an accompaniment to main courses, but in other rather unusual ways. For example, they produce an *Empanada Gallego*, which is something like the Cornish pasty produced in the southwest of England. It is a long, cigar-shaped pie filled with an assortment of very young, choice vegetables and flavored with fish, meat, poultry, or sausage. As a one-dish meal or luncheon snack, it is extremely popular.

## NAVARRE AND ARAGON

The cooking in these two smaller provinces which lie along the Pyrenees concentrates on the use of strong, rich sauces. The favorite method of preparing chicken or meat is *a la Chilindron*, made by stewing the main ingredient with ground pepper, red peppers, tomatoes, and garlic. Trout is also given emphasis in the recipe *Trucha a la Navarra* in which it is stuffed with either Serrano ham or a local chorizo.

2

# 2 THE WINES OF SPAIN

I f you are an oenophile (don't worry, it only means wine lover), then Spain is the country for you. Spain is the third largest wine producer in the world, being topped only by France and Italy. She has more vines under cultivation than any other country. Few other countries have such a wide range of wines, most of which are blended and sold under brand names in the inexpensive to medium price range.

Because Spanish climate is ideally suited for viniculture, it has always been possible to produce vast quantities of wine cheaply. A high proportion of this yield was, in the past, sold to other European countries to strengthen their own local wines. Even today, Spain still exports considerable quantities of wine for blending (called *vinos de mezcla*), and anonymous Spanish wines lend to many foreign brand names virtues they may otherwise lack.

Until fairly recently, the Spanish wine industry was poorly organized and much of the equipment used for producing their wines was out-of-date. Wine from different areas was mixed, not always in the same proportions, with the result that one could not always be certain that two bottles with the same label would be alike. For this reason more than any other, Spain had a reputation for producing only inferior wine.

Now, however, new equipment is being introduced rapidly and stringent laws have been drawn up and, moreover, are being strictly enforced, with the result that certain red wines, especially from the Rioja area, can compete with many from Bordeaux. Rioja wines are indisputably among the nation's best, and a bottle that carries a *Guarantia de Origen* is a reliable indication that it will be very good indeed.

However, the ordinary table wines (*vinos de mesa*) are the type you will probably drink with your meals in Spain, that is unless you happen to prefer a sparkling wine (*vino de espumoso*). These table wines are quite superior to, and have a higher alcoholic level than, their equivalents in France or Italy, and, of course, they are inexpensive. But at this level the white wines tend toward blandness and close similarity in flavor within their dryness or sweetness group. Some of the regional wines are of exceptional quality and

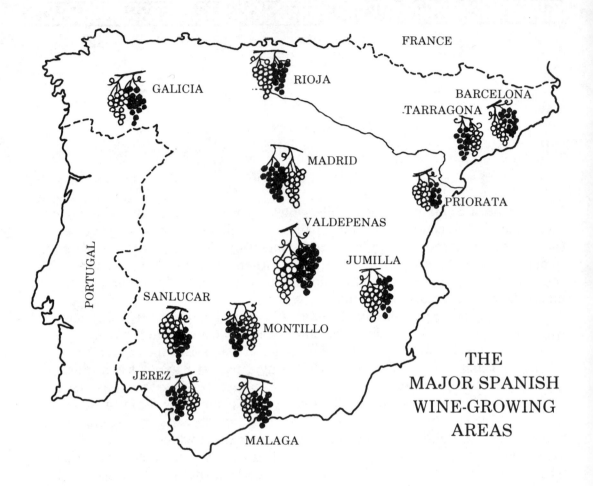

FRANCE

GALICIA

RIOJA

BARCELONA

.TARRAGONA

MADRID

PRIORATA

VALDEPENAS

JUMILLA

SANLUCAR

MONTILLO

JEREZ

MALAGA

PORTUGAL

THE
MAJOR SPANISH
WINE-GROWING
AREAS

value, but many that are sold locally are so restricted, only because they do not travel well.

Besides the vinos de mesa, there are a number of wines termed common wines (*vinos corriente* or *vinos comunes*) that are sold in the less expensive restaurants, in wine lodges (*bodegas*), and in considerable quantities to Spanish households for daily consumption.

## SHERRY

There are a number of regions throughout the country that produce wines of special character, perhaps the most famous of which is the area around Jerez de la Frontera, which produces Sherry: always spelled with a capital S!

Sherry was first exported to England during the reign of Elizabeth I and in those days it was known as "sack," a derivation of the Spanish word *seco* (dry).

Sherry is divided into two main types—*finos* and *olorosos*—and from these two come a number of derivatives.

*Finos* are without exception light and bone-dry, and are created when the *flor* (a floating layer of yeast cells) settles on the top of the vats and feeds on any trace of sugar that is left in the wine after fermentation. This leaves the wine with a very pale golden color and with a slightly earthy flavor and bouquet. These wines are made entirely from the Palamino grape and are regarded with great esteem in Spain. They are usually considered to be *aperitivos* (aperitif wines), but one often sees a Spanish family drink a fino throughout a meal, especially if they are eating shellfish.

*Oloroso*, which in Spanish means "fragrant," is the second basic type of Sherry and is richer and darker than the fino. It is often aged in oak casks for anything up to fifteen years before bottling, and in its natural state is as dry as a fino. However, for foreign markets it is sometimes sweetened.

*Amontillado* starts life as a fino, but after the flor disappears, the wine takes on a deeper color and a pronounced nutty flavor. It is therefore an older wine than a fino and is usually more expensive. Again in its original state it is a dry wine but is also sometimes sweetened for the export market.

*Amoroso* is a lightish-style oloroso with a deep-brown color and a very full flavor.

*Cream Sherries* are always mixtures, similar in style to amorosos and of varying quality.

*Brown Sherries* are heavily sweetened olorosos.

## SHERRY CHARACTERISTICS

All Sherries that require sweetening have the juice of the Pedro Ximenez grape added. This variety grows in the lowlands and in sandy soil. After picking, the grapes are spread out on plastic sheets to dry in the hot sun. This process turns them into an almost raisinlike fruit which produces highly concentrated, sweet juice.

All Sherries are blended to a remarkable consistency by the use of the *solera* system. Huge butts of Sherry are arranged in tiers one above the other, the older Sherries being at the bottom of the tier and the new Sherries at the top. Pipes connect the butts one to the other. Sherries for bottling are taken from the lowest butt, and as the wine is withdrawn, Sherry from the next higher butt replaces the wine so removed, and so on until each butt of Sherry (except the top one) gets a sort of promotion to a higher grade. The top butt is then filled with new vintage Sherry, and eventually after perhaps twelve or fifteen years, will reach the bottom butt and be ready for bottling.

Just outside the immediate area of Jerez de la Frontera is the coastal town of Sanlucar de Barremeda. This town is renowned for a special fino called *Manzanilla*. It is light and dry, as are all finos, but with a slight "salty" flavor possibly due to the proximity of the vineyards to the sea. It is very popular as an aperitif and is also drunk as an accompaniment to shellfish.

In respect of quality and value, one cannot overlook the excellent wine produced in the area of Montilla. Situated just south of Córdoba, the area was considered part of the Sherry region until 1933 when the government decided to revoke the cachet of Sherry country and make it a separate region as far as wine production was concerned. The wines of this area are somewhat different from Sherry, although their style is quite similar to fino and oloroso. They do have one tremendous advantage over Sherry. Because they are less well known, these wines are approximately 50 percent cheaper and are usually of excellent quality.

## Serving Sherry

Despite what one reads to the contrary and despite the tradition of serving Sherry in a small glass, this is quite wrong. A Sherry should be able to brag about its fragrance and its character, and this is impossible if served in a glass with a smaller capacity than 6⅔ fluid ounces (200 ml). The Spanish serve Sherry in *copitas*, those tall glasses which are widest at the bottom and gradually taper toward the top. In a glass of this design, the fragrance may gather and be sniffed with a great deal of pleasure, even before the drink is sipped.

Fino Sherry, Manzanilla, and the dry Montillas should be served chilled—about 50°F (10°C). Both Amontillados and medium Sherries should be slightly less chilled—55°F (11°C). Olorosos are at their best when served at room temperature.

Most Spanish buy their Sherry from a local bodega, bringing their own container and having them filled from the gigantic butts which line the walls. Here, among the other wines, spirits, and liqueurs, a range of excellent Sherries is obtainable, always in excellent condition in their wooden casks. The Spanish do not care to buy Sherry in bottles because when a bottle is opened, on contact with the air, the wine begins to oxidize and deteriorate. So they buy enough for only a day or two.

Finos are particularly sensitive to bottling. Once in bottle, the wine deteriorates slowly but steadily, even after just a few months. Fortunately of all Sherries, finos are alone in this. Amontillados and others do not suffer any loss of flavor or character in an unopened bottle.

## THE WINES OF GALICIA

Far to the north of Spain is the province of Galicia, damp and green with a stunning coastline. In addition it has three other claims to fame. The town of El Ferral del Caudillo in the northeast of the province was the birthplace of General Franco. A little further south lies the important port of La Coruña, reported to be the ugliest city in Spain, and west of La Coruña is Cape Finisterre. This was the name by which Galicia was known until the New World was discovered, for previously, all God-fearing people believed that nothing lay west of this spur of land except the sea. The heretics who sailed west past this point would undoubtedly slip over the edge of the world and into the pit of hell! Yet today, this part of Spain should be renowned for yet another reason. For it produces some of the most delightful wines of the country—the *vinos verdes*.

The three main wine growing centers in Galicia—Ribeiro, Valdeorras, and Monterrey—lie well south of the province, below Santiago de Campostella and even Pontevedra. North of these two cities the climate is harsh, even for the hardy Albariño vines to flourish. In winter it is a hard, cold land with heavy rain and almost continual mists rolling in from the sea. Even in summer the temperature is much lower than in any other part of Spain.

The beauty of this northern part of Galicia lies in the attractive whitewashed houses with their windows framed with flecked granite and the doors painted blue or green. Some of the older houses in the area have protected balconies, enclosed by panes of glass set in tiny wooden frames (something like the mullioned windows of Tudor England) as a protection against the biting winds.

The white-flecked granite, which is seen in almost every rock formation, is used in considerable measure for houses, offices, barns, and stores and even for fences that divide the tiny fields, which are a feature of Galician husbandry.

Further to the south, beyond Pontevedra, the weather is kinder. It is still a region of granite-strewn heights, but the boulders have a rounder and less ridged appearance. During the summer the area resembles a gigantic rock garden with masses of mountain flowers in yellow, mauve, and red covering the huge gray stones.

Along the coastal route south toward Vigo, one sees a succession of deep inlets which cut sharply into the land and create areas of breathtaking beauty. These are the *rias*, the lush, green fjords where the air smells of salt and seaweed. Sometimes the waters cut around low hills to produce a necklace of small islands with sandy beaches miles inland from the rocky coast.

The port of Vigo is built in a gracious semicircle and is one of the most pleasant in Spain. It is defended from the sea by a series of inlets and sandbars which camouflage the deep-water channel from the unwary, and which have thwarted many past invaders. However, Sir Francis Drake captured and pillaged the town, and as a result of the many battles between the British squadrons and the huge flotillas of Spanish treasure ships that sought to gain protection of the port, the seabed is covered with gold.

A few miles west of Vigo one reaches the first of the main wine-growing areas—the Ribeiro. This area produces most of the Galician wines and is centered around the town of Ribadavia. From here come some of the better known brands such as Pozo, Lar, and Xeito.

It is in this area that one will see, perhaps for the first time, the Galician method of training vines on posts set well clear of the ground or on wires strung between rows of sturdy trees. It is quite common to see thick curtains of growing vines up to 200 yards long and 30 feet high. This unique method of viniculture keeps the grapes clear of the ground and also reduces their exposure to reflected sunlight. Thus they retain a high proportion of acid which, when broken down during the second fermentation, results in the distinctive flavor of the vinos verde. These "green wines" are so-called, not because the wine is green in color, in fact the best of this type is lemon-yellow, but because they are wines that should be drunk young and fresh.

The fruit from the high-growing vines is picked in very late summer when it contains a low percentage of sugar and more malic acid than would be found in normal growth vines. If these grapes were vinified in the usual manner, it would result in wines that were very harsh and over-acid. So a special form of secondary fermentation is produced by naturally occuring yeasts, and thus the bulk of the excess malic acid is broken down into a milder and smoother lactic acid, and at the same time carbon dioxide is produced. Some of this natural gas is retained in the wines, with the result that a slight, impermanent sparkle is characteristic of many young vinos verdes.

Most of these wines are low in alcohol (between 9 and 12 percent) and the whites are dry, slightly astringent but not unduly acid. They have a flowery bouquet and a light, delicate flavor of fruit. The slight sparkle (*pétillance*) to which I have referred can, in some cases, be described as a prickling sensation; slightly peppery would be a good description in some of the better wines. As has been mentioned, all white wines should be drunk young, the best time is in the spring following the harvest, and they should of course be served chilled.

The best and most famous of the Galician grape varieties is the Albariño, which is used in varying percentages in most of the white vinos verdes. The other favored variety, Loureiro, is also used extensively. Sometimes these two are mixed to produce a wine that is heavier on the palate and much deeper in color than the true, young vinos verdes. Perhaps the best wine produced is the *Albariño del Palacio*, which is light, distinctly flowery, and has all the other delightful characteristics previously mentioned.

Some others, however, like the famous *Pefinanes Palacio* are not true vinos verdes, since the *reservas* are matured in cask for anything up to six years, and come out a golden wine, very well flavored and with considerably less bite than the young wines.

Up to now we have been discussing the excellent white wines of the province and it is somewhat surprising that they have managed to retain such a low profile, for they are similar to the popular Portuguese vinos verdes and are equally good, if not better than those produced by their next-door neighbor. Of course, part of the reason they are less well known than almost any other wine in Spain is that the Galicians themselves drink their own wines almost exclusively, and they seem to want to keep a good thing to themselves. As the Galicians have mighty thirsts, they consume almost all of the 300,000 hectoliters produced each year.

In Galicia as in Portugal, considerably more red wine is produced than white. But while the whites are fermented *au virgen*, the reds are treated in the first place with the pips, skins, and some of the stalk, and are so high in tannic acid they make the teeth screech in protest, unless one is accustomed to their hardness. But again, except for the very light seafood dishes, the cuisine of the province makes these wines acceptable to the residents, for the cooking of Galicia is strong and robust, and many dishes require a very hearty wine to complement their flavors.

To visit other wine-growing areas of the province, one leaves the town of Ribadavia and travels east toward the lovely town of Orense. The name comes from *oro* (gold)—not the gold from the New World that was a blessing and also a curse to Spain, but the gold from the River Sil that was panned there for centuries.

A few miles from Orense, by a long and tortuous route, we come to the almost inaccessible town of El Barco de Valedorras. In this area are produced both red and white wines, some of superior quality but without the pétillance of the young vinos verdes.

South to the valley of Tamega, near the town of Verin, is the area where the Monterrey wines are produced. Here, in contrast to the rest of Galicia, the vines are trained *a la castillana* (close to the ground) and produce strong wines of up to 14 percent alcohol.

It is common in this part of Galicia for the very full-bodied red wines to be drunk from shallow earthenware bowls, about four inches in diameter (something like the shape and size of a French tastevin) and glazed on the inside, to set off the deep ruby color of the wines. These wines are drunk exclusively by local residents who relish the almost raw quality of the product without batting an eye.

## THE WINES OF RIOJA

Apart from Switzerland, the Iberian peninsula, which spreads over some 225,000 square miles, is the most mountainous region in Europe. The main geographical feature of this vast area is the high, barren plateau shaped something like an inverted soup plate, in the center of which stands Madrid, and from which a series of mountain massifs and formidable rocky spurs runs from the capital toward the coastal regions. It is almost impossible to travel to the sea in any direction from Madrid without crossing a mountain barrier.

This unusual topography makes Spain a country of great climatic contrasts. It is difficult to imagine greater extremes than the lush pastures of Navarre; the parched scrubland of Extremadura with roving herds of sheep and goats; the wide, rolling terrain of the wheatlands of La Mancha; and the semitropical area around Valencia with its rich harvests of oranges, sugar cane, and rice.

But there is one thing that every province has in common: its vineyards. Each province produces wine in considerable quantities, but because of the great differences in climate, soil, and terrain, the wines produced are all different in character, quality, and alcoholic strength.

Of all the growing areas, the Rioja—which stretches along the northern part of Spain—is the best known and is capable of producing not only wines of individual character and very high quality, but also some that can compete with all but the very top-ranked Bordeaux. The Rioja region, which is approximately 75 miles (120 kilometers) long and 19 miles (30 kilometers) wide, lies in a broad valley running from east to west, through which flows the River Ebro. At the western end, in the areas of Rioja Alvesa and Rioja Alta, tall hills line the valley on both sides, and here the vineyards are planted both on the comparatively flat ground and are also terraced up the sides of the hills.

In these two regions the best of the Rioja wines are produced, for the soil is a mixture of sandstone, limestone, chalk, and granite, ideal for viniculture. The climate also helps the production of quality wines. The temperature in the spring is mild and damp, the summers are short and hot, and the fall long and mellow, thus allowing the grapes ample time to reach their full excellence.

The main advantage that this area has over the Rioja Baja (lower Rioja) is that during the height of summer, the hills protect the vines from too much sun and so keep the ratio of sugar to other ingredients in the grapes in correct balance. Sugar content in the grapes is directly proportionate to alcoholic content after fermentation. Thus the strength of the wines in this area is between 11 and 13 percent.

In Rioja the vines are grown a la castillana: pruned low and unsupported by wires. A dozen or so grape varieties are used to produce the wines, although only six are used extensively. The white wines are made from just two varieties—*Malvasia,* a variety originally imported from Greece, and the homegrown variety called *Viura.* Four varieties are used to make the excellent Rioja reds, and each variety makes its individual contribution to produce a balanced wine. The *Garnacho* is a cousin of the famous Grenache from France and the grape that is used to produce the delicious Tavel Rosé and as a blend in the popular Chateauneuf-du-Pape. It is a high-yield grape which gives a wine with both alcoholic strength and lightness. Then there is the *Tempranillo,* a Spanish variety which, if used on its own produces a "must" that is too low in acidity, but is very attractive when blended. The *Graciano* provides freshness, flavor, and aroma, and the *Mazuelo* is rich in tannin and so ensures long life and stability in a red wine that requires a lot of maturing.

The center of the Rioja wine trade is around the village of Haro, although the business center is further east in the town of Lorogno. Both reds and whites are produced here and some of the whites, especially those produced by the Marquess de Murrieta at Castillo Ygay, are justly renowned.

The reds are kept in cask for a number of years, and in fact a minimum of six years in cask is required to earn the coveted *reserva* title, which indicates that the wine was laid down in an exceptional year. Even the youngest wine must spend two years in cask in order to qualify for the deckle-edged stamp of authenticity. Rioja wines that are kept in cask for four years or more have the legend *vino de crianza* (wine from the nursery) displayed on the label at the back of the bottle. In red wines this indicates a better quality than those that do not show this designation.

Many of the bodegas produce a bordeaux-style wine (*tipo burdeo*) and a fuller, richer version in the style of Burgundy (*tipo burgoña*). Each type is put into appropriately shaped bottles: square shoulders for the burdeo and sloping shoulders for the burgoña. The vintages of 1970 and 1968 were exceptional: those of 1974, 1975, and 1976 were rated good.

In contrast to the wine-growing regions of France—with their hundreds of *domaines* and *chateaux* producing Burgundy and Bordeaux—in the Rioja area there are only about fifty bodegas permitted to export wine with the government *denominación de origen* label attached to each bottle.

Most of the larger bodegas in the Rioja Alta (high Rioja) produce *tintos* (reds) and *claretes* (lighter red wines) of various ages and vintages as well as *blancos* (whites) both dry and sweet. Often there is a *rosado* (rose) in the list also. Spaniards usually bracket the red Murrietas and the Riscals as the best Riojas, and of the two the Murrieta is a softer, fruitier wine while the Riscal is lighter and with more astringency. Their reservas are quite outstanding, but almost impossible to obtain, especially those over twenty years old.

Other red reservas, upward of ten years old, and excellent wines by any standard are C.U.N.E.'s Imperial Gran Reserve, Santiago's Condal, and the outstanding Vendimia Especial from Bodegas Bilbainas. Let's not forget also the Royal from Bodega Franco Españolas.

Next in age and quality to the reservas are a group of red wines usually about six years old. A short list of some of the best that you should try would probably include the Viña Zaco from Bilbainas, and a wine produced by Lopez de Heredia called Vina Tondonia 6 año. Sexto año means that the wine was bottled in the sixth year after the harvest. Finally, one must not forget the dry and mature Vina Doraña from Gomez Cruzado.

Of the younger fine quality wines, the 4 año Murrieta and Riscal must head the list: both quite outstanding for their age, while the popular wines in the 3 año range come from C.U.N.E.

## THE WINES OF CATALONIA

The wine-growing region of Catalonia stretches from just north of Barcelona some one hundred miles south to a point well below Tarragona, where the River Ebro meets the sea. Along this coastline, and for a few miles inland, there are five growing areas each producing wines of different character and each of them of more than passing interest. In total, Catalonia produces almost 275 million gallons of wine each year.

### Alella

Alella, with its hard, granite soil, is the most northerly of the regions and the smallest of the five, covering in all no more than perhaps fifteen square miles. Consequently its wine production is small, although of good quality. The best known of the wines in this area are produced by Alella Vinicola Bodegas Cooperativas. Their reds are soft and full, while the white wines are fresh and fairly fruity with some having a slight resemblance to certain Moselles.

This cooperativa markets its wine under the brand name Marfil (ivory). Their Marfil Blanco is a luscious wine, very slightly on the sweet side, while the Marfil Seco is less full but much drier. The light-colored Marfil Tinto is a strong-flavored wine with a good bouquet, and the Marfil Rosado is slightly heavier than one would expect.

All Alella wines are aged in cask for one to two years before bottling, and none are allowed on the market until they are at least three years old, which is sufficient time for them to develop their full flavor and bouquet.

All the wines conforming to the Denominación de Origen are so marked on the bottle, together with the phrase *Alella Legítima.*


## Penedes

Penedes is the most important and most interesting of the wine-growing areas, running from the Mediterranean coast inland to the hills of Monserrat, some two thousand feet up. Here the vines drape the sloping hills and its mainly limestone soil produces rather different wines from other areas within the region.

It is divided into growing areas somewhat similar to those in the Rioja, and in the coastal area, the Baja Penedes near the resort of Sitges, most of the sweet wines are produced from the *Sumoll* and *Malvasia* (Malmsey) grapes. Some of the best wines are made in Villafranca de Penedes, and here the big name is Torres, for this company has done much to bring the reputation of the better Spanish wines to their present high position.

For many years Torres has been experimenting with a number of grape varieties and very sophisticated vinication methods. One of their out-standing successes is the production of a quite beautiful Spanish Gewürztraminer. The grape from which this delicious wine is produced is the pinkish-white cousin of the Traminer family, which yields a rather soft, slightly spicy, and very heavily perfumed white wine and is more usually found in Luxemburg and Germany.

Most of the Torres grapes come from independent farmers although the company does own considerable vineyard acreage. One of the best selling of the younger wines, Sangre de Toro, is a blend. It is full-bodied, deep red, and one of the better examples of a medium-priced Catalan wine. The older Coronas Reservas are vintage wines, and the best of them are up to the standard of second-growth clarets, with excellent body and intense bouquet. However, they do need to be kept longer than a modern French claret.

The white, still wines of Torres are, I think, about the best in Cat-alonia and are justifiably popular. This is especially true of the Viña Sol and the quite excellent Gran Viña Sol Reserva. These wines are made from slightly underripe *Macabeo* and *Parellada* grapes. The younger of the two wines is kept in cask for a few months, then bottled and allowed to rest for at least another year before being sold. The reservas however are given a much longer maturing period to develop their distinctive characteristics before being sold.

## Tarragona

Tarragona is the largest wine-growing district in this part of Spain with a huge production of vermouths and liqueurs. It also manufactures vast quantities of inexpensive, blended wines for export and for use by other exporting bodegas in Spain.

Most of this wine is transported by road in giant tankers, and daily along the streets leading to the harbor one may see these tankers being filled and sent on their way. Beneath the roads of each of these bodegas are rows and rows of huge oak *tinas*, each holding thousands of gallons of various wines. Under the floors are the *depósitos* of stainless steel or cement which are used for blending the different wines to match a customer's requirements. The skills of Tarragona chemists in matching wines from a customer's sample is world renowned and demands no less skill than that required of a tea blender.

As in Portugal and a few other countries, these large bodegas and the cooperativas throughout Spain play an important part in the prosperity of the wine industry by buying grapes from independent farmers to produce vast quantities of medium to good wines, which make up by far the greater proportion of the total production of the country.

In this respect, Spain is fortunate in being able to produce a wider range of better quality, low-priced wines than any other country in the world. Export of bulk wines is big business and those that are sent abroad improve the quality of the national product, imparting to those wines qualities which they may not otherwise have enjoyed.

## Priorato

Within the region of Tarragona, in the mountain area to the south, is the small enclave of Priorato. With its lava and slate soils, Priorato produces some highly potent deep-red wines which are more usually sent to the large bodegas, but may also be bought in local bars.

Here, as in other parts of Catalonia, one may dispense with drinking from a glass and use the round-bottomed bottle fitted with a spout (called a *porron*), which when tipped at a correct angle, sends a stream of wine into the mouth. However, some practice is required and a little skill to boot, to prevent the wine from splashing over one's shirt front.

Priorato also produces some white dessert wines with such tremendous viscosity that they cling to the glass like honey and contain up to 20 percent alcohol. Among the best of these is the Blanco Licoroso which is made from the *Garnacho Blanco*, the *Macabeo*, and the *Pedro Ximinez* grapes.

## Sparkling Wines

About 90 percent of all Spanish sparkling wines is made in the Penedes area, the center of which is the town of Sadurni de Noya. Here the wine is produced by the champagne method. Although there are a number of companies making wine in this manner, the largest in the business is Codorniu, which made its first bottle of sparkling wine in 1872, and now produces about 40 million bottles each year. This puts the 24 million bottles of French champagne produced by Moët et Chandon, the largest producer, somewhat in the shade. Codorniu also has something like 100 million bottles racked and resting in its 10 miles of underground cellars.

Another excellent producer of sparkling wines by the *méthode champenoise* is Freixenet, and their Cordon Negro is an outstanding wine. This producer uses three types of grapes to produce their wine—*Xarello* which gives color and vinosity, *Macabeo* giving finesse and delicacy, and *Paralleda* for bouquet and fragrance.

Most other of these better quality wines are similar to the French blanc de blanc in being made only from white grapes, mainly *Sumoll*.

There are two other methods of producing sparkling wines. First, carbon dioxide gas is introduced into still white wines, giving them a fizz. These are the cheap, very popular but nonetheless inferior *gasificados* of which quantities are made in Tarragona. Second, with the tank—or cuve close—method, fermentation takes place in sealed tanks. Although the latter does not have the character of the wines made by the *méthode champenoise* nor indeed the fullness, they are still quite acceptable wines, although they tend to froth when opened rather than bubble.

## OTHER REGIONS

South of Tarragona lies a group of less important wine-growing areas. All of these (except Valencia) are quite small, but together contribute very substantially to the overall wine production of Spain.

## Urtiel-Requena

This area is situated between the two towns of Urtiel and Requena and lies approximately 43 miles (70 kilometers) due east of Valencia. This area produces some light and well-balanced wines with a low alcoholic content, mainly from the *Bobal* and *Macabeo* grapes.

## Jumilla and Yecla

These areas are south of Valencia and produce slightly coarse wines with a very high alcoholic content—up to 18 percent. Both reds and whites are produced, some of which are known with very good reason as *vinos valientes*—strong man's wines.

## Valencia and Alicante

Here large quantities of rather earthy wines are produced, again having a high alcoholic content.

## Valdepeñas

Traveling 300 kilometers west of Valencia, we come to the largest wine growing area in Spain. This is La Mancha, and Valdepeñas is the wine center of the area. Most of the wines are drunk while still young and are generally the carafe wines (*vinos corrientes*) served in many restaurants. Many of the better wines in this category are made from *Menastrel* and *Tintorera* grapes and have a strength of up to 15 percent. The white wines are slightly less alcoholic.

## Málaga

In Andalucia, from the port of Málaga inland to the hillside town of Antequera, lies the area which produces the dessert wines of Málaga. They range from very sweet to medium sweet, with one or two rare examples of a slightly drier wine, somewhat reminiscent of port.

# DRINKING YOUR SPANISH WINE

When at last you get to the point of choosing and drinking Spanish wine, do not be intimidated by the endless arguments about which wine should go with which food. All sensible people who love wine agree that to "drink what you enjoy" is the only maxim to follow.

Of course some purists will tell you that you should only drink red wine with meat or game and white wine only with chicken or fish. As an inflexible rule, this is nonsense. Though it may be true that a well matured Rioja or a good but rather lighter Penedes will complement a steak or partridge, what happens if you have the misfortune to be served a red wine so green, so poor, or so harsh that it makes your teeth squeak? Then again, suppose you don't like the dryness that is characteristic of most red wines. Suppose they make you ill or increase your blood pressure, what then? Do you stop drinking wine with meat or game? Of course not! You simply choose a full-bodied white wine that, as far as possible, can hold its own with the flavor of the meat—and then you enjoy your dinner.

Again, there are many excellent very dry white wines (from the Alicante region for example), one of which would be an excellent accompaniment for a grilled sole. But what if you have a strong preference for red wine? Do you stop drinking wine with fish? Of course you don't. You simply choose a light, young red or perhaps a dry *rosado* (rosé). It may not be ideal for everyone, but it's just *great* for you. And that's what matters.

There is yet another point which the pundits tend to overlook. Even if one does enjoy red wines with meat or game and white wines with fish or chicken, the wine that should accompany a dish depends to a very large extent on the *style* of the dish being served. For example, should a chicken dish be served in which slices of strong, piquant sausage play an important part, the chances are that a white wine (usually recommended to accompany chicken) would be too delicate and too subtle to provide the necessary contrast. Similarly, when eating the first lamb chops of the season, a heavy red wine would ruin the delicate flavor of the meat. So the whole business of choosing and drinking wine depends solely upon a little intelligent thought, coupled with a person's *individual* preference.

Apart from the pleasures derived from drinking wine with a meal, one of the duties of that wine is to refresh the palate and allow the taste buds to absorb the flavors of the food. So the wine should never overpower the food, but by its very nature provide a delightful contrast.

As many Spanish dishes have strong and distinctive flavors, you may find that a few experiments with different wines may be necessary before you can match your preferences to the dishes you prepare. And, of course, this is a fascinating pursuit. Getting acquainted with different wines is like being introduced to a new community. Each wine is a different family, although they may be cousins under the skin. The Rioja family is different from the Castilian; the Galicians are different from those which come from Valdepeñas. Within each family you will meet members you will like more than others. You may also meet whole families that you won't like at all. But if wine is important to you, the only way to find out is to experiment in this way, and the best way to do this is through wine tasting.

## Wine Tasting

There is nothing complicated or mystical about tasting wine; you certainly don't have to be an expert to enjoy a wine tasting. However, before one starts to taste and test wine it is necessary to know what features and characteristics to look for.

The ingredients of wine are a subtle combination of alcohol, aroma, bouquet, acid, sugar, and tannin. The purpose of a wine tasting is to evaluate these features, relate them to one another, and decide if the amalgamation of features is pleasant or unpleasant—as far as *you* are concerned.

Most wine is consumed with food. When the marriage of wine and food take place in the mouth, the wine will change slightly in character. But during tasting, without food, the good or bad characteristics will show.

It's important to taste wines in suitable order. Basically that is: dry before sweet; cheap before expensive; young before old; and white before red.

Judge each wine on flavor and character. For a start, note these features:

*Dry or Sweet?* This will depend upon the amount of sugar left in the wine.
*Sharp or Soft?* This will depend largely upon the acidity of the fruit. Too much acidity and the wine may taste sour; too little and it may taste "flabby."
*Fruitiness?* This does not mean that the wine is "grapey," but that it has preserved a fresh taste and smell of good, ripe fruit.

Overall, every wine should be well balanced with none of the general features absent or exaggerated. Of course, in the cheapest wines, these characteristics may well be absent, for the wines are often produced with little finesse, though they may be quite drinkable. But if we speak of the better wines from Rioja and Catalonia, where factors of quality in wines may be judged and compared, then it is usual to call a wine that has plenty of taste "robust" or "full-flavored" or "big." Such a wine may also have a high alcoholic content.

Less flavored wines are often described as "light," and this in itself is not a bad thing. There are many good, light wines on sale. The problem arises when the wine that should be robust is in fact light. Wine with little flavor and a lot of acidity is described as "thin."

## Background of Table Wines

Before embarking on your first wine tasting session it is a good thing to know something about the general background of table wines.

First, remember that wine is an end product of a perfectly natural process. Wine making is not a manufacturing process, as is, for example, making sausages, where the flavor and texture can be altered by adding more pork or less seasoning, more fat, or less rusk. Wine grapes are simply taken from the vine and pressed; then the juice is fermented.

When this is done, the vintner is stuck with the results, and there is little that can be done to improve a poor wine. The hundreds of different variations in wines, which range from diabolical to excellent, are the result of the type of grapes grown, the area of growth, the amount of rainfall and sunshine, the skill of the vintner, and the soil on which the vines grow.

In the south of Spain the summers are long and hot and the winters provide inadequate rain for good table wines to be made, although the Sherries and the sweet wines of Malaga flourish. Around the area of Madrid, the summers are still hot but the winters are colder than in the south, and here the cheaper wines of La Mancha and Valdepeñas are produced. But it is in the north of Spain where the best wines are made. Running in a broad sweep from around the area of Logrono and Haro across the east of Catalonia, we find that the summers are ideal and the rainfall adequate.

Throughout the spring and summer the vines sprout their leaves, then blossom. The fruit is formed and grows to maturity. During this period, airborne yeasts gather on the grape skins as a white or gray bloom. These act as a natural fermenting agent when the grapes are pressed.

In early autumn the grapes are fat and full; and around the middle of October the pickers with large gathering baskets clip off the ripe bunches as they pass along the rows of vines. Even when ripe, most wine grapes are tart, so that the pickers do not judge the fruit by the taste, but rely upon their years of experience to decide which bunches to pick and which to leave for the next time. The vineyards are combed for ripe fruit many times during the harvesting season: a laborious and costly business.

When the baskets are full they are taken to the collection sheds. From the sheds, the grapes are tipped into the huge wine presses. Slowly at first, pressure is applied and the white juice gushes into the vats. More pressure is applied and the flesh, skins, pips, and some stalk fall into the vat with the juice.

Incidentally, whatever color skin the grapes may have, the juice is always white. The depth of color of new red wine depends upon how long the skins of the red grapes have been left in the juice during fermentation. White wine may be made either from red or white grapes, but the skins are removed immediately after pressing to avoid staining.

When pressing is completed, the "must"—that is the juice, flesh, skins, and so on, together with the yeasts—is left to ferment in the vats. The vintner must control the fermentation very carefully; too little fermentation gives an unfinished product. Overfermentation spoils the wine, which eventually turns into vinegar.

The process of fermentation takes several weeks and during this time the new wine is constantly tested. When the correct level of alcohol is reached, fermentation is stopped. This is perhaps the most crucial stage in wine making, as it is at this point that good and bad features of a wine begin to show.

The wines are then clarified and, if necessary, blended with other wine, then filtered and stored in oak barrels to mature. Cheap wines are allowed a very limited period in cask, but the better wines spend many years in the barrel, gradually maturing to bring out their flavor and character. When ready, wine is filtered, bottled, and corked or capped. The cheap wines are sent to the market while some of the more expensive wines are kept in bottle at the bodega for further aging.

## Evaluating Wines

Wines are judged on three criteria: appearance (examine the color, tone or depth, and clarity); bouquet (look for cleanliness, youth or age, depth, and fruit); and taste (dryness or sweetness, body, flavor, tannin, acid, elegance or finesse). In other words, you examine the wine with three senses: you look at it, you smell it, and finally you taste it—in that order.

APPEARANCE.   Examine the color. The hue can be very important. It is best to tilt the glass over a white background and examine the rim. Red wine will vary in hue from purple through various shades of red to mahogany, depending upon maturity, district, and vintage.

*Purple* indicates extreme youth or immaturity.
*Ruby* is found in fullish Rioja and other good wines.

*Red* is the transitional period between youth and maturity.

*Red-brown* indicates the wine is maturing well. Can be found in red wines five years or more in bottle.

*Mahogany* is a more mellow color, indicating considerable maturity.

*Brown-amber* indicates a wine that is either very old or is prematurely old (oxidized).

White wines vary from pale yellow-green through deeper yellow to gold and amber. Dry white wines usually start with little color and darken with age. Sweet wines start with a fuller color.

*Green-tinged* is a particular characteristic of some of the vinos verdes of Galicia and fairly common in many young wines.

*Straw* is a pleasant lively yellow with a slight touch of green. A good color for most dry white wines.

*Yellow-gold* is quite normal for any white wine.

*Gold* generally indicates a sweet or more luscious wine, or one with bottle age. Some of the Catalan and Riojan wines develop a golden sheen after about six years in bottle.

*Yellow-brown*, or any brown tinge, implies considerable age in the bottle. However, it can also indicate that the wine has broken up and oxidized.

Rosados vary in color enormously—from orange to pink.

*Orange*, especially pure orange is not a desirable hue, although a pleasant orange-pink is quite normal in some rosados.

*Pink* is perfectly acceptable. However a suspicion of blue is not desirable.

*Rose* should be positive, clear, and appealing. It should not look like watered-down red wine.

Now examine the "tone." Remember that although the basic fullness or paleness will depend to a certain extent upon the origin of the wine, its depth will give some indication of its component parts. A very full, almost opaque, red-purple wine will usually have more than its fair share of tannin, acid, natural sugar, and other extractives. Tone, together with the color, will give an indication of the wine's maturity.

Next observe the clarity. This is of prime importance in the various stages of wine development from fermenting to bottling to final decanting. When selecting wines for testing, handle them carefully; don't shake them or move them about too much. This will only tend to cloud the wine, especially if it has age.

A dull cloudiness or obstinate haze or suspended matter in the bottle is the danger signal, but tiny pieces of floating cork and loose sediment are usually quite harmless. Flakes of tartaric acid crystals are sometimes seen in both fortified and white wines. They are caused by a sudden change of temperature and are harmless.

BOUQUET.   The importance and value of the nose is generally underrated. A good deal of valuable information can be obtained from the bouquet.

*Cleanliness.* The wine should smell like wine. Anything at all like vinegar, bad cabbage, almond kernels, or pear drops should be regarded as a danger signal.

*Youth or age.* It is almost impossible to describe bottle age. The physical components of young wines tend to be pronounced and raw; they have had little time to settle down and blend smoothly together. Youthful acidity has a mouth-watering effect. A raw cooking apple smell indicates excess malic acid, often found in young white wines of poor vintage. The bouquet mellows with age and is noticeably softer and more harmonious.

*Fruit.* This is a desirable quality, but remember that a wine can be described as "fruity" without having any trace of "grapiness." A distinct grapey bouquet is only found in wines made from certain characteristic grape varieties, such as the Muscatel.

*Depth.* A bouquet can be described as light or deep, nondescript, superficial, full, or rounded. These descriptions apply to the degree of development of the bouquet. Some poor quality wines have a full bouquet, and conversely some wines may have a dumb, or underdeveloped, bouquet.

TASTE.   The taste should generally confirm opinions drawn from the nose.

*Dryness or sweetness.* This is basic and easily judged constituent particularly important in white wines. Don't be misled by thinness or excessive acidity which tend to make one underestimate the actual sugar content.

*Body.* The weight of wine in the mouth is basically due to the alcoholic content. It is an important binding and keeping quality. The weight of a wine can be felt by taking a sip and holding it in the closed mouth, then moving the jaw up and down and juggling the wine with the tongue.

*Flavor.* This is all important. Even if it is impossible to describe, at least record whether it is agreeable or not.

*Tannin.* Although disagreeable in a young wine (it is harsh and dry in the mouth, something like strong, cold tea), tannin is an essential preservative extracted from the grape skins during fermentation. It precipitates proteins, acts as a general preservative, and is essential to long life in a red wine.

*Acid.* After dryness and flavor, acidity is the most noticeable factor. It gives a wine purpose and finish. Extremes are of course undesirable. Excess sugar, natural or otherwise, tends to mask the true degree of acidity.

*Elegance.* The final seal, as it were. It is judged by the completeness and balance of the component parts; the length of time the flavor lingers in the mouth; and its aftertaste.

RATING WINE.    Making notes is a good habit even if they appear feeble or nonsensical at first. Note the date of the tasting, the name of the wine, district, vineyard, year of vintage (if applicable), and the price. Although price is not a tasting quality, it is difficult to conceive of any tasting where price is of no consideration.

Rate the *appearance* on a scale of 1 to 10; the *bouquet* also from 1 to 10; and the *taste* from 1 to 20. Use as a model the tasting card that refers to a Rioja Reserva red wine.

*Tasting Card for Rioja Reserva*

| | | | |
|---|---|---|---|
| *Appearance* | Red-brown with a pronounced brown rim; medium-deep tone; fine, very clear.    9 points | SUMMARY | A beautiful wine, very pleasant to drink now, with plenty of bottle life left. |
| *Bouquet* | Clean, fruity, full, and mature.    9 points | Date_____    Price_____ | |
| *Taste* | Dryish, full-bodied, well balanced (tannin and acid present but not predominant). Excellent full flavor; fine finish.    18 points | Details_____ | |
| | TOTAL = 36 points | _____ | |

Because of the wide range, the variety, and the low price of wine in Spain, wine-tasting parties are a very popular social occasion, especially in the warm weather. So the following "Glossary of Terms" is for those who would like to take their tasting and testing a step further. If all participants in the wine tasting use the same vocabulary to describe their reactions to each wine, everyone will know exactly what is meant, and the comparisons and opinions will be that much more valuable.

## THE LANGUAGE OF WINE TASTING

*Acetic:* vinegary; the wine will be undrinkable and past repair.

*Almond kernels:* probably due to poor handling.

*Baked:* distinct smell of burnt and shrivelled grape due to excess sun.

*Clean:* absence of foreign odors.

*Cooked:* result of overuse of sugar in poor vintage.

*Deep:* well-developed; opposite of dumb.

*Dumb:* underdeveloped, but likely to be fuller and better in time.

*Fragrant:* attractive and flowery; could be quite superficial however.

*Grapey:* a rich, Muscatel-like aroma produced by varieties of that grape.

*Green:* young and raw; youthful acidity prominent.

*Little:* scarcely any bouquet apparent; either dull or underdeveloped.

*Meaty:* heavy; rich, almost "chewable" quality.

*Pear drops:* (in young, white wine) badly made and in dubious condition.

*Peppery:* sharpness due to raw, young components (among others, alcohol, acid) which may not have had time to marry; noticeable on some big, young red wines.

*Piquant:* fresh and mouth-watering acidity.

*Pricked:* excess volatile acidity; probably tart but just drinkable.

*Spicy:* rich and herblike.

*Stalky:* a smell of damp twigs; not derogatory, merely descriptive.

*Sulphury:* a sharp, acrid smell which prickles the back of the throat due to excess sulphur treatment during bottling.

*Sweet:* self-explanatory. Note that a dry wine can have a sweet smell.

*Tart:* a trifle overacid. Similar to piquant but probably too acid for the average drinker.

*Woody:* a particular aroma derived from the cask due to late racking or contact with a poor (or fresh) cask.

*Volatile:* often used but does not mean much; rather high acidity. Bouquet is the result of volatile esters, acids, and aldehydes.

The following terms are used to describe the *flavors* and general effects in the mouth.

*Acid:* the essential, natural quality which can be detected on the tongue. Not only an essential keeping quality, but gives the wine the necessary bite and bouquet. Degrees of acidity vary. It is high in some Galician wines and low in many of the wines coming from the south of Spain. Lack of acidity results in a flabby wine with a watery finish, while excess acid leads to tartness and undrinkability.

*Bite:* a combination of tannin and acid, expected in young wines, but unpleasant if found in excess.

*Bitter:* a sign of a very poor wine.

*Body:* the weight of wine in the mouth. Some wines, especially those in the south, tend to be heavier than those from the north.

*Breed:* a quality of flavor and texture due to its origin.

*Cloying:* sweet and heavy; lacking crisp acidity to make it interesting.

*Coarse:* rough and indifferently made. Not to be confused with the immaturity of a fine, young wine.

*Delicate:* a light and charming balance of quality and flavor.

*Dry:* absence of sugar; a wine fully fermented out.

*Fat:* medium- to full-bodied, allied to a soft, rounded texture.

*Full-bodied:* filling the mouth; heavy in alcohol and extractives; probably over 14 percent alcohol.

*Finish:* a pleasing and firm end to the taste. Good balance with a reasonable degree of acidity is required for a firm, crisp finish.

*Grip:* firm and emphatic combination of physical characteristics.

*Hard:* severity is due to overprominence of tannin and acid, both of which may mellow in time.

*Heavy:* full-bodied and overpowering. Note the context (a strapping, red Rioja wine would appear heavy with a light summer lunch, but not with a good, solid dinner in winter).

*Light:* implying lack of body; probably under 12 percent alcohol.

*Luscious:* soft, sweet, fat, fruity, all beautifully balanced.

*Piquant:* a degree of acidity which makes the mouth water, but not unpleasantly.

*Rich:* a full and not necessarily sweet ensemble of fruit, flavor, and body.

*Silky:* between firm and soft; describes the texture in the mouth.

*Sweet:* considerable natural sugar.

*Tough:* a full-bodied wine of overpowering immaturity; not necessarily youthful.

*Vigorous:* lively, healthy, and developing well.

*Well-balanced:* satisfactory blend of physical characteristics (fruit, alcohol, tannic acid) and the less tangible elements of breed and character.


## COOKING WITH WINE

In addition to its important place in Spanish gastronomy, wine has another function in the cuisine of the country, for it not only gives added zest to flavors, but also is beneficial in other ways. It supplies mineral salts lacking in meat and other foods rich in protein. It is a terrific tenderizer, a natural marinade for those extra lean cuts of meat. Much of Spanish beef (*carne*) and veal (*tenera*) falls in this category. In addition, wine also acts as an auxiliary agent for aiding the digestion of foods.

All of these are very good reasons for using wine in cookery. Remember also that wine used in cooking does not make a person inebriated, for during the cooking process the alcohol evaporates, leaving the most desirable flavor and aroma of the wine itself. So never add wine to a dish just before serving. Then even the youngest member of the family can eat food that has wine as an ingredient.

Use porcelain, glass, or earthenware containers for marinading. Some metals, especially aluminum, give food and wine an off-flavor.

All red meat and game improve by being marinaded for a period of up to 24 hours. The pieces of meat, placed in a dish, are covered by the wine. If you do not have sufficient wine for this, remember to turn the meat halfway through the marinading time to allow both sides to be equally treated. This wine is, of course, used in the actual cooking of the dish.


### Sauces

White fish sauces use a young, dry white wine which will enhance the flavor of the fish. Sweet wines tend to turn the sauce gray and sometimes taste unpleasant. Dry white wines also should be used for cooking most white meats (there are exceptions of course). Young red wines should be used for sauce in which red meats or game are cooked.

When using red wine in sauces, it should be boiled first until it is well reduced. Combine it with the aromatic ingredients—for instance, mushrooms, shallots, herbs—after which the natural pan juices of the meat or game should be added. If there is too little of this in the pan, you may care to add a little stock or a bouillon cube to give the extra volume. Mix all together; boil rapidly for a minute only; and then if you wish to thicken the sauce, add a little arrowroot or cornstarch premixed with cold water to form a smooth, runny paste.

Another pointer: It is useful to remember that cloves and cinnamon do much to enhance the flavor of red wine in cooking. (These ingredients are used in some of the recipes that appear in the latter part of this book.) Of course, garlic blends well also and loses much of its potency when used in a rich, red wine sauce. Fennel and cayenne pepper do great things for a white wine sauce; and bay leaves and thyme are excellent with both red and white wines used in sauce making.

When making white wine sauces for use with fish, a slightly different technique is used than when making a red wine sauce. As the fish will have to be cooked for a very short time in order to keep its succulence, the wine in which it is being cooked will not have had time to reduce to the required degree. Therefore remove the cooked fish from the pan or casserole, and boil rapidly the remaining liquor over a high flame to reduce it to the proper proportion. It may then be used as a base for the sauce or, if very considerably reduced, may be poured directly onto the dish itself, just before service.

To give any sauce a fuller, richer flavor, you should add a little Spanish brandy. For one pint of sauce, heat a tablespoon of brandy over a flame until the brandy catches fire. Allow it to burn for about ten seconds (this eliminates the alcohol), then pour it into the sauce while still flaming. Mix well.

## SPIRITS AND LIQUEURS

The range of obtainable Spanish-produced liqueurs is formidable. Almost every type which originated in France, Germany, and Italy is now produced in Spain under license. All are very good and cost far less than the imported originals.

Liqueurs are used not only in the preparation of hot desserts but are used as an accompaniment to vanilla ice cream. Try Crème de Menthe over a serving of vanilla ice cream; or Crème de Cacaō or Gran Marnier. . . .

## Chartreuse

This liqueur, originally produced in France, is now manufactured by the Carthusian monks in a small distillery just outside Tarragona. It is said to contain over 130 different herbs which are infused in a wine spirit. The manufacture is in the hands of just three monks, each knowing just a part of the complete recipe. Thus, the secret will always be well kept.

## Vermouth (*Vermout*)

While not a spirit or even a liqueur (but strictly an aperitif), Vermouth is included in this list, as again, it is a drink that is produced from an original Spanish recipe (rather than being made under license). It is an extremely popular drink in Spain and is made in considerable quantities in Tarragona by the universally accepted method of infusing wine with a variety of herbs and fortifying the mixture with brandy. There are a number of national brands available both in the pale "dry" style and the red "sweet" style. Flavors of the same style differ between brands.

## Gin (*Ginebra*)

Spanish gin has a somewhat different flavor from that of a traditional London gin. The better brands of Spanish gin, such as Larios, M & G, and Gallardon are very palatable and are made from pure neutral spirit which is further purified by redistillation, and then flavored (mainly with juniper). Sometimes however a variety of other herbs are added in the most minute quantities to various different brands to produce the distinctive flavors. This method of production is common to all countries.

## Rum (*Ron*)

Little need be said about Spanish white rum, for it is produced in exactly the same manner as in the West Indies. It is an excellent product and many brands are sold in the United States. As with all other locally produced spirits it is inexpensive.

## Vodka (*Vodka*)

This is another excellent product which, while not having the style, character, and flavor of the expensive Russian vodka, is by no means a poor relation.

## Brandy (*Conac*)

Many brands are manufactured in Spain, some being produced by firms that are better known for their wines and Sherries. There is a wide range of qualities available from the very inexpensive, young, and slightly raw brandies to the smooth, mature, and quite excellent Carlos Primero and many others. The vintage brandies are all of high quality and are fairly expensive, but less so than imported French brandies. For everyday drinking, Fundador and "103" (Ciento y Tres) are popular brands.

## A QUESTION OF PROOF

Visitors to Spain will be interested in comparing the alcoholic strength of Spanish wines, spirits, and liqueurs with those of either the United States or United Kingdom.

There are three different scales in use throughout the world for indicating the alcoholic content in any liquid. These methods are referred to as the "Proof Systems," and since each differs from the other two, complete understanding of the situation may sometimes be complicated. The proof systems are: American (U.S. proof); Sykes (British, Canadian, and Commonwealth generally); Gay Lussac (Metric proof used in the rest of Europe).

In the United States absolutely pure 100 percent spirit is rated 200 and proof spirit is rated 100, which is therefore 50 percent pure spirit and 50 percent water.

The Gay Lussac (metric) system is simplicity itself. If the proof is 50, then the alcoholic strength is 50. And as the Gay Lussac system is used in Spain, you will want to know about this one.

The Sykes system is much more complicated. No simple mathematical formula can enable one to translate British proof into U.S. proof or Gay

### PROOF SYSTEMS

| Gay Lussac (Metric) | American (U.S. proof) | Sykes (British, etc.) | % alcohol (by volume) |
|---|---|---|---|
| 100 | 200 | 175 | 100 |
| 57 | 114 | 100 | 57 |
| 50 | 100 | 88 | 50 |
| 45 | 90 | 80 | 45 |
| 43 | 86 | 75 | 43 |
| 40 | 80 | 70 | 40 |
| 37 | 74 | 65 | 37 |

*Note: These are approximate comparisons.*

Lussac. Under the British system, absolute alcohol is 175.25 and proof spirit is 100.

To most drinkers, the single important factor to know is the alcoholic strength of the liquor in the bottle. The Proof Systems table should allow you to compare with reasonable accuracy.

# All About Pots, Pans, and Cooking Utensils

# 3

# 3  ALL ABOUT POTS, PANS, AND COOKING UTENSILS

T here is very little difference in the basic kitchen utensils sold in Spain and those of any other western European country. Styles, materials, and costs vary as much as anywhere else, and of course the same general rule follows: the better the product, the more expensive it will be.

Before deciding on your basic utensils, several points should be considered: what type of food you prefer; what entertaining you will do and how often; what type of cooker you are working with and so on. In this respect you will find that because of the nature of Spanish cuisine, and often the lack of space in many Spanish kitchens, cooks prefer utensils that may be used both on top of the stove and in the oven. Thus few cooking pots and pans have long handles.

## COOKWARE MATERIALS

At its simplest, cooking is the transfer of heat from one medium to another, and this factor is therefore important to your choice of cookware. Look for a degree of porosity, which helps heat to spread rapidly and evenly, and also see that the internal surfaces are easy to clean. To this end, most cooking utensils are made from one material only, or from two or more sandwiched together. Here are the characteristics of most of the common materials used.

### Aluminum

Strong and durable, aluminum is an excellent conductor of heat. There are two types of aluminum utensils:

*Cast aluminum* is made by pouring molten metal into molds. These pieces are fairly thick and heavy and provide full heat conduction. They are therefore excellent for cooking over a low flame. A great deal of professional cookware is made in this manner and is quickly identified by its clean, simple, yet very functional lines and flat bottoms. Most cast aluminum cookware is hammered or polished outside and burnished on the inside.

*Sheet aluminum* is made by stamping or spinning the metal sheet over a die. A dull satin finish on the base gives maximum heat absorption while the interior may be plain (natural) or buffed out to give fine parallel lines around the interior surfaces. The price of sheet aluminum utensils is governed to a great extent by the thickness of the metal. Thickness is measured by gauges: the higher the gauge the thinner the metal. Utensils made of heavy-gauge metal have edges that are flat and smooth while the edges of lightweight utensils are often bent back (rolled) to strengthen the rim.

Aluminum utensils that are to be used inside the oven should have sturdy, heavy-duty handles made of malleable iron or steel, riveted through the pan so that they will not chip, crack, break, or come loose. Most utensils of this nature have twin handles for balanced lifting when they are full of food.

Almost without exception, covers should be flat, very secure, and have an easy-to-hold metal loop which is big enough to accommodate a pot holder in hand.

## Copper

Copper, one of the oldest metals used for cooking because it has the highest conductivity, was for years traditional in haute cuisine. Since mild poisons may be produced when copper comes in contact with some foods, utensils should be lined, usually with chrome or tin. They are very expensive but worth the price if you plan to use them as part of your kitchen decor.

## Stainless Steel

This metal stands wear and tear better than others. It is one of the easiest to clean and is entirely acid resistant. But it does not conduct heat as well as aluminum or copper and often has other metals bonded to it in a "sandwich" construction, giving added conductivity and durability.

In order to get the best of all worlds, some cookware is produced with a two-layer construction of stainless steel and copper or stainless steel and aluminum; a three-layer construction of either carbon steel or copper between stainless steel layers; four layers, comprising one of carbon steel, two stainless steel, and an outer of copper.

## Cast Iron

Cast iron is very popular in Spain, especially as a skillet or frying pan. Although very heavy, this type of utensil is an excellent conductor of heat.

As broilers (grills) are not universal in Spanish domestic kitchens, cast-iron skillets with raised internal ridges on the bottom of the pan are used to obtain a similar effect to that of broiling. The piece of meat or fish rests on the ridges, allowing any surplus fat to drain from the food. It is of course cooked "from the bottom, upwards"; in other words, the heat source is from below rather than from above, as in broiling, but the effect is similar. The food is cooked "dry."

The traditional paella dish is always made of cast iron and is flat bottomed with no internal ridges.

New cast-iron utensils should be matured before use. Wash the utensil and scrub thoroughly, then dry and rub the surface with oil. Heat the oven to 400°F (200°C) and bake the pan for an hour at this temperature. If the utensil rusts after you have used it for cooking, repeat the maturing process again.

The more expensive cast-iron pans are lined with vitreous enamel or a nonstick coating. While still very heavy, they have the advantage of conducting heat quickly and evenly and being very easy to clean. Internal chipping can be a problem if the cook is careless and uses heavy metal spoons to stir or remove food, but with moderate care they last for years.

## Fired Clay Ware

Ideal for casseroles and dishes requiring slow cooking, fired clay ware has a low rate of heat conduction. Utensils retain heat well, so are ideal to be transferred from oven to table.

## Glass

Glass, either clear, opaque, or with colored designs, can be specially made to overcome extremes of heat and cold. Quite inexpensive and therefore very popular, glass must not be used directly on a flame.

## Glass Ceramic

This type of cookware may be transferred from deep freeze to direct flame, making it ideal for all-purpose use. This material retains heat well, has a

## CAPACITY CALCULATIONS

| No. in Family | Item | Shape | Approx. Capacity U.S. | Approx. Capacity Metric | Height In. | Height Cms. | Width or Diam. In. | Width or Diam. Cms. | Length In. | Length Cms. | Number Required |
|---|---|---|---|---|---|---|---|---|---|---|---|
| 2 | Casserole | — | 1 qt/32 fl oz | 1 Liter | — | — | — | — | — | — | 1 |
| 4 | " | — | 2 qt/64 fl oz | 2 Liters | — | — | — | — | — | — | 1 |
| 6 | " | — | 3 qt/96 fl oz | 2 Liters | — | — | — | — | — | — | 1 |
| 2 | Baking Dishes | Oval | 1½ qt/48 fl oz | 1½ Liters | 1¾ | 4 | 6 | 15 | 10 | 25 | 1 |
| 2 | " | Round | 1½ qt/48 fl oz | 1½ Liters | 2 | 4 | 8 | 20 | — | — | 1 |
| 4 | " | Oval | 2 qt/64 fl oz | 2 Liters | 1¾ | 4 | 7½ | 18 | 11¾ | 29 | 1 |
| 4 | " | Round | 2 qt/64 fl oz | 2 Liters | 1¾ | 4 | 10 | 25 | — | — | 1 |
| 6 | " | Oval | 3 qt/96 fl oz | 3 Liters | 1¾ | 4 | 8½ | 22 | 13½ | 34 | 1 |
| 6 | " | Round | 3 qt/96 fl oz | 3 Liters | 1¾ | 4 | 12 | 30 | — | — | 1 |
| 2 | Saucepans | Round | 1 qt/32 fl oz | 1 Liter | — | — | — | — | — | — | 2 |
| 2 | " | " | 1½ qt/48 fl oz | 1½ Liters | — | — | — | — | — | — | 2 |
| 2 | " | " | 2 qt/64 fl oz | 2 Liters | — | — | — | — | — | — | 2 |
| 2 | " | " | 3 qt/96 fl oz | 3 Liters | — | — | — | — | — | — | 1 |
| 4 | " | " | 1 qt/32 fl oz | 1 Liter | — | — | — | — | — | — | 1 |
| 4 | " | " | 1½ qt/48 fl oz | 1½ Liters | — | — | — | — | — | — | 3 |
| 4 | " | " | 2 qt/64 fl oz | 2 Liters | — | — | — | — | — | — | 3 |
| 4 | " | " | 3 qt/96 fl oz | 3 Liters | — | — | — | — | — | — | 2 |
| 6 | " | " | 1 qt/32 fl oz | 1 Liter | — | — | — | — | — | — | 2 |
| 6 | " | " | 1½ qt/48 fl oz | 1½ Liters | — | — | — | — | — | — | 2 |
| 6 | " | " | 2 qt/64 fl oz | 2 Liters | — | — | — | — | — | — | 4 |
| 6 | " | " | 3 qt/64 fl oz | 3 Liters | — | — | — | — | — | — | 3 |

| Servings | Item | Shape | Capacity (fl oz) | Capacity (Liters) | | | | | | | Qty |
|---|---|---|---|---|---|---|---|---|---|---|---|
| 2 | Skillet | Round | — | — | — | — | 8 | 20 | — | — | 1 |
| 4 | " | " | — | — | — | — | 9 | 23 | — | — | 1 |
| 6 | " | " | — | — | — | — | 8 | 20 | — | — | 1 |
| 6 | " | " | — | — | — | — | 9 | 23 | — | — | 1 |
| 2 | Omelette Pan | " | — | — | — | — | 6 | 15 | — | — | 1 |
| 4 | " | " | — | — | — | — | 6 | 15 | — | — | 1 |
| 6 | " | " | — | — | — | — | 6 | 15 | — | — | 1 |
| 2 | Roasting Pan | Oblong | — | — | 2 | 5 | 8 | 20 | 12 | 30 | 2 |
| 4 | " | " | — | — | 2 | 5 | 8 | 20 | 12 | 30 | 2 |
| 6 | " | " | — | — | 2 | 5 | 9 | 22½ | 14 | 35 | 2 |
| 2 | Soup Kettle | Round | 4 qt/128 fl oz | 4 Liters | — | — | — | — | — | — | 1 |
| 4 | " | " | 4 qt/128 fl oz | 4 Liters | — | — | — | — | — | — | 1 |
| 6 | " | " | 6 qt/192 fl oz | 6 Liters | — | — | — | — | — | — | 1 |
| 2 | Deep Fryer (with basket) | Round | 2 qt/64 fl oz | 2 Liters | — | — | — | — | — | — | 1 |
| 4 | " | " | 3 qt/96 fl oz | 3 Liters | — | — | — | — | — | — | 1 |
| 6 | " | " | 3 qt/96 fl oz | 3 Liters | — | — | — | — | — | — | 1 |
| 2 | Paella Dish | Round | — | — | 1¾ | 4 | 8 | 20 | — | — | 1 |
| 4 | " | " | — | — | 1¾ | 4 | 10 | 25 | — | — | 1 |
| 6 | " | " | — | — | 1¾ | 4 | 12 | 30 | — | — | 1 |

smooth surface, and can be cleaned by abrasive and detergent. While more expensive than plain glass, glass ceramic cookware offers an excellent value.

## Earthenware

This is one of the most widely used materials for dishes and casseroles. In Spain, this material is usually given a rough internal glaze. These utensils are ideal for slow cooking in the oven, and if used in conjunction with an asbestos pad, may be used over an open flame.

## Pestle and Mortar

The single item in a modern Spanish kitchen that seems to relate to the Middle Ages and touches upon alchemy is the pestle and mortar. In every Spanish kitchen, both commercial and residential, this piece of equipment is found and is still used with great regularity, as it has been for many hundreds of years.

A great many Spanish cooks have two such utensils in constant use: one made of stone or heavy ceramic for crushing garlic or anything wet (like a maceration of spices and wine) or pounding baby crab for use in a soup or sauce; the other made of wood, when dry spices alone are required.

Crushed or ground spices have become available only recently, and while they may be regarded as one further small step in the emancipation of the cook, most Spanish cooks will not have them in the kitchen. They regard these seasonings as quite inferior, and truth to tell, many do lose their potency quite quickly even when stored under the best possible conditions. No modern cook is expected to grind his or her own mustard, but once the rich, natural fragrance of hand-ground anise or cumin seed are inhaled, even the most casual cook will want to own a pestle and mortar.

## CAPACITY REQUIREMENTS

The number and capacity of cookware required depends on the number of persons in your family. These calculations do not take into consideration any guests you may wish to entertain. The capacities shown in the table will be required when cooking Spanish recipes.

# MEASURE FOR MEASURE

The following is an explanation of the metric system of weights and measures with their American equivalents. There are just a few points to remember always when working to metric weights and measurements.

1. Metric units replace but do not *equal* imperial units.

2. Therefore metric units are rounded off to the nearest convenient figure to be practical. For example: 1 oz = 28.352 g. Obviously, it would be impractical to try to measure this metric amount accurately, so 1 oz is rounded off to 30 g.

## Common Metric Measures

$$Volume = (L)\ liter$$
$$Mass = (g)\ gram$$
$$Length = (m)\ meter$$
$$Temperature = (C)\ degrees\ Celsius;\ centigrade$$

## Metric Relationships

$$(Volume)\ 1000\ mL = 1\ (L)\ liter$$
$$(Mass)\ 1000\ g = 1\ (Kg)\ kilogram$$
$$(Length)\ 10\ mm = 1\ (cm)\ centimeter$$
$$(Length)\ 100\ cm = 1\ (m)\ meter$$

The following are the conversions that will be used in the recipes in this book:

## Volume

$$30\ mL = 1\ fl\ oz$$
$$250\ mL = 1\ cup$$
$$500\ mL = 1\ pint\ or\ 16\ fl\ ozs$$
$$1½\ dcL\ (deciliters) = 5\ fl\ ozs$$

## Dry Measure

$$
\begin{array}{rcl}
1 \text{ mL} & = & \tfrac{1}{4} \text{ teaspoon} \\
2 \text{ mL} & = & \tfrac{1}{2} \text{ teaspoon} \\
5 \text{ mL} & = & 1 \text{ teaspoon} \\
15 \text{ mL} & = & 1 \text{ Tablespoon} \\
25 \text{ mL} & = & \tfrac{1}{8} \text{ cup } = 1 \text{ oz} \\
50 \text{ mL} & = & \tfrac{1}{4} \text{ cup} \\
125 \text{ mL} & = & \tfrac{1}{2} \text{ cup} \\
250 \text{ mL} & = & 1 \text{ cup}
\end{array}
$$

## Mass

$$
\begin{array}{rcl}
15 \text{ g} & = & \tfrac{1}{2} \text{ oz} \\
30 \text{ g} & = & 1 \text{ oz} \\
120 \text{ g} & = & 4 \text{ ozs} \\
250 \text{ g} & = & 8 \text{ ozs} \\
500 \text{ g} & = & 1 \text{ lb} \\
750 \text{ g} & = & 1\tfrac{1}{2} \text{ lbs} \\
960 \text{ g} & = & 2 \text{ lbs} \\
1 \text{ kg} & = & 2\tfrac{1}{4} \text{ lbs}
\end{array}
$$

## Length

$$
\begin{array}{rcl}
25 \text{ mm (millimeters)} & = & 1 \text{ inch} \\
30 \text{ cm (centimeters)} & = & 1 \text{ foot} \\
1 \text{ m (meter)} & = & 1.1 \text{ yards}
\end{array}
$$

## Temperature

| °Fahrenheit (F) | °Celsius (C) |
| --- | --- |
| 300 | 150 |
| 325 | 160 |
| 350 | 180 |
| 375 | 190 |
| 400 | 200 |
| 425 | 220 |
| 450 | 230 |
| 500 | 260 |
| 525 | 270 |
| 550 | 290 |

**FREEZING POINT.**   Celsius = 0 degrees
Fahrenheit = 32 degrees

**BOILING POINT.**   Celsius = 100 degrees
Fahrenheit = 212 degrees

# METRIC KITCHEN UTENSILS

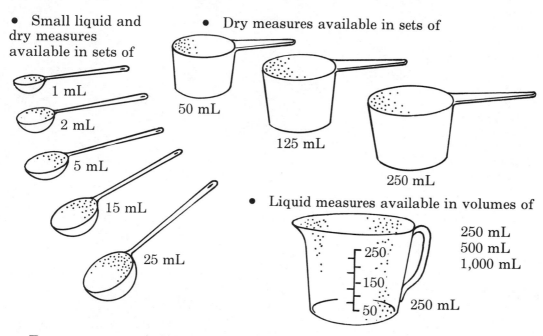

- Small liquid and dry measures available in sets of

  1 mL
  2 mL
  5 mL
  15 mL
  25 mL

- Dry measures available in sets of

  50 mL
  125 mL
  250 mL

- Liquid measures available in volumes of

  250 mL
  500 mL
  1,000 mL

  250 mL

- Temperature replacement chart for oven heat control unit.

- Metric ruler.

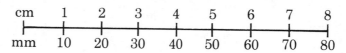

| cm | 1 | 2 | 3 | 4 | 5 | 6 | 7 | 8 |
| mm | 10 | 20 | 30 | 40 | 50 | 60 | 70 | 80 |

# APPROXIMATE EQUIVALENT MEASUREMENTS
## (Tablespoon/Cup/Gram)

|  | Tablespoon | Cup |
|---|---|---|
| Almonds (blanched, whole) | 10 g | 150 g |
| Almonds (ground) | 11 g | 180 g |
| Almonds (slivered) | 6 g | 100 g |
| Beans (dried, navy) | — | 200 g |
| Breadcrumbs (dry) | 10 g | 160 g |
| Breadcrumbs (fresh) | 5 g | 80 g |
| Broad Beans (dried) | — | 300 g |
| Broad Beans (fresh) | — | 120 g |
| Butter | 15 g | 250 g |
| Cheese (cottage) | 15 g | 250 g |
| Cheese (dry) | 7 g | 120 g |
| Cheese (freshly grated) | 6 g | 100 g |
| Chickpeas | — | 180 g |

| | *Tablespoon* | *Cup* |
|---|---|---|
| Flour | 8 g | 125 g |
| Lentils | — | 250 g |
| Meat (cooked, cubed) | — | 150 g |
| Meat (raw, minced) | — | 250 g |
| Mushrooms (chopped) | — | 90 g |
| Parsley (fresh, chopped) | 3 g | 50 g |
| Peas (dry) | — | 180 g |
| Peas (fresh) | — | 150 g |
| Rice (cooked) | — | 180 g |
| Rice (raw) | 15 g | 200 g |
| Sugar (brown) | 11 g | 180 g |
| Sugar (granulated) | 15 g | 250 g |
| Walnut meats | — | 120 g |

# The Basics of Spanish Cuisine

4

# 4  THE BASICS OF SPANISH CUISINE

Anyone who has read a few foreign cookbooks will be aware that while many countries produce many of the same foods, especially those geographically close to each other or having similar climates, certain characteristics in every national cuisine distinguish one style from the others. For example, soy sauce is the basis of many Far Eastern cuisines, but if we examine some of the recipes we find that there are quite considerable differences between Japanese, Korean, Chinese, and Indonesian cooking. This is of course due to the various flavor additions that are made by each country to the basic soy sauce. The Japanese additions are sugar and sake; the Indonesians add garlic, sugar syrups, and peanuts; in some Chinese cooking ginger root and Sherry are common additions; while Korean cuisine adds sesame seeds, garlic, and brown sugar. These combinations of ingredients give to each country the characteristic flavor of a national cuisine that is easily recognizable.

And so it is with Mediterranean and southern European cooking. Both Italy and Spain grow similar crops, so that one might reasonably think there would be a similarity in the end results. Yet after tasting Italian and Spanish foods, one could never confuse the different ethnic styles. The fundamental flavors that are common to western Mediterranean cooking are olive oil, garlic, herbs, and tomatoes. In the Provence region of France (and Spain's next-door neighbor) garlic and tomatoes predominate; in Italy, olive oil, garlic, tomatoes, and oregano are the main flavoring ingredients; while in Spain, *all* these fundamental items are used, but in a very different manner. In Spain, herbs play a very prominent part in the national cuisine. Of course, nearer the borders of any two countries recipes and techniques do tend to overlap, and in this particular instance, for example, there are similarities in Catalan and Provencal cooking and in the recipes of Galicia and Portugal. In order to get the best results from Spanish recipes, it may be wise to learn a little about the basics of the cuisine.

## OLIVE OIL

Spain, the world's largest producer of olive oil, is far ahead of Italy, which holds second place. A great deal of oil is exported, although home consumption is naturally very considerable—and for good reason. Olive oil provides the body with an all-important and highly concentrated source of energy. Its chemical composition is almost identical to the fat contained in the human body, and therefore is very easily digested; it is able to emulsify easily; and, finally, it is rich in unsaturated fatty acids.

Throughout Spain one sees grove after grove of gnarled twisted olive trees with their gray-green leaves, set in a meticulously cared-for land. Not a weed, not a tuft of grass is allowed to intrude between the carefully tilled rows, for in Spain the culture of olives is as important as growing grapes for wine.

There are over one hundred different varieties of olive tree, and the choice of varieties used in any particular area depends upon climate, soil, use of the fruit, and so on. Some olives are grown for eating, some for the production of oil. Unripe green olives, those used for eating, are harvested around September; fully ripe olives, used for oil production, are cropped as late as January.

The flavor and quality of oil produced varies considerably. These factors depend not only on soil and climate, which are of course important, but also on the care taken when harvesting the crop. Olives must be individually picked to be at their best; if the fruit falls to the ground and is bruised, the oil produced will be more acid.

The rather strong flavor of some poor quality oil tends to intrude when used in cooking, and sometimes overwhelms the natural flavor of these foods, spoiling the overall effect of the dish. On the other hand, good quality oil imparts a delightful and characteristic flavor. There are four grades of olive oil sold in most parts of Spain.

*Aceite extra virgen de oliva* (Super quality): This is pure oil obtained from the first pressing. It has a mild, delicate aroma and is much prized by experts. It is the best quality available. Note the word "extra" on the label when purchasing.

*Aceite superfino virgen de oliva* (First quality): This grade is similar to extra but containing no more than 1½ percent by weight of acid. Note the word "superfino" on the label.

*Aceite fino virgen de oliva* (Fine quality): The difference between superfino and fino is that fino may contain between 1.6 percent and 3 percent by weight of acid. Note the word "fino" on the label.

*Aceite de oliva* or *oliva virgen* or *oliva refinado* (Good quality): This product is obtained by blending virgin oil with olive oil that has been refined. It must not contain more than 2 percent by weight of acid.

## Vintages

The experts are of course able to distinguish between the various vintages of olive oil. They know immediately not only from what area the oil was produced but what year it was made. The most unexpected people are experts. Not only are they producers, sales agents, and similar professionals as one would suppose, but also farmers, housewives, bank clerks, and postmen! Further, the testing and evaluation of a new pressing is a very serious occasion, reaching almost ritualistic status.

Around February, when the raw olive oil is about to be produced, the manufacturers visit their customers and other people whose judgment they value and invite them to taste the new oil and give an opinion. The function is a little like a wine tasting.

On these occasions, guests are provided with thick slices of bread which they toast over hot coals. The toasted bread is then rubbed with freshly crushed garlic and then dipped in the fresh oil that comes trickling into the vat, warm and golden. At this early stage the oil has not developed its distinctive flavor, and the taste is something like toasted nuts. But this is the time when the experts give their opinion and the future of this particular pressing is decided. What the criteria are by which the oil is judged I have no idea—and the experience for me held very little charm—but then I am no connoisseur.

## GARLIC

The characteristic flavor of all Mediterranean cooking is garlic. Like all good things, it should be used in moderation. Almost every savory recipe that is cooked in a covered pot or casserole contains garlic. Therefore it is very important to be able to judge the degree of flavor that garlic will give, under certain circumstances. You will then be able to cook authentic Spanish dishes, but adjust the flavor of garlic to suit your palate requirements.

For a very subtle flavor, the whole clove of garlic should be fried first of all in the oil in which the meat, poultry, or fish will be browned (or cooked). The deeper the color of the fried garlic, the stronger will be the resultant flavor. But even if the garlic is cooked to a dark brown stage, the flavor will not be intrusive. After cooking, the garlic is discarded.

For a stronger flavor, the garlic clove may be crushed (but not sufficiently for it to disintegrate) and then it may be fried in a similar manner to that described above. Again, the garlic is discarded after frying.

For true garlic lovers, as many cloves as desired should be chopped finely, fried in a little oil or fat until golden, and then left in the hot fat while the meat is seared. The oil and garlic is then transferred to the cooking dish together with any other ingredients, to continue adding flavor during the entire cooking process.

If oil is not used in a recipe, a mild flavor may be obtained by blanching the peeled clove in boiling water for about 3 minutes, then adding it to the cooking container. The garlic should be removed before the food is served. Some cooks tie the garlic in a piece of muslin so that it may easily be identified for removal.

When using garlic in an oil/vinegar/herb/lemon juice dressing, it is a good plan to put half a peeled bulb (or as little as one clove, if preferred) in a bottle of oil and allow it to remain there for a few days. This will impregnate the oil which will then be used in making the dressing.

Although a garlic press is often seen in a kitchen, I do not use one as I feel that with a press one loses the best part of the bud. A similar (and perhaps preferable) method may be achieved by placing the clove of garlic under the flat of a broad-bladed French knife, then applying firm pressure with the heel of the hand. The tissue-thin skin bursts and the cream-colored clove slides out. Should you wish to crush the clove of garlic, then just hit the blade sharply with rather more force.

## TOMATOES

In most Spanish recipes that call for the use of tomatoes, they are always peeled prior to being put into the cooking pan. Of course, if they are being used to make a sauce, and the sauce is to be strained before serving, then there is no need to skin them beforehand. Tomatoes form the base of many sauces, and one of the better methods of producing a rich and flavorful base is by combining them with onions, garlic, and paprika. The Spanish term for this base is *sofrito*.

## *Sofrito*

1 lb (500 g) tomatoes
½ lb (250 g) onion, finely chopped
2 cloves garlic, finely chopped

3 Tbsp. (3 × 15 mL spoon) olive oil
salt and pepper
paprika

1. Blanch the tomatoes in boiling water to remove their skin.

2. Fry the onions and garlic in the oil until soft and golden, then add the peeled and chopped tomatoes.

3. Cook the mixture over a low heat until the liquid from the tomatoes has evaporated and the sauce has become thick.

4. Season with salt and pepper, remove the pan from the stove, and stir in the paprika.

*Note: The sofrito is now ready for any other ingredients called for in the recipe. When cool, it should be packed in a glass jar with an airtight screw lid and stored in the refrigerator. It will keep for up to three months. Should you wish to save time and trouble, there are a number of good brands of commercial sofrito obtainable everywhere.*

# HERBS AND SPICES

The variety of herbs used in everyday Spanish cooking is generally wider than in either American or British cuisine. Spaniards have become accustomed to a wide variety of flavors and to the intriguing contrasts that the judicious use of herbs and spices can provide. The recipes in this book use these ingredients as the Spanish would and give the authentic flavor one would experience in Spain.

Most herbs are pungent and the whole secret (if indeed it is a secret) when flavoring a dish, whether with herbs or anything else for that matter, is to see that no single flavoring is so intense as to become intrusive. Each herb has a volatile oil that gives it its distinctive flavor. The longer an herb is in a food, the more oil it releases (heat causes a faster release). Therefore it takes a little time for the flavor to work into a dish. So be patient, but don't overdo it; if left too long, the dish becomes bitter. So if in doubt, use half the quantity of herbs indicated, then taste the food as it is cooking to learn just how the different herb flavorings develop under heat and moisture. You can always add more next time. The exception to this rule is when using bay leaves. Use in the quantity suggested: the flavor will not intrude.

Use fresh herbs if possible. In Spain these are usually obtainable at the vegetable markets, although many Spanish grow their own. Dried herbs are readily available in packets or glass jars in every supermarket, and for the sake of convenience and practicality, the herbs mentioned in the recipes are dried, unless otherwise stated. As a general rule it is safe to calculate that dried herbs are three times as potent as fresh (1 teaspoon dried herb is equal to 1 tablespoon fresh herb). See the table on Uses of Herbs and Spices for ways to employ these ingredients.

# USES OF HERBS AND SPICES

| English | Spanish | Use |
|---------|---------|-----|
| **HERBS** | | |
| Basil | *Albahaca* | Stews, fish, soup, cheese, stuffings |
| Bay | *Laurel* | Stews, marinades |
| Chives | *Cebollinos* | Salads, potatoes, eggs |
| Dill | *Eneldo* | Fish, lamb, cauliflower |
| Fennel | *Hinojo* | Fish, sauces, marinades |
| Garlic | *Ajo* | Almost every type of savory dish |
| Marjoram | *Mejorana* | Soups, stews, stuffings |
| Mint | *Hierbabuena* | Sauce, lamb, potatoes, soup |
| Oregano | *Oregano* | Mushrooms, sauces, fish, stews |
| Parsley | *Perejil* | Sauces, fish, salads, garnishes |
| Rosemary | *Romero* | Shellfish, pork, lamb |
| Sage | *Salvia* | Baked fish, cheese dishes |
| Tarragon | *Estragon* | Meat, chicken, fish, sauces |
| Thyme | *Tomillo* | Stews, tomatoes |
| **SPICES** | | |
| Capers | *Alcaparras* | Mutton, fish, vegetables |
| Chili | *Chili* | Sauces |
| Cinnamon | *Canela* | Puddings, beverages, sauces |
| Cloves | *Clavos* | Beef stews, soup, ham, onions |
| Cumin | *Comino* | Cabbage |
| Dill (seeds) | *Eneldo* | Oil/lemon and vinegar dressing |
| Ginger | *Jengibre* | Casseroles |
| Mustard | *Mostaza* | Dressings, as condiment |
| Nutmeg | *Moscada* | Chicken, eggs, soups (pulse bases) |
| Paprika | *Paprika, pimentón* | Chicken, stews, and as a coloring |
| Pepper (black) | *Piminta* | As seasoning and condiment |
| Pepper (red) | *Pimiento* | |
| Peppercorn | *Pimenta Entero* | Soups, stews, steak |
| Saffron | *Azafrán* | Rice, fish, soup. |

In many towns and villages throughout Spain, the spice man makes his weekly visit to the local market, setting up his stall and displaying his selection of herbs and spices. His stock usually includes up to sixty different forms of the various herbs and spices; whole, ground, chopped, and flaked. He sells his goods in quantities as small as one ounce (approximately 30 g). He sells genuine saffron, which is obtained from the stamen of a special crocus, and is, incidentally, the most expensive spice in common use, in bags weighing one-third ounce (10 g). His prices are lower than if one bought similar products bottled or packaged from a store, and, consequently, he does a brisk business. In addition, he is also the local herbalist and his wares are particularly popular with the older generation.

During the Spanish Civil War (1936–1939), and in fact until the early 1950s, manufactured drugs and modern remedies were not readily available to many Spaniards and recovery from an illness depended more upon the toughness of the person than on health care. Their only aid was the use of herbs and other natural remedies. So, even today, despite the availability of modern drugs, the herbalist is still a welcome sight in the market.

In a section of his display, next to the herbs and spices, are plastic packets of carefully dried flowers and grasses, roots and barks, all home-produced natural cures for most common ills, and some for a few rather mysterious complaints. There are cures for arthritis, asthma, upset stomach, blood pressure, kidney trouble, constipation, gall bladder attacks, and so on. You name it and the spice man has a cure. Moreover, he also carries cures for sweating, for over-heated blood, for surges, and other interesting and undefinable complaints. When I asked just exactly what was a surge, the reply was a lugubrious shake of the head and a deep sigh. He most certainly was not telling! The impression he gave was that such a complaint was far too intimate and tragic to discuss with a layman.

## TOASTED FLOUR

This is used to a considerable extent in Spanish cooking as a thickener for soups, stews, and sauces. It is produced by putting a thin layer of flour on a piece of aluminum foil and browning it in the oven for about ten minutes at a temperature of 350°F (180°C). The toasting process cooks the flour, thus eliminating the raw flavor and producing an excellent nonfat thickener. Its inclusion in a dish imparts a slightly nutty flavor. Once again, this product may be purchased in most stores.

## BREADCRUMBS

Both toasted and plain breadcrumbs also play an important part as a thickening agent and are used in almost every type of savory dish. Toasting gives a similar nutty flavor as does toasted flour, the main difference being that the absorption quality of breadcrumbs is much greater. As another change of flavor and texture, seasoned breadcrumbs may be used. For example, one simple idea when thickening sauces containing chicken is to mix in a blender one ounce (30 g) of poultry stuffing with four ounces (120 g) of fine breadcrumbs.

## TOASTED ALMONDS

Almonds are used in soups, sauces, and as an accompaniment to meats and fish. All almonds should be blanched before further treatment, and this is done by plunging them into boiling water, allowing them to remain until the water has cooled sufficiently for them to be taken out with the fingers. The loose skin may then be easily slipped off with the finger and thumb.

To toast blanched almonds, place them on a baking tray in a preheated oven at 350°F (180°C) until browned. Should salted almonds be required (for tapas, for example), sprinkle salt over the nuts as they come from the oven.

## SAUSAGES

There are, of course, dozens of different types of sausage produced in Spain. Some are used as a major part of a dish; such as *butifara catalonia*, others are used purely as a flavoring agent, such as *chorizos*.

*Chorizo* is the generic name for literally dozens of savory sausages, either smoked or unsmoked, but all containing pork and pimiento. Each region has a slightly different recipe made by adding extra ingredients such as juniper berries, pig liver, etc.

*Butifara catalonia* is made from fat pork, salt, pepper, cloves, cinnamon, nutmeg, and white wine.

*Butifara negra* is similar to butifara catalonia, with the addition of pig' blood and chopped mint.

*Lomo embuchado* is a smoked whole loin of pork in a casing which may be cut into slices and fried or eaten cold.

*Longanzia* is a large sausage containing lean pork, garlic, marjoram, powdered pimiento, salt, and pepper.

*Longanzia en manteca* is similar to longanzia; this type has been preserved in lard.

*Morcilla negra*, blood sausage, similar to the French *boudin noir*, is best when produced in Asturias. It is made from pork, garlic, and spices, but the main ingredient is pig's blood.

*Morcilla blanca* has chicken, fat bacon, hardboiled eggs, parsley, and seasoning as ingredients.

*Mortadella*, originally an Italian sausage, is now produced in Spain. It contains lean pork, spices, seasonings, brown sugar, saltpeter, and aguadente.

*Salami* is similar to the French and Italian versions although the flavor varies greatly from area to area. If you enjoy salami, ask to taste a sample before buying.

*Salchichas* is the generic name for small pork sausages made from pork, lamb, or veal and sometimes flavored with nutmeg and/or rum.

*Salchichon* is a large variety of sausage made from filet of pork, a little bacon fat, and pepper, then lightly smoked.

*Salchicas aragonesas* are made from lean pork, diced pork fat, pimiento, raisins, and spices.

*Sobresada* is a sausage of finely ground pork (like a pâté) and a high proportion of pimiento.

*Botillo con repello* is a highly seasoned pork sausage with a small proportion of crushed pork bone included.

*Morcilla de mi pueblo* is a black sausage containing minced pine kernels.

## CHEESES

Although a wide variety of foreign cheeses are available in Spain, the number of domestic varieties is limited. This is because many of the areas and provinces do not have the pastures available to feed the flocks of cows, sheep, and goats that are required to produce a good variety of cheeses. However, those that are home-produced have character and most of them have more than a little bite. Many are the equivalent to a matured cheddar or a Cheshire.

The main varieties are:

*Asturias* is a strong fermented cheese with a very sharp flavor.

*Bola* is similar to the Dutch Edam in style and flavor.

*Burgos*, a soft cheese with a creamy texture, is produced in the town of that name.

*Cabrales*, made from goat's milk (sometimes from cow's milk), is similar to Roquefort.

*Cebreto* is another variety of veined cheese with a good, creamy texture and a pale yellow rind.

*Cincho* is a hard cheese made from ewe's milk.

*Manchego*, a hard cheese made from ewe's milk and made in La Mancha, has a sharp flavor and may be white or pale yellow.

*Mancha pok* is a hard cheese made from cow's milk with a less sharp flavor, and is more like a mild cheddar.

*Perilla* is a firm but rather bland cheese made from cow's milk.

*Queso* is the Spanish name for cheese. (For example: *queso de cabra*, made from goat's milk; *queso de oveja*, made from ewe's milk; *queso del pais*, locally made cheese; *queso fresco*, curd cheese.)

*Requeson* is a soft curd cheese with a mild flavor made in Catalonia.

*Roncal*, a close-grained, hard cheese, has a piquant flavor and is made from ewe's milk.

*San Simon* is similar to perilla in consistency and flavor.

*Tertilla*, made either from sheep's or goat's milk, is soft and creamy with a rather mild flavor.

*Teta* is a firm, bland cheese made from cow's milk.

*Ulloa*, a soft cheese made in Galicia, has a strong resemblance to Camembert.

*Villalon*, sharp cheese made from ewe's milk, is usually rather salty.


## HOW TO USE THE RECIPES

Now that you have read about ingredients common to Spanish cuisine, here are some guidelines for following the Spanish recipes given in this book.

1. Read through the entire recipe before commencing and be sure you have all the necessary ingredients and utensils.

2. The ingredients are listed in the order in which they will be required and all instructions are in sequence.

3. All ingredients mentioned in the recipes are in a cleaned or preprepared state: for example, onions and garlic are peeled; meat is trimmed of excess fat and gristle.

4. Prepreparation techniques are given for each item in the relevant section.

5. The United States has chosen to adopt the International Metric system and so, where applicable, alternative weights and measurements on this scale have been shown in parentheses. Keep in mind that cooking is not an exact science and one should not always be totally precise over anything except perhaps in some baking recipes. What is more, when converting American weights and measures to metric, it is impossible to be entirely accurate and practical at the same time. So the metric weights and measures have been rounded off to a practical alternative. Should you wish to convert tablespoons (15mL) into grams, a list of the major items used in this book is shown on page 51. Finally, the golden rule is never to mix the two types of measurement. Use either American *or* metric throughout any one recipe.

6. When salt is mentioned in a recipe, it refers to ordinary table salt, although garlic salt may be substituted if preferred. Pepper should be freshly ground black pepper. Although in some cases specific amounts of these two seasonings are given, this is meant as a guide, rather than a quantity to be blindly followed. So as in all things, use your own discretion.

# Tapas *and* Entremeses

5

# 5  *TAPAS* AND *ENTREMESES*

Visitors to Spain have always been enchanted by the custom of serving *tapas* (appetizers) with the prelunch or predinner drinks. Residents, too, enjoy the custom and regard it as yet another good reason for living in Spain. Seville is noted for the excellent display of tapas served in bars and *tascas* (taverns) throughout the city. In Madrid, also, they make a great thing of this premeal snack. In some bars, like Chicote's in Avenida Jose Antonio, one does not only see a bar that provides a truly wondrous selection of these foods, but is fascinating for the thousands of rare wine bottles displayed around the walls.

"Tapa-time" is when the lethargy, which is Spain's first gift to the visitor, descends. It is also the time when some of the characteristic events take place each day that give Spain its individuality. At noon or soon after, while one is sitting under a shady tree away from the hot sun, happily munching the selection of tapas that the waiter has brought and sipping a cool, dry Sherry, an aperitivo, or even a chilled glass of beer, you may well be approached by begging gypsy children. Of ages from about four years up to six or seven, they will come up to you with completely blank faces, without a smile or any expression at all. They will tug on your sleeve, extend their hand, and sometimes mutter *"peseta."* If you ignore them or just shake your head, they will remain, hand outstretched, and looking around them, without a care in the world.

They know quite well that visitors especially tend to be embarrassed by a dirty, scruffy child holding out a hand for the equivalent of ten cents, while they are enjoying their tapas and a drink. If one wishes to get rid of these beggars, one just says *"virse"* (go away). The Spaniards, and especially the gypsies, see nothing wrong in begging. They believe that it gives the donor the opportunity to show Christian charity, and so the child beggar confers upon the donor just as great a favor as one does to them by giving money.

As a change of pace, the bootblacks circulate continually looking for customers. The Spaniard regards spotless footwear as an indication to the rest of the world that he is not engaged in hard or dirty work. To call a Spaniard a working man is a deadly insult.

During the tapa session before dinner, one will be treated to music by a peripatetic guitarist who usually has more enthusiasm than musical skill. If one is lucky, a troupe of students from the local university dressed in medieval costume will serenade your table with guitar, mandolin, and harmonious voices. They usually collect more for their efforts than others. Anyhow, the whole period is very relaxing.

Of course, tapas are obtainable in every city, town, and village in Spain. Some are very simple (*tapas naturales*) and consist of a few olives, toasted almonds, etc.; others may produce *especialidades de la casa*, that is house specialties, such as *empanditas* (small savory patties containing meat, fish, or vegetables and served hot) or perhaps deep-fried squares of marinated fish.

Although the word tapa means top, and these snack dishes were originally served only on top of the counter, nowadays they are presented in small oval or kidney-shaped dishes. The skill in their choice and presentation is to include as much color and variety of shape and texture as possible. Both cold and hot items should be included. The cold are eaten first, then the hot tapas are brought to the table.

## A SHORT LIST OF *TAPAS NATURALES*

*Lettuce hearts* are served with an oil and lemon dressing or a plain or garlic-flavored mayonnaise.

*Artichoke hearts* are prepared with a plain or garlic dressing.

*Blanched pimiento* in vinaigrette or a piquant sauce.

*Canned sardine*, in oil, is garnished with rings of raw, sweet onion.

*Shrimp* are grilled and seasoned with salt and lemon juice.

*Oysters* are on half-shell.

*Mussels* are on half-shell with garlic and lemon dressing.

*Tunafish* is in olive oil.

*Pickled tunafish* is served with sliced onion and garlic.

*Pickled cucumbers* are sliced and served with diced ham.

## Olives

Black or green olives may be served plain or stuffed with garlic, pimiento, anchovy, or almonds. Often raw olives are put in brine with herbs added, and these are a change from the more common method of pickling. Incidentally, when the last of the olives has been used from the jar, don't throw the brine and herb liquor away. Save it to season fillings for stuffed eggs or add a little to scrambled eggs.

TO PIT OLIVES.   Place olives on a paper towel and roll gently with a rolling pin to loosen the pit. Press the olive with the heel of your hand and the pit will pop out.

　　　　　With typical frugality, Spanish villagers use the pits of olives for fuel. In some of the small towns and villages one will see a table fitted with a brazier underneath, and heavy chenille or velour curtains around the edge. These may be tightly drawn around the legs so that, no matter how the rest of the body freezes in winter, the legs and feet are in their own oven. This brazier is fueled with pulverized olive pits!

## Toasted Almonds

There are three classic methods of toasting almonds, each giving a different flavor to the finished article and each being so very much better than those obtainable even from the best supplier.

*Method 1:* The almond kernels are placed in a preheated oven at 275°F (170°C) for 40 minutes until the nuts are dark brown. The almonds are done when the skin slips off easily.

*Method 2:* Crack the almonds and blanch them in boiling water to remove the brown skin. Dry well on a towel then bake in the oven as for Method 1.

*Method 3:* The almond in its shell is put in the oven and baked for about 40 minutes. Test one nut after baking for 30 minutes to determine if the batch is sufficiently cooked.

SALTED ALMONDS.   These may be made by blanching the nuts first, then frying them in moderately hot oil to allow the almonds to cook without burning. They are then drained and dried on paper towels, then salt is shaken over the batch. They may be stored for a long period in an airtight glass jar. A variation to the above may be made by adding a little cumin powder, curry powder, or crushed coriander seed to the salt.

## HOUSE SPECIALTIES

### *Empanditas* (Em-pan-dee-tass)

These dainty little patties are quickly and easily made with the paste recipe given here, and may be stuffed with a variety of savory fillings. The practice in Spain is to cut the pastry into various shapes—round, triangular, square, oblong—to indicate the different fillings (see drawing, opposite page).

These fillings are usually made from whatever is left over in the kitchen, plus a little imagination. You will need one mixing of pastry to produce 20 to 24 patties and about 1¼ lbs (620 g) of filling, using a teaspoon for each patty. Further, you will need to add a binding agent, such as a little cream, sauce, mayonnaise, or dry white wine so that the filling may be moist and remain so after cooking.

## *Paste for Empanditas*

2½ cups (600 mL) flour
½ tsp. (1 × 2 mL spoon) salt
1¼ cups (300 mL) shortening
7 Tbsp. (7 × 15 mL spoon) ice water
   (approximately)

1. Sift the flour and salt together in a bowl.
2. Cut the shortening into small pieces and put them in the flour. Work shortening into flour until the mixture reaches the consistency of breadcrumbs.
3. Add water gradually, so as not to overmoisten. Gather paste into a ball. Divide into two pieces.
4. Roll out each piece to approximately 9 inches (22.5 cm) square.
5. Trim and cut paste into desired shape.
6. Moisten edges with beaten egg, fold, and bake in preheated oven at 375°F (190°C).

When making empanditas, use these suggested fillings:

1. Ground, cooked chicken with minced celery, minced olives, and coffee cream to bind.
2. Ground, cooked ham with sweet pickle and minced raw onion, and a little prepared mustard to bind.
3. Flaked, cooked fish and lemon juice with a pinch of chopped mint, and a very little cream to bind.
4. Cream cheese with chopped, stuffed olives and chopped nuts.
5. Cream cheese, chopped pineapple, and chopped nuts.

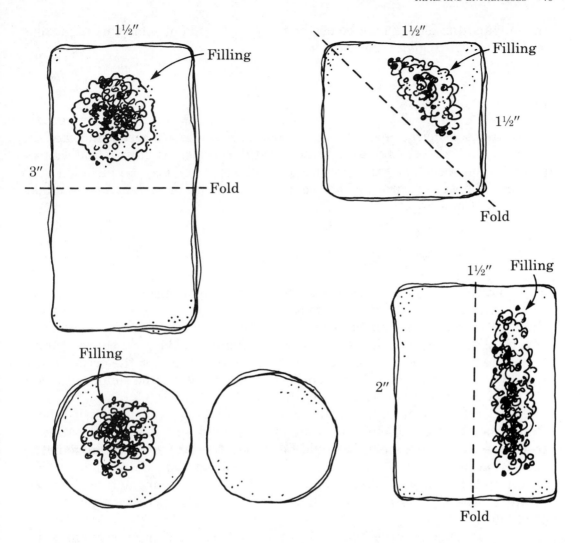

6. Chopped hard-boiled egg with chopped ham and minced onion, moistened with mayonnaise.

## *Tartaletas*

Open-faced tartlets or barquettes are even more versatile than the savory patties, for the base may be made from the same recipe given before. The tarts may be made beforehand and cold filling added when required. Any of the empanditas fillings may be used with the addition of some sort of garnish on top of each to give a good finish.

## *Palitos*

These are toothpicks upon which various cold foods are stuck and may be comprised of almost any colorful and tasty morsels. Anything that can be threaded on a cocktail stick and used as an appetizer may be included such as ham, cheese, chorizo, pickled vegetables, mushrooms, salt fish, seafood, and cooked molluscs.

## STARTERS AND HORS D'OEUVRE *(ENTREMESES)*

Your choice of menu for an occasion at home can make or break your reputation as an entertainer. Each gastronomic step from the premeal drink to the last sip of coffee must be planned beforehand, first as single items, then as parts of a total effect. You can see that the importance of the first course cannot be overlooked, for it must be just right to set the stage for the occasion and equally right for the menu it precedes. You may want it to be simple and even if it is, it can nevertheless be glamorous.

When planning a starter, consider what type of food will follow. Remember that each course on your menu should lead easily and naturally to the next. For example, it would be wrong to serve oysters immediately before sausages and white beans. The two courses just do not match. Far better to serve, say, a simple soup which is unpretentious and more appropriate to the dish it precedes. Save the oysters for a more sophisticated occasion.

Be sure that the items you serve are varied and interesting and give the menu sufficient color. Let each course be individually colorful, and allow the whole menu to provide contrast. For example, don't start with asparagus soup and follow with a casserole of chicken served with boiled potatoes and cauliflower: the colors are too much alike. And a meal where one basic color predominates—such as pâté, broiled steak, and chocolate ice cream to follow— even *sounds* as dreary as it looks. So keep the colors bright and as different as good taste and good sense allow.

When color monotony becomes unavoidable, give the meal a lift with a vivid garnish. Parsley and lemon may be commonplace but are always useful, as is a garnish of tomato on appropriate dishes. But accompaniments to the main item also can be chosen for contrast. Spanish cooks very often use these combinations: green peas with chopped red peppers added to rice; baked tomatoes stuffed with sweet corn; chopped red peppers and chives sprinkled over potatoes; sliced, fried eggplant still in its skin; zucchini, chopped tomatoes, and wafer-thin slices of onion as a garnish to broiled fish or meat.

The well-balanced meal provides a balanced progression of flavors from the starter, which is designed to whet the appetite, to a main course to be eaten with zest, to a dessert that clears and refreshes the palate. If more than three courses are served, the problem becomes even more tricky, but the principle still applies. Don't kill the palate or the appetite with heavy flavors or huge portions.

Contrasts of flavor are essential for adding zest and piquancy, so you should never let one ingredient dominate. Do not, for example, serve mushroom soup followed by steak with mushrooms (or indeed *any* dish containing mushrooms). Do not serve a meat-flavored soup before a meat course. Neither is it a good idea to start with a strongly flavored soup or a game pâté and follow with a delicate main course, such as grilled sole. And if you do decide to serve a piquant sauce with any dish, be sure the flavor does not overpower the main item.

Just as we serve fried croutons with consomme to provide a contrasting texture to the soup, so must we contrast interesting textures throughout the meal. Avoid serving a soup, then a stew or casserole (although this is done in parts of Spain, especially in the villages), and then a puree of fruit. All these courses are wet in texture and offer no variety. If the main dish is smooth, accompany it with vegetables that are crisp and firm. If two of your courses are firm, say, avocado pear to start and a praline ice cream for dessert, choose a main dish that is soft in texture.

Ideally, appetizers or starters should not be difficult for the single-handed host or hostess to prepare or serve but, at the same time, should give the guests an interesting talking point. So as a start, here are four simple bases and some easy ways to prepare and serve each.

## Avocado Pear or *Aguacate* (Awa-cat-ay)

It was only fairly recently, certainly within the last fifteen years, that avocado pears became known in Spain. Now both the smooth green and the dark rough-skinned varieties are grown extensively. Because of their fairly recent introduction into Spanish cuisine, there are not too many original recipes to be found. However, local chefs have taken traditional ideas from other countries and adapted them to national tastes. So while the following ideas may not be entirely Spanish or entirely ethnic in origin, they are all very good indeed.

Avocado pears make an ideal base as a starter. They are very high in vitamin content, and the bland but distinctive flavor makes them very adaptable for a number of different treatments. To prepare, slice the pear lengthwise, then give a slight twist to separate the halves. Remove the large stone. Each half is sufficient for one person.

The exposed flesh changes color quite quickly, so if you intend to keep them in the cut condition for more than an hour or two, sprinkle the flesh with a citrus juice to stop any discoloration. Pears should be eaten when ripe, and this can be ascertained by pressing the top gently with a finger. Should the flesh feel soft, the pear should be ready for immediate eating. However, it is usually a better idea to purchase them while still hard and mature them at home. This may be done by putting the pears in a thick paper bag and keeping them at room temperature. Test each day for ripeness and use when the flesh is soft.

The most common way to serve avocado pears, even in Spain, is with an oil and lemon juice dressing or with a filling of shrimp in mayonnaise. But for a change, try these interesting variations. Each recipe serves four people.

## Aguacate y Consomé

(Awa-cat-ay e Kon-som-ay)
Avocado with jellied consomme

Thoroughly chill a can of beef consomme (*consome de buey*) so that it sets to a light jelly. Just before serving, remove from can and chop jelly into small cubes, then pile into serving dishes and top with peeled and sliced avocado.

## Aguacate con Pollo

(Awa-cat-ay kon Poll-yo)
Avocado with chicken

4 ozs chopped chicken meat
2 Tbsp. (2 × 15 mL spoon) mayonnaise
3 Tbsp. (3 × 15 mL spoon) finely
   chopped celery
1 Tbsp. (1 × 15 mL spoon) chopped
   green pepper
½ tomato, skinned, seeded, and
   chopped
salt and pepper

1. Combine all ingredients and adjust seasoning if necessary.
2. Split avocados lengthwise, remove stone, and fill cavities with the chicken mixture. Garnish with sprigs of celery leaves.

## Aguacate con Frutas

(Awa-cat-ay kon Froo-tas)
Avocado with fresh fruit

Fill each pear half with a few fresh strawberries and several black and green grapes.

## Ensalada Aguacate

(En-sal-ar-da Awa-cat-ay)
Avocado with salad

Combine small cubes of fresh pineapple with larger pieces of avocado pear. Sprinkle a little lemon juice over and chill. Serve with a mixture of half whipping cream and half mayonnaise.

# *Aguacate en Parilla*

(Awa-cat-ay n Par-ill-ya)
Grilled avocado

Scoop the flesh from 2 ripe avocados, mash with some chopped shrimp and a little whipping cream. Replace mixture in shells, sprinkle with breadcrumbs, dot with butter, and put under a preheated grill until the crumbs are golden.

## Tomatoes

One of the most neglected starter bases is the tomato, and in Spain, where the tomatoes are absolutely excellent, they should be used as often as possible. If using medium to large tomatoes, they should be skinned (see index for instructions); if small, the skin may be left on.

*Tomates Rellenos* is the name for Stuffed tomatoes, and here are a few ideas for the stuffing:

1. Mix 4 ozs of curd cheese or cottage cheese with 2 Tbsp. (2 × 15 mL spoon) mayonnaise and 2 ozs (60 g) chopped walnuts. Blend together until smooth and fill the tomatoes.

2. Combine 2 sieved hard-boiled eggs with 2 Tbsp. (2 × 15 mL spoon) mayonnaise, 2 chopped anchovies, and 2 tsp. (2 × 5 mL spoon) anchovy paste. Mix together and fill tomato shells.

3. Mix together 2 ozs (60 g) cooked green peas with 2 ozs (60 g) chopped cooked ham and a little mayonnaise. Add 1 Tbsp. (1 × 15 mL spoon) grated hard cheese. Mix thoroughly and fill tomato shells.

4. Peel 3 ozs (90 g) cucumber and chop it finely. Mix with one small carton of plain yogurt, a little salt and pepper, and lemon juice to taste. Fill shells with this mixture.

5. Mix 6 ozs (180 g) peeled shrimp with 3 Tbsp. (3 × 15 mL spoon) mayonnaise and a lick of mustard. Fill tomato shells.

## Eggs

The hard-boiled egg presents a paradox: at the same time it is both an ordinary part of the diet and a food for festive occasions. The egg may be eaten any day of the week, yet on special occasions, it becomes an attraction.

Stuffed eggs, *Huevos Rellenos*, make easy-to-prepare but attractive starters. They may be served simply with a sardine stuffing or a tuna mayonnaise filling or given a party look with Danish or Swedish caviar. The usual filling for stuffed eggs is most often composed of the mashed yolks with the preferred seasoning and additives. For a lavish effect, pile the fillings high in the white, and for decorative effect, use a piping tube.

Before filling, eggs may be sliced in two ways:

1. Remove shells after cooking and cut the eggs in half lengthwise, in which case the half eggs will look a little like small boats.

2. Cut off the narrow end and take a slice off the rounded end, then halve the eggs crosswise, so the two halves will stand upright. Carefully squeeze the yolk out from the white, without splitting the white.

Here are a few ideas for stuffing eggs:

1. Mash the yolks of four hard-boiled eggs and combine with 3 tsp. (3 × 5 mL spoon) chopped chives, 2 Tbsp. (2 × 15 mL spoon) mayonnaise, a dash of mustard, and salt and pepper to taste. Fill the whites generously and sprinkle lightly with paprika. Serve on a lettuce leaf.

2. Mash the yolks of four hard-boiled eggs and mix with the contents of a small can of sardines in olive oil that has been drained. Add a little prepared mustard, mayonnaise, grated lemon rind, and a squeeze of lemon juice. A little minced onion is good too. Blend thoroughly, add salt and pepper to taste, then fill the whites and garnish with a sprig of parsley and a twist of lemon.

3. Combine the yolks of the four eggs with 4 ozs (120 g) crabmeat, 2 Tbsp. (2 × 15 mL spoon) mayonnaise, a dash of prepared mustard, a little minced onion, and salt and pepper to taste. Fill the whites and garnish with a strip of blanched pimiento on each half. Serve each on a single lettuce leaf.

## Artichokes

Only French artichokes are obtainable in Spain and are most popular served as a vegetable. However, stuffed artichokes (*Alcachofas Rellenas*) are served in a number of good restaurants. I will give the basic procedure needed to trim, cook, and prepare the artichoke to be ready for stuffing and then add a few suggested fillings.

**BASIC PREPARATION OF ARTICHOKES.**    In addition to the artichokes, you will need 2 quarters of lemon and a large pan of salted water.

1. Cut the stems off the artichokes.

2. Bring the water to boiling point, add the lemon then the artichokes, and cook uncovered for about 25 minutes (until the leaves from the center come away easily).

3. Remove and cool, then turn upside down to drain.

4. When cool, part the outer leaves, and pull the center leaves so that the outer leaves remain intact and the artichoke resembles the petals of a flower.

5. With a teaspoon, scrape the heart which lies at the base of the artichoke and remove the choke (the thistle-like growth in the center of the heart).

6. Trim the bottom of the artichoke, so that it will sit easily on a dish.

You now have your hollow artichoke, sitting flat, and your stuffing may then be made and inserted.

**STUFFINGS FOR ARTICHOKES.**    Use these fillings to stuff the prepared artichokes.

## Egg and Anchovy Stuffing

Beat 4 large eggs in a bowl with a little pepper. Set aside. Wash 4 anchovy fillets in cold water and pat dry. Mash the anchovy to a paste. Place artichokes in a colander over a pan of hot water, cover with foil, and reheat. Just before serving, melt about 1 oz (30 g) butter in a saucepan and dissolve the anchovy paste. Add the beaten eggs and stir while they cook. When creamy, add 1 oz (30 g) butter, check the seasoning, then spoon the mixture into the warm artichokes.

## Pork and Bacon Stuffing

¼ lb (120 g) minced pork fillet
2 ozs (60 g) finely chopped smoked
    bacon

1 small onion, finely chopped
1 clove garlic, finely chopped
1 sprig of parsley, chopped
oil for frying
1 small tomato, peeled, seeded, and
    finely chopped
pinch of nutmeg

1. Prepare artichokes as explained in the preparation instructions. Keep hot.

2. In the hot oil, fry the pork and bacon for a few minutes. Add the onion, garlic, and tomato. Cook till soft and the meat is done.

3. Add nutmeg and parsley and cook for another minute. (If the mixture is too dry, moisten with a little dry white wine.)

4. Fill artichokes with mixture and serve at once.

## Asparagus

A considerable amount of wild asparagus is sold in Spain and one finds that often the stalks are very mixed: some young and tender, others large and woody. It is best to avoid this type and buy the cultivated asparagus. Here is one good recipe that I like.

## Espárragos con Nuezes

(Es-pah-rah-go kon Nwaythes)
Asparagus with walnut butter

1 lb (480 g) fresh asparagus
2 Tbsp. (2 × 15 mL spoon) butter
2 ozs (60 g) chopped walnut meat

1. Scrape the sides of asparagus to remove the spurs and scales, then cut off thick, tough ends.

2. Boil in slightly salted water until just tender.
3. Heat butter in a pan until it turns slightly golden, add walnut meat, and cook over a very gentle heat for another minute.
4. Pour over asparagus and serve.

## Fresh Figs

The expensive, dark, and very large figs called *Brevas* come onto the market in June. Wait for another five or six weeks and the smaller, brownish-purple variety are cheap and plentiful. There are two nice methods of serving figs as a starter. The first is to peel them, then chill for about 1 hour and serve them with slices of the famous Serrano ham. Or you may care for *Higos Rellenos*.

## Higos Rellenos

(Ig-os Rell-ay-nos)
Stuffed fresh figs

12 ripe, fresh figs
5 ozs (150 g) curd cheese or cream cheese
2 Tbsp. (2 × 15 mL spoon) chopped almonds

1. Cut the tops off the figs and make a pocket in each.
2. Cream the cheese and mix in the nuts.
3. With a teaspoon, fill each fig with the mixture.

## Other Entremeses

## *Pimentos Fritos*

(Pee-men-toss Free-tos)
Fried green peppers

The small green peppers are the ideal
size for this Spanish specialty.

Wash and dry several small green
peppers, but leave the stem attached to
the top. Cut slits in the bottom end and
sprinkle a little salt inside each. Fry
them in hot oil in a skillet. Serve hot.
Hold the stem and eat them whole.

## *Champiñones au Gratin*

(Sham-p-ni-ones o Gra-tan)
Mushrooms au gratin
serves 4

12 ozs whole mushrooms (360 g)
1 Tbsp. (1 × 15 mL spoon)
    breadcrumbs
1 large sprig of parsley, finely chopped
2 Tbsp. (2 × 15 mL spoon) grated
    cheese
salt and pepper
1 Tbsp. (1 × 15 mL spoon) olive oil
1 glass (1½ dcL) dry white wine
butter for greasing dish

1. Wash the mushrooms, and remove
and chop the stems.
2. Mix stems with the breadcrumbs,
parsley, and cheese.
3. Lay mushrooms, heads down, in a
buttered baking dish and cover with the
crumb/parsley mixture. Sprinkle well
with salt and pepper, then with the
olive oil.
4. Preheat oven to 350°F (180°C).
5. Pour wine in baking dish and cook in
oven for about 20 minutes.

## *Gambas a la Plancha*

(Gam-bass a la Plan-sha)
Broiled shrimp

Allow about ½ lb (250 g) of large
shrimp per person. Wash in cold water
but do not remove the shells. Sprinkle
with salt, lemon juice, a dash of pepper,
and a little olive oil. Preheat broiler.
Prepare ½ cup (120 mL) cold water and
mix a little lemon juice and salt with
the water. Place prepared shrimp on
broiler rack and put under the heat.
Drizzle this mixture over the shrimp
from time to time as the shrimp are
cooking. The fish will be ready when
the shells turn bright orange, usually
about 3 minutes cooking on each side.

## *Gambas al Ajillo*

(Gam-bass al A-hill-yo)
Shrimp in garlic sauce

Again allow about ½ lb (250 g) of
shrimp per person. Place the washed,
peeled, and deveined shrimp in
individual casseroles and sprinkle with a
little finely chopped garlic and a very
small quantity of hot chili powder. Heat
about 1 Tbsp. (1 × 15 mL spoon) olive
oil per portion and pour over the
shrimp and cook for a few minutes over
the fire.

## *Gambas del Casa*

(Gam-bass del Ka-sa)
Shrimp of the house

¾ lb (360 g) shrimp
salt and pepper
pinch nutmeg
¼ cup (60 mL) chicken stock
½ cup (120 g) butter
4 whole cloves of garlic, crushed
1 cup (160 g) dry breadcrumbs
2 Tbsp. (2 × 15 mL spoon) chopped
    parsley

1. Heat oven to 400°F (200°C).
2. Shell and remove black vein from shrimp.
3. Divide shelled shrimp into 4 portions and place into individual casseroles or ramekin dishes.
4. Add nutmeg and chicken stock and pour over shrimp.
5. Heat the butter in a pan and saute the garlic until brown. Remove the garlic and discard.
6. Mix breadcrumbs and parsley with the butter and spoon the mixture over the shrimp.
7. Bake for about 12 minutes. Do not overcook.

# Ostras al Horno con Almendras

(Os-tras al Orno kon Al-men-dras)
Baked oysters with almonds

½ cup (120 mL) butter
4 Tbsp. (4 × 15 mL spoon) ground
    blanched almonds
1 clove garlic, crushed
3 Tbsp. (3 × 15 mL spoon) brandy
salt and pepper
1 Tbsp. (1 × 15 mL spoon)
    breadcrumbs
24 oysters on the half-shell

1. Cream together the butter and ground almonds, blend in the garlic, brandy, salt and pepper, and breadcrumbs.
2. Preheat oven to 450°F (230°C).
3. Cover each of the oysters with some of the mixture and bake for about 5 minutes.

# Pastel de Conejo

(Pas-tel day Kon-ay-ho)
Rabbit pâté

This is quite an outstanding recipe for a pâté and well worth the trouble to prepare.

## MARINADE

2 onions, chopped
3 wine glasses or 15 fl ozs (3 × 1½ dcL)
    dry white wine
large pinch oregano and dried basil
2 bay leaves

1 skinned rabbit about 4½ lbs (2 Kg)
about 1 lb (500 g) *tocino* or belly pork
6 ozs (180 g) lean veal, ground
6 ozs (180 g) lean pork, ground
3 Tbsp. (3 × 15 mL spoon) Sherry
1 tsp. (1 × 5 mL spoon) garlic salt
black pepper (essential)
1 Tbsp. (1 × 15 mL spoon) chopped
    parsley
1 Tbsp. (1 × 15 mL spoon) thyme

1. With a sharp knife cut along the spine of the rabbit from head to tail and continuing along the thighs and down to the leg, separating the meat from the bones. Go to the front of the rabbit and take meat from the front legs.
2. Dice all the meat and put in a large bowl with the marinade. Put in refrigerator for 24 hours.
3. When ready to prepare the pâté, preheat oven to 375°F (190°C).
4. Take half the tocino and cut it into thin strips; then with this, line the pâté mold or ovenproof casserole.
5. Remove the diced rabbit from marinade and drain. Cut the remaining tocino into *very* small dice and mix with the rabbit, veal, pork, Sherry, and seasonings.

6.  Fill the mold with this mixture then cover with the remaining strips of tocino.

7.  Place mold in a roasting pan with 2 in (5 cms) water and bake in oven for 1¾ to 2 hours.

8.  Allow to cool completely, then refrigerate.

## Queso Frit

(Kay-tho Frit)
Fried cheese

This is served at the Meson del Conde Restaurant in Marbella. It is quite unusual and very, very good.

Dip wedges of firm Brie cheese in beaten egg seasoned with a little salt and pepper, then drop into breadcrumbs. Then deep-fry the pieces in hot oil for about 1 minute until the crumbs are golden.

# 6

# 6  SOUPS

$S$opa (soup) is a basic Spanish food and in towns and villages throughout the country is seen on the table almost every day. Vegetable soups predominate, partly because such a wide variety is available and, of course, because vegetable soups are most economical. Like the French, the Spanish cook is thrifty and little food is thrown away, be it meat trimmings, bones, leftover pasta, or rice.

When one thinks of Spanish soups, one's mind usually leaps to *gazpacho*, the peasant soup that has become known internationally. Originally made only with vinegar, water, garlic, onions, and bread, gazpacho was supposed to have originated from the *posca* (the sponge of vinegar and water) carried by Roman legionnaires during their campaigns. This also was the drink that the soldiers gave to Christ on the Cross, and although generally regarded as a cruel joke, was indeed the only refreshment they had to offer. Thousands of retired Roman soldiers settled in Spain and were to a large extent responsible for colonizing much of the country.

## GAZPACHO

There are now as many recipes for gazpacho as for paella and cocido, and the recipe will differ depending on the area from which one hails. But in *all* recipes four ingredients appear without fail: tomatoes, garlic, olive oil, and vinegar.

The peasant-style gazpacho always contains breadcrumbs; the restaurant version seldom does. In Andalucia they serve side dishes of finely diced hard-boiled egg, cucumber, tomato, fried croutons, onion, green peppers, and sometimes chive. A spoonful of each (or all) is sprinkled over the soup as a floating garnish.

This is not the habit elsewhere. Other recipes call for the tomatoes to be mashed with the oil, vinegar, water, and garlic while the other ingredients are finely chopped and added to the mixture to give the soup a fresh, crisp quality. Needless to say, while the textures may be different the flavors tend to be somewhat similar. Andalucia and Extremadura tend to specialize in gazpacho and these two different recipes will illustrate the variations possible in a soup called by the same name!

## Gazpacho Andaluz

(Gath-pash-o An-da-luth)
Andalucian gazpacho
serves 4

2 slices white bread with crusts
    removed
2 cloves garlic
2 green peppers, seeded and chopped
3 ripe tomatoes, chopped
3 Tbsp. (3 × 15 mL spoon) olive oil
4 cups (1 liter) ice water
2 Tbsp. (2 × 15 mL spoon) wine
    vinegar
salt and pepper to taste

GARNISH

hard-boiled egg
cucumber
tomato
fried croutons
onion
green pepper
chive

1. Prepare garnish. The items are served in small dishes and guests serve themselves as desired.

2. Soak the bread in cold water, then squeeze almost dry.

3. In a mortar, crush the garlic and peppers together with a little salt, then add the chopped tomatoes and squeezed bread. Mix well.

4. Blend in the olive oil and when this is absorbed, add one cup of ice water.

5. Strain the mixture through a sieve into a deep bowl and with the back of a wooden spoon, force as much of the solids through the mesh as possible.

6. Add vinegar and the rest of the water, season to taste, and serve at once with the garnish.

*Note: If you have a blender you may mix all the ingredients together at the same time (except the water) and blend on low speed for a few seconds. Then sieve as described in Step 5. Add water, season, and serve.*

## Gazpacho Extremaduro

(Gath-pash-o Eth-tray-ma-duro)
Gazpacho from Extremadura

2 slices white bread with crusts
    removed
2 cloves garlic
1 onion
1 green pepper, seeded and chopped
¼ tsp. (1 × 1 mL spoon) cumin seed
salt and pepper
1 egg, lightly beaten
4 Tbsp. (4 × 15 mL spoon) olive oil
3 Tbsp. (3 × 15 mL spoon) white wine
    vinegar
4 cups (1 liter) ice water

1. Soak bread in water and squeeze almost dry.

2. In a mortar, crush the garlic, onion, green pepper, and cumin seed with a little salt.

3. Add the squeezed bread and blend in the beaten egg.

4. Gradually add olive oil, stirring all the time and when absorbed, strain the mixture into a deep bowl, forcing as much of the solids as possible through the mesh.

5. Stir in the ice water and serve very cold.

*Note: If using a blender, proceed exactly as for previous recipe. A garnish is NOT served with this recipe.*

## Ajo Blanco con Uvas

(A-ho Blan-ko kon Oo-vass)
Malagueñan gazpacho
serves 4

The gazpacho which originated from Malaga is not a true version, for it does not contain tomatoes. Yet it is an interesting variation and a delicious cold soup for lunch on a hot Andalucian summer day. It may almost be described as an iced drink with almonds and grapes.

3 slices of white bread with crusts
    removed
white wine vinegar
6 ozs (180 g) blanched almonds
2 cloves garlic
1 small onion
½ cup (120 mL) olive oil
24 peeled, seeded white grapes
4 cups (1 liter approx.) ice water

1. Soak the bread in vinegar and squeeze almost dry.
2. In a mortar, pound the almonds to a fine paste, add garlic and onion and continue pounding until smooth.
3. Add the bread, then gradually pour in the olive oil and mix thoroughly.
4. Put the mixture through a sieve into a deep bowl, and with the back of a wooden spoon force as much of the solids through the mesh as possible.
5. Peel and seed the grapes.
6. Pour the ice water into the soup mixture, stir to amalgamate, then drop 6 grapes into each bowl and serve at once.

*Note: If you use an electric blender, mix all ingredients (except the grapes) and blend until the almonds are as fine as you would like. Then strain as described in Step 4 and continue with Steps 5 and 6.*

## Gazpacho Aguacate

(Gath-pash-o Awa-cat-ay)
Avocado gazpacho
serves 4

This is yet another gazpacho that is, strictly, *not* one. Yet it won first prize for Chef Enrique Martell who is in charge of the kitchens at the Marbella Club, as the best original recipe.

2 ripe avocados
2 ozs (60 g) crushed blanched almonds
½ cup (120 mL) olive oil
salt and pepper to taste
1 tsp. (1 × 5 mL spoon) vinegar
4 cups (1 liter) cold water,
    approximately

1. Peel the avocados, chop them and either mash them in a mortar together with the almonds, or obtain the same result in an electric blender, to obtain a smooth paste.
2. Add the oil, seasonings, and vinegar gradually, then finally the water until the soup has acquired a good consistency.

*Optional: The finished soup may be garnished with small cubes of avocado or chopped parsley. Serve very cold.*

## OTHER VEGETABLE SOUPS

## *Sopa Fria de Pepinos*

(So-pa Freer day Pep-ee-nos)
Cold cucumber soup
serves 4

Still on the subject of cold soups for hot days, this is a delicious idea from Valencia.

4 cups (1 liter) chicken broth
4 Tbsp. (4 × 15 mL spoon) Sherry
2 small cucumbers, peeled and finely
   diced
pinch nutmeg
salt and pepper to taste
small sprig of mint, chopped very fine

1. Chill the chicken broth, then skim and remove any fat from the surface.
2. Heat the broth slightly to liquify, then add Sherry, cucumber, nutmeg, and mint. Adjust seasoning.
3. Whisk well to amalgamate, then chill again for about 1 hour. Serve in cups.

## *Crema de Aguacate*

(Kray-mer day Awa-cat-ay)
Avocado cream
serves 4

The flavors of chicken and avocado seem to go together like ham and eggs. This is another very simple soup that is so good, it should be saved for special occasions.

4 cups (1 liter) chicken broth
2 avocado pears
lemon juice
1 cup (250 mL) light cream
salt and pepper to taste

1. Chill chicken broth and remove any solidified fat from surface.
2. Peel avocados and mash the flesh.
3. Heat broth to liquify, then blend in avocado pulp and lemon juice. Stir in the cream and season to taste.
4. Mix thoroughly and chill well before serving. Garnish with chopped parsley or parsley and zest of lemon mixed.

## *Sopa de Tomate*

(So-pa day Tom-arte)
Fresh tomato soup
serves 4

3 very ripe tomatoes, peeled and
   chopped
1 small onion, finely chopped
3 stalks celery, finely chopped
2 whole cloves
1 wine glass or 5 fl oz (1½ dcL) dry
   white wine
2 Tbsp. (2 × 15 mL spoon) butter
2 Tbsp. (2 × 15 mL spoon) flour
2 cups (½ liter) milk
salt and pepper

1. Combine tomatoes, onion, celery, cloves, and wine in saucepan, cover pan, and bring to the boil.
2. Reduce heat and simmer for 15 minutes, still covered.
3. Melt butter in a pan, stir in flour and cook for 1 minute, thus making a roux. Stir in milk gradually, beating well between each addition, then simmer until mixture thickens.
4. Season to taste.
5. Pass the tomato mixture through a sieve, then stir it into the sauce. Heat but do not boil for a few more minutes.
6. Serve with garlic croutons (see *Croutons de Ajo*).

## Croutons de Ajo

(Croutons day Ar-ho)
Garlic croutons

3 Tbsp. (3 × 15 mL spoon) butter
1 clove garlic, crushed
6 slices white bread

1. Melt butter in saucepan with garlic,
then remove from heat.
2. Cut crusts from bread, then brush
with the garlic butter.
3. Toast in preheated oven at 300°F
(150°C) for 45 minutes or until bread is
golden brown and crisp.
4. Cut into small croutons and serve.

## Sopa Maria

(So-pa Maria)
Maria's soup
serves 4

1 oz (30 g) butter
1 lb ripe tomatoes, peeled and chopped
1½ quarts (1½ liters) water
2 Tbsp. (2 × 15 mL spoon) tomato
   puree
2 Tbsp. (2 × 15 mL spoon)
   breadcrumbs
¼ cup (30 mL) light cream
salt and pepper

1. Melt the butter in a saucepan and
saute the tomatoes very gently, then
add the water and cook for 20 minutes.
2. Stir in the tomato puree and
continue to cook for 5 minutes more.
3. Pass the mixture through a sieve,
then add the breadcrumbs.
4. Put soup back into pan and bring
back to the boil stirring all the time.
5. Finally just before serving, remove
pan from stove and stir in cream.
Season to taste.

## Sopa Verde

(So-pa Ver-day)
Green soup
serves 4

1 large cabbage leaf, finely sliced
1 quart (1 liter) chicken stock
1 clove garlic, minced
1 medium-size onion, finely chopped
1 lb (500 g) mashed potatoes
salt and pepper
1 Tbsp. (1 × 15 mL spoon) chopped
   parsley

1. Simmer the cabbage in the stock
until tender. (*Note:* add the cabbage to
*boiling* stock.)
2. Add garlic and onion and continue
simmering until soft.
3. Slowly blend in the mashed potatoes
by adding some of the stock in the pan
to the potatoes until they become
almost liquid, then pouring back into
the stock.
4. Season to taste and continue to
simmer for about 10 minutes until the
soup is creamy.
5. Add chopped parsley, stir in and
serve.

## Sopa de Nuezes

(So-pa day Nwaythes)
Walnut soup
serves 4

1½ pints (¾ liter) chicken broth
1 Tbsp. (1 × 15 mL spoon) butter
1 Tbsp. (1 × 15 mL spoon) flour
2 egg yolks
4 ozs (120 g) peeled, chopped walnuts
4 Tbsp (4 × 15 mL spoon) light cream
a squeeze of lemon juice

1. Heat but do not boil the chicken
broth.

2. In a separate saucepan, melt the butter and add the flour to make a roux. Cook for one minute.

3. Gradually stir in the heated broth, stirring until the mixture is smooth and without lumps of any sort.

4. Bring to a boil and cook for 5 minutes until the sauce thickens.

5. Remove from heat. In a cup mix the egg yolks with a little of the sauce, then add that mixture to the remainder of the sauce.

6. Mix the chopped nuts with the cream and lemon juice and stir into the soup, blending thoroughly. You *may* require a little salt and pepper.

*Note: To remove the skin from the nuts, drop them in a bowl of boiling water. Then the skin will come away easily.*

## FISH SOUPS

Some of the best soups you will encounter in Spain are the fish soups, many of which are similar to the French *bouillabaisse* but generally are not so difficult to prepare. They are, however, delightful brews. The fish used depends on what is available at the time, but includes at least three different varieties and always two varieties of shellfish. Some recipes call for the addition of ham (particularly the cured, Serrano ham); others use either breadcrumbs or mashed potato for thickening. The first recipe is for a soup called Quarter-of-an-Hour Soup. Why it goes by this name I have yet to discover, for it takes considerably longer to prepare than its name implies—but it's worth it.

Let me reiterate: you may use any white fish that is available and any shellfish obtainable. The flavor comes from using different varieties of fish and shellfish combined with the ham, egg, and seasonings.

## *Sopa al Quarto de Hora*

(So-pa al Quart-o day Ora)
Quarter-hour soup
serves 4

### SUGGESTED FISH

¼ lb (120 g) shrimp
½ lb (240 g) hake
12 mussels

1 Tbsp. (1 × 15 mL spoon) olive oil
1 large onion, finely chopped
2 cloves garlic, finely chopped

2 very ripe tomatoes, peeled, seeded, and chopped
2 slices of smoked bacon, diced fine
2 Tbsp. (2 × 15 mL spoon) breadcrumbs
1 oz (30 g) Serrano ham cut in thin strips
2 hard-boiled eggs, roughly chopped

1. Peel and devein the shrimp, then chop them. Cut the hake into small bite-sized pieces.

2. Put the fish, shellfish, and mussels into a large pot containing about 1 quart (1 liter) cold water and bring to a

boil. When boiling, reduce heat and add a little salt.

3. Meanwhile in a frypan, heat the olive oil and saute the onion, garlic, tomatoes, and bacon until the onions are tender and slightly golden.

4. With a slotted spoon, remove the mussels, then take away their top shells and discard. Put mussels back into pot.

5. Put the onion/tomato mixture into the fish pot, then add the breadcrumbs, Serrano ham, and the eggs.

6. Cook the mixture over a low heat for a further 5 minutes to amalgamate flavors.

## A Special Fish Soup

Have you even wondered why a young man should wish to spend eight or ten years slogging over a hot stove for up to ten hours a day in order to become a chef, when with possibly less effort and probably much greater financial reward he could become a deep-sea diver, a coal miner, or perhaps even a ballet dancer? This was the question I put to Chef Jose Ramos who was elected Chef of the Year in 1978 and is in charge of the kitchens at La Fonda Restaurant in Marbella.

He told me that he came into the business for the very practical reason that it was the only job around at the time. At the start, he hated it: the hours were very long and the financial rewards were paltry. But it gave him the opportunity to learn his profession from some of the best chefs in the country.

He recalled the long periods of hot, sweaty work, the endless months of pure drudgery, the countless hours of boring, repetitive labor—such as cutting tons of potatoes into barrel-like shapes of equal size; slicing vanloads of onions; washing fields of lettuce; shucking acres of peas; pulling the entrails of endless fowl—then fetching and carrying the heavy cooking pots, and doing other rotten jobs for the particular chef he was assigned to at the time. But he gradually got accustomed to the work, it all became easier, and he gained confidence as his skills developed.

"Now," he said, "after fifteen years, I have this job which is mainly supervisory and managerial. I don't work too hard, but I have to assume the greater burden and the continual stress associated with the production of food for the most discriminating guests. There is always an inner stress every single day; a feeling of self-doubt. The higher up you are, the heavier the responsibility. In this profession, there is no excuse for errors.

"On the lighter side," he continued, "the pay for a good *chef de partie* is not bad. He would make about 130,000 pesetas a month, and in common with other workers in Spain, gets fourteen months pay each year. The hours he works are of course, antisocial, not to say deplorable, for the Spanish seldom think about dinner until 10:30 at night and many restaurants only become busy toward midnight. But that is what it's all about," he concluded. During quiet periods, Chef Ramos spends time working out new recipes with which to delight his clients. This next is his latest creation.

## Sopa Costa del Sol

(So-pa Kosta del Sol)
Mussel soup with cream
serves 4

4 cups (1 liter) dry white wine
1 bay leaf
2 stalks of young, tender celery, finely
  chopped
2 Tbsp. (2 × 15 mL spoon) chopped
  parsley
1 clove garlic, crushed
30 (approximately) large mussels,
  washed and scrubbed
2 egg yolks, beaten
2 Tbsp. (2 × 15 mL spoon) light cream
½ wine glass or 2½ fl ozs (¾ dcL)
  brandy
salt and pepper to taste

1. Boil together in a covered pan the first five ingredients.
2. When boiling, add the scrubbed mussels, reduce heat, cover the pan again and cook for about 6 minutes (until the mussels open).
3. Remove the mussels with a slotted spoon, discard the shells, and pull away and discard the black cord that runs around the edge of each mussel. Then chop the remaining mussel flesh finely.
4. Allow the stock to cool slightly, then strain.
5. Add the beaten egg yolks, the cream, brandy, salt, and pepper.
6. Mix thoroughly by beating gently for two or three minutes so that the yolks blend throughout the mixture.
7. Finally, toss in the chopped mussels, then refrigerate.
8. Serve very cold.

## Other Fish Soups

## Crema de Almejas

(Kray-mer day Al-may-hath)
Cream of clams
serves 4

1 lb (500 g) baby clams
1 small onion, chopped fine
1 carrot, chopped fine
3 glasses or 15 fl oz (4½ dcL) dry white
  wine
½ cup (120 mL) water
juice of 1 lemon
2 egg yolks, well beaten
1 wine glass or 5 fl ozs (1½ dcL) brandy
½ wine glass or 2½ fl ozs (¾ dcL)
  Malaga wine (or sweet Sherry)
1 pint (½ liter) light cream

1. Put the clams in a pot with the onion and carrot, the wine, and the water. Bring to a boil.
2. Lower the heat and continue simmering until clams open. Then add the lemon juice.
3. Strain the broth into a large bowl, then remove as many of the loose clam shells as possible and discard.

4. Add the beaten egg yolks to the broth and mix well, then add the brandy and Malaga wine. Finally add the cream and mix very well.

5. Put in the refrigerator for about 1 hour and serve chilled with a garnish of chopped parsley.

## Sopa de Gambas

(So-pa day Gam-bass)
Cold shrimp soup
serves 4

1 lb (500 g) fresh shrimp
1 small onion
½ lemon, cut in two pieces
2 Tbsp. (2 × 15 mL spoon)
   breadcrumbs
1 egg yolk
pinch nutmeg
pinch of fresh oregano
1 cup (250 mL) milk
salt and pepper to taste
lemon slices for garnish

1. Wash and then cook the fresh shrimp. Allow to cool, then shell and remove the intestinal tract from each.

2. In a pot containing 1 quart (1 liter) cold water, put the shells, onion, and lemon pieces and cook for about 20 minutes.

3. Then strain the mixture into a large bowl. Now add the breadcrumbs and mix.

4. In an electric blender, put the peeled shrimp, the egg yolk, nutmeg, and oregano. Then add the milk and about ½ cup of the stock, taken from the bowl.

5. Give the mixture a good whirl in the blender, then return to the bowl containing the rest of the stock, adding a little at a time, amalgamating between each addition.

6. Return the whole mixture to the pot and heat for about 5 minutes or so, but do *not* let the soup boil.

7. Press through a fine sieve. Chill for 2 hours and serve with a garnish of parsley or thin slices of lemon floating on top of the soup.

## Sopa de Pescado

(So-pa day Peth-kar-doo)
Fish soup
serves 4

Once again, any kind of fish and shellfish may be used, but as mentioned earlier, the authentic Spanish fish soup, *Sopa de Pescado*, always has three varieties of fish and two of shellfish. Buy your fish whole if possible or, if the fishmonger fillets it or cuts it into pieces, bring home the head and bones to use as stock. Use shrimp and mussels or shrimp and clams, which are equally good.

2 lbs (1 Kg) assorted fish, cleaned and
   cut into slices; and shellfish shelled,
   peeled, and cleaned
1 small onion, minced
4 Tbsp. (4 × 15 mL spoon) olive oil
1 large ripe tomato, peeled and chopped
1 bay leaf
large sprig parsley
2 Tbsp. (2 × 15 mL spoon) white
   breadcrumbs
2 cloves garlic, minced
salt and pepper

1. In a pot containing 1½ quarts (1½ liters) water, put the heads, bones, etc. of the white fish and the shells of the shrimp, add a little salt, and boil for 15 minutes.

2. Strain this stock into another pot and discard the bones, etc.

3. In the pot containing the stock, put the cut fish and shellfish and the mussels (or clams) and cook for 15 minutes.

4. Meanwhile, heat the olive oil in a frypan and gently saute the onion until it takes on a little color.

5. Then add the tomato and let the mixture reduce as much as possible. Then add to the soup pot, together with the bay leaf, parsley, breadcrumbs, and raw minced garlic.

6. Cook all together for another 10 minutes, adjust seasoning, and serve very hot.

*Note: In southern Spain it is very common for both the Sopa de Pescado and Sopa de Mejillones to have saffron as an ingredient. This colorful extra is added to the stock at the last minute. A pinch is sufficient.*

## Sopa de Mejillones

(So-pa day Meh-e-lyoan-es)
Mussel soup
serves 4

The nearest U.S. equivalent to many Spanish fish soups is Manhattan chowder, in that they both contain diced ingredients and include tomato. This is such a soup which uses diced pork as a flavor and texture contrast.

3 wine glasses or 15 fl ozs (4½ dcL) dry
   white wine
1 lb (500 g) scrubbed mussels
1 green pepper, chopped
2 Tbsp. (2 × 15 mL spoon) olive oil
½ lb (250 g) lean pork (preferably
   fillet), diced
1 medium-size onion, chopped
1 stalk celery, chopped
1 bay leaf
½ Tbsp. (½ × 15 mL spoon) tomato
   paste

2 Tbsp. (2 × 15 mL spoon)
   breadcrumbs
1½ pints (¾ liter) chicken stock
salt and pepper

1. Put the wine in a deep saucepan and bring to the boil. Add mussels and cook, covered, until shells have opened.

2. Meanwhile, blanch the green pepper in boiling water for 2 minutes, then rinse under very cold water. Reserve.

3. Remove mussels from the pan with a slotted spoon and take them out of their shells. Discard the shells.

4. In a deep frypan, heat the oil and fry the diced pork over a gentle heat until it takes on a color, then add the onion, celery, and bay leaf. Cook until the pork is tender.

5. When ready, strain the mussel/wine stock into the frypan containing the pork mixture, then add the green pepper and stir in the tomato paste. Cook over a low heat for 10 minutes.

6. Add the breadcrumbs, then the chicken stock, to extend the soup to the desired consistency.

7. Add the cooked, shelled mussels, adjust seasoning, and simmer for a few minutes.

## Calderada

(Kal-dee-radah)
Galician fish soup
serves 8

This recipe comes from Galicia and is a variety of bouillabaisse.

2 lbs (1 Kg) assorted white fish
½ lb (240 g) shelled shrimp
½ lb (240 g) or about 30 shelled mussels
3 onions, finely chopped
3 cloves garlic, finely chopped
1 Tbsp. (1 × 15 mL spoon) flour
½ cup (120 mL) olive oil

1 Tbsp. (1 × 15 mL spoon) vinegar
1 Tbsp. (1 × 15 mL spoon) chopped
parsley
1 bay leaf
salt and pepper
8 slices of toast

1. Clean the white fish and cut into pieces of equal size.

2. Shell the shrimp, then discard the shells.

3. Drop the mussels into 1 pint of boiling, slightly salted water, cover the pot, and cook the mussels for 5 minutes until the shells open. Remove with a slotted spoon, discard shells, and reserve liquor.

4. In a large pot put the onions, garlic, flour, oil, vinegar, parsley, and bay leaf, then the pieces of fish and shellfish. Mix gently, cover the pot, and let rest in a cool place for 2 hours. This is a form of marinade.

5. When ready, pour over the liquor in which the mussels were cooked plus approximately 3 pints (1½ liters) cold water.

6. Cook over a high heat for 15 minutes or so until fish is tender.

7. Season the stock and then strain it off. Reheat the stock and pour it over the slices of toast in a large tureen or into individual bowls.

8. Serve the fish separately.

## OTHER SOUPS

I want to end this section by giving two interesting and extremely good recipes for soups made with dried vegetable base. The first is a rather rich, very satisfying soup suitable for cold days; the second is a much lighter puree with ham added.

## *Pure de Garbanzos*

(Pur-ay day Gar-ban-thoth)
Puree of chickpeas
serves 4

¾ lb (360 g) chickpeas, soaked
overnight
1½ pints (¾ liter) water
1 onion, whole
1 carrot, whole
1 leek, whole
1 bay leaf
sprigs of parsley
pinch thyme (or sprig of fresh, if
available)
pinch nutmeg
3 eggs
1 oz butter

1. Drain the chickpeas and put them in another pot with 1½ pints of fresh water.

2. Cook them together with all the other ingredients, except the eggs and butter, until the peas are soft.

3. Remove the onion, carrot, leek, bay leaf, and sprigs of herb, then pass the soup through a fine sieve.

4. Reheat the soup, which will be quite thick, and gradually stir in the beaten eggs and butter, making sure that you keep the pot over a low flame. Cook for 2 minutes only as the eggs must scarcely be set. Serve.

*Note: If the soup is too thick, it may be extended by adding a little chicken stock or water to reach the desired consistency.*

## Pure de Lentejas

(Pur-ay day Len-tay-hass)
Puree of lentils
serves 4

¾ lb (360 g) lentils
1 quart (1 liter) water (approximately)
1 carrot, chopped
1 onion, sliced
1 clove garlic, minced
1 bay leaf
3 Tbsp. (3 × 15 mL spoon) olive oil
3 ozs smoked bacon, cut in fine strips
1 onion, chopped
2 tomatoes, peeled, seeded, and
   chopped

1. In a large pot cook the lentils together with the other ingredients in the first group until tender but not mushy. Ideally, the lentils should have just a little bite in them. Add more water if the puree is becoming thick and heavy.

2. When cooked, pass through a sieve or put in an electric blender, and return to cooking pot.

3. Heat the oil in a pan and saute the bacon, then the onion until soft. Finally add the tomatoes and cook for a further 10 minutes.

4. Add bacon mixture to the puree, mix well, and reheat. Should more water (or stock) be required, add this to obtain the desired consistency.

*Eggs, Omelettes, and Tortillas*

7

# 7   EGGS, OMELETTES, AND TORTILLAS

T here can be little doubt that the egg is one of the most useful and versatile of all foods. The egg can be cooked in many different ways and is thus as much at home as part of classical dishes as it is in more mundane catering. Indeed, the egg is one of the basics of classical cookery, and aside from there being over 1,200 different egg dishes in classical cuisine, it also plays a vital part in enriching soups and sauces, bonding minced meats, and coating food ready for deep frying. Yet so often we treat the egg as a poor relation in cookery. Perhaps because it is such a commonplace food, we tend to disregard the more exciting ways of serving eggs and concentrate more on its usefulness as a breakfast food.

Of course, eggs have not always had such a high reputation. In England in the fifteenth century they were blamed (quite wrongly of course) for the outbreak of the Great Plague that swept London in 1665, and then spread to Europe. Of course it was not eggs that carried or spread the disease, but rats that reached epidemic proportions prior to the plague. Now let's go back to eggs.

First, a few tips about using eggs:

1. Salt toughens eggs, so add it to egg dishes only after they are cooked.

2. Avoid beating eggs directly into hot liquids or they may very well curdle. Just add small amounts of the hot (not boiling) mixture to the eggs, beating well between additions. Then you may slowly stir the egg mixture into the remaining liquid.

3. If you plan to unmold a baked custard, beat the eggs only *slightly* before adding to the liquid. This will help the eggs stay firm when baked. Too much beating will produce a light, porous custard that may break when being turned onto a serving dish.

4. In order to produce hard-boiled eggs without a black or green ring around the yolk, put the raw eggs into cold water, bring to the boil, and allow the eggs to cook for no more than 1 minute. Turn off heat and let the eggs stay in the water for 15 minutes.

5. To peel hard-boiled eggs smoothly, crack while still hot against a hard surface. The more cracks you make in the shell, the more easily the pieces will come off.

6. To make a very light omelette, do not use eggs straight from the refrigerator. They should be cold but not very cold. To give an extra lift, add a pinch of cornstarch to the eggs before beating.

7. Brown eggs have the same nutritive value as white-shelled eggs, but their yolks do tend to be darker.

Much of the egg cookery in Spain is based on the simple cooking methods: boiling, baking, and, of course, in the form of an omelette (tortilla). When eggs are used as a first course (entremeses) they are often soft-boiled, shelled, and served on a savory base. They are also baked in the oven, again on a base of vegetables or rice. Poached eggs (*huevos escalfados*) are not commonly seen in Spain.

## SOFT-BOILED EGGS *(HUEVOS PASADOS POR AGUA)*

In order to obtain the correct flavor/texture relationship when using soft-boiled eggs in conjunction with other ingredients, the eggs must indeed be soft boiled—the yolk soft and creamy and the white set firm. This is how Spanish cooks obtain this correct degree of firmness.

Place the cool (but not cold) eggs into a saucepan with cold water and bring gently to the boil. Remove pan from heat and allow the egg to rest in the water for 3 minutes. Rap the shells against a hard surface very gently to obtain fine cracks, then remove shell with care.

In central and northern Spain, soft-boiled eggs are given several elaborate preparations:

*Barcelona:* Diced, peeled tomatoes and chopped green pepper are sauteed in butter and are used as a base for soft-boiled eggs. Eggs are served in individual casseroles or on a large serving dish.

*Cadiz:* Mashed potato and fried onion are formed into cakes. A slight hollow is made in the center of each and the egg is slipped into the depression, then covered with tomato sauce.

*Granada:* Eggs are placed on a bed of cooked rice, coated with cheese sauce, and garnished with flaked crabmeat or chopped shrimp.

*Gitano:* Eggs are served on a bed of saffron rice and coated with a curry sauce.

*Eugenie:* Eggs are served on a large, flat field mushroom which has been grilled and smeared with a little liver pâté.

*Florentine:* Eggs are served on a bed of cooked, drained spinach coated with a cheese sauce and quickly glazed under the broiler.

## SCRAMBLED EGGS *(HUEVOS REVUELTOS)*

To keep scrambled eggs from becoming hard, the Spanish method is to break the required number of eggs in a bowl, season with pepper, and beat while the pan is warming on the stove. Drop a piece of butter in the pan, and just when it starts to froth, pour in the eggs and immediately reduce the heat. Stir with a wooden spoon until the mixture reaches a creamy consistency. When light and creamy, add just a little warmed light cream to the mixture, stir to blend, and remove from the heat. This technique gives a quite excellent consistency.

These are some special preparations for scrambled eggs:

*Bilbao:* The scrambled eggs are mixed with diced shellfish and asparagus tips and covered with a shellfish (lobster) sauce.

*Asturian:* Mixed with diced eggplant, tomato, and favas that have been sauteed in butter, then drained.

*Princesse:* Mixed with finely diced, cooked chicken meat and garnished with asparagus tips.

*Don Juan:* Mixed with chopped green peppers and mashed anchovy fillets, sauteed in butter.

*Maria:* Mixed with stewed tomatoes and grated hard cheese, garnished with chopped chives.

## OMELETTES

Ask chefs what they eat for lunch and more often than not their choice will be an egg dish. This may surprise many people who believe that chefs live off the fat of the land and usually choose the best item on the menu. Not so. In most kitchens, the junior and semiskilled staff eat before the restaurant opens for lunchtime business, thus leaving them free for clearing and cleaning after the mealtime rush is over. The chefs eat at the end of the service period.

Eating before service starts is not so bad, since the kitchen is fairly cool and relatively calm. But for senior staff it is different. After working for about four hours in a kitchen at a temperature of around 120°F (about 50°C), testing and tasting dozens of different dishes, the idea of eating anything at all is, to many chefs, slightly repugnant.

Although the upper hierarchy of the kitchen may indeed choose any item they wish from the menu, and also any item that is not listed which they may care to prepare (or ask their apprentices to prepare), simple foods are generally their preference. So they turn to eggs, often omelettes.

The traditional Spanish Omelette is a monster, about 1 inch (2.5 cm) thick and containing only potato and onion as a filling. Many recipes contain additional ingredients such as cooked red and green peppers, green peas, and in fact, almost any savory bits and pieces that the cook can find. And, of course, there is nothing at all wrong with using these items. But for the purist, this will not be a true Spanish Omelette.

So let us start on the right foot by not upsetting these perfectionists and prepare the traditional recipe. As you will observe, the technique is quite different for preparing a Spanish-type omelette than when cooking a conventional French omelette. So follow the instructions carefully.

## Tortilla Española

(Tor-tee-ya Eth-pan-yola)
Spanish omelette

olive oil for frying
1 large onion, finely chopped
2 potatoes, finely diced
a little salt
a pinch of pepper
6 whole eggs
2 Tbsp. (2 × 15 mL spoon) cold water

1. In a deep 10 inch (25 cm) omelette pan or skillet, heat the oil and saute the onions and potatoes until tender (they should not be browned in any way). Then sprinkle the mixture with salt and pepper. Remove onion and potatoes from pan and keep to one side.

2. In a bowl, beat the eggs and water together thoroughly.

3. Pour about one-third of the eggs into the pan and allow about 10 seconds to elapse for some of the egg to set on the bottom of the pan.

4. Spoon about one-third of the potato and onion mixture onto the egg in the pan, then with the back of a fork, lift the crust that has set from around the edge of the pan to allow more of the liquid egg to run under the omelette, forming another crust on the bottom of the pan.

5. When this one-third of the egg is almost firm and the vegetables are set in the mixture, add a further one-third, shaking the pan to keep the sides and bottom free, and a further one-third of the potatoes and onion.

6. Again, lift the cooking omelette with a fork or spatula so the liquid egg reaches the bottom of the pan.

7. When the omelette is almost set, once again repeat the procedure with the remaining egg and potato mixture, all the while cooking over a low heat.

8. When the final part of the omelette is firm, loosen it from the sides and base of the pan, invert a large plate over the frypan, then turn upside down on the plate.

9. Remove any pieces of omelette that may be sticking to the bottom of the pan, brush the pan with just a little more oil, and return the omelette to the pan, moist side down. Cook until a golden crust is formed.

*Note: Spanish omelettes are served either hot or cold. If served hot, they are cut into wedges; if served cold (very often seen on a tapa bar), the omelette is sliced thinly.*

The conventional French-style omelette is also very popular as a first course for dinner or as part of a luncheon menu. This is especially true of stuffed omelettes (*tortillas rellenas*) about which we shall speak later. A French-style omelette is very simple to prepare. The secret of making a tender omelette (if secret it is) is to move the beaten eggs from the bottom of the hot pan with the back of a fork as soon as they start to set. This allows more of the remaining liquid egg to reach direct heat, to cover the bottom of the pan, and to set, when again you move the set egg to make room for yet more liquid to hit the bottom. As the omelette is cooking, it tends to look something like scrambled egg in the center of the pan, while the base will become a golden brown.

Omelettes cooked in this manner are much more tender that those that are just allowed to bake slowly through to a stage when the omelette looks like chamois leather. Further, the degree of firmness can more easily be controlled when the former technique is used. Remember also that a pinch of cornstarch will give you a lighter, more fluffy omelette.

## Tortilla Sencillo

(Tor-tee-ya Sen-seel-yo)
Plain omelette
serves 1

2 eggs
1 Tbsp. (1 × 15 mL spoon) cold water
pinch black pepper
a little butter

1. Break eggs in a bowl, add water and pepper, and beat.

2. Heat a 7 inch (17.5 cm) omelette pan or skillet over moderate heat. When hot, add the knob of butter and swirl around pan to cover the bottom. Do not put the butter into a *cold* pan.

3. As soon as the butter is foaming, pour in the eggs, leave for just a few seconds to allow the base to set for the first time, then stir the center as described above.

4. When the omelette is cooked to the degree desired, flip one side of the

omelette toward the center of the pan with a fork or spatula, then flip the other side in a similar manner.

5. Take a warmed plate or serving dish in your left hand and the handle of the pan in your right, place the plate over the pan, and invert the pan to transfer in onto the plate. Serve at once.

### *Tortillas Rellenas* (Tor-tee-yas Rell-ay-nas) or Stuffed omelettes

Flavorings, herbs, and spices added to a plain omelette broaden its scope tremendously. The variations are extensive and mainly commonplace. However, there is one national technique which, while not exclusive to Spain, adds considerable interest to the dish.

Rather than add raw or cooked items to a plain omelette just prior to serving as is most usual, a very pleasant alternative is to coat them with a little white sauce (see Thick White Sauce recipe, page 123), to which a spoonful of cream has been added. The procedure is as follows:

1. Fry the desired ingredients (if necessary) in a little butter or oil until soft. Drain on a paper towel.

2. Take a small quantity of white sauce (thick) and gently warm it in a saucepan. Add cream and mix.

3. Place the cooked ingredients in a dish and mix in just a little of the sauce to make a thick mixture.

4. When the plain omelette has set, spread the mixture over the whole surface with a spatula.

5. Roll the omelette from one side to the other, so it takes the shape of a large cigar. Serve at once.

The three regional recipes for omelettes that follow do not use this technique, but there is no reason why you may not treat the fillings *a la crema*.

### *Tortilla de Higado*

(Tor-tee-ya day Ig-a-doe)
Chicken liver omelette Andalucian style
serves 2

3 chicken livers
2 tsp. (2 × 5 mL spoon) olive oil
1 Tbsp. (1 × 15 mL spoon) flour
1 Tbsp. (1 × 15 mL spoon) dry Sherry
1 Tbsp. (1 × 15 mL spoon) chicken stock

pinch each of garlic salt and black pepper
1 tsp. (1 × 5 mL spoon) chopped parsley
4 eggs

1. Saute chicken livers in the oil over a brisk heat until browned on the outside but pink inside. Remove from pan.

2. Slice the livers, toss them in the flour, and return to the pan.

3. Add Sherry, stock, and seasonings. Simmer until livers are cooked and the liquid is almost evaporated. Then sprinkle with the parsley.

4. Make a plain omelette using four eggs (for 2 people) and spoon in the mixture just before folding.

## Tortilla de Calabaza

(Tor-tee-ya day Kal-a-batha)
Zucchini omelette from Barcelona
serves 2

1 Tbsp. (1 × 15 mL spoon) olive oil
1 clove garlic, minced
1 small onion, minced
1 whole scallion, finely chopped
2 small, young zucchini, thinly sliced
1 ripe tomato, peeled, seeded, and
   chopped
pinch of marjoram
salt and black pepper
4 eggs

1. Heat a skillet, pour in the oil, and gently saute the garlic, onion, and scallion until soft.

2. Add zucchini, tomato, and marjoram. Cover pan and cook until tender. Then season to taste.

3. Make a plain four-egg omelette and spoon the above mixture onto the omelette before folding.

## Tortilla de Almejas

(Tor-tee-ya day Al-may-hath)
Clam omelette from Cadiz
serves 2

½ lb (240 g) tiny clams (*coquinas*)
1 Tbsp. (1 × 15 mL spoon) brandy
1 Tbsp. (1 × 15 mL spoon) dry Sherry
2 egg yolks
1 Tbsp. (1 × 15 mL spoon) whipping
   cream

garlic salt and black pepper
4 eggs

1. Read instructions for preparing clams, page 194.

2. Remove clams from shells and discard shells.

3. In a saucepan, heat the brandy, clams, and Sherry but do not boil.

4. In a bowl, combine the egg yolks and cream, then stir into the clam mixture *off* the heat.

5. Continue stirring over a very low heat until mixture thickens. Season to taste.

6. Make a four-egg omelette and spoon in the mixture just before folding.

*Note: This is a variation of the Tortilla a la Crema but somewhat richer. It is a speciality of Cadiz.*

## Tortilla de Gambas

(Tor-tee-ya day Gam-bass)
Shrimp omelette from Galicia
serves 2

½ lb (240 g) cooked shrimp
1 Tbsp. (1 × 15 mL spoon) olive oil
1 scallion, chopped
½ tsp. (1 × 2 mL spoon) chopped fresh
   tarragon (or a pinch of dried herb)
1 tsp. (1 × 5 mL spoon) chopped
   parsley
1 Tbsp. (1 × 15 mL spoon) dry Sherry
garlic salt and black pepper
4 eggs

1. Devein, shell, and cook shrimp as explained on page 180.

2. Mash the shrimp in a mortar with just a little of the oil (or use an electric blender for this purpose).

3. Heat a skillet, pour in the remainder of the oil, and saute the scallion until soft.

4. Stir in the shrimp, herbs, and Sherry and cook gently until the mixture is well heated and the Sherry almost evaporated. Season to taste.

5. Make a four-egg plain omelette and spoon the mixture into the center just before folding.

## Other Omelette Fillings

*Algerian:* Filled with diced, sauteed onion, red peppers, and garden peas.

*Eva:* Filled with sliced mushrooms and chopped cooked hearts of artichokes mixed with a little tomato sauce.

*Vasca:* Filled with cooked sliced leeks, smoked bacon pieces, and diced cooked potato.

*Valencia:* Filled with creamed sweet corn and mushrooms.

*Segovia:* Filled with chopped mussels and shrimp.

*Francés:* Filled with chopped cooked shallot mixed with chopped raw tomato.

## BAKED EGGS

When it comes to baked eggs, the Spanish are very inventive. Perhaps the most famous dish cooked in this style is *Huevos a la Flamenca*.

## *Huevos a la Flamenca*

(Wave-oth a la Fla-men-ka)
Andalucian baked eggs
serves 4

3 red peppers, diced
1 green pepper, diced
1 large onion, chopped
2 cloves garlic, fine chopped
2 Tbsp. (2 × 15 mL spoon) olive oil
3 ripe tomatoes, peeled, seeded, and chopped
4 ozs (120 g) diced cooked ham
2 ozs (60 g) chorizo, thinly sliced
pinch of basil
½ cup (150 mL) chicken stock
salt and black pepper
8 whole eggs
½ cup (80 g) cooked green peas
a few asparagus tips
2 Tbsp. (2 × 15 mL spoon) chopped parsley

1. Heat a large skillet and gently saute the peppers, onion, and garlic in the hot oil, until mixture is soft.

2. Add tomatoes, ham, chorizo, and basil. Cook for 5 minutes longer.

3. Preheat oven to 375°F (190°C).

4. Now add the chicken stock to the onion and tomato mixture. Season to taste and heat thoroughly.

5. Divide the hot mixture into 4 portions and place each into an individual casserole or ramekin.

6. Break 2 eggs into each container and arrange the cooked peas and asparagus tips around each set of eggs.

7. Bake in oven for about 15 minutes, until eggs have set.

8. Sprinkle with chopped parsley and serve.

## Huevos Vasca

(Wave-oth Vass-ka)
Baked eggs, Basque style
serves 4

The vegetable base for this dish is similar to a French *ratatouille* except that it contains more garlic and a little diced chorizo.

1 eggplant
2 red peppers, chopped
2 green peppers, chopped
2 onions, chopped
3 cloves garlic, minced
4 ripe tomatoes, peeled, seeded, and chopped
4 ozs (120 g) chorizo, diced
3 Tbsp. (3 × 15 mL spoon) olive oil
1 sprig fresh mint, chopped
8 eggs

1. Slice, then chop the eggplant, and place in a bowl with the peppers, onions, garlic, tomatoes, and chorizo.

2. In a large skillet, heat the oil, then tip the vegetable mixture into the pan and saute gently until the vegetables are soft. Should the mixture be a little dry, add chicken stock or, if you prefer, tomato juice to moisten.

3. Preheat oven to 375°F (190°C).

4. When cooked, add the chopped mint, mix well, and divide the vegetable mixture into 4 individual casserole dishes or ramekins.

5. Break 2 eggs into each dish and bake until eggs are set.

## Cazuela de Habas

(Kaz-whaler day Hab-as)
Casserole of lima-type beans
serves 4

2 large onions, chopped
2 cloves garlic, chopped
¼ cup (60 mL) olive oil
3 Tbsp. (3 × 15 mL spoon) sofrito or tomato paste
¼ tsp. (¼ × 5 mL spoon) cumin seed
½ cup (120 mL) chicken stock
3 cups (360 g) cooked fresh broad beans
salt and pepper
4 whole eggs

1. In a deep skillet, saute the onions and garlic in the oil until soft. Add the sofrito and cumin seed.

2. Meanwhile, preheat oven to 350°F (180°C).

3. When vegetables in the skillet are soft, add the stock and beans, mix thoroughly, and season to taste.

4. Transfer the whole vegetable mixture to 4 shallow dishes. Break 1 egg into each dish and bake in the oven until eggs are set.

## Huevos Cardenal

(Wave-oth Kar-day-nal)
Eggs, Cardinal
serves 4

This is a most attractive starter and is also very popular with children.

4 large, ripe tomatoes
4 eggs
2 cloves garlic, minced
salt and pepper
1 tsp. (1 × 5 mL spoon) chopped parsley
2 Tbsp. (2 × 15 mL spoon) melted butter

1. Preheat oven to 425°F (220°C).

2. Cut top from the tomatoes and scoop out most of the pulp. Place in oven for 15 minutes.

3. Remove tomatoes from oven and break 1 egg into each. Sprinkle with garlic, salt and pepper, and finally the parsley.

4. Melt butter in a saucepan, then pour over tomatoes.

5. Return to oven and bake for about 10 minutes until eggs are set.

## TARTAS APETITOSAS (SAVORY TARTS, QUICHE)

In Madrid perhaps more than any other city in Spain, savory tarts (something like the French quiche) are very popular. They are made with almost any filling—meat, fish, or vegetable—or indeed with a mixture of all three. However, the basis is always the same—eggs, cheese, and cream or yogurt. In summer they are served cold in slices as a tapa or in larger wedges as a first course. In winter they are served hot as a luncheon dish or as a second course for dinner. The following recipes are representative of Spanish savory tarts.

You will notice that the first recipe uses yogurt instead of cream. This ingredient provides a really excellent flavor contrast against the slight sweetness of the Spanish onions. However, the yogurt needs to be treated (i.e., the excess of liquid must be removed) before it can be used as a substitute for cream, sour cream, or cottage cheese.

### To Treat Yogurt

Line a wire or plastic strainer with a double layer of cheesecloth or fine-woven cotton cloth. Tip the yogurt into the strainer, lift the ends of the cloth, and squeeze the cloth into a fairly tight ball to force out the excess liquid. Place a small plate on top of the yogurt package, and on the plate place a weight. Leave in the strainer so that any extra liquid may drain off. Put in refrigerator and leave for about 12 hours.

## Tarta de Cebolla

(Tar-ta day The-bowl-ya)
Onion tart

### PASTRY

1½ cups (180 g) flour
1 tsp. (1 × 5 mL spoon) baking powder
½ tsp. (1 × 2 mL spoon) salt
⅔ cup (180 g) butter
1 Tbsp. (1 × 15 mL spoon) lard or shortening
ice water to mix

### FILLING

4 or 5 medium-size Spanish onions
2 Tbsp. (2 × 15 mL spoon) butter
1 tsp. (1 × 5 mL spoon) sugar
2 whole eggs, well beaten
a very good pinch nutmeg

1 cup (250 mL) treated yogurt
½ cup (125 mL) whipping cream
salt and pepper

1. To make pastry, sift the flour, baking powder, and salt together. Cut in the butter and lard, then add enough ice water to make a stiff dough. Let pastry rest for 20 minutes.
2. To make the filling, saute the onions in the butter. Add the sugar and cook until soft, tender, and golden brown. Allow to cool slightly.
3. Roll out pastry and fit into a 9 inch (22 cm) flan tin.
4. Preheat oven to 400°F (200°C).
5. In a bowl combine the eggs, nutmeg, yogurt, and cream.
6. Arrange the cooked onions on the bottom of the pastry in the flan tin and sprinkle with salt and pepper.
7. Pour the egg/yogurt mixture over the onions.
8. Bake in oven for 10 minutes. Then reduce heat to 300°F (150°C) and bake for a further 20 minutes or so until the filling has set.

## Tarta de Calabaza

(Tar-ta day Kal-a-batha)
Zucchini tart

2 Tbsp. (2 × 15 mL spoon) olive oil
3 cups (180 g) unpeeled zucchini, thinly sliced
1 large onion, finely chopped
2 Tbsp. (2 × 15 mL spoon) chopped parsley
½ tsp. (1 × 2 mL spoon) dried basil
¼ tsp. (1 × 1 mL spoon) oregano
½ tsp. (1 × 2 mL spoon) garlic salt
good pinch of pepper
3 whole eggs
3 Tbsp. (3 × 15 mL spoon) cream
2 cups (500 mL) grated mild cheese

made pastry for flan tin
2 tsp. (2 × 5 mL spoon) prepared mustard

1. Preheat oven to 375°F (190°C).
2. In a large skillet, heat the oil and cook the zucchini and onion until tender. Do not mash the zucchini.
3. Stir in the herbs and season to taste with salt and pepper.
4. In a large bowl, blend the eggs, cream, and cheese, then stir in the cooked onions and zucchini.
5. Line a 9 inch (22 cm) flan tin with pastry and spread the bottom with prepared mustard. Then pour egg mixture on top.
6. Bake for 20 minutes or until a knife inserted in the center of the flan comes out cleanly.
7. Let the cooked tart stand for at least 10 minutes before serving.

## Tarta de Gambas

(Tar-ta day Gam-bass)
Shrimp tart

1 Tbsp. (1 × 15 mL spoon) olive oil
1 large onion, finely chopped
1 clove garlic, minced
1 lb (500 g) raw shrimp, shelled and deveined
1 cup (90 g) sliced mushrooms
salt and pepper
3 eggs
3 Tbsp. (3 × 15 mL spoon) light cream
2 cups (240 g) grated hard cheese
1 Tbsp. (1 × 15 mL spoon) brandy
1 Tbsp. (1 × 15 mL spoon) chopped fresh tarragon (or 1 tsp. dried herb)
short pastry for flan tin

1. Preheat oven to 375°F (190°C).
2. Heat a skillet, pour in the oil, and gently cook the onions and garlic until tender.

3. Meanwhile, chop the shrimp and add them to the onions, etc. during the last 5 minutes of cooking time, then drop in the mushrooms. Allow to cool. Season to taste.

4. In a bowl, blend the eggs, cream, cheese, brandy, and tarragon.

5. Line a 9 inch (22 cm) flan tin with short pastry. Spread the shrimp and onion mixture over the bottom, then pour in the egg mixture.

6. Bake for about 20 minutes or until mixture is set.

Despite the fame of Madrid in the production of these delicious tarts, there is a restaurant in Estepona which challenges this superiority. The Restaurante Libro Amarillo (The Yellow Book) is one to which guests return again and again, and not only for their savory tarts. Members of the Rothschild family have chartered a plane to visit this quite outstanding restaurant, and its guest list reads like an international Who's Who.

The kitchen is run by Jose Citrano, a young chef who was trained at the Hotel Metropole in Marbella, which at that time had a brigade of French chefs. Work was done on the traditional *parti* system, where each section of the kitchen was the responsibility of a *chef de partie* under the supervision of the *chef de cuisine*.

Citrano started, as do most young aspiring cooks, in the boring and laborious vegetable section, then went on to learn about roasts, grills, and soups. He went on to the fish section, then the cold room for aspics, hors d'oeuvre, and cold dishes which included canapes and tapas. Here also he learned the arts of decoration and sculpting birds, fish, and flowers out of solid blocks of ice for use as decorative centerpieces on a buffet. Finally he went on to the sauce partie, the final section in his training, supervised by the "crown prince" of the kitchen—the sous-chef. During all this time he was mastering the finer points of his profession: how to balance flavors and textures; the affinities of various foods; how to chop, slice, bake, braise, broil, and so on to a standard of excellence acceptable in a first-class establishment.

After his years at the Metropole he left to gain further experience, but as with many, the experience of changing employment was a shock. Citrano shudders to remember the first time he was put in charge of a kitchen in a modest Spanish restaurant. This was on the first day of a new job, just after leaving the Metropole. He had, of course, acquired a wealth of knowledge from his previous tutors and had mastered the subtleties of producing a perfect souffle or a duck *a l'Orange*. But he was at a loss when he saw an item on the menu called *Cocido Madrileño*.

"I'd never cooked anything Spanish in my life," he told me. "That was the reason I came to this place—to learn ethnic cooking." But the head waiter saved the day. "He was an amateur cook of considerable ability who remembered his mother's recipe, so we were able, between us, to produce a decent *cocido* after all." His recipe for Tarta Citrano which follows is classic.

## Tarta Citrano

(Tar-ta Sit-ra-no)
Jose Citrano's quiche

pie dough for crust
1 pint (½ liter) light cream
6 ozs (180 g) diced cooked ham
½ cup (60 g) cubed cheese
5 eggs
1 tsp. (1 × 5 mL spoon) chopped chives
garlic salt and pepper
½ cup grated cheese

1. Prepare pastry and arrange in 9 inch (22 cm) flan tin.
2. Preheat oven to 375°F (190°C).
3. In a saucepan, warm the cream over low heat but be sure it does not boil.
4. Let the cream cool slightly, then add the ham and the cubed cheese and the eggs. Mix together.
5. Now add the chives and seasonings, mix together, then pour into pie shell.
6. Sprinkle the grated cheese over the surface and bake in oven until set (approximately 40 minutes).

*Sauces*

8

# 8  SAUCES

Thdis is another aspect of Spanish cookery that is rather limited, for not too many sauces are basically and traditionally Spanish. Many of the sauces served with meat, fish, or chicken are those that are incorporated in the dish itself and are formed while the main ingredient is cooking. However, there are some typically Spanish sauces that are prepared apart. Of course, the best known of these is mayonnaise (*mahonesa*) in its various forms.

## MARINADES

Marinades, however, are a different matter, and most often meat used in *cocidos*, or stews, or casseroles is put in a marinade prior to further treatment. There is something rather exotic and exciting about marinades. The beauty of using them where necessary is that they are so simple to make, and yet the results are so very worthwhile.

Possibly because the beef sold in Spain is not as tender and flavorful as that seen in the United States (although many Spanish butchers are beginning to adapt to the idea of aging their beef and older veal), Spanish cooks use the marinade to add both flavor and succulence to their meats. The more tender cuts such as sirloin (*lomo bajo*) and rump (*tapa, contratapa,* and *redondo*) should not need to be tenderized, but the cheaper cuts will undoubtedly improve if they are marinated.

To be effective a marinade must contain acid of some sort, be it vinegar, cider, wine, or, in some cases, fruit juice. The acid in these liquids acts on the connective tissue in the joints and they become softened. However the marinade can only work on the parts of the joint it can reach, so it is necessary on occasion to pierce holes in the joint with a metal or wooden skewer, so that the marinade can infiltrate into the meat. Ideally, a marinade should be prepared and kept in the refrigerator about twenty-four hours before the meat is laid in it, so that the flavors may amalgamate.

Naturally, large pieces of meat require longer marinating than smaller pieces. For example, steaks up to 1½ inches (3.75 cm) will require only about three or four hours in the marinade, as will cubes of meat that are going to be stewed. Large joints for pot-roasting or oven-roasting will require up to twenty-four hours in the marinade (and the joint should be turned frequently) to impart flavor and give it tenderness.

It is preferable if the marinade covers the meat, so a bowl just large enough to hold the joint is the first requirement. Too large a container will mean that more marinade than is really necessary will have to be made. Turn the meat at least once during the period and cover and refrigerate the meat during the entire time. A marinade used for large joints should not include strong individual elements such as soy sauce or sage as these are powerful and distinctive flavors which will penetrate the meat or fowl and possibly kill the natural flavor.

All Spanish marinades are made with a wine base (usually red wine for meat), olive oil, garlic, and perhaps a little wine vinegar; and with some of the less pungent herbs such as thyme, rosemary, basil, and fennel. Some marinades for chicken use nutmeg, dry Sherry, and tomato juice, giving the chicken dishes a stunning flavor.

Below are three Spanish marinades you may care to try. Notice that they are not too acidic, as this would spoil the flavor of the meats. Note that:

1. A marinade prepared in advance may be kept in the refrigerator for two weeks, providing it has not been used.

2. A marinade should only be used twice providing it is used within two or three days, and with the same type of meat. It must then be thrown away.

3. Do not use a marinade on a second occasion with a different type of meat than used the first time. The flavor of the first meat may permeate the second meat and spoil the flavor.

## Marinade No. 1 (uncooked)

1 wine glass or 5 fl ozs (1½ dcL) white
   wine
6 peppercorns
1 bay leaf
2 cloves garlic, crushed
2 cloves
salt and pepper

pinch nutmeg
juice of 1 lemon

Use for meat. Place the meat in a container (preferably earthenware or glass) and pour the premixed marinade over it. Place in refrigerator.

*Note: Should there be insufficient marinade to cover the meat, it should be turned at least once during the period of marinating.*

## Marinade No. 2 (uncooked)

This is a mild marinade for chicken and veal.

1 onion, finely chopped
2 shallots, finely chopped
1 carrot, finely chopped
1 stick of celery, finely chopped
1 clove garlic, finely chopped
sprig of fresh thyme (or pinch dry herb)
1 bay leaf
2 cloves
6 whole peppercorns
½ tsp. (1 × 2 mL spoon) salt
pinch of coriander seed
3 wine glasses or 15 fl ozs (4½ dcL) wine
½ wine glass or 2½ fl ozs (¾ dcL) tarragon vinegar
½ cup (120 mL) olive oil

Use this marinade in a similar way to that described in the recipe for Marinade No. 1.

*Note: This recipe will produce approximately 1 quart (1 liter) of marinade.*

## Marinade No. 3

This is a cooked marinade and is used when the cook needs to speed the tenderizing and flavoring process. The recipe is exactly the same as in Marinade No. 2 but a little of the olive oil is used to saute gently the finely chopped vegetables for 5 minutes or so to soften them and impart a deeper flavor to the marinade. Then add the remainder of the ingredients and allow to simmer for ¾ hour. Be sure to allow the marinade to cool completely before using.

## MAYONNAISE

This classic cold sauce originated in the island of Mahon. While being prepared, it can be as temperamental as an opera singer if handled incorrectly or as gentle as a baby if handled correctly. And there is little to remember to achieve success.

1. All ingredients must be at room temperature. The sauce will curdle if any of the ingredients are too cold or too warm or even if the temperature in the kitchen is too hot.

2. The oil must be added a few drops at a time when you start; the rate of addition can be slightly accelerated as the mayonnaise thickens.

3. The yolks should be mixed with some of the mustard *before* the addition of any oil. This will help the sauce to form a firm emulsion.

4. When the mayonnaise has been made, whisk in a little boiling water. This will lighten the sauce and help the emulsion to hold.

The most common whisking appliances used when making mayonnaise are:

*Blender:* this appliance makes up to 1 pint (½ liter) of quite excellent mayonnaise, and has the further advantage that it is easy to scrape the sauce out of the container.

*Rotary hand whisk:* ideal for making small quantities, but preparation takes a relatively long time because the oil has to be added drop by drop.

*Electric whisk:* a fast method for making larger quantities, suitable only for recipes using egg yolk (as in the recipe that follows). It is useless in recipes using *whole eggs*.

Should you find the flavor of virgin olive oil a little too strong or heavy, use olive oil for perhaps one-quarter of the total oil required, and use corn, peanut, or sunflower oil for the remainder.

The following recipe will produce 1 pint (½ liter) of thick, yellow mayonnaise.

## Mahonesa

(Mahon-aysah)
Mayonnaise

2 egg yolks
1 tsp. (1 × 5 mL spoon) dry mustard
1 tsp. (1 × 5 mL spoon) French
  mustard
1 tsp. (1 × 5 mL spoon) salt
1 tsp. (1 × 5 mL spoon) sugar
½ tsp. (1 × 2 mL spoon) pepper
pinch of cayenne pepper
2 tsp. (2 × 5 mL spoon) lemon juice
1½ cups (370 mL) oil, mixed as
  preferred
2 tsp. (2 × 5 mL spoon) white wine
  vinegar
1 Tbsp. (1 × 15 mL spoon) boiling
  water

1. Separate the yolks from the whites.

(Reserve the whites for another purpose.)

2. In a bowl, beat the yolks until creamy. Add the mustard and other seasonings together with 1 teaspoon of the lemon juice.

3. When these are well mixed, you may now start adding the oil. If using an electric mixer or blender, the oil may be trickled down the side of the bowl so that it will be absorbed gradually. If using a hand whisk it will take longer as, at the beginning, the oil must be added drop by drop.

4. As soon as the sauce begins to thicken to the consistency of whipping cream, the oil may be added in a gentle stream.

5. During this process, the sauce should be thinned down with the remainder of the lemon juice and the vinegar.

6. When all has been absorbed, whisk in the boiling water.

This method should give you foolproof mayonnaise. If for any reason the mixture curdles, the following steps should be taken:

1. Start the process again using just one egg yolk, whisking it in another bowl.

2. Then very gradually whisk in the separated mayonnaise, in small quantities, being sure that each addition is combined before more of the curdled mayonnaise is added.

## *All-i-oli*

A Spanish specialty, garlic mayonnaise (*All-i-oli*) dates back over one thousand years and is said to have originated in Egypt and been introduced into Spain by the Romans. The original recipe did not include egg yolks and was perhaps somewhat crude for a contemporary palate. Now the generally accepted method of producing this sauce incorporates egg yolks.

A similar set of rules applies to preparing all-i-oli as to mayonnaise, in regard to temperature of the ingredients and the gradual addition of the oil.

The first recipe is a plain garlic mayonnaise used in many restaurants and homes; the second recipe is more commonly found in Andalucia.

# *All-i-oli*

(Alley-o-lee)
Plain garlic mayonnaise
makes about ¾ pint (360 mL)

2 cloves garlic
1 Tbsp. (1 × 15 mL spoon) lemon juice
a little cold water
2 egg yolks
¾ pint (360 mL) olive oil
salt and pepper to taste

1. In a mortar or blender, put the garlic, a little of the lemon juice, and a little water, and mash all together well.
2. Then add the lightly beaten egg yolks and blend.
3. Gradually add the oil, whisking all the time until the mixture begins to thicken, then the oil may be added more rapidly. During this latter step add the remaining lemon juice, then season to taste.

# *All-i-oli con Tomates*

(Alley-o-lee kon Tom-at-es)
Andalucian all-i-oli
makes about ¾ pint (360 mL)

2 cloves garlic
a good pinch of salt
2 egg yolks
1 cup (250 mL) olive oil
2 ripe tomatoes, peeled, seeded, and
  mashed

1. Mash garlic in a mortar with the salt.
2. Stir in the lightly beaten egg yolks
3. Gradually add the olive oil, stirring all the time until the sauce begins to thicken.
4. Last, add the well-mashed tomatoes. Beat to mix.

# BEARNAISE

The Spanish have their own variety of Bearnaise which they call by the same name as the French and is not too different from the classical recipe. It is usually served with grilled fillet (*solomillo*) or sirloin steak (*entrecote*).

## *Salsa Bearnaise*

(Salsa Beer-naise)
Bearnaise sauce

3 Tbsp. (3 × 15 mL spoon) wine
    vinegar
2 Tbsp. (2 × 15 mL spoon) water
1 shallot, finely minced
pinch of salt and pepper
2 Tbsp. (2 × 15 mL spoon) chopped
    fresh chervil
2 Tbsp. (2 × 15 mL spoon) chopped
    fresh tarragon
3 egg yolks
4 Tbsp. (4 × 15 mL spoon) butter

1. Put the vinegar, water, shallot, salt, and pepper, and half the chervil and tarragon in a saucepan, bring to a boil and continue boiling until the volume is reduced by one-third.

2. Remove from the heat and when slightly cooled, stir in the egg yolks.

3. Transfer the saucepan to a double boiler, the bottom half containing boiling water. Set stove to low heat.

4. In another saucepan, heat the butter gently, just enough to melt it. The butter should not be too hot.

5. Add the melted butter gradually to the other ingredients, whisking between each addition.
*Note:* This part of the process is similar to making mayonnaise and must be done gradually, with continual whisking, as the sauce thickens due to the gentle heat of the water.

6. When thick, strain the sauce into a sauce-boat, then stir in the rest of the chervil and tarragon.

# HOLLANDAISE SAUCE

Despite the awe in which most cooks hold this most beautiful sauce, it is one of the easiest to produce if a proper recipe is followed. Just try it and see.

## *Salsa Hollandaise*

½ cup (120 g) butter (salted *or*
    unsalted)
2 egg yolks
1 tsp. (1 × 5 mL spoon) lemon juice

⅓ cup (85 mL) boiling water
salt and white pepper

1. Divide the butter into 3 equal parts.
2. Put the first part into the top section

of a double boiler, over hot but *not* boiling water. Add the egg yolks and lemon juice.

3. Stir until butter is melted.

4. Add the second part of the butter, and as the mixture thickens, add the third part.

5. When all the butter has melted, add the boiling water *very* gradually, whisking constantly.

6. Continue to cook for 2 or 3 minutes longer.

7. Finally, add the salt and pepper to taste.

*Note: The French tend to prefer their Hollandaise made with unsalted butter, which gives the sauce a very bland flavor. In Spain, salted butter is preferred. Also, should the mixture curdle, beat in 2 Tbsp. (2 × 15 mL spoon) of boiling water.*

## WHITE SAUCE

The Spanish, in common with most cooks throughout Europe, find many occasions when a white sauce (*salsa blanca*) is useful. It is called a *Bechamel* in Spain, although it is not exactly a true (classic) recipe that is used. Depending on its consistency—thick, medium, or thin—it may be used for a number of purposes. The thick white sauce should be used for coating croquettes, etc. The medium white sauce should be used for creamed chicken, fish, or vegetables. The thin white sauce should be used for thinly coating vegetables and as a base for soup.

The following recipe is based on one cup (250 mL) of milk, with the two variable factors being the fat and flour.

## *Basic White Sauce*

### THICK WHITE SAUCE

1 cup (250 mL) milk
4 Tbsp. (4 × 15 mL spoon) butter
4 Tbsp. (4 × 15 mL spoon) flour
pinch of salt, pepper, and nutmeg

### MEDIUM WHITE SAUCE

1 cup (250 mL) milk
2 Tbsp. (2 × 15 mL spoon) butter
2 Tbsp. (2 × 15 mL spoon) flour
pinch of salt, pepper, and nutmeg

### THIN WHITE SAUCE

1 cup (250 mL) milk
1 Tbsp. (1 × 15 mL spoon) butter
1 Tbsp. (1 × 15 mL spoon) flour
pinch of salt, pepper, and nutmeg

1. Melt the butter in a saucepan over a low heat. When melted, remove butter from stove before stirring in flour. This will ensure a smoother sauce.

2. Stir in the flour, mixing thoroughly to ensure all the butter is absorbed into

the flour. The mixture should look something like marzipan and should leave the sides of the saucepan cleanly.

3. Add the cold milk a little at a time, again *off* the heat when making the additions, beating rapidly and constantly between additions, and scraping the bottom of the pan as you stir and beat. *Note:* The mixture *must* be perfectly smooth (with no lumps at all) before you add more milk.

4. When all the milk has been absorbed, stir in the seasonings and simmer the sauce very gently for 10 minutes to allow the grains of flour to burst and the sauce to become rich and full. The more you beat the sauce, the more glossy it will be.

I have gone into rather more detail on this question of making a white sauce, as many young cooks seem to have a problem producing a good, glossy, well-cooked sauce. As a sauce of this type is required very often, it would be helpful to explain just what happens to the ingredients as they are being combined and cooked.

In the first place, the butter is melted so that it may be absorbed by the flour, to soften the grains, and to give them flavor. When the milk is added and heat applied, each tiny granule of flour absorbs the liquid and begins to expand. This expansion is more rapid if hot liquid is used, so since the cook needs to control the rate of gradual expansion, the milk is added *cold*. If the grains of flour expand too quickly (before the cook can beat the mixture smooth between each addition of milk), the grains of flour will tend to stick together in groups and produce a heavy, lumpy sauce. Many poor sauces are due to the liquid being added hot (possibly in an attempt to save time), and this very often spoils the sauce altogether.

The recipe and method just given will ensure success. You will appreciate just why equal quantities of butter and flour are used; the one is able exactly to absorb the other. You will also understand just why beating the sauce constantly is the other secret of success.

## TOMATO SAUCE

Tomato sauce is possibly the most popular sauce in every region of Spain, mainly because Spanish tomatoes give such an excellent flavor to the sauce and also because a tomato sauce may be used as an accompaniment for so many dishes. The following recipe will please you, and the few variations that are included will give the sauce greater possibilities.

# Salsa de Tomate

(Sal-sa day Toh-mah-tay)
Spanish tomato sauce
makes 2 quarts (2 liters)

5 lbs (2 Kg) ripe tomatoes
2 Tbsp. (2 × 15 mL spoon) olive oil
1 large onion, finely chopped
2 cloves garlic, finely chopped
1 large red pepper, seeded, and finely
   chopped
1 tsp. (1 × 5 mL spoon) salt
a good pinch of black pepper
1 tsp. (1 × 5 mL spoon) dried basil
½ tsp. each (1 × 2 mL spoon) oregano,
   rosemary

1. Put tomatoes into boiling water to help loosen the skins; then peel the tomatoes and core them.
2. Heat the oil in a deep frypan and gently saute the onion, garlic, and red pepper until soft. Do not allow the vegetables to color at all.
3. Add the tomatoes, salt, pepper, dried basil, oregano, and rosemary. Simmer over a very low heat for one hour. The mixture will have become thick and begin to look like a tomato sauce. If sauce is too thin, continue simmering until it has reached the thickness you like.
4. Allow to cool, then spoon into glass jars and keep in the refrigerator.

# Variations

# Salsa Cristina

Sauce Cristina

This is very good with fish or any seafood. It is a mixture of tomato sauce and mayonnaise.

1 cup (250 mL) mayonnaise
2 tsp. (2 × 5 mL spoon) tomato sauce
4 Tbsp. (4 × 15 mL spoon) dry Sherry
2 tsp. (2 × 5 mL spoon) dry mustard

Mix all ingredients together.

# Salsa Roja

Red sauce

Another sauce good with fish or any type of seafood, especially mussels, this is often used with cold mixed vegetables.

1 pint (½ liter) tomato sauce
1 large Spanish onion, minced

Mix the two ingredients and allow to stand for 12 hours before using.

# Piri-Piri

Hot Sauce

This is a variation on the authentic Piri-piri and is made simply by adding about ½ tsp. (1 × 2 mL spoon) dried red pepper to 1 pint (½ liter) tomato sauce. More or less dried red pepper may be used, depending on personal taste.

# Salsa Diablo

(Salsa Dee-ab-lo)
Hot sauce (but not scorching!)

1 pint (½ liter) tomato sauce
2 Tbsp. (2 × 15 mL spoon) red wine
   vinegar
good dash of pepper
2 tsp. (2 × 5 mL spoon) Dijon mustard
2 Tbsp. (2 × 15 mL spoon) brandy
1 Tbsp. (1 × 15 mL spoon) butter

1. In a saucepan mix the tomato sauce, vinegar, pepper, mustard, and brandy. Whisk well so that the mustard is completely blended with the rest of the ingredients.
2. Heat the mixture over a very low flame and simmer for 10 minutes.
3. Now add the butter, stirring until melted.
4. Keep warm and serve with shrimp, lobster, crayfish, etc.

## OTHER SAUCES

## *Salsa Verde*

(Salsa Vaird-hay)
Green sauce

This is an excellent sauce to be served with fish, especially broiled or baked.

1 cup (30 g) freshly chopped parsley
¼ cup (60 mL) olive oil
1 small clove garlic, minced
salt and pepper
1 Tbsp. (1 × 15 mL spoon) lemon juice
1 Tbsp. (1 × 15 mL spoon) dry Sherry

1. In a bowl add the olive oil to the parsley, then mix in the garlic. Beat well until amalgamated.
2. Then add salt and pepper, lemon juice, and Sherry.

## *Salsa Armada*

(Salsa Ar-ma-da)
Navy sauce

Use this sauce for grilled or baked fish.

2 anchovy fillets
24 capers, washed and dried

3 shallots, minced
1 medium-size onion, minced
½ lb (250 g) butter
salt and pepper
juice of 2 lemons
pinch of nutmeg

1. Mash the anchovies and capers and mix with shallots and onion.
2. Melt butter and gently simmer the above ingredients until the anchovy dissolves.
3. Just before serving, add lemon juice and nutmeg, stir to combine, then heat the sauce so that it comes to the table very hot.

## *Salsa S'agaro*

(Salsa S-agar-o)
S'Agaro sauce

This is yet another excellent fish sauce.

1 red pepper, minced
1 green pepper, minced
6 large tomatoes, peeled and seeded
8 toasted almonds, crushed
4 cloves garlic, minced
2 small onions, minced
1 cup (250 mL) (approximately) olive oil
¼ cup (60 mL) wine vinegar
2 Tbsp. (2 × 15 mL spoon) brandy
salt and pepper

1. In a blender (or using a mortar and pestle) mash the peppers, tomatoes, almonds, garlic, and onions to a paste.
2. Gradually add the oil, a little at a time, and when one-quarter of the oil has been added, pour a little of the vinegar into the mixture, alternating oil and vinegar until a good consistency has been reached.
3. Add the brandy and seasoning. Mix well.

# Salsa Tartare

(Salsa Tar-tar)
Tartar sauce

2 hard-cooked egg yolks
salt and white pepper
1 cup (250 mL) olive oil
2 tsp. (2 × 5 mL spoon) white wine
    vinegar
1 tsp. (1 × 5 mL spoon) each: finely
    chopped chives, parsley, onion,
    gherkins, capers, olives

1. In a bowl, pound the egg yolks to a
paste and season with salt and pepper.
2. Gradually add the oil, beating all the
time and alternating with a few drops
of vinegar between each addition.
3. When the sauce is thick, stir in the
finely chopped herbs, etc.

Note: For a quick tartar sauce, use a cup
of mayonnaise and stir in the flavorings.

# Salsa de Almendras

(Salsa day Al-men-dras)
Almond sauce

This recipe is another great favorite
and is used to accompany eggs, cold
meats, chicken, or liver.

yolks of 2 hard-boiled eggs
8 toasted almonds
2 tsp. (2 × 5 mL spoon) chopped
    parsley
1 pint (½ liter) milk
salt and pepper

1. Grind the yolks, almonds, and
parsley together in a mortar (or mix in
an electric blender).
2. Then add the milk and seasoning.
3. Transfer the entire mixture to a
saucepan and simmer until the sauce
has been reduced by half.
4. Pass through a sieve and serve hot.

# Salsa al Jerez

(Salsa al Her-eth)
Sherry sauce

This sauce is suitable for any meat,
chicken, or mild game.

4 Tbsp. (4 × 15 mL spoon) butter
2 onions, chopped
2 stalks of celery, finely chopped
2 Tbsp. (2 × 15 mL spoon) flour
1 glass (1½ dcL) dry Sherry
a little chicken stock (or water)
1 bay leaf
3 cloves
salt and pepper

1. Heat the butter gently, then saute
the onions and celery until soft.
2. Stir in the flour and, stirring
constantly, let the mixture cook for a
few minutes. Add Sherry and stock.
3. Continue stirring until sauce has
thickened. Add bay leaf, cloves, and
season to taste. Note: You may need
more liquid if the sauce is very thick.
Use a little more stock or water to get
it to the right consistency.
4. Cook for about 30 minutes, then
adjust consistency as explained in Step
3.
5. When cooked, pass the sauce
through a sieve. Reheat and serve.

# Salsa de Anchoas

(Salsa day An-cho-ass)
Anchovy and walnut sauce

This is a very good sauce when spread
over grilled meats; the contrast of
anchovy and nuts is both unusual and
quite delightful.

4 fillets of anchovy
1 clove garlic
¼ cup (30 g) shelled walnuts          (cont.)

2 tsp. (2 × 5 mL spoon) wine vinegar
¼ cup (60 mL) olive oil

1. In a mortar, crush the anchovies, garlic, and walnuts, then add the vinegar to make a paste.
2. Then blend in the olive oil drop by drop, maintaining a smooth paste before adding further oil.

## Salsa Amarilla

(Salsa Am-ar-ill-ya)
Yellow sauce

This sauce is good with chicken, ham, or almost any cold meats.

4 hard-boiled eggs
1 Tbsp. (1 × 15 mL spoon) Madeira or Malaga wine
1 Tbsp. (1 × 15 mL spoon) brandy
2 Tbsp. (2 × 15 mL spoon) oil
salt and pepper
1 cup (250 mL) chicken stock
1 Tbsp. (1 × 15 mL spoon) wine vinegar
good pinch of dry mustard powder

1. Separate egg whites from yolks. Chop whites finely and put to one side.
2. Mash the yolks and mix them with the wine and brandy.
3. When thoroughly mixed, add the oil, drop by drop.
4. Season with salt and pepper, then stir in the stock and wine vinegar.
5. Finally add the mustard powder in the strength you prefer.

## Salsa de Vinagre

(Salsa day Vin-ag-ray)
Vinegar sauce

Use this sauce with salads and boiled fish. This is a "vinegar sauce" that does not contain vinegar. Vinegar may be used, however, to replace the lemon juice.

1 small onion, finely chopped
1 clove garlic, finely chopped
1 Tbsp. (1 × 15 mL spoon) chopped parsley
4 Tbsp. (4 × 15 mL spoon) olive oil
a little cold water
juice of one lemon
1 Tbsp. (1 × 15 mL spoon) chopped green olives
salt and pepper

1. In a bowl mix the onion, garlic, and parsley. Mix in the oil.
2. Mix the cold water with the lemon juice, then add to the sauce.
3. Pour this mixture into a pan and heat over a low flame; it will thicken slightly. Then remove from heat. Do not allow it to boil.
4. At the last moment, mix in the chopped olives. Allow to cool and serve.

## Salsa de Aguacate

(Salsa day Awa-cat-ay)
Avocado cream sauce

This sauce is used for egg dishes, salads, and vegetables

1 tsp. cornstarch (1 × 5 mL spoon)
½ cup (120 mL) light cream
salt and pepper
1 avocado
lemon juice

1. Mix cornstarch with a little cold water, then blend it with the cream.
2. Cook over a low heat, beating well, until smooth and thickened. Then add salt and pepper.
3. Peel avocado, mash it, and add a little lemon juice. Pass it through a sieve and blend into the warm cream mixture.

# Salsa Romesco

(Salsa Ro-mes-coe)
Romesco sauce

This is a hot sauce and a specialty of Catalonia. It is mainly used with fish, but is equally good on vegetables.

1 ripe tomato, seeded and peeled
1 oz (30 g) toasted hazelnuts
1 oz (30 g) toasted almonds
½ tsp. (1 × 1 mL spoon) chili powder
3 cloves garlic, minced
salt to taste
¾ cup (200 mL) olive oil
¼ cup (60 mL) wine vinegar

1. In a mortar grind the tomato, nuts, chili powder, and garlic. (Use a blender if you have one.)
2. Add salt and then gradually incorporate the oil.
3. The sauce will gradually thicken. When thick, beat the vinegar into the mixture to obtain a good consistency.

## SAVORY BUTTERS

These mixtures of softened butter and seasoning agents may be used in three ways. First, savory butters can be used as a dip for bite-sized pieces of shellfish. In this case, the butter and seasonings are first mixed, then heated gently in a pan and poured into individual bowls for use by the guests. Second, savory butters may be spread on baked or grilled fish, grilled meat, or plain vegetables just prior to serving. The third use for these butter mixtures is as a spread for making sandwiches, which lends a subtle and most interesting flavor.

For whichever purpose you decide to use them, savory butters may be prepared in advance, wrapped in foil, and kept in the refrigerator until required. Of course, dozens of permutations are possible for these creamed butters, but the recipes noted here are the most popular in Spain.

# Anchovy Butter

Cream 2 Tbsp. (2 × 15 mL spoon) of butter with 2 tsp. (2 × 5mL spoon) anchovy paste. (The strength of the seasoning may be altered according to taste.)

*Note: Use on meat or fish.*

# Almond Butter

Pound 8 blanched almonds as finely as possible and mix with 2 Tbsp. (2 × 15 mL spoon) butter.

*Note: Use for fish or vegetables.*

# Crayfish Butter

Pound together equal quantities of crayfish meat and butter. (Any other shellfish may be substituted.)

*Note: Use for fish.*

# Garlic Butter

Blanch 2 cloves of garlic in a little boiling water. Drain, dry, then pound with 2 Tbsp. (2 × 15 mL spoon) butter.

*Note: Use for meat, fish, or vegetables.*

## Herb Butter

Mix together ½ tsp. (1 × 2 mL spoon) *each* of finely chopped chervil, parsley, tarragon, and chives. Cream with 2 Tbsp. (2 × 15 mL spoon) butter.

*Note: Use for meat, fish, or vegetables.*

## Mustard Butter

Cream 1 scant tsp. (1 × 5 mL spoon) prepared mustard with 2 Tbsp. (2 × 15 mL spoon) butter.

*Note: Use for meat.*

## Paprika Butter

Cream 2 tsp. (2 × 5 mL spoon) of paprika with 2 Tbsp. (2 × 15 mL spoon) butter.

*Note: Use for meat or fish.*

## Nutmeg Butter

Blend ¼ tsp. (1 × 1 mL spoon) nutmeg and a little lemon juice, a dash of white pepper, and 1 tsp. (1 × 5 mL spoon) chopped chives, with 2 Tbsp. (2 × 15 mL spoon) butter.

*Note: Use for fish, broccoli, cauliflower, or green beans.*

## Tarragon Butter

Pound enough fresh tarragon leaves to make 1 tsp. (1 × 5 mL spoon), then rub through a fine sieve. Mix with 2 Tbsp. (2 × 15 mL spoon) butter. (Dried herb may be used if more convenient.)

*Note: Use for fish.*

## Salsa Negra

(Sal-sa Negra)
Black butter

1 Tbsp. (1 × 15 mL spoon) butter
1 tsp. (1 × 5 mL spoon) tarragon
   vinegar

1. Melt the butter in a small pan, then increase the heat until the butter turns brown.
2. Remove from heat at once and stir in the vinegar.
3. Pour over the fish while still very hot.

*Note: Use with skate (raya).*

*Rice*

9

# 9 RICE

**M**ore rice is eaten throughout the world than any other vegetable. This fact is not surprising when one realizes that rice requires less labor to prepare than any other major raw vegetable, it has no preparation loss (and in fact increases its weight between three and four times when cooked), it is easy to store, and does not easily deteriorate. It was perhaps the first natural convenience food. Further, it contains all the essential amino acids in proper proportion and is easily digested, taking only about an hour in the process while other foods take up to four hours. That is why rice is so good when eaten at a late evening meal.

In most Eastern countries and Asia, rice is cooked with loving care. In Spain, too, where rice has been growing since the sixteenth century, it is treated like an old and trusted friend, and there are many delightful and creative ways of cooking it. Seldom is the rice washed in running water. Instead it is cleaned by placing it in cold water for a few minutes and picking out any dirt or stones or grit, then rubbing it dry between the folds of a cloth.

South of Barcelona lies the rice-growing area of Spain, and we find that rice dishes are popular in the cuisine of the Levante, Murcia, and Andalucia. In the central and northern parts of the country, rice is used in small quantities and, of course, the ever popular *paella* is found everywhere. But apart from this, one seldom sees a section of the menu in a restaurant that is devoted to rice dishes.

But in the three provinces named, they often combine rice with butter, finely chopped onion, and rich chicken stock, and simmer it gently until it is delightfully tender. Sometimes they mix the stock with a little dry white wine, and, when cooked, they season it with such ingredients as chive, chopped parsley, sesame seeds, various herbs, and grated cheese. Spanish cooks also combine rice with fruits, nuts, mushrooms, pimientos, and chopped ham: not all together of course! They add rice to salads, soups, stuffings, and creamed dishes.

Three types of rice are readily available in Spain:

*Long-grain:* grains are light and fluffy when cooked and tend to separate naturally.

*Short-grain* (called "round" or "Valencia"): short, plump grains tend to cling together when cooked.

*Brown rice* (called "integral"): becoming more and more popular because of its better, natural flavor.

In addition to these types, one is able to obtain parboiled rice, sold under brand names and similar to the brand Uncle Ben's found in the United States. This type of rice is partly cooked before the brown cover is removed and this process transfers some of the goodness from the cuticle to the grain. Instant rice is also obtainable. This is fully cooked and then dried. Complete reconstitution is effected by adding about two and a half times its weight in liquid and cooking for a very short period.

The most common fault in the preparation of rice is overcooking. The best principle to follow is, I think, to cook rice to be used for dessert (the short-grained or Valencia rice) very thoroughly so that it is quite soft. However, for savory rice it is better to stop cooking at a point when the rice just starts to get soft. This gives a very slight nuttiness to the grains, which often adds a great deal to the texture contrast of the whole dish.

The usual method of preparing simple boiled rice is to put the rice in a pan with twice its volume of water and a teaspoon (1 mL) of salt for each quart of liquid used. The water is brought to the boil; the rice stirred once very gently with a fork; then the pan is tightly covered and simmered (without removing the lid) for about twelve minutes. After this time, the rice is tested, and if more time is required, then cooking continues.

In Spain however, plain white rice is cooked as follows: it is a two-step process. There is no point in giving a specific recipe as the quantity of flavoring ingredients may be varied according to your own particular taste. You will need onion, cut in large pieces; garlic, crushed but left whole; bay leaves; rice; oil for frying; salt; and chopped parsley.

1. In the oil, fry the onions, garlic, and bay leaves until the onion and garlic is golden, then add the rice. Lower the heat, stir the mixture, and continue cooking. The rice absorbs most of the flavor of the other ingredients and also the oil.

2. Meanwhile in a saucepan put double the volume of water as there is rice, add salt, and bring to the boil.

3. When the water is boiling, add the mixture from the frypan, and allow it to boil over a strong heat for about 5 minutes, stirring frequently.

4. Then cover the saucepan, remove it from the heat and leave it on the side of the stove for another 15 minutes.

5. When the rice is cooked, remove the bay leaves, large pieces of onion, and the garlic. The cooked rice should be dry and each grain fluffy. Sprinkle with chopped parsley before serving.

Instead of using salted water, rice may be cooked in a variety of different liquids to enhance its flavor and to give it added color. For example, fruit juices may be used for puddings and dessert rice: the rice takes on the color and flavor of the juice used, providing an interesting variation. Spanish children love this sort of dessert. Diluted tomato juice (equal quantities of juice and stock or water) may also be used for savory dishes, as may various stock cubes (chicken, beef, and vegetable). Some cooks vary the method given above for Spanish rice and fry the rice first in butter, adding a little dry Sherry. Then when the rice has absorbed the butter, chicken stock is added and the rice is cooked until tender. This is a superb method!

Let us start this recipe section with a really stupendous dish from Andalucia. You will notice that the method of cooking the rice is somewhat different from that used for white rice. The reason for this is that white rice is used as an accompaniment to a number of dishes rather than as an *intrinsic* part of a dish as is the case here. However, notice that the basic principle of flavoring the rice is still used.

## Arroz con Gambas

(Arr-oth kon Gam-bass)

Rice with shrimp
serves 4

¾ lb (360 g) large shrimp

### SHRIMP BUTTER

6 Tbsp. (6 × 15 mL) butter
1 small onion, finely chopped
1 stalk celery, coarsely chopped
1 bay leaf
2 Tbsp. (2 × 15 mL spoon) chopped parsley
1 glass (1½ dcL) dry white wine

### THE RICE

2 Tbsp. (2 × 15 mL spoon) butter
2 Tbsp. (2 × 15 mL spoon) olive oil
1 small onion, finely chopped
2 cups (360 g) rice
½ glass (¾ dcL) dry white wine
shrimp stock
salt and pepper
2 Tbsp. (2 × 15 mL spoon) grated hard cheese

1. Prepare the shrimp as explained (see index), shell, devein, and keep to one side but reserve the shells and liquor.

2. Make the shrimp butter. Melt 4 Tbsp. of butter and saute the onion and celery with the bay leaf and parsley for

about 2 minutes. Then add shrimp shells and cook for a few minutes, stirring continually.

3. Moisten with dry white wine and simmer the mixture until the wine is almost evaporated.

4. Now pound the mixture to a smooth paste or put in a blender to obtain the same result.

5. Return the paste to the pan, and with the remaining 2 Tbsp. of butter, cook for 2 minutes more, stirring all the time. Strain and reserve.

6. Now prepare the rice. In another pan, heat the butter and oil and saute the onion until transparent. Add the rice and cook, stirring continuously, for about 5 minutes until the rice is golden. Then add the wine.

7. When rice has absorbed the wine, add 2 cups (500 mL) of the strained shrimp liquor, and continue to cook until the rice is tender, adding more shrimp liquor (or water) when necessary.

8. When rice is almost cooked to the desired consistency, add the cooked shrimp, and just before serving, stir in the shrimp butter and the grated hard cheese.


## Arroz con Pescado

(Arr-oth kon Peth-kar-doo)
Rice with white fish
serves 4

You will find this cold dish of rice and fish delightful for lunch on a hot day.

½ lb (250 g) rice

### DRESSING

6 to 8 Tbsp. (6 to 8 × 15 mL spoon) olive oil
2 Tbsp. (2 × 15 mL spoon) wine vinegar
2 Tbsp. (2 × 15 mL spoon) finely chopped parsley
1 or 2 cloves of garlic, crushed
dry mustard, to taste
4 fillets of anchovy, chopped fine
¾ lb (360 g) cooked, flaked white fish
salt and pepper, to taste

### GARNISH

4 ripe tomatoes
2 green peppers
1 small cucumber
French dressing
chopped hazelnuts (or almonds)
ripe black olives

1. Cook the rice as directed for white rice. It should be quite dry when cooked and the grains should be fluffy.

2. Place rice in a sieve and pour cold water through it to remove any starch. Allow to drain thoroughly and become quite cold.

3. Make a pungent dressing by combining the oil, vinegar, parsley, garlic, dry mustard, and anchovies.

4. Put the rice and fish in a bowl. Mix in the dressing and season with pepper and salt. Place in the center of a serving dish.

5. Chop the tomatoes, peppers, and cucumber, season with French dressing, and place around the mound of rice and fish.

6. Decorate the top of the rice with chopped nuts and the black olives.

## Arroz con Mejillones y Almejas

(Arr-oth kon Meh-e-lyoan-es e Al-may-has)
Rice with mussels and clams
serves 4

24 mussels
2 cups (½ liter) clams
5 Tbsp. (5 × 15 mL spoon) olive oil
3 cloves garlic
2 Tbsp. (2 × 15 mL spoon) chopped
    parsley
1 ripe tomato, peeled, seeded, and
    chopped
½ lb (250 g) rice
water, if required
salt and pepper to taste

1. Put to boil on the stove 1 quart of slightly salted water. When boiling, drop in the mussels and clams and cook over a moderate heat until the shells open.

2. Remove the fish with a slotted spoon, take off all the shells, and discard them. Put fish to one side.

3. Continue to boil the cooking liquid until it is reduced to half the original quantity.

4. Meanwhile heat the olive oil in a frypan; add the garlic and cook gently until it begins to color; then put in the parsley, tomato, clams, and mussels. Let the mixture fry for a few minutes.

5. Now add the reduced shellfish juice and, as soon as it begins to boil, add the rice and seasoning. Cook over a high flame until the rice begins to absorb the liquid, then reduce heat and cook for 15 minutes or until rice is done.

6. Should the mixture become too dry, add a little boiling water, as required.

7. Place on a serving dish, garnish with lemon slices, and serve.

## PAELLA

Paella is undoubtedly the one dish that has become an international classic. The ingredients change for each section of Spain, and indeed almost every family has its own favorite way of preparing this dish. It is by no means a difficult dish to prepare, but it does take time and the proper ingredients.

Natural rice must be used in order to give the necessary flavor to the other ingredients. Saffron, that most expensive coloring in the world, or the more commonly used saffron color called *azafrán de color*, is a must. Olive oil is necessary also.

It is also a good plan to purchase a *paellera*, the special dish used only to make paella. As explained in a previous chapter, this is a shallow iron pan with sloping sides and two side handles. However, if you wish, a shallow frying pan with sloping sides may be used.

When cooking the paella, it is important that the flame of the stove should cover the whole bottom of the pan. All the ingredients for the paella may be prepared beforehand, except of course for the rice, so really it only takes the time required to cook the rice for the paella to be ready for the table; about twenty minutes.

The paella from Valencia is famous and is made from a mixture which includes seafood, chicken, pork, and sometimes pork sausage. Paella Valenciana is the only paella that has a particular recipe. For variety, you can experiment with any other ingredients you prefer.

## Paella a la Valenciana

(Pay-ell-ya a la Val-en-ci-ana)
The original paella
serves 4

2 breasts of chicken
½ lb (250 g) pork loin
⅓ cup (85 mL) olive oil
2 ripe tomatoes, peeled, seeded, and
    chopped
2 cloves garlic, minced
½ cup (80 g) green beans, cut finely
½ cup (80 g) shelled green peas
½ tsp. (1 × 2 mL spoon) paprika
1½ cups (360 mL) rice
1 quart boiling chicken stock (or water)
pinch of saffron color
8 large shrimp
12 mussels
½ pint (¼ liter) clams
salt and pepper to taste

1. Put clams in cold water for an hour to eliminate sand prior to use.
2. Cut the chicken breasts and the pork into small pieces, season them with salt and pepper, then fry in olive oil heated almost to smoke point. The oil must be very hot.
3. Brown the meats over this heat for about 5 minutes, then add the tomatoes, garlic, beans, and peas. Cook for 5 minutes longer.
4. Take the pan off the stove and mix in the paprika.
5. Return the pan to the fire. Put in the rice and fry until the rice has taken on some color. Meanwhile heat the stock or water to boiling.
6. Mix the saffron color in with the water or stock. Add to the pan and cook on high flame for 5 minutes. Stir to mix.
7. Reduce heat to moderate and cook for a further 15 minutes.
8. When the rice is half-cooked (about 6 minutes), add the shrimp, mussels, and clams, and bury them under the cooking rice.
9. When all is cooked, let the dish rest for a few moments on the side of the stove so that the fish juices may blend with the rice.

*Fish and Shellfish*

# 10

# 10 FISH AND SHELLFISH

With more than 46,000 miles of rivers, Spain offers a variety of freshwater fish for the gourmet. The geography of the peninsula determines the various watersheds which spill into the Atlantic, the Cantabrian Sea, and the Mediterranean. With few exceptions, Spanish rivers are relatively short, with fast running water, and are rich in salmon, trout, carp, shad, and mullet. These varieties of fish are readily available, especially in the towns that are near a river.

Naturally, there is also an abundance of saltwater varieties caught on both the Atlantic and Mediterranean coasts. Many of these varieties, while unknown outside the waters of continental Europe, make quite excellent eating. Others of course are not so good, either because they have too many bones or because their flesh is coarse. These we shall discuss a little later.

## MARKET FORMS OF FISH

The market forms of fish in Spain are similar to those found in the United States and United Kingdom.

### Whole (Round) Fish

The fish, as it comes from the sea, will at least need to be eviscerated. In Spain the fishmonger will do this for you if you ask, but many Spanish buy the fish whole and make use of the intestines (especially the liver). The head of a large fish, such as mero or grouper, is also prized, and in many peasant recipes is regarded as the best and sweetest part of the fish.

AMOUNT TO BUY.   Allow 1 pound (500 g) of whole fish per serving.

## Cleaned (Eviscerated) Fish

For this kind of fish, the intestines have been removed but the head and fins are still attached. This form is not often seen in Spanish markets, as most fish are sold and weighed whole. So you pay for the intestines, etc. whether you want them or not. One exception to this rule is trout: they are always cleaned prior to weighing.

AMOUNT TO BUY.   Again, 1 pound (500 g) per serving is usual, or with trout, one 10 ounce (300 g) fish is adequate.

NOTE.   Large, whole fish, weighing from 4 to 5 pounds (2 Kg to 2½ Kg), will have about 1¼ to 1¾ pounds (620 g to 840 g) waste from head, bone, fins, and intestines. An exception is a John Dory. This fish has a gigantic head, which accounts for almost three-quarters of its total weight.

## Dressed Fish

Fish that are being sold as cutlets or steaks are dressed by the fishmonger before cutting. This means that the fish have been cleaned and scaled, and usually the gill covers have been removed.

AMOUNT TO BUY.   One-half pound (250 g) per serving is usual.

## Fish Fillet

These are fish that have been cleaned and the flesh removed from both sides of the backbone. But remember, most fish is sold whole. If you ask the fishmonger to fillet it for you, the price you pay will be for the whole fish. The only fillets that are sold are frozen fillets of fish.

AMOUNT TO BUY.   Between 5 ounces (150 g) and ½ pound (250 g) is sufficient.

## Wings

This only applies when buying skate (*rai*). The body is discarded and the two wings are the portions sold. In Spain, rai is the only fresh fish sold in parts.

AMOUNT TO BUY.   One-half pound (250 g) is a good serving.

# COOKING METHODS

In Spain, as in most other countries, fish for the most part is cooked in four basic ways: deep-fried, pan-fried, poached, or baked. Broiling (under a grill or salamander) is not usual in the Spanish home, although a broiling effect is obtained by using the ridged cast-iron skillet.

## Fried Fish

In Andalucia, fried fish is extremely popular, and cooks are expert at making it. Small fish, such as *chanquettes* (similar to whitebait but smaller) and tiny whole fresh anchovy (*boquerones*) are often simply dipped in seasoned flour and then quickly deep-fried. With this technique, only a few fish are cooked at one time so that the oil temperature will remain constant, the pan will not be crowded with fish, and the coating will not be rubbed off. The trick of course is to have the frying oil at the right temperature—365°F (185°C)—and the fish sufficiently moist so the sifted and seasoned flour will stick. When frying these fish, the flour is sifted each time a fresh batch is dredged, so that no tiny lumps of flour that may have stuck together from the moisture in the previous batch of fish will adhere to the next batch. This technique ensures a fine, even coating which does much to enhance the eating qualities of the fish. The flour used for dredging is also kept warm, as a further precaution against lumping.

Fillets of fish are dipped first in seasoned flour and then in a coating batter after which they are fried in the usual way. The frying oil is kept at the ideal temperature of 365°F (185°C) and again, only a few pieces of fish are cooked at the same time. In this way the oil retains its efficient frying heat and seals the fillets immediately. The batter does not absorb the oil and become soggy as would be the case if the temperature were lower or too many pieces of fish were cooking at the same time. Finally, the fish will not overlap, knocking off the coating so it sinks to the bottom of the pan.

Now although olive oil is used extensively in Spain, it is *not* used as a deep-frying medium. This is because the temperatures required for successful deep-frying are too high for olive oil to be effective. Each oil and fat has a smoke point—the temperature at which a thin, blue-white haze rises from the medium, and the point at which it starts to break down. Olive oil will start to smoke at between 300 and 315°F (150 to 155°C), a temperature much too low for successful deep-frying. So Spaniards use a more suitable product.

# SMOKING TEMPERATURES OF FRYING COMPOUNDS

|  | (°F) | (°C) |
|---|---|---|
| Hydrogenated vegetable compound | 440–460 | 225–235 |
| Standard vegetable shortening | 420–440 | 210–225 |
| Cottonseed oil | 410–430 | 205–225 |
| Chicken fat and corn oil | 400–430 | 200–225 |
| Lard | 340–350 | 175–180 |
| Olive oil | 300–315 | 150–158 |
| Bacon fat | 290–300 | 145–150 |

The coating batters commonly used in Andalucia are slightly unusual and have something to do with the excellence of their results. Both of the following batters produce a beautifully light and crisp finish.

## Coating Batter No. 1

½ cup (125 mL) all-purpose flour
½ tsp. (2 mL) salt
1 Tbsp. (1 × 15 mL) olive oil
1 whole egg
3 Tbsp. (3 × 15 mL) milk
    (approximately)
2 Tbsp. (2 × 15 mL) soda water

1. Sift the flour and salt into a bowl.
2. Add the oil, egg, and milk. Beat until smooth.
3. Finally add the soda water and beat again until blended.

*Note: The soda water (club soda) is the secret ingredient!*

## Sifted, Seasoned Flour

Basically this is sifted flour seasoned with salt and pepper.

1 cup (250 g) all-purpose flour
1 tsp. (1 × 5 mL spoon) salt
¼ tsp. (1 × 1 mL spoon) pepper

## Coating Batter No. 2

This batter has a beer base. Use either fresh or flat beer.

1 cup (250 g) all-purpose flour
1 cup (250 mL) beer

1. Mix the two ingredients very thoroughly, preferably using a rotary beater.
2. Cover bowl and allow batter to stand for at least 4 hours before using.

*Note: Spanish cooks often add a pinch of nutmeg or ground cloves to this recipe; and either garlic salt or celery salt is substituted for plain salt.*

## Breaded Fish

This is popular the world over, and here again, in most parts of Spain the product is exceptional. There are three steps to follow for perfect results.

1. *Flouring:* The seasoned flour must be sifted so that no small lumps adhere to the fish.

2. *Moistening:* This is done by dipping the dry fish in very well-beaten egg to which 1 Tbsp. (1 × 15 mL spoon) of cold water has been added. Beat well together. Do not use an egg straight from the refrigerator as it is harder to beat and amalgamate.

3. *Breading:* Use fine breadcrumbs. The finer the crumb, the firmer (and better) the coating.

> *Note:* In some restaurants where fish is a specialty, the cooks often substitute dry Sherry for the cold water in the moistening agent. This gives the fish a much fuller flavor.

## Baked Fish

In many coastal areas, baked fish is also a specialty. What makes some of the Spanish recipes so good and so different is the imaginative use of a variety of flavoring agents which are added. This gives an extra gastronomic dimension to even the most simple recipe for a food which, on the face of it, seems to be quite dull.

## *Seasoning Mix for Baked Fish*

This is an excellent seasoning mix which is sprinkled over the fish just before being placed in the oven.

2 Tbsp. (2 × 15 mL spoon) parsley flakes
1 Tbsp. (1 × 15 mL spoon) dried grated lemon rind
1 Tbsp. (1 × 15 mL spoon) celery seed
1 Tbsp. (1 × 15 mL spoon) thyme
1 Tbsp. (1 × 15 mL spoon) marjoram
1 Tbsp. (1 × 15 mL spoon) savory
1 tsp. (1 × 5 mL spoon) dried chives

½ tsp. (1 × 2 mL spoon) crushed bay leaf
½ tsp. (1 × 2 mL spoon) grated nutmeg

Mix all ingredients thoroughly and store in an airtight container until required.

Makes about 3 ounces (90 g).

As you know, there is an entirely different principle involved when cooking meat and when cooking fish. In the former case, the cooking process is used to tenderize the meat sufficiently for it to become edible and more easily digestible. In the case of fish, it is cooked just sufficiently to break down the tender flakes and develop the natural flavor of the fish itself and to extract the flavor and aroma of any herbs and spices used in the preparation. Consequently you will notice that all baked fish recipes call for a preheated oven, so that the correct temperature is maintained from start to finish of the cooking process. All fish is baked at a moderate temperature, just sufficient to firm up the flesh, but not high enough to toughen the delicate protein.

Cooks in Spain are as adamant about temperatures when baking fish as they are concerning the flavoring ingredients (such as vegetables or herbs). All vegetables are chopped finely so that they will be *just* cooked (and with a slight crispness to them) at the same time as the fish is ready. When chopped, the vegetables are mixed and half the quantity is placed under the fish to be cooked, the remainder on top. The whole is moistened with a little wine, fish stock, or water; the casserole is covered and placed in the oven.

The recipe for *Pescado Blanco a la Malagueña* is a typical example of this principle. The recipe may be used for any type of white fish either baked whole or in cutlets. Test for doneness by sliding the blunt end of a spoon or fork between the natural divisions (or flakes) of the fish.

Spanish cooks use another interesting two-step technique to introduce flavor into their fish cookery. The first step is making what is, in effect, a thick vegetable sauce by gently stewing a mixture of vegetables, herbs, wine, and perhaps other flavorings. When cooked, the mixture is passed through a sieve and reduced (if necessary) to the consistency of a thick sauce. Meanwhile, the fish is *partly* baked in an oiled casserole.

In step two, when the sauce has been made, the fish is removed and the sauce placed in the casserole; the fish is then replaced on top of the sauce. Both fish and sauce are then baked together for a few minutes to finish cooking the fish and for the flavor of the sauce to permeate the flesh. Spanish cooks all agree that this technique produces a dish that emphasizes both the flavor of the fish and also the perfume of the vegetables, and is, by far, better than cooking fish and vegetables together in the sauce from the start. Three recipes that use this technique are included in this chapter and are indicated by the note "two-step."

A number of vegetable combinations may be used for the sauce and will, of course, depend on personal preference. But the important fact to remember is that whatever vegetables are used, they should not be too highly seasoned, otherwise the delicate flavor of the fish will not come through. Finally, if you make your sauce just a little too sharp, it may be brought back by the addition of a small quantity of brown sugar; if the sauce is too sweet, then sharpen it with lemon juice or a teaspoon or so of wine vinegar.

# FRESHWATER FISH

Some freshwater fish, particularly carp and mullet, need to be treated with salt before cleaning and cooking, to remove the slight muddy flavor which they sometimes have. This is a very simple process and necessitates hanging the fish on a hook stuck into the under jaw, then putting a tablespoon of rock salt in the mouth. Leave the fish to hang from the hook for about two hours. The salt will dissolve and pass through the fish. It will then be ready for further preparation. The fish will need to be cleaned, so follow the instructions in the diagram on p. 149.

### *Trucha* (Troo-cha) or River trout

There are a number of different varieties of river trout sold in Spain, and although they differ somewhat in appearance, their mild yet distinctive flavor is the same in all species. Trout are almost always sold whole/cleaned, although some restaurants insist that their fish should be left whole/uncleaned with the entrails left in the fish. The trout are then fried or grilled and when cooked, the entrails are easily removed. The flavor imparted to the fish by this cooking method is quite fantastic.

The most simple method of cooking trout is pan-frying in a little olive oil and lemon juice together with a spoonful of blanched almonds. The following recipe is also very simple to make, but it is quite an outstanding dish.

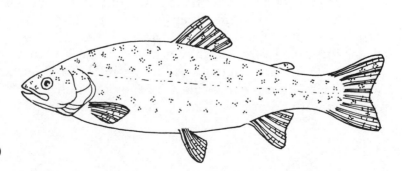

*Trucha* (River Trout)

# *Trucha con Gran Marnier*

(Troo-cha kon Gran Mar-nee-ay)
River trout with Gran Marnier
serves 4

1 Tbsp. (1 × 15 mL spoon) cognac
salt and pepper

slivered, toasted almonds
¼ cup (60 g) butter
4 fresh river trout
½ cup (120 mL) double cream
3 Tbsp. (3 × 15 mL spoon) Gran
  Marnier

1. Melt butter in a thick-bottomed skillet and saute the trout until cooked. Turn once only.

2. Meanwhile, heat the cream in a saucepan over a gentle heat. Do not let it boil.

3. When hot, stir in the Gran Marnier and cognac.

4. Place cooked trout on a heated serving dish; sprinkle with a little salt and pepper; then pour the cream sauce over. Sprinkle with almonds just prior to serving.

## Trucha a la Navarra

(Troo-cha a la Na-var-ah)
Trout, Navarre style
serves 4

This recipe is something different and very good indeed.

1 Tbsp. (1 × 15 mL spoon) olive oil
½ lb (250 g) lean ham, chopped
¼ lb (125 g) mushrooms, chopped
4 river trout, cleaned
1 Tbsp. (1 × 15 mL spoon) flour
pinch salt and pinch pepper
1 Tbsp. (1 × 15 mL spoon) chopped
  parsley

1. Quickly saute the ham and mushrooms in the oil over a brisk heat.

2. Remove with a slotted spoon and divide the mixture into four equal parts. Stuff each trout.

3. Dust the stuffed fish with flour.

4. Reduce heat and, in the same oil, saute the fish for about 5 minutes on each side. Turn once, allowing the skin to become an attractive golden color.

5. Remove from pan. Place on a serving dish. Sprinkle with salt and pepper, then chopped parsley.

## Carpe (Kar-pay) or Carp

The carp is a round fish with a small mouth, two barbels hanging from under the chin, and no teeth. Members of the carp family are particularly abundant in the upper and middle reaches of almost every river in Spain and are available all year round. However, they are best between November and March.

The most common size found in the fish markets will weigh about two pounds (1 Kg). When this size, they are delicious filleted, sprinkled with fresh fennel, and broiled. Larger fish may be stuffed and baked.

## Lisa or Mujol (Lee-zer or Mu-hol) or Gray mullet

This is a fairly large fish, up to a length of fifteen inches (38 cms). It has a gray, scaly back, stripes on the sides, and a white belly. The flesh is a little coarse, but firm. Avoid very large fish with flabby flesh. Bake, poach, or grill.

# CLEANING FISH

1. *Slit the skin open from the vent (near the tail) to the gills.*

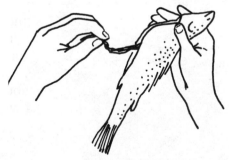

2. *Make a cross-cut at the head to separate the lower junction of the gills from skin.*

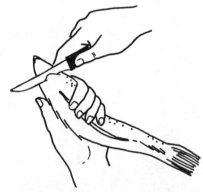

3. *While holding the gills firmly, pull the fish backwards to release the gills and other internal organs. Be sure to clean out the body cavity thoroughly.*

4. *Along the backbone you will see a black streak covered by a membrane. Cut this membrane by scratching the length of the backbone with a knife. Then push out the black material with your thumb.*

*Salmón* (Sal-moan) or Salmon

These delectable fish are available from the first Sunday in March until the twenty-first of July, when the season closes. The river salmon is smaller than the Pacific salmon, is slightly more mottled in appearance, and has excellent flavor. The popular cooking method used in the United States and Britain, that of serving it poached, is seldom used in Spain. Their favorite method is oven baking in a marinade.

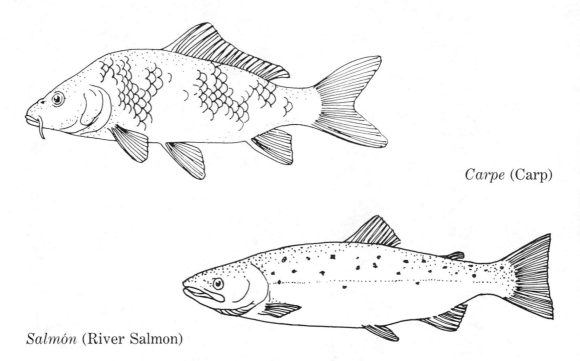

*Carpe* (Carp)

*Salmón* (River Salmon)

## *Salmón al Horno*

(Sal-moan al Orno)
Salmon baked in a marinade

3 Tbsp. (3 × 15 mL spoon) oloroso
  Sherry
3 Tbsp. (3 × 15 mL spoon) olive oil
1 Tbsp. (1 × 15 mL spoon) wine
  vinegar
1 tsp. (1 × 5 mL spoon) salt
½ tsp. (1 × ½ mL spoon) thyme

4 peppercorns, crushed
1 Tbsp. (1 × 15 mL spoon) chopped
  parsley
1 Tbsp. (1 × 15 mL spoon) chopped
  fennel
4 salmon steaks, each weighing about ½
  lb (250 g)

1. Combine the ingredients in a bowl and marinade the salmon steaks for a minimum of 6 hours (overnight is better).

2. When ready to cook, first preheat oven to 375°F (190°C).

3. Cut four pieces of heavy aluminum foil large enough to completely enfold each steak.

4. Lay fish on foil and spoon 1 Tbsp. of the marinade over each fish.

5. Crimp and fold the foil to seal, and bake in oven for 30 minutes.

## SALTWATER FISH

The Spanish coast, with its almost 2,000 miles of lovely and varied terrain, is the habitat of a rich and diverse marine life. Most of the fish caught from these shores are excellent. Some, however, because of a high bone content or coarse flesh, should be avoided. The following fall in this latter category:

| | | |
|---|---|---|
| Angelote | Cabella | Faneca |
| Arana | Corballo | Rato del Mar |
| Boga | Corvina | Rascasio |
| Cabrilla | Doncella | Vaquita |

Quite obviously, these are the Spanish names for the fish. Unfortunately there are no English translations by which you would recognize them. Of course, if they were on display in the market, their local name would be given.

This next group of saltwater fish may be tried with confidence:

*Abejedo* (Abbay-hay-doe) or Pollack

*Abejedo* is yellowish in color and rather similar to *Pescadillo* (whiting) but somewhat darker. It has good quality white flesh but is less delicate than whiting. It is usually baked or pan-fried.

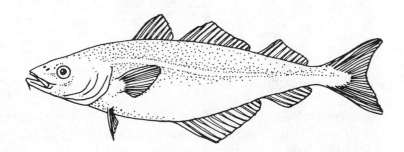

*Abejedo* (Pollack)

## *Busego* (Bus-ay-go) or Pink bream

This medium-sized fish grows up to 18 inches long (45 cms), with a slightly pink head and a red-gray back. Large fish are marked with a black spot on the shoulder. These are best served whole if small or may be filleted, crumbed, and pan-fried.

## *Boquerón* (Bock-er-own) or Fresh anchovy

This is a specialty of the Mediterranean, especially around the Costa del Sol. They may be distinguished from the sardine by their projecting snout and large mouth, which reaches almost to the gills. These fish are caught when they are between 1½ and 2½ inches long (38 mm and 65 mm). If small, they are washed, dredged with seasoned flour, deep-fried, and eaten whole. If larger, they are usually gutted, the heads are removed, and the tails are joined together in groups of four or five, with the fish spread out in the form of a fan. The whole fan is then deep-fried in very hot oil, which causes the tails to stick permanently.

*Boquerón* (Anchovy)

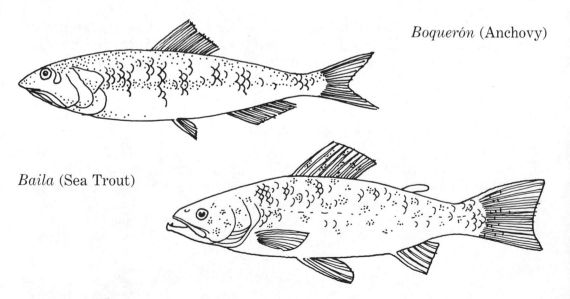

*Baila* (Sea Trout)

## *Baila* (Bile-yer) or Sea trout

Baila resembles salmon in many respects, having silvery scales when freshly caught and often displaying dark spots on the top half of the body. The flesh is usually pale pink, but may sometimes be white. It has a mild flavor with tender yet firm flesh. The usual market weight is between 1½ pounds (750 g) and 5 pounds (2.5 Kg). Simple preparation methods are best for this fish and one of the better methods is given in the following recipe.

## Baila al Horno

(Bile-yer al Orno)
Baked sea trout
serves 4

1 Tbsp. (1 × 15 mL spoon) butter
1 whole cleaned sea trout,
   approximately 3 lbs (1½ Kg)
4 peeled and finely chopped shallots
½ tsp. (1 × 2 mL spoon) salt
¼ tsp. (1 × 1 mL spoon) pepper
2 Tbsp. (2 × 15 mL spoon) lemon juice

1 Tbsp. (1 × 15 mL spoon) chopped
   parsley

1. Preheat oven to 375°F (190°C).
2. Place the whole fish in a buttered, ovenproof casserole, and sprinkle with the shallots and seasoning. Cover and bake in oven for 20 minutes.
3. Remove carefully from the casserole and place fish on a serving dish. Sprinkle with lemon juice and chopped parsley. Use the cooking liquor from the dish as a sauce.

CUTTING A WHOLE FISH AT THE TABLE.    Cut directly to the bone, then slide a wide spatula between the flesh and the ribs and lift off each portion. When top half has been served, lift and remove the backbone (cutting it at the point where it joins the head, if necessary). Then serve the remaining half of the fish.

*Carpón/Gallina del Mar* (Kar-poan/Gall-e-ner del ma) or Redfish, rosefish, rockfish

This is a red fish with a very large head and a fierce expression. They make excellent eating and have a mild flavor and tender flesh. One very simple method to present this delicious fish is to poach the whole fish in a little white wine together with a dab of butter and a hint of oregano. Or try the following outstanding recipe.

## Pasteles de Carpón

(Pas-tay-less day Kar-poan)
Fillet of redfish in puff pastry
serves 4

1½ lbs (750 g) fillet of carpón
¾ lb (375 g) puff pastry
pinch of nutmeg

½ lb (250 g) cooked, well-drained
   spinach
1 egg yolk

1. Cut fillets into 4 neat pieces of equal size, then gently poach them in milk and water. Drain well.

2. Preheat oven to 375°F (190°C).

3. Roll out pastry to an approximate square 16 in. × 16 in. (40 × 40 cm). Then cut into 4 equal squares.

4. Wrap each fish fillet in some of the spinach, then place on the puff pastry. Sprinkle with a dash of nutmeg.

5. Fold pastry around the fish to make a neat parcel, paint with egg yolk, and bake until pastry is cooked.

*Carpón* (Redfish)

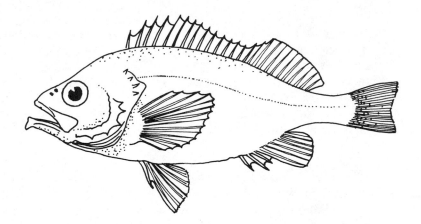

## *Cherne* (Cher-na) or Stone bass, Wreckfish

Similar in appearance to rock bass (*mero*), cherne has very good flavor. The main difference between cherne and mero is that the former has prominent cheekbones behind the eye sockets. It is a large fish, sometimes up to 5 feet (150 cm) long, and is sold in cutlets or fillets.

## *Chopa* (Cho-pa) or Sea bream, Black bream

This fish is a little like pink bream (*busego*) but has a dark gray skin and black markings, and many yellow longitudinal stripes. The fish must be scaled prior to cooking, and a whole fish may be baked or broiled. These are medium-sized fish, seldom reaching more than 18 inches (45 cm) in length.

## *Chanquettes* (Shan-kettiz) or Whitebait

These fish are smaller than the whitebait served in the United States or United Kingdom, seldom reaching more than 1½ inches (4 cm) in length. Usually they are caught when ¾ inch long. They are a very popular dish along the Costa del Sol where they are dredged in seasoned flour and fried for a few moments only, until they are golden brown. They are served at once with lemon.

## Dorada (Dor-arder) or Gilthead

This member of the bream family has a golden lateral stripe along its sides and a black spot near the shoulder. The skin is silvery and it is a most attractive fish: very good to eat as well. It may be cooked in any way applicable to bream, but I particularly liked this fish when I had it in a restaurant in Ronda where this was their specialty. The dish was called *Dorada Rellena* (Stuffed gilthead).

The little town of Ronda is set in the hills twenty-five miles (40 kilometers) from the Mediterranean coast, and clings stubbornly to the two shoulders of the ravine which is nearly one thousand feet (300 meters) deep. This "nest of eagles" is reached by one of three bridges, one of which, the Puento Nuevo (New Bridge), was built in 1755 and gives one a paralyzing view of the gorge dividing the town. It has a lantern-lit parapet, and leaning over the stone railings is a dizzying sight.

Apart from being one of the oldest towns in Spain, Ronda has other claims to fame, for it was here that the Moors rallied in their last rising against Ferdinand and Isabella. But more important still, to present-day Spaniards at least, is that Ronda was the site (at the beginning of the eighteenth century) where Ferdinand Romero, a carpenter, fought the first bull—*on foot!*

Until that time, bullfighting was the exclusive sport of princes and noblemen who sharpened their eyes and strengthened their wrists by killing wild bulls on horseback. During one such exhibition in 1710, the bull charged horse and rider, knocking both to the ground. The nobleman was trapped under his struggling mount with the bull's horns a few inches from his chest. As the bull was ready to drive the horns into the prostrate rider's body, Romero leapt into the circle in an attempt to distract the bull's attention from the fallen rider. Waving his broad Andalucian hat as a lure, he drew the bull away from the noble rider, then continued to hold the huge beast's attention by slow movements of his hat. Time and again he lured the bull past his body, to the admiration of the onlookers and the frustration of the beast. So was born the ritual of modern bullfighting.

## Dorada Rellena Romero

(Dor-arder Rell-ay-ner)
Stuffed gilthead, Romero style
serves 4

4 whole fish, 1 lb (500 g) each
 (approximately)

1 Tbsp. (1 × 15 mL spoon) butter
1 Tbsp. (1 × 15 mL spoon) lemon juice
¼ tsp. (1 × 1 mL spoon) pepper
1 Tbsp. (1 × 15 mL spoon) chopped
 parsley

STUFFING

4 Tbsp. (4 × 15 mL spoon) breadcrumbs

4 Tbsp. (4 × 15 mL spoon) chopped mushrooms

⅛ tsp. (½ × 1 mL spoon) ground nutmeg

⅛ tsp. (½ × 1 mL spoon) marjoram

1 wine glass or 5 fl ozs (1½ dcL) dry white
   wine

1 Tbsp. (1 × 15 mL spoon) butter

1. Preheat oven to 350°F (180°C).

2. Make a stuffing by mixing all the dry ingredients and moistening with sufficient wine to make a soft mixture.

3. Stuff the cleaned fish with the mixture.

4. Place the stuffed fish in a buttered ovenproof dish. Sprinkle with lemon juice, then pepper, and bake for about 30 minutes.

5. Serve the cooking liquor as a sauce. Garnish with the chopped parsley.

## *Estorino* (Es-tor-eeno) or Spanish mackerel

The flesh is slightly pink and very good and is not to be mistaken for the *caballa* which has dark red flesh (like beef) and is not a very good buy. The mackerel is a long, slender fish with a striped blue and green body and a silver belly and gray smudgy spots. The flesh is firm, but deteriorates fairly quickly. Bake, broil, fry, or pickle.

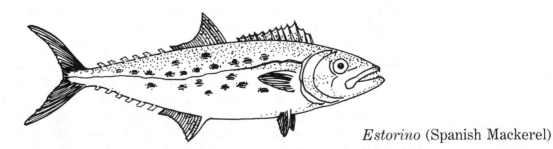

*Estorino* (Spanish Mackerel)

A quick and easy way with these fish is to put them in an ovenproof dish (no butter or oil) but with just a little white wine, three whole cloves, a bay leaf, and a good pinch of salt. Bake in a preheated oven at 375°F (190°C) for 25 minutes. Serve with a good piquant sauce or a tart fruit sauce. (See index for sauce recipes.)

Mackerel fillets are popular when pickled and served as a first course (entremeses). One small mackerel per serving is usual.

# Estorino en Escabeche

(Es-tor-eeno n Es-cab-esh)
Pickled mackerel
serves 4

4 mackerel, 12 ozs (360 g) each
  (approximately)
1 small onion, sliced
8 whole cloves
1 chili pepper
6 crushed peppercorns
1 bay leaf
1 sprig of tarragon
wine vinegar and water, to cover fish

1.  Preheat oven to 325°F (160°C).
2.  Roll each fillet around a piece of raw onion, starting from the tail and rolling toward the shoulders.

3.  Fasten the flaps by inserting two whole cloves into each flap and into the rolled flesh.
4.  Place the rolled fillets in a baking dish, flap-side down. Add the other ingredients to the dish.
5.  Add equal amounts of wine vinegar and water just to cover the fish, then bake in oven for about 25 minutes.
6.  Remove dish from oven and allow fish to cool in the cooking liquor.

*Note: Ask the fishmonger to fillet the mackerel crosscut (butterfly cut). In Spanish this is called mariposa. The head and backbone are removed, but the two fillets are left joined together. This recipe can be made up to 5 days before required if the fish is refrigerated.*

## *Lenguado* (Len-gwar-do) or Sole

A similar variety to that sold in the United States and United Kingdom, this fish can reach a weight of up to 5 pounds in the Mediterranean (2½ Kg). Unless the fish is required for baking, a better size is under 1½ pounds (750 g) as the flesh is less coarse. In Spain it is common to see sole as small as 4 inches (10 cm), which in most countries would be thrown back into the sea. However, these small fish are very inexpensive and the fishmonger will skin them for you while you wait. Although the proportion of bone to flesh is high in these little fish, the flavor is outstanding. I buy them whenever possible and treat them in the following manner.

      Cut off the head at an angle (as the flesh extends further down one side than the other). Wash the small pocket so exposed and remove black membrane. With a pair of kitchen scissors, cut away the fins around the fish. Wash, dip in beaten egg, then breadcrumbs. Fry for a few minutes turning once. Incidentally, I always cut the fins from any sole that I am pan-frying or broiling so my guests will not need to scrape the tiny side bones from the fish after it has been served. A fish in its prime, weighing 10 to 12 ounces

(300 g to 360 g) is sufficient for one serving and will provide four substantial fillets if required.

Sole lends itself to many exotic treatments and has always been regarded as a fish for gourmets. Spanish cooks agree with this philosophy and have produced a number of first-class recipes. One of the best was invented by Chef Diego Godoy at El Conquistador Restaurant in Fuengirola.

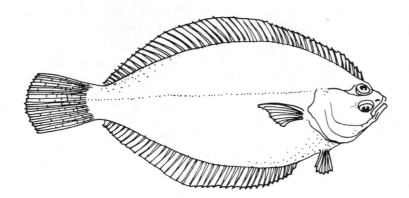

*Lenguado* (Sole)

This young man is one of the youngest *chefs de cuisine* along the Costa del Sol. It seems he started cooking at the age of nine, helping his mother prepare some of the simple but excellent dishes of Andalucia. It then became just a matter of time before he decided to make cooking his profession.

He started as an apprentice (*pinche*) and quickly found that kitchen work was truly his vocation; cooking fascinated him. At the Hotel Fenix in Madrid he learned the basic elements of preparation and presentation of all the food items on their extensive menu, and the character of all the ingredients used. Later, at the famous fish restaurant Horno de Santa Teresa, he learned more about fats and oils, about cooking temperatures, about the physical construction of foods (especially fish), and the dozens of other pieces of information which together form the fundamental culinary skills required to become competent in each department.

He told me that his most shattering experience as a pinche was when he realized that there were at least three hundred ways to cook and serve sole, at least one hundred and twenty classical recipes for the humble potato, and more than four hundred varieties of soup. And this was just part of the repertoire required of a first-class chef. As an Andalucian, fish continued to be his specialty and this is his recipe for sole.

## Filetes de Lenguado al Champaña

(Fill-et-ays day Len-gwar-do al Sham-
pan-ya)
Sole in champagne
serves 4

2 ozs (60 g) butter
16 fillets of sole (4 whole fish)
juice of 1 lemon
2 glasses or 10 fl ozs (3 dcL) dry
   champagne
½ pint light cream
pinch of dill seed

1. Melt the butter in a large frypan
over a medium heat and brown the
fillets to an attractive golden color.

2. Remove from pan and keep warm.

3. Reduce heat, then add lemon juice
and champagne. Simmer over a low
heat until liquid is reduced by half.

4. Add the cream and the dill. Beat
well to combine, then return sauce to
stove and reheat but do *not* boil.

5. Place sole fillets on a hot serving
dish in 8 piles of 2 each.

6. Pour the sauce over the fish and
serve.

*Note: Chef Godoy decorates the center of
the serving dish with a pile of seeded
black grapes.*

## Lenguado Tropical

(Len-gwar-do Trop-e-kal)
Sole with bananas
serves 4

Flavor and texture contrast are still
very evident in this delightful
combination of fish, fruit, cheese, and
vegetable.

1 cup (250 mL) prepared Bechamel
   sauce (See index for recipe.)

1 lb (500 g) fresh spinach
¼ tsp. (1 × 1 mL spoon) salt
dash of nutmeg
1 Tbsp. (1 × 15 mL spoon) light cream
2 Tbsp. (2 × 15 mL spoon) olive oil
2 large ripe bananas
½ tsp. (1 × 2 mL spoon) salt
1 lb sole fillets
2 Tbsp. (2 × 15 mL spoon) grated hard
   cheese

1. Prepare Bechamel sauce as directed.

2. Wash and drain spinach, place in a
saucepan, sprinkle with ¼ tsp. salt, and
cook until leaves are limp.

3. Drain thoroughly, chop spinach fine,
then rub through a sieve or put in
blender to make a puree.

4. Add nutmeg and cream, mix well,
and arrange mixture on the bottom of
an ovenproof dish. Keep warm.

5. In a frypan, heat the olive oil and
saute the bananas, which should be
sliced into rondels (rings), over a brisk
heat until lightly browned. Drain on
paper towel and put on the bed of
spinach.

6. Now sprinkle the fillets of sole with
a little extra salt, reduce the heat under
the pan, and saute the fish until cooked
(about 2 minutes on each side).

7. Remove fish from pan, drain on
paper towel, and place them over the
bananas.

8. Pour the prepared Bechamel sauce
over all, sprinkle with the grated
cheese, and lightly glaze under the
broiler.

## Filetes de Lenguado con Vermouth

(Fill-et-ays day Len-gwar-do kon Ver-
moot)
Sole in vermouth
serves 4                              *(cont.)*

From Tarragona, the home of Spanish vermouth, comes this very simple supper dish.

1 oz (30 g) butter
8 large fillets of sole
1 wine glass or 5 fl oz (1½ dcL) dry
    vermouth
cold water
salt and pepper

1.  Preheat oven to 325°F (160°C).
2.  Butter an ovenproof casserole and place in it the fillets folded in half.
3.  Add vermouth and enough water to cover the fish.
4.  Bake in oven for 20 minutes.
5.  Remove fish, put on a serving dish, and keep warm.
6.  Pour cooking liquid into a saucepan and reduce to about half over a brisk heat. Season to taste, then pour over fish just before bringing the dish to the table.

## Filetes de Lenguado, Linette

(Fill-et-ays day Len-gwar-do, Lin-et)
Sole with cream and mushrooms
serves 4

This final dish using sole illustrates once again the flair that Spanish cooks have for mixing colors and flavors to make yet another exciting presentation.

1 oz (30 g) butter
8 large fillets of sole
salt and pepper
4 ozs (120 g) chopped mushrooms
3 large tomatoes, skinned and chopped
2 wine glasses or 10 fl oz (3 dcL) dry
    white wine
¾ cup (200 mL) whipping cream
2 tsp (2 × 5 mL spoon) chopped parsley

1.  Preheat oven to 375°F (190°C).
2.  Butter a casserole, fold the fillets in half, season with salt and pepper, and place in casserole.
3.  Sprinkle mushrooms and chopped tomatoes over the fish, then pour in the wine.
4.  Bake in the oven for about 15 minutes.
5.  Carefully remove the fillets and keep them warm.
6.  Add the cream to the liquor in the casserole, sprinkle in the parsley, and mix. Heat slightly if necessary, but do not boil.
7.  Replace the fillets in the hot sauce and serve.

*Lubina* (Lu-beaner) or Common sea bass

Although there are a number of varieties of sea bass throughout the world, some averaging up to 300 pounds (150 Kg) in weight, the two varieties most seen in Spain are relatively small fish, weighing little more than 5 pounds (2½ Kg). These fish have a silvery-gray back and a white belly with delicate, tender, and slightly pink flesh. They are an admirable fish, but need scaling before cooking. Depending on size, they may be baked whole, pan-fried as cutlets, or filleted and deep-fried. As these fish hold their shape so well after cooking, they are often used for the restaurant specialty *Lubina a la Sal*. This is served along the three coasts of Spain and is much in demand. However, it is simple to prepare.

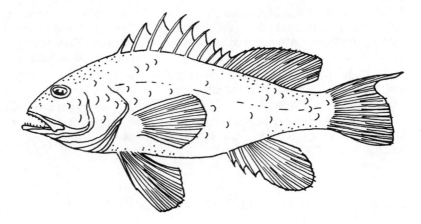

*Lubina* (Sea Bass)

# Lubina a la Sal

(Lu-beaner a la Sal)
Sea bass in salt
serves 4

All that is required for this dish is a whole ungutted fish weighing about 3 pounds (2½ Kg) and a supply of rock salt.

1. In an oven dish or a roasting pan, spread a layer of rock salt to a depth of at least ½ inch (1.25 cm).
2. On top of this salt, place the whole fish, then cover it completely with a further layer of salt. Press the salt firmly onto the top and sides of the fish, so that it will not slide off during cooking.
3. Bake in a preheated 425°F (200°C) oven for about 30 minutes.

The salt will form a hard crust around the fish and will need to be broken. If you work from the side of the fish and break the salt crust with a fork, it will lift off in one large piece, taking away the skin and revealing the steaming, white succulent flesh. Place the one flank of the fish onto two plates, then lift the backbone, and serve the lower flank. This dish is usually served with two or three kinds of sauce such as mayonnaise, salsa verde, and a garlic, lemon, and parsley sauce. (See index for recipes.)

# Lubina en Papel Aluminio

(Lu-beaner n Pap-el Alumin-eo)
Sea bass in foil
serves 4

8 ozs (250 g) soft breadcrumbs
2 Tbsp. (2 × 15 mL spoon) chopped
    parsley
8 Tbsp. (8 × 15 mL spoon) olive oil
1 medium-size onion, minced
4 ozs (125 g) sliced mushrooms
8 stuffed green olives, sliced
4 bay leaves
4 cutlets of sea bass, 6 oz (180 g) each
    (approximately)
salt and pepper
1 ripe tomato, cut into 4 slices
4 pieces of aluminum cooking foil, each
    approximately 10 × 10 inches (25 ×
    25 cms)

1. Preheat oven to 400°F (220°C).

2. Mix the first six ingredients, blending well to make a moist dressing. Divide dressing into 8 equal parts.

3. Place one part of the dressing on each of the pieces of foil, dust with salt and pepper, then put one cutlet over each portion of dressing.

4. Put the remaining portions of dressing over each cutlet, put a bay leaf on top, then a slice of tomato.

5. Draw the corners of each piece of foil together and twist the top to make secure. Now fold the edges of the foil to retain the steam and juices.

6. Bake in the oven for 30 to 35 minutes.

7. Serve each portion in its foil wrapper.

## *Mero* (Mare-o) or Rock bass, Grouper

This is a rounder fish than the lubina with a grayish-black back and a white belly. This fish is delicious, having firm, delicately flavored flesh, and is suited to any standard method of cooking. Some species of this fish have a yellowish-brown or a slightly reddish skin, and these are equally good to eat.

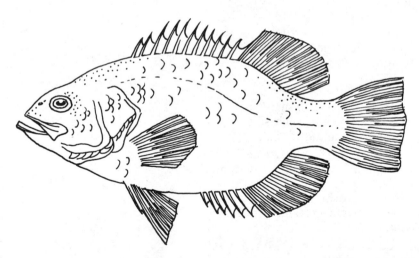

*Mero* (Rock Bass)

## *Mero a la Naranja*

(Mare-o a la Nar-an-ha)
Rock bass with orange sauce

⅛ cup (30 g) butter
⅛ cup (20 g) flour
1 cup (250 mL) chicken stock
salt and pepper
pinch of nutmeg

juice of 2 oranges
juice of 1 lemon
4 cutlets of mero
olive oil, to moisten
1 whole orange, sliced

1. Make a roux with the butter, flour, and chicken stock. Season.

2. When cooked, it should have the consistency of a thick sauce. Take off

the stove. Add the nutmeg and the juice of oranges and lemon. Mix to make a smooth sauce, and keep warm.

3. Dab the fish cutlets with a little oil and broil under a preheated grill (or pan-fry if preferred).

4. When cooked, transfer to a warm serving dish and strain the fruit sauce over the fish. Garnish with slices of whole orange.

*Note: Taste the sauce while adding the juices: you may prefer more (or less) orange, or more (or less) lemon. Adjust the flavor to suit.*

# Mero con Tomates

(Mare-o kon To-mat-ays)
Rock bass with tomatoes
serves 4

This is the first of the "two-step" recipes.

## TOMATO BASE

1 Tbsp. (1 × 15 mL spoon) olive oil
2 cloves garlic, finely chopped
1 small onion, finely chopped
4 large tomatoes, skinned, seeded, and chopped
2 wine glasses or 10 fl ozs (3 dcL) dry white wine
2 whole cloves
1 tsp. (1 × 5 mL spoon) salt
¼ tsp. (1 × 1 mL spoon) pepper
½ tsp. (1 × 2 mL spoon) sugar
1 Tbsp. (1 × 15 mL spoon) chopped parsley
3 Tbsp. (3 × 15 mL spoon) fine breadcrumbs

## FISH

4 cutlets (2 fish) mero (or similar white fish)
flour for dusting
1 Tbsp. (1 × 15 mL spoon) olive oil

### FIRST STEP

1. Prepare the tomato base in a saucepan as follows: Heat the oil and gently fry the garlic and onions until soft. Add the chopped tomatoes, wine, cloves, salt, pepper, sugar, and parsley. Cook over a low flame for about 20 minutes, stirring occasionally.

2. While this base is cooking, prepare the fish as follows: Dip the cutlets in flour and cook them in a frypan with a little olive oil. Cook them slowly, until they are just over half-cooked, and the surface of the fish is brown. Remove fish from pan and keep warm.

### SECOND STEP

3. Preheat oven to 350°F (180°C).

4. In the oil in which the fish was cooked, fry the breadcrumbs. Add them to the tomato base still cooking in the saucepan. Mix to make a smooth sauce. Pass the cooked base through a sieve, adjusting the seasoning if necessary.

5. Pour half of the base into an ovenproof dish. Place the fish cutlets on top of the base. Pour the remainder over the fish. Bake uncovered in the oven for about 15 minutes, until the fish is cooked. Serve in the ovenproof dish.

# Mero Pastelera

(Mare-o Pastel-airer)
Rock bass, baker's style
serves 4

2 Tbsp. (2 × 15 mL spoon) olive oil
1 Tbsp. (1 × 15 mL spoon) finely chopped onion
1 clove garlic, finely chopped
8 boiled potatoes, thickly sliced
4 cutlets of rock bass

*(cont.)*

4 thick slices of lemon
2 tsp. (2 × 5 mL spoon) salt
1 Tbsp. (1 × 15 mL spoon) chopped
  parsley
¼ tsp. (1 × 1 mL spoon) pepper
2 Tbsp. (2 × 15 mL spoon)
  breadcrumbs
1 Tbsp. (1 × 15 mL spoon) tomato
  paste

1.  Preheat oven to 375°F (190°C).
2.  Pour half the oil into an ovenproof
dish and sprinkle the chopped onion and
garlic on the bottom. Then place the
sliced cooked potatoes over this base.
3.  Arrange the cutlets on top of the
potatoes, put a slice of lemon on each,
and sprinkle with salt and a little of the
remaining olive oil.
4.  In a bowl, mix the parsley, pepper,
breadcrumbs, and the rest of the oil to
make a paste.
5.  Spread this paste over each of the
cutlets; cover and bake in the oven for
30 minutes.
6.  Ten minutes before removing from
the oven, put a dab of tomato paste on
each of the cutlets. Remove cover and
continue baking. Serve the fish in the
baking dish.

## Mero con Jerez

(Mare-o kon Her-eth)
Rock bass with Sherry
serves 4

2 Tbsp. (2 × 15 mL spoon) olive oil
4 fillets of rock bass (or alternative fish)
1 wine glass or 5 fl oz (1 dcL) dry
  Sherry
1 tsp. (1 × 5 mL spoon) salt
½ tsp. (1 × 2 mL spoon) sugar
2 Tbsp. (2 × 15 mL spoon)
  breadcrumbs
6 stuffed olives, finely chopped
2 Tbsp. (2 × 15 mL spoon) blanched,
  chopped almonds

1.  Preheat oven to 350°F (180°C).
2.  Oil an ovenproof dish with a little of
the olive oil and place the fish fillets in
it.
3.  Pour Sherry into the dish, then dust
the fillets with the salt and sugar.
Sprinkle the remaining oil over the fish.
4.  Mix together the breadcrumbs,
chopped olives, and nuts and arrange on
top of the fish, pressing it into the flesh
to hold it in place.
5.  Bake uncovered for about 25
minutes, gently basting the fish
occasionally with the liquid in the dish.

*Merluza* (Mare-lootha) or Hake, White salmon

This is a fish that is particularly plentiful in Spanish waters and is suitable
for baking, poaching, or steaming. It is a long, large slender fish with a silver-
gray skin and tender, white flesh, with very few bones. Small specimens of
Merluza are sometimes called *Pescadillas*.

   One of the pleasures of visiting the Asturias, the province that lies
between the Basque country and Galicia, is drinking the delicious cider made
from local apples, in one of the picturesque taverns called *chigres*. Here one

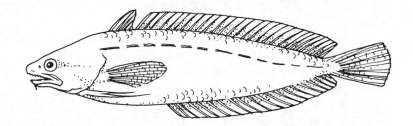

*Merluza* (Hake)

can sit, glass in hand, and, if one is lucky, listen to folk songs sung by one of the many male choirs that are a feature of this area. This experience is very reminiscent of the Welsh choirs in Britain and the small local choirs heard in the southern part of the United States. The following recipe uses cider as a moistening agent, and the dish will certainly leave you "with a song in your heart."

# *Merluza Asturiana*

(Mare-lootha As-tur-e-arah)
Hake, Asturian style
serves 4

3 Tbsp. (3 × 15 mL spoon) olive oil
4 cutlets or fillets of merluza
½ tsp. (1 × 2 mL spoon) salt
¼ tsp. (1 × 1 mL spoon) pepper
1 small onion, chopped
1 clove garlic, crushed
2 red pimientos, seeded and chopped
1 green bell pepper, seeded and
    chopped
1 bay leaf
1 wine glass or 5 fl ozs (1 dcL) dry cider
    or unsweetened apple juice

1. Preheat oven to 375°F (190°C).
2. Put 1 Tbsp. of the oil into an ovenproof dish. Season the 4 pieces of fish with salt and pepper. Bake covered for about 15 minutes.
3. Meanwhile, in the remaining oil, saute the onion and garlic until soft and light brown. Add the red and green peppers and the bay leaf and cook over a very low flame until the peppers are soft.
4. Drain the oil from the frypan, add the cider, and continue cooking until a fairly thick sauce is produced.
5. Test for seasoning, then pass the sauce through a fine sieve.
6. Take fish from the oven, cover with the strained sauce, and continue cooking for a further 15 minutes.

In complete contrast to the above is a recipe for Merluza that uses the fish in an entirely different manner. This dish was served to me one lunchtime in Toledo, after I had visited the Palace of Lerma just outside the town.

The palace is full of fascinating furniture and paintings, but to my mind the most outstanding item on display was the portrait by the artist Riber of Madame Ventiera. She was a seventeenth century charmer who married twice and had seven children. Her main claim to fame however was that she sported a full spade beard, and the portrait shows this bearded lady suckling one of her babies! A little disconcerting for any onlooker, one may think, but not sufficient to stop me from enjoying my lunch.

## Merluza con Jamon y Huevos

(Mare-lootha kon Ham-on e Wave-oth)
Hake with ham and eggs
serves 4

1 Tbsp. (1 × 15 mL spoon) butter
1 Tbsp. (1 × 15 mL spoon) olive oil
4 slices cooked ham, 2 ozs (60 g) each
　(approximately)
1½ lbs (750 g) hake fillets
1 wine glass or 5 fl ozs (1½ dcL) dry
　white wine
1 Tbsp. (1 × 15 mL spoon)
　breadcrumbs
4 Tbsp. (4 × 15 mL spoon) water
　(approximately)
½ tsp. (1 × 2 mL spoon) salt
¼ tsp. (1 × 1 mL spoon) pepper
3 whole eggs, well beaten
1 Tbsp. (1 × 15 mL spoon) chopped
　parsley

1. Preheat oven to 400°F (200°C).
2. Melt butter in a frying pan, add the oil, and brown the slices of ham over a brisk heat.
3. Remove ham and pour the fat and oil into an ovenproof dish.
4. Place the fish fillets in the dish. Add the wine, breadcrumbs, water, and seasoning.
5. Cover the dish and bake in oven for about 15 minutes.
6. Remove from oven, place the ham slices over the fish, and pour over the beaten eggs.
7. Cover the dish again, return to the oven, and bake about 5 minutes until the eggs are set.
8. Sprinkle with parsley and serve at once.

## Pargo (Par-go) or Red bream

Another type of sea bream and superior to both the Busego and Chopa, this variety has a rose or red tint along its sides and back and white tips to its tail. It is very good cut into cutlets, then baked or broiled.

## *Pescado* (Peth-kar-doo)

*Pescado* is not a variety of fish, but the generic term of all fish (but usually white fish) in Spanish. So on a restaurant menu you may see *"Pescado a la something-or-other"* which indicates that the dish has a fish base, probably merluza or one of the less expensive fish, certainly not rapé or mero or any of the more expensive varieties. The following recipes show how white fish is treated in five different provinces. Each recipe is typical of the area.

# *Pescado Blanco a la Malagueña*

(Peth-kar-doo Blan-ko a la Mal-a-gway-nyer)
White fish, Malaga style
serves 4

Notice in this recipe that the oil is used as the cooking agent, rather than wine or fish stock. This gives the white fish a fuller flavor and is typical of this area of Andalucia.

4 cutlets of white fish
4 medium-size tomatoes
1 Tbsp. (1 × 15 mL spoon) blanched, chopped almonds
½ tsp. (1 × 2 mL spoon) salt
¼ tsp. (1 × 1 mL spoon) pepper
2 medium-size onions
2 cloves garlic
3 green peppers, seeded

1 Tbsp. (1 × 15 mL spoon) chopped parsley
2 Tbsp. (2 × 15 mL spoon) olive oil

1. Preheat oven to 350°F (180°C).
2. Skin, seed, and chop the tomatoes. Place in a mixing bowl with the almonds, salt, and pepper.
3. Chop the onions, garlic, and green peppers finely. Add the parsley and mix with the other ingredients in the bowl.
4. Pour the oil into a casserole, then place half the tomato mixture at the bottom of the dish.
5. Lay the fish on top of the mixture and cover them with the remaining half of the mixture.
6. Put a lid on the casserole and bake in oven for 30 minutes.

The next recipe comes from around the Sitges area in Catalonia. Sitges is a very popular resort town and during the summer months is crowded with vacationers. However, before summer really begins, the townsfolk have a day to themselves and really put on a show. This is the Feast of Corpus Christi (May 29th) when the streets literally become a carpet of flowers.

On that day, many of the thoroughfares are cordoned off and a competition is held by the city's officials to judge the most beautiful floral carpet. The competitors, either individuals or groups of friends or neighbors, start at dawn to execute the most dazzling displays. On hands and knees they place hundreds of thousands of blooms, mostly carnations, to create intricate designs along the winding streets. The competitors must follow strict rules regarding the subject and composition of the designs. There must be no advertising or anything that can be regarded as bad taste or the entry is immediately disqualified.

Hours before the judging, thousands of visitors pour in by road and rail to see the dazzling creations. A special train, known as the "Floral Express," comes from Barcelona. On arrival at Sitges station the visitors are greeted with gifts of carnations by the townsfolk.

Yet the glory of the floral carpets is short-lived, for after the judging and the prize giving, the road barriers are removed and a religious procession travels the route. When it has passed, all that is left are the broken blooms waiting to be swept away by the street cleaners.

## Pescado al Horno, Costa Brava

(Peth-kar-doo al Orno Costa Brava)
Baked white fish
serves 4

2 Tbsp. (1 × 15 mL spoon) olive oil
4 white fish fillets or cutlets
1 medium-size onion
1 tsp. (1 × 5 mL spoon) salt
½ tsp. (1 × 2 mL spoon) pepper
1 clove garlic, crushed
1 wine glass or 5 fl ozs (1½ dcL) dry
    white wine
2 Tbsp. (2 × 15 mL spoon) lemon juice
pinch marjoram
2 Tbsp. (2 × 15 mL spoon or 60 g)
    breadcrumbs
1 Tbsp. (1 × 15 mL spoon) chopped
    parsley

1. Preheat oven to 350°F (180°C).
2. Pour half the olive oil into an ovenproof casserole and place the portions of fish in it.

3. Chop the onion finely and sprinkle over the fish, add garlic clove, then season with salt and pepper.
4. Pour in the wine and lemon juice; add the pinch of marjoram. Drizzle the remaining tablespoon of olive oil over the fish.
5. Sprinkle the whole with the breadcrumbs, cover the casserole, and bake for 25 minutes. Sprinkle chopped parsley over the dish before serving.

## Pescado al Horno con Patatas y Almendras

(Peth-kar-doo al Orno kon Bat-at-as e Al-men-dras)
Baked white fish with potatoes and almonds
serves 4

Cooks along the Costa Brava often include peeled oranges with the herb and wine. This recipe comes from Galicia, that province of hearty eaters.

2 medium-size onions
4 medium-size peeled potatoes
2 Tbsp. (2 × 15 mL spoon) olive oil
½ tsp. (1 × 5 mL spoon) salt
dash of pepper
1 wine glass or 5 fl ozs (1½ dcL) dry
  white wine
4 cutlets of white fish
1 Tbsp. (1 × 15 mL spoon or 30 g)
  slivered almonds

1. Preheat oven to 350°F (180°C).
2. Chop onions and potatoes finely and line the bottom of a casserole with the mixture.
3. Sprinkle one tablespoon of the oil over the vegetables and season with salt and pepper.
4. Pour in the wine and then place the fish on top of the vegetables.
5. Drizzle the remainder of the oil over the fish, then sprinkle with the almonds.
6. Cover the casserole and bake for about 35 minutes.

*Note: If you prefer to use oily fish such as trout, swordfish, or fillets of mackerel, the cooking time should be extended by about 10 minutes. Incidentally, unsalted peanuts or hazelnuts may be substituted for almonds.*

The next recipe comes from Castile and was served to me in the city of Burgos. Quite near the city, and well worth a visit, is the monastery of Las Huelgas. On either side of the main altar are the kneeling figures of Alphonso and his wife Elenor, daughter of Henry II of England. Another quite extraordinary feature to be seen in the Capella de Santiago, which is attached to the monastery, is the figure of St. James seated on a throne and holding a sword in his right hand. The body is articulated, so that the sword arm may move when required.

The story is told that the kings of Castile were too proud to receive the accolade of knighthood from another mortal, so they built this statue of St. James (Santiago) with movable arms. By pressing a lever, the gilded sword descends, the point touching the candidate's shoulder, and so the dubbing is accomplished. Edward I of England received the accolade in this chapel.

## Filetes de Pescado, Castilliana

(Fill-et-ays day Peth-kar-doo Kas-till-e-arner)
Fillets of fish, Castilian

Notice that this dish is somewhat unusual in its use of red wine as a flavoring, which gives it an attractive appearance and a greater depth of flavor. The flavor is also emphasized by the use of anchovy paste. It's well worth trying.

1 clove garlic
2 small onions
1 Tbsp. (1 × 15 mL spoon) olive oil
4 portions of white fish fillet
flour for dusting
½ tsp. (1 × 2 mL spoon) salt
¼ tsp. (1 × 1 mL spoon) pepper
4 tsp. (4 × 5 mL spoon) anchovy paste
  (or, 2 whole anchovies, each cut in
  half)
4 medium-size tomatoes
12 pitted black olives, chopped
pinch thyme

*(cont.)*

1 wine glass or 5 fl ozs (1½ dcL) red wine

1 Tbsp. (1 × 15 mL spoon) chopped parsley

1. Preheat oven to 350°F (180°C).

2. Chop garlic and onion finely.

3. Pour the oil into a casserole and sprinkle the onion mixture over the bottom.

4. Dust the fish fillets with flour and put them on the onion mixture, then season with salt and pepper.

5. Spread the anchovy paste over each fillet of fish (or place half an anchovy on each piece). Slice the tomatoes thickly and distribute them over the fish together with the black olives. Sprinkle with thyme.

6. Add the red wine, cover the casserole, and bake for approximately 35 minutes.

7. Just before serving, sprinkle the whole with the chopped parsley.

*Note: The anchovy will provide added salt, so don't use more than recommended.*

## Pescado en Vino Blanco

(Peth-kar-doo n Vee-no Blan-ko)
Fish in white wine and cream

Finally, this rather luxurious dish using white fish originates from Aragon.

1 clove garlic
4 portions of white fish
½ tsp. (1 × 2 mL spoon) salt

¼ tsp. (1 × 1 mL spoon) pepper
2 Tbsp. (2 × 15 mL spoon or 30 g) butter
1 small onion, finely chopped
4 ozs (120 g) mushrooms, finely chopped
2 wine glasses or 10 fl ozs (3 dcL) dry white wine
2 egg yolks
4 Tbsp. (4 × 15 mL spoon) light cream
chopped parsley

1. Preheat oven to 350°F (180°C).

2. Crush clove of garlic and rub over bottom of a casserole. Leave garlic in the dish.

3. Place fish on top and dust with salt and pepper.

4. Dot the fish with the butter. Sprinkle the onion over the fish, then add the mushrooms and the white wine.

5. Bake covered in the oven for about 25 minutes.

6. When cooked, remove the fish carefully from the casserole and keep warm.

7. Pour the cooking liquor into a small saucepan. Remove and discard the garlic and over a brisk heat, reduce the liquor to about half the original quantity.

8. In a bowl, mix the egg yolks with the cream.

9. Remove the reduced liquor from the heat and allow to cool for a minute or two, then add the egg/cream mixture and stir away from the heat until the sauce thickens.

10. Pour this over the fish, sprinkle with parsley, and serve.

### Pez Espada (Peth Es-parda) or Swordfish

This is a very large fish weighing up to 600 pounds (250 Kg) with very rich, distinctive, and close-grained (almost meatlike) flesh. It is especially good sliced in ½ inch (12 mm) steaks, and broiled or pan-fried. This fish requires very little in the way of added flavoring and usually when broiled, the steaks are dressed only with lemon juice or a little wine vinegar. The recipe that follows (from San Sebastian) uses a preliminary marinade.

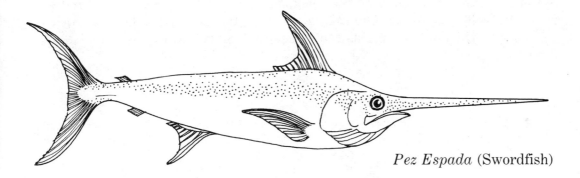

*Pez Espada* (Swordfish)

## Pez Espada Grillado

(Peth Es-parda Grill-yardo)
Grilled swordfish
serves 4

4 swordfish steaks, each 6 ozs (180 g)
   (approximately)
8 Tbsp. (8 × 15 mL spoon) olive oil
3 Tbsp. (3 × 15 mL spoon) lemon juice
1 Tbsp. (1 × 15 mL spoon) red wine
   vinegar
1 Tbsp. (1 × 15 mL spoon) chopped
   parsley
1 clove garlic, crushed
1 medium-size onion, minced
dash of nutmeg

1. In a bowl marinate the fish steaks in the other ingredients. Cover with foil and refrigerate for about 12 hours.

2. Preheat broiler to maximum temperature.

3. Remove fish steaks from marinade and place them on aluminum foil. Drizzle a little of the marinade over each and put under broiler, about 4 inches (10 cms) from the heat.

4. Immediately reduce heat to moderate and cook fish until light golden, about 4 minutes on each side. Turn once only during cooking.

*Note: Be sure that the fish steaks are no more than ½ inch (12 mm) thick.*

## *Rapé* (Rapp-ay) or Angler, frogfish, monkfish, toadfish

This variety is one of the very best to be caught in Spanish waters. Although its appearance is formidable, its white flesh has the most excellent flavor, something like that of lobster. The fish has a huge mouth and very sharp teeth, a grayish skin, and a chalk-white belly. It is a favorite fish served cold with a salad, when the similarity of flavor between angler and lobster is striking. The recipe is simplicity itself, for all that is required is to bake the fillets of fish in the oven together with a small quantity of white wine and a dusting of salt. Depending on the thickness of the fillet, the cooking time will range between 15 and 25 minutes in a 375°F (190°C) oven. Allow the fish to cool in its own juice, then cut into pieces and serve with a mayonnaise or a light vinaigrette.

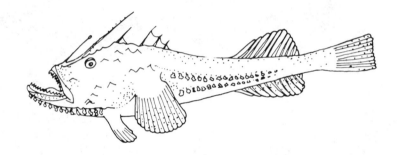

*Rapé* (Anglerfish)

## *Rapé al Horno*

(Rapp-ay al Orno)
Baked angler-fish
serves 4

This is a recipe from Málaga.

4 fillets of angler of equal thickness
½ tsp. (1 × 2 mL spoon) salt
¼ tsp. (1 × 1 mL spoon) pepper
2 Tbsp. (2 × 15 mL spoon) olive oil
1 clove garlic, chopped
1 medium-size onion, chopped
1 Tbsp. (1 × 15 mL spoon) chopped
    almonds
1 Tbsp. (1 × 15 mL spoon) crushed,
    salted peanuts
2 peeled and seeded tomatoes, chopped
4 Tbsp. (4 × 15 mL spoon)
    breadcrumbs
pinch of saffron or artificial egg yellow
    color

1. Preheat oven to 375°F (190°C).
2. Season the fish fillets with salt and pepper and place in a casserole with half the olive oil. Cook covered for about 10 minutes.
3. Meanwhile, in the remaining oil, gently fry the garlic, onion, nuts, and tomatoes. When onions are soft, add the breadcrumbs and mix well to obtain a smooth, soft paste, then add saffron or yellow color.
4. Drain the liquor from the fish in the oven and add this to the breadcrumb mixture. Beat the sauce again to mix. Pour over the fish still in the casserole.
5. Return to the oven and bake for 15 minutes at the same temperature.

## *Raya* (Ray-er) or Skate

The thornback is the most usual variety of skate seen in Spain and is by far the best of the three varieties caught around the coasts. All three types have a characteristic smelly skin and are one type of fish that should not be eaten when entirely fresh. Two-day old fish will give a better flavor, but after three days, the ammonia smell may be too strong for all but the most determined skate-lover.

The skin of skate is always removed before serving and it requires being scrubbed before cooking to remove the heavy slime that sometimes coats the skin. Only the wings are used, and these are bought ready-dressed from the fishmonger. The flesh is creamy and very digestible and may be pan-fried and served with black butter, which tends to counteract the ammoniac smell, or deep-fried, which also counters the slightly disagreeable smell. (See index for recipe for Black Butter.)

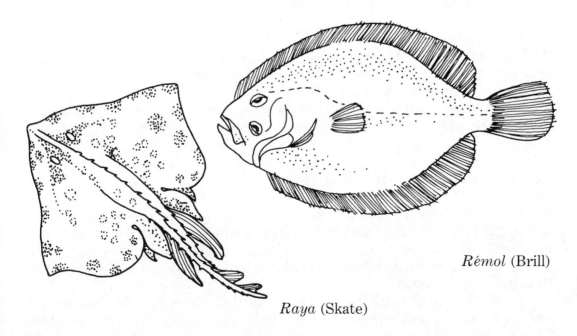

*Rémol* (Brill)

*Raya* (Skate)

## *Rémol* (Ray-mol) or Brill

Rémol is a fish similar to the *Rodaballo* (turbot) but does not have the bony knobs that characterize the turbot. The color is variable but most often dark brown or green-brown on the upper skin. It is an excellent fish with flesh rather more delicate than turbot.

Popular ways of cooking this fish are to simmer it in white wine and water in the proportion of one-third to two-thirds, and then serve it with Hollandaise sauce or a Sauce Tartare. (See index for recipes.)

## *Rodaballo* (Rod-a-bal-yo) or Turbot

A fish with dark mottled spots on the upper side (similar to brill), rodaballo usually has an almost black upper side. It is seldom seen whole in the United States, whereas in Spain, small fish weighing about 3 pounds (1½ Kg) are very common. The fish may be baked whole or cut into portions and pan-fried, poached, or baked. Cutlets should be soaked in cold water to which a little lemon juice and salt has been added to whiten the flesh.

## *San Pedro* (San Pedro) or John Dory

San Pedro is an oval-shaped fish with a very large, spiny head. The skin is thick and covered with small scales. The black mark on the shoulder is surrounded by a light gray circle. The head and intestines account for almost two-thirds of its total weight, a fact to remember when purchasing. It has an excellent flavor, with firm flesh that separates easily into four fillets, free of bone. It is equal to brill in quality and may be prepared in a similar manner.

## *Salmonette* (Sal-mon-ette) Red Mullet

There are two common varieties of this fish, the smaller measuring about 9 inches (23 cm) and the larger about 18 inches (45 cm). This latter also may be identified by the stripes on the first dorsal fin and a touch of yellow on the flanks. Furthermore, the larger variety is generally of a much deeper red than its smaller cousin.

These fish have a long pedigree, for they were reared as food by the ancient Egyptians and have been used for this purpose through the centuries. These fish are still among the most prized along the Mediterranean coast and are one of the few fish that are baked whole (not gutted). Small salmonette are usually grilled, pan-fried, or baked, but never poached.

The following is an excellent recipe from Seville, the spiritual home of *flamenco*, the dance beloved by each and every Andalucian. The Galicians may have their *muneira*, the Aragonese their *jota*, and the natives of Leon their *giraldilla*, but to every Andalucian, these pale into insignificance against the "fantastic flamenco."

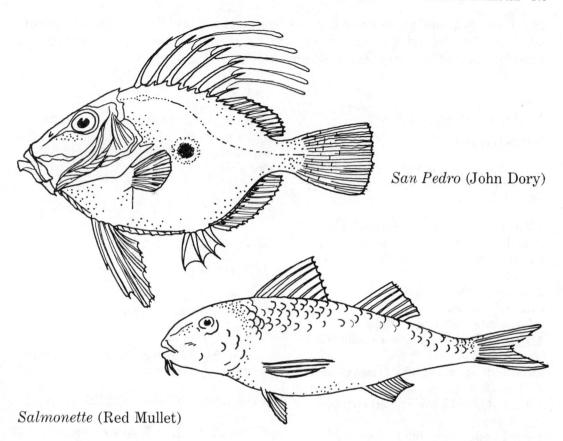

*San Pedro* (John Dory)

*Salmonette* (Red Mullet)

Easter is the time, most experts agree, when the best flamenco is heard. For during Holy Week in April, groups and individuals perform in the open with a passion and devotion seldom seen on the stage or in nightclubs. Flamenco falls into two categories: *Cante Chico* which includes light songs and tinkling music, reflecting the gay, happy side of life; and *Cante Tondo* which is used to reflect the sorrow, anguish, and despair so dear to the Spanish heart and temperament.

Flamenco has a noble heritage, for it was first performed over 2,000 years ago in Cadiz and over the years has absorbed Byzantine, Moorish, and Jewish musical cultures. In the troublesome Middle Ages, when the Moors and Jews were expelled from Spain, the musical traditions of the flamenco were taken over by the gypsies, who added their own characteristic rhythms, and thus the dance became associated in many people's minds as a gypsy dance.

Each part of the dance follows a particular pattern: from the foot-stamping (*zapateado*), the hand-clapping (*palmada*), to the snapping of the fingers (*pito*), all are performed to predetermined patterns and traditional rhythms. It takes up to twelve years to become a truly professional dancer, accepted by the critics, and many who enter this gruelling profession fail through lack of subtlety, the trademark of the expert.

## Salmonettes a la Sevillana

(Sal-mon-ettes a la Sevill-e-arner)
Red mullet, Seville style
serves 4

4 Tbsp. (4 × 15 mL spoon) olive oil
2 medium-size onions, chopped
1 wine glass or 5 fl ozs (1½ dcL) dry
    white wine
2 cloves garlic, minced
salt and pepper
2 large ripe tomatoes, chopped
1 Tbsp. (1 × 15 mL spoon) tomato
    paste or sofrito
4 red mullet, about 10 oz (300 g) each
2 Tbsp (2 × 15 mL spoon) breadcrumbs
1 Tbsp. (1 × 15 mL spoon) chopped
    parsley
1 hard-boiled egg, finely chopped

1. Heat half the oil in a frypan and cook the onions. When light brown and soft, add the white wine and continue cooking until the wine has reduced to half the original quantity.
2. Add garlic and seasonings, then the tomatoes and paste, and continue to simmer for a further 15 minutes.
3. Meanwhile, preheat oven to 350°F (180°C).
4. Mash the tomato mixture while still in the pan to a coarse paste.
5. Place the fish in an ovenproof dish; pour the sauce over, sprinkle with breadcrumbs; then drizzle the remainder of the oil over the breadcrumbs.

6. Bake in oven for about 30 minutes.
7. Just before serving, sprinkle the dish with chopped parsley and the chopped egg.

## Salmonettes con Salsa Romesco

(Sal-mon-ettes kon Sal-sa Romesko)
Grilled red mullet with Romesco sauce
serves 4

This is from Tarragona, where Sauce Romesco is a specialty.

4 red mullet, 8 to 10 ozs (250 to 300 g)
    each
4 Tbsp. (4 × 15 mL spoon) olive oil
2 Tbsp. (2 × 15 mL spoon) white wine
    vinegar
juice of 2 lemons

SAUCE

1 small onion, chopped
2 Tbsp. (2 × 15 mL spoon) olive oil
3 tomatoes, peeled, seeded, and chopped
4 cloves garlic
24 roasted almonds
a little lemon juice
salt and pepper
1 tsp. (1 × 5 mL spoon) paprika
chopped parsley for garnish

1. Clean and wipe the fish inside and out, but do not wash them. Make a few horizontal gashes in the sides.

2. Place them in a bowl with the olive oil, vinegar, and lemon juice and allow them to marinate for four hours.

3. Now make the sauce. Fry the onion in the olive oil until soft. Remove from pan and put into a blender or mortar the cooked onions, tomatoes, garlic, and almonds. Mix in the blender (or pound in the mortar with a pestle), adding sufficient olive oil to make a puree.

4. Finally add the lemon juice, salt and pepper, and the paprika and mix thoroughly.

5. Preheat the broiler, then drain the fish and place under the hot grill.

6. When cooked, garnish with the parsley and serve the sauce separately.

## *Sardinas* (Sar-deen-as) or Fresh sardines

Perhaps the most common and certainly the most inexpensive fish in Spain is the sardine. When freshly caught and either broiled or barbequed over charcoal, they are absolutely excellent, with delicate flesh and delicious flavor. This is the manner in which they are most often served in restaurants or in beachside cafes and tavernas. One eats them with one's fingers, nibbling the flesh from first one side then the other. New bread and a huge salad usually accompany this marvelous meal.

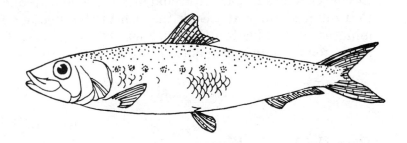

*Sardinas* (Sardine)

## Dried Fish

One of the favorite fish of the people on the Iberian peninsula is *bacalao* (back-laow), which is salted cod dried in the sun. Until the advent of modern roads and fast motor vehicles, this fish was a dietary standby for many Spanish and Portuguese living miles from the seashore, for it could be transported by mule or cart for many days in the hot climate without deterioration—a tremendous asset fifty (or even thirty) years ago.

When purchased it looks exactly like a grayish-yellow kite, as the fish has been split from head to tail before being salted and left in the sun to dry. It is as hard as a board and quite unappetizing to look at. But handled properly it becomes the basis of a number of interesting dishes.

Despite the fact that the Basque province has an extensive coastline and the freshest fish are always available, the Basques are particularly fond of bacalao and have produced undoubtedly one of the best recipes for this type of fish to be found throughout Spain. The one that originates from the area known as Vizcaya is perhaps the best of all. Vizcaya is one of the two Spanish Basque areas (the other is Guipuzcoa) which lie on the Bay of Vizcaya (or Biscay as it is known to foreigners).

Legend has it that the Basques are descendants of Noah's third son, Japhet, who after the Flood left the mountains of Armenia where the Ark had come to rest. He settled with his family in the valley of Roncal, at the foot of the Pyrenees. But whatever their antecedents, the Basques are hearty eaters and drinkers and, to show their continued independence and individuality, have a language of their own which is totally unlike Spanish.

PRELIMINARY PREPARATION. First wash it in cold water, then cut it into pieces, the size of which depends on the recipe used. Leave the pieces to soak in cold water for 36 hours. Then drain and put the pieces into a pan. Cover with fresh, cold water and bring to a boil. Reduce the heat immediately to a quiet simmer and cook the fish in this manner for between 12 and 15 minutes, depending on the thickness of the pieces. Then drain it. It is now ready for further treatment, according to the recipe to be used.

## Bacalao a la Vizcaya

(Back-a-laow a la Bis-kyer)
Dried cod, Basque style
serves 4

The recipe is completed in two steps.

STEP 1: SAUCE

1 clove garlic, crushed
1 Tbsp. (1 × 15 mL spoon) olive oil
1 small onion, chopped
4 tomatoes, peeled, seeded, and chopped

6 red peppers, seeded and chopped
salt and pepper
2 Tbsp. breadcrumbs

1. Fry the garlic in the oil over a gentle heat until golden brown. Remove and discard.

2. Put the onions in the oil and allow to stew slowly without browning. When soft, add the tomatoes, red peppers, and a little salt and pepper. Continue cooking over a very low heat for three-quarters of an hour. Note: If the sauce

gets too thick, moisten with a little water.

3. When the vegetables are well cooked, pass them through a sieve, then add the breadcrumbs and mix well.

## STEP 2: FISH

2 lbs (1 Kg) dried cod, weighed dry
2 Tbsp. (2 × 15 mL spoon) olive oil
4 green peppers, seeded and thinly sliced
2 large onions, thinly sliced
6 large tomatoes, skinned, seeded, and chopped

1. Prepare the fish as described earlier and fry carefully in the oil over a moderate heat.

2. When cooked and the flakes are soft, drain the fish well, dry on paper towels, and keep warm.

3. In the same oil, slowly stew the peppers, onions, and tomatoes.

4. Preheat oven to 375°F (190°C).

5. When the vegetables are cooked, combine with the mixture in the other pan.

6. Then in a casserole, place enough of the total sauce mixture to cover the bottom. Place the fried bacalao on top and pour the rest of the sauce over.

7. Cover the casserole and bake in the oven for a further 15 minutes to blend the flavors.

# SHELLFISH AND MOLLUSCS

## Shrimp and Prawns

In Spain, there are five different species of shellfish which in the United States would be known as "shrimp" and in the United Kingdom as "prawns," and the generic term for *four* of these varieties is *gambas*. They range in size from the very small shrimp to the large deep-sea variety, which is rose-colored and may be identified by its long head and beak and black spots on the shell. In fact, this variety is the true gamba. The fifth species of shellfish in Spain is a very large, almost 8-inch (20-cm) variety with a blood-red shell, known as a *carabinero*.

One of the best treatments of large gambas or carabineros is the style known as *Gambas a la Plancha* (Grilled deep-sea shrimp). They are washed in cold water, brushed with a mixture of olive oil and lemon juice, and placed on a hot griddle to cook for five minutes on each side, turning once. The oil and lemon juice are frequently dripped over the cooking fish. The shrimp are served with lemon butter or a garlic mayonnaise.

DEVEINING PRAWNS. Prior to cooking and serving prawns, one should remove the sand vein, which runs down the back of each fish. This is

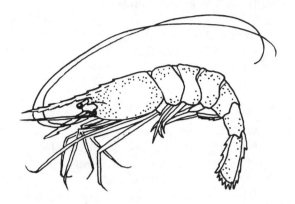

*Gamba* (Deep-Sea Prawn)

easily done by removing the head and then inserting a skewer or cocktail stick between the joint of the shell. Lift the skewer carefully to extract the vein in one piece. If the vein breaks, repeat at another point along the back. Alternatively, if appearance is not important, the fish may be shelled and a shallow cut made lengthwise along the back. Rinse the vein out with cold water.

TO SHELL GAMBAS.   Remove the legs, turn the gamba on its back, and with your thumbs, peel the shell from the underside. This will leave the tail shell intact. You may either gently pull this off or let it remain as required in some recipes.

In addition to gambas you will see the carabinero, which is even larger but is caught in more shallow waters. This variety is also bright red in color, but does not have the black spots on the shell. This type also may be treated in a similar manner to gambas. Both are very suitable for the following recipe.

## *Gambas Rellenos*

(Gam-bass Rell-ay-nos)
Stuffed butterfly shrimp
serves 4

1½ lbs (750 g) gambas or carabineros
2 small onions, finely chopped

2 cloves garlic, minced
2 ozs (30 g) butter
pinch thyme
½ cup (125 mL) light cream
3 ozs (90 g) breadcrumbs
1 Tbsp. (1 × 15 mL spoon) tomato
   paste or sofrito

salt and pepper
1 Tbsp. (1 × 15 mL spoon) chopped
    parsley
1 egg yolk
2 ozs (60 g) Manchego or other grated
    hard cheese

1. Prepare the shellfish by shelling
them as previously described, leaving
the tail shell in place. Remove the sand
vein.
2. With a sharp knife, butterfly the
prawns by carefully splitting the
outside curve where the vein is located,
almost through to the inside curve, and
along the entire length of the prawn.
3. Flatten the prawns carefully and

place on a flat pan lined with aluminum
foil and brushed with oil. Sprinkle
prawns with salt.
4. Prepare the stuffing. First, cook the
onions and garlic in the butter with the
thyme. Add the cream, breadcrumbs,
tomato paste, and salt and pepper (to
taste).
5. Mix thoroughly and simmer for 5
minutes, then beat in the parsley and
egg yolk. (The stuffing should be firm,
but not dry.)
6. Preheat the broiler. Spoon a dab of
stuffing on each prawn, sprinkle each
with a little grated cheese, and broil
until the cheese is melted and golden
brown.

In addition to the two varieties of shrimp and prawn mentioned, you
will come across the delightful *langostino*, another large variety distinguished
by its brownish color with pink tints; and the *camerón* which is the smallest
of the group and is pinkish-gray with a rather short body. For smaller shrimp,
the following recipe is ideal.

## Caserola de Gambas

(Ka-tha-ro-lah day Gam-bass)
Prawn/shrimp casserole
serves 4

1½ lbs (750 g) fresh small prawns
4 dozen mussels
2 wine glasses or 10 fl ozs (3 dcL) dry
    white wine
3 ozs (90 g) butter
1 medium-size onion, minced
2 cloves garlic, minced
4 mushrooms, chopped
2 ozs (60 g) flour
salt and pepper
4 ozs breadcrumbs
1 Tbsp. (1 × 15 mL spoon) chopped
    parsley

1. Cook fresh shrimp in sufficient
simmering salted water to cover for 3
minutes (until they change color).
2. Drain and plunge into cold water.
3. Prepare the mussels for steaming as
described on p. 196.
4. Cook the mussels in a saucepan with
the wine until shells open (about 8
minutes).
5. Remove mussels and keep on one
side; discard shells, but strain and keep
the cooking liquor.
6. With 1 oz (30 g) of the butter, fry
the onion, garlic, and mushrooms over a
low heat.
7. In a saucepan, make a roux with the
remaining butter and the flour using
the fish stock to extend to a smooth

sauce. Season with salt and pepper.

8. Preheat oven to 450°F (230°C).

9. Add the onion mixture to the white sauce, then the mussels, and finally the cooked prawns.

10. Pour the mixture into an ovenproof dish, sprinkle the breadcrumbs over the top, and bake uncovered for about 15 minutes or until the crumbs are browned.

11. Sprinkle with parsley before serving.

Another simple dish served in some of the restaurants in Cuenca is *Gambas a la Crema*. Situated right in the heart of Spain, the town of Cuenca has the reputation of being the one place in the entire country where the purest Spanish is spoken, and truth to tell, it is easier to understand the language here than in most other locations.

The houses in the old part of the town hang over the craglike edges of rock which have, over the centuries, been eaten away by the two rivers, Jucar and Huecar. The houses were built some time in the fourteenth century as summer residences of kings, but now looking over a gaping void, are still inhabited by local residents.

## Gambas a la Crema

(Gam-bass a la Kray-mer)
Creamed shrimp
serves 4

1 Tbsp. (1 × 15 mL spoon or 30 g)
    butter
1 lb (500 g) peeled raw shrimp
salt and pepper
pinch of nutmeg
½ cup (125 mL) milk
½ cup (125 mL) light cream
½ cup (80 g) ready-cooked peas
¾ cup (120 g) dry breadcrumbs

1. Preheat oven to 400°F (200°C).

2. Use a little of the butter to grease 4 individual casseroles, souffle dishes, or empty scallop shells.

3. Divide the shrimp into these containers, dust each container with salt, pepper, and nutmeg.

4. Mix milk and cream and pour into the containers.

5. Sprinkle the cooked peas into each, cover with the breadcrumbs, then cover the crumbs with the remaining butter and bake for about 15 minutes until crumbs are golden brown.

## Gambas Tostadas

(Gam-bass Tos-tar-dash)
Deep-fried shrimp toasts
serves 4

This is an exciting and unusual luncheon dish that may be served as a first course for dinner or as a hot snack when the toasts are cut into quarters.

1 tsp. (1 × 5 mL spoon) medium Sherry
½ tsp. (1 × 2 mL spoon) salt
1 egg white
1 tsp. (1 × 5 mL spoon) cornstarch
1 lb (500 g) deveined shrimp, minced
8 slices white bread, cut from a square
    loaf
2 Tbsp. (2 × 15 mL spoon) sesame
    seeds

oil for deep-frying
parsley for garnish

1. Make a smooth paste with the Sherry, salt, egg white, and cornstarch. Then mix in the minced shrimp.

2. Remove crusts from bread slices. Divide the shrimp mixture between the slices.

3. Press the mixture firmly into each bread slice using the back of a spoon. Sprinkle each slice with sesame seeds.

4. Heat oil to 350°F (180°C).

5. Fry the toasts one or two at a time, putting the *shrimp side downward* first. (This will set the mixture and seal it to the toast.) When the edges of the bread turn slightly golden, turn carefully with a slotted spoon, and fry the other side.

6. Drain on paper towels. Arrange on a serving dish and garnish with parsley sprigs.

# Fritura de Gambas

(Frit-ura day Gam-bass)
Deep-fried shrimp
serves 4

This recipe is rather special in that the batter is made with beer, rather than water. The batter *must* be allowed to stand for four hours before using. But the shrimp it produces is worth the waiting time.

1 cup (250 mL) flour
1 cup (2½ dcL) beer
1 lb (500 g) large raw shrimp
oil for deep-frying

1. Mix flour and beer in a large bowl and blend thoroughly using a rotary beater if available. Allow to stand at room temperature for about 4 hours.

2. Wash, shell, and devein the shrimp,

but leave tail shell intact.

3. Heat oil to 375°F (190°C). Holding the shrimp by the tail, dip them one by one into the batter, then drop them into the hot oil, a few at a time.

4. Fry until golden brown, about 2½ to 3 minutes, then drain on paper towels and keep warm.

# Poached Gambas

Shrimp of all sizes are used extensively in salad and as a constituent in many first course dishes (entremeses). When used in this way, the shrimp are most often poached very gently in an appropriate liquor. Besides the very common salted water, many Spanish cooks use a spiced liquor which imparts a subtle flavor to the shrimp without in any way masking its taste. The whole secret, of course, is not to overcook. This is a poaching liquor you will enjoy, and the recipe is sufficient to poach one pound (500 g) of shrimp.

1 cup (250 mL) dry white wine
1 pint (500 mL) water
2 Tbsp. (2 × 15 mL spoon) wine vinegar
2 crushed whole peppercorns
2 cloves garlic, crushed
¼ tsp. (1 × 1 mL spoon) oregano
2 bay leaves

1. In a large saucepan, combine all ingredients, bring to the boil, and allow to simmer for 30 minutes.

2. Strain the liquor and, if required at once, bring back to the boil, then drop the shrimp (shelled or unshelled) into the liquor and cook for between 5 and 8 minutes, depending on their size.

*Note: The crucial point when poaching gambas of any size is when the fish begin to curl. When this occurs they are cooked just right! Stop cooking at once, and plunge the gambas into cold water.*

## The Lobster Family

Again, some confusion may arise regarding nomenclature. As already explained, the Spanish langostino is a large shrimp, whereas in France, the similar word—langoustine—refers to a member of the lobster family: called in Spanish *cigala*. And don't mistake this fish for the *cigarra*, which is the flat lobster.

The *cigala (see-ga-la)* is the smallest of the lobster group and is known as the Dublin Bay prawn or sea crayfish. It may be recognized by its light coral color (when alive) and long, white-tipped claws and legs. The preferred way of eating these delightful crustaceans is to cook them in salted water for 10 minutes, then serve the tails hot with melted butter or in a mild garlic mayonnaise.

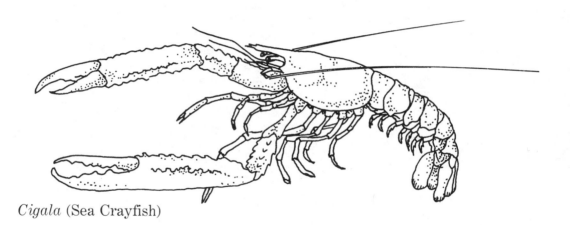

*Cigala* (Sea Crayfish)

In the well-known Madrid restaurant Tres Encinas, they serve these cigalas steaming hot after being cooked in a herbed wine liquor. One may eat them at the table, served with an assortment of savory butters, or standing at the counter in the noisy bar.

Spain is a noisy country, and this is not only due to the motorists who sound their horn at the slightest impediment to their progress, but also to the constant noise made by the Spaniards themselves. And in this, Madrid, being the capital, seems to outdo any other city. Every customer in a bar, for example, must raise his voice so as to be heard at the other end of the room, although speaking with two or three friends. There is always a television going at full blast, yet often it seems the sound is turned off, due to the great noise of conversation. The waiters bawl their orders; the service hands bawl confirmation.

As the bar becomes more crowded, so the decibel level rises louder and louder, until each speaker must shout louder and louder to be heard. His colleagues will be standing just inches from his side, nodding and showing acute interest and often speaking at the same time, so each little group is yelling and thoroughly enjoying themselves.

I mention this in passing, for I had just visited such a bedlam prior to going into Tres Encinas to eat the delectable crayfish cooked in their style. The peace and charm of the restaurant and the tender cigalas did much to restore my shattered nerves.

## Cigalas en Vino Hierba

(See-ga-las n Vee-no He-air-ba)
Sea crayfish in herbed wine
serves 4

2 cups (500 mL) dry white wine
3 medium-size onions, sliced
2 large carrots, sliced
4 cloves garlic, crushed
small bunch parsley
10 whole cloves
1 large lemon, sliced
4 bay leaves
1 Tbsp. (1 × 15 mL spoon) fresh mint, chopped
24 cigalas (live)

1. Fill a large kettle (6 quart/6 liter capacity) two-thirds full with cold water. Add all the ingredients except the crayfish. Cover and bring to boil, then reduce heat and simmer for 20 minutes.

2. Drop about 6 cigalas head first into the boiling liquid. When liquid returns to the boil, cook them 6 or 7 minutes until the shellfish become bright red. Lift them out with a slotted spoon and keep warm.

3. Repeat process until all fish are cooked.

4. Serve warm with individual dishes of savory butter. (See index for savory butter recipes.)

Langosta (lan-gos-ter) is the clawless lobster species, known as spiny lobster, rock lobster, or crayfish. It has a reddish-brown body with yellow and white markings. Cigarra (see-garra) is the flat lobster, recognized by the lumps on the shell and its very short claws. Bogavante (bog-a-vantay) is the Spanish name for the clawed lobster, the largest of the species. When alive, it is dark blue to black in color, with some yellow or green blotches.

There are very few Spanish recipes that involve cooked, hot lobster together with other ingredients. The Spanish tend to agree that the best way to eat these fish is just plainly broiled or freshly grilled, with a good sauce to give flavor contrast.

When buying lobster, select green (when uncooked) langosta, cigarra, or bogavante that are heavy for their size and weigh 1½ to 2 pounds (750 g to 1 Kg). They should be active when purchased, preferably straight from a tank of seawater.

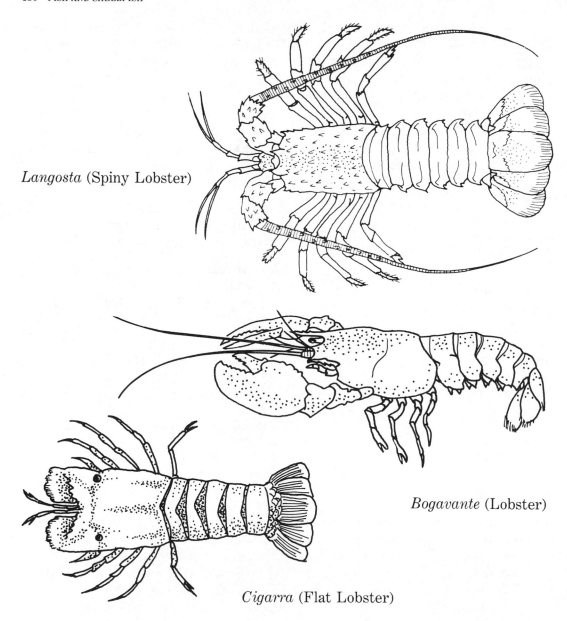

*Langosta* (Spiny Lobster)

*Bogavante* (Lobster)

*Cigarra* (Flat Lobster)

TO BOIL LIVE LOBSTER.   Use a large boiling kettle and fill with sufficient cold water to cover the lobsters. Add 1 Tbsp. (1 × 15 mL spoon) salt for each gallon (4 liters) of water, and add a few bay leaves. When the water is boiling briskly, grab each lobster (or crayfish) behind its head and plunge it head first into the boiling water. This will kill it instantly. Bring the water back to boiling, then reduce the heat and simmer for 15 minutes if the lobsters are under 2 pounds (960 g), or 12 minutes if much smaller. When cooked, plunge them into cold water, then drain before serving.

TO SHELL AND REMOVE MEAT.   Place the cooked lobster on its back and break off the legs and, if a bogavante, the large claws. Separate the body from the tail by arching the back until it breaks. Hold the tail in the left hand and with kitchen scissors cut the thin shell under the tail lengthwise. Remove the solid tail meat in one piece and with a small knife remove and discard the blue vein which runs the entire length. Split the body shell and remove the white meat which lies in four small pockets where the legs are attached. In this area also are the tomalley (liver), which looks like a greenish paste, and the coral (roe), if the fish is female. (Both these parts are edible.) Discard the remainder of the shell which contains the stomach, lungs, etc. Crack the large claws with the back edge of a heavy kitchen knife, and remove the meat in one piece.

TO SPLIT AND SERVE COOKED LOBSTER.   Cut through the heavy shell from head to tail. Remove the stomach, which lies just behind the head, then pull out the black intestinal vein which runs from the lower part of the body down to the tail. Remove the liver, which is regarded as choice, and is

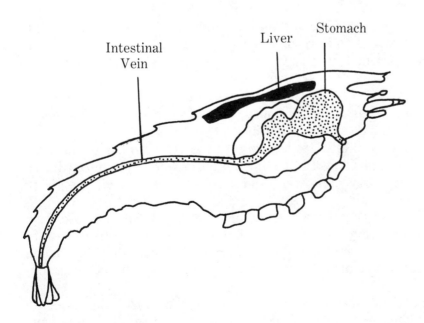

*The Split Lobster*

used in flavoring seafood sauces, and the roe, also used for flavoring and coloring sauces. Finally, crack the large anterior claws (if applicable to the variety), and remove the meat. Twist off and discard the spiny legs.

HOW TO EAT A WHOLE LOBSTER.   Follow these procedures:

1. Twist off the claws and crack each claw with a nutcracker. (In Spain, some restaurants provide a small wooden block and a hammer to break the claws.)
2. Separate the body from the tail by arching the back.
3. Bend back and then break flippers off the tail.
4. Insert a fork into the cavity where the flippers broke and push the meat out.
5. Take the body in one hand and lift off the heavy back shell to obtain the tomalley, which will be adhering to the top shell.
6. Now crack the lower body apart sideways, to obtain the remaining meat.
7. Finally, twist off the small claws and remove the succulent (but very small amount of) meat by sucking on the broken ends.

## The Crab Family

There are three main species of crab found around the coasts of Spain. The tiny ones are called *nécoras* and are used either as a base for shellfish soup and sauce or are seen cooked on a tapa bar as a snack. The technique used to get at the meat when they are served as a tapa is to pull off the legs and top shell and suck out the meat. A pretty messy business, but the meat is quite delicious. When used in a sauce or soup, nécoras are crushed in a mortar, then added to the stock. The liquid is strained prior to finishing.

The main variety of crab, called *cangrejo*, is very similar to the type known as dungeness found along the California coast and elsewhere. These have the characteristic dusty pink shell, and a good specimen will weigh up to 3½ pounds (1.75 Kg).

Finally, there is the *centolla*, the spider crab, which is recognized by its furry legs and the very rough top shell. The color ranges from rose to almost a mahogany. Both cangrejo and centolla are best when freshly boiled and dressed, although there are some provincial recipes which are outstanding.

Select crabs that are active and heavy for their size. Lightness in proportion to size indicates that the crab has been out to sea for some time and has lived on its own stored nourishment. The flesh therefore will be stringy and lack flavor. Also reject all crabs with damaged shells or missing claws or legs. If you buy cooked crab, test for weight and size. When you pick them up, shake them to see that some of the weight is not water that has entered the crab during the cooking process.

TO COOK LIVE CRAB.   Use a similar method to that for cooking live lobster. After putting the crab into the boiling water, wait for the liquor to return to boiling, then cook the crab for 25 minutes for a weight of 1¾ pounds (850 g), and proportionately more or less depending on size. When cooked, remove from the water and plunge it into cold water to stop the cooking process immediately. When the crab is quite cold it is ready to be dressed or served whole for guests to open and extract the meat.

TO EXTRACT THE MEAT.   Remove the legs and claws by twisting them away from the body. Crack the claws by hitting them with the back of a kitchen knife or if at table, use a nutcracker. Remove the soft meat and discard shells and membrane. Should there be any soft, creamy curd, this will indicate the crab is very fresh. Now separate the body from the upper shell. To do this, lay the crab on its back with the tail end facing you. Hold the top shell down firmly with the fingers and use thumbs to lever the body section out of the top shell. Set the body section aside while you deal with the top shell. Remove and discard the stomach which is located at the head end, and scrape the meat from the shell using the handle of a small spoon.

Return to the body section and pull off and discard the gray gills which are attached to the other side. Now split the body section in half and with a larding needle, a skewer, or a knitting needle, pry out the meat that lies in the various cavities of the body. Discard the empty shell.

*Note:* If you wish to use the top shell as a container for the crab, it should be trimmed by tapping along the natural curved lateral line which separates the very hard shell from the much thinner part. The trimmed shell should then be washed, dried, and rubbed with a little oil.

## *Txangurro*

(Shan-gurr-o)
Stuffed crab, Basque style
serves 4

4 live spider crabs
2 medium-size onions, minced
2 cloves garlic, minced
4 Tbsp. (4 × 15 mL spoon) olive oil
2 ripe tomatoes, peeled and chopped

1 Tbsp. (1 × 15 mL spoon) sofrito
1 wine glass or 5 fl ozs (1½ dcL) dry white wine
1 tsp. (1 × 5 mL spoon) sugar
1 tsp. (1 × 5 mL spoon) salt
pinch of paprika
½ cup (120 mL) brandy
½ cup (120 mL) breadcrumbs
¼ cup (60 g) butter

1. Cook the crab in the manner described previously (see *To Cook Live Crab*). Remove the meat from the claws and body. Retain the shells after trimming.

2. In a large pan, fry the onions and garlic in olive oil until soft, then add the tomatoes and sofrito. Let the mixture simmer until the liquid evaporates and the sauce is firm, almost solid.

3. Now add the wine, sugar, salt, and paprika and again allow the liquid to evaporate and the sauce to become firm.

4. Preheat oven to 400°F (200°C).

5. Add the chopped crabmeat to the sauce and heat through, then add the brandy and simmer for 5 minutes.

6. Spoon the mixture into the cleaned, oiled crab shells, sprinkle with breadcrumbs, dot with butter, and bake until brown in the hot oven.

## Tarta de Cangrejo

(Tarta day Kan-ray-ho)
Crabmeat tart
serves up to 8

1 prebaked pastry shell (9 inch/22 cm dia.)
1½ cups (360 mL) fresh grated mild cheese (such as Mancha Pok)

2 Tbsp. (2 × 15 mL spoon) butter
1 medium-size onion, minced
1 clove garlic, minced
8 ozs (250 g) crabmeat
4 whole eggs
1 cup (250 mL) light cream
2 Tbsp. (2 × 15 mL spoon) lemon juice
½ tsp. grated lemon peel (1 × 2 mL spoon)
¼ tsp. (1 × 1 mL spoon) each dry mustard and salt
16 cooked asparagus tips

1. Sprinkle half the cheese over the bottom of the precooked pastry shell.

2. In a frypan, melt the butter and gently cook the onion and garlic until soft without browning. Add the crabmeat, mix well, and carefully spoon over the cheese in the pastry shell.

3. Preheat oven to 325°F (160°C).

4. In a bowl, beat the eggs together with the cream, lemon juice, lemon peel, salt, and mustard. Then pour over the crab mixture.

5. Sprinkle evenly with the remaining cheese, and arrange the asparagus tips in the form of spokes of a wheel.

6. Bake for approximately 60 minutes, until the center of the egg mixture is firm.

7. Remove from oven, allow to cool for 15 minutes, then serve warm.

## Calamares (Squid)

The very name "squid" tends to send shivers down the spine. To tell the truth, squid are not glamorous or even very attractive fish, but properly prepared are most certainly a Mediterranean treat. Large specimens do sometimes reach a little over 18 inches (48 cms) in length, but usually they are seen in

# CLEANING AND PREPARING SQUID

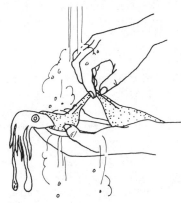

1. *Hold the fish under running water and with the fingers pull away and discard the spotted skin that covers the head.*

2. *Turn back the edge of the hood where it meets the body and carefully pull out the sword-shaped, transparent shell. Discard this also.*

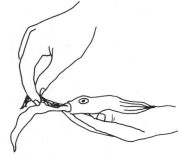

3. *Hold the head in one hand, the body and tentacles in the other, and pull gently to separate.*

4. *Remove and discard all material including the ink sac (unless it is being used in the recipe), which is situated behind the body. Then remove the eyes.*

5. *With the body upside down, so the tentacles are spread, open them to disclose the mouth. Then squeeze gently so that the hornlike beak will pop out. Discard.*

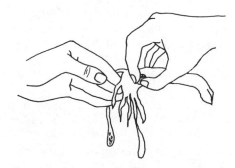

*The squid is now ready for further preparation.*

the market very much smaller than this. As with most fish in Spain, they are bought *entiero* (whole), and need to be cleaned prior to cooking. See diagram (previous page) for instructions.

## Calamares Frit

(Kal-a-mar-eth Frit)
Deep-fried squid
serves 4

Served all along the Mediterranean coast, this dish is very popular as a hot tapa as well as a main dish. The tender, nutty pieces of golden squid are served with half a lemon and accompanied by a green salad and warm, buttered rolls.

4 squid, ½ lb (250 g) (approximately) each
1 tsp. (1 × 5 mL spoon) powdered garlic
1 tsp. (1 × 5 mL spoon) salt
½ tsp. (1 × 2 mL spoon) pepper
1 cup (250 mL) fine breadcrumbs
1 cup (250 g) sifted flour
dash of nutmeg
oil for deep frying

1. Clean and prepare squid as already described.
2. Cut the hood crosswise into ½ in. (12 mm) strips, thus forming rings. Dry on paper towels and keep separate.
3. Leave bodies and legs whole and put them to dry on paper towels. Keep separate from hood rings.
4. Preheat frying oil to 360°F (185°C).
5. In a plastic bag, add powdered garlic, salt, pepper, crumbs, flour, and nutmeg. Shake well to mix.
6. Drop the dry rings a few at a time into the breading mixture. When coated, remove with a skewer or a fork and drop the rings, a few at a time, into the hot fat.
7. Cook for about 25 seconds or until the rings are a light golden brown.

8. Remove with a slotted spoon, drain on paper towels, and keep warm.
9. Coat the legs and bodies in a similar manner and proceed as for cooking the rings.

*Note: The bodies and legs of squid tend to retain a quantity of their natural body liquor. Consequently when they are deep-fried, these parts tend to make the hot oil splatter. It is for this reason that the legs and body are cooked separately from the rings.*

## Calamares Rellenos

(Kal-a-mar-eth Rell-ay-nos)
Stuffed squid
serves 4

4 squid, ½ lb (250 g) (approximately) each
4 ozs (120 g) ham, finely chopped
12 stuffed olives, finely chopped
3 ripe tomatoes, peeled and chopped
salt and pepper
1 Tbsp. (1 × 15 mL spoon) chopped parsley
2 medium-size onions, chopped
2 cloves garlic, chopped
2 Tbsp. (2 × 15 mL spoon) olive oil

1. Clean the squid, discarding the ink sac and intestines.
2. Remove the tentacles and chop finely, then mix with the ham, olives, tomatoes, salt and pepper, and half the chopped parsley.
3. Stuff the squid about three-quarters full with this mixture and fasten each opening with a cocktail stick.
4. Gently fry the onions and garlic in the olive oil and when soft, lay the

stuffed squid on the onion mixture and cook for 30 minutes, turning occasionally.

*Note: If the mixture in the frypan becomes too dry, add a little water (or dry white wine).*

## Pulpitos a su Tinta

(Pul-pee-toss ar su Tin-tah)
Baby squid in their own ink
serves 4

1 lb (500 g) baby squid
¼ cup (60 mL) olive oil
1 clove garlic, chopped
1 Tbsp. (1 × 15 mL spoon) flour
¼ cup (60 mL) red wine
chopped parsley
salt and pepper
1 onion, chopped

1. Clean squid. Remove the ink sac and reserve.

2. Cut the body into rings and the tentacles into pieces.

3. In a pan heat the oil and saute the garlic until soft. Add the pieces of squid and cook for a further 3 minutes or so, turning the squid frequently.

4. Sprinkle the flour into the pan and allow the oil to absorb. Add the red wine gradually, continually stirring. Mix in the parsley, salt, and pepper. Allow the mixture to simmer very gently until it thickens.

5. Meanwhile, dissolve the ink sac in a little cold water and add the black liquor to the rest of the ingredients in the pan.

6. Finally, add the chopped onion, then cover the pan and allow the squid to simmer for 15 minutes.

*Note: If the sauce is too thick, add a little more red wine. Serve on a bed of white rice.*

### Angulas (An-goo-las) or Baby eels

These tiny eels are a great delicacy in many parts of Spain and are served at parties, receptions, and on very special occasions. They are caught at the mouth of some of the larger rivers in Spain and kept alive until the moment of cooking.

They are prepared as follows. Take about 2 pounds (1 Kg) angulas, wash them in running water, then dry them gently on a towel. Heat sufficient olive oil in a wide-mouthed saucepan to take the eels, and in it toss 3 or 4 cloves of garlic. Heat the oil until it bubbles. Throw the eels into the hot oil, put on the pan lid at once (to stop them jumping out), and cook for no more than a minute. Serve at once in a little of the cooking oil.

### Almejas (Al-may-has) or Clams

These come in all sizes, from varieties measuring up to 5 inches (12 cm) to the very tiny ones the size of a nickel, called *coquinas*. The larger ones are usually eaten raw with a squeeze of lemon, the smaller are steamed open and used in soups, stews, sauces, or perhaps as a tapa. There are a few recipes which combine them with other ingredients such as pork, and these make an unusual and interesting dish.

After purchase, all bivalves should be examined and broken or open shells discarded. The remainder are then washed in running water and left to soak in brine for an hour to let them disgorge any sand that may have accumulated in the shell.

The major varieties of clams are:

*Navaja* (razor shell): a species which reaches a length of 6 inches (15 cm). It is quite distinctive in that it is the only long, rectangular bivalve. Eaten raw.

*Concha Fina* (carpet shell): up to 3 inches across (8 cm) with a yellowish to slightly cinnamon-colored shell and darker lines, both concentric and running from back to front. Eaten raw.

*Amayuela* (clovisse): smaller than the previous variety but with similar concentric lines running around the shell.

*Coquinas* (wedge shell): pearly shelled with rather flat base. Sizes from very small up to 1 inch (2½ cm). As mentioned, the smaller ones are cooked, and the larger are most often eaten raw.

## *Berberecho* (Bear-bear-ay-cho) or Cockles

This is a medium-size mollusc reaching up to 2 inches (5 cm) in diameter, with a creamy-yellowish shell with deeply ridged radiating lines. It is eaten raw or may be cooked until the shell opens in a wine/water solution.

## *Concha de Peregrino* (Kon-sher day Pear-i-green-o) or Pilgrim scallop

Similar to the larger sea scallop found in many parts of the world, including the United States, the pilgrim (or bay) scallop is found most particularly in Galicia and is inextricably associated with St. Tiago de Campostella (St. James of Campostella). Both the powerful white muscle, with which the mollusc propels itself across the floor of the sea and with which it opens and closes its shell to feed, and the orange tongue are eaten. In the United States the orange part is usually thrown away, although there is no logical reason for this.

SCALLOP PREPARATION. To open scallops, you first clear any beard (a dark frill around the edge of the shell) by pulling it away with the fingers.

Now put the scallop in a hot oven for a few moments, rounded part down, and the shells will open. Remove the white muscle and the orange tongue, wash in cold water, and use as instructed in recipe. Although the muscle is powerful when the mollusc is alive, when cooked it is very tender, providing the cooking heat is gentle. So do not poach in boiling liquid; just let the fish rest in very hot stock or milk and gently simmer on the side of the stove. If you wish to saute, this must be done over a moderate heat, using butter rather than oil.

## Peregrinos con Crema y Uvas

(Pear-i-green-os kon Kray-mer e Oovas)
Creamed scallops with grapes
serves 4

This recipe comes from San Sebastian.

2 cups (500 mL) chicken stock
1 tsp. (1 × 5 mL spoon) lemon juice
dash of nutmeg
12 shelled scallops
¼ cup (60 mL) butter
1 onion, minced
flour
1¼ cups (300 mL) light cream
6 ozs (180 g) seeded green grapes
½ well-blanched red pepper, finely
    chopped
salt and pepper

1. In a saucepan bring the chicken stock, lemon juice, and nutmeg to simmer.

2. Add the washed scallops and cook very gently for about 5 minutes. Remove them and set aside.

3. Raise heat under the stock, bring to a fast boil, and reduce volume to about half.

4. In another pan, melt the butter and fry the onion until soft.

5. Stir in flour to make a roux. Extend the roux first with ½ cup (120 mL) stock, then with the cream, beating between additions. Simmer until sauce is cooked.

6. Remove from heat, add scallops and grapes, then stir in the chopped red pepper.

7. Return to heat until all ingredients are hot. Season to taste.

8. Serve on a bed of saffron rice.

*Note: If sauce is too thick, add a little more stock.*

### Mejillones (Meh-e-lyoan-es) or Mussels

Mussels are prolific around each coast and are the cheapest of all shellfish. They are simple to prepare and the bright orange flesh is both delicious and highly nutritious. In Spain they are purchased by weight. After purchase, put them in the refrigerator until needed. When required, place them in a wide bowl ready for preparation. You may find that due to the chill of the refrigerator the shells may have opened. If this is so, pick up each one and tap it sharply against the side of the bowl. If the shell does not close, the fish is dead and must be discarded.

To prepare, each mussel must be bearded in a similar manner to that described for scallops. The shells also should be scrubbed with a hard brush under running water to remove any sea moss or tiny barnacles that may be attached. They are then ready for further preparation.

## Caldereta Asturiana

(Kal-der-etta As-tur-e-arnah)
Fish stew, Asturian style
serves 4

12 cleaned mussels
24 cleaned clams
2 lbs (1 Kg) assorted white fish, cleaned
2 Tbsp. (2 × 15 mL spoon) olive oil
2 onions, finely chopped
1 quart (1 liter) boiling water
salt and pepper
5 whole peppercorns
sprig of fresh mint
1 wine glass or 5 fl ozs (1½ dcL)
   medium Sherry
large pinch of ground nutmeg
2 Tbsp. (2 × 15 mL spoon) chopped
   parsley
pinch of saffron or yellow color

1. Open the mussels and clams and discard the shells.
2. Cut the white fish (which should be a mixture of three different varieties) into pieces about 2 inches (5 cm) square.
3. In a deep pan, heat the oil and gently saute the onions over a low heat until soft but not colored.
4. Place the pieces of fish on the onions, cover the pan, and allow to cook on a low heat for about 10 minutes without stirring.
5. Now add the boiling water to the pan together with the rest of the ingredients, *except* the parsley and saffron, and cook for another 15 minutes until the fish is tender.
6. Remove a cupful of the cooking liquor, add the saffron and the parsley to it, and mix. Then pour back into the pot. Stir to combine and serve from the pot.

## Mejillones a la Marinhera

(Meh-e-lyoan-es a la Mar-in-air-ah)
Mussels, sailor style
serves 4

The Spanish equivalent to the classical French dish *Moules Mariniere* is the similarly named *Mejillones a la Marinhera*. The oil and breadcrumbs included in the Spanish version give the dish a completely different flavor and texture.

4 Tbsp. (4 × 15 mL spoon) olive oil
2 large onions, minced
4 cloves garlic, minced
2 wine glasses or 10 fl ozs (3 dcL) dry
   white wine
2 lbs (1 Kg) ripe tomatoes, peeled and
   seeded
3 Tbsp. (3 × 15 mL spoon) chopped
   parsley
salt and pepper

6 lbs (3 Kg) live mussels
2 Tbsp. (2 × 15 mL spoon)
   breadcrumbs

1. Pour the oil into a very large saucepan or kettle with a lid and gently stew the onions and garlic until soft.

2. Add the wine, tomatoes, parsley, salt, and pepper and bring to a fast boil.

3. Now add the cleaned mussels, place the lid tightly on the saucepan, reduce heat, and simmer gently for about 5 minutes, until the shells are open.

4. With a draining spoon, remove the cooked mussels and transfer them to four serving dishes.

5. Add breadcrumbs to the cooking liquor, mix well, and pour over the fish.

6. Serve with chunks of hot bread, which are used to dip into the sauce.

## Mejillones al Horno con Queso

(Meh-e-lyoan-es al Orno kon Kay-tho)
Baked mussels with cheese
serves 4

6 lbs (3 Kg) live mussels
1 quart (1 liter) salted water
4 Tbsp. (4 × 15 mL spoon) olive oil
½ cup (120 mL) minced onions
2 cups (500 mL) minced mushrooms

1 Tbsp. (1 × 15 mL spoon) chopped
   parsley
salt and pepper
2 cups (500 mL) fresh breadcrumbs
2 Tbsp. (2 × 15 mL spoon) butter
4 Tbsp. (4 × 15 mL spoon) hard cheese,
   grated

1. Scrub, beard, and test all mussels as previously explained.

2. In a large covered kettle, heat the water to a brisk boil, then drop in the mussels, close the lid tightly, reduce the heat, and steam for about 6 or 7 minutes until the shells have opened.

3. Remove the mussels with a draining spoon and shell them.

4. In a frypan, heat the oil and saute the onions gently until soft. Add the mushrooms.

5. Drain off any excess oil from the pan. Then add the parsley and a little salt and pepper to the mixture.

6. Preheat oven to 425°F (220°C).

7. Arrange the shelled mussels in a 2 quart (2 liter) baking dish or four individual dishes.

8. Spread the onion mixture over the mussels. Cover with breadcrumbs and melted butter, then the grated cheese.

9. Bake in oven for about 10 minutes until the cheese is melted and the crumbs are brown.

### Ostras (Os-tras) or Oysters

Many of the oysters one purchases in Spain are the Portuguese variety, identified by the large oval to oblong and very irregular shell. This is in contrast to the almost fan-shaped shell of the Pacific and Olympic oysters of the United States and the Colchester and Helford oysters found in the United Kingdom.

  Portuguese oysters have yet another distinctive characteristic in that their flesh has a distinct greenish tinge, rather than the more usual gray-white. Don't let this difference in color put you off: the flavor is very good indeed.

Generally, most oysters are eaten raw either as a prelunch snack or as a first course at dinner. On these occasions, the Spanish seldom drink spirits, as this tends to pickle the tender flesh of the oyster in the stomach, causing some difficulty in digestion. On some occasions, however, one finds cooked oysters offered in restaurants and these either have been gently poached in fish or chicken stock and then used in salads or as an ingredient in an entree, such as the very excellent *Solomillo Relleno* (Fillet steak stuffed with oysters).

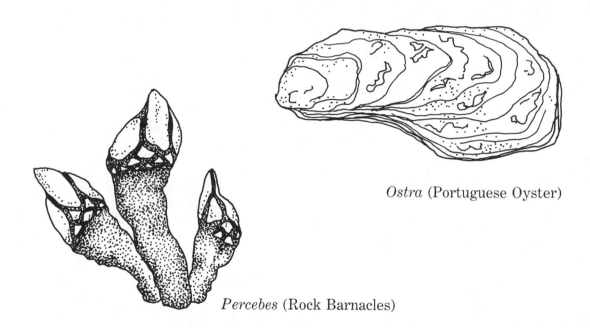

*Ostra* (Portuguese Oyster)

*Percebes* (Rock Barnacles)

TO PREPARE OYSTERS.   To clean and open oysters, first scrub the shells under cold running water, then drain. Fold a damp cloth into an oblong shape and place the oyster (rounded side down) on one end of the cloth. Cover the top shell with the other end of the cloth to protect your hand from the rough shell. With a sturdy, sharp-pointed knife, force the tip of the blade into the apron of the shell and cut toward the hinge until the muscle is cut. Remove the top shell, cut the oyster free from the bottom shell and serve it raw in its natural juices which lie in the bottom shell. Wedges of fresh-cut lemon are all that is required to accompany them.

POACHED OYSTERS.   For one dozen oysters (shucked) bring to a boil 2 cups (½ liter) chicken or fish stock. Add the oysters and simmer on the lowest possible heat for no more than 2 minutes. The oysters will become plump and somewhat firm and the edges will corrugate. They are now ready for further preparation or use in salads.

## *Ostion* (Os-tee-on) or Special oyster

This is a very small member of the oyster family found mainly around the coast near Cadiz. This variety *cannot* be eaten raw, and is most often shucked, then coated with egg and crumbs, and fried in deep oil.

## *Percebes* (Per-thay-beth) or Rock barnacles

These quite unlikely looking shellfish are approximately 4 inches (10 cm) in length and look something like witch's fingers. They are eaten raw with an oil, lemon, and garlic dressing. These are quite delicious once one has taken the plunge.

# 11

# 11   MEATS

I n Spain, one rarely sees a roast of beef—roast lamb, certainly; suckling pig, very often; but roast beef, seldom.

Many experienced cooks believe that in order to be perfect, a roast must overcome five obstacles. The meat must be *choice:* it must be properly *aged* and roasted at the *correct* temperature by an *expert* cook in a *good* mood. Should any of these essentials be missing, we are told, the roast will fail.

This perception about roasts may well be true. Meats reach flavorful maturity at different ages: lamb first, pork next, beef last. And in Spain, as far as beef is concerned, this presents a problem.

## BEEF AND VEAL

Owing to the lack of good grazing land in many parts of Spain and the prohibitive cost of animal feed, many of the beef animals are slaughtered either as suckling calves or when they are between one and two years of age. This means that the beef is not allowed to reach gastronomic maturity, and consequently, prime cuts do not have the marbling and other joints often do not possess the flavor or conformation of say, U.S. Prime or Choice. However, the milk-fed veal is a very superior product.

In Spain the word *vaca* literally means cow, *toro* means bull, and *buey* means bullock. In some shops they still advertize beef as *carne de vaca*, which is generic for beef, and is often of poor quality.

In most cities and towns, butchers now work to a standard classification regarding the cuts of meat. While it may seem, when first entering a butcher's shop, that one is viewing the result of a massacre—with the various lumps and chunks of meat of no recognizable shape or cut—the classification as explained below will take some of the gamble out of a purchase.

1. *Ternera de Avila* or *Ternera de Lechal* is milk-fed veal similar to that which American and British cooks are accustomed to and is most often of superior quality.

2. *Ternera* is young beef approximately one year old.

3. *Añojo* is a young steer up to approximately two years old.

4. *Vacuno* is a beast that is slaughtered between two and three years old.

5. *Lidia* is meat from a bull fought in the bullring. So beware—the meat will certainly be tough.

In addition to the classifications shown above, beef is also categorized by price, according to the cut. In the shops you will often see the meats displayed with price tags showing the cost per kilogram, with some explanation of the cut displayed (such as *extra, lomo, Primera 'A,'* etc.). The following descriptions indicate the areas of quality and are in descending order:

*Extra* or *Solomillo* is the fillet of beef or tenderloin.

*Lomo* refers to the whole loin section consisting of up to 12 ribs. The cut therefore can be either from the sirloin end or from the fore-rib end, so watch how it is cut. The sirloin end is better quality and the price for a piece from either end will usually be the same.

*Primera 'A'* refers to the five cuts taken from the area which is equivalent to the U.S. rump and round, and the English topside, silverside, rump, and round. The Spanish names for these five cuts are: *tapa, cadera, redondo* or *babilla*, depending on the part of the rump-end from which the cut is taken, and finally the *contratapa*.

*Primera 'B'* refers to the *culata de contra* and the *rabillo de cadera*, both of which come from the hindquarter in the area roughly equivalent to the thick flank. This category also applies to three cuts from the forequarter—the *aguja*, the *espadilla*, and the *pez*. This last cut comes from the area between the shoulder and the neck.

*Secundo* is the *morcillo* (shin); *brazuelo* (top of the shoulder); *falda gorda* or *aleta* (the flank or plate).

*Tercera* is the third quality, the lowest, and includes the *costillar* (short ribs), *pecho* (brisket), *rabo* (tail), and *pascuezo* (neck meat).

Do not be misled by a ticket on a piece of meat which says *biftek*. This does not necessarily mean that the piece is beefsteak, although that is the literal translation. In a similar way, a piece of meat marked *rosbif* can come from any part of an animal, sometimes but not usually considered suitable for roasting. So make your purchases (1) according to the classification (age of the animal), and (2) according to category (part of the animal). See the diagram showing Spanish cuts of beef and veal.

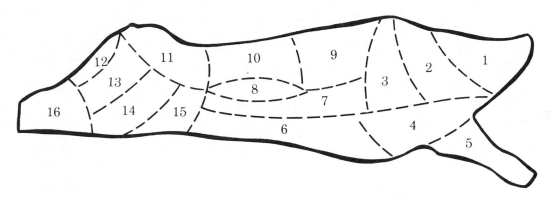

*Beef and Veal (Spanish Cuts)*

1. *Pezcuezo* = neck
2. *Aguja* = shoulder
3. *Espadilla* = shoulder
4. *Pecho* = brisket
5. *Brazuelo* = top of shoulder
6. *Falda* = flank
7. *Costillar* = short ribs
8. *Solomillo* = fillet
9. *Lomo alto* = fore-ribs
10. *Lomo bajo* = sirloin
11. *Cadera* = part of rump/round
12. *Tapa* = part of rump/round
13. *Contratapa* = part of rump/round
14. *Redondo* = part of rump/round
15. *Babilla* = thick flank
16. *Morcillo* = shin/shank

If you must have a roasting joint, it is better to buy a piece from *lomo bajo* (sirloin) or possibly from the *lomo alto* (toprib), and see to it that the meat is in the Ternera classification. If you are prepared to hang the meat for a week, then you may try Añojo. Remember, meat is sold fresh in Spain as a general rule (although there are now some butchers who age their meat to sell to foreigners), so always buy meat beforehand, as any aging you require must be done at home.

Other cuts from the hindquarter, such as *babilla, redondo, tapa, cadera,* and *contratapa,* and also the *espadilla* from the forequarter, are most suitable for pot-roasting or braising. Most other joints are more suitable for stews or for long, slow cooking. With all the cheaper cuts of meat, it helps if they are marinated for up to six hours prior to cooking. All Spanish marinades contain wine or vinegar, and sometimes both, as well as herbs and spices. (Refer to index for recipes for marinades.)

Partly because the price of meat in Spain is always high and also because the quality of the more expensive cuts is often indifferent, the most popular type of dish throughout the country—the *cocido*—uses the cheaper cuts together with an abundance of fresh vegetables. The cocido is part soup, part stew. The broth is usually served first and then the meat and vegetables will follow as the main dish. The name for this type of dish differs in various parts of the country. In the Asturias it is called *pote;* in Catalonia it is *olla;* in La Mancha they call it a *punchero;* and in Galicia it is called a *caldo.*

Cocido literally means "boiled," and whatever local or regional name is given the dish, the base is always an assortment of boiled meats, using whatever is available and inexpensive together with fresh and dried vegetables, and slices of spicy sausage or smoked ham, to give it added piquancy. Often the meat is marinated in wine with crushed peppercorns and herbs. such as rosemary, oregano, or bay leaves, then dipped in flour, fried in a little oil to seal the meat juices within each piece of meat, then simmered for an hour or two. Should you wish to use the browning technique for making a cocido or stew, remember that red meats should be browned quickly, uncovered. Remember also that the pieces of meat should not touch each other as they brown or they will stew rather than saute. There must be air space around them to seal the juices; so cook them a few at a time in the pan.

## Cocidos

There is an area around the Puerto del Sol (the Sun Gate) in Madrid which still has some of the best, inexpensive restaurants in the city. It is an area of narrow streets, intimate tavernas, and tiny bodegas—the very heart of a great city—and from which radiate ten streets like spokes of a wheel. No other place in Spain has been more important than this rather ugly square, and since 1606 when Philip III made it the official capital of Spain, the Sun Gate has been the scene of revolts and revolutions, proclamations and assassinations.

In one of these small restaurants in Calle Carmen one may sit in winter—when the weather can be miserable, bitterly cold, and perhaps snowing—and be served with a very special cocido named after a very special man: Santiago Pelayo. Now the name Pelayo may not mean much to the average foreigner, but to a Spaniard, especially a bullfight *aficionado,* the name has a magic ring. For Señor Pelayo is perhaps the most exclusive tailor in the world. He makes the *traje de luces* or "suit of lights" for the *torreros*—the men who kill the bulls.

When one is invited to visit his workshop just off the Puerto del Sol, the entrance is not impressive. But once through the doors at the bottom of the stairs, one enters a world of beauty, color, and inordinate skill. Each garment for each torrero is hand cut, hand stitched and hand finished, and in the over fifty years since Pelayo started business, no machine of any kind has been used to take over these duties.

As one enters the basement room, the bolts of silk and satin stacked along the wall flash their beauty in literally every color in the rainbow under the harsh electric lights. The material is woven in a convent near Barcelona and is produced for only two purposes—to make holy vestments for the church and for the matador to wear when he goes to meet and kill the bulls: each a ritual in its own different way.

The broad workbenches behind which the seamstresses sit are covered with pieces of silk and partly finished coats and breeches. The room is quiet as the women industriously sew each section of the suit, padding a part, if necessary, to give the wearer a better figure. The sleeves and breeches are piped and encrusted with heavy gold braid; the shoulders are decorated with epaulettes. The breeches must be skintight, and the coat must hug the shoulders and be sufficiently heavy to stay in position, no matter what physical movement the matador makes in the ring. It takes over one thousand hours to make a traje de luces to a standard of perfection seldom seen outside the premises of this most exclusive tailor in the world.

## Cocido Pelayo

(Ko-the-doe Pay-lay-o)
Pelayo's stew
serves 4

1 cup (180 g) chickpeas
1 lb (500 g) boned shoulder of lamb
6 slices of chorizo
4 slices smoked bacon, cut into pieces
4 bay leaves
salt and pepper
5 pints (2½ liters) cold water
1 lb (500 g) small potatoes
1 lb (500 g) onions, chopped
1 large leek, chopped
½ lb. (250 g) carrots, chopped
1 lb (500 g) cabbage, rough chopped
½ cup (120 mL) cooked rice
salt to season

1. Soak the chickpeas overnight. Drain the peas and discard the water.

2. In a deep saucepan, put the lamb (in one piece), the chickpeas, chorizo, bacon, and bay leaves. Season with a little salt and pepper. Cover with the cold water, and bring to a rapid boil.

3. Remove the scum from the top of the water, reduce the heat, and simmer for about 1 hour.

4. Then add the potatoes, onions, leek, and carrots and continue to simmer for 20 minutes.

5. In a separate saucepan with a little slightly salted water, cook the cabbage until tender. Drain and keep hot.

6. Take most of the liquid from the larger pan, add the cooked rice, adjust seasoning, and serve this soup as a first course.

7. Place the meat on a warm serving platter, slice into four pieces, and arrange the vegetables around the meat in such a way that every person gets a little of everything.

Notice that this last recipe had lamb as the meat base. In Andalucia they use beef, searing the meat in a little oil before putting it in the pot with sausage, green beans, garlic, and a touch of saffron to color the dish. In Cordoba their *carne d'olla* is a very simple dish of cabbage, bacon, sausage, and chickpeas. The punchero of La Mancha is based on pork and chicken with bacon, chorizo, cabbage, garlic, and chickpeas. In Galicia the caldo uses white beans with both veal and chicken and a special type of aged ham called *unto* or *anto*, only obtainable in that area. Smoked bacon is an acceptable substitute and is used in the following recipe.

## Caldo Gallego

(Kal-do Gal-yay-go)
Galician cocido
serves 4

¼ lb (120 g) smoked bacon, chopped
1 thick slice of salt pork, chopped
½ lb (250 g) veal, cut into cubes
½ stewing chicken, cut into 4 pieces
½ cup (100 g) dried navy beans
salt and pepper
8 cups (2 liters) cold water
2 white turnips, each cut into 2 pieces
1 whole chorizo, cut into 4 pieces
½ small cabbage, rough chopped
a handful of turnip greens

1. In a large pot put the bacon, salt pork, veal, chicken, and beans. Season with salt and pepper and cover with water.
2. Cook on a very slow heat for 2½ hours.
3. Then add the turnips, chorizo, and cabbage and cook for 15 minutes.
4. Add the chopped turnip greens and cook 15 minutes longer.
5. Serve the liquor first as a soup, then the meat and vegetables as the main course.

The two examples of cocidos give a good idea of the character and ingredients in these somewhat peasanty dishes. Their main attraction is that they are piquant, filling, and originally contained almost any ingredient that was available. Over the past twenty-five years, cocidos have become somewhat more sophisticated and now have been promoted to regional dishes with actual recipes.

The cocidos are different from the *estofadas* (stews) which are more like the meat and vegetable mixtures popular in most parts of the world. Estofadas may be made from beef, veal, lamb, pork, or chicken but always include some singular ingredient, often chorizo, to give it a vivid flavor contrast. Furthermore, you will notice that the cooking times for estofadas are much shorter than for cocidos, and the meal is served as one course rather than as a soup followed by a main dish. The following is a good example of a flavorful beef stew.

## Estofada de Vaca Española

(Esto-far-dah day Vacker Eth-pan-yola)
Spanish beef stew
serves 4

1½ lbs (750 g) stewing beef, cut into pieces
4 ozs (120 g) smoked bacon, cut into strips
1 large onion, chopped
4 cloves garlic, chopped
2 Tbsp. (2 × 15 mL spoon) olive oil
2 wine glasses or 10 fl ozs (3 dcL) dry white wine
1 wine glass or 5 fl ozs (1½ dcL) wine vinegar
1 pint (½ liter) stock
¼ tsp. (1 × 1 mL spoon) *each*, rosemary, basil, and oregano
½ tsp. (1 × 2 mL spoon) paprika
4 ripe tomatoes, peeled, seeded, and chopped
2 white turnips, rough sliced
1 leek, sliced
salt and pepper
1 lb (500 g) small new potatoes
1 sprig fresh mint

1. Put the beef, bacon, onion, and garlic in a stewpan and cover with the oil, wine, vinegar, and stock. Cook briskly for 15 minutes and remove scum from top of pan.
2. Then add the herbs, paprika, tomatoes, turnips, and leek. Lower the heat to obtain a simmer, skim the top of the liquor when necessary, and cook for about 1 hour or until the meat is tender.

3. Add salt and pepper, then the potatoes and mint. Cook for ½ hour.

*Note: The stew will not have a great deal of liquor when the dish is finally cooked. Should you wish a somewhat looser stew, add a little more stock.*

## Ternera con Alcachofas

(Tear-near-er kon Al-ka-cho-fas)
Veal with artichokes
serves 4

This dish originates from Seville, one of the most beautiful cities in the whole of Spain. The cathedral is the largest Christian church after St. Peter's in Rome and St. Paul's in London. The Giralda tower dominates the city like a sacred lighthouse and is a focal point for residents and visitors alike. Inside the gigantic cathedral, dozens of Spanish women dressed in black bow in prayer before the many altars, like devout ravens. The main altar is awe-inspiring, and even the young Spanish children are silent before its majesty. For this most interesting dish you will need:

2 Tbsp. (2 × 15 mL spoon) pork or beef drippings
1½ lbs (750 g) lean veal, cut into 4 thick slices
2 large onions, sliced
salt and pepper
1 wine glass or 5 fl ozs (1½ dcL) dry white wine

(cont.)

2 Tbsp. (2 × 15 mL spoon) brandy
1 cup (250 mL) stock
4 tomatoes, peeled, seeded, and
   chopped
8 cooked artichoke hearts (*See index for recipe.*)

1. Melt the drippings in a large deep pan and brown the veal slices, then remove from pan.
2. Saute the onions until soft, then

drain the excess fat and replace the veal slices. Dust with salt and pepper.

3. Add the wine and brandy and the stock, cover the pan, and simmer on top of the stove for about 1½ hours until meat is tender.

4. During the last half hour, add the tomatoes and artichoke hearts.

5. Remove veal onto a serving dish and keep warm.

6. Reduce cooking liquor (if necessary), then pour over meat and serve.

The restaurants in Cadiz serve a stew-type dish which is tremendously popular. Its secret is that the dish is finished off with yogurt and caraway seeds. Historians agree that Cadiz is the oldest continually inhabited city in Europe and was founded by the Phoenicians in about 1100 B.C., Across the Bay of Cadiz lies the site of the very ancient city of Tartessos which was known in biblical times as Tarshish. This city was founded about 2500 B.C., demolished by the Carthaginians in about 600 B.C., and was lost sight of from that time.

Cadiz is also the birthplace of Manuel de Falla, the composer of such masterpieces as "The Three-Cornered Hat" and "Nights in the Gardens of Spain." He is buried under a gigantic slab of granite in the cathedral and his image is printed on the 100 peseta note.

## *Ternera Gaditana*

(Tear-near-er Had-it-arner)
Veal, Cadiz style
serves 4

1¼ lb (625 g) lean veal
flour to dredge
salt and pepper
2 Tbsp. (2 × 15 mL spoon) olive oil
2 large onions, sliced
2 cloves garlic, minced
4 ripe tomatoes, peeled, seeded, and
   chopped

1 pint (½ liter) chicken stock
1 wine glass or 5 fl ozs (1½ dcL) dry
   white wine
3 Tbsp. (3 × 15 mL spoon) plain yogurt
½ tsp. (1 × 2 mL spoon) caraway seeds

1. Cut the veal into bite-size pieces, dredge with seasoned flour, and saute quickly in the olive oil, a few pieces at a time.

2. When all pieces of meat are seared and golden, remove them from the pan and keep to one side.

3. Saute the onions in the same oil and, when soft, replace the meat, add the garlic, tomatoes, stock, and wine.

4. Cook covered on a very low heat for about 1½ hours (or until the meat is tender), then adjust seasoning if required before adding the yogurt and caraway seeds. Take the pan from the stove, but keep covered.

5. Let the contents rest for 10 minutes, then serve.

## Ternera Elegante

(Tear-near-er Ellay-ganty)
Elegant veal
serves 4

This is a delightful dish to be served on very special occasions.

4 thin pancakes, made without sugar
  (*See index for recipe.*)
2 Tbsp. (2 × 15 mL spoon) butter
4 fillets of veal about ¾ inch (18 mm)
  thick
salt and pepper
¼ lb (120 g) mushrooms, finely chopped
1 clove garlic, minced
1 wine glass or 5 fl ozs (1½ dcL)
  medium Sherry
grated hard cheese

1. Make the pancakes in an 8 inch (20 cm) pan and remove.

2. Melt the butter, season the veal fillets, and saute gently until cooked. Keep to one side.

3. Preheat oven to 400°F (200°C).

4. In the same pan, saute the mushrooms and garlic, then add the Sherry. Cook a little to reduce the Sherry and obtain a coarse paste.

5. Put a fillet on each pancake with some of the mushroom mixture underneath and some on top.

6. Fold the pancake so that it envelopes the fillet and place in a buttered fireproof dish.

7. Sprinkle the grated cheese on top of each pancake and put in the oven for 5 minutes or so, until the cheese has glazed.

## Rollitos Fantasia

(Rol-e-toss Fan-ta-sia)
Stuffed veal fillets
serves 4

4 eggs
4 fillets of lean veal
8 thin slices of smoked bacon
8 small bay leaves
flour
2 Tbsp. (2 × 15 mL spoon) butter
1 Tbsp. (1 × 15 mL spoon) olive oil
1 wine glass or 5 fl ozs (1½ dcL) dry
  white wine
approximately 1 cup (250 mL) stock

1. Prepare the eggs as follows: Place 4 eggs in cold water, bring to a boil, turn off heat, and allow eggs to sit in the water for 5 minutes.

2. Meanwhile, beat the fillets of veal to ⅛ inch (3 mm) thickness and on each fillet lay 2 slices of bacon and 2 bay leaves.

3. Gently crack the eggs, put in cold water for a minute, then carefully remove the shells. *Note:* The eggs will not be hard-boiled, just firm.

4. Place one whole boiled egg at the edge of each fillet and enclose the egg, bacon, and bay leaves by rolling the fillet around the other ingredients.

5. Secure with toothpicks, but *don't* pierce the egg, then roll each fillet in flour.

6. Melt the butter in a pan, add the oil, and fry the rolled fillets until they are golden.

7. Now add the wine. Increase the heat a little and cook until the wine has evaporated.

8. Reduce heat again, add the hot stock and cook for about 20 minutes, turning the fillets occasionally to get even color and adding a little more stock if required to keep the pan moist.

9. Remove toothpicks before serving on a bed of creamed potatoes.

## Chuletas de Ternera, Blanca

(Choo-lett-as day Tear-near-er Blanka)
Veal cutlets with cheese and
mushrooms
serves 4

1 Tbsp. (1 × 15 mL spoon) olive oil
4 veal cutlets
salt and pepper
2 egg yolks
1 Tbsp. (1 × 15 mL spoon) melted
    butter
juice of 1 lemon
a little warm water

2 Tbsp. (15 g) grated hard cheese
3 medium-size onions, sliced
12 mushrooms, rough chopped
1 Tbsp. (1 × 15 mL spoon) chopped
    parsley

1. In a pan heat the oil, then dust the cutlets with salt and pepper and brown them quickly.

2. Preheat oven to 400°F (200°C).

3. In a saucepan mix the egg yolks, melted butter, lemon juice, and a little warm water. Heat over a very low flame to thicken the mixture *slightly*.

4. Put the glazed cutlets in an ovenproof casserole and pour the egg/butter mixture over the cutlets.

5. Sprinkle the grated cheese on top and cook for 20 minutes.

6. In the pan in which you glazed the cutlets, gently fry the onions and when soft, add the mushrooms and cook for a further 5 minutes. Sprinkle with fresh chopped parsley and mix all together in the pan.

7. Remove cooked cutlets from oven, pour the onion/mushroom mixture over and bring to the table.

One of the simplest dishes made with veal cutlets was served in Soria when I was on my way to the fiesta at San Pedro Manique, a nearby village. The fiesta is held each year, the highlight of which is the occasion when local youths walk across a pit of red-hot wood embers. The feast and the occasion commemorate the time, twelve centuries ago, when an Arab chieftain installed himself in the area and demanded one hundred virgins for his harem. Three were selected from San Pedro Manique but their fiances pleaded with the emir and said they would "go through fire, water, and storm to save the girls." The emir then ordered the three young men to walk over a pit of live embers carrying their fiancees on their backs. The boys did just that, their fiancees were saved, and this exploit has been reenacted each year since then.

I am told that there is no trick; the boys actually do walk over the burning embers, and believe me, they are red hot and the boys do walk barefoot. So, is it faith or is there a technique?

## Chuletas de Ternera San Pedro

(Choo-lett-as day Tear-near-er San Pay-dro)
Veal cutlets, San Pedro
serves 4

4 veal cutlets 6 ozs (180 g) each, approximately
flour
salt and pepper
2 Tbsp. (2 × 15 mL spoon) butter
1 wine glass or 5 fl ozs (1½ dcL) medium Sherry

1 Tbsp. (1 × 15 mL spoon) ground almonds
¼ tsp. (1 × 1 mL spoon) dried sage

1. Flour and season the veal cutlets, then put them in a pan with about half the butter and cook quickly until golden on each side. Reduce heat and cook gently until tender.
2. Remove the cutlets from the pan and keep hot on a serving dish.
3. Add the remainder of the butter to the pan, then the Sherry, almonds, and sage. Cook together for one minute, then pour over the cutlets.

A certain affinity exists between veal and Sherry, and the Spanish combine these two ingredients in many of their better meat dishes. Similarly with cheese: this too is popular, especially as an ingredient for stuffing veal cutlets. The cutlets are in a butterfly cut, the slice of cheese is laid on the base slice of the veal, and the flap covers the cheese. The whole cutlet is dipped in flour, beaten egg, and breadcrumbs, then fried to a golden brown.

There is only one dish made with ground beef (or veal) that I really enjoy and I have no idea of its correct name, so perhaps we may call it Hamburgers with cheese.

## Hamburguesas con Queso

(Amburg-esas kon Kay-tho)
Hamburgers with cheese
serves 4

1½ lbs (750 g) of the best minced beef you can afford
a little cold water
1 whole egg, beaten
1 Tbsp. (1 × 15 mL spoon) finely minced onion
1 good sprig of parsley, chopped fine

salt and pepper
¼ lb (120 g) blue cheese (Cebrero, Roquefort, or blue)
1 Tbsp. (1 × 15 mL spoon) butter
1 Tbsp. (1 × 15 mL spoon) brandy

1. Mix the minced beef with 2 Tbsp. cold water until the water is absorbed.
2. Now mix the beef, beaten egg, onion, parsley, salt, and pepper thoroughly and form into eight patties about ½ inch (12 mm) thick.

3. Now blend the cheese, butter, and brandy and mix until smooth. Form into four balls and chill until needed.

4. Preheat broiler.

5. When required, press one cheese ball between two beef patties. Press edges firmly together and grill quickly 3 to 5 minutes each side or to the degree of doneness required.

*Note: The secret of a juicy grilled hamburger is the addition of just a little cold water to the beef before cooking.*

## LAMB

Away from the towns and cities, the shepherd is a very familiar sight throughout Spain, for the Spanish are lovers of lamb. From the foothills of the Sierra Nevada, near Granada, with their snow-capped tops that glisten in the sun even in summer, over the rolling hills and lush green valleys or across the harsh, dry plains of Extremadura and La Mancha, thousands of flocks of sheep will roam the land, tended by their patient and skilled protectors.

The Spanish shepherds are perhaps the most skillful in the world. Even in the scorching heat of summer, they will find the best and most succulent pastures, and lead their flocks toward this grazing. They will know just where there are pools of freshest water that are quiet and still. For sheep have not changed their habits or instincts since biblical times. The phrase from Psalms—"He leadeth me beside still waters"—refers to the fact that sheep will not drink from rivers, streams, or any running water.

These men lead a quiet, introspective life, and after the solitude and peace of the countryside and days alone with their flock, they find it difficult to adapt to the noise and good humor found in a typical village taverna. Their relationship with their charges is ambivalent. They give many of their sheep pet names, but do not appear to have favorites in the flock. When asked how they felt when some of their charges had to be taken to the slaughterhouse, it seems they have a fatalistic attitude. "We are all born to die," they say, "some sooner than others: it is God's will." They don't think death is scary, but they do have an infinite belief in the hereafter. To them, life and death simply form a predetermined cycle.

With this attitude, they cull their flock, picking first the young lambs that in any circumstances will not grow into sturdy animals. These are known as *cordero lechal* or milk-fed lambs and are no more than one month old. Their flesh is very delicate and requires careful cooking to preserve it. Overcooking kills the flavor effectively, so light roasting of the major joints and grilling the loin is the best method.

As with all young meat, the bone content is high. A leg from this type of lamb weighing about 3½ pounds (1.75 Kg) will be sufficient for two servings. The majority of the remaining lambs that are to be killed is allowed to grow somewhat larger and is called *cordero pascual* or spring lamb and has a carcass weight of between 20 and 27 pounds (9 and 12 Kg).

The shepherd has no conscience about eating members of his flock, and, in fact, many of his meals consist of lamb. Over the years the shepherds have evolved a recipe which partly pickles the meat so that it may be carried in a skin bag for a number of days without spoiling. By reducing the pickling ingredients and amending the original recipe, we come up with a quite excellent dish that is not so highly spiced yet is full of flavor.

## Cordero Pastor

(Kor-dare-oo Pas-tor)
Shepherds' lamb
serves 4

4½ lb (2¼ Kg) leg of lamb
  (approximately)
2 cloves garlic, slivered
a little olive oil
salt and pepper
2 wine glasses or 10 fl ozs (3 dcL) red
  wine
2 Tbsp. (2 × 15 mL spoon) tarragon
  vinegar
3 whole cloves
flour, for thickening
stock or water, as required

1. Preheat oven to 400°F (200°C).
2. Trim all fat and any thick skin from lamb. Make a few incisions in the flesh and insert the slivers of garlic into the cuts. Rub joint with a little olive oil and salt and pepper.
3. Place lamb on a rack in a roasting dish and cook in the oven for 15 minutes.
4. After this period, reduce the temperature to 325°F (160°C). Add the wine, vinegar, and cloves and cook for 1¼ hours, basting the meat every 20 minutes or so.
5. When the joint is tender, remove it to a serving dish and keep hot.
6. Add sufficient flour to the pan drippings to make a roux and extend with stock or water to make a good pouring sauce. Adjust the seasoning if necessary.
7. Strain the sauce, slice the meat, and pour sauce over.

Despite the tender, loving care that the sheep receive from their shepherds, sometimes young lambs die at birth. Then the shepherd takes advantage of this bounty to roast the tender meat over a wood fire—occasionally tossing a bunch of wild marjoram or any other aromatic into the flames to give the meat an enticing flavor. There is one dish that was invented by the local shepherds from the Cuenca area called *Chuletas Asadas al Sarmiento* (Lamb chops roasted over a fire of vine shoots) which has become so popular that it is often featured on the menu of many local restaurants.

Now we come to a bit of a problem concerning nomenclature. The word *caldereta* used in the next recipe usually means a "fish or shellfish stew." Here, for some reason, the word is applied to a *lamb* stew. Don't let it bother you—the dish is easy and very good.

## Caldereta de Cordero

(Kal-der-etta day Kor-dare-oo)
Lamb stew
serves 4

4 medium-size onions, chopped
1 clove garlic, crushed
1 Tbsp. (1 × 15 mL spoon) olive oil
1½ lbs (750 g) boned shoulder of lamb
4 ozs (120 g) lean ham, chopped
3 peppercorns
1 bay leaf, crushed
1 wine glass or 5 fl ozs (1½ dcL) dry
  white wine
1 cup (250 mL) chicken stock
  (approximately)
2 tsp. (2 × 5 mL spoon) cornstarch
water to mix

1. Place the onions and garlic in a frypan with the oil and cook until golden brown, but not dark.
2. Cut the meat into bite-size pieces and put into a stewpan.
3. Remove the garlic from the frypan and discard. Then put the oil and onions in the stewpan with the meat.
4. Add all the other ingredients, except the cornstarch, and simmer for about 1¼ hours until the meat is tender. (Test after one hour—often the meat is just right.)
5. A few minutes before serving, mix the cornstarch with sufficient water to pour, then add to the stew. Stir to distribute the thickening, then serve.

## Estofada Valenciana

(Esto-far-dah Val-n-c-arner)
Lamb stew, Valencia style
serves 4

In many areas of Spain, cooking reaches truly great heights, and in the Valencia area this is the case with another variation of stewed lamb. This recipe combines two of the province's excellent products—almonds and lemon.

¼ lb (120 g) smoked bacon, cut into
  small pieces
1 Tbsp. (1 × 15 mL spoon) olive oil
1½ lbs (750 g) boned shoulder of lamb
flour for dredging
1 large onion, chopped
1 pint (½ liter) stock or water
1 bay leaf
12 small, whole new potatoes
salt and pepper
1 Tbsp. (1 × 15 mL spoon) grated
  lemon rind
1 cup (150 g) fresh green peas
1 Tbsp. (1 × 15 mL spoon) chopped,
  toasted almonds
1 Tbsp. (1 × 15 mL spoon) chopped
  parsley

1. Preheat oven to 325°F (160°C).
2. In a pan, fry the bacon pieces in the olive oil, then remove bacon to ovenproof casserole.
3. In the same oil, fry the pieces of floured lamb until colored, then put in casserole with bacon.
4. Fry the onions in the same oil until tender but not colored, then drain off surplus oil and put onions in casserole.

5. Pour stock over contents in casserole, add bay leaf, potatoes, seasonings, and lemon rind. Cover and cook in oven for about 1 hour.

6. After this time, add the peas and cook for a further 15 minutes.

7. Just before serving, sprinkle the almonds and parsley over all.

## Preparing Lamb Chops

Lamb chops are a great delicacy, and Spanish cooks prepare them when cut either from the loin or the rack (i.e., loin chops or rib chops). In Spain the loin and rack are considered as one single joint (containing 14 chops) and the chops you buy may come from either end of the joint. While the better chops come from the loin end, you may be charged the same price if they are cut from the rackend.

These chops (*chuletas*) are either broiled or pan fried. One important point to remember is that if you propose to pan-fry the chops, the preliminary step is to dip them in *beaten egg* prior to covering in breadcrumbs. If the chops are to be broiled, they should be dipped in *melted butter* before being crumbed.

## Chuletas Empanadas Alicante

(Choo-let-as Em-pan-a-das Ali-kantay)
Breaded lamb chops, Alicante style
serves 4

1 whole egg
8 trimmed lamb chops
breadcrumbs to coat
1 Tbsp. (1 × 15 mL spoon) olive oil
½ wine glass or 2½ fl ozs (¾ dcL) dry white wine
¼ cup (50 mL) stock or water
2 Tbsp. (2 × 15 mL spoon) grated orange rind
1 Tbsp. (1 × 15 mL spoon) toasted flour (approximately)

1. Beat the egg with a little cold water until mixed.
2. Dip the chops into the beaten egg. Coat them with the crumbs, patting them into the chops to ensure adequate covering.

3. Pan-fry them over a moderate heat in the olive oil until they reach the degree of doneness you require. Remove them from the pan and keep warm.
4. Add the wine, stock, and orange rind to the pan and cook together for about 5 minutes over a low heat.
5. Thicken the sauce with the toasted flour, then pour over the chops.

## Chuletas Empanadas con Almendras

(Choo-let-as Em-pan-a-das kon Al-mendras)
Lamb cutlets with almonds
serves 4

These chops/cutlets may be either pan-fried or broiled. Depending on the cooking method, they will be either dipped in beaten egg or in melted butter, before being coated with breadcrumbs.

2 Tbsp. (2 × 15 mL spoon) toasted
   almonds
breadcrumbs
salt
8 lamb chops, trimmed

1. In a blender, grind the toasted
almonds finely.
2. Add them to the breadcrumbs and
salt and mix thoroughly.
3. Treat the chops with beaten egg or
melted butter as explained in the
introduction to the recipe.
4. Coat the chops in the crumb
mixture, then broil or fry.

## Asado de Cordero, Jerez

(A-sar-doe day Kor-daer-oo Her-eth)
Roast lamb with Sherry
serves 4

One of the most outstanding lamb
dishes uses strong coffee, sweet sherry,
and dark chocolate to provide the
basting liquor. Of course it should not
work, but believe me, it does, and for
"rave notices" this is the party dish.

1 leg of lamb, 4 lbs (2 Kg)
   (approximately)
1 clove garlic, slivered

salt and pepper
½ cup (120 mL) strong black coffee
1 wine glass or 5 fl ozs (1½ dcL) sweet
   Sherry
1 small square dark, unsweetened
   chocolate
stock or water

1. Preheat the oven to 400°F (200°C).
2. Make incisions around the leg of
lamb and insert the slivers of garlic in
the cuts. Rub the leg with salt and
pepper.
3. Put the leg on a rack in a roasting
pan and place in the oven for 20
minutes.
4. Reduce heat to 325°F (160°C) and
add *all* the other ingredients to the
roasting dish.
5. Cook at this temperature for about
1¾ hours or until meat is tender, but
be sure to baste the lamb with the pan
liquor every 15 minutes. (I know it's a
bore, but it makes *all* the difference.)
6. If the liquor is insufficient toward
the end of the cooking period, add stock
or water to extend.
7. After the meat is cooked, the liquor
may be thickened (if required) with
toasted flour, or strained and served
without thickening.

Easter Week (*Semana Santa*) begins on the previous Saturday and
ends on Good Friday. In Malaga, as in a number of towns and cities, Semana
Santa is very special. For it is here that religious processions take over the
city, and perhaps only Seville can surpass the splendor and the magnificence
of the show Malaga presents to her faithful.

From Palm Sunday to Good Friday these processions take place,
winding their way through the main streets and the narrow alleys so that as
many people as possible may see the show. Dozens of gigantic floats (*paseos*)
representing incidents in the life of Jesus pass before the gaze of the huge
audiences. Many of these floats depict the Virgin Mary and the child Jesus,
the stations of the Cross, and madonnas seated on golden thrones and dressed
in satin with jewel-encrusted diadems. And the procession goes on for hours
and hours.

Sometimes as many as ten or twelve figures are depicted on a single float, all life-size and swaying from side to side as they are carried on platforms by up to fifty hefty volunteers. In front and behind each float, penitents walk wearing their robes of black or gray which cover them from head to foot. Only their eyes can be seen staring through the slits cut in their painted hoods, reminiscent of heretics and the Spanish Inquisition.

Many foreign visitors fail to realize that these processions are not just another excuse for dressing up and having a good time. The people who act as penitents really do seem to share the agony of Christ on the Cross, and many hang their heads with shame for what they feel they did to their Savior. The whole feast is simple and sincere, even if at times it does seem a little irreverent. For example, one of the men carrying a float may dash from under the canopy to gulp wine from a bottle held by a friend or a member of his family, or to grab a piece of bread and smoked sausage, before he ducks back under the float to shuffle forward for another hour or so.

This is all part of the total experience, and those taking part seem to gain tremendous spiritual benefit from their participation. Many are in tears, and all who are weeping do so quite openly. There is nothing unmanly in weeping during Semana Santa, although at other times it is considered an open indication of weakness.

Of course, after the procession is over for the day, and the mixture of emotional liberation and spiritual purge is complete, the penitents set out to enjoy themselves. And part of that enjoyment is, of course, to eat. The following recipe is a specialty served during Semana Santa.

## Cordero Asado con Albaricoques Secos

(Kor-daer-oo A-sar-do kon Al-bar-e-coke-kays Say-kos)
Lamb with dried apricots
serves 4

½ lb (250 g) dried apricots
1 cup (250 mL) chicken stock
1 boned loin-end of lamb, just over 2½ lbs (1 Kg)
salt and pepper

1. In a saucepan stew the dried apricots until tender with the chicken stock.
2. Preheat oven to 325°F (160°C).

3. Strain the apricots and use them as a stuffing, wrapping the boned loin around the mashed apricots and tying with kitchen string. Rub with salt and pepper and cook for about 1¼ hours.

## Roast Loin

This recipe is the most simple, yet certainly one of the best ways of cooking roast loin.

Preheat the oven to 350°F (180°C), insert slices of garlic under the skin of the joint of lamb, and cook until tender. Remove from the oven. Sprinkle the outside with freshly chopped mint, then with breadcrumbs, pressing them into the skin. Brown the crumbs under a hot grill and serve.

## Chuletas de Cordero, Granada

(Choo-lett-as day Kor-dare-oo)
Lamb cutlets, Granadan style
serves 4

Granada was the Spanish city most beloved by the Moors and was the last citadel to which they retreated before their final expulsion in 1492. This recipe presents the lamb chops in a pastry case shaped like a curving Moorish sword. This arrangement is meant to honor Isabella's final victory when she promised that her army would make the Moors "eat their swords."

4 lamb cutlets, trimmed (large cutlets)
2 Tbsp. (2 × 15 mL spoon) olive oil
¼ lb (120 g) mushrooms, finely chopped
short pastry
4 small pieces of lean cooked ham
1 egg yolk

1. Saute the chops in the olive oil over a brisk heat without completely cooking them. Remove and allow them to get cold.

2. In the same oil, fry the mushrooms, then drain them on absorbent paper and keep to one side.

3. Preheat oven to 375°F (190°C).

4. Roll out a thin layer of short pastry (see index for recipe) and place on it the 4 cutlets, allowing sufficient paste to wrap around each.

5. Divide the mushroom mixture into 4 portions and put one part on each cutlet, then cover with a piece of ham.

6. Wrap pastry around each cutlet, leaving the rib bone sticking out.

7. Paint each with beaten egg yolk and cook in the oven for about 30 minutes. Before serving dress with a paper frill on each bone.

## Cordero Asado La Mancha

(Kor-dare-oo A-sar-do La Man-cher)
Roast lamb, Castilian style
serves 4

Lamb in any form has a great affinity with cumin, also, as this last recipe will show.

1 leg lamb
olive oil
2 cloves garlic, minced
1 Tbsp. (1 × 15 mL spoon) ground almonds
a good pinch each of powdered cumin seed, rosemary, and oregano
a little red wine

1. Preheat oven to 325°F (160°C).

2. Brush lamb with a little olive oil.

3. Mix all the other ingredients together with a little red wine to make a paste.

4. Cut fairly deep incisions in the lamb and spread the paste in the cuts and on the surface of the meat.

5. Place on a rack in a roasting dish and cook for about 2 hours or until meat is tender.

6. Keep basting every half hour to impregnate the flavor into the meat.

# PORK

Pork is available throughout the year in every part of Spain and is usually of consistent good quality and the least expensive of animal meats.

Select flesh that is pale pink and with a rather light coating of back fat. Darker meat and a high proportion of surface fat indicate age and possible toughness. The fat should be firm and the bones of the loin should be soft and red at the ends.

## Roast Pork

Since pork contains a high proportion of fat, all joints may be roasted, and because of the fairly high fat covering, are self-basting. The exception to this is when roasting suckling pig. Pork should be roasted in an oven preheated to 350°F (180°C) and allowed 35 minutes per pound (500 g) weight for joints cooked with bone-in; and 45 minutes per pound for joints that have been boned and rolled, or boned, stuffed, and rolled.

## Suckling Pig

Throughout Spain these pigs are killed when they are little more than three weeks old and weigh about 6 to 8 pounds (3 to 5 Kg), sufficient for 8 servings. When roasted whole and brought to the table on a platter decorated with fresh bay leaves and garnished with baked whole tomato and lemon baskets, this is undoubtedly a party dish requiring no more trouble to prepare (and less time to cook) than a large turkey.

Many regional specialties have been built around pork and the following recipe, which originates from just outside Zafra, is famous and over four hundred years old. Zafra is a small town a little over 40 miles south of Merida, with narrow streets, turrets and towers, and a general air of tranquility and calmness.

To some visitors the town is of considerable interest, as it was to Zafra that Jane Dormer, a close friend of Mary Tudor, came from England in 1565 as the bride of the Duke of Feria. She had met her future husband when he was in attendance on Philip II of Spain, who had come to England for his marriage to Mary Tudor. The duke must have been a handsome suitor and also very persuasive, for he succeeded in winning Jane's favors against the competition of such noblemen as the Duke of Norfolk, the Earl of Devonshire, and the Earl of Nottingham.

Being a devout Catholic, Mary Tudor was enthusiastic about the forthcoming marriage of her close friend Jane, but regretfully, the queen died before the marriage ceremony could take place. However, after a suitable period of mourning, Jane and the Duke married and set off for Spain. Their journey through Flanders and northern Spain to Zafra took two years, as in almost regal splendor the cavalcade of coaches and outriders, baggage wagons and servants (over two hundred strong), travelled in a very leisurely fashion toward their destination. One can imagine Jane's excitement as she travelled south, across the big, broad landscapes, seeing for the first time the masses of asters and peonies growing wild along the wayside, and the herds of wild pig roaming the slopes, feeding on the huge crop of acorns.

Finally, on reaching Zafra, her gilded coach climbed the hill and swept through the imposing arch, under the crest of five fig leaves, the badge of the Figueros family of which the duke was head. Then the coach proceeded into the courtyard with its central fountain, the strutting peacocks, and the columned balconies, for her first glimpse of her own castle in Spain.

She spent the rest of her life in the region, and after her husband died when their only child, a son, was seven years old, she managed the estate so successfully that she became one of the richest landowners in Spain. Both Jane and her husband are buried in a somber tomb at the nearby convent of Santa Clara, with the nuns of the order keeping vigil to this day over the tomb of the friend of Mary Tudor.

The area around Zafra has always been famous for its pork, hams, and sausage, produced perhaps from the descendents of the wild pig that roamed the region so many years ago. Roast suckling pig flavored with wild thyme and rosemary has always been a popular dish in the area and must have made a regular appearance on the table of the duke and duchess. The following dish is named after the convent where Jane is buried.

## Cochinillo Asado, Santa Clara

(Kosh-in-ill-yo As-ardo)
Roast suckling pig, Santa Clara style

suckling pig, 6 to 8 lbs (3 to 4 Kg)
   (approximately)
1 clove garlic, slivered
salt and pepper
1 tsp. (1 × 5 mL spoon) dried rosemary
1 tsp. (1 × 5 mL spoon) dried thyme

juice of 1 lemon
1 Tbsp. (1 × 15 mL spoon) olive oil
1 wine glass or 5 fl ozs (1½ dcL) dry
   white wine
cold water

1. Wash inside and outside of the pig.
2. Preheat oven to 400°F (200°C).
3. With a sharp knife, make a number of nicks in the outer skin along the backbone and insert the slivers of garlic. (Use more garlic if you wish.)

4. Turn the pig on its back and with a fork, prick the inside in a number of places. (This will allow the herbs and seasonings to permeate the flesh.)

5. Sprinkle the inside with salt and pepper, then the herbs, and, finally, with the lemon juice.

6. Place the piglet on its back on a wire rack in a deep roasting pan and cook in this position for 30 minutes.

7. Then after this period, turn the piglet onto its belly and brush with olive oil. Return to the oven, reduce oven heat to 350°F (180°C), and cook for 2½ hours.

8. During the final hour, add the wine and a little cold water to the pan, and baste the piglet occasionally with the pan liquor.

TO CARVE SUCKLING PIG.   Use a firm knife with a pointed blade. First remove the shoulder by making a half-circular cut through the crisp skin around the top of the shoulder blade. With the point of the knife, separate the ball and socket joint and then continue the circular cut to remove the whole joint. Proceed in a similar manner to remove the other shoulder and the two leg joints. Now sever the head from the body by inserting the point of the knife between the base of the skull and the backbone. With a firm twist of the wrist, the bones will separate. Now cut a strip of skin about 1 inch (2½ cm) wide along the whole length of the loin from shoulder to tail. This will expose the entire backbone and allow you to separate the two sides of the carcass into the two long loin joints, and then to cut them into neat cutlets. Work from the center backbone to the outside, toward the belly of the piglet.

## More Pork Recipes

## *Lomo de Cerdo, Aragonesa*

(Lo-mo day Sare-do Ara-gon-ayser)
Loin of pork, Aragon style
serves 4

Cooks in the province of Aragon tend to give many of their foods a slightly sharp flavor, and when this principle is applied to pork, the result is perfect. Here, it is produced by using wine vinegar during the early stages of the cooking process.

loin of pork, 2 lbs (1 Kg)
   (approximately), prepared
3 Tbsp. (2 × 15 mL spoon) olive oil
6 medium-size onions, chopped
1 Tbsp. (1 × 15 mL spoon) white wine
   vinegar
salt and pepper
½ cup (120 mL) stock or stock cube in
   water
1 wine glass or 5 fl ozs (1½ dcL) dry
   white wine
4 whole cloves
few grains of saffron

1. Chop the pork loin into 8 slices and marinate for 12 hours.

2. When ready, preheat oven to 375°F (190°C).

3. In a frypan, saute the pork chops in the olive oil until well browned on both sides. Transfer the chops to ovenproof casserole.

4. In the same oil, fry the onions under a reduced heat until soft. Strain off surplus oil.

5. Add the wine vinegar to the onions in the pan and allow the mixture to boil until all moisture has evaporated. Then season with salt and pepper.

6. Transfer onions to casserole. Add stock to the frypan to remove any residue and pour over the onions and pork.

7. Add the white wine, cloves, and saffron.

8. With a wooden spoon, stir thoroughly just once to mix all the ingredients and put in the oven for 45 minutes or until chops are tender.

*Note: This dish requires prepreparation in that the pork needs to lie in a marinade for 12 hours before cooking. (See index for marinade recipe.)*

## Lomo de Cerdo Asado

(Lo-mo day Sear-do As-ardo)
Roast loin of pork
serves 4

Another technique guaranteed to produce excellent results with a roast loin of pork is to prepare what may be termed a "dry marinade." It works equally well with a veal joint and gives the meat a beautiful depth of flavor.

1 piece of pork loin, 2 lbs (1 Kg)
  (approximately)

DRY MARINADE

small bunch parsley
1 clove garlic
1 tsp. (1 × 5 mL spoon) dried marjoram
juice of 1 lemon
salt and pepper

1. Bone the loin of pork and trim off any surplus fat, but keep the fat for use later on.

2. On the inside of the loin, make a number of vertical cuts about ½ in (12 mm) deep into which you will work the marinade.

3. Make the dry marinade as follows. Chop the parsley and garlic as finely as possible, then sprinkle the marjoram over and moisten with a little lemon juice to make a soft paste. Then add the salt and pepper to taste.

4. Now spread the marinade paste over the inside of the loin and into the incisions that you have made.

5. Tie the loin with string, wrap it in foil, and keep in the refrigerator for 24 hours so that the flavor of the savory paste can be absorbed into the meat.

6. Remove the loin from the refrigerator an hour before you start cooking process, and remove the foil.

7. Preheat oven to 350°F (180°C).

8. Place the loin on a rack in a roasting pan, spread the retained fat over the meat (or if there is no fat, rub with a little oil), and roast for about 1¾ hours.

## Chuletas de Cerdo Rellenos

(Choo-lett-as day Sear-do Rel-ay-nos)
Stuffed pork chops
serves 4

Simple dishes are always attractive to the busy cook, even if only to keep you from bending over a hot stove for hours on end. This one is an excellent example of a "half-hour gourmet" dish.

4 pork chops, ¾ inch (18 mm) thick (approximately)
4 slices of liver pâté
a little olive oil
salt and pepper

1. Preheat broiler to maximum 500°F (250°C).

2. Make an incision about 2 inches long into each chop. Cut well into the flesh to make a deep pocket.

3. Press a generous amount of liver pate into each pocket, then brush with olive oil, and season with salt and pepper.

4. Place under very hot broiler for 3 minutes, then reduce the heat and cook gently for 10 minutes more, turning twice.

Mixing pork and shellfish is a habit dearly loved by both Spanish and Portuguese cooks. The two recipes that follow will convince you just how right they are. The first recipe is Andalucian; the second Basque.

## Lomo de Cerdo con Almejas

(Lo-mo day Sear-do kon Al-may-has)
Loin of pork with clams
serves 4

1½ lbs (750 g) boned loin of pork
Marinade No. 1 (See index for recipe.)
1 Tbsp. (1 × 15 mL spoon) olive oil
1 Tbsp. (1 × 15 mL spoon) pork lard or pork drippings
1 lb (½ Kg) fresh baby clams in shell

1. Trim the loin of pork of excess fat and cut into bite-size pieces. Place the pork in about 1 pint of marinade and refrigerate for 4 hours, turning the pieces every hour.

2. When ready, drain the meat but keep the marinade.

3. Heat the oil and lard in a heavy pan and gently saute the pork until cooked.

4. Meanwhile, heat the marinade in a saucepan with a lid.

5. Wash the clams in cold water, then toss them into the hot marinade.

6. Raise the heat to boiling, cover the pan, and cook the clams for about 5 minutes (until they open).

7. Strain clams through a sieve, pouring the hot marinade over the pork pieces still in the deep pan.

8. Remove any discarded clam shells and any top shells, then add the clams to the pork.

9. Gently heat the mixture for a few minutes to allow the flavors to blend, then serve.

## Lomo de Cerdo Marinhera

(Lo-mo day Sear-do Mar-in-air-ah)
Loin of pork sailor style
serves 4

1½ lbs (750 g) loin of pork
Marinade No. 1 (See index for recipe.)

(cont.)

1 wine glass or 5 fl ozs (1½ dcL) dry white wine
1 wine glass or 5 fl ozs (1½ dcL) water
pinch of salt
1 lb (½ Kg) fresh baby clams in shell
2 Tbsp. (2 × 15 mL spoon) olive oil
1 medium-size onion, finely chopped
1 clove garlic, finely chopped
2 tomatoes, skinned and chopped
salt and pepper
juice of two oranges
1 Tbsp. (1 × 15 mL spoon) chopped parsley

1. Trim the boned loin of excess fat and cut into bite-size pieces. Marinate for 12 hours.
2. When required, heat the wine and water in a saucepan with a lid, add the salt, and when boiling toss in the clams. Cook for about 5 minutes (until clams open).
3. Drain the clams, then continue boiling liquor until reduced to half the volume. Reserve.
4. Remove any discarded shells from clams and any top shells. Put clams to one side in a dish.
5. Remove pork from the marinade, heat the olive oil in a deep frypan, and saute the pork pieces until they are tender. Remove to a side dish and keep warm.
6. In the same oil, saute the onion and garlic gently until transparent. Add the chopped tomatoes. Cook until the mixture is quite soft and combined to form a thick sauce.
7. Add enough of the reduced marinade to give the sauce a good consistency, then the fried pork pieces, and the clams.
8. Mix the sauce, meat, and shellfish. Place on a serving dish.
9. Sprinkle the orange juice and parsley over the platter before serving.

*Note: If after adding the reduced marinade the sauce is too thin, you may resolve this by mixing the sauce with a few breadcrumbs to thicken it. If the sauce is too thick, add a little more dry white wine.*

## Cerdo en Cazuela

(Sear-do n Kath-whaler)
Pork chops in casserole
serves 4

4 pork chops
paprika
salt and pepper
2 medium-size onions, chopped
2 ripe tomatoes, peeled, seeded, and chopped
1 Tbsp. (1 × 15 mL spoon) chopped parsley
1 wine glass or 5 fl ozs (1½ dcL) dry white wine
1 clove
1 bay leaf

1. Preheat oven to 350°F (180°C).
2. Sprinkle chops with paprika, salt, and pepper, and sear them in a very hot, dry pan. Then remove to casserole.
3. In the small amount of pork fat left in the pan after searing the chops, gently fry the onions, tomatoes, and parsley. (You *may* have to use a very little oil also, but the idea is that the vegetables should be as dry as possible.)
4. When all the fat (and any oil) has been absorbed, add the white wine and let cook for a few minutes more. Pour the mixture over the chops. Add the clove and the bay leaf on top.
5. Cover the casserole and cook for about 1 hour.

# Lomo de Cerdo con Granada

(Lo-mo day Sear-do kon Gra-nada)
Loin of pork with pomegranate
serves 4

1½ lbs (750 g) loin of pork, cut into 4
    chops
1 Tbsp. (1 × 15 mL spoon) olive or corn
    oil
2 ozs tocino (60 g) cut into small pieces
2 wine glasses or 10 fl ozs (3 dcL) red
    wine
2 ripe pomegranates
1 liqueur glass or 2½ fl ozs (¾ dcL)
    *aguardiente* or brandy
salt and pepper

1. In a large frypan, brown the pork
chops in the oil and tocino. When
sufficiently browned, reduce the heat
and continue cooking, adding the red
wine from time to time to moisten the
pan.
2. While the pork is cooking, peel the
pomegranates, discarding the mem-
branes and outer skin. Put the ripe
flesh into a small saucepan.
3. When the chops are cooked, remove
them to a warm serving dish.

4. Pour the cooking liquor from the pan
into the saucepan with the pomegranate
flesh, add the aguardiente or brandy
and heat through under a gentle flame
for just a few minutes.
5. Spoon a little of the sauce over the
chops and serve. Bring the remainder
of the sauce in a sauce-boat.

# Lacon con Grelos

(Lack-on kon Gray-los)
Shoulder of pork with turnip greens

This famous Galician dish is very simple
to prepare. The whole dish may sound a
little crude, but the flavor contrast is
quite outstanding and most agreeable,
providing one likes the strong flavor of
turnip greens (a little like spinach, but
more so!).

Boil the pork shoulder in salted water
until it is almost falling off the bone.
Remove and cut into large serving
pieces. Wash turnip greens and cook in
the liquor, removing when tender.
Drain, chop, season, and serve with the
boiled pork. Boiled potatoes may
accompany this dish also.

# VARIETY MEATS

## Liver

Only in the more sophisticated butchers' shops is one able to buy lamb liver
alone. One usually has to buy the whole "pluck"—that is the liver, kidney,
and lungs which one sees hanging from hooks, all looking rather messy. If
one can overcome this first shock, the whole pluck is worth buying, for prices
usually are very reasonable. Although one has to discard the lungs, there is

the added bonus of having the lamb kidney for breakfast.

Calf and pig liver is available in the more conventional manner—that is, one may buy it separately—so there are no soggy pieces to remove. Chicken liver too is sold but often has the heart attached, so you may wish to detach this before using the livers.

The most tender liver is obtained from calf and chicken, although lamb liver is usually almost as tender. Pig liver is improved if soaked in milk for an hour or so before being cooked.

## Higado con Aguacate

(Ig-ad-o kon Awa-cat-ay)
Liver (calf or lamb) with avocado pear

I really enjoy this dish: the flavor contrast is delightful and most unusual. Another plus: since it takes so little time to prepare, only 15 minutes, it is just the dish for a small dinner party.

2 ripe avocado pears
lemon juice
flour (for dredging)
salt and pepper
2 Tbsp. (2 × 15 mL spoon) butter
8 thin slices of liver
½ wine glass or 2½ fl ozs (¾ dcL) dry
    white wine
pinch oregano

1. Cut avocados in half, remove the inner stones, and peel (as explained in the vegetable section). Slice each half avocado into 4 pieces (total 16 pieces) and brush with lemon juice to preserve the color.
2. Season the flour well with salt and pepper, and dip the pieces of avocado and the liver into the flour mixture.
3. In a frypan, melt half the butter and quickly saute the liver first, then the pieces of avocado. Then place the cooked food on a serving dish.

4. Add the remaining butter to the pan and heat until it begins to change color to light golden.
5. Add the wine and oregano, heat through, and pour the sauce over the liver and avocado pieces.

## Higado Basquaise

(Ig-ad-o Bask-ayse)
Liver, Basque style
serves 4

1 Tbsp. (1 × 15 mL spoon) olive oil
1 Tbsp. (1 × 15 mL spoon) butter
2 cloves garlic, minced
1 red pepper, diced
1½ lbs (750 g) calf liver
12 mushrooms, chopped
1 Tbsp. chopped parsley
juice of 1 lemon
salt and pepper
a little red wine

1. Put the oil and butter in a deep frypan and heat. Then saute the garlic until golden.
2. Add the red pepper and cook until soft.

3. Chop the liver into bite-size pieces and add to the mixture in the frypan. Cook gently for 6 or 8 minutes, stirring occasionally.

4. Now add the mushrooms, parsley, and lemon juice, and cook for a further 5 minutes.

5. Add salt and pepper to taste, then remove contents to a warmed serving dish.

*Note: If the mixture becomes too dry, moisten with a little red wine before seasoning.*

The next recipe comes from Seville, and how it got its name is somewhat of a mystery. The Alcazar was a famous garden linked to the Tower of Gold by a subterranean passage that fell into disuse when the Moors were finally driven out of Spain. Pedro the Cruel installed himself in the Alcazar and had the gardens restored at great expense. He held court there and built a small pool in which his mistress, Maria de Padilla used to bathe. To flatter the king, his courtiers offered to drink the bathwater. Pedro was delighted. However, one of the group refused to drink. "Sire," he explained, "it is unwise for me to drink the gravy, lest I desire the meat."

## Higado del Alcazar

(Ig-ado dell Al-ka-zar)
Calf liver, Alcazar
serves 4

½ lb (250 g) fresh mushrooms
4 Tbsp. (4 × 15 mL spooon) butter
juice of 1 lemon
salt and pepper
1½ lb (750 g) sliced calf liver
flour to dredge
2 Tbsp. (2 × 15 mL spoon) olive oil
4 slices cooked ham
2 Tbsp. (2 × 15 mL spoon) brandy
1 cup (250 mL) light cream

1. Wash the mushrooms quickly in cold water, roughly chop them, then saute them in a large saucepan with half the butter. Add lemon juice and season with salt and pepper. Keep warm until serving time.

2. Season the liver with salt and pepper, dip into flour, and keep to one side.

3. In a second saucepan heat the olive oil and the remaining butter and saute the ham slices until they begin to turn brown. Then remove ham from the pan and keep warm.

4. In the same pan, saute the liver for 2 or 3 minutes on each side. Remove and keep in a warm place.

5. Add the brandy to the pan and increase heat, tipping pan toward flame so the spirit ignites. When the flame subsides, add the cream plus the mushrooms and any liquor from that first pan.

6. Heat the second pan now containing the mushrooms and cream.

7. Place a slice of ham under a slice of liver and pour the mushroom sauce over. Repeat for the other 3 portions.

## Kidney

Kidneys may be obtained from lamb, veal, pork, and kid. They need a little preparatory treatment to be at their best. So they should be soaked in cold water to which the juice of a lemon or a tablespoon of vinegar has been added, then they should be blanched in boiling water for 3 minutes. Kidneys are then ready for further preparation.

## *Riñones Asturiana*

(Reen-yon-ays As-tur-e-arnah)
Veal kidney, Asturian style
serves 4

1¼ lb (625 g) veal kidney
2 Tbsp. (2 × 15 mL spoon) olive oil
4 slices smoked bacon, cut into strips
1 small onion, sliced
1 Tbsp. (1 × 15 mL spoon) chopped parsley
1 wine glass or 5 fl ozs (1½ dcL) dry Sherry
pepper
1 Tbsp. (1 × 15 mL spoon) tomato paste
salt to taste

1. Wash the kidneys and remove center core. Cut them into small pieces and saute them quickly in the olive oil.
2. Remove the kidney and keep warm.
3. In the same oil, fry the pieces of bacon, then add the onion, cooking until onion is soft and the bacon crisp.
4. Now add the parsley and the glass of Sherry, then the kidneys, pepper, and tomato paste. Mix well and continue cooking until there is no blood visible in the kidney.
5. Serve with the sauce on a bed of rice with salt to taste.

## *Riñones Basquaise*

(Reen-yon-ays Bass-kayze)
Kidney, Basque style
serves 4

1¼ lb (625 g) veal kidney
1 Tbsp. (1 × 15 mL spoon) butter
1 clove garlic, minced
flour
1 glass or 5 fl ozs (1½ dcL) cider
1 Tbsp. (1 × 15 mL spoon) brandy
salt

1. Wash and clean the kidney as described in previous recipe.
2. Melt the butter and saute the kidney pieces quickly until brown, then remove to a warm dish.
3. Put the garlic in the frypan and cook for a few moments until soft, then add sufficient flour to the fat in the pan to make a roux. Leave the garlic in the pan.
4. Extend the roux with the cider and the brandy, then cook gently for 5 minutes until thickened and clear. Season to taste, then pour over kidneys, and serve.

## Sweetbreads

These too are popular and inexpensive. They should be first soaked for an hour in cold water. Then sweetbreads should be dropped into boiling water, to which 1 Tbsp. of lemon juice or vinegar has been added to each pint of water (acidulated water), and blanched for three or four minutes. Drain the sweetbreads and rinse again in cold water. Cut away any membrane adhering to them, then dry them between two kitchen towels.

## Pinchos a la Navarra

(Pinch-os a la Navarra)
Cocktail kebabs, Navarra style
serves 4

6 ozs (180 g) sweetbreads
6 ozs (180 g) chicken livers
⅓ cup (80 g) butter
salt and pepper
4 ozs (120 g) hard cheese
8 small mushrooms
1 cup (¼ liter) bechamel sauce (See
   index for recipe.)
2 whole eggs
breadcrumbs
oil for deep frying

1. Prepare the sweetbreads as previously described, then cut them into bite-size pieces. Prepare the chicken livers in a similar manner.

2. In a frypan melt the butter and gently fry the chicken livers and sweetbreads for about 8 minutes. Remove from pan.

3. Cut the cheese into squares, then on long wooden toothpicks, assemble a piece of sweetbread, a piece of cheese, a piece of liver, and a mushroom. Assemble as many pinchos as there are ingredients available.

4. Dip the pinchos into bechamel sauce, then deep-fry for two minutes until the sauce is golden and forms a crisp batter.

5. Allow the pinchos to cool, then dip in beaten egg and roll in breadcrumbs, then deep-fry once more until golden. Serve with quarters of lemon.

## Mollejas al Jamon

(Moll-ay-has al Ham-on)
Sweetbreads with ham
serves 4

1 lb (500 g) veal sweetbreads
a little butter
2 ozs (60 g) Serrano ham, chopped
1 small onion, minced
salt and pepper
a little stock

1. Prepare sweetbreads as previously explained and cut into bite-size pieces.

2. In the butter, fry the ham and the minced onion until the onion is light brown, then add the sweetbreads, salt, pepper, and a little stock.

3. Cover the pan and slowly cook the mixture for about 20 minutes, stirring frequently to stop sticking, and adding more stock if required to keep sweetbreads moist.

4. Toward the end of the cooking period, add more salt and pepper as required.

## Brains

These meats have a bland flavor and need some preparatory work before they may be used. First wash the brains in cold water, remove the skin and veins, and then soak in acidulated water for about 1 hour. Remove, place in fresh, cold water which is brought to the boil, and allow the brains to blanch for about 20 minutes. The most usual way of serving this meat is in slices, deep-fried.

## *Sesos Fritos*

(Say-sos Free-tos)
Deep-fried brains
serves 4

2 sets of calf brains
flour, beaten egg, breadcrumbs
oil for deep frying

Slice the brains into small pieces, dip in flour, beaten egg, then breadcrumbs, and deep-fry in hot oil.

## *Callos a la Madrileña*

(Kall-yos a la Mad-ree-layn-yer)
Tripe, Madrid style
serves 4

1½ lbs (750 g) tripe
4 Tbsp. (4 × 15 mL spoon) vinegar
2 Tbsp. (2 × 15 mL spoon) salt
1 lemon, cut in half

1 pig's foot, cut lengthwise
1 onion, sliced
2 cloves garlic
1 carrot, chopped
2 tsp. (2 × 5 mL spoon) marjoram
1 wine glass or 5 fl ozs (1½ dcL) dry Sherry
1 wine glass or 5 fl ozs (1½ dcL) dry white wine
2 cups (½ liter) stock
1 leek, chopped
1 bay leaf
3 Tbsp. (3 × 15 mL spoon) olive oil
2 ozs (60 g) smoked bacon, chopped
2 ozs (60 g) chorizo, sliced
2 Tbsp. (2 × 15 mL spoon) tomato paste
salt and pepper
parsley, chopped

### TO PREPARE THE TRIPE

1. Wash the tripe in water (to cover) and half the vinegar.

2. Lay the tripe flat on a board, sprinkle with the salt, and rub the salt into the tripe using the halves of lemon.

3. Then soak the tripe in water to cover, adding the remainder of the vinegar and leave for an hour.

4. Remove tripe after this time. Throw the water away.

5. Boil the tripe in fresh water for 15 minutes.

## TO PREPARE THE DISH

1. Cut the parboiled tripe into bite-size pieces and put in a deep saucepan with the pig's foot, onion, garlic, carrot, marjoram, Sherry, wine, stock, leek, and bay leaf.

2. Bring to the boil, skim top of the pan, and simmer for 2 hours. Allow to cool slightly.

3. Bone the pig's foot, chop the meat and skin together, and put this back into the saucepan.

4. Heat the oil in a frypan and saute the bacon and chorizo until browned. Add the tomato paste and simmer for 15 minutes.

5. Transfer this mixture to the saucepan containing the tripe and simmer together for a further 30 minutes.

6. Add salt and pepper to taste, then just before serving throw in some chopped parsley.

*Poultry and Game*

12

# 12  POULTRY AND GAME

Until quite recently, most people living in the smaller towns and villages in Spain always kept a few hens and a cockerel in their backyard. Not only did this provide them with a fairly regular Sunday dinner, but the eggs were useful as well. For this reason, there are more recipes in Spain for cooking chicken than for any other dish.

In many parts of the country, game such as pheasant, partridge, wild duck, hare, and rabbit is abundant and, of course, very popular. There are many unusual but delightful ways of preparing game.

## CHICKEN/*POLLO* (POLL-YO)

### Market Information

Despite the fairly recent advent of intensive egg production in many parts of Spain, and the consequent deluge of hens on the market from this source, a considerable proportion of chickens on sale are still free-range birds as opposed to battery raised. However, in general, all poultry tend to be thinner and sometimes less tender than those generally obtainable in the United States, although the flavor is most often superior.

When you see these birds in the shops, you will notice first of all the distinct yellow pigment of their skin, in contrast to the milky-white, cellophane-wrapped chicken sold in the stores at home. With few exceptions, the poultry is sold *entero*—that is with its head and feet still attached—although the bird has been opened and some of the entrails removed. What does remain inside the chicken is the liver, heart, gizzard, and gall bladder, and these should be withdrawn before cooking the bird. Chickens sold in this condition are called *pollo entero* (poll-yo en-tair-o). Cleaned birds, with head and legs removed, are sold in large towns and in supermarkets and are known as *pollo limpio* (poll-yo lim-pee-o).

237

One more point: chickens are killed at a much later age than is usual in either France or the United States and normal market weights are something between 3½ and 4½ pounds (1¾ and 2 Kg). Seldom does one see such a bird as a *poussin* or a very young broiler bird. Spanish boiling or stewing fowl called *gallina* (gall-een-ya) are also sold somewhat heavier than seen in most other Western European countries, and weights of around 8½ pounds (4 Kg) are common.

When you buy your chicken, the shopkeeper will weigh the bird entero. He will then chop off the head and feet and if you wish, will wrap them up in the bag with the rest of the bird. This is common practice, for the Spanish cook always includes the neck in a chicken stew (and often the scrubbed feet), as the latter provide a gelatinous ingredient to thicken the stew. The shopkeeper will also quite readily chop any chicken in half or quarters, and sell you any individual portion you require. So one does not have to buy a whole bird to produce a chicken stew for two persons.

Select birds with compact bodies and broad breasts and with the fat as close to white as possible. Inspect the fat at the vent to determine color. Scrawny, elongated chickens with flat breasts are to be avoided.

**TO PREPARE CHICKEN FOR ROASTING.**  Remove and retain the internal organs, and wash the interior with cold water. Remove fat from both sides of the rear vent and reserve. Peel a medium-size onion, cut in half, and insert in cavity. Slice a lemon in two and insert this in the carcass also. Crush 4 cloves of garlic. Make a small nick in the skin of the chicken where the legs join the thighs and on both sides of the breast. Insert a clove of garlic into each aperture.

**TO CLEAN GIBLETS.**  Clear the blood and membrane from around the heart. Cut off fat and membrane from around the gizzard and carefully remove and discard the inner lining. Separate the liver from the green gallbladder and discard any part of the liver that may have a greenish tinge through contact with the gall bladder. Wash all the prepared giblets and they are now ready for further preparation. They may be put in cold water with the neck and cooked until tender, the resulting stock being used as a base for gravy or sauce; or they may be cooked with the bird, then finely chopped and added to pan drippings to make a different type of gravy.

**TO ROAST CHICKEN.**  Preheat oven to 325°F (180°C). Place untrussed bird on a roasting rack. Arrange the liver across the breastbone and the internal fat from the vent over the liver. This will self-baste the breast during roasting and also prevent the liver from becoming hard. Put the neck, gizzard, and heart on the rack also to prevent burning. Finally, cover the breast with aluminum foil, but leave the legs and thighs exposed, and roast for about 2¼ to 2½ hours.

TO PREPARE A STUFFED BIRD.   Cut off the neck at the base and fill the front cavity two-thirds full with the selected stuffing. Pull the neck skin over the cavity and tuck it under the front of the bird. Fill the rear cavity two-thirds full and secure with skewers; or alternatively, cut a large onion in half and insert one half into the hole to stop the stuffing from oozing out. Now you may truss the bird if you wish.

TO TRUSS A CHICKEN.   Tie the feet together with a long piece of string, leaving two long ends of the string on either side. Turn the wings in under the back and pull the neck skin under the bird. Place the chicken on its back and draw the strings across the bird to hold the legs close to the body and also to keep the neck skin in place. Tie the string ends together tightly. Cut off surplus string.

CUTTING A CHICKEN FOR STEWING.   It is usual to cut a bird into 14 portions. When just 8 pieces are required for a casserole, for example, the chicken is divided as follows: 2 drumsticks; 2 thighs; and the 2 breasts are each cut into 2 pieces including the wings. Should you need to separate a roast chicken into 6 portions, with light and dark meat equally divided, the procedure is described in the drawing (following page).

## Stewed Chicken

In many areas throughout Spain, the most popular method of cooking chicken (or meat of any sort) is as a stew. As explained previously, this is because unlike most kitchens in other parts of western Europe, many houses in Spain, especially the older ones (and these predominate), are not equipped with full-size baking or roasting ovens. This applies more to houses in small towns and villages than to those in the cities.

This lack of oven capacity is not because the modern Spanish family cannot afford to buy a stove, for Spain is now an affluent country, but most often because in so many houses there is literally no room in the kitchen. In the past, and to some extent even now, kitchens in Spain are much smaller than those in, say, France or Italy. Consequently, the cook has to do the majority of the cooking on a four-burner boiling ring. In such houses it is not uncommon to see a brand-new refrigerator in the living room, next to a gigantic color TV!

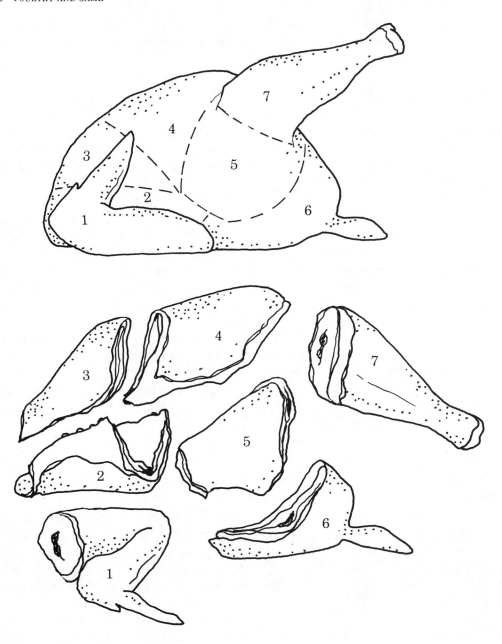

*Cutting a half chicken into 7 portions, or 14 portions for a whole bird.*

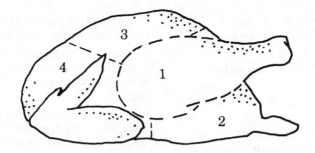

*Cutting chicken when eight pieces are required.*

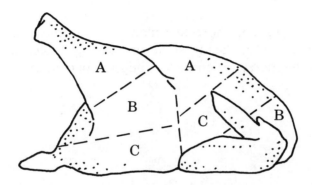

*Cutting a chicken when six pieces are required (light and dark meat equally divided).*

## Puchero de Pollo

(Pu-chair-o day Poll-yo)
Chicken stew
serves 4

There are many, many permutations of stewed chicken, all quite similar but each called by a different name depending on the province or district from which it originated. This is a typical example of a well-flavored stew.

1 4-lb (2 Kg) chicken cut into pieces
4 Tbsp. (4 × 15 mL spoon) olive oil
2 medium-size onions, rough chopped
3 cloves garlic, crushed *(cont.)*

5 carrots, rough chopped
2 white turnips, rough chopped
12 green olives, pitted
1 wine glass or 5 fl ozs (1½ dcL) dry white wine
1 pint (1½ liter) chicken stock or water
salt and pepper
1 generous sprig of fresh mint
1 Tbsp. (1 × 15 mL spoon) chopped parsley

1. In a large stewpan, brown the pieces of chicken in the oil. Then remove from pan.

2. Put in the pan the onions and garlic, and stew gently until soft.

3. Replace chicken pieces, add the rest of the ingredients except the parsley, cover the saucepan, and simmer for 1½ hours.

4. Just before serving, remove the sprig of mint, sprinkle the chopped parsley over the stew, then bring to the table.

*Note: For the best results, chicken pieces should be browned slowly, covered or uncovered. (Red meats should be browned quickly, uncovered.)*

As you will realize, there are many variations of this first simple dish that can be made by replacing some of the vegetables mentioned with others, such as red peppers, green peas, chopped bacon, almonds, etc.

## Stuffed Chicken

Many chicken dishes include stuffing as a flavoring agent for the bird and I include two of the best I have tasted.

The first dish I had in the Parador at Santo Domingo de Calzado when I was doing a tour of the Rioja vineyards. Santo Domingo is a little town about 37 miles (60 kilometers) west of Burgos and must be one of the smallest towns in Spain to have its own cathedral.

The day I arrived there I decided to visit the cathedral, and pushing open the sanctuary door, entered the cold, dark building. A few candles were burning in wrought-iron sconces attached to huge gray stone pillars, providing a pale, flickering light and deep, dark shadows. There was also slight illumination around the ornate altar and a few votive lights burned in the various recesses by the chapel entrances. Waxen effigies of the long-dead saints and bishops lay in glass coffins inside each chapel, their pale lifelike hands crossed over their breast or with palms together in silent supplication. I was quite alone in this huge building and the silence and stillness was complete.

Suddenly, there was a slight noise: like a fingernail tapping on a glass coffin. The hair on the back of my neck rose almost straight up. One could imagine almost anything in the dimly lit building. Then the noise was repeated, tap! tap! A wild thought struck me; those *were* waxen effigies in the chapels, weren't they? With my heart thumping, I turned for the door.

Suddenly, without any warning, a raucous crowing filled the cathedral and echoed round and around the building. Cock-a-doodle-do, cock-a-doodle-do. I must have jumped a foot into the air. My head jerked round to locate the source of the noise and there before my startled gaze, in a glass cage set over the main doorway, was a white cockerel and a white hen! They were happily pecking at the corn which was lying on the floor of their unusual coop. Their pecking had almost given me a heart attack. Chickens in a church, I thought as I hurried out into the warm sunshine. Why do they keep chickens in a church? I crossed the square to the Parador and asked the receptionist if he could explain the incongruity. He told me the following legend.

Sometime in the Middle Ages, a prosperous French family paused at Santo Domingo on their way to pay homage at the shrine of Santiago de Campostella. While staying at the inn, a local girl working in the tavern became enamored with the handsome son. He spurned her, and in revenge she stole a silver chalice from the cathedral and hid it in the young man's luggage.

The family left the inn to continue on their pilgrimage, the young man quite unaware of the stolen chalice in his baggage. The loss of the goblet was discovered by a priest who raised the alarm, upon which the young woman volunteered the information that she had seen the young Frenchman slip out of the cathedral hiding something under his cloak. A chase was immediately instigated and soon the pilgrims were caught and their baggage searched. Naturally, the missing chalice was found, the young man arrested and brought back to town. He was tried, found guilty of theft and sacrilege, and was promptly hanged!

The sorrowing parents continued on their way to Santiago de Campostella. On their return they again had to pass through Santo Domingo and to their great distress found that the body of their son was still hanging on the gibbet. However, imagine their astonishment when on going near the body, their son spoke to them. He told his parents that he had prayed to San Tiago (St. James) and through his intercession had been saved. The angels had fed him each day and that was why he was alive.

Overjoyed, the parents rushed to the house of the mayor who at that time was just sitting down with his family to a meal of two stuffed chickens. He naturally didn't believe the story, pointing out that it was as impossible that their son was alive as for those two chickens sitting in the dish to start to crow. At once the two birds obliged!

Of course it all turned out well. The girl confessed, the young man was released, and the happy family returned to France, but not before the father endowed the cathedral with sufficient money to commemorate the wondrous occasion. So in memory of this miracle, a white cock and hen have been kept in a glass cage within the cathedral for over 450 years.

## Pollo Relleno, Santo Domingo

(Poll-yo Rell-ay-no)
Stuffed chicken, Santo Domingo

STUFFING

½ cup (90 g) raisins, seedless
2 Tbsp. (2 × 15 mL spoon) brandy
1 cup (180 g) cooked white rice
½ cup (60 g) chopped walnuts
¼ cup (40 g) cooked green peas

1 4 lb (2 Kg) (approximately) chicken
1 medium-size onion
1 medium-size carrot, chopped
1 Tbsp. (1 × 15 mL spoon) olive oil
1 bay leaf
1 Tbsp. (1 × 15 mL spoon) flour
salt and pepper
1 wine glass or 5 fl ozs (1½ dcL) medium
   Sherry

1. Marinate the raisins in the brandy for 2 hours or so.
2. Mix the raisins and the brandy with the other ingredients listed for the stuffing.

3. Preheat oven to 375°F (190°C).
4. Stuff the cleaned chicken as previously described.
5. Place the stuffed bird on a wire rack, breast upwards, and cook in the oven for about 2 hours.
6. During this cooking period, saute the onion and carrot in the olive oil, add the bay leaf, and continue cooking slowly until the carrot is soft. Set aside.
7. When the chicken is cooked, remove from oven and keep warm.
8. Drain off surplus fat from roasting pan, leaving the chicken drippings.
9. Chop chicken liver finely.
10. Add the flour, salt, and pepper to the pan drippings together with the chopped liver and the Sherry, and mix to make a sauce. Simmer gently to allow the sauce to thicken, then add the previously cooked onion and carrot. The sauce should not be too thick, so dilute with a little water or stock should this be necessary.
11. Strain the sauce, and serve with the carved chicken.

The other outstanding stuffed chicken dish is produced at a restaurant in Mijas. Mijas (Mee-hass) is a small town that nestles in the hills above Torremolinos. Until about fifteen years ago it was just a quaint and very typical village with nothing very much to recommend it except perhaps a wonderful view of the sea.

Today all that has changed, for because of its quaintness and the growth of Torremolinos as a tourist town, Mijas too has become a tourist attraction, full of gift shops and bars. From the gastronomic point of view however, it does have certain compensations, for just ouside the town is an excellent restaurant, La Molina del Cura (The Mill of the Priest), whose kitchens are run by an inventive young chef, José Cuevas Villalba.

Villalba came into the profession through somewhat romantic circumstances. When he was a young man, the kitchen in his fiancee's house was the only place where he could be alone with his future wife and away from the suspicious eyes of her mother. So during the eight years of courtship, he spent hours and hours in the kitchen helping to prepare meals, and fell in love with cooking.

The story has a happy ending, as it should after eight years. Not only is he now happily married to the young lady but also has two children, and is head chef at this well-known and popular restaurant. But as with all good cooks, he feels the pressure of producing top quality dishes day after day.

"Cooking for discriminating guests is always a nerve-wracking business," he said. "We are always behind the scene and do not know whether our efforts are entirely successful. It makes one very tense."

This feeling of stress under kitchen pressures brought to mind the story of Vatel, the major-domo to King Louis XIV, one of the better-known gourmets in history. The main duty of Vatel, so we are told, was to supervise the royal meals especially to maintain the king's prowess in the bedchamber. On one important occasion, the king demanded that a special effort be made. When the oysters chosen did not arrive in time, Vatel was so deeply ashamed that he went outside and killed himself. One seriously doubts if a modern chef-de-cuisine would take such drastic steps should even a king be unhappy about a dish, but something of this sentiment is shared by every good cook I have known.

However, there is nothing for Villalba to be ashamed about with his excellent recipe for stuffed chicken.

## Pollo Relleno del Molino

(Poll-yo Rell-ay-no dell Mo-le-no)
Stuffed chicken
serves 4

2 roasting chickens, 3 lbs (1½ Kg) each
  (approximately)

STUFFING

2 cups (500 g) freshly cooked spinach
½ cup (120 g) raisins
1 small onion, finely chopped
½ tsp. (1 × 2 mL spoon) each thyme and
  oregano
salt and pepper

*(cont.)*

2 cloves garlic, minced

1 cup (100 g) grated sharp cheese (try Manchego)

1 whole egg

2 slices toast, cut into dice

½ cup (120 mL) light cream

2 Tbsp. (15 g) blanched, chopped almonds

¼ cup (60 mL) chopped parsley

4 slices of smoked bacon or tocino

1. Preheat oven to 375°F (190°C).

2. Cut the chicken in half on either side of the backbone and discard the backbone. Then remove wing-tips and discard these also. (Use these offcuts for stock.)

3. Mix the rest of the ingredients (except the bacon) in a bowl to make a firm but not dry stuffing. Add a little milk to the mixture if too dry.

4. Separate the skin from the breast of each of the four portions to make a large pocket.

5. Divide the stuffing into four portions and stuff the pocket of each breast with most of the stuffing.

6. Arrange the chicken pieces on a slightly oiled roasting pan and put the extra stuffing under each portion.

7. Wrap each breast with a slice of bacon, cover lightly with aluminum foil, and bake for about 1¼ hours. Remove foil during last 20 minutes of cooking period.

## Roasted Chicken

For a quick and simple meal the Spanish, like the rest of the world, often turn to a plain roasted chicken. In many towns there is at least one shop that cooks these birds on a gas-fired spit to a delicious golden brown. It is a very popular take-out item.

A restaurant in Almeria specializes in broiled chicken pieces and has gained a reputation by sprinkling a little granulated sugar over each portion before putting it under the grill, making especially sure that the sugar goes into the crevices in the wings and legs. This does not make the cooked chicken sweet, as one would expect, for in fact as the sugar melts it makes the skin moist and succulent.

It is quite common practice to sprinkle a little gin over a roasting bird after it has been in the oven for about 20 minutes, and to baste the bird from time to time with the pan drippings. Gin is a great tenderizer and helps in the development of flavor.

In the Balearic Islands—Majorca, Minorca, and Ibiza—chicken pieces are smeared with mayonnaise before being put under the broiler. This gives the skin a really crisp finish and an unusual but attractive flavor. Although the province of Aragon does not have a highly distinctive cuisine, there are a few interesting chicken specialties, one of the best being *Pollo al Chilindron*, said to have been invented in the provincial capital, Zaragoza, about

300 years ago. This dish also has the reputation of being the favorite of Goya, the painter, who was born near that town in 1746. Zaragoza is one of Spain's oldest cities, and the name is a corruption of Caesar Augustus who made it his headquarters while carrying out a campaign to conquer Spain.

## Pollo al Chilindron

(Poll-yo al Shil-in-dron)
Chicken with peppers and tomatoes
serves 4

4 individual portions of chicken
salt and pepper
2 Tbsp. (2 × 15 mL spoon) olive oil
6 large red peppers, seeded and
    chopped
6 large ripe tomatoes, peeled, seeded,
    and chopped
1 large onion, finely chopped
4 ozs (120 g) diced cooked ham
1 bay leaf
pinch of rosemary

1. Season the chicken pieces with salt and pepper. Slightly brown them in the hot olive oil until crispy.

2. Blanch the chopped red peppers in boiling water for 2 minutes, then add them to the chicken pieces in the pan. Add the chopped tomatoes, onion, ham, bay leaf, and rosemary.

3. Stew the whole mixture over a low heat until the chicken is tender.

*Note: The legs and thighs will take longer to cook than the breasts. The vegetables will reduce to a moist paste and are served with the chicken. If the mixture needs extra moisture, add a little dry white wine as required.*

## Other Chicken Recipes

Spain has always honored her artists, be they painters, sculptors, or bull-fighters. In 1577, the painter Domenikos Theotokopoulos, later known as El Greco (The Greek), came to Toledo. He was enchanted by this beautiful city that had, until a few years prior to his arrival, been the capital city of Spain. He loved the quiet squares, the maze of steep, narrow lanes, and the massive stone buildings with their crests and coats of arms above the entrance gates. It was in Toledo that he produced his greatest works, and the city still owns most of his masterpieces.

      The house where he lived for many years is still standing and nearby is a museum devoted to his works. He is not only remembered in Toledo as one of her most famous adopted sons and the greatest artist of his period, but his name has been given to an excellent chicken dish containing red wine and anchovies. So even the cooks in Toledo pay respect to his name!

## Pollo al Vino, El Greco

(Poll-yo al Vee-no)
Chicken in red wine
serves 4

2 Tbsp. (2 × 15 mL spoon) olive oil
1 Tbsp. (1 × 15 mL spoon) butter
2 medium-size onions, chopped
4 cloves garlic, crushed
4 individual chicken portions
¼ pint (120 mL) chicken stock
1 wine glass or 5 fl ozs (1½ dcL) red
    wine
2 fillets anchovy, cut into strips
1 Tbsp. (1 × 15 mL spoon) tomato
    paste
½ tsp. (1 × 2 mL spoon) dried basil
salt and pepper

1.  Heat the oil and butter in a large
pan over a moderate flame and gently
saute the onions and garlic until tender.
2.  Add the chicken pieces and slightly
brown them.
3.  When the chicken has taken on a
good color, add the remaining
ingredients and simmer covered for
about an hour or so until the chicken
pieces (especially the legs and thighs)
are tender.
4.  Remove the chicken, strain the sauce
through a sieve, and pour over the
portions just prior to serving.

*Note: As with the previous recipe, should
the vegetable sauce become too thick,
moisten with a little red wine or chicken
stock to achieve a good consistency.*

## Pollo Asturiana

(Poll-yo As-tour-ree-arnah)
Chicken in the Asturian style
serves 4

The province of Asturias lies in the
northern part of Spain between the
Basque country and Galicia, although
nothing about its cooking or the
personality of its natives is similar to
that of either of its neighbors.
However, among other things, the area
is noted for its apples from which an
excellent cider is made. The following
dish brings out the best both in the
chicken and the apples.

1 Tbsp. (1 × 15 mL spoon) butter
1 Tbsp. (1 × 15 mL spoon) olive oil
4 individual portions of chicken
salt and pepper
2 lbs (1 Kg) apples, peeled and cored
1 wine glass or 5 fl ozs (1½ dcL) dry
    cider
2 Tbsp. (2 × 15 mL spoon) brandy

1.  Preheat oven to 325°F (160°C).
2.  In a pan on top of the stove, melt
the butter, add the oil, and lightly
brown the chicken pieces while
seasoning them with salt and pepper.
3.  Place chicken pieces in a casserole
with the drippings and cook, covered,
for 30 minutes.
4.  After this period, add the chopped
apples, cider, and brandy. Cook for a
further 40 minutes.
5.  When the chicken pieces are tender,
remove from the casserole and keep
warm.
6.  Put the apple puree and the liquid in
the casserole through a sieve. Mix
thoroughly, adjust seasoning, and serve
with the chicken.

# Pollo Piquante

(Poll-yo Pee-kan-tay)
Savory chicken
serves 4

This is the first of four good recipes using chicken breast. It is a very simple dish which may be served hot or cold.

8 whole breasts of chicken
pinch basil
3 cloves garlic, minced or very finely chopped
1 stalk crisp celery, very finely chopped
1 Tbsp. (1 × 15 mL spoon) chopped parsley
7 ozs (210 g) cooked ham, thinly sliced
2 Tbsp. (2 × 15 mL spoon) butter
1 Tbsp. (1 × 15 mL spoon) olive oil
1 wine glass or 5 fl ozs (1½ dcL) medium Sherry

1. After washing the breasts and removing any membrane and sinew, pound them to a thickness of ¼ inch (6 mm).

2. In a bowl, mix the basil, garlic, celery, and parsley and scatter a spoonful of the mixture over each breast.

3. On top of the flavorings, place one slice of ham, roughly the same shape and size as the chicken breast.

4. Roll the chicken breast, enclosing the ham and seasonings. Fasten with one or two toothpicks.

5. In a frypan, melt the butter over a low heat, add the oil, and gently fry the chicken breasts for about 15 minutes, turning frequently so they brown evenly. Cook until tender.

6. During the last 5 minutes of cooking, pour the Sherry into the frypan and turn breasts so they absorb the flavor.

7. Serve hot or cold. If cold, this makes an ideal picnic dish.

# Pechugas de Pollo, Margarhita

(Pay-chew-gas day Poll-yo)
Fried chicken breasts
serves 4

1 Tbsp. (1 × 15 mL spoon) butter
2 Tbsp. (2 × 15 mL spoon) olive oil
8 whole chicken breasts
½ lb (250 g) chicken livers
1 large onion, finely chopped
2 cloves garlic, minced
juice of 1 lemon
2 Tbsp. (2 × 15 mL spoon) breadcrumbs (approximately)

1. In a large pan melt the butter over a gentle heat, then add the olive oil and saute the chicken breasts until lightly glazed and sealed. Remove from pan.

2. Cut away any yellow membrane from the chicken livers, chop roughly, and put into the pan with the onion and garlic. Cook gently until the onion is soft and transparent.

3. Return chicken breasts to pan and continue cooking until tender. Remove breasts to a serving dish and keep warm.

4. With a fork, squash the chicken livers until they become a mash. Add the lemon juice, then the breadcrumbs to the pan to thicken the sauce. Mix well with a fork to combine.

5. Spoon sauce over breasts before serving.

*Note: To stop the livers from splattering during the frying process, they should be perforated all over by sticking them with a fork.*

## Pechuga de Pollo con Naranjas

(Pay-chew-ga day Poll-yo kon Nar-an-has)
Chicken breasts with oranges
serves 4

This recipe from Valencia is simplicity itself.

2 Tbsp. (2 × 15 mL spoon) butter
8 chicken breasts
2 large navel oranges, peeled and
  chopped
1 Tbsp. (1 × 15 mL spoon) fresh mint,
  chopped
pinch nutmeg
salt and pepper

1. In a deep frypan, melt the butter and brown the chicken breasts until crispy. When golden, remove from pan.
2. Put the chopped orange segments (and any juice obtained while chopping) in the pan and gently stew for a few minutes until cooked to a pulp.
3. Return the breasts to the pan and cook gently for about 15 minutes, until tender. Remove and keep warm.
4. Add the chopped mint and the nutmeg to the orange pulp in the pan and stir to mix well. Heat to bubbling, then season with salt and pepper to taste.
5. Strain the sauce, then pour over breasts just before serving.

## Pechuga Alhambra

(Pay-chew-ga Al-am-bra)
Chicken breasts, Moorish style
serves 4

I was informed by the restaurant owner in Granada that this dish originated in Morocco. As the Moors occupied some parts of Spain for eight hundred years,

I suppose the recipe may be regarded as ethnic. It is unquestionably middle eastern, but so very good.

oil for deep frying
1½ tsp. (1½ × 5 mL spoon) salt
pinch pepper
2 Tbsp. (2 × 15 mL spoon) dry Sherry
6 ozs (180 g) finely chopped blanched
  almonds
1 lb (500 g) chicken breasts
2 egg whites
3 Tbsp. (3 × 15 mL spoon) cornstarch

1. Preheat frying oil to 360 to 370° F (185 to 190°C).
2. In a bowl mix salt, pepper, and Sherry.
3. In a second bowl, put the chopped almonds.
4. Cut chicken breasts into bite-size pieces and put them in the bowl with the Sherry mixture.
5. Beat egg whites lightly, add cornstarch, and mix well.
6. With a fork, dip chicken pieces into cornstarch mixture, then into the chopped nuts.
7. Drop the covered chicken pieces one by one into the hot fat and fry until golden. Remove from oil and drain on paper towels, then place on serving dish.
8. Serve with pineapple rice (rice cooked in pineapple juice).

## Pollo Maria

(Poll-yo Ma-rear)
Chicken Maria
serves 4

There is nothing like a good chicken casserole for an easy and flavorful meal. This one provides a beautiful visual contrast as well as a treat for the palate.

## SAUCE

2 Tbsp. (2 × 15 mL spoon) butter
2 Tbsp. (2 × 15 mL spoon) flour
1 cup (2 dcL) milk
salt

1 Tbsp. (1 × 15 mL spoon) butter
2 cups (180 g) chopped mushrooms
½ wine glass or 2½ fl ozs (¾ dcL) dry
    white wine
8 ozs (250 g) cooked chicken in pieces
4 sticks celery, chopped
½ cup (50 g) blanched, slivered almonds
½ blanched green pepper, diced
1 blanched red pepper, diced
12 stuffed olives, sliced
pinch pepper

1. Make a sauce with first four ingredients. Cook for 10 minutes.

2. While the sauce is simmering, saute the mushrooms in the butter over a moderate heat.

3. Preheat oven to 350°F (180°C).

4. Drain mushrooms and add to the cooked sauce, then mix in the wine.

5. Pour the wine and mushroom sauce into an ovenproof casserole, then add the remainder of the ingredients.

6. Cover the casserole and bake in the oven for 30 minutes.

*Note: This is a very good dish when served with plain boiled rice.*

## Pollo con Estragon

(Poll-yo kon Es-tra-gon)
Chicken with tarragon
serves 4

This recipe produces a dish that proves the point "simplicity is a virtue."

½ cup (120 g) butter
1 large bunch fresh tarragon
1 roasting chicken
1 wine glass or 5 fl ozs (1½ dcL) dry
    white wine

1. Preheat oven to 375°F (190°C) and melt half the butter in a roasting pan while the oven is heating.

2. Chop half the tarragon very finely and mix with the other half of the butter. Put this inside the chicken.

3. When the oven is hot and the butter in the pan has melted, put the chicken in the pan *lying on its side.*

4. Turn the bird onto the other side after cooking for 15 minutes, add the wine, and cook for a further 15 minutes.

5. Now place the bird breast upward and cook for a final 45 minutes, basting frequently.

6. Serve the chicken with the remainder of the chopped tarragon sprinkled over the portions.

## GAME

After Switzerland, Spain is the most mountainous country in Europe. This broken terrain provides many different types of wildlife. So it is no wonder that from October 12th, when the hunting season starts, the sport is enjoyed by thousands of Spaniards and visitors alike.

Among the more unusual game, wolf, wild boar, and mountain goat are hunted quite frequently, as are deer and roebuck. Rare sightings of bear and lynx occur, but these latter species are protected and may not be shot.

## Partridge

Of the smaller game which are hunted for the larder, partridge are the most popular and the most prolific target, and each region has its own favorite method of preparation. There are four varieties of partridge in Spain, of which the red partridge with its gray breast with red below, snow-white back, and red bill and legs, is the most common and also the most succulent.

Select young, plump birds weighing about 1¼ pounds (625 g), each with soft feet and pliable bills, if you wish to roast them. Larger birds are preferable for stewing.

TO DRESS PARTRIDGE.  In common with all wild game birds (except quail), partridge should be hung, undrawn, in a cool, dry place from between 2 and 7 days, depending on the degree of flavor or ripeness desired. Most often the bird will have to be plucked and cleaned and dressed at home. This is done by taking the feathers (a few at a time) between the thumb and first finger and pulling sharply, following the lie of the feathers. If you pull them back, away from the direction in which the feathers lie, you may tear the skin of a young bird. Start plucking at the feet and legs, then across the back, then around the sides and neck, leaving the breast until last. When cleanly plucked, cut off the head. To remove the feet, cut through the inside skin at the joint where the leg (drumstick) meets the foot. Bend the foot joint back and break the ball and socket joint. Take the foot in the left hand and holding the bird firmly with the right hand, pull the foot with a long, steady pull. Repeat with the other leg.

TO DRAW AND CLEAN PARTRIDGE.  Make a horizontal cut through the skin at the vent end of the bird, just below the end of the breast-bone, just large enough to admit your hand. With your forefinger, trace around the inside of the bird, starting from one side, moving over the breast, to the other side, and pulling away the membrane, skin, veins, etc., which hold the insides in place. Remove the insides and reserve the gizzard, heart, and liver (the giblets) for gravy making if required. Remove the gallbladder, which is on the surface of the right lobe of the liver and throw this away. Do not break or split the gallbladder as the green bile contained inside will give a bitter flavor to any part of the bird it touches. Pull away every particle of the lungs, which are pinkish-red and spongy and lie on either side of the backbone. These are discarded also.

TO CUT PARTRIDGE FOR STEW.   A small partridge weighing about 1¼ pounds (625 g) is sufficient for one serving. After plucking and cleaning it is cut into two halves along the length of the backbone. A large bird weighing 1¾ to 2 pounds (850 to 950 g) is cut into four joints: two legs and thighs and two breasts including the wings.

TO ROAST PARTRIDGE.   Cook in a preheated oven at 400°F (200°C) for 15 minutes, then increase the temperature to 450°F (230°C) and cook 10 minutes longer.

The woods and fields around Toledo are full of red partridge and a good day's hunting with only two guns can bag up to 60 brace of these excellent birds. Toledo stands on an enormous craggy ledge and from some viewpoints seems to defy gravity. As the hunters return homeward they see in the distance the Imperial City standing high above the surrounding countryside, like some vast cathedral pointing heavenward and shimmering in the violet twilight. The red earth and the green fields surrounding Toledo are a complete contrast to the steel-gray stone walls and slate roofs that give the city a hard, metallic look. The men will cross one of the bridges over the fast-flowing River Tegus which surrounds the city walls, like a natural moat, and then they will proceed on into the city with its tortuous network of cobbled alleys and austere-looking houses and buildings. The famous specialty of Toledo is the local partridge stewed in the red wine from Mentrida.

## Perdiz a Toledo

(Pear-deez a Toledo)
Stewed partridge, Toledo style
serves 4

2 large, cleaned partridge
1 large onion, with two whole cloves
    stuck in it
4 cloves garlic, crushed
2 Tbsp. (2 × 15 mL spoon) olive oil
4 wine glasses or 20 fl ozs (6 dcL) red
    wine
2 Tbsp. (2 × 15 mL spoon) tarragon
    vinegar
salt and pepper

1. Cut each partridge into four pieces as previously directed.
2. In a stewpan place all the ingredients and allow to simmer over a low heat for about 1½ hours until the leg and thigh joints are tender.
3. Remove partridge from pan and keep warm. Remove the onion and discard.
4. Heat the cooking liquor rapidly to reduce to about a quarter of the original volume.
5. Strain the reduced sauce over the partridge before serving.

PICKLED PARTRIDGE.    In the Soria area, which lies northeast of Madrid, pickled partridge is a great delicacy. There does not seem to be any specific recipe for this dish, each cook having his or her own particular preference as to quantities of ingredients. There does however seem to be a general consensus of opinion of what the ingredients should be. The following is the general principle for pickling these birds, and I will give it to you as it was told to me.

Young birds are cleaned and trussed and placed in a large earthenware pot, then covered with seasoned stock, red wine, chopped onion, garlic, a few whole cloves, some crushed peppercorns, and a generous sprig of bay. The birds are gently stewed in this mixture until tender and then allowed to cool thoroughly in the cooking liquor. They are then removed, well dried with a cloth, and placed in a clean earthenware container. Sufficient red wine is then poured over them to cover completely, then olive oil to a depth of ½ to ¾ inch (12 to 18 mm) is added. The wine pickles the partridge and the oil—which rises to the top of the container—keeps out the air, and prevents the birds from going bad. They may be stored in this condition for up to three months if kept in a cool larder. When required for use they are drained and served cold with hot bread and a mixed salad.

## Perdiz con Col

(Pear-deeth kon Kol)
Partridge with cabbage
serves 4

This is a quite exceptional dish from Barcelona, somewhat similar to that served in the Languedoc area of France.

### STUFFING

3 cups (250 g) breadcrumbs
6 ozs (180 g) lean ham, diced
2 cloves garlic, minced
1 Tbsp. (1 × 15 mL spoon) chopped parsley
1 whole egg, beaten
4 raw partridge livers, chopped

4 young partridge, cleaned and dressed
½ cup (120 mL) olive oil
4 cloves garlic, finely chopped
½ cup flour (120 mL)
bouquet of parsley, thyme, bay leaves, and a large piece of orange peel
4 wine glasses or 20 fl ozs (6 dcL) red wine
2 Tbsp. (2 × 15 mL spoon) tomato puree
1 wine glass or 5 fl ozs (½ dcL) stock or water
1½ lbs (750 g) prepared cabbage

1. Make a fairly dry stuffing by combining all the ingredients listed in the first section.

2. Stuff the partridge with this mixture and truss as you would a chicken.

3. In a large, deep pan on top of the stove, heat the oil and fry the garlic until soft. When soft, put the trussed birds in the oil to lightly glaze and stiffen them.

4. Remove from pan and keep to one side.

5. In the pan, shake in the flour, mix with the oil, and allow to cook for a few minutes over a gentle heat.

6. Tie the sprigs of herbs together with thread or fold them in a square of muslin and tie at the top.

7. Add the wine, tomato puree, and stock to the pan to produce a sauce, then add the herbs and orange peel and cook all together for about 15 minutes over a low heat.

8. Remove the herbs and peel, and strain the sauce.

9. Chop the cabbage roughly, put in a deep saucepan, place the partridge on top, and pour the strained sauce over.

10. Return to top of stove and simmer, covered, for about one hour.

11. When tender, place birds on serving dish and spoon cabbage/sauce over.

As we have observed, in Spain as in France, it is not regarded as unusual to name a particularly good dish after a saint, a national hero, or a greatly admired person. Such examples from the French cuisine as Pêche Melba, Crème du Barry, and Coquilles St. Jacques come readily to mind. In the United States this is not the accepted custom and there are few dishes which commemorate an event or applaud the name of famous and worthy Americans. Pity! The Spanish regard this form of honor as a lasting memorial to the person and of more value than having a marble plaque set in the wall of a church.

The following dish is named after one of Spain's greatest monarchs. The name Felipe Secundo (Philip II) has been given to a number of quite excellent dishes as a tribute not only to a revered king, but also to a person with exquisite culinary taste. His attitude toward food was in complete contrast to that of his father Carlos V, who was (to put it mildly) a glutton, and whose interest in matters of state was minimal. His eating habits can hardly be believed. It is said that his breakfast at 5 AM consisted of meats, fowl, and pastries. At noon he lunched on as many as twenty different meat dishes followed by huge quantities of sweetmeats, washed down with quarts of wine. At dusk, he consumed fish, meats, and fruit. Again at around midnight he required yet another meal to stave off hunger until the following dawn.

As if to compensate for this gross behavior, Philip II was a discriminating, fastidious person—and a gourmet.

## Perdiz Felipe Secundo

(Pear-deeth Fay-lee-pay Se-coon-doe)
Partridge, Philip II style
serves 4

3 ozs (90 g) cooked ham, finely chopped
1 small onion, minced
4 slices of chorizo, finely chopped
½ cup (120 mL) breadcrumbs
salt and pepper
1 cup (2 dcL) orange juice
    (approximately)
4 partridge breasts

2 Tbsp. (2 × 15 mL spoon) olive oil
4 ozs (120 g) seeded white grapes
6 ozs (180 g) rice
1½ pints (¾ liter) chicken stock
½ lb (250 g) fresh raspberries
2 tsp. (2 × 5 mL spoon) cornstarch

1.  Preheat oven to 350°F (180°C).

2.  Combine ham, onion, chorizo, breadcrumbs, and salt and pepper to taste. Moisten with some of the orange juice to make a loose, but not sloppy, stuffing.

3.  Make an incision along the side of each of the breasts, cutting to within ¾ inch (18 mm) of each end and ¾ inch (18 mm) of the back. This will make a pocket for the stuffing.

4.  With a spoon and fingers, stuff the pockets, forcing the stuffing in to produce a puffed breast.

5.  Brush the filled breasts with a little olive oil and place in a casserole with the grapes.

6.  Bake uncovered in the oven for about 40 minutes, basting with the remainder of the oil and orange juice every 10 minutes. The breasts should be delicately browned.

7.  Meanwhile, in a saucepan, cook the rice in the seasoned chicken stock. Drain and arrange on a serving dish.

8.  Crush the raspberries through a sieve to remove any seeds. Retain the flesh and juice.

9.  Remove the cooked partridge breasts and grapes from the casserole and arrange on the bed of rice. Keep warm.

10.  Thicken the juices in the casserole with the cornstarch mixed with a little cold water. The sauce should be just slightly thickened. Stir over low heat until cooked.

11.  Now add the crushed raspberries to the sauce, mix well, and heat again, but do not boil. Serve sauce separately.

## Quail

Quail are more common in Spain than in the United States, and Spaniards make good use of these delectable little birds, which weigh about 4 ounces (120 g) when cleaned and dressed. Two or three per person is the usual serving.

In September and October they migrate to the hot climate of India and then in the spring they return to the Mediterranean area in huge flocks.

On their return they are trapped alive and put into cages for fattening.

The method of trapping these tiny birds is unique and relies for its success upon the fact that the returning flocks, each numbering many thousands of birds, travel *exactly* the same route year after year, and always return to the same few fields from which they departed. The trappers bait the center of the field with grain and the returning birds, starving and almost exhausted from their incredible journey, land and feed voraciously, almost oblivious to what is going on around them. And a lot is going on.

Prior to their arrival, the stage has been set. To one side of the field a huge net of fine mesh nylon, of a size to blanket the field, is carefully folded in pleats. To the two corners of the folded net are attached short-fuse rockets. The other two corners are securely pegged to the ground. When the birds are safely feeding, a signal is given, the two fuses are lit, and the rockets roar over the field dragging the light nylon net with them, to land on the other side of the field. The whole process takes no more than *three* seconds.

Hundreds of the quail escape in that short time before the net traps them, but many more hundreds are caught to end up on a gourmet's table. When cooking quail, select plump, compact birds with dull, slightly matt skin.

TO PREPARE QUAIL.   No preparation is necessary. In Spain all quail are ready for the oven. Unlike other game birds, quail should never be allowed to get "high." Keep them no longer than two days.

## Codornices Asadas

(Kod-or-niece Ass-a-das)
Pot roast quail
serves 4

Roast quail (it's pot roast, really) is a dish often served in many of the good Marbella restaurants.

3 Tbsp. (3 × 15 mL spoon) olive oil
2 cloves garlic, crushed
12 plump quail
1 cup chicken stock (250 mL)
2 wine glasses or 10 fl ozs (3 dcL) dry
    white wine

3 bay leaves
pinch of *each*, thyme, basil, rosemary
½ cup (40 g) fine, fresh breadcrumbs

1.  Preheat oven to 350°F (180°C).
2.  Heat the oil in a casserole and brown the crushed garlic, then remove the cloves and discard.
3.  Lightly glaze the quail in the hot oil. This will take about 10 minutes, and you should turn the birds once or twice to obtain equal glazing.

4. Now add the rest of the ingredients (except the breadcrumbs), cover the casserole, and cook for 30 minutes.

5. Place the cooked quail on a warm serving dish, strain the cooking liquor, and thicken to a desired consistency with the breadcrumbs.

6. Pour this sauce over the birds before serving.

A few miles west of the town of Marbella is Estepona with its white houses glistening in the sun, wide sandy beaches, blue skies, and swaying palms. It was founded by the Romans who built the aqueduct nearby, and the ancient town was further developed by the Moors. It still retains the characteristic narrow streets that isolate the old part of the town from the new.

It is a town of contrasts, with modern buildings and a brand-new yachting marina next to the old fish market and harbor. Recent office blocks stand next to squat Moorish houses, yet everything blends in a sympathetic manner.

## Codornices con Coñac

(Kod-or-niece kon Ko-nyack)
Quail in Spanish brandy

In Estepona they have this outstanding recipe for quail which first stews the birds in chicken stock, thus giving them an unparalleled flavor.

12 trussed quail
1 quart (1 liter) concentrated chicken stock
2 Tbsp. (2 × 15 mL spoon) butter
3 Tbsp. (3 × 15 mL spoon) Spanish brandy

1. Stew the quail in the chicken stock very gently for 20 minutes, after the stock has come to the boil.

2. Remove the birds and dry them on paper towels.

3. In a large saucepan, melt the butter and lightly glaze the birds, a few at a time. Keep warm.

4. When all are glazed, return them to the large pan and pour the brandy over them all.

5. Increase the heat and tilt the saucepan toward the flame so it catches fire.

6. When the flames have subsided, the quail are set on a platter and the butter/brandy sauce is poured over.

Note: If you use an electric stove, flaming in the manner described is not possible. As an alternative, heat the brandy in a metal soup ladle, then set the brandy alight and pour over the birds in the saucepan.

## Pigeon

Very young and tender pigeons are a true delicacy and as such are highly esteemed. Select young, plump birds with soft, tender feet. If serving roast pigeon, allow one bird per serving. Older, larger birds should be casseroled, allowing one-half bird per serving. Prepare as described for partridge.

TO ROAST PIGEON.   Truss the bird, then sear by pouring a tablespoon of very hot oil over the breast of each bird. Then wrap with strips of smoked bacon or tocino, place in a preheated oven at 375°F (190°C), and cook for 1 hour.

## *Pichones Granada*

(Pee-cho-nays Gra-nada)
Casserole of pigeon
serves 4

Larger birds may be used in this recipe.

2 large pigeons
2 Tbsp. (2 × 15 mL spoon) olive oil
4 slices of smoked bacon, chopped
3 large onions, finely chopped
4 ozs (120 g) white flour
   (approximately)
1 cup (2 dcL) chicken or veal stock
2 wine glasses or 10 fl ozs (3 dcL) red
   wine
1 small smoked sausage (chorizo)

1. Clean the pigeons if necessary (see instructions for cleaning partridge), then chop each bird in two pieces from neck to vent.
2. Heat the oil in a deep pan and quickly sear the 4 portions.
3. Remove the pigeon to a casserole, then fry the chopped bacon until crisp. Add that to the casserole.
4. Gently stew the onions in the oil and bacon fat until soft but not colored, then add these to the pigeon in the casserole.
5. Preheat oven to 350°F (180°C).
6. Sprinkle sufficient flour into the pan to absorb the oil and fat (thus making a roux). Add the stock and wine gradually, beating well between additions.
7. When the sauce has reached the desired consistency so that it may be easily poured, put this in the casserole too.
8. Slice the chorizo thinly, spread over the pigeon portions, cover the casserole, and cook in oven for about 1¼ hours.

## Wild Rabbit

Rabbit is often shot in many parts of the country. One of the most popular ways that the hunters in the field cook young rabbit (and they are only good when young) is to clean and skin the animal on the spot, rub it all over with olive oil in which crushed garlic has been soaked, then barbeque it on four stout sticks over a wood fire. During the roasting process they throw generous bunches of wild rosemary on the flames so the flavor will penetrate the flesh of the rabbit. When cooked they eat this tender, succulent meat with new bread washed down with the local red wine.

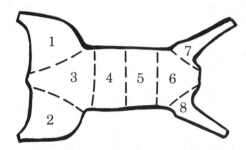

*Cutting a rabbit.*

A similar result, but by no means so dramatic, may be achieved with commercially raised rabbits which are sold throughout Spain, clean and skinned and almost ready for the oven, but with the head still attached.

## *Roast Rabbit*

1 rabbit, cleaned and skinned
olive oil
salt and pepper
pinch of dried rosemary
1 wine glass or 5 fl ozs (1½ dcL) red
   wine
1 clove garlic, crushed

1. Preheat the oven to 375°F (190°C).
2. Cut off the head of the rabbit and chop the carcass into serving pieces as shown in the illustration.
3. Rub each piece with a little olive oil, sprinkle with salt, pepper, and a pinch of dried rosemary.
4. Place rabbit pieces on a wire rack, then into a roasting pan.
5. Put a little olive oil, a glass of red wine, and a clove of crushed garlic in the roasting pan.
6. Cook rabbit pieces for about 45 minutes, basting at regular intervals.

Note the use of rosemary in the Roast Rabbit recipe. Rosemary is one of the most adaptable herbs that grow wild in Spain. It is also one of the most ancient. Rosemary was well known in ancient Egypt and was the favorite flower of Queen Nefertiti. She had a garland placed around her neck at her coronation as Queen of Egypt in 1360 B.C., and on her tomb when she died. This fragrant plant with its gray, evergreen leaves and soft blue flower was regarded as sacred by the priests in ancient Egypt and was used as an ornamental shrub in their temples and in the royal palaces of the Pharaohs.

Rosemary was growing wild in Spain at the time Caesar Augustus came to conquer the country, and it is still seen extensively in this wild state. The flowers are edible and are used in the most exotic salads, and the leaves are used for seasoning soups, stews, and meats. Both Henry VIII of England and Lord Byron loved their meats seasoned with this herb.

## Wild Duck

Wherever there is an area of quiet water and peaceful surroundings, it is there that one is likely to find wild duck. A few miles north of Tortosa (Catalonia) is an area which fulfills these idyllic conditions, for at Flix, some 47 miles (75 kilometers) from the town is the new dam which has made the River Ebro into an artificial lake. Here, among the olive groves and green hills which surround the water are flocks of wild duck, mostly mallard.

For cooking, select young, plump birds with soft feet and pliable beaks. Clean as for partridge.

TO ROAST WILD DUCK.   Place the cleaned bird in a preheated oven at 350°F (190°C) and cook until tender. In common with other game birds, wild duck have very little natural fat and it is necessary to coat each bird with bacon or tocino before putting them in the oven.

Note that wild game birds of the same size vary considerably in their degree of tenderness and are therefore very different from commercially reared birds. Thus no specified roasting time can be given. Each bird must be tested for doneness.

## *Pato con Nabos*

(Par-toe kon Nar-bos)
Duck with white turnips
serves 4

This recipe uses the flavor of two distinctive ingredients to produce an excellent contrast.

2 ducks

salt and pepper
2 Tbsp. (2 × 15 mL spoon) pork fat, chicken fat, or similar fat
4 ozs (120 g) flour (approximately)
1 wine glass or 5 fl ozs (1½ dcL) red wine
1 pint (½ liter) stock
¼ tsp. (1 × 1 mL spoon) ground ginger
4 carrots, roughly chopped
8 small, whole onions                    *(cont.)*

2 slices smoked bacon, chopped
1½ lbs (750 g) white turnips
1 Tbsp. (1 × 15 mL spoon) olive oil

1. Take the cleaned duck and cut each into six pieces. Dust pieces with salt and pepper.

2. In a deep pan heat the pork fat over a good flame and glaze the duck pieces until light golden. Remove from pan.

3. Add sufficient flour to make a roux (see page 123), then add the wine and stock to make a thin sauce.

4. Now add the ginger, carrots, whole onions, and bacon. Place the duck pieces over and cook covered over a gentle heat for about 45 minutes.

5. Meanwhile, peel the turnips and cut them into thick rings. In a frying pan with the hot olive oil, brown them quickly.

6. Drain the turnips. Add them to the duck and continue cooking for a further 45 minutes.

*Note: Total cooking time is 1½ hours.*

## Pato con Aceitunas

(Par-toe kon Ass-e-tu-nas)
Duck with olives
serves 4

Again using the flavor contrast principle to produce an exciting taste experience, this is another success story.

2 young, wild ducks
4 Tbsp. (4 × 15 mL spoon) olive oil
3 cloves garlic, crushed
4 red peppers, roughly chopped
2 medium-size onions, sliced
1 lb (500 g) tomatoes, peeled, seeded, and chopped
1 tsp. (1 × 5 mL spoon) granualted sugar
1 wine glass or 5 fl ozs (1½ dcL) dry Sherry
1 bay leaf
¼ tsp. (1 × 1 mL spoon) dried rosemary
1 cup (¼ liter) chicken or veal stock
24 pimiento-stuffed olives

1. Cut each cleaned duck into 6 pieces.

2. In a pan, heat the oil and lightly glaze the duck until golden, then remove the pieces to an ovenproof casserole.

3. In the pan, saute the garlic, red peppers, onions, and the tomatoes until all are very soft.

4. Preheat oven to 375°F (190°C).

5. Drain off excess oil from the cooked vegetables and sprinkle with the sugar. Then add to casserole.

6. Add the Sherry, herbs, and stock. Cook covered for about 1 hour (until legs and thighs of the duck are tender).

7. Remove duck pieces and place on a warm serving dish to keep warm.

8. Strain sauce, then add the chopped olives to the sauce. Reheat, then pour sauce over the duck.

## Guinea Hen

These flavorful birds, with a dressed weight of approximately 1 pound (500 g) when young and about 2 pounds (approximately 1 Kg) when older, are specialties of a number of prestigious restaurants throughout Spain. At the Restaurante Hacienda in Marbella, they produce an exquisite dish with this bird.

To be awarded a two-star rating in Guide Michelin is an honor many restaurant owners would give a great deal to possess. Yet Paul Schriff, the *chef-patron*, takes all his accolades and compliments in stride, determined that praise shall not be an excuse for lowering standards. Born in Luxembourg, he studied first at the hotel school in Namur, Belgium, then gained further experience at the renowned Maison du Cygnes in Brussels. He became the protege of the *maitre chef*. He recalls that his most significant experience as a young cook was when the maitre took him to market.

The maitre, he recalls, was dressed in black with a white shirt and a starched wing collar. He carried gray kid gloves and wore a gray velvet fedora set squarely on his head. He walked the streets with professional majesty, the young cook scurrying after him. Lesser mortals like doctors, lawyers, and tradesmen doffed their hats as the maitre passed, and received a benign nod and a smile in response.

They proceeded into the bustle of the market where dozens of small merchants, many of them local growers and producers, offered a complete range of the freshest foods. Crates of vegetables were there for inspection, as were carcasses of beef, lamb, and pork, their flanks stuck with colored ribbons fluttering in the breeze to attract the attention of prospective buyers.

Then they went on to the fish market, crammed with such a variety it seemed the buyer must be spoiled for choice. The maitre inspected, rejected, touched, tasted, smelled, prodded, poked, argued, frowned, and, when some item pleased him, occasionally smiled. All during this performance, the maitre explained to his protege the "factors of quality" to look for in each item.

"At the end of this glorious morning, which I remember so very clearly," Schriff told me, "the maitre gave me this valuable piece of advice. Use fresh, local produce of the best possible quality, *always!* It is one of the fundamentals of fine cuisine in any country. Never settle for second best or your cooking will only be second best."

This philosophy has guided Paul Schriff over the years, and when he came to Spain in 1969, he reconstructed his classic dishes using the best foods available locally.

## Pintada Hacienda

(Pin-ta-dah Has-e-n-da)
Guinea fowl, Hacienda style
serves 4

This is Paul Schriff's outstanding recipe for guinea hen.

2 guinea fowl, 2 lbs (1 Kg) each
a little butter
1 cup (2 dcL) light cream
2 Tbsp. (2 × 15 mL spoon) minced raisins
1 wine glass or 5 fl ozs (1½ dcL) port wine
salt and white pepper

1.  Preheat oven to 400°F (200°C).

2.  Brush the breasts and legs of the guinea hens with a little melted butter.

3.  Roast the birds for 45 minutes, covering the breasts with aluminum foil.

4.  Meanwhile, in a saucepan heat the cream over a very low flame, then add the raisins and a little of the port wine.

5.  When the birds are cooked and tender, remove from the oven, add the remainder of the port wine to the pan drippings, and with a fork, scrape the bottom of the pan to obtain any residue.

6.  Now add the cream mixture and season to taste.

7.  With kitchen shears, split each bird in half lengthwise, place the 4 halves on a warm serving dish, and pour the cream sauce over.

*Fruits and Vegetables*

# 13

# 13 FRUITS AND VEGETABLES

Possibly the greatest difference between purchasing fruits and vegetables in Spain and doing the same thing in a U.S. supermarket is that in America, much of the produce is graded by size and quality. In Spain, the fruits and vegetables are seldom graded and, consequently, one sees produce of varying size and quality and degree of maturity for sale in the same box. It is necessary to pick over the items and inspect them for suitability. The ability to choose from a box of produce is one very good reason why many shoppers prefer to buy their goods from small stalls rather than from shops, where the owner prefers to serve you with items that are not all of the same degree of maturity. Some are even overripe. It is therefore even more important that the shopper knows more about purchasing standards than would be the case in the United States or United Kingdom, and be able to recognize the factors of quality in each item to be purchased.

## FRUITS

In the case of fruit, the visitor may find it somewhat difficult to assess the usefulness of some of the Spanish produce, for there are no varietal names displayed on any produce. And in some cases the greengrocer has little knowledge of the characteristics of the produce being sold.

Fortunately, most of the fruits sold are strains of well-known, international varieties, and their characteristics are fairly easily recognizable. But to help the reader distinguish the more common varieties of fruits available in most parts of Spain, where possible, names and distinguishing features are noted. See the Fruit Availability Calendar for an overall view of seasonal availability.

Let us start with some general rules to follow when buying fruit.

1. Generally, fruit should be ripe or matured or very close to maturity. Never select overripe fruit or very ripe fruit as it is often mealy and lacking flavor.

## FRUIT AVAILABILITY CALENDAR

| | | J | F | M | A | M | J | Ju | A | S | O | N | Dec |
|---|---|---|---|---|---|---|---|---|---|---|---|---|---|
| Apples | *Manzanas* | X | X | X | X | X | X | X | X | X | X | X | X |
| Apricots | *Albaricoques* | X | X | X | X | X | X | X | X | X | X | X | X |
| Avocados | *Aguacates* | X | X | X | X | X | X | X | X | X | X | X | X |
| Bananas | *Plátanos* | X | X | X | X | X | X | X | X | X | X | X | X |
| Blackberries | *Zarzamoras* | | | | X | X | X | X | X | | | | |
| Cherries | *Cerezas* | | | | | X | X | X | | | | | |
| Currants (Black) | *Grosellas negras* | | | | X | | | | | | | | |
| Custard Apples | *Chirimollas* | X | X | | | | X | X | X | X | X | X | X |
| Figs | *Higos* | | | | | | X | X | X | X | | | |
| Gooseberries | *Uvas espinas* | | | | | | X | X | | | | | |
| Grapefruit | *Pomelo* | X | X | X | X | X | X | X | X | X | X | X | X |
| Grapes | *Uvas* | | | | | X | X | X | X | X | X | X | X |
| Lemons | *Limónes* | X | X | X | X | X | X | X | X | X | X | X | X |
| Limes | *Limas* | | | X | X | X | X | X | X | X | X | X | |
| Melons | *Melónes* | | | | | X | X | X | X | X | X | X | X |
| Mangos | *Mangos* | | | | | X | X | X | X | X | | | |
| Oranges | *Naranjas* | X | X | X | X | X | X | X | X | X | X | X | X |
| Peaches | *Melocotónes* | | | | | X | X | X | X | X | X | X | X |
| Pears | *Peras* | X | | X | X | X | X | X | X | X | X | X | X |
| Persimmons | *Nísperos* | X | X | X | X | X | X | X | X | X | X | X | |
| Pineapples | *Piñas* | X | X | X | X | X | X | X | X | X | X | X | X |
| Plums | *Ciruelas* | X | | X | | X | X | X | X | X | X | X | X |
| Pomegranates | *Granadas* | X | | X | | | | X | X | X | X | X | X |
| Raspberries | *Frambuesas* | | | | X | X | X | X | X | X | X | X | |
| Strawberries | *Fresas* | | | | X | X | X | X | X | X | X | X | X |
| Tangerines | *Mandarinas* | X | X | X | X | X | X | X | X | X | X | X | X |

2. Fruit should be well formed and developed. It can be slightly misshapen, but not to the point where appearance is greatly affected.

3. Fruit should be free from damage. This damage includes growth irregularities or deformities, limb rub, skin break and scars, decay or rot, mold, disease, insect infestation, bird damage, or handling bruises.

4. The largest sample is not always the best flavored or the most economical. Consider the purpose for which the fruit is to be used (e.g., buy cooking apples for culinary purposes and eating apples for dessert).

## Apples (*Manzanas*)

Historians tell us that the apple (in a somewhat different form) was known to the caveman and to the ancient Greeks and Romans. It is, of course, mentioned in the Bible, although some people have put forward the suggestion that the "apple" in the Garden of Eden was in fact an *apricot*. However, the apple has been cultivated in Europe for over 2000 years. There are literally thousands of different varieties, the vast majority of which are produced by accidental pollination rather than by commercial decision. Those that are commercially grown are tried and true favorites (some fifty varieties) and are heavy croppers. Among the varieties found in Spain are:

*Golden delicious:* a medium-size dessert apple sometimes used for culinary purposes. Slightly conical shape with a yellow/gold skin and slightly waxy appearance. The flesh is crisp, tender, and very juicy with possibly a slight yellow tinge.

*Red delicious:* medium size with either deep red or striped red skin. Crisp, juicy white flesh, sometimes with a slight pink tinge. This is a dessert variety.

*Rome beauty:* a cooking apple with round, slightly flattened shape, usually large with a yellow skin and a mottling of bright red. White flesh, tender and juicy. Used extensively in Spain, especially for baked apples.

*Grimes golden:* a dual-purpose variety, popular in Spain. It is a medium to large apple with a deep yellow skin and yellow flesh.

*Granny Smith:* a medium-size to large dual-purpose apple with a flattened, conical shape. The flesh is white, crisp, and juicy and very well flavored when mature. It keeps very well and is excellent for culinary purposes when green, easily recognizable by its bright skin. For dessert purposes, it is better if the fruit is tinged with yellow.

*Gravenstein:* medium size with a greenish-yellow skin, often turning to orange-yellow with red striping. White to yellow flesh, crisp and juicy. Another excellent dual-purpose fruit.

*Purchasing Standards: Select:* firm, heavy fruit, bright, and characteristically colored. This will almost certainly guarantee maturity and good flavor. *Refuse:* soft, shrivelled, or bruised fruit.

*To store:* in a cool place. Warm temperatures hasten the ripening (or overripening) process and cause apples to lose their crispness and flavor. So in Spain, buy what you will need for a day or two only. If kept for later use, be sure to refrigerate.

*To prepare:* wash and peel then slice, etc.


## Apricots (*Albaricoques*)

Freshly picked, tree-ripened apricots are just like a ball of honey. They are an extremely delicate fruit, so avoid those samples that are very soft to the touch as this feature probably indicates some degree of decay. Apricots do not ripen well off the tree, and after picking gain little flavor and only a small amount of sugar. In Spain, apricots are picked almost at their peak of maturity, so the flavor is outstanding. Two main varieties are available:

*Royal:* medium size with an orange-yellow skin and a faint red blush. Deep orange flesh and a sweet, full flavor.

*Tilton:* larger fruit, yellow to orange with a red blush and a rather flat appearance. Light orange flesh and good flavor.

*Purchasing Standards: Select:* unblemished fruit (this is most important) with a pronounced aroma. *Refuse:* bruised samples, split skins, or fruit with a greenish tinge.

*To prepare* (for cooking): wash, halve, and remove stone. Poach in a little syrup (1 lb [500 g] sugar to 1 pint [½ liter] water) flavored with vanilla. Remove skins after gentle cooking.


## Avocados (*Aguacates*)

A native of Mexico, this fruit has been cultivated for centuries, but has only made its appearance in Spain during the last fifteen years or so. It is also known as the alligator pear. Three main varieties are grown in Spain.

*Fuerte:* a pear-shaped fruit with a shining green skin and weighing between 8 and 12 ounces (250 to 360 g).

*Hass:* a smaller variety, has the same early skin color but turns black when fully matured.

*Alligator:* another small variety similar to Hass, but the skin is covered with nodules which give it the appearance of alligator skin.

*Purchasing Standards: Select:* firm to slightly soft fruit, heavy for their size, that will yield to gentle pressure. *Refuse:* misshapen samples or fruit with broken skin or bruising. Irregular scab marks are superficial and do not affect the quality of the fruit (only the appearance).

*To store:* not in a refrigerator but keep in a cool place.

*To prepare:* do not use until the flesh is fully ripe, soft, and buttery. Halve lengthwise, discard the black seed, and, with the blunt end of a teaspoon, remove the flesh. Slice or chop as desired. If you wish to use peeled halves, cut them in two before peeling, again with the back of a spoon. After cutting through the skin, work the blunt end of the spoon along the cut between the skin and the flesh until the skin comes away easily. Dip peeled pieces of avocado in lemon juice to avoid discoloration.

## Bananas (*Plátanos*)

Bananas are one of the fruits that tastes better when it is not tree-ripened. Color and condition of the skins are good indications of the use that should be made of the banana. When the skin is yellow, the banana is firm enough to cook and ripe enough to eat as dessert. If the yellow peel is flecked with brown, the fruit is fully ripened and ideal for immediate serving in salads or for dessert. Black skins denote poor quality and, generally, the flesh inside is turning brown also. Three varieties are most often seen in Spain:

*Gros Michel:* large fruit in big, compact bunches. The fruit has tapering ends, excellent flavor, and smooth-textured flesh.

*Cavendish:* a large type with rather blunt ends. Good flavor and texture.

*Canary:* small fruit in small bunches, usually with a considerable amount of brown speckling. Different flavor than either of the other two varieties.

*Purchasing Standards: Select:* firm bananas in a bunch (not loose) and with a bright appearance. *Refuse:* split or heavily bruised fruit or those with noticeably uneven marking.

*To store:* in a cool place, not a refrigerator. Bananas do not resume ripening once they have been chilled in a refrigerator.

*To prepare:* no preparation necessary.

*Note:* The *plantain* is a species of banana used only for culinary purposes. It is an extra-large variety with a coral-colored pulp. So don't be misled: in Spain all bananas are called plátano.

## Berries

Since all berries (except strawberries) are highly perishable, they should be bought for immediate consumption.

*Purchasing Standards: Select:* berries that are firm, plump, and full colored. Remember also that only strawberries are privileged to wear a cap as a sign of maturity. All other berries that are mature should be free of their hull. *Refuse:* crushed, wet berries, those in a stained container, or those with hull attached.

*To store:* refrigerate with as much ventilation as possible.

*To prepare:*

*Blackberries (zarzamoras):* hull any fruit that needs it, then wash and drain at once. If fruit is slightly overripe, mash it and use as a topping for ice cream.

*Raspberries (frambuesas):* similar treatment to blackberries. Overripe berries should be used in a sauce.

*Gooseberries (uvas espinas):* pick over and discard damaged fruit, then top and tail to remove stalks at either end. Wash and drain at once. Overripe berries make an excellent sauce for grilled (broiled) fish.

## Cherries (*Cerezas*)

Dessert cherries are one of the most delicate fruits and cannot stand very much handling. Major varieties available are:

*Bigarreau:* large, heart-shaped fruit with a bright red color and full flavor.

*Emperor Francis:* dark red, heart-shaped fruit; one of the best varieties.

*Roundel:* larger than the two previous varieties, purplish in color with dark red and very juicy flesh.

*Purchasing Standards: Select:* fruit with a bright appearance, firm, and well colored for their variety. It is preferable to buy fruit with the stalk attached. *Refuse:* small, light, hard fruit or any showing split skin or any sign of decay.

*To store:* refrigerate with stalk attached; give them as much room as possible.

*To prepare:* remove stalk, examine for damage etc., wash and drain well.

## Currants

The name is derived from the Grecian city of Corinth where dried currants originated. Both black (*grosellas negras*) and red currants (*grosellas rojas*) are a species of grape.

*Purchasing Standards: Select:* bright, plump currants with a good characteristic color. *Refuse:* broken, split, or wet fruit or any in stained containers.

*To store:* sort, cover, and refrigerate.

*To prepare:* inspect fruit, remove stalks by gently running a fork down the fruit from the stem. Wash picked fruit, drain well, and use as soon as possible. Ideal fruit to combine with raspberries in an open flan.

## Figs (*Higos*)

Historians are somewhat uncertain just where the fig first was grown, but it is thought they were brought westward from Asia Minor. The fruit is extremely perishable and should be bought for immediate use. Two major varieties are available:

*Brevas:* large, plump, and oval-shaped with a delicious flavor. These are on the market in June.

*Calimyrna:* a green fruit turning to a good, deep purple to brown. These are ready in August. Excellent flavor.

*Purchasing Standards: Select:* firm, plump fruit with a characteristic color. *Refuse:* split or squashed fruit; overripe figs have a sour smell caused by fermentation.

*To store:* refrigerate.

*To prepare:* after washing, figs may be eaten with the skin on, or may be peeled and sliced.

## Grapefruit (*Pomelo*)

Originally from China, this citrus fruit is now cultivated in most countries with a warm climate. Color does not necessarily indicate flavor, for the fruit can range from pale yellow to almost bronze. Minor skin blemishes do not affect the flavor or eating quality, although bruising is a detriment. Two major varieties are available:

*Duncan:* medium to large fruit with a yellow skin, very juicy, and with excellent flavor. Seeded variety.

*Marsh pink:* a smaller fruit, seedless, with a light yellow skin sometimes faintly tinged with pink. Pink flesh, very juicy.

*Purchasing Standards: Select:* firm fruit with a good shape and even color. *Refuse:* split or misshapen fruit or samples with bruises.

*To store:* room temperature for a short period; refrigerate for longer periods.

*To prepare:* inspect, then wipe fruit: cut horizontally and loosen sections with a special knife. Remove and discard center fiber; or, cut skin away with a sharp knife following the contour of the fruit. (See illustration under "Oranges.")

## Custard Apple (*Chirimolla*)

This is a fruit about the size of a large apple with a very attractive pale green skin with indentations all over. When opened, the ripe fruit has a pulp which looks like and has the texture of custard with flat, black seeds which are inedible. It is extremely sweet and delicious when ripe and is used for a dessert, or the pulp may be put through a sieve and used as a topping for ice cream or as a filling for a prebaked flan.

*Purchasing Standards: Select:* good, bright, clean fruit, fairly soft to the touch, and with few brown patches. *Refuse:* badly browned fruit.

*To store:* refrigerate, but if quite ripe, use as soon as possible.

*To prepare:* cut open, spoon out pulp, and use as required or serve whole.

## Grapes (*Uvas*)

Dark varieties of grapes should be free from a green tinge and green grapes should have a very slight amber tint for them to be completely ripe. However, Almeria grapes are quite delightful just prior to maturity and have a crisp, refreshing texture and flavor. The varieties are:

*Red emperor:* very attractive variety with large, oval, ruby-red fruit; very sweet and juicy.

*Cardinal:* a large red variety often with a strong hint of purple in the bunches; extra sweet.

*Malaga:* Another red variety of round, large fruit and good flavor.

*Almeria:* white variety, oval shape; excellent keeping qualities and very good flavor.

*Muscat:* large, rather compact bunches of round white fruit of excellent quality with a slightly musk flavor.

*Purchasing Standards: Select:* plump, full grapes that are firmly attached to the stem. If stem is dry and brittle it is likely the bunch will shatter badly when shaken. Must have good color characteristic of the variety. *Refuse:* loose grapes or those that are sticky or have tiny brown marks where the stalk meets the fruit: this is the first sign of decay.

*To store:* refrigerate in a perforated plastic bag.

*To prepare:* inspect, remove from stem, wash, and drain.

## Lemons (*Limones*)

Lemons are grown extensively in Spain where the quality is extremely varied. One tends to find lemons of many sizes in the same box, so choose with care.

*Purchasing Standards: Select:* fruit with a fine-textured skin, heavy for their size, moderately firm. These points indicate juiciness. *Refuse:* very large lemons and those with a coarse skin.

*To store:* at room temperature for a few days or refrigerate if being kept for a longer period.

*To prepare:* inspect fruit for blemishes, wash well, and use in appropriate manner.

*Note:* Since lemons (like all citrus fruit) are composed largely of water, they tend to shrivel after being kept over a week or so. Immersing them in water for half an hour helps to restore their freshness and will increase their juiciness to an appreciable extent.

## Limes (*Limas*)

*Purchasing Standards: Select:* small fruit, heavy for their size and with a good shape and a total bright green skin. *Refuse:* limes that are blemished or badly misshapen or odd colored.

*To store:* as for lemons.

*To prepare:* as for lemons.

## Mango (*Mango*)

This fruit varies considerably in size from about 8 ozs (250g) to over 3 lbs (1.5 Kg) and the shape may be from round to oblong, sometimes pear-shaped. The color too can vary and may be green to yellow and sometimes tipped with red.

*Purchasing Standards: Select:* fruit firm to the touch; clean and bright with a heady aroma. *Refuse:* wrinkled specimens or those with a grayish discoloration.

*To store:* refrigerate.

*To prepare:* peel with a sharp knife and cut the flesh into pieces, including that clinging to the stone. If to be served as dessert, leave the fruit in the skin as it is exceptionally juicy. Half a mango is a good portion.

## Melon (*Melón*)

All melons (except watermelon, *sandia*) are called by the one name. There is no sure guide for determining quality in melon, but the following indications are fairly dependable.

*Cantaloupe:* the fruit is gray-green in color and round to oval in shape.

*Purchasing Standards: Select:* fruit that has the netting standing out like whipcord. There should be no trace of a stem at the blossom end and the melon should have a delicate, aromatic smell. *Refuse:* fruit with a very soft blossom end (often caused by overhandling) and loose, watery seeds that swill around the inside when the melon is shaken.

*To store:* refrigerate. Wrap in airtight material to keep aroma from other foods.

*To prepare:* inspect for ripeness, then cut with a stainless steel knife. Remove seeds and proceed as required.

*Honeydew:* creamy color varying from green to pale yellow; slightly oval in shape.

*Purchasing Standards: Select:* fruit with a distinct fragrance, for this is a sure indication of maturity, as is a slight oily film noticeable on the rind. Large fruit is always better than small specimens. If the melon is underripe, it will attain softness and aroma if kept in a warm temperature, away from sunlight. *Refuse:* cut or scarred fruit.

*To store:* as for cantaloupe.

*To prepare:* as for cantaloupe.

*Charentais:* a small round variety with a flat top and bottom and an attractive green skin with pale yellow stripes. It has exceptional flavor and a delightful aroma. The flesh tends toward an amber-gold-orange color.

*Purchasing Standards: Select:* fruit with a high perfume and softness around the blossom end. *Refuse:* cut or badly scarred fruit; hardness at both ends; great variation in overall color.

*To store:* as for cantaloupe.

*To prepare:* as for cantaloupe.

*Watermelon:* a very large variety with a glossy dark skin, scarlet to red flesh, and prominent black seeds.

*Purchasing Standards: Select:* a thin outer skin which will peel easily when a fingernail is scraped along the side. The underside should be a good yellow color, *not* white. *Refuse:* cut or badly scarred fruit; uneven or blotchy color on top skin.

*To store:* as for cantaloupe.

*To prepare:* trim, then cut into pieces.


## Oranges (*Naranjas*)

Five main varieties of oranges are grown in Spain and are used for different purposes. The first sign of a good orange is a lustrous skin, which may either be orange in color or sometimes green—the orange develops as the fruit ripens. The skin should fit tightly and should be fine grained. Puffy skins and a coarse grain indicate overmaturity and lack of juiciness.

*Navels:* are an almost round variety, although sometimes they are slightly oval, and have the distinctive dimple at one end. They are very juicy with few pips and are an ideal dessert orange.

*Valencias:* are thin-skinned, round, and sweet and are used mainly as juice oranges, rather than dessert oranges.

*Seville:* a bitter orange used for marmalade-making.

*Ortanique:* a cross between an orange and a tangerine, it is similar in size to a Navel orange. It has a thin orange-yellow skin and sweet, juicy flesh.

*Satsuma:* similar to a tangerine, it is round and squat with a smooth, fairly thick skin and pale orange flesh without pips.

*Purchasing Standards: Select:* firm fruit, heavy for size with a fine-textured skin in all varieties (except Satsuma). Color does not indicate maturity and heavy black markings seen on some crops of oranges do not affect flavor. *Refuse:* fruit with coarse skin, puffy or shrivelled.

*To store:* at room temperature for a few days.

*To prepare:* two methods of peeling are 1) in a spiral or 2) following the contour of the fruit. (See illustration.)

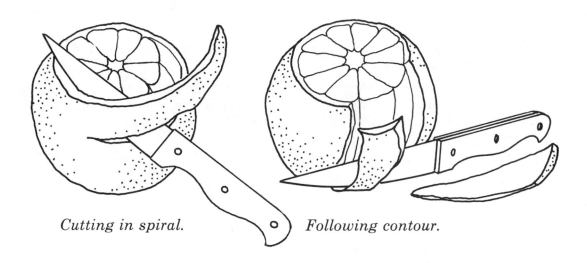

*Cutting in spiral.*          *Following contour.*

## Peaches (*Melocotones*)

Peaches may be yellow- or white-fleshed, although this makes no difference to their sweetness providing they are ripe. Two main types are grown: the Clingstone, so-called because the stone clings to the flesh; and the Freestone, so-called because the stone is easy to remove. Clingstones are most often used for culinary purposes and Freestones are the dessert variety. Select fruit on the basis of ground color, not blush. They all should have a creamy-yellow background with no green tinges. Peaches do not gain sugar after they are picked and will only get softer, not sweeter. Three of the major varieties are:

*Red Globe:* small to medium-size, round fruit with orange to deep red skin.

*Amsden:* medium-size, slightly flattened with a red flush and some mottling. Greenish-white flesh, very juicy.

*Sunhigh:* medium to large, oval shape, orange skin with red flush. Excellent.

*Purchasing Standards: Select:* bright, well-formed fruit with a strong fragrance. Color of underside should be creamy-white to yellow, blushed with red. *Refuse:* bruised fruit with shades of brown on the skin and an oversoftness.

*To store:* refrigerate unwashed.

*To prepare:* examine for maturity and any blemish. Skin with stainless steel knife or blanch first, then skin immediately.

## Pears (*Peras*)

Most of the pears sold in Europe today are the result of a horticultural spree by the landed gentry of France, who around the 1850s had a fierce competition to see who could produce the finest species. As a result, scores of new types of pears were introduced and many of them were quickly forgotten. However, some of their efforts proved very worthwhile and are with us today in such excellent varieties as D'Anjou, Comice, Bosc, and Bon Cheretin—all rich in sugar and with very good flavor.

In making your selection, do not be put off by a scar or a minor blemish, as this will in no way affect inner delicacy. In fact many excellent varieties have a marked russeting. If a pear is hard to the touch at the time of purchase, allow it to stand at room temperature until the flesh responds to gentle pressure. The following are important varieties sold in Spain (see illustration):

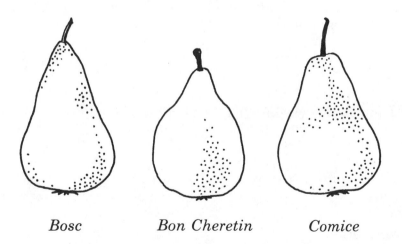

*Bosc*        *Bon Cheretin*        *Comice*

*Bosc:* medium to large dessert pear, with skin covered with a brown russeting, which gives the fruit a greenish-brown appearance. This will change to a dark cinnamon when fully ripe. It has an elongated shape with a long, tapering neck. Flesh is white and juicy with an aromatic, slightly tart flavor.

*Comice:* a large, rounded pear with a short neck. Color green to yellow, changing to a deeper yellow when fully mature, and often showing russet spots. Flesh is yellowish-white with an excellent perfumed flavor. One of the best dessert pears.

*Bon Cheretin:* also known as the Bartlett, this is a medium- to large-sized fruit, equally good for dessert or cooking. It has a regular shape, is green in color changing to yellow when fully ripe, and sometimes with a blush on the underside. Buttery, white flesh with a sweet, slightly aromatic flavor. This variety will not keep.

*Agua:* a small light green pear that retains its distinctive color when ripe. The flesh is crisp and has an excellent flavor. Will keep for a week or so.

*Anjou:* large size and regularly shaped pear, with a green to greenish-yellow skin when ready to eat. Often has a red flush on one side and is inclined to show some russeting. Flesh white, tender, and juicy with a good flavor.

*Purchasing Standards: Select:* fruit with a good appearance and fairly firm to the touch. Pears ripen from the *inside* outwards! Color must be characteristic for variety. *Refuse:* soft or bruised pears or those showing brown marks around the stalk end, for this often indicates a diseased core.

*To store:* refrigerate.

*To prepare:* examine for disease and blemishes. Cut and peel. They are now ready for further treatment.


## Persimmons (*Nisperos*)

These have the appearance when ripe of orange tomatoes. They also have a leathery skin which turns from yellow to almost an orange-red when ripe. The soft flesh has a sharp flavor.

*Purchasing Standards: Select:* plump fruit with a glossy skin and with the stem firmly attached. *Refuse:* split or cracked skins or unripe fruit which means it is very acid.

*To store:* refrigerate

*To prepare:* wash carefully, remove stem, serve on a plate, and eat with a spoon or put through a sieve and use the pulp.


## Pineapple (*Piña*)

Color and aroma are the factors indicating quality and maturity. A ripe pine-apple in good condition has a fresh, clean appearance and is slightly soft to the touch and with a fragrant odor. The eyes are flat and almost hollow. Immature fruit will not ripen properly once picked. There are two main varieties:

*Piña Morada/Piña Roja:* a somewhat squat, heavy variety with a red blush when ripe.

*Cayenne:* a tall variety with a yellow-orange color.

*Purchasing Standards: Select:* plump, heavy-for-size fruit, firm to the touch and with a clean fragrance. *Refuse:* soft fruit, fruit with spiked or underdeveloped eyes, or with a dull appearance.

*To store:* use as soon as possible and refrigerate only just before needed. Long periods of refrigeration induce brown spots on the flesh.

*To prepare:* the easiest method is to slice the fruit from the frond down, cutting into wedges and then, if necessary, slice the flesh from the rind. If rings are required, cut the bottom off the fruit, then slice diagonally at an angle of about 45 degrees. The eyes can then be cut away in strips quite easily.

## Plums (*Ciruelas*)

There are two major types of plum: the Japanese, which can be medium to large and come in a number of colors but *never* black or dark-blue skinned; and the European variety, which are *always* either blue or black skinned. Both types need to be mature when harvested for they do not continue to ripen after being picked nor do they gain sugar. Consequently a check on sweetness is necessary. Some of the better known varieties are:

*Santa Rosa:* purplish-red with yellow, juicy flesh; ideal cooking plum.

*President:* oval, purplish skin, yellow flesh, good for tarts and pies.

*Gaviota:* heart-shaped with an orange to light red skin; an excellent dessert plum.

*Italian:* small, oval fruit with a purplish skin and slightly green flesh; good for tarts and pies.

*Purchasing Standards: Select:* firm fruit, slightly soft at the tip and with a good overall color. *Refuse:* hard, poor-colored, shrivelled fruit, or split or blemished skins.

*To store:* refrigerate immediately if you do not wish them to soften more. If not soft enough, leave at room temperature.

*To prepare:* if pitted plums are required, cut along the seam with a stainless steel knife and twist the plum in half to remove the stone. To peel a whole plum, hold it with a fork in boiling water until the skin cracks, then peel as for a peach or tomato.

## Pomegranate (*Granada*)

The emblem of the city of Granada, this fruit was introduced into Spain by the Moors. The fruit does originate from biblical times. It is about the size of an apple with a thin, hard skin which is inedible. The inside consists of many seeds surrounded by a bright crimson pulp with a slightly tart flavor. Pomegranates may be eaten fresh or used in sauces or in jelly making.

*Purchasing Standards: Select:* fresh looking fruit, heavy for size with a thin, almost unblemished skin. *Refuse:* split or broken fruit.

*To store:* refrigerate and it will keep indefinitely.

*To prepare:* break open, remove kernels with a fork or spoon, and suck the pulp from the seeds. Or, cut in half and press the juice from the fruit with a reamer. Sweeten and dilute with water as a summer drink. Use as a sauce or sprinkle a few seeds over a salad.

## Tangerines (*Mandarinas*)

The tangerine is a small member of the citrus family and a great deal like a satsuma, except for its color which is a waxy bright orange. The skin is always loose and puffy (quite different from a good quality orange). The inner sections are easily pulled apart and used as dessert or as a garnish for salads.

*Purchasing Standards: Select:* bright-colored fruit, heavy for size, which indicates juiciness. *Refuse:* poor-colored or dull-skinned fruit.

*To store:* refrigerate.

*To prepare:* peel and use or serve unpeeled in a bowl of fresh fruit. An ambrosia made with chilled segments sprinkled with Gran Marnier and shredded fresh coconut can be a simple but most attractive dessert.

## VEGETABLES

In Spanish homes, vegetable dishes are most often served as a separate course at lunch or dinner. While a few potatoes may accompany a meat dish or a baked tomato may be served with a piece of liver or a pork chop, it is usually only hotels, catering to a wider clientele, that serve a choice of vegetables with meat or fish. In the recipes that follow the description, selection, and basic preparation of vegetables, it will be indicated which is suitable to accompany a main course and which may be served as an entree.

Quality of vegetables on the table starts with quality bought from the market. In Spain, this quality can vary considerably, for much of the produce is ungraded and often the storage conditions are not of the best. So shop with care, for there is no sauce that can give the right taste and texture to vegetables that are poor quality. For this reason, purchasing standards for each type of vegetable are included in this chapter. Unlike fruits, varietal differences are not important for most vegetables. In instances where variety is of some importance, a few notes are included in the appropriate section. See the Vegetable Availability Calendar for an overall view of seasonal availability.

Touching briefly upon cooking techniques, here is a reminder that will help you produce successful results. First and foremost: Do not overcook fresh vegetables. They should be served crisp and tender to be at their best.

BOILING VEGETABLES.   Cook in a minimum of water needed to prevent scorching. Salt the cooking water and bring to a boil *before* adding vegetables. After the vegetables have been added, bring to the boil again, then simmer gently. Cook all green vegetables in an uncovered pot to allow the destructive acids to escape and help maintain the natural color. Red vegetables are cooked covered, for the presence of acid intensifies the color: the exception is red cabbage which is cooked uncovered to release some of the sulphur content through evaporation. Red vegetables also can be improved by adding a little vinegar to the water about 5 minutes before cooking is completed. If vinegar is added too soon, it tends to toughen the cellulose. White vegetables tend to take on a gray color when overcooked, and although yellow vegetables do not seem to be much affected by long periods of cooking as far as appearance is concerned, their crispness is generally lost. Root vegetables and habas are cooked in a covered pot.

BAKING VEGETABLES.   Vegetables that are baked have very interesting flavors produced by caramelizing the sugar and browning the starch. It is by this method that many Spanish dishes obtain such unusual effects. Baking can be used to advantage with plain vegetable cookery. Preparation is simple. Wash and peel (or scrape) the vegetables, then pour over them a little melted butter, season with salt and pepper, and bake for an hour in a moderate oven, about 375°F (190°C). The following recipe is a favorite Spanish accompaniment to roast meats, especially pork or chicken.

## VEGETABLE AVAILABILITY CALENDAR

| | | J | F | M | A | M | J | Ju | A | S | O | N | D |
|---|---|---|---|---|---|---|---|---|---|---|---|---|---|
| Artichokes | *Alcachofas* | ● | X | X | X | X | | | | | X | ● | X |
| Asparagus (purple) | *Espárragos (trigueros)* | | X | X | X | X | X | | | | | | |
| Asparagus (green) | *Espárragos (blancos)* | | | | X | X | X | | | | | | |
| Beans, broad | *Habas* | X | X | ● | X | X | ● | | | | | | |
| Beans, string | *Judías verdes* | | X | X | X | X | X | X | X | X | | | |
| Beet | *Remolacha* | X | X | X | X | X | X | X | | | | | |
| Broccoli | *Brécol* | X | X | X | X | | | | | | X | X | X |
| Brussels Sprouts | *Coles de Bruselas* | X | | | | | | | | | X | X | X |
| Cabbage | *Repollo, Col* | X | X | X | ● | X | X | X | X | X | X | X | X |
| Carrots | *Zanahorias* | X | X | X | X | X | X | X | X | X | ● | X | X |
| Cauliflower | *Coliflor* | X | ● | X | ● | | | | | X | X | X | X |
| Celery | *Apio* | X | X | X | X | X | X | | | X | X | X | X |
| Chard | *Acelga* | ● | X | X | X | X | X | X | X | X | X | X | X |
| Cucumber | *Pepino* | | | | | ● | X | ● | X | X | X | | |
| Eggplant | *Berenjena* | | | | | ● | X | X | X | X | X | | |
| Endive | *Endibia* | X | X | X | X | X | | | | | X | X | X |
| Leek | *Puerro* | X | X | X | X | ● | X | X | ● | X | X | ● | X |
| Lettuce | *Lechuga* | X | X | X | X | X | X | X | X | X | X | X | X |
| Mushrooms (wild) | *Champiñones* | | | | X | X | | | X | | X | X | |
| Onion | *Cebolla* | X | X | X | X | X | X | | | ● | X | | |
| Pepper (red) | *Pimento (rojo)* | X | | | | X | X | X | X | X | X | X | |
| Pepper (green) | *Pimento (verde)* | X | X | X | X | X | ● | X | X | X | X | | |
| Pumpkin | *Calabaza* | | | | X | X | X | | X | | X | X | X |
| Radish | *Rábano* | | X | X | X | X | X | | | | | X | X |
| Spinach | *Espinaca* | X | ● | X | X | X | | | | | X | X | X |
| Tomatoes | *Tomates* | X | X | X | X | X | X | ● | ● | X | X | | X |
| Turnip | *Nabo* | X | X | X | X | | | | | | X | X | X |
| Turnip greens | *Grelos* | X | X | X | X | | | | | | | X | X |
| Watercress | *Berro* | X | X | X | X | X | X | X | X | X | ● | X | X |
| Zucchini | *Calabacín* | X | X | X | X | ● | X | X | ● | ● | X | X | X |

Potatoes (*patatas*) are in season all the year round.
Cheapest available vegetables are shown by ●.

# Mezcla de Legumbres Asados

(Meth-kla day Lay-goom-bres As-ar-dos)
Baked mixed vegetables

Bake together equal quantities of medium-size whole carrots, onions, parsnips, turnips, and potatoes, each stuck with a whole clove. Pour over the melted butter, and add a crushed clove of garlic and 2 Tbsp. (2 × 15 mL spoon) medium Sherry to the pan. Bake in a moderate oven for an hour or until the vegetables are brown and potatoes crisp.

STEAMING VEGETABLES.   Although this method of vegetable cookery is not often used by the Spanish, for anyone interested in retaining vitamins and minerals, it has a great deal to recommend it. Since vegetables in a steamer are not exposed to air, and since only the smallest amount of water is used, the retention of ascorbic acid, thiamine, riboflavin, niacin, and carotene is significant, as is the retention of minerals which would be lost if a large amount of water were used and then the water discarded.

## Artichokes (*Alcachofas*)

Only the globe (or French) artichoke is available in Spain. This is a thistle-type vegetable comprising a base (fond) and a choke (a conical, hairy center) with overlapping leaves, the bottom of which are edible. The fond (*fondo*) is the most important part of the vegetable, while the choke is inedible, except in very young artichokes when it may be eaten raw, usually with a vinaigrette sauce or boiled with the fondo and then fried. Size has little to do with flavor or texture, but look for worm damage at the base.

*Purchasing Standards: Select:* samples that are uniformly green in color with green leaves that are closed around the base. They should be heavy for their size and the outside leaves should be supple. *Refuse:* those with brown leaves (although this may be due to frost, so take into consideration the weather, or to age). Hard-tipped outer scales are a sign of old stock, and look for worm holes at the base.

*To store:* cut stem off base and refrigerate; use quickly.

*To prepare:* trim base, then put in cold salted water for half an hour. This will move any insects that may be in the vegetable.

**TO COOK ARTICHOKE HEARTS** (*FONDOS DE ALCACHOFAS*). Pare the base of the artichoke and remove the lower leaves by pulling them backwards and then away from the base. This will show the edge of the saucer-shaped heart and the side of the hairy choke. Now cut the artichoke horizontally about 1 inch (2½ cm) from the bottom. This will then show you the choke. With a sharp knife, trim away the remainder of the leaves adhering to the base, beginning at the center and working toward the edges of the heart. Trim the base so it assumes a uniform, round shape. With a small spoon carefully scoop out the choke, being sure that the edges of the heart are not broken. Drop the cleaned heart into cold water to which a little vinegar has been added. This will help retain the color of the heart. Then cook (or blanch) as required.

**TO BLANCH VEGETABLES.** A point about blanching: Many Spanish cooks favor blanching vegetables such as artichoke hearts, asparagus, brussels sprouts, green beans, broccoli, peas, peppers, and pimiento, for it gives these vegetables a firmer texture and flavor in addition to fixing their natural color. No more dull-looking vegetables if you blanch first!

To blanch, wash and prepare vegetables. Toss them in slightly salted boiling water to cover. Bring water back to boiling and cook for 2 minutes, then drain the vegetables and place them at once in very cold (preferably ice) water. When vegetables are quite cold, drain them again and put in refrigerator until required.

Should you wish to serve vegetables with just a plain butter sauce, they may be cooked in boiling salted water to the point when they are *just* tender, drained, and chilled as described and held in the refrigerator. When you need them, they need only be heated in a saucepan with the butter over a brisk flame until the vegetables are warm.

**TO BOIL ARTICHOKES.** This is a delightful luncheon dish as a first course. Cut the leaves from the top of the artichoke to a depth of about 1 inch (2½ cm). (This will then allow the vegetables to float base down in the boiling salted water.) Trim the base evenly, then put into the boiling water. Cook for about 25 minutes or until the base leaves come away easily from the bottom of the artichoke. Put the cooked artichokes into cold water, then invert them to allow water to drain out and serve. If served warm, then a mayonnaise or a Hollandaise sauce is the usual accompaniment; if served cold, then a piquant vinaigrette is most often served.

**TO BRAISE ARTICHOKES.** These vegetables are often braised and stuffed, and for this method of preparation, the artichokes are trimmed and then blanched in boiling water for 8 minutes only to prevent them going black.

Then cool them quickly and remove the choke as previously described. (This is the preliminary preparation for the following recipe.)

## Alcachofas Rellenas

(Al-ka-cho-fas Rell-ay-nas)
Stuffed artichokes
serves 4

1 Tbsp. (1 × 15 mL spoon) olive oil
2 Tbsp. (2 × 15 mL spoon) chopped
  onion
3 cloves garlic, minced
½ lb (250 g) lean ground pork
salt and pepper
1 Tbsp. (1 × 15 mL spoon) tomato
  puree
¼ cup (60 mL) chicken stock
2 Tbsp. (2 × 15 mL spoon) light cream
12 artichoke hearts
½ cup (40 g) fresh breadcrumbs
½ cup (60 g) grated cheese

1. Preheat oven to 375°F (190°C).
2. Heat a pan or skillet, add the oil, and gently saute the onion and garlic for 2 minutes.
3. Add the meat and a little salt and pepper, and continue to cook for 5 minutes, stirring the mixture to keep it from sticking.
4. Now add the tomato puree and the stock and cook for another 5 minutes, timed after the mixture has come to the boil.
5. Remove from heat and blend in the cream, and with a spoon, fill the blanched artichoke hearts.
6. Sprinkle with breadcrumbs, then with grated cheese, and bake in the oven for 20 minutes.

WHOLE STUFFED ARTICHOKES.   Whole stuffed artichokes make a most attractive display on a cold buffet table. Trim the base of the artichoke flat so it stands firmly on a plate. Cook in boiling salted water as described, then cool and drain. In this case, do not cut the top off the vegetable: leave the whole artichoke intact until cooked. Then remove the inner leaves and a good many of the side leaves, starting from the center. Take away the choke with a small spoon, leaving the heart and the surrounding leaves. There will be a cavity where the leaves have been removed. Fill this with a seafood or meat mixture to which you have added a little cream. Garnish the top with a sprinkle of chopped parsley.

## Alcachofas Frit

(Al-ka-cho-fas Frit)
Fried artichokes
serves 4

12 baby artichokes
flour for dusting
salt and pepper
oil for frying

1. Clean the artichokes and slice off tops so that only about 1 inch (2½ cm) remains above the heart. Trim stems and cook in boiling salted water until tender.

2. Cut the cooked vegetables into four pieces, roll them in flour seasoned with salt and pepper, and fry them in very hot olive oil. Drain on paper towels and serve immediately.

*Note: This may be served as an accompanying vegetable.*

## Asparagus (*Espárragos*)

The first asparagus one sees on the market in February is the wild variety (*espárragos trigueros*), and young boys and girls scour the fields in the early morning to sell their crop to local markets. Quality varies considerably, and thin, delicate spikes may be in the same bunch as those that are thick and woody. Later, in March, the cultivated crop is ready and the quality is better, with the stalks more consistent in size. Only the green part of the stem is usually tender, so the relative amount of green and white on the stalk is an important factor.

*Purchasing Standards: Select:* tender, brittle stalks with close, compact tips. *Refuse:* tall, flat stalks or those with a broad, woody base or with open tips.

*To store:* in the lower part of the refrigerator, covered to prevent drying.

*To prepare:* cut off any woody or white ends, then scrape thick green stems. Tie in convenient bunches and cook in slightly salted water. When cooked, drain well.

## *Espárragos de Gitanos*

(Es-par-a-goth day Hit-anos)
Gypsy's asparagus
serves 4

Wild asparagus is most often used for this dish. It is an entree.

1 bundle asparagus
oil for frying
2 red peppers, seeded and chopped
small bunch of parsley, chopped
1 large onion, chopped
1 clove garlic, minced
salt and pepper
½ cup (40 g) breadcrumbs

2 tsp. (2 × 5 mL spoon) wine vinegar
8 eggs

1. Prepare asparagus and cook as described above. Drain and put in ovenproof dish.

2. Preheat oven to 375°F (190°C).

3. Heat oil in deep pan and gently saute all the vegetables until tender. Season to taste.

4. When vegetables are soft, add breadcrumbs, and at the last minute, the vinegar. Stir to mix.

5. Pour mixture over asparagus.

6. Break eggs over the vegetables and bake in the oven until the eggs are set.

# Espárragos con Jamón al Horno

(Es-par-a-goth kon Hamon al Orno)
Baked asparagus and ham
serves 4

This is also an entree.

2 cups (500 mL) Bechamel sauce (See
  index for recipe.)
good pinch each, nutmeg and oregano
1½ lbs (750 g) fresh cooked asparagus
3 large cooked potatoes, sliced
2 hard-boiled eggs, sliced
2 cups (180 g) diced cooked ham
6 slices of chorizo
1 cup (250 mL) breadcrumbs

1. Prepare Bechamel sauce, add herbs.
2. Preheat oven to 375°F (190°C).
3. Place half the cooked asparagus in an ovenproof dish, then the sliced potatoes on top, then the sliced egg.
4. Now put the rest of the asparagus on the egg, sprinkle the diced ham over, then lay the chorizo on the ham.
5. Cover with the warm Bechamel sauce and sprinkle with breadcrumbs.
6. Bake in oven for 25 minutes until crumbs are golden.

# Espárragos Isabella

(Es-para-agoth Isabella)
Asparagus with cheese
serves 4

This is an entree.

1½ lbs (750 g) asparagus
2 ozs (60 g) butter
½ cup (120 mL) grated cheese

1. Prepare asparagus.
2. Tie into 4 equal bundles and cook in boiling salted water until tender.
3. Meanwhile, melt the butter and heat until slightly golden.
4. Preheat broiler.
5. Place cooked asparagus on a heat-proof serving dish, pour over melted butter, and sprinkle with grated cheese. Then brown lightly under the broiler before serving.

## Eggplant (*Berenjena*)

A member of the squash family and a native of Asia, eggplant is a popular vegetable in Spain. The main variety grown is the long purple, although the variety with a white background and attractive purple stripes is often seen. Either type is equally good, and shape has no relation to quality. Eggplant can be bitter when cooked, especially when the skin is left on. To avoid this, the vegetables should be sliced, then sprinkled with salt and left half an hour, then drained. Rinse the slices in cold water after draining. This process is known as *dégorger* and is used with large zucchini also. It improves the flavor of both vegetables very considerably.

*Purchasing Standards: Select:* shiny, bright-colored, and firm vegetables, heavy in relation to size, with a taut skin and a good color. *Refuse:* withered samples with scars or cuts or with visible worm injury.

*To store:* hold very briefly in a cool place; do not refrigerate.

*To prepare:* wipe with a damp cloth and remove stem and calyx. Cut according to requirements and dégorger before proceeding further. Eggplant discolors quickly, so unless using immediately, sprinkle with lemon juice after dégorger.

## Berenjenas al Horno

(Ber-en-hay-nas al Orno)
Baked Eggplant

Add cubed eggplant to the pan in which pork is roasting about 15 minutes before the joint is done.

## Berenjenas con Judias

(Ber-en-hay-nas kon Hoo-dee-as)
Eggplant with green beans
serves 4

This is a vegetable accompaniment.

2 medium-size eggplants
4 Tbsp. (4 × 15 mL spoon) olive oil
1 small onion, finely chopped
1 clove garlic, finely chopped
4 ripe tomatoes, peeled and chopped
pinch of oregano
6 fillets anchovy, chopped
pinch of sugar
pepper
1 Tbsp. (1 × 15 mL spoon) butter
1 lb (500 g) freshly cooked green beans
chopped parsley

1. Cut eggplant into slices or fingers and prepare as described previously.
2. Heat oil in skillet or frypan and saute onions, garlic, and eggplant until onion is tender.
3. Add tomatoes, oregano, anchovy, sugar, then pepper to taste.
4. Cook mixture together until fairly dry. Drain as much oil as possible.

5. Return to pan with the butter and toss over a moderate heat until butter is melted and mixture is nicely hot.
6. Arrange in center of serving dish and surround with the hot, freshly cooked snap beans.
7. Sprinkle with chopped parsley and serve.

## Berenjenas en Pudín

(Ber-en-hay-nas n Pu-deen)
Eggplant pudding
serves 4

This is an entree accompanied by pieces of fried bread cut into triangles which surround the dish.

2 medium-size eggplants
2 lbs (1 Kg) very ripe tomatoes
1 lb (500 g) onions, minced
3 eggs
3 cups (¾ liter) Bechamel sauce
chopped parsley

1. Preheat oven to 350°F (180°C).
2. Peel the eggplants and cut them into slices or chunks. (There is no need to dégorger.)
3. Cook in salted water until tender, then drain.
4. Pass the tomatoes through a sieve into a bowl containing the minced onion, then toss in the cooked eggplant.
5. Beat the eggs in a separate bowl and mix with the tomatoes, onions, and eggplant.
6. Pour the mixture into a buttered mold and put in the oven for 20 minutes.

7. Remove from oven after this period, wait for 5 minutes, then unmold the cooked mixture onto a serving dish.

8. Pour the hot Bechamel sauce over, sprinkle with chopped parsley, and serve.

## Berenjenas Camposino

(Ber-en-hay-nas Cam-po-see-no)
Eggplant, peasant style
serves 4

This is an elegant dish which belies its name and is an excellent vegetable to accompany meat or fowl.

1½ lbs (750 g) eggplant
1 tsp. (1 × 5 mL spoon) salt
½ cup (125 mL) olive oil
1 large onion, sliced
¼ tsp. (1 × 1 mL spoon) crushed cumin
1½ lbs (750 g) tomatoes, peeled and seeded
1 cup (250 mL) cooked chickpeas
1 wine glass or 5 fl ozs (1½ dcL) red wine

1. Cut the eggplant into bite-size pieces and dégorger.

2. In a skillet pour half the oil and fry the eggplant until lightly browned.

3. Transfer to an ovenproof dish.

4. Preheat oven to 400°F (200°C).

5. In the remainder of the oil, saute the onion until transparent then toss in the cumin, tomatoes, and chickpeas.

6. Add the wine and bring the mixture to a gentle boil.

7. Transfer to a casserole, season to taste, and bake uncovered for 35 minutes.

## Caserola de Berenjenas

(Ka-tha-ro-la day Ber-en-hay-nas)
Eggplant casserole
serves 4

This is an entree.

4 eggplants
2 Tbsp. (2 × 15 mL spoon) olive oil
1 Tbsp. (1 × 15 mL spoon) butter
salt and pepper
¼ teasp. (1 × 1 mL spoon) thyme
8 Tbsp. (8 × 15 mL spoon) grated cheese
¾ cup (200 mL) light cream
6 tomatoes, peeled and sliced
4 Tbsp. (4 × 15 mL spoon) breadcrumbs

1. Peel the eggplants, cut into slices ½ inch (12 mm) thick, and dégorger.

2. Wipe slices dry and fry in the olive oil over a brisk heat until they are lightly glazed, but not fully cooked.

3. With a little of the butter, grease an ovenproof dish.

4. Preheat oven to 375°F (190°C).

5. Place a layer of eggplant slices on the bottom of the dish. Season with salt, pepper, and thyme. Sprinkle half of the cheese and half of the cream over the eggplant.

6. Add a layer of tomatoes, then a little more cheese and a little cream; then more eggplant, more tomatoes, cheese, and cream until ingredients are used. Finish with cream on top.

7. Sprinkle with breadcrumbs, dot the surface with the remaining butter, and bake in the oven for about 45 mintues.

## Broad Beans (*Habas*)

Many American readers will not be familiar with broad beans, usually called *habas* but sometimes known as *favas*. Although they look something like fresh lima beans, their flavor is quite different and the skins are tougher. Taken out of the pod, most Spanish cooks remove this outer skin to reveal a delicate green bean which is both very tender and flavorful. Broad beans are not used as an accompaniment to a dish, only as the basis of an entree. Allow 1 pound (250 g) per serving when buying these beans.

*Purchasing Standards: Select:* pods that are bright in color and as light green as possible. This will depend upon their being an early or late crop. *Refuse:* late season, heavily swollen pods; if late crop blanch after podding, then remove outer skin of beans.

*To store:* refrigerate.

*To prepare:* shuck, inspect for insect damage, then cook in boiling salted water.

## *Habas Catalana*

(Hab-ath Cat-a-lar-nah)
Broad beans, Catalan style
serves 4

2 Tbsp. (2 × 15 mL spoon) white lard
½ lb (250 g) smoked bacon cut into 4
    pieces
4 lbs (2 Kg) broad beans
1 large onion, chopped
2 cloves garlic, minced
2 ripe tomatoes, peeled and chopped
1 wine glass or 5 fl ozs (1½ dcL) dry
    Sherry
½ wine glass or 2½ fl ozs (¾ dcL)
    brandy
pinch each, oregano, thyme, rosemary
sprig of fresh mint
¼ lb (125 g) chorizo cut in slices
chicken stock or water
salt and pepper

1. Melt the lard in a large pan and fry the pieces of bacon over a brisk heat until brown on the outside. Then remove from pan. Meanwhile, shell the beans.

2. Fry the onion and garlic in the same pan, and when the onions begin to turn golden, add the tomato and the beans.

3. Cook for 5 minutes. Mix in Sherry, brandy, and herbs.

4. Return bacon to the pan. Add the sliced chorizo and enough stock or water to cover the mixture. Season with salt and pepper.

5. Put a lid on the pan and cook over a low heat for about 40 minutes until beans are quite tender.

# Habas con Salchichas

(Hab-ath kon Sal-chee-chas)
Beans with sausages
serves 4

½ cup (120 mL) minced onion
¼ cup (60 mL) olive oil
6 fresh tomatoes, peeled and diced
2 lbs (1 Kg) broad beans
salt and pepper
1 Tbsp. (1 × 15 mL spoon) chopped
    parsley
1½ lb (750 g) pork sausages

1. Fry the onions in the oil until soft.
Do not brown.

2. Add the tomatoes, prepared beans,
salt, and pepper. Stew, covered, for 30
minutes.

3. Mix in parsley and keep warm.

4. In another pan, fry the sausages
gently until cooked.

5. Transfer the tomato/bean mixture
onto a serving dish, arrange the cooked
sausages on the sauce, and serve.

# Habas con Jamón

(Hab-ath kon Ham-on)
Broad beans with ham
serves 4

4 lbs (2 Kg) broad beans
1 Tbsp. (1 × 15 mL spoon) olive oil
½ lb (250 g) cooked ham, diced
salt and pepper
chopped parsley

1. Shell, blanch, and remove outer
skins of the beans (if necessary). Boil
the beans until tender.

2. Heat the oil and put the ham and
beans to fry quickly over a brisk heat.
Season to taste, add chopped parsley,
and serve at once.

## Snap and French Beans (Judias Verdes)

Both the stringless (snap) beans and the stringed (French) beans are called
*judias verdes*. The snap bean is recognized by its round flute-like shape (called
a *flagolet* in French), and the French bean is flat. The quality of both types
is good in Spain.

*Purchasing Standards: Select:* (Snap beans) bright, crisp beans of a good color.
Break a sample before purchasing to test both for crispness and lack of string,
which occurs with old beans. (French beans) young pods with a good color
and no coarse string along the edges. *Refuse:* limp beans of both types, any
with worm damage; and French beans over 5 inches (12 cm) long.

*To store:* can be held at a low temperature for a short period after which they tend to go limp.

*To prepare:* snap beans require only the ends to be cut off and then may be left whole or cut into two or three pieces. French beans require that the strings along both edges be cut away, then they may be sliced thinly or cut into two or three pieces. Both varieties are then put into boiling salted water and cooked until just tender.

## *Judias Verdes con Queso*

(Hude-e-as Vaird-ess kon Kay-tho)
Green beans with cheese
serves 4

1 Tbsp. (1 × 15 mL spoon) butter
1 lb (500 g) snap or French beans,
  cooked and halved
½ cup (120 g) grated cheese (save a
  little for later)
pinch nutmeg
¼ cup (60 mL) milk
1 Tbsp. (1 × 15 mL spoon) olive oil

1. Preheat oven to 400° F (200°C).
2. Butter an ovenproof dish and arrange cooked beans in the bottom.
3. Sprinkle with most of the grated cheese, then the nutmeg and the rest of the butter in small pieces.
4. Mix the milk and oil and pour into casserole.
5. Sprinkle with the remaining cheese and bake in oven for 15 minutes.

## Beets (*Remolachas*)

In Spain, beets are mainly used as a relish or part of a salad, hardly ever as a vegetable accompaniment. However, there is no reason why they should not be so used. The root should be typically dark red without fanging (double root) or splitting; the stem should be clean and firm and should not have begun to flower.

*Purchasing Standards: Select:* small roots (these have better texture) and unbroken skin, otherwise beets may bleed when cooking. *Refuse:* any badly scarred or misshapen or with long whiskers.

*To store:* should be kept in a fairly moist atmosphere as they tend to dry out in a warm room.

*To prepare:* wash carefully; don't cut stem or root too near the bulb or they will bleed and lose color. Cook in boiling water until tender (about 3 hours) and leave in cooking water to cool if possible.

## Broccoli (*Brécol*)

Developed in Italy in the sixteenth century from a species of cauliflower, broccoli is not too often seen in Spanish markets. When available, the color should be dark to sage green. Stalks should be firm and tender. Within reason, the size of the stalk does not affect the eating quality, providing that the stalk is green.

*Purchasing Standards: Select:* bunches with bright green flowers and a good colored stalk. Thick stalks may be peeled and the central inner flesh chopped and cooked with the florets. *Refuse:* any that show yellowing of flowers, dryness, or branches with white, woody stalks.

*To store:* use as soon as possible, as warm conditions cause wilting.

*To prepare:* trim to service portions; split large stalks vertically to allow faster cooking. Wash each stalk in cold water and cook in boiling water until stalks are just tender. Proceed as required.

## *Brécol con Almendras*

(Breyk-ol kon Al-men-dras)
Broccoli with almonds
serves 4

1 lb (500 g) broccoli
3 Tbsp. (3 × 15 mL spoon) butter
2 Tbsp. (2 × 15 mL spoon) slivered
  almonds
1 tsp. (1 × 5 mL spoon) lemon juice

2 Tbsp. (2 × 15 mL spoon) toasted
  breadcrumbs

1. Cook broccoli as instructed. Drain and place on serving dish. Keep warm.

2. Heat butter in saucepan and brown almonds. Stir in lemon juice, then pour over broccoli.

3. Sprinkle breadcrumbs over the vegetable and serve.

## Brussels Sprouts (*Coles de Bruselas*)

This is yet another vegetable that originated in China and was first grown in Europe (in Brussels) in the thirteenth century. You will find in Spain that the cropping is uneven, and both large and small buds are on sale in the same box. So you should pick them out for yourself.

*Purchasing Standards: Select:* small, hard, compact buds with a good, bright color. These will have the characteristic nutty flavor when cooked. *Refuse:*

full-blown, large, and puffy buds, or those with yellow leaves or a wilted appearance.

*To store:* hold briefly in refrigerator.

*To prepare:* trim buds after removing any soiled outer leaves; cut the stem and pierce with the end of a sharp knife. Do not make a deep criss-cross cut at the base of the stem as this tends to loosen the leaves and open the buds during cooking. Wash well and cook in boiling salted water. Drain.

## Coles de Bruselas Valenciana

(Col day Broo-say-lahs Valenciana)
Brussels sprouts, Valencia style

Cook brussels sprouts as explained. In the meantime, saute a few blanched almonds in a little butter until golden. Pour almonds and butter over the sprouts before serving.

## Coles de Bruselas con Crema

Brussels sprouts with cream

Cook as explained. Drain and chop the sprouts. Season to taste, then mix with a little light cream. Do not overcook: be sure that the sprouts are *just* tender.

## Cabbage (*Repollo* or *Col*)

Two types of cabbage most often seen are those known in the United States as Danish (or Holland) (solid, tight-headed cabbage, usually pale green, and with a thick heavy stalk) and the pointed variety which has a looser head with darker leaves.

*Purchasing Standards: Select:* heads that are reasonably heavy for their size and well trimmed, with a bright color for their variety. *Refuse:* wilted, flabby leaves or those tinged with yellow.

*To store:* in a cool place. Cabbage wilts in dry storage.

*To prepare:* trim base, cut into quarters or strip leaves from stalk, then remove central stem and any large veins. Wash well, then cut into smaller pieces and cook in boiling salted water until just tender.

## Col con Queso

(Kol kon Kay-tho)
Cabbage with cheese

Combine freshly cooked, shredded cabbage with a Bechamel sauce (2 lbs/ 1 Kg cabbage to 2 cups/½ liter sauce). Spread layers of cabbage in a baking dish, sprinkled between with grated cheese. Cover with buttered breadcrumbs. Bake in oven until lightly browned.

# Col Relleno

(Kol Rell-ay-no)
Stuffed cabbage
serves 4

2 young Danish-type cabbage
2 bay leaves
1 egg
½ cup (250 mL) milk
¼ lb (120 g) ground lean pork
¼ lb (120 g) ground lean veal
¼ lb (120 g) fine chopped chorizo
1 medium-size onion, finely chopped
1 clove garlic, finely chopped
a little chopped parsley
1 pint (½ liter) meat stock
2 carrots, rough chopped

1. Trim cabbage and boil whole in salted water with the bay leaves for about 10 minutes.

2. Meanwhile, beat the egg and milk together. Mix in the pork, veal, chorizo, onion, garlic, and parsley. This is the stuffing for the cabbage.

3. Remove cabbage from pot and drain well. Allow to cool a little, then discard any coarse outer leaves.

4. Loosen remaining leaves and put the stuffing between them, spreading it throughout the whole cabbage.

5. Tie the cabbage with kitchen string (like a parcel) so the stuffing will not fall out.

6. Return to boiling pot, add the meat stock, throw in the carrots, bring all to the boil, and simmer for about 45 minutes.

## Carrots (*Zanahorias*)

All carrots, however young, are sold without their green stems, and again varying sizes will be offered in the same box.

*Purchasing Standards: Select:* young, smooth, clean roots with no whiskers if being used as a vegetable or in a salad; larger, clean samples if needed for flavoring in stock. *Refuse:* fanged (double-rooted), discolored, or scarred roots, pale color or tinged with green at the head, or any samples with soft areas.

*To store:* in a cool, dark place.

*To prepare:* trim, wash, and scrub young vegetables; peel older ones, if not being used for stockpot. Then cut into rondels, fingers, or slice at an angle. Blanch or cook in boiling salted water.

# Zanahorias a la Casa

(Thah-na-oa-ryah a la Kar-za)
Home-style carrots
serves 4

1 lb (500 g) young carrots
2 Tbsp. (2 × 15 mL spoon) butter
1 small onion, finely chopped
1 Tbsp. (1 × 15 mL spoon) flour
1 pint (½ liter) milk

*(cont.)*

pinch of oregano
salt and pepper
1 egg yolk, well beaten

1. Clean, slice, and blanch carrots for 2 minutes, then drain well.

2. Melt the butter in a saucepan, drop the carrots in the pan, and saute gently until soft and tender. Remove from pan and keep warm.

3. In the same butter, saute the onion, and when soft but not browned, stir in the flour. Cook together for a minute or so.

4. Then add the milk gradually, but stirring all the time. Allow the sauce to cook until thickened. Then add herbs and seasoning to taste.

5. When the sauce is cooked, add the carrots. Just before serving stir in the well-beaten egg. Mix over a gentle heat for a minute or two only. Then serve.

## Cauliflower (*Coliflor*)

Originally developed in Asia and now grown almost universally, cauliflower is closely related to broccoli.

*Purchasing standards: Select:* white or creamy curd. *Refuse:* stained or loose, open flower clusters.

*To store:* in a cool place, head down to stop moisture forming on the curd.

*To prepare:* after the outer leaves are removed and the vegetable is washed (upside down), cauliflower is best cooked whole. Cut a cross into the base, then plunge in boiling salted water, curd-side upwards. Cook until core is just tender. The florets may then be separated into serving portions.

## *Coliflor Frit*

(Kol-e-flor Frit)
Fried cauliflower

Discard the leaves and central stalk, using only the florets without stalk. Marinate in oil and wine vinegar for about half an hour. Drain well, dip each floret in beaten egg, and fry in hot oil.

## Celery (*Apio*)

Mainly green celery is grown in Spain, similar to the variety known in the United States as pascal.

*Purchasing Standards: Select:* heads that are compact and crisp, with fairly small individual stalks if required for salad or a vegetable; large stalks are suitable as flavoring. *Refuse:* soft, pliable heads indicate coarseness and hard stems may be stringy or woody. Internal injury, such as blackheart, may be detected by opening the stalks and examining the heart.

*To store:* keep cold and moist.

*To prepare:* stalks are trimmed down to about 6 inches (15 cm) from the base so the tender stems and root remain. The root is trimmed and the stalks are well washed to remove any dirt that may lie between the closed stems. When required as a vegetable, the stalks are cut into two or four pieces and blanched in acidulated water, refreshed in ice water, then finished as desired. Coarse stalks are used in the stock pot or as a flavoring in cooking water. When eaten raw, it is cleaned as described, then the stalks are placed in ice water until required. Leave the small tender leaves attached.

# Apio con Queso

(R-p-o kon Kay-tho)
Celery with cheese

Cut sticks of celery into 2 inch (5 cm) lengths and cook in boiling salted water until tender. Place them in a lightly buttered baking dish and sprinkle with a little pepper and grated cheese. Dot with knobs of butter and bake in a 350°F (180°C) oven until cheese is browned.

## Chard (*Acelgas*)

In the south of Spain true spinach is not grown. Swiss chard (or beet spinach) is substituted, and in fact is often called spinach, although it is a very different vegetable but with a similar flavor. Chard has much longer, larger, and tougher leaves, and a long white stalk that looks like a fleshy celery stalk. Both the stalk and leaves are used, but are cooked separately.

*Purchasing Standards: Select:* bright, fresh, green bunches with clean stalks and deep-colored leaves. *Refuse:* limp, wilted bunches.

*To store:* keep in a very cool place.

*To prepare:* cut stalks from leaves. Prepare separately.

*Stalk:* remove any strings or bruised parts, chop into sections, wash, and cook in boiling salted water.

*Leaves:* tear leaves away from ribs, wash well; chop and cook in a very little water. Drain, chop, and use as desired.

## *Acelgas Malagueña*

(Ass-el-gas Ma-la-gway-nyer)
Chard, Malaga style

1 bunch chard, 2 lbs (1 Kg)
   (approximately)
oil for frying
1 clove garlic, chopped
1 red pepper, seeded and sliced
4 Tbsp. (4 × 15 mL spoon)
   breadcrumbs
chopped parsley
pinch nutmeg
1 tsp. (1 × 5 mL spoon) paprika
½ Tbsp. (½ × 15 mL spoon) wine
   vinegar
salt to taste

1. Prepare the stalks as described, then cook in boiling salted water. Drain and reserve.
2. Now prepare the leaves of the chard. Cook, drain, and chop.
3. Put both leaves and stalk in a casserole or a deep serving dish. Keep warm.
4. Heat the oil in a skillet and gently fry the garlic, pepper, breadcrumbs, parsley, nutmeg, and paprika until the red pepper is soft.
5. Pound this mixture in a mortar or whip in a blender, then add vinegar and salt to taste.
6. Pour over chard and serve hot.

## Chicory (*Achicoria*)

This vegetable is known as Belgian endive in the United States. It is a blanched vegetable and is grown in darkness. The stems should be well bleached but in some cases the characteristic primrose color will run to about one-third of the stem area.

*Purchasing Standards: Select:* crisp, clean, firm heads, tightly fastened. *Refuse:* limp or wilted stems.

*To store:* hold briefly in a very cool place.

*To prepare:* cut a thin slice off the base of each head, then run the head under cold water: do not allow it to soak. With a pointed knife, remove the core from the base of each head. The vegetable is now ready for hot or cold preparation. If used for salads, individual leaves are removed and served whole or in pieces as desired. Cooked chicory is always stewed in butter with a little lemon juice and just a dash of water.

## Cucumber (*Pepino*)

The cucumber is a member of the gourd family and related to the pumpkin. It is usually served as a salad ingredient, in which case the skin should first be removed. If required to be cooked, dégorger will help improve the flavor. In Spain the variety seen is the short, outdoor kind (similar to a zucchini) which may be identified by the pimples on the outer skin.

*Purchasing Standards: Select:* young, firm cucumber with a good, clear overall color. *Refuse:* any with brown markings (showing decay), or limp and soft specimens. Examine the length of each before buying.

*To store:* keep moderately cold. Very cold temperatures cause injury.

*To prepare:* peel and slice or cut into desired shapes. If to be cooked, dégorger, then proceed.

### Fennel (*Hinojo*)

This is a light green stalk and shoot vegetable which has the appearance of a heavy rooted celery (without the tall stalks). It imparts a flavor of anise (licorice) and is used most often in sauces, but occasionally as a vegetable, usually with fish or ham.

*Purchasing Standards: Select:* tight roots, clean yellow-white color. *Refuse:* damaged roots shown by open stalks or brown discoloration.

*To store:* briefly in a cool place.

*To prepare:* as for celery.

## Hinojo con Jamón

(Hin-o-ho kon Ham-on)
Fennel with ham
serves 4

1½ lbs (750 g) fennel
3 Tbsp. (3 × 15 mL spoon) olive oil
4 ozs (120 g) chorizo, diced
6 ozs (180 g) cooked lean ham, chopped
salt and pepper

1. Wash fennel and boil in salted water for 40 minutes, then drain and chop.

2. In a skillet, heat the oil. Gently saute the chorizo and ham for 5 minutes.

3. Add the chopped fennel, stir well, and heat through. Season. Serve at once as an entree.

## Garlic (*Ajo*)

Garlic is of Egyptian origin and is used extensively in all Mediterranean and most western European cuisine. The white bulb consists of several separate cloves, each encased in a light purplish skin. The flavor of garlic in any cooked dish may be regulated according to the method used. See details on page 57. The smell of garlic on the breath may be dispelled by chewing on a whole coffee bean.

## Leeks (*Puerros*)

A member of the onion family, leeks are mainly used as an ingredient in some types of cocido.

*Purchasing Standards: Select:* those with broad white bulbs and long white stems, clean and free from discoloration. *Refuse:* limp plants with badly wrinkled outer skin or with brown patches.

*To store:* in a cool place.

*To prepare:* trim off the tap root at base. Remove top green leaves at the point where they fork. The outside skin should then be removed and discarded and a deep cross-cut made in the top of the green leaves toward the base, so the inside may be washed. Washing is done by holding the split leek under running water to dislodge any inner dirt. Then cut as required and blanch or cook in boiling salted water.

## Lettuce (*Lechuga*)

Much of the lettuce in Spain is of the stemmed variety, which does not have a firm heart and unless young can be somewhat tough. The other major variety is very similar to Romaine lettuce and is generally of better quality.

*Purchasing Standards: Select:* young, crisp, green lettuce with no discoloration. *Refuse:* limp, dirty, or wet samples.

*To prepare:* trim any discolored leaves and cut slice from base. Wash well in advance, drain very well, and keep in refrigerator until required.

## Mushrooms (*Champiñones* or *Setas*)

Most mushrooms now sold are cultivated in local farms and are the white-capped variety. None of these mushrooms are trimmed at the base when seen in the market, so are purchased with some base dirt and spore ends attached.

*Purchasing Standards: Select:* clean, white-capped samples with short stems. *Refuse:* damp or discolored caps.

*To store:* as briefly as possible in a very cool place. They turn dark if not used quickly, and damp and smelly if not stored so that air can circulate around them.

*To prepare:* trim base, then wipe caps with a damp cloth. Do not peel or soak in water. Cut the stalk level with the cap. This helps the cap retain its shape during cooking. Use the stalks for another purpose.

## *Champiñones al Horno*

(Sham-pee-nee-o-ness al Orno)
Baked mushrooms
serves 4

Preheat oven to 300°F (150°C). Wipe and trim large mushrooms and place on a tray cap downwards. Sprinkle a little salt into each cap and bake for no more than 15 minutes. A pool of liquor will form in each cap, keeping it moist. Be sure not to spill this liquor when removing the caps from the oven. Serve with broiled meats or other entree.

## *Setas con Crema*

(Say-tas kon Kray-mer)
Creamed mushrooms
serves 4

1 lb (500 g) mushrooms
salt and pepper
3 Tbsp. (3 × 15 mL spoon) light cream
1 Tbsp. (1 × 15 mL spoon) butter

1. Preheat oven to 450°F (230°C).
2. Trim and wipe mushrooms and place them cap upwards in a shallow pan.
3. Sprinkle with salt and a little pepper, then pour cream over them.
4. Dot with butter and bake for 10 minutes.
5. Serve with steak or other appropriate meat.

## *Champiñones Frit*

(Sham-pee-nee-o-ness Frit)
Deep-fried mushrooms

Trim and wipe mushrooms. Make a beer batter (see index) and with a fork dip each mushroom into the batter. Deep-fry in hot oil. Serve as an appetizer.

## Onions (*Cebollas*)

The most widely seen onions are similar to three varieties grown in the United States.

*Bermudas:* a flat, thick variety, brown-skinned and with a fairly mild flavor.

*Globes:* a medium- to large-size round onion with a brown skin and a fairly strong flavor. An excellent cooking onion.

*Spanish:* a round variety with brown and purple skin, purple-white flesh, and a sweet, mild flavor.

*Purchasing Standards: Select:* hard onions with dry skins. *Refuse:* any with soft patches or those with open necks which indicate over-maturity; also beware of those that have dampness at the neck which indicates internal decay.

*To store:* must be in a dry place and preferably cold or cool.

*To prepare:* trim, peel off brown outer skin and one skin beneath the outer. Remove any discolored parts. Cut or slice as required.

A favorite method of serving whole onions with a roast meat is to wash but *not* peel whole onions and cook them in a moderate oven until tender. When cooked, peel and pour over a good cream sauce.

## *Caserola de Cebollas*

(Ka-tha-ro-la day The-bowl-yas)
Onion casserole
serves 4

4 large Spanish onions
3 Tbsp. (3 × 15 mL spoon) butter
salt and pepper to taste
pinch of thyme
½ cup (40 g) fresh breadcrumbs
¼ cup (30 g) grated cheese
pinch paprika

1. Preheat oven to 350°F (180°C).
2. Skin and slice onions.
3. Heat a skillet, melt the butter, and saute onions until transparent.
4. Season with salt, pepper, and thyme. Place in a shallow ovenproof dish.
5. Sprinkle with breadcrumbs and cheese, then paprika.
6. Bake until the breadcrumbs are brown.

## *Cebollas Rellenas*

(The-bowl-yas Rell-ay-nas)
Stuffed onions
serves 4

4 large onions
¼ cup (60 mL) olive oil
2 eggs, beaten
3 Tbsp. (3 × 15 mL spoon) grated cheese
1 Tbsp. (1 × 15 mL spoon) brandy
2 Tbsp. (2 × 15 mL spoon) breadcrumbs
salt and pepper
1 Tbsp. (1 × 15 mL spoon) butter

1. Preheat oven to 350°F (180°C).

2. Peel onions and cut one-third from the top of each.

3. Remove most of the inside of the onion with a fork to make a cup.

4. Boil these cups in salted water for 5 minutes, then drain upside down.

5. Heat the oil in a skillet. Chop onion centers finely and saute until tender.

6. Add eggs, cheese, brandy, and breadcrumbs. Season the mixture to taste and stuff the onion cups with this filling.

7. Place the filled cups in an ovenproof dish, dot them with butter, and bake for about 30 minutes.

## Peas (*Guisantes*)

For best results, after having been picked, peas should be quickly cooled and kept cool throughout the marketing process. This is somewhat difficult in Spain as in a warm climate or temperature, peas quickly lose their sugar and flavor.

*Purchasing Standards: Select:* young, tender peas with a fresh appearance and a bright color. The color is most important. *Refuse:* dark green peas, those with swollen or puffy pods, and any that are touched with brown soft spots.

*To store:* keep in pod, and store in the refrigerator.

*To prepare:* remove from pod, inspect for faulty peas. Cook in boiling salted water until just tender. A touch of sugar in the water is a good idea unless the peas are very young, and a sprig of mint in the water will also improve the flavor.

## Peas with Ham

Saute 2 chopped onions and 4 ozs (120 g) of chopped ham in 2 Tbsp. (2 × 15 mL spoon) of butter until onion is transparent. Stir in ½ lb (250 g) cooked peas and heat through. Sprinkle with fresh-chopped mint, and serve with fish.

## Peas and Cucumber

Peel and dice one cucumber. Shell 1 lb (500 g) peas and cook in slightly salted boiling water. Approximately 3 minutes before the peas are cooked, add the diced cucumber. Drain vegetables well and toss with a little melted butter and a pinch of pepper. Serve with chicken or fish. Serves 4.

## Peas and Onions

Chop 2 small onions finely and add to 8 ozs (250 g) shelled peas. Cook together in boiling salted water until peas are almost soft. Now add a few leaves of finely shredded lettuce and cook together for only 1 minute longer. Drain through a sieve and return the vegetables to the cooking pot with a knob of butter. When butter is melted, transfer all to a vegetable dish. Serve with chicken or meat. Serves 4.

## *Menestra de Guisantes*

(Men-es-tra day Ghee-san-tays)
Pea stew
serves 4

3 Tbsp. (3 × 15 mL spoon) butter
2 lbs (1 Kg) garden peas
2 ozs (60 g) cooked ham, chopped
8 ozs (250 g) cooked cold meat (chicken, veal, pork, etc.)
2 artichokes, heart and tender inside leaves only
4 ozs (120 g) mushrooms, chopped
boiling water
3 cloves garlic, chopped
salt and pepper
2 Tbsp. (2 × 15 mL spoon) flour (approximately)

1. Melt the butter in a saucepan and gently stew the peas, ham, cooked meat, artichokes, and mushrooms for about 10 minutes.

2. Then add sufficient boiling water, just to cover the ingredients in the pan.

3. Bring the water back to the boil; add the garlic and salt and pepper. Cover the pan and simmer until artichokes are cooked.

4. Then gradually add the flour, stirring all the time until the mixture thickens to the degree you like. The amount of flour required will naturally depend on the amount of liquor in the pan and the thickness of the sauce you desire.

5. Serve at once as an entree.

## Peppers (*Pimentos*)

The large red and the green sweet bell peppers so well known in the United States are both called *pimentos* in Spain. *Pimento verde* is the green; *pimento morrón* or *pimento rojo* is the red pepper. Green peppers ripen into red and sometimes turn slightly yellow during this process. There are two types of sweet peppers, one larger than the other. The former is a variety having three or four lobes and tapers slightly toward the blossom end. This variety is used for stuffing as well as other purposes. The smaller type is thinner and funnel-shaped and is only used for purposes other than stuffing. Both varieties have similar flavor. The hot chili pepper called *guindilla* is a member of the same capsicum family and from this pepper, when it is dried, comes the red pepper known as cayenne: *pimenta de cayena*. The dried, powdered sweet red pepper becomes paprika.

Red peppers are usually skinned before using and this is done by splitting them; removing the seeds and white ribs inside; rubbing them with olive oil; then putting them under a hot broiler for 15 or 20 minutes, being sure to turn them over periodically. They are thus broiled until the skins become black, after which they are cooled and the skins are carefully removed. Green sweet peppers do not require skinning.

*Purchasing Standards: Select:* bright, shining peppers with firm, tight skins, thick flesh, and fresh-looking stalks. *Refuse:* wrinkled or very dull or soft samples.

*To store:* in a cool, not cold temperature.

*To prepare:* remove stalk, seeds, and white ribs. Skin (if red) then use as required.

## Stuffed Peppers

This recipe is for a salad or tapa.

Remove top and seeds from a whole green pepper. Stuff firmly with a mixture of cottage cheese and walnuts. Chill for an hour, then cut crosswise to show green pimento rings filled with a white savory mixture.

## Pimentos Rellenos

(Pim-entos Rell-ay-nos)
Stuffed peppers
serves 4

4 large green peppers
1 Tbsp. (1 × 15 mL spoon) olive oil
1 medium-size onion, finely chopped
6 mushrooms, chopped
1 ripe tomato, peeled, seeded, then
  chopped
½ cup (60 g) lean ham, diced
1 cup (180 g) precooked rice
a little chicken stock

1. Preheat oven to 375°F (190°C).
2. Make an incision down the side of each pepper and remove the seeds with a teaspoon. Cut off the stalk.
3. Heat the oil in a skillet and cook the onions gently until transparent.
4. Then add the mushrooms, tomato, ham, and rice. Mix well and heat through.
5. Stuff the peppers with this mixture through the side where you have removed the seeds.
6. Tie the peppers with thread and place in a slightly oiled casserole.
7. Add a little chicken stock (or water), cover, and bake in oven for 50 minutes.

8. Remove thread before serving as an entree.

*Note: Many alternative stuffings may be used based on the same principle.*

## Pimentos Royale

(Pee-men-tos Roy-alay)
Rolled peppers
serves 4

This is a very attractive summer luncheon dish.

½ lb (250 g) cooked, shelled shrimp
1 Tbsp. (1 × 15 mL spoon) butter
a few stuffed olives
4 large red peppers, skinned
chopped parsley and lettuce leaves for
  garnish

1. In a mortar (or electric blender) make a paste with the shrimp, butter, and chopped olives.
2. Spread the mixture on the halves of red pepper and roll like a cigar.
3. Place on a serving dish with lettuce and chopped parsley.

## Pisto

(Pees-to)
Spanish vegetable medley

1 large onion
1 zucchini, dégorger
2 large, ripe tomatoes
1 lb (500 g) green peppers
1 lb (500 g) potatoes
oil
salt and pepper

1. Cut all the vegetables into small chunks.

2. Heat oil and fry potatoes for several minutes, then add the onions. After a few minutes, mix in the zucchini and, finally, the tomatoes.

3. Add salt and pepper. Cook until all vegetables are tender.

## Potatoes (*Patatas*)

Both red-skinned and white-skinned potatoes are available throughout the year. Quality is generally good, although between seasons and for a very short time they may have such defects as blackheart or have internal black spots which cannot be detected by ordinary visual inspection. Potatoes that have been exposed to light will have a green tinge on their skin and this should be cut off before using.

*Purchasing Standards: Select:* relatively hard, smooth, and well-shaped potatoes. *Refuse:* badly cut, shrivelled, or sprouting samples.

*To store:* away from light and in a cool place.

*To prepare:* peel or scrape and cook as recipe demands.

## Spinach (*Espinaca*)

Spinach is mainly sold in central and northern Spain and is of the crumpled-leaf variety.

*Purchasing Standards: Select:* crisp, well-developed, and stocky bright plants with a good color. *Refuse:* overgrown, straggly, discolored, or wilted leaves.

*To store:* in refrigerator.

*To prepare:* remove any coarse stems, wash very well, and cook at once without any additional water. Season after cooking and chopping with a little nutmeg and, if you like, a little minced raw onion. Melted butter is optional.

## *Espinaca con Romero*

(Espeen-aka kon Ro-mero)
Spinach with rosemary
serves 4

1 lb (500 g) spinach
1 Tbsp. (1 × 15 mL spoon) butter
1 clove garlic, minced
4 young scallions, chopped

salt and pepper
½ tsp. (1 × 2 mL spoon) dried
   rosemary
chopped parsley

1. Wash and prepare spinach.

2. In a saucepan melt the butter. Fry garlic and scallion in it for one minute.

3. Add spinach, salt, pepper, rosemary, and parsley. Mix well with a wooden spoon and cook over a low heat for about 7 minutes, until spinach wilts.

## Squash (*Calabaza*)

A number of different types of squash are available: turban, butternut, and pumpkin which are hard shelled; and crookneck, cocozelle, and patty-pan which are soft shelled. Zucchini or Italian squash is included in this category, although it is only a cousin to the others. The pumpkin is used in many Spanish soups and cocidos as a thickener. The other varieties of hard-shell squash are normally peeled before using, and often served mashed with some butter, brown sugar, and a touch of cinnamon. Another treatment of this type of squash is to mix the cooked vegetable with a little pork fat, chopped bacon, and cooked broad beans. The soft-shelled varieties simply need to be cut into slices and cooked. Zucchini, unless very young, needs to be dégorger before cooking.

*Purchasing Standards: Select:* soft-shell squash that are small, crisp, and free from cuts or bruising. Hard-shell varieties *should* have hard shells and no soft spots. *Refuse:* bruised or soft samples in either variety.

*To store:* soft shell in cool temperature; hard shell in a less cool, but dry temperature.

*To prepare:* soft shell are sliced with skins often left on if young. Hard shell are halved, the seeds removed, the rind cut off, cut into pieces, and cooked as required.

## Sweet Potatoes (*Boniatos*)

The soft-fleshed variety are most common in Spain: the variety which has an orange- to salmon-colored flesh.

*Purchasing Standards: Select:* clean, smooth, firm, and bright specimens. *Refuse:* those with cracks or holes (wireworm damage).

*To store:* at a moderate temperature: not below 55°F (13°C).

*To prepare:* this vegetable is always boiled first before it is mashed or baked in the oven. Wash and scrub, but do not peel. Cook in slightly salted water for between 25 and 40 minutes depending on size. Drain, then peel and mash.

TO BAKE SWEET POTATOES.   Boil for 10 minutes, then place in a hot oven 425°F (220°C) and bake for 30 minutes.


## Tomatoes (*Tomates*)

A number of varieties are available including the Italian plum and a round-shaped mature red. Both are good dual-purpose varieties. A third variety, which has irregularly shaped ridges, is marketed while still having a large proportion of green skin. Even with this color, it is a mature vegetable and is outstanding for salads. In the south of Spain especially, tomatoes may need to be skinned before use as the skins can be quite tough.

*Purchasing Standards: Select:* firm, well-shaped tomatoes with tight skins. *Refuse:* those with splits, uneven contour, soft to the touch, or with uneven development.

*To store:* do not refrigerate; keep at moderate temperature for a short time.

*To prepare:* wash, remove stem, peel if necessary. Use as required in recipe.


## Turnips (*Nabos*)

The white turnip is a vegetable related to the mustard family from which it gets its slightly hot flavor. In Spain most turnips are elongated, rather than round, and look like gigantic white radishes. Young turnips have a mild flavor; older ones develop considerable flavor.

*Purchasing Standards: Select:* young, well-shaped samples without fangs (double roots) or growth splits. *Refuse:* old, whiskery turnips or any with cuts or brown spots.

*To store:* they should be kept in a cool place.

*To prepare:* trim off top leaves, peel away thick skin, then chop or slice, and cook as described in the recipe.


## DRIED VEGETABLES (*LEGUMBRES SECOS*)

The quality of dried vegetables can vary considerably. The quality factor applies to age, size, and grading of the vegetables. Good quality stock which is the product of the current year's crop need not be soaked before cooking, except for chickpeas. Just cover them completely with water, and set to simmer gently until tender. Salt is added after cooking.

Older and poor quality vegetables need to be soaked for a few hours. Completely cover with warm water and leave until ready, then drain off. Rinse in cold water, cover with stock, and cook with aromatic herbs and vegetables. Cook until tender, remove garnish, drain, season, and, just before serving, add a little butter.

In many recipes one reads that dried vegetables should have long periods of presoaking. This practice is mistaken, as extended periods of soaking cause the beans to begin fermenting, making them more difficult to digest and affecting their flavor. A quick way to tenderize white beans is to put them in cold water and bring to the boil rapidly, then keep on the edge of the stove, with the pan lid fitting tightly, for an hour.

## Basic Bean Preparation

2 cups (250 mL) beans
2 cloves
1 onion
2 large carrots, whole
2 bay leaves
sprig of thyme

1. Wash beans or peas and remove any stones and dirt.
2. Stick the cloves into the whole onion.
3. Cover with cold water or stock, add the onion, carrots, bay leaves, and thyme.
4. Cook as instructed.

You will find the following dried vegetables available in most stores and supermarkets.

Lentils (*Lentejas*): the brown variety is most common
Chickpeas (*Garbanzos*)
Navy beans (*Judias blancas*)
Red beans (*Judias pintas*)

14

# 14 DESSERTS

U ntil a comparatively short time ago, most Spanish families served the simplest desserts, consisting mainly of fresh fruits. Sometimes, if fruit was not cheap, almonds or dried figs would be substituted. The Moors introduced the very rich, sweet confection made from honey, egg yolk, and almonds. For centuries these were served toward the conclusion of a meal. But when the Moors were finally driven from Spain, the practice of eating such sweet items after a meal fell into disuse, and today they appear as a tea-time luxury rather than a dessert. The rich, dry biscuits which are another Spanish confection often come with a morning glass of Sherry.

But, of course, as is the case with most things in Spain, when one makes a statement, it has to be qualified. And this is no exception. There are still areas in the north where the guest is just as likely to be offered a *yema* made with egg yolk, honey, etc., and in the south, the ubiquitous caramel cream or *flan* is on every menu. However, in most areas of Spain times have changed. The Spanish have evolved a series of desserts, most of which are still based on fresh fruits, to suit the growing sophistication of the Spanish people and to charm the foreign visitor. A number of these desserts use egg whites (in souffles and meringue) left over after the yolks have been used to make the biscuits and cakes.

Tarts and other desserts made with pastry are popular, and I have included a recipe for making pastry on p. 320 which is most unconventional, to say the least, but which for some reason works like a charm. Sherbets and home-made ice cream naturally come into their own in such a country and such a climate, and I have offered a number of ideas in this section for your enjoyment.

## Easy-to-Prepare Desserts

# *Naranjas en Caramelo*

(Nar-an-has n Kar-a-mello)
Caramel oranges
serves 4

In this first recipe, one makes a caramel from sugar and water which is allowed to cool. The recipe is in two parts: making the caramel and preparing the orange peel. The rest is simple.

1 cup (250 g) sugar
½ cup (120 dcL) cold water
½ cup (120 dcL) warm water
8 navel oranges

1. In a heavy saucepan dissolve the sugar in ½ cup of water over gentle heat. Dissolve the sugar very slowly to prevent crystallization. Keep the pan at a very low heat so the water will not boil. *Do not stir* the mixture.
2. When every grain of sugar has dissolved, the syrup may be boiled and should cook steadily until it has a rich brown color.
3. When this color is reached, remove the pan from the stove and dip the base in cold water to prevent further cooking.
4. Now pour the ½ cup of warm water into the sugar syrup. Mix, then return to the heat, and bring back to the boil to dissolve the caramel.
5. Pour the syrup into a bowl and cool.
6. Using a potato peeler, thinly slice the peel from one orange. Cut this peel into needle-like strips.
7. Cook in boiling water for 5 minutes. Drain and dry on paper towels.
8. Cut the peel, pith, and outer membrane from all oranges, leaving the flesh exposed.
9. On a plate to catch the juice, slice each orange across into segments.
10. Reshape the oranges by spearing the slices together with a toothpick; arrange in a deep glass dish.
11. Pour the cold caramel over them and sprinkle with the cooked orange peel.

*Note: You can separate the white membrane from the orange sections if you cover the unpeeled orange with boiling water, let it stand for 5 minutes, then peel.*

# *Fresas Sorpresa*

(Fray-sas Sor-pray-sa)
Surprise strawberries
serves 4

2 Charentais melons
1 lb strawberries
½ wine glass or 2½ fl ozs (¾ dcL) sweet Málaga wine
a little caster (fruit) sugar

1. Cut melons in half and remove the pips.
2. Fill the cavities with strawberries that have been washed and hulled, then sprinkle with the wine and a little caster sugar.
3. Leave in refrigerator for about 2 hours before serving.

*Note: Wash strawberries before hulling, otherwise water will get into the berries, dilute their flavor, and make them mushy.*

## Melocotónes a la Parrilla

(Mel-o-cot-on-es a la Par-ill-ya)
Grilled peaches
serves 4

4 large fresh peaches
1 Tbsp. (1 × 15 mL spoon) caster
   (fruit) sugar
2 Tbsp. (2 × 15 mL spoon) Gran
   Marnier or Orange Curaçao
1½ cups (365 mL) whipping cream
1 cup (200 g) brown sugar
   (approximately)

1. Peel the peaches by dropping them into boiling water for 2 minutes, after which the skins will slip off easily.
2. Cut the flesh into ½ inch (12 mm) slices and place them in a souffle dish. Discard the pits. Sprinkle the slices with caster sugar and Gran Marnier.
3. Whip the cream until stiff and spread over the peaches in the dish. Leave in refrigerator overnight.
4. When ready to serve, preheat broiler to maximum.
5. Sprinkle the brown sugar to a depth of about ½ inch (12 mm) all over the cream and put under the very hot grill until the sugar caramelizes.
6. Serve at once while the crust is very hot.

## Melocotónes en Champaña

(Mel-o-cot-on-es n Sham-pan-ya)
Peaches in Spanish champagne
serves 4

This is a wonderful dessert for a patio luncheon on a hot summer's day.

8 medium-size fresh peaches
½ cup (120 mL) sugar
½ bottle champagne (dry)

1. Skin the peaches as described in the previous recipe.
2. Cut the peaches in half and remove the pits.
3. Sprinkle caster sugar over the fruit and mix well.
4. Place in refrigerator and chill thoroughly. At the same time, chill the champagne.
5. When ready to serve, pour the champagne over the peaches.

## Melocotónes en Vino

(Mel-o-cot-on-es n Vee-no)
Peaches in red wine

8 medium-size fresh peaches
½ cup (120 mL) caster (fruit) sugar
2 wine glasses or 10 fl ozs (3 dcL) red
   wine

1. Peel peaches as previously described.
2. Cut them in half and put them in a bowl, then sprinkle with sugar and pour in wine. Chill for a few hours before serving.

## Plátanos en Cazuela

(Plat-a-noss n Kath-wale-ah)
Bananas in casserole
serves 4

4 large, ripe bananas
1 Tbsp. (1 × 15 mL spoon) butter
1 wine glass or 5 fl ozs (1½ dcL) dark
   rum
1 Tbsp. (1 × 15 mL spoon) brown sugar

1. Preheat oven to 375°F (190°C).
2. Peel, then cut bananas in half lengthwise.

3. Butter a fireproof dish, put in the bananas, drizzle with the rum, then sprinkle on the sugar.

4. Bake in oven for 25 to 30 minutes.

*Note: This method of cooking bananas gives an effect similar to that achieved when bananas are cooked and flamed over a spirit-lamp. For a more dramatic effect, you may heat more rum in a ladle over a flame, set fire to it, and pour the flaming spirit over the bananas before bringing them to the table.*

## Dulce de Melón

(Dul-say day Mel-on)
Melon puree

1 large, ripe melon
sugar

1. Peel the melon and remove and discard skin and pips.

2. Cut into small pieces and put into a large pan. Add about half its own weight in sugar. Allow to stand for three hours.

3. After this time, place the pan over a low heat so that the sugar forms a syrup.

4. When the sugar has entirely dissolved, raise the heat and cook until the syrup has a golden color.

5. Remove the pan from the fire, turn the puree into a dish, and allow to cool thoroughly.

6. Serve with a sprinkling of ginger and whipped cream.

This next recipe is for a cold sweet served in the government-owned Parador just outside Segovia. The Parador was a monastery from the middle of the fifteenth century until 1835. In 1895, a few days before Christmas, a party of Englishmen were walking toward Segovia from the village of San Idelfonso when darkness fell and they became lost. They knocked on the door of the monastery and were let in by a monk, who said they could shelter, but could not be provided with food or drink. The three travellers had their own supplies, so that did not trouble them, and soon they were being escorted through a large hall where monks were eating in absolute silence, as their order demanded. They were shown into a cell where they stayed the night.

In the morning, the travellers heard sounds of singing, and rather than disturb the monks at prayer, they left a polite note of thanks for their shelter. On reaching Segovia, they told of the experience at the monastery and were informed that the monastery had not been occupied for over 50 years! Now to the recipe.

## Albaricoques el Paular

(Al-bar-e-koke-s el Pow-lar)
Cold apricot meringue
serves 4

½ lb (250 g) dried apricots
¼ cup (120 g) sugar

1 Tbsp. (1 × 15 mL spoon) Gran Marnier
1 Tbsp. (1 × 15 mL spoon) brandy
4 egg whites, beaten until stiff

1. Soak the apricots in cold water overnight. Put them in a pan with the water and simmer until tender.

2. Drain off the liquid and sieve the apricots. Then add the sugar, Gran Marnier, and brandy.

3. When the puree is quite cold, fold in the stiffly beaten egg whites and turn into a souffle dish.

4. Put the dish, covered with foil, in a pan of water and steam for about 40 minutes.

5. Meanwhile, preheat oven to 300°F (150°C).

6. Still in its pan of water, remove the foil cover and transfer the mousse to the oven and bake for a further 20 minutes until the top is golden and firm to the touch.

7. Turn off the heat and leave the dish in the oven to cool gradually. If exposed to the air at once, it will collapse.

8. When quite cold remove from oven and keep in a cool place until needed.

## Manzanas con Ron

(Man-zan-as kon Ron)
Baked apples with rum
serves 4

This dish of baked apple is one of the most popular desserts throughout Spain, partly because it is so very easy to prepare and partly, of course, because apples are among the least expensive fruits during most of the year.

4 large baking apples
1 Tbsp. (1 × 15 mL spoon) raisins
1 Tbsp. (1 × 15 mL spoon) brown sugar
½ wine glass or 2½ fl ozs (¾ dcL) dark
   or light rum
a little cold water

1. Preheat oven to 375°F (190°C).
2. Core apples and stuff them with raisins.
3. Sprinkle with brown sugar, then put them in a casserole and pour over the rum and a little cold water.

4. Cook for about 35 minutes, until apples are soft.
5. Serve with whipped cream.

## Dulce de Aguacate

(Dul-say day Awa-cat-ay)
Sweet avocado
serves 4

2 large, ripe avocados
2 Tbsp. (2 × 15 mL spoon) caster
   (fruit) sugar
1 wine glass or 5 fl ozs (1½ dcL)
   medium Sherry
nutmeg

1. Cut the avocados in half lengthwise, remove and discard the large pit, and taking great care, remove the soft flesh from the shell with the back of a small spoon. Be sure not to break the skins.

2. Mash the flesh with the sugar, then stir in the Sherry and grate in a little nutmeg.

3. Spoon the mixture back into the shells and chill. Serve garnished with a thin slice of twisted lemon or lime, if desired.

## Frambuesa Sierra Nevada

(Fram-bu-ay-sa See-air-a Nevada)
Raspberry cream
serves 4

3 egg whites
4 ozs (60 g) confectioner's sugar
1 lb (500 g) fresh raspberries

1. Beat the whites together with the sugar until stiff.
2. Add crushed raspberries by folding them into the mixture.

*Note: If you have a blender, put all ingredients into bowl and beat enough to hold shape. Chill and serve.*

## Desserts with Pastry

I am sure everyone has a favorite recipe for short crust, so I will not bother to give a conventional one. But I will, as promised earlier, give a most unconventional recipe used by some cooks in Spain and with the greatest success. You may care to try it, or to stick to your own tried-and-true pastry formula.

## Pastel Español

(Pas-tell Eth-pan-yola)
Spanish short crust

1 cup (250 g) shortening
¼ cup (60 g) butter
¼ cup (50 g) sugar
3 cups (500 g) plain flour + 1 tsp. (5 mL) salt
¼ cup (60 mL) cold water (approximately)

1. Cream the shortening, the butter, and sugar thoroughly.
2. Add the flour and salt gradually, mixing well between each addition.
3. Add all the water at once and mix.
4. Use plenty of dusting flour when rolling out.

*Note: The dough will take considerable stirring, as the mixture will be very sticky at first, but will gradually become a fairly firm paste.*

## Tarta de Melocotón

(Tar-ter day Mel-o-co-ton)
Open peach tart

pastry for an 8-inch (20 cm) flan
skinned fresh peach halves
1 tsp. (1 × 5 mL spoon) cinnamon
2 egg yolks
1 cup (250 mL) plain yogurt

1. Roll out the prepared pastry and line the flan tin.
2. Arrange the skinned peach halves in the flan and sprinkle with the cinnamon.
3. Preheat oven to 350°F (180°C).
4. Bake the flan in the oven for 20 minutes.
5. Meanwhile beat the yolks and yogurt and pour over the partly cooked flan.
6. Bake 20 minutes. Serve warm.

*Note: If the peaches are not entirely ripe, you may need a little sugar. Sprinkle this over the peaches at the same time as the cinnamon.*

## Tarta de Nata

(Tar-ta day Na-ta)
Open flan with candied fruits

prepared pastry for 8-inch (20 cm) flan
1½ cups (420 mL) milk
¼ cup (60 g) sugar
3 eggs
6 ozs (180 g) candied fruits, chopped finely
2 drops vanilla

1. Line the flan tin with the pastry and put in refrigerator.
2. Preheat oven to 375°F (190°C).
3. In a saucepan, heat the milk and sugar over a low flame but do not allow to boil. Set on side of stove.
4. In a bowl, beat the eggs well, add the candied fruits, the hot milk in a thin stream, and finally the vanilla. Mix thoroughly and pour the warm mixture into the uncooked pie shell.
5. Bake for 20 minutes. Serve cold.

## Tarta de Albaricoque

(Tar-ta day Al-bar-e-kokay)
Apricot and cheese flan

8 ozs (250 g) cottage cheese (Burgos
   cheese or any *queso fresco*)
¼ cup (60 g) confectioner's sugar
¼ cup (90 g) blanched almonds, finely
   chopped
1 prebaked 8-inch (20 cm) pie shell
about 6 or 7 skinned fresh apricots
½ cup *crema de limón* (recipe follows)

1. Beat cottage cheese, sugar, and
almonds until smooth and well blended.
Spread onto the cold pie shell.

2. Cut fresh apricots in half, discard
pits and place the halves, pitted side
down onto the cheese mixture.

3. In a saucepan, heat the *crema de
limón* until fluid, then pour over the
apricots. Allow to cool and serve.

*Note: The cheese used in this recipe may
be any low-fat, curd cheese, the two
varieties mentioned being very suitable.*

## Crema de Limón

(Kray-mer day Lee-mon)
Lemon preserve

This is a confection similar to the
traditional British Lemon Curd and is
used as a preliminary layer on a cold
pastry shell, prior to adding other
sweet ingredients such as fruit. In the
recipe given previously, it is being used
in an alternative manner as a topping.

zest of 2 lemons
3 Tbsp. (3 × 15 mL spoon) butter
1 lb (500 g) granulated sugar
6 egg yolks
3 egg whites
juice of 3 lemons

1. Grate the skins of the lemons to
obtain the zest.

2. Then put all the ingredients into a
pan with a thick base and heat over a
low flame, whisking well. The sauce will
thicken as the sugar dissolves and the
eggs begin to firm.

*Note: The mixture may be used at once
or can be stored for some weeks in a
sealed jar kept in the refrigerator.*

## Desserts Using Meringue

## Merengue de Manzana

(Mer-en-gay day Man-za-na)
Apple meringue

3 cups (750 mL) apple sauce or puree
3 egg whites
¼ tsp. (1 × 1 mL spoon) cream of
   tartar
6 Tbsp. (6 × 15 mL spoon) caster sugar

1. Put the apple puree in a deep baking
dish.

2. Preheat oven to 450°F (230°C).

3. Make meringue by whippping egg
whites with cream of tartar until light
and frothy, then gradually add the
sugar and continue beating until the
meringue becomes stiff.

4. Pile over the apple puree, set in the
hot oven, and bake for about 4 minutes
until meringue is tinged with gold.

## Merengue de Castañas

(Mer-en-gay day Kas-tan-yas)
Meringue with chestnut puree

BASIC MERINGUE

4 egg whites
½ tsp. (1 × 2 mL spoon) salt
½ cup (120 g) caster sugar

1. Whisk the whites until they achieve a stiff foam. Then add the salt and sugar and fold into the whites.

2. With a pastry bag, pipe the meringue to the desired size and shape on a buttered and floured baking sheet.

3. Sprinkle with a little more sugar and bake in a very low oven until firm.

*Note: Use this recipe to make meringue nests or, if you prefer, these may be bought from most confectioners: they make them in a number of shapes and sizes.*

1 8 oz (250 g) tin of chestnut puree
2 tsp. (2 × 5 mL spoon) orange
   marmalade
½ cup (120 mL) light cream
4 meringue nests
chocolate chips

1. Put the puree in a bowl with the marmalade and cream and mix thoroughly.

2. Spoon mixture into the meringue nests just prior to serving.

3. Sprinkle with chocolate chips at the last minute.

*Note: If you wish to use fresh chestnuts for this recipe, the puree may be made as described in the following recipe for Soufle de Castañas.*

# Soufle de Castañas

(Su-flay day Kas-tan-yas)
Chestnut souffle

## PUREE

12 ozs (360 g) chestnuts
1 cup (250 mL) milk
1 Tbsp. (1 × 15 mL spoon) sugar
½ tsp. (1 × 2 mL spoon) vanilla

## SOUFFLE

2 Tbsp. (2 × 15 mL spoon) butter
4 egg yolks
3 Tbsp. (3 × 15 mL spoon) sugar
¼ tsp. (1 × 1 mL spoon) salt
6 egg whites, beaten until stiff

1. To remove the skins of the chestnuts, slit them halfway around with a knife and place them in a hot oven until they open. They may then be easily peeled.

2. Simmer the peeled chestnuts in the milk, sugar, and vanilla until tender.

3. Now mash them or put in a blender to make a cream. Then add the butter, egg yolks, the 3 tablespoons of sugar, and the salt, mixing well. Heat at a low temperature for a few minutes to combine the flavors. Refrigerate.

4. Preheat oven to 425°F (220°C).

5. When puree is cold, fold in the beaten egg whites and pour into a buttered souffle dish. Bake for 20 minutes. Serve immediately.

# Soufle de Plátanos

(Su-flay day Plat-a-nos)
Banana souffle

1 Tbsp. (1 × 15 mL spoon) butter
4 bananas, sliced
½ cup (120 g) sugar
4 whole eggs
2 Tbsp. (2 × 15 mL spoon) brandy
3 maraschino cherries, chopped

1. Melt the butter in a frypan over gentle heat. When hot, add the sliced bananas and half the sugar.

2. Cook for a few minutes until the sugar is dissolved and the bananas take on a slight glaze. Set aside.

3. Separate the eggs. Preheat the oven to 400°F (200°C).

4. Beat the rest of the sugar and the egg yolks until well mixed. Then beat the whites and fold into the mixture.

5. Butter a shallow ovenproof dish or a souffle dish and spread about one-third of the mixture on the dish.

6. Bake in oven for about 5 minutes, then remove.

7. Arrange the glazed bananas on the cooked portion of the souffle and cover them with the uncooked mixture. Decorate with the chopped cherries.

8. Return to the oven and bake for 8 minutes or until the souffle is golden.

9. For a special occasion, flame with brandy when bringing to the table.

# Flan

Caramel custard

Perhaps the most popular of Spanish desserts, the *flan* is little more than a custard cream with a lining of caramelized sugar. Special two-handled pans are sold for making this dessert, although a saucepan (for making the caramel) may be used just as well.

## CARAMEL

4 Tbsp. (4 × 15 mL spoon) sugar
2 Tbsp. (2 × 15 mL spoon) water

## CUSTARD

1 pint (½ liter) milk
1 tsp. (1 × 2 mL spoon) vanilla
½ cup (120 mL) sugar
2 eggs

## THE CARAMEL

1. In the special tin mold (or in a small saucepan), boil the sugar and water together until the mixture becomes dark brown.

2. Hold the mold by the handles and tilt the syrup around the inside until the whole area is covered. (If using a saucepan and independent molds, pour the caramel into each mold and tilt to allow the caramel to cover the base.)

## THE CUSTARD

1. Preheat oven to 400°F (200°C).

2. Heat the milk with the vanilla and sugar and allow to simmer for 5 minutes.

3. Meanwhile, beat the eggs thoroughly.

4. Allow the milk to cool slightly, then strain into the beaten eggs and blend well.

5. With a fork, break any bubbles in the mixture, as these will cause the cooked custard to break when removed from the mold.

6. Pour the mixture into the prepared molds or dishes.

7. Put the filled molds into a deep baking dish and fill the dish with sufficient water to reach two-thirds of the way up the sides of the molds.

8. Put in the oven and bake for about 30 minutes.

9. Invert mold and serve with the caramel on top.

*Note: Do not let the water in the baking dish reach the boiling point or it will spoil the custard. If the custard is not cooked when water reaches boiling, add more cold water. The custard is done when it is firm to the touch and has a brown skin on top.*

## Sorbets, Frozen Assets

Among the many pleasures of the table both in summer and winter, one of the most subtle and delicious is the sherbert or sorbet. Colorful and tempting, cooling as a breeze, it provides the ideal menu item for many occasions. And it's easy to make too.

The contemporary sorbet, called in Spain *sorbete*, has come a long way from the mixture of freshly gathered snow and fruit juice which constituted the original oriental sorbet. Furthermore, our contemporary palates would not accept the addition of rosewater or spices which, in the fifteenth century, was favored by the Turks and Persians. Today, our tastes are such that we require less exotic flavors.

In the horse and carriage days of one hundred years ago, when banquets and feasts consisted of many courses and the palate became sated with strong, rich flavors, the sorbet was a welcome introduction to the bill of fare. It was served immediately before the roast course, and the object was to refresh the palate and prepare the guest to better enjoy the succeeding dishes. Indeed, the sorbet continued in this role and as a symbol of the grand occasion until 1914; then made a reappearance during the 1920s and 1930s, to disappear again in 1939.

Today, homemade sherbet has gained a tremendous popularity when served on almost any occasion, except perhaps the most ordinary. The very simplicity of the water-ice makes a fitting end to a good and perhaps rich meal, either at luncheon or dinner. And as has been said, it is easy to make. All that is required is a refrigerator with a freezing compartment. Try these recipes to enchant your family and friends.

## *Sorbete de Limón*

(Sor-betty day Lee-mon)
Lemon sorbet

1 quart (1 liter) water
12 ozs (360 g) sugar
juice of 4 lemons
2 ozs (60 g) sugar
2 egg whites, beaten to a peak

1. Put the water and sugar in a saucepan over a gentle heat until sugar is dissolved. Then add lemon juice and allow to cool for just a minute or two, then strain through a fine sieve.

2. Pour into a refrigerator tray and freeze until mushy, about ½ hour.

3. Remove and pour semifrozen mixture into a chilled bowl. Beat with a rotary mixer until smooth, but not melted.

4. Add the 2 ozs (60 g) of sugar to the beaten egg whites, then stir in the half-frozen lemon mixture.

5. Return to freezer and freeze until firm—about 2 to 3 hours—stirring two or three times during this period.

## Sorbete con Ron

(Sor-betty kon Ron)
White rum sorbet

A slightly different technique is required when the sorbet contains alcohol. The following is a basic preparation and the spirit used may vary according to preference. One thing to remember however: use no more than ¼ cup or 2 fl ozs (60 mL) of spirit to 1 cup (250 mL) of water base or the sorbet will not freeze.

1 cup (250 mL) water
4 ozs (120 g) sugar
juice of two lemons
¼ cup (60 mL) white rum
1 egg white, beaten until stiff

1. Put the water and sugar in a saucepan over a gentle heat until sugar is dissolved. Add lemon juice, mix and cool. Pour into refrigerator tray and freeze for about ½ hour, until mushy.

2. Remove from tray and put mixture into chilled bowl.

3. Add rum and beat with rotary mixer until smooth but not melted. Return to freezer tray and rechill for 20 minutes.

4. Turn out again into a chilled bowl, beat again with the rotary beater, then fold in the stiff white of egg.

5. Spoon back into refrigerator trays and freeze until firm, stirring occasionally to get a smoother consistency.

## Ice Cream

Of course, even greater interest can be achieved at the dinner table by serving homemade ice cream. The technique is slightly more difficult than making sherbet, but once you have accomplished it, you will never be tempted to serve any ice creams other than your own.

Here are a few rules to remember before attempting your first batch:

1. Be sure that your freezer compartment in the refrigerator is really cold. If in doubt, set it at the lowest temperature about 30 minutes before the mixture is first placed in the freezer.

2. Add the exact amount of sugar called for in the recipe. Do not add extra sugar as it will prevent the mixture from freezing.

3. Add fruit and finely chopped nuts when the ice cream is partially thickened.

4. Heavy cream, evaporated milk, and homogenized milk will make ice cream very creamy.

5. Unless heavy cream is used, a thickening agent such as eggs, gelatin, or cornstarch is required to prevent crystals from forming. This will absorb part of the liquid and will result in a very creamy and smooth-textured ice cream.

6. Freeze partially for 30 minutes. Remove the mixture from the tray and turn into a chilled bowl. Beat with a rotary mixer until smooth but not melted, then return to the ice tray and spread evenly. Freeze until firm, stirring occasionally. As soon as the ice cream is firm, wrap in aluminum foil to prevent ice crystals from forming.

## Helado de Vainilla

(Hell-ah-doe day Vain-eel-ya)
Vanilla ice cream

1¼ quarts (1¼ liters) heavy cream or 1
    quart (1 liter) evaporated milk
2 tsp. (2 × 5 mL spoon) vanilla
pinch salt
6 ozs (180 g) sugar

Combine all ingredients in a bowl and stir until well blended. Strain mixture into freezer trays, then proceed as directed in instruction no. 6 in the preceding list.

## Helado con Chocolate

(Hell-ah-doe kon Choc-o-lat-ay)
Chocolate ice cream

3 eggs
6 ozs (180 g) sugar
1 quart (1 liter) milk
1 tsp. (1 × 5 mL spoon) instant coffee
½ lb (250 g) unsweetened chocolate
2 tsp. (2 × 5 mL spoon) almond extract

1. Beat the eggs in a saucepan until thick and lemon colored. Stir in the sugar and blend well.

2. Add milk, coffee, and chocolate. Cook over a very low heat until the mixture boils, stirring all the time. Keep boiling for 10 minutes, then add almond extract at end of cooking period.

3. Remove from heat and beat until quite smooth. Allow to cool.

4. Spoon the mixture into freezer trays and partially freeze for 30 minutes.

5. Then turn mixture into chilled bowl and beat again until smooth, but not melted.

6. Return to freezer trays and freeze for 2 to 3 hours, stirring occasionally.

*Variations: An exciting change from the recipe above can be made as follows: Add 3 Tbsp. (3 × 15 mL spoon) Sherry, 2 ozs (60 g) candied cherries, and 2 ozs (60 g) candied pineapple (both candied fruits finely chopped). Fold this mixture into the partially frozen mixture (step 5). Reduce the almond extract to ½ tsp. (1 × 2 mL spoon).*

ICE CREAM TOPPINGS. These few suggestions for ice cream toppings are served in Spanish homes and restaurants: they make for a delightful change of flavor.

1. Mix apricot jam with a little apricot brandy. Use on vanilla ice cream.
2. Sprinkle a pinch of nutmeg on vanilla or peach ice cream.
3. Sprinkle a pinch of ginger on ginger or chocolate ice cream.
4. Pour white rum and orange juice on vanilla ice cream.
5. Pour a little crème de cacāo over coffee or chocolate ice cream.
6. Pour creme de menthe over lemon ice cream.
7. Finally, use liqueurs as a topping to make any ice cream a party piece.

# English/Spanish Dictionary of Kitchen Utensils

| *English* | *Spanish* |
|---|---|
| Blender | *Batidora* |
| Bottle opener | *Abrebotella* |
| Brushes | *Capillos* |
| Can opener | *Abrelatas* |
| Carving knife | *Trinchante* |
| Casserole | *Cacerola* |
| Chopping board | *Tabero* or *Tabla* |
| Colander | *Coladera* or *Colador* |
| Corkscrew | *Sacacorchos* |
| Cutlery | *Cuchillería* or *Cuberteria* |
| Double boiler | *Olla de doble fondo* |
| Egg beater | *Batidor de huevos* |
| Egg slicer | *Rebanador de huevos* |
| Enamelware | *Cosas esmaltadas* |
| Food mill | *Molinilla de verduras* |
| Foil (aluminum) | *Hojas de aluminio* |
| Frying pan | *Sartén* |
| Funnel | *Embudo* |
| Garlic press | *Exprimidor* or *Triturador de ajo* |
| Glasses | *Vasos* or *Copas* (wine glasses) |
| Grater | *Rallador* |

| *English* | *Spanish* |
|---|---|
| Ice cube trays | *Bandejas para hielo* |
| Kitchen string | *Cuerda (de cocina)* |
| Knife sharpener (butcher's steel) | *Chaira* |
| Kitchen knives | *Cuchillos de cocina* |
| Ladle | *Cuchara* or *Cucharón* |
| Liquidizer | *Licuadora* |
| Measuring cups | *Tazas de medida* |
| Measuring jugs | *Vasos* or *probetas graduados* |
| Measuring spoons | *Cucharas de medida* |
| Mincer | *Máquina para picar carne* |
| Mixing bowls | *Fuentes ondas* |
| Mold (jelly) | *Molde* |
| Mortar and pestle | *Mortero y majadero mano* |
| Pastry board | *Tablero para repostería* |
| Pastry bag (piping bag) | *Manguera de repostería* |
| Pastry brush | *Cepillo de repostería* |
| Pepper mill | *Molinillo de pimiento* |
| Pie plates | *Platos para tartas* |
| Potato peeler | *Pelador de patatas* |
| Potato ricer | *Rallador de patatas* |
| Pressure cooker | *Olla a presión* |
| Roasting pan | *Fuente para asar* |
| Rolling pin | *Rodillo de pastelero* |
| Salad bowl | *Ensaladera* |
| Salt shaker | *Salero de mesa* |
| Sauceboat | *Cacerola* or *cazo* |
| Scales | *Balanza* |
| Scissors | *Tijeras* |
| Serving spoon | *Cuchara grande* |
| Sieve | *Tamiz* |
| Skewer | *Brocheta* |
| Skillet | *Sarten* |
| Skimmer | *Espumadera* |

| *English* | *Spanish* |
|---|---|
| Spatula | *Espátula* |
| Squeezer | *Exprimidor* |
| Stew Pot | *Olla* |
| Strainer | *Colador* |
| Teapot | *Tetera* |
| Thermometer | *Termómetro* |
| Tongs | *Tenazas* |
| Tray | *Bandeja* |
| Wire whisk | *Batidor de alambre* |
| Wooden spoons | *Cucharas de madera* |

# Glossary of Cooking Terms

Bake (*hornear*): to cook in dry heat in an enclosed oven

Barbecue (*asar*): to cook over hot embers, usually in the open air

Bard (*lardear*): to cover uncooked lean meat (and sometimes fish) with slices of pork fat or bacon to prevent surface drying during cooking

Baste (*pringar*): to moisten foods (usually baking or roasting in the oven) with melted fat or pan juices

Beat (*batir*): to incorporate air in a mixture or to make it smooth or to mix well after adding additional ingredients

Bind (*unir*): to unite ingredients with a sauce

Blanch (*blanquear*): a) to precook foods for a very short time by plunging them into boiling water
b) to plunge fruit, nuts, and some vegetables into boiling water to assist in the removal of outer skin

Blend (*mezclar*): to mix ingredients thoroughly

Boil (*hervir*): to bring liquids to a temperature of 212°F (100°C) or to cook foods in boiling liquid

Braise (*asar con doble fuego*): to cook foods in a small quantity of fat, then add liquid and continue to cook in a tightly covered utensil

Broil (*asar en parrillas*): to cook by dry heat under a broiler or grill

Coat (*cubrir*): to cover food with a glaze or other covering

Chop (*tazar* or *cortar*): to separate into pieces by cutting with a knife or cleaver

Dredge (*polvorear*): to coat with flour, breadcrumbs, etc.

Drizzle (*rociar*): to sprinkle small quantities of liquid such as oil, vinegar, wine, etc., over food

Flake (*triturar* or *formar hojuelas*): to pull apart foods such as fish which when cooked falls into natural divisions; to shred into small pieces

Flambé (*flamear*): to ignite a hot alcoholic spirit after adding to a dish

Fricasse (*guisadar*): to prepare food in a cream sauce based upon the cooking liquid

Gratinate (*gratinar*): to cover cooked food with cheese/breadcrumbs and brown the dish under a grill or in the oven

Marinade (*marinar*): to let food stand in a flavoring or tenderizing liquid

Macerate (*macerar*): to let fruits stand in a wine or liqueur to absorb flavor

Pan fry (*freir*): to cook in a small amount of oil over direct heat

Poach (*escalfar*): to cook food gently in a simmering liquid

Preheat (*precalentar*): to allow the oven or other cooking appliance to reach the required temperature prior to cooking

Roast (*asar*): to cook in an enclosed oven by dry heat; similar to bake

Sauté (*saltear*): to cook in a small amount of hot oil or fat, similar to pan fry

Scale (*desescamar*): to remove the scales from a fish with the back of a knife before treating it further

Season (*sazonar*): to add salt, pepper, or other condiments and spices to give the dish more flavor

Simmer (*hervir a fuego lento*): to cook just below boiling point

Skim (*quitar espuma*): to remove from the surface of a liquid any undesirable froth or foam; to remove a layer of fat from the top of a dish

Stew (*estofar*): to cook by simmering in sufficient liquid to cover

Strain (*colar*): to remove solid food from any liquid by passing the solids through a sieve, colander, or muslin

Stir (*agitar*): to mix ingredients uniformly

# Index

All-i-oli. *See* Mayonnaise
Almejas. *See* Clams
Almond(s)
  broccoli with, 295
  butter, 129
  salted, as appetizer, 71
  sauce, 127
  toasted, 62; as appetizer, 71
Anchovy(ies)
  butter, 129
  fresh, 6; how to prepare, 152
  sauce, 127
Angler (fish), how to prepare,
  171
Appetizers (tapas), 69–71.
    *See also* Hors d'Oeuvre
  almonds, salted, 71; toasted,
    71
  clams in wine, 4
  Empanditas (savory filled
    patties), 72
  olives, black and green, 70
  Palitos, 74
  peppers, stuffed, 307
  scallions, grilled, 4
  tapas naturales (artichokes,
    mussels, oysters, etc.), 70
  tartlets (barquettes), 73
Apple(s), about, 269; varieties,
  269
  baked with rum, 319
  custard, 274
  meringue, 321
Apricot(s), about, 270
  and cheese flan, 321
  cold, meringue, 318
  dried, lamb with, 219
Arroz. *See* Rice
Artichoke(s) French, about,
  285–287
  fried, 287
  hearts, as appetizer, 70
  how to prepare, 78, 286
  as starter, 78

stuffings for, 79, 287
veal with, 209
Asado. *See* Pork
Asparagus, 4; about 288–289
  baked and ham, 289
  with cheese, 289
  Gypsy's, 288
  as starter, 80
  with walnut butter, 80
Avocado (pear), about, 270–271;
    varieties, 270
  with chicken, 76
  cream sauce, 128
  cream soup, 90
  with fresh fruit, 76
  gaspacho, 89
  grilled, 77
  with jellied consomme, 76
  liver with, 228
  with salad, 76
  as starter, 75
  sweet, 319

Bananas, about, 271; varieties,
  271
  in casserole, 317
  souffle, 322
Barnacles, rock, 199
Bass, rock (Grouper), 162–164
  baker's style, 163
  with orange sauce, 162
  with Sherry, 164
  with tomatoes, 163
Bass, sea, 160
  in foil, 161; in salt, 161
Beans, broad, 3; about, 292
  casserole, 109
  Catalan style, 292
  with ham, 293
  with sausages, 293
Beans, dried, basic preparation,
  311; varieties, 311
Beans, green
  with cheese, 294

eggplant with, 290
Beans, snap (French), about, 291
Bearnaise sauce, 122
Beef, about, 203–206
  cuts, what to buy, 204–205
  hamburgers with cheese, 213
  stew, Spanish, 209
Beets, about, 294
Berries, about, 272; varieties,
  272. *See also* individual
  names
Blackberries, about, 272
Black butter (Salsa Negra), 130
Brains, deep-fried, 232
Brandy, about, 39
  quail in, 258
Bream, how to prepare, 152,
  154, 166
Brie (cheese), as starter, 83
Broccoli, about, 295
  with almonds, 295
Brussels sprouts, about, 295
  with cream, 296
  Valencia style, 296
Butters, savory, 129–130

Cabbage, about, 296
  with cheese, 296
  partridge with, 254
  stuffed, 297
Calamares. *See* Squid
Caldo verde. *See* Green soup
Calf liver. *See* Liver
Cantaloupe, about, 276
Caramel, orange, 316
Caramel custard (flan), 323
Carp, how to prepare, 149
Carrots, about, 297
  home style, 297
Cauliflower, about, 298
  fried, 298
Celery, about, 298
  with cheese, 299

Chard, about, 299
  Malaga style, 300
Charentais (melon), about, 276
Cheese, about, 63; varieties,
    63–64
  and apricot flan, 321
  asparagus with, 289
  cabbage with, 296
  celery with, 299
  fried, as starter, 83
  green beans with, 294
  hamburgers with, 213
Cherries, about, 272; varieties,
    272
Chestnut
  puree, meringue with, 321
  souffle, 322
Chicken, 237–251; about, 238
  Asturian style, 248
  with avocado, 76
  fried breasts, 249; with
      oranges, 249
  how to prepare, 238–239
  liver, cocktail kebabs, Navarra
      style, 231
  liver, omelette, Andalucian
      style, 106
  marinade for, 119
  with peppers and tomatoes,
      247
  in red wine, 248
  roasted, 246
  sauces for, 127–128
  savory, 248
  stew, 241
  stuffed, 245; Santo Domingo,
      244
Chickpeas, puree of (soup), 97
Chicory, about, 300
Chocolate ice cream, 326
Chorizo. See Sausages
Clam(s), about, 193; varieties,
    194
  as appetizer, 4
  cream of (soup), 94
  fish stew, Asturian style, 196
  loin of pork with, 225
  and mussels, rich with, 136
  omelette from Cadiz, 107
Cocidos. See Stews
Cockles, about, 194
Cod, dried, Basque style, 178
Cooking terms, glossary of,
    333–334
Cookware, about, 43–48
Cordero. See Lamb
Crab(s), varieties of, 188
  how to prepare, 189
  stuffed, Basque style, 189
  tart, 190

Crabmeat, as stuffing for eggs,
    78
Crayfish, 184–185. See also
    Lobster
  butter, 130
  in herbed wine, 185
Croutons, garlic, 91
Cucumber(s), about, 300
  peas and, 305
  pickled, as appetizer, 70
  soup, cold, 90
Currants, about, 272
Custard apple, about, 274

Desserts, 7, 315–327
  about, 315
  apple meringue, 321
  apples, baked with rum, 319
  apricot and cheese flan, 321
  apricot meringue, cold, 318
  avocado, sweet, 319
  banana souffle, 322
  bananas in casserole, 317
  caramel custard, 323
  caramel oranges, 316
  chestnut souffle, 322
  flan with candied fruits, 320
  ice cream, 325–326: chocolate,
      326; toppings for, 327;
      vanilla, 326
  lemon preserve, 321
  lemon sorbet, 324
  melon puree, 318
  meringue with chestnut puree,
      321
  with pastry, 320–321
  peach tart, 320
  peaches, grilled, 317
  peaches in red wine, 317; in
      Spanish champagne, 317
  raspberry cream, 319
  rum sorbet, 325
  short crust, Spanish, 320
  sorbets, as frozen assets,
      324–325
  strawberries, surprise, 316
Diablo (hot) sauce, 125
Dictionary (English/Spanish) of
    kitchen utensils, 329–331
Dried vegetables. See Vegeta-
    bles, dried
Duck
  with olives, 262
  with white turnips, 261
  wild, 261; how to roast, 261

Egg(s), about, 101
  almond sauce for, 127
  and anchovy stuffing for arti-
      chokes, 79

avocado cream sauce for, 128
  baked, Andalucian, 108
  baked, Basque style, 109
  cardinal, 109
  and ham, hake with, 166
  lima-type bean casserole, 109
  omelettes, 103–108
  scrambled, 103
  soft-boiled, 102–103
  as starter, 77
  stuffed, 78
Eggplant, 289–291
  baked, 290
  casserole, 291
  with green beans, 290
  peasant style, 291
  pudding, 290
Empanditas, as appetizer, 9, 72
Entremeses. See Hors d'Oeuvre
Equivalent measurements,
    49–51
Estofadas. See Stews

Fennel, about, 301
  with ham, 301
Figs, about, 273; varieties, 273
  as starter, 80; stuffed, 80
Fish, 141–179. See also Shell-
    fish; individual names
  about, 141–142, 146, 153
  anchovy, fresh, 152
  angler (frogfish, monkfish),
      171
  baked, 146; seasoning mix for,
      145
  bass, rock (grouper), 162–164
  bass, sea, 161
  bass, stone (wreckfish), 154
  breaded, 145
  bream: pink, 152; red, 166; sea
      (black), 154
  butters, savory, for, 129–130
  carp, 149
  cod, Basque style, 178
  dried, about, 177–178
  eels, baby, 193
  fillets, 153, 169–170
  freshwater, 148–151
  fried, 143–144; batters for, 144
  gilthead, 155–156
  hake (white salmon), 164–166
  John Dory, 174
  mackerel, Spanish, 156–157
  mullet, gray, 149
  mullet, red, 174–177
  pollack, 151
  redfish (rosefish, rockfish), 153
  salmon, 150–151
  saltwater, 151–177
  sardines, fresh, 177

sauces. *See* Sauces
savory butters for, 129–130
sole, 157–160
soup (pescado), 95. *See also* Soups
stew, Asturian style, 196
swordfish, 170–171
trout, river, 148–149
trout, sea, 153
turbot, 174
white, 167–168; with rice, 136
whitebait, 154
in white wine and cream, 170
Flans
apricot and cheese, 321
caramel custard, 323
open, with candied fruits, 320
Fruits, 267–282. *See also* Desserts; individual names
about, 267–269
availability calendar, 268
candied, open flan with, 320
fresh, with avocado, 76
Frying liquids, smoking temperatures of, 144

Gambas. *See* Shrimp
Game, 251–252. *See also* individual names (e.g. Partridge, Rabbit)
Sherry Sauce for, 127
Garbanzos. *See* Chickpeas
Garlic, about, 302
butter, 130
in cooking, 57–58
croutons, 91
Gazpacho, 6, 87–89
garnishes for, 87
Gilthead, about, 155
stuffed, Romero style, 155
Gin, about, 38
Glossary of cooking terms, 333–334
equivalent measures, 49–51
wine language, 34–35
Gooseberries, about, 272
Grapefruit, about, 273; varieties, 273
Grapes, about, 274–275; varieties, 274
Green (verde) sauce for fish, 126
Green soup, 9, 91
Grouper. *See* Bass, rock
Guinea fowl, Hacienda style, 263

Habas. *See* Beans, broad
Hake (white salmon), 164
Asturian style, 165
with ham and eggs, 166

Ham
asparagus and, 289
broad beans with, 293
and eggs, hake with, 166
with fennel, 301
peas and, 305
sweetbreads with, 231
yellow sauce for, 128
Hamburgers with cheese, 213
Herb butter, 130
Herbs and spices, varieties of, 59–61
Hollandaise sauce, 122
Honeydew, about, 276
Hors d'Oeuvre (Entremeses), 74–83. *See also* Appetizers
artichokes, 78; stuffings for, 79
asparagus, 80; with walnut butter, 80
avocado (pear), 75; variations, 76–77
cheese, fried, 83
eggs, 77; stuffed, 78
eggs cardinal, 109
figs, 80; stuffed, 80
mushrooms au gratin, 81
oysters, baked with almonds, 82
peppers, green, fried, 81
rabbit pate, 82
shrimp, broiled, 81; in garlic sauce, 81; of the house, 81
tomatoes, 77; stuffed, 77
Huevos. *See* Eggs

Ice cream, about, 325
chocolate, 326
toppings, 327
vanilla, 326

John Dory (fish), how to prepare, 174
Jose Citrano's quiche, 113

Kidneys, veal, 230
Asturian style, 230
Basque style, 230
Kitchen utensils, English/Spanish dictionary of, 329–331

Lamb, 214–220
chops, breaded, Alicante style, 217
cutlets, Granada style, 220
cutlets, with almonds, 217
with dried apricots, 219
liver, with avocado pear, 228
roast, Castilian style, 220
roast, with Sherry, 218
roast loin, 219

shepherds, 215
stew, 216; Valencian style, 216
stew, Pelayo's, 207
Leeks, about, 302
Lemon(s), about, 275
preserve, 321
sorbet, 324
Lentils, puree of, 98
Lettuce, about, 302
hearts, as appetizer, 70
Lima-type beans. *See* Beans, broad
Limes, about, 275
Liqueurs and spirits, 37–39; proof systems, 39–40
Liver, about, 227
almond sauce for, 127
calf, Alcazar, 229
calf (or lamb), with avocado pear, 228
calf, Basque style, 228
chicken, cocktail kebabs, Navarra style, 231
chicken, omelette, Andalucian, 106
Lobster, about, 185–188

Mackerel, Spanish, about, 156
pickled, 157
Mango, about, 275
Marinade(s), how to use, 117–118
for baked salmon, 150
cooked (#3), 119
dry (for pork), 224
for rabbit, 82
uncooked (#2) for chicken and veal, 119
uncooked (#1) for meat, 118
Mayonnaise, about, 119–120
basic, 120
garlic (all-i-oli), 121; with tomatoes, 121
Meat. *See also* individual names (e.g. Pork, Veal)
about, 203–206
butters for, 129–130
marinades for, 117–118
sauces for, 127–128
soups. *See* Soups
stews. *See* Stews
Mejillones. *See* Mussels
Melons, about, 4, 276–277; varieties, 276. *See also* individual names (e.g. Cantaloupe, Honeydew)
Meringue desserts (basic), 321
apple, 321
apricot, 318
with chestnut puree, 321

Metric measurements, 49–51
Molluscs, 193–199. *See also*
    Shellfish
Mullet, gray, how to prepare,
    149
Mullet, red, 174–177
    with Romesco sauce, 176
    Seville style, 176
Mushrooms, about, 5, 303
    au gratin, as starter, 81
    baked, 303
    creamed, 303
    deep-fried, 303
Mussels, about, 195–196
    as appetizer, 70
    baked, with cheese, 197
    and clams, rice with, 136
    fish stew, Asturian style, 196
    prawn/shrimp casserole, 181
    sailor style, 196
    soup, 96; with cream, 94
Mustard butter, 130

Navy (Armada) sauce, 126
Nutmeg butter, 130

Olive oil, in cooking, 56–57
Olives (black and green)
    as appetizer, 70
    duck with, 262
    how to pit, 71
Omelettes, 103–108
    chicken liver, 106
    clam, 107
    fillings for, 108
    plain, 105
    shrimp, 107
    Spanish, 7, 104
    stuffed, 106–108
    zucchini, 107
Onions, about, 304; varieties,
    304
    casserole, 304
    peas and, 305
    stuffed, 304
    tart (savory), 110
Orange(s), about, 277; varieties,
    277
    caramel, 316
    chicken breasts with, 249
    sauce for rock bass, 162
Ostion (special oysters), 199
Ostras. *See* Oysters
Oysters, about, 197–199
    as appetizer, 70
    baked with almonds, as
        starter, 82
    poached, 198
    special (Ostion), 199

Paella, 137; a la Valenciana
    (original), 5, 138

Palitos, as appetizer, 74
Paprika butter, 130
Partridge, 252–256
    about, 252–253
    with cabbage, 254; stuffing
        for, 254
    Philip II style, 256
    pickled, 254
    stewed, Toledo style, 253
Pastry, Spanish short crust, 320
Pate, rabbit, 82
Pato. *See* Duck
Peaches, about, 278; varieties,
    278
    grilled, 317
    in red wine, 317
    in Spanish champagne, 317
    tart, open, 320
Pears, about, 279; varieties,
    279–280
Peas, about, 305
    and cucumber, 305
    with ham, 305
    and onions, 305
    stew, 306
Pelayo's stew (lamb), 207
Peppers, about, 306; varieties,
    306
    fried, green, as starter, 81
    rolled, 307
    stuffed, 307
    and tomatoes, chicken with,
        247
Perdiz. *See* Partridge
Persimmons, about, 280
Pescado. *See* Fish; White Fish
Pickled cucumber, as appetizer,
    70
Pickled partridge, 254
Pickled tunafish, as appetizer, 70
Pig, roast suckling, Santa Clara
    style, 222
    how to carve, 223
Pigeon, casserole of, 258
Pil-Pil (simmering technique), 8
Pimento, blanched, as appetizer,
    70
Pineapple, about, 280; varieties,
    281
Piri-Piri (hot sauce), 125
Pisto (Spanish vegetables), 307
Plums, about, 281; varieties, 281
Pollack, how to prepare, 151
Pollo. *See* Chicken
Pomegranate, about, 282
    loin of pork with, 226
Pork, 221–227
    and bacon stuffing for
        artichokes, 79
    chops, in casserole, 226
    chops, stuffed, 224
    loin, roast, 224

loin, with clams, 225; sailor
    style, 225
loin of, Aragon style, 223
loin with pomegranate, 226
shoulder, with turnip greens,
    227
suckling pig, Santa Clara
    style, 222
Potatoes, about, 308
    baked, white fish with, 168
    sweet, about, 309; to bake,
        310
Pot roast quail, 257
Poultry. *See* individual names
    (e.g. Chicken, Duck); Game
Prawns. *See* Shrimp and Prawns

Quail, about, 257–258
    pot roast, 257
    in Spanish brandy, 258
Quarter-hour (fish) soup, 6, 92
Queso. *See* Cheese
Quiche. *See* Tarts, savory

Rabbit
    pate, 82
    roast, 260
    wild, about, 260
Raspberry(ies), about, 272
    cream, 319
Recipes, how to use, 64–65
Redfish fillet in puff pastry, 153
Red mullet. *See* Mullet, red
Read sauces. *See* Tomato sauces
Regional specialties, 3–10
    Andalucian, 6–7
        calf liver, Alcazar, 229
        eggs, 102, 106–108
        garlic mayonnaise (all-i-oli),
            121
        gaspacho, 6, 88–89
        lamb cutlets, Granada, 220
        mullet (red), Seville style, 176;
            Romesco sauce, 176
        pigeon casserole, Granada, 259
        quarter-hour soup, 6, 92
        rice with shrimp, 135
        sole in champagne, 159
        veal, Cadiz style, 210
        veal with artichokes, Seville,
            209
    Asturian
        chicken, 248
        fish stew, 196
        hake, 165
        kidney, veal, 230
    Basque, 8
        cod, dried, 178
        crab, stuffed, 189
        eggs, 109
        kidney, veal, 230
        liver, 228

pil-pil (technique), 8
scallops with grapes, San
    Sebastian, 195
squid, in own ink, 193
Castile and Madrid, 7–8
fish fillets, 169
lamb roast, 220
partridge, Toledo, 253
tripe, 232
Catalonian, 3–5
broad beans, 292
Romesco sauce, 129
wines, 22–25
zucchini omelette, Barcelona,
    107
Costa Brava, baked white fish,
    168
Extremadura, gaspacho, 88
Galician, 9
cocido (stew), 208
fish soup, 96
shrimp omelette, 107
wines, 17–20
Rioja, wines of, 20–22
Valencian, 507
brussels sprouts, 296
chicken breasts with oranges,
    249
cucumber soup, 90
lamb stew, 216
paella, 138
Rice, 5, 133–138
how to prepare, 133–135
with mussels and clams, 136
paella, 137–138
with shrimp, 135
with white fish, 136
Rock bass. See Bass, rock
Rockfish. See Redfish
Romesco sauce, 129, 177
with grilled red mullet, 176
Rosefish. See Redfish
Rum, about, 38
white, sorbet, 325

S'agaro sauce, 126
Salad
with avocado, 76
avocado cream sauce for, 128
stuffed peppers, 307
vinegar sauce for, 128
Salmon, baked in marinade, 150
Salmon, white. See Hake
Salmonette. See Mullet, red
Salsa. See Sauces
Salsa Negra (black butter), 130
Sardines
as appetizer, 70
fresh, how to prepare, 177
as stuffing for eggs, 78
Sauces, 119–129. See also Mari-
    nades

almond, 127
anchovy and walnut, 127
avocado cream, 128
Bearnaise, 122
green (verde), 126
Hollandaise, 122
hot, 125; diablo, 125
mayonnaise, 119–121; garlic,
    121; with tomatoes, 121
navy (armada), 126
red, 125
Romesco, 129, 177
S'agaro, 126
Sherry, 127
Sofrito (tomato base), 58
tartar, 127
tomato, 124–126
vinegar, 128
white sauces, 123–124
yellow (amarillo), 128
Sausages, varieties, 62–63
beans with, 293
chorizo, 7
Savory butters, 129–130
Savory chicken, 248
Savory tarts. See Tarts, savory
Scallions, grilled, as appetizer, 4
Scallops, 194–195
creamed, with grapes, 195
how to prepare, 194
Sea bass. See Bass, sea
Seafood. See Fish and Shellfish
Shellfish, 179–196. See also
    Fish; individual names
clams, 193–194
cockles, 194
crab, 188–190
crayfish, 184–185
lobster, 185–188
molluscs, 193–196
mussels, 195–196
oysters, 197–199
sauces. See Sauces
scallops, 194–195
shrimp and prawns, 179–183
soups. See Soups
squid, 190–193
Sherbet. See Sorbets
Sherry(ies), about, 14–17; vari-
    eties, 15
roast lamb with, 218
rock bass with, 164
sauce, 127
Shrimp and Prawns, about,
    179–183
as appetizer, 70
broiled, as starter, 81
butter, 135
casserole, 181
creamed, 182
deep-fried, 183
deep-fried toasts, 182

in garlic butter, as starter, 81
grilled, deep-sea, 179
of the house, as starter, 81
omelette from Galicia, 107
poached, 183
rice with, 135
soup, cold, 95
stuffed, butterfly, 180
tart (savory), 111
Sofrito, 58. See also Tomato
    sauces
Sole, 157–160
with bananas, 159
in champagne, 159
with cream and mushrooms,
    160
how to prepare, 157
in vermouth, 159
Sopa. See Soups
Sorbets, as frozen assets,
    324–325
lemon, 324
white rum, 325
Souffles
banana, 322
chestnut, 322
Soups, 87–98
avocado cream, 90
chickpeas (garbanzos), 97
clams, cream of, 94
cucumber, cold, 90
fish and seafood, 92–96
Galician, 96
garlic croutons for, 91
gazpacho, 6, 87–89; garnishes,
    87
green (verde), 9, 91
lentil, 98
Maria's (tomato), 91
mussel, 96; with cream, 94
pescado (authentic), 95
quarter-hour, 92
shrimp, cold, 95
tomato, fresh, 90
vegetable, 90–91
walnut, 91
Spanish omelette, 7, 104
Spanish short crust, 320
Spanish vegetable medley,
    307
Spices. See Herbs and Spices
Spinach, about, 308
with rosemary, 308
Spirits and liqueurs, 37–39;
    proof systems, 39–40
Squash, about, 309
Squid, 190–193
deep-fried, 192
stuffed, 192
in their own ink, 193
Starters. See Hors d'Oeuvre;
    Appetizers; Tarts, savory

Stews
  beef, Spanish, 209
  chicken, 241
  fish, Asturian style, 196
  Galician cocido, 208
  lamb, 216; Valencian style, 216
  partridge, 253
  pea, 306
  Pelayo's (lamb), 207
Strawberries, surprise, 316
Stuffings for:
  artichokes, 79
  chicken, 244, 245
  eggs, 78
  fish, 156
  partridge, 254
Suckling pig, roast, Santa Clara
  style, 222
Sweet potatoes. *See* Potatoes,
  sweet
Sweetbreads, 231
  cocktail kebabs, Navarra
    style, 231
  with ham, 231
Swordfish, 170; grilled, 171

Tangerines, about, 282
Tapas. *See* Appetizers; Hors
  d'Oeuvre; Tarts, savory
Tapas naturales, 70
Tarragon butter, 130
Tart, open peach, 320
Tartaletas (barquettes), as appe-
  tizer, 73
Tartar sauce, 127
Tarts, savory, 110–113
  Jose Citrano's quiche, 113
  onion, 110
  shrimp, 111
  zucchini, 111
Ternera. *See* Veal

Thickeners, in cooking, 61
Tomato(es), about, 310
  all-i-oli with, 121
  and peppers, chicken with, 247
  rock bass with, 163
  sauces, 125–126
  sofrito (sauce base), 58
  soup, fresh, 90; sopa Maria, 91
  as starter, 77; stuffed, 77
Tortillas. *See* Omelettes
Tripe, 7; Madrid style, 232
Trout (river), 148–149
  with Gran Marnier, 148
  Navarra style, 149
Trout (sea), baked, 153
Tunafish, as appetizer, 70;
  pickled, 70
Turbot, how to prepare, 174
Turnip(s), about, 310
  duck with, 261
  greens, shoulder of pork with,
    227

Vanilla ice cream, 326
Veal, 209–213
  with artichokes, 209
  Cadiz style, 210
  cutlets, San Pedro, 213
  cutlets with cheese and mush-
    rooms, 212
  elegant, 211
  fillets, stuffed, 211
  marinade for, 119
Vegetables, 282–311. *See also*
  individual names
  availability calendar, 284
  baked, mixed, 285
  beans, basic preparation, 311
  blanching, 286
  butters for, 129–130
  dried, about, 310

  how to prepare, 282–285
  sauces for, 128–129
  soups, 90–91
  Spanish medley, 307
Vermouth, about, 38
Vinegar sauce, 128
Vodka, about, 38

Walnut butter, 80
Walnut soup, 91
Watermelon, about, 277
Whitebait, how to prepare, 154
White fish
  baked (Costa Brava), 168
  baked with potatoes and
    almonds, 168
  fillets, Castilian, 169
  fillets, in wine and cream, 170
  Malaga style, 167
White sauce, 123–124
Wild duck, 261
Wild rabbit, 260
Wines, 13–40. *See also* Regional
  specialties
  choosing, 27–29
  cooking with, 36–37; sauces,
    36–37
  evaluating, 30–34
  glossary of terms, 34–36
  making, 29–30
  proof systems of, 39
  Sherries, 14–17
  spirits and liqueurs, 37–39

Yellow (amarillo) sauce, 128
Yogurt, how to treat, 110

Zucchini omelette, 107
Zucchini tart (savory), 111

# THE
# ARABIAN
# NIGHTS

# THE ARABIAN NIGHTS

*Or Tales Told by
Sheherezade During a Thousand
Nights and One Night*

---

RETOLD BY **Brian Alderson**

ILLUSTRATED BY **Michael Foreman**

---

BOOKS OF WONDER

MORROW JUNIOR BOOKS

*New York*

For Sheherezade herself

Asie, Asie, Asie,
Vieux pays merveilleux des contes de nourrice . . .

First published in Great Britain in 1992 by Victor Gollancz Ltd. First published in the United States in 1995 by Morrow Junior Books.

Brian Alderson and Michael Foreman have asserted their right to be identified as authors of this work.

Printed in Hong Kong
1  2  3  4  5  6  7  8  9  10

Library of Congress Cataloging-in-Publication Data
Alderson, Brian.   The Arabian nights, or, Tales told by Sheherezade during a thousand nights and one night/retold by Brian Alderson; illustrated by Michael Foreman.    p.    cm.—(Books of wonder)
Summary: An illustrated collection of stories from the "Arabian Nights," including those of Sindbad, Ali Baba, and Aladdin.
ISBN 0-688-14219-2  [1. Fairy tales.   2. Folklore—Arab countries.   3. Arabs—Folklore.]   I. Foreman, Michael, ill.   II. Title.
III. Title: Arabian nights.   IV. Title: Tales told by Sheherezade during a thousand nights and one night.
V. Series.   PZ8.A36Ar  1995  398.22—dc20  94-40945  CIP  AC

# CONTENTS

Invocation     7

THE TWO KINGS, SHAH SHAHRYAR AND SHAH ZAMAN,
AND THE WAZIR'S DAUGHTER SHEHEREZADE who told
these tales during a thousand nights and one night     9

THE TALE OF THE FISHERMAN AND THE JINNI     17
The Tale Which the Fisherman Told of the Sage Duban,
in which King Yunan tells:     21
    *The Tale of the Loyal Falcon and*     24
    *The Tale of the Faithful Parrot*     26

THE TALE OF THE PORTER OF BAGHDAD     31

THE TALE OF THE HUNCHBACK     34
    *His Lamentable Death*     34
    *What Happened at the Sultan's Court*     39

THE FABLE OF THE BIRDS AND THE BEASTS
AND THE CARPENTER     43

THE FABLE OF THE WOLF AND THE FOX     48

THE FABLE OF THE MONGOOSE AND THE MOUSE     51

THE TALE OF THE EBONY HORSE     55
    *His Coming*     55
    *What Happened to the Prince*     58
    *The Homecoming of the Ebony Horse*     64
    *What Happened to the Princess*     66
    *And How it All Ended*     70

THE TALE WHICH ALI THE PERSIAN TOLD
TO AMUSE HARUN AL-RASHID     73

MA'AN BIN-ZAIDAH, THE DONKEY AND THE CUCUMBERS     76

THE STORY OF SINDBAD THE PORTER
AND SINDBAD THE SAILOR,
in which Sindbad the Sailor tells:     79
    The Tale of the Vanishing Island, and his     80
    Adventure of the Valley of Diamonds, and his     81
    Adventure with The Old Man of the Sea     85

THE TALE OF THE CITY OF BRASS     91
    *Of the Jars of Solomon*     91
    *Of the Black Castle*     92
    *Of the Ifrit Dahish*     97
    *Of the City of Brass*     101
    and *Of the Ending of the Journey*     110

THE TALE OF THE MAN WHO STOLE
THE DOG'S GOLDEN DISH     111

THE TALE OF THE RUINED MAN AND HIS DREAM     114

THE TALE OF THE SIMPLETON AND HIS DONKEY     116

THE TALE OF JA'AFAR THE BARMECIDE
AND THE AILING BEDOUIN     117

THE STORY OF ALI BABA AND THE FORTY THIEVES     120
    *The Cave*     120
    *The Kitchen Scales*     125
    *Kasim's Come-uppance*     126
    *Coping with the Corpse*     127
    *Calcification*     130
    *The Captain's Craft*     133
    *The Kitchener's Craft*     137
    *How it Ended*     139

THE STORY OF ALADDIN AND THE SLAVE OF THE LAMP     142
    *The Uncle*     142
    *The Cave*     144
    *The Lamp*     150
    *The Princess*     154
    *Bridegroom Number One*     158
    *Bridegroom Number Two*     163
    *The Wizard*     168
    *How It Ended*     177

HOW IT ALL ENDED     182

Editor's Remarks     185

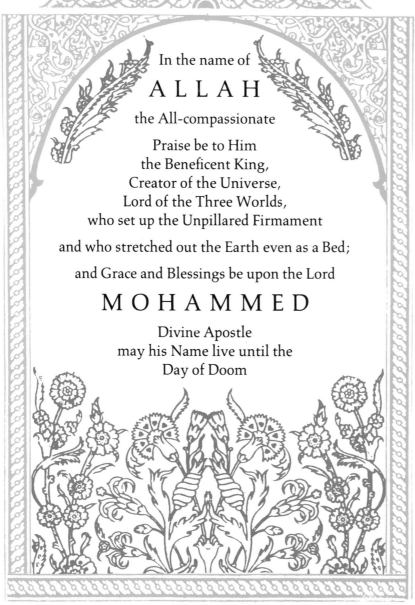

In the name of

# ALLAH

the All-compassionate

Praise be to Him
the Beneficent King,
Creator of the Universe,
Lord of the Three Worlds,
who set up the Unpillared Firmament

and who stretched out the Earth even as a Bed;

and Grace and Blessings be upon the Lord

# MOHAMMED

Divine Apostle
may his Name live until the
Day of Doom

# THE TWO KINGS, SHAH SHAHRYAR AND SHAH ZAMAN, AND THE WAZIR'S DAUGHTER SHEHEREZADE

**I**n past times, in the far history of the world there was a great king who ruled over all the lands of Arabia and Persia, even to the shores of India, and when this king died he left his kingdom to his two sons, Shahryar and Zaman. These brothers were as close to one another as the nut within its shell and they divided their inheritance equally between them; Shahryar becoming king of land towards the west, with his palace at Baghdad, and Zaman becoming king of lands towards the east, with his palace at Samarkand.

For many years the brothers ruled their two kingdoms with justice and mercy until one day the Shah Shahryar felt a longing to see the Shah Zaman once more, so he called to him his chief minister, or Wazir, and he ordered that a great caravan be prepared to journey to his brother. There were to be camels and horses, laden with rich gifts of jewels and silks, there were to be white slaves and brown slaves, bearing precious ointments and sweetmeats, and in their midst the Wazir should journey with a letter full of loving greetings, in which the Shah Shahryar invited the Shah Zaman to return to Baghdad to be his honoured guest.

All came to pass as the Shah Shahryar intended. The Wazir and the caravan of horses and camels and body slaves brought the letter to the Shah Zaman, and after a week of feasting the Shah Zaman prepared a like baggage train to travel to his brother's palace. Loaded with many presents of gold and ivory, with rich carpets and with hangings of brocade, the caravan assembled and amid the rejoicings of the people of Samarkand it left the great gate of the city and encamped the first night within view of the city walls.

Now it so happened that, in the deepest part of the night, the Shah Zaman awoke in his tent and recollected that he had left

in his chamber in his palace a great ruby that was to be a present from himself to his brother. So he secretly arose and made his way back to the city, gaining entrance to the palace through a private postern, and climbing by a hidden staircase to his own chamber. What should be his horror however, when, on entering the room, he beheld his wife sleeping in the arms of a giant slave on his own carpet-bed.

"By Allah!" cried the Shah to himself, "how can it be that such a thing can happen, with the baggage train even yet within sight of the city walls? And if it can happen thus, what else may take place during the time that I am at my brother's court?" And in rage and sorrow he drew his scimitar and with one blow sliced the sleeping lovers into four pieces. Then he seized the forgotten ruby from its place and returned to his encampment in secret as he had come.

With expectation and longing the caravan now travelled its way across the mountains and the deserts to the city of Baghdad where it was greeted by the lords and the people alike, and the Shah Shahryar himself came down to open the city gates for his brother and to lead him in honour to the imperial palace. But through all the journeyings and the rejoicings the Shah Zaman was cast down, unable to think of anything beyond the death of love and the faithlessness of humankind. And although his brother prepared for him a great feast—the first in a long line of feasts—and although he was lodged in a wing of the palace resplendent with rich hangings and carpets and overlooking the Shah's own pleasure garden, there could be no raising his despondent spirits. His eye paled and his skin turned yellow with grief and nothing that his brother could do would revive him. "I am tired after my long journey," was all that he would say.

One day it came about that the Shah Shahryar prepared a great hunting expedition. Hoping that it would distract his brother from his sorrows he called upon him to mount and join them in the chase. But the Shah Zaman refused, asking only to be allowed to rest, and so the king and his huntsmen departed and left him to be cared for in his own quarter of the palace.

As he made his way dolefully from room to room it so happened that he came upon a little lattice window overlooking

a secluded glade of the Shah's pleasure garden. Peering out through a corner of the window he was surprised to see the Shah's wife, who was a woman of great beauty, traversing the lawns, surrounded by a company of twenty slave girls in their robes and hoods. When they reached a fountain in the centre of the glade they cast off their robes and behold! they were not all slave girls, but girls and men too, and as they began to disport themselves naked beside the water the captain of the slave-guard leapt from a nearby tree and joined with the Queen herself.

In amazement the Shah Zaman watched the secret joys of the Queen and her slaves. "Truly," he said to himself, "the trustlessness and depravity of man stretches even to Baghdad!" and from that time on he began to recover his spirits. His eye brightened, his walk took on a new vigour, and when his brother returned from the hunt he was surprised and delighted at the change that he saw.

"Alhamdohlillah!" he cried, "when I departed the flower was fading, when I came back the flower was flourishing. What is the meaning of this riddle?" But the Shah Zaman kept his own counsel, not wishing that his brother too should be cast into the despair that had been his.

As the days passed however, the Shah Shahryar would not let the matter rest. He urged and urged his brother to tell him the reason for the sudden reversal of his fever and eventually the Shah Zaman gave way and told everything: the faithlessness of his wife, the killing of the wretched pair, the discovery that the Queen of Shah Shahryar was faithless too.

"By Allah!" cried the Shah, "can such a thing be possible?" And once more he ordered a hunting party to be prepared, and one which this time both he and his brother would attend; so the next day they set off for the chase. This time though, at their first encampment, the Shahs Shahryar and Zaman left their Wazirs to guard their tents, with orders that none should be admitted on pain of death, and they returned in secret to the palace. There, the next day, they placed themselves by the lattice window and observed how, once more, the Shah's wife and the slave-guard, the slaves and the handmaidens took their pleasure in the pleasure garden.

"Truly, my brother," cried the Shah Shahryar in despair, "there is no faith to be found in humankind. Let us betake ourselves from this evil place, to walk the world as poor pilgrims, never to return unless we should find one who is more wretchedly treated than ourselves. Then shall our wrath be without appeasement."

So the two Shahs left the palace and the hunting camp, where the Wazirs still stood their guard, and they walked as pilgrims across the world. Eventually they came to the line of the sea and here they took their rest in the shade of a tall tree beside a brook that ran down into the ocean.

While they were sitting there a great cloud began to form across the horizon and before long it took the shape of a huge black Jinni, or earth spirit, whirling towards them with the noise of a thousand hurricanes. In terror the two Shahs climbed into the branches of the tree where they had been sitting, and they beheld how the Jinni swirled down to the shore below them, carrying with him a huge chest made of crystal. This chest he opened, taking from it a broad casket locked with seven padlocks, and these locks he opened with a steel key, and out of the casket there stepped a girl as serenely beautiful as the sailing moon.

"Love of my heart," said the Jinni, "I would sleep." And she

knelt down on the sandy shore, and the Jinni placed his head on her lap and fell at once into a deep sleep.

When she saw that he truly was asleep she looked up into the tree and commanded the two kings to come down or else she would wake the Jinni who was with her. In fear and trembling Shah Shahryar and his brother descended to the ground, and then, gently moving from the sleeping Jinni, she commanded that each of them should come to her as a man comes to his wife. In vain they protested, in vain they sought to escape; there was nothing for it but to do as she required, under pain of her waking the Jinni.

When she had had her way with them she demanded that each should give her the ring of office that he carried on his finger, and when they had done so she went to her casket and drew from it a string on which were knotted five hundred and seventy of such similar rings. "You should know," she said, fastening their tokens in place, "that this Jinni snatched me away for himself the night I was to be married and he keeps me locked within my casket in a chest of crystal at the bottom of the sea, so that none but he may enjoy me. Even so—such is my cunning—I have betrayed him no less than five hundred and seventy—now five hundred and seventy-two times, and here is my proof. But go your way now, my Lords, before this creature should awake and slay us all."

So the Shah Shahryar and the Shah Zaman left the Jinni and his lady beside the line of the sea, and the Shah Shahryar said, "Is not this Jinni more wretched than ourselves? Just as he is more mighty, so his humiliation is the greater at the hands of this woman. Let us return to the palace and take our just revenge." And the two Shahs made their way back to the hunting camp, and returned to the palace with all their train, and the Shah Shahryar ordered forthwith that his faithless wife should be done to death. He then swore a great oath, that, from that day on, he would every night marry a new bride and every morning he would slay her, and so he would be avenged on the faithlessness of women.

Thus it came about. Every night a girl was brought to the bridal bed with great pomp, and every dawn the Wazir was called to lead her to her execution; but it was not long before the people began to cry out at such cruelty. Men hid their

daughters, or carried them over the sea to other lands, for fear
that they should become brides of the Shah Shahryar, until
eventually the Wazir could find no girl to bring to the Sultan.
The only ones left in all the city were the Wazir's own two
daughters, Sheherezade and Dunyazad.

Now Sheherezade was a girl of quick wits, richly versed in
the lore and fables of Arabia, and when she saw her father cast
down and fearful for his life, because there was no bride for the
king, she said, "By Allah, O my father, do not grieve, but send
me to be partner to the Shah Shahryar. Either I shall live, or I
shall die a death for all women, and whichever happens there
should be nothing but pride for you." And however strongly
the Wazir urged her not to be so foolish, the more strongly
Sheherezade determined to pursue her course.

So in heavy dejection the Wazir took his way to the Shah's
throne room and casting himself before his master's feet he
revealed the intention of his daughter. "Wonder upon
wonders!" cried the Shah, "how can this be? My oath is an
oath for all time and all women. It cannot be denied for the
favours of my Wazir's daughter." For he had long known and
loved Sheherezade and had no desire to visit on her the
punishment of all the others. But the Wazir wept and told him
that she was not to be diverted from her aim—that she must
and would marry the Shah and die the death of her kind; and
the Shah, with admiration for her comeliness and for her
courage, bade his servants prepare the wedding feast, and bade
his headsman test his sharpest axe, that her death in the
morning should be swift and sure.

But Sheherezade rejoiced in her fate and called to her
younger sister, Dunyazad.

"Listen well, O sister," she said. "Tonight I go to the Sultan
Shahryar to be his bride and his wife. Now after he has taken
me to the marriage bed I will send for you to be with me—for
at dawn I shall be beheaded—and you must say to me, 'Tell
me, O sister, for the night is long and we cannot sleep, some
story that will while away the hours before the sad sunrise',
and then I shall tell a tale which, Allah willing, shall be the
saving of us all."

"With all my heart," said Dunyazad. And so it came to pass
that the Wazir brought Sheherezade to the Shah and they were

married, and in all joy he brought her to the marriage bed where, after much pleasure, they fell asleep. But in the middle of the night Sheherezade woke and called upon her husband, saying, "My Lord, I cannot sleep for fear of the daylight hour when I shall lose my life. Permit me to send for Dunyazad, my sister, that she may be with me in this time of trial." So the Shah gave his leave, and when Dunyazad came she said, "Tell me, O sister, for the night is long and we cannot sleep, some story that will while away the hours before the sad sunrise."

"If my Lord permits," said Sheherezade; and the Shah—who dearly loved a tale—agreed, and so Sheherezade began the tale of:–

# THE FISHERMAN AND THE JINNI

I have heard, O auspicious King, that there was once an aged fisherman who lived in great poverty with his wife and six children. Each day he would go down to the sea-shore to fish and it was his habit to cast his net into the water three times and three times only.

So one afternoon he went down to the tide-line, set down his basket, waded into the sea and cast his net. When it had settled to the bottom he gathered the cords together and tried to haul it in, but however much he pulled it would not budge an inch, so he drove a stake into the ground, fastened the cords of the net to it and dived into the water to see what the burden was. Eventually he released the net and brought it to land, only to discover that all it contained was a dead jackass which had torn the meshes.

"Truly," said the fisherman, "there is no Majesty and there is no Might save in Allah, but this is strange winnings to get from the sea," and he cast his net a second time. Once more he brought it to land only with great difficulty, diving to free the burdened net from the sea-bottom. And once more he found that it contained not a shoal of fish but rubbish—a large pitcher full of sand and mud, potsherds and broken glass.

"Lord!" cried the fisherman, "You know that I cast my net only three times in each day. Twice have I cast now and You have rendered me nothing; pray give me my daily sustenance." And calling again upon Allah he threw his net the third time and watched as it sank and settled.

But this cast was no different from the others. The net stuck and there was nothing for it, but the fisherman had to dive down and free its tangles from the bottom—and this time when he brought it to land he found that it contained a jar of brass, shaped like a cucumber and stoppered with a leaden cap that bore the seal of the Emperor Solomon, the son of David.

"Praise and blessings to Allah!" cried the fisherman, "for here is a fish that will bring me ten golden dinars in the brass market. But first I must know what riches it may contain." And he took out his knife and worked at the sealed stopper till he had loosened it from the jar. Then he carefully tipped the vessel to see what might be inside.

There was nothing. But as he gazed at the jar, marvelling greatly that Solomon or his agents should have sealed it without anything inside, he saw issue from the neck a black smoke which began to pour out across the surface of the shore and then to billow heavenward in a huge, thick vapour. And slowly the vapour condensed into a shape and the shape into the solid figure of a Jinni whose crest touched the clouds while his feet were yet planted on the

ground. His head was as a dome, his hands like pitchforks, his legs long as mizzen masts, his mouth big as a cave, his teeth like tombstones and his eyes burning like two brilliant lamps.

"There is no God but *the* God!" cried the Jinni, "be of good cheer, O fisherman!"

But the fisherman, far from being of good cheer, was shaking in his shoes. His teeth chattered, the spittle dried in his mouth and he became blind about what to do.

"Why biddest thou me to be of good cheer?" he asked.

"Because in this very hour thou must die a chosen death."

"Whyso?" cried the fisherman. "Why shouldst thou kill me, who have brought thee up out of the sea to dry land and freed thee from thy jar?"

"Ask not," said the Jinni. "Ask only by what kind of death thou seekest to die and by what manner of slaughter I shall slay thee. For thou must know that I am one of the Jann that sinned against Solomon, the son of David, and that when I refused to embrace the True Faith he shut me up in that jar and had me cast into the midmost ocean.

"Know also, fisherman, that I lay in that ocean an hundred years, and I said in my heart, 'Whoso shall release me, him will I enrich for ever and ever,' but no one came. So I lay there four hundred years more, and I said in my heart, 'Whoso shall release me, to him I will grant three wishes,' but still and still and still nobody came. Thereupon I waxed wroth with exceeding wrath and I swore to myself that whoso should release me, him would I slay, giving him only the choice of death that he should die."

But with this speech of the Jinni, Sheherezade perceived the coming of the day and fell silent.

"What a strange tale this is," said her sister Dunyazad.

"Indeed so," said Sheherezade, "but it is as nothing to what must follow if my Lord will permit me to live until the coming night and will spare me from his wrath."

And the Sultan said to himself, "By Allah, I shall not kill her until the tale be told." So he went forth into his court. He gave edicts and he granted suits, and when his Wazir came to him with a shroud made for Sheherezade he said no word but left the hall. And when night came he joined Sheherezade once more in the marriage bed.

After they had caroused and slept, and when the first part of the night was over, Dunyazad came to them once more, saying,

"O my sister, continue now thy story of the Fisherman and the Jinni." And without more ado Sheherezade went on:–

It hath reached me, O auspicious King, that the Jinni had held forth in a long speech, threatening death to the fisherman. But during his words the fisherman gradually resumed his senses and determined in his mind that, as a man of contrivance and intelligence, he might yet encompass the destruction of the Contumacious One.

"Then is it so," he asked, "that my only injury toward thee is that I let thee out of thy brass bottle?"

"That is so," said the Jinni.

"Then is it so," he asked again, "that for the good I have done thee thou returnest only evil?"

"Indeed it is so," said the Jinni, "but I have endured enough of this talk. Die thou must, and without delay."

"Then tell me," cried the fisherman, "by the Most Great Name, graven on the seal of Solomon, the son of David, if I question thee on one more matter wilt thou give me a true answer?"

"Yea," answered the Jinni (for he trembled at the mention of the Most Great Name), "but ask it briefly."

"Very well," said the fisherman. "Tell me, however was it that thou couldst fit into this brass jar which would not now hold even the toenail of thy big toe?"

"What?" said the Jinni, "dost thou not believe that I was trapped in that bottle a thousand years or more?"

"Nay," said the fisherman, "how could I believe it, when I see that thou ridest above me in the clouds and this jar so small? Thou couldst not do it."

So at that the Jinni shook himself and became again a black vapour and shrank and little by little flowed back into the jar; and when he was well inside the fisherman sprang for the stopper and the seal and stoppered up the mouth of the jar, crying out, "A boon! A boon! Ask me by what kind of death thou seekest to die and by what manner of slaughter I shall slay thee; for by Allah, I will throw thee into the sea and will post a warning to all that come here that in these waters there dwells a Jinni who gives as a favour a choice of death to those who rescue him!"

Now when the Jinni realized that he had been outwitted and was once more under the seal of Solomon he became lowly and submissive.

"I did but jest," he said, speaking through the sides of the jar.

"Thou liest," said the fisherman, "thou vilest of the Jann. There is nothing

for it but I shall throw thee back into the sea where thou mayst be housed and homed another thousand years . . . ''

"Ah!" cried the Jinni, "say not so. Open for me and I shall serve thee well."

"Thou liest!" said the fisherman. "It will be no better with thee than it was with the Wazir of King Yunan and the Sage Duban."

"And who was the Wazir of King Yunan and the Sage Duban?" asked the Jinni; and there followed:—

## THE TALE WHICH THE FISHERMAN
## TOLD OF THE SAGE DUBAN

Know thou, O Jinni, that in ages long past there was a King in Persia by the name of Yunan. He was a powerful ruler, but his body was afflicted with leprosy and although doctors and physicians and leeches came from every nation, with medicines and powders and unguents, not one of them could cure the King.

Now one day there came to the land an ancient sage who was called Duban, a man versed in the books of Greece and Rome, and of Persia, Arabia and Syria, one who knew all the skills of healing with herbs and potions. Nor was it long before he heard of the sufferings of the King, and after a night of contemplation he betook himself to the court, where he knelt before the King and kissed the ground between his hands.

"O King," he said, "tidings have reached me of your misfortune and of how a great host of physicians have found no way to mitigate it. But lo! I can cure thee, even though I make thee drink no draught nor anoint thee with no ointment."

And when King Yunan heard these words he marvelled greatly and said, "By Allah, if thou make me whole I will enrich thee down to the sons of thy sons, and I will give thee rich gifts and call thee friend."

So the sage took his way and hired a house in the city for the better storage of his books and scrolls and his medicines and aromatic roots. And there he fashioned a wonderful polo mallet with a curiously-wrought wooden handle, and he took the mallet to the King and brought him to the palace yard, there to play a chukka of polo. "Take the mallet," said Duban to the King, "and grip it as I do, so! Then ride into the game and strike the ball mightily up and down and as the palm of thy hand sweats upon the mallet so shall the cure be proved."

Then the King rode his pony into the polo match and played a vigorous chukka, striking the ball from one end of the ground to the other and sweating like any common man. And when the chukka was done he betook himself to the bath house and as he bathed he observed his body and saw that it was clean as virgin silver. The leprosy had gone.

 At this point Sheherezade once more left off her story, for the day was dawning. But once more the Sultan spared her life for the sake of the tale that she was telling. And the next night she continued:–

It hath reached me, O auspicious King, that the fisherman was telling the Jinni the tale of how the Sage Duban had come to King Yunan and cured him of his leprosy. Great was the rejoicing of King Yunan and of his court at this miraculous cure and when the Sage Duban appeared for an audience the King greeted him with due honour, set before him gifts of jewels and money and fine robes and treated him as friend.

But not everyone at the court was filled with such delight. For there was among the King's Wazirs, a Wazir of frightful aspect, shrunken with envy and malice, and when he saw the honours bestowed upon the Sage Duban his jealousy knew no bounds. That night he came before the King privily in his chamber and laid charges against the sage, that he was plotting the downfall of the King.

"How can this be?" said King Yunan. "Why, the sage cured me of my illness without drowning me in draughts or boiling me in ointments. How should I not reward him? Indeed, if I were to heed your warning and have him done to death I would surely repent of the deed as King Sindibad repented of killing his falcon."

"Pardon me, O King," said the Wazir, "but I know nothing of King Sindibad or of his falcon." So King Yunan recounted:—

# THE TALE OF THE LOYAL FALCON

There was once a King of the Kings of Persia who loved hunting. He had reared a falcon, whom he took with him everywhere, and he had made for this falcon a golden cup which was hung about her neck that he might himself give her to drink therefrom.

Now one day the King and his men were out hunting and as they were staking their nets there came towards them a proud gazelle. "Stay!" cried the King, "whosoever allows that gazelle to spring over his head, that man shall I surely slay." But the gazelle advanced slowly towards the King himself, and when she reached him she sank back on her haunches, and crossed her forehoof over her breast as though to salute the King. And as he bowed in acknowledgement she suddenly bounded high over his head and sped off into the desert.

"By Allah!" cried the King, "my life is upon my own head!" and he galloped off in pursuit of the gazelle with his falcon on his fist. The chase carried them to the foothills of a row of mountains where the gazelle made for a cave in the rocks, but the King unleashed his falcon who swooped upon it and drove her talons into its head so that the King was able to come up and slay the beast with his mace; and after he had quartered it he packed it into his saddle bags and set off to return to his men.

By now though, it was the hottest time of the day, and both the King and his horse were athirst, so they sought about among the foothills for water. Nor was it long before they heard a plashing noise and found a tree which was dropping water as though it were melted butter.

At once the King took the golden cup from about his falcon's neck and filled it with the water; but before he could drink the bird struck with her pounces

and upset the lot. So the King filled the cup a second time, and again the bird overturned it with her talons. At this the King was wroth with exceeding wrath and when his falcon tipped the cup a third time he pulled out his sword and struck off one of her wings.

At this the creature raised its head and seemed to motion to the King to look up at the tree, and when he did so he saw there, enmeshed in the branches, a brood of vipers from whose fangs had dropped the streams that he took to be water. So without more ado he rode back to his camp with the slain gazelle, but when he came to attend to his injured bird it turned up its eyes at him and died.

"Thus," said King Yunan to his Wazir, "thus does ingratitude foster calamity, just as it did in the case of the husband and the parrot."

"Pardon me, O King," said the Wazir, "but I know nothing of the husband and the parrot." So King Yunan proceeded to tell:—

## THE TALE OF THE FAITHFUL PARROT

There was once a certain merchant who married a woman of perfect beauty. "Happy for him," you may say, but because of her loveliness he was mad jealous that she might come to know some other man, so he kept to his house with her day and night.

Eventually, however, it came about that he must attend to business in a distant city, so he went to the bird market and bought for an hundred dinars a speaking parrot whom he put in the house to watch over his wife and to report to him when he returned.

Now his wife had indeed fallen in love with another man—a young Turk—and once the husband had gone he came to join her and they feasted by day and slept together by night. So when the merchant returned home he questioned the parrot about what had been going on and the bird told everything.

At once rage and violence entered the merchant's heart and he thrashed his wife as though she had been a dog in the street, and she, in her turn, called up her slave girls to punish whomsoever (as she believed), had told tales about her. But the slave girls all swore that they had kept her secret and they pointed to the parrot as the cause of all the trouble.

So the next time that the merchant went from home his wife made different plans, and before her lover arrived she arranged for the girls to attend around the parrot's cage. One sat underneath it with a hand-mill, grinding and grinding for all she was worth. One stood over the cage sprinkling water through its roof. And one ran about the room flashing the lamplight into the cage with mirrors of polished steel.

Thus, when the husband returned, he inquired of the parrot what might have happened in his absence, and the bird replied, "Pardon, O my master, but I can tell you nothing by reason of the thunder and lightning and pouring rain that assailed me all night."

"How can this be?" cried her master, "for we are in the season of high summer and there is neither cloud nor rain the whole time long." And with that he deemed that a bird who could lie once might lie twice and he hauled the parrot from its cage and dashed its brains out on the floor. Only later, when a slave girl confessed, did he discover the trick that had been played on the bird and he mourned greatly that such faithfulness should be rewarded with death.

King Yunan's Wazir refused to be moved by these stories however and he continued day and night to turn the King's mind against the Sage Duban. "For after all," said he, "if he cured thee by so innocent a means as holding a polo

stick, who is to say that he may not choose his time and slay thee with a like simplicity?"

And as water will wear rock, so these speeches wore away the King's faith in the Sage Duban and eventually he sent for him to attend his court.

"Knowest thou why I have summoned thee?" he said; and the sage answered, "Allah alone, the Most High, knows the secrets of the heart."

"I have summoned thee only to take thy life and utterly destroy thee."

"O King, wherefore so; and what ill have I done?"

"Men tell me that thou art a spy come hither to slay me, and lo! I will kill thee ere I be killed by thee." And the King called forth his Sworder to strike off the sage's head. But the sage pleaded that he might be spared (said the fisherman to the Jinni, 'Even as I pleaded with you when I let you out of the jar'), but the King was adamant: "There is no help for it; die thou must, and without delay."

Now when the sage realized that there was no turning the King from his purpose, he said, "O King, if truly there be no help, then grant me some little time that I may go down to my house and make all preparations against my death, and on my return I will bring thee a parting gift that is the rarest of all rarities and that shall be a treasure for your treasury."

"And what may that be?" asked the King.

"It is a book that shall reveal to thee all the secrets of the world. For if—when thou hast cut my head off—thou open three leaves of the book and read three lines of the page on thy left hand, my head shall speak and shall answer every question thou choose to ask."

Well, the King wondered much at this strange present and he sent the sage, closely guarded, to his house and all was settled as he desired. And the next day the King went to his audience hall, among his Emirs and his Wazirs, his Nabobs and his Chamberlains, and the Sage Duban stood before him bearing a worn old volume and a little flask of metal full of powder.

"Give me a tray," he said, and when they brought him one he spread the powder on it, smoothed it out, and said, "O King, take this book but do not open it until my head falls; then set it on the powder of this tray and forthwith the blood will cease to flow and the time will be at hand to open the book."

So the King took the objects and made a sign to the Sworder, who struck off the head of the Sage Duban and placed it on the tray. Straightway the blood stopped flowing and the head unclosed its eyes and said, "Now open the book, O King."

The King opened the book, but found that the leaves were stuck together; so he licked his finger and turned the first leaf. There was no writing to be seen. So with much difficulty and in the same way he opened six leaves of the book,

but could find nothing on them.

"O Physician," he said, "there is no writing here."

"O King," said the head, "turn over yet more." And so the King proceeded, licking his finger at each leaf to separate it from its fellows. On all the pages he found neither guidance nor wisdom—but on all of them his finger discovered, unbeknown, a rare and subtle poison and within minutes of his having opened the book the King fell into violent convulsions.

*"So ends the pride of mortal things,"* said the head.

*"So ends the tyranny of Kings."*

And it spoke no more.

"Thus you may see, O Jinni," said the fisherman, "that if King Yunan had spared the Sage Duban, Allah would have spared him. Likewise if thou hadst spared me then Allah would have spared thee; but nothing would satisfy thee save my death; so now I will render thee the same service and cast thee back into the ocean, with warnings to whomsoever shall find thee to toss thee back again, and thou shalt abide in these waters till the End of Time."

Then began a great argument between the fisherman, shouting on the shore, and the Jinni, booming in his brass jar. And the end of it was that the Jinni swore a solemn oath by Allah, the Most High, that if the fisherman released him, so far from slaughtering him he would reward him with an abundance of riches.

Once more therefore the fisherman lifted the stopper from the jar and the Jinni flared into the air like a smoke. Then, when he had once more resumed his gigantic state he kicked the brass jar with its stopper and seal and sent it flying an hundred miles into the sea. At this the fisherman feared once more for his life and trembled so that he wet his britches, but the Jinni laughed like the roaring of a tribe of desert lions and bade the fisherman follow him into the hills that lay at the back of the sea-shore.

There he took him into a hidden pass that led to a secret lake where fish were to be seen so thick that those on the surface were lying on the fins of those below.

"Here thou mayst fish in peace," said the Jinni, "and with thy three casts a day bring home neither jackasses, nor broken pots nor brass bottles, but a wealth of merchandise." And with that he made off to see the world that he had not seen for a thousand years while the fisherman lived to enjoy a long and prosperous life.

Now this tale of the fisherman and the Jinni was concluded during the fourth night of Sheherezade's storytelling, and because there was yet more time before the day dawned she went on to begin:—

## THE TALE OF THE PORTER OF BAGHDAD

Who carried a great basket of provisions to the house of three wealthy ladies in the city and for his reward, he was allowed to stay and drink and eat with them and disport with them naked as they took their evening bath. And as Sheherezade told this story to the Shah

Shahryar the nights passed by and turned themselves to days, and
Sheherezade continually embroidered her tale so that:
the porter and the three ladies were joined by three Persian Kalandars (which
is to say Holy Men who live by begging), and each of these Kalandars had only
one eye;

and the porter and the ladies and the one-eyed Kalandars were then joined by
none other than the Caliph Harun-al-Rashid, and his Wazir, and Masrur his
Swordsman—all in disguise—who were walking through the town in quest of
adventures,

and the ladies prevailed upon the three Kalandars to tell the company how
each had come to lose his eye. Thus:
The First Kalandar lost his eye in revenge for an accident. For he was the son
of a king and one day, out hunting, he had shot an arrow into the eye of his
father's Wazir. Then, some years later, when that Wazir himself came to
power he caused the prince to be likewise blinded.

The Second Kalandar lost his eye through the violence of the Ifrit Jirjaris of
the seed of Iblis. For he, too, was the son of a king, but by ill fortune he roused
the wrath of the Ifrit who changed him into an ape. Only by the magical
shape-shiftings of another emperor's daughter was he able to recover his form,
but as he watched her battle with the Ifrit, the fire of their fury touched him
and he was blinded in one eye.

The Third Kalandar lost his eye in the manner that Bluebeard's wives lost
their heads. For in travelling the world he discovered a great palace, where
dwelt forty damsels of amazing beauty. They made him welcome and
entertained him as the king's son that he was, but after some time had passed
they had, perforce, to leave him on his own for the space of forty days. They
gave him keys to the doors of forty rooms in the palace, with injunctions that
he might go into thirty-nine of them but not the fortieth. But pride and
curiosity got the better of him and when he came to the fortieth door he
opened it and found within a black horse of majestic size. This he mounted,
and before he could command it, it flew off up into the air and carried him to a
mountain far from the palace and there it left him—flicking out one of his
eyes with its tail as it flew away.

Such were the stories told by the Kalandars to the Caliph of Baghdad and his
servants and the three ladies and their porter, and they pleased their audience
as much in the telling, as did Sheherezade the Shah Shahryar; and when those
stories were done she went on to recite:–

# THE TALE OF THE HUNCHBACK

## *His Lamentable Death*

Once upon a time, long years ago, in a city in China there lived a hunchback who was court jester to the sultan of that place. One night he was walking through the streets when he fell in with a tailor and his wife—a jovial pair who liked any excuse for a party. So the tailor and his wife invited the hunchback home for supper and the tailor went down to the bazaar and laid in a stock of fried fish and bread and lemons and sweetmeats for dessert.

While they were feasting off these good things, the tailor's wife, by way of a joke, picked up a chunk of fish and stuffed it into the hunchback's mouth, saying:

> "Now, by Allah, swallow, swallow;
> If you do not, naught will follow,"

and the hunchback duly gulped it down. But the Lord looked not kindly on the joke. There was a bone stuck in the chunk of fish, which lodged in the hunchback's gullet, and without more ado he choked—and died.

Great was the consternation of the tailor and his wife. "Truly, there is no Majesty and no Might, save in Allah!" cried the man. "How should such foolishness fashion such a fate?" But his wife said, "Leave thy wailing, this is what we must do . . ." and she schemed a scheme by which they would wrap the hunchback in a silken shawl and carry him to the doctor's, crying all the while that he was an infant child overcome with plague.

So this they did and the people on the streets avoided them everywhere. And when they came to the doctor's house they knocked at the door and told the slave who answered it, that they had brought a child who was sick with an unknown sickness. "Here is a silver piece," they said, "go and tell thy master to come down at once," and while the slave girl hastened off they took the hunchback into the hallway, propped him up neatly at the top of the staircase and hurried home as fast as they could.

Now the doctor was at supper with his wife, but when he saw the silver piece that the slave girl brought him he jumped up and rushed to meet the customers who were like to prove such valuable patients; and bustling along in the dark he did not notice the hunchback's corpse leant up against the top of the stairs. He banged into it and straightway it tumbled over and rolled down to the bottom, flump!

"Lights!" he cried, "lights!"—and when the girl brought a lamp and he saw the hunchback lying there stone dead he believed that he had died from the fall. "By Hippocrates!" he said, "I have killed a hunchback," and he rushed back up the stairs to his wife, moaning and flapping his arms. "Leave thy blethering," she said, "all things can be turned to good account. We will carry him up to the terrace roof and lower him down into the dinner-man's garden, and the dogs will come down and eat him up."

For it so happened that the doctor and his wife lived next door to the reeve who had control over the sultan's kitchen, and this reeve—whom they liked to call the dinner-man—was wont to bring home great stores of oil and fat and leftover meat and sheep's tails which he stored in his garden, where he was thus much plagued by the local rats and mice and cats and dogs, who broke in to steal the food. So the doctor and his wife carried the dead hunchback up to their open roof and then carefully lowered him down into the dinner-man's garden, where they contrived to prop him against the wall of the shed where he stored his foodstuffs.

Before long the dinner-man returned home from an evening reading of the Koran and what should he see but a shadowy figure skulking by his store-room. "Wah! By Allah," he said, "so it is men that rob me;" and he seized a hammer and knocked the hunchback on the head, clunk! At once the hunchback fell over and the dinner-man shone a lamp on him and discovered to his horror that he must have knocked him dead. "Aieee!" he cried, "a curse upon all sheep's tails and hunchbacks. Was it not enough that thou shouldst be a man of crumpled stature, and must thou be a robber too? Alas, alas, may the Veiler of all Secrets be with me in this enterprise." And he picked up the hunchback and carried him through the dark of the night to the bazaar, where he leant him against a wall as though he were a drunkard resting on his homeward way.

Soon after, along came the sultan's steward (who was indeed drunk), and stopped by the wall to attend to some urgent business. But when he saw this figure looming beside him, he thought it to be an assassin and he straightway smote him. "Actions first, questions later," said he to himself. But no sooner had he struck the hunchback once than he toppled over and the steward fell upon him and began pummelling him and shouting for help.

This brought the watchman of the bazaar with his lamp and his cudgel, and even though the drunken steward explained the provocation he had suffered from a hunchback who sought to steal his turban and all his worldly goods, there was no doubt that the hunchback himself was dead. So the steward was taken away for trial and was condemned to be hanged that very morning.

The gallows were put up; the torch-bearer came, who was also the local hangman; the governor came to approve the execution; and a great crowd assembled to watch the fun. But no sooner was it revealed that the steward was to be hanged for killing the hunchback in the bazaar than the dinner-man came forward crying, "Stay! stay! it was not he who killed the hunchback; it was I," and he related how he had found the marauding fellow in his garden, lurking to steal his meat.

"Very well," said the governor to the torch-man, "change 'em round. Hang up this man on his own confession."

But no sooner was the dinner-man ready to be hanged than up came the doctor, crying, "Stay! stay! it was not he who killed the hunchback; it was I," and he told how he had knocked him down the staircase in his haste to lay hands on his clients' silver pieces.

"Very well," said the governor to the torch-man, "change 'em round. Hang up this man on his own confession."

But no sooner was the doctor ready to be hanged than up came the tailor crying, "Stay! stay! it was not he who killed the hunchback; it was I," and he related the sad joke of the chunk of fish.

"Very well," said the governor to the torch-man, "change 'em round. Hang up this man on his own confession."

But by this time the torch-man on the scaffold was getting a trifle weary of all the chopping and changing and was beginning to lose interest in hanging anyone that day; while up at the court the sultan was beginning to wonder what had become of his hunchback jester, for he'd done all his duties for the morning and wanted some amusement. So when they told him that his hunchback was down at the scaffold, stone dead, while the torch-bearer was put to a deal of trouble because so many people had claimed to have killed him, the sultan decided he was being deprived of some curious entertainment. So he sent for his chamberlain and bade him go down to the scaffold, pay off the torch-bearer, and bring the variety of murderers before him.

## What Happened at the Sultan's Court

Well—
    There's no avail
    In a twice-told tale;
so we do not need to hear again the explanations that were given to the sultan, but when they were over he was mightily pleased and called for the whole to be written in letters of liquid gold. "For," said he, "did you ever hear a more

wondrous story than the four-times killing of my hunchback?"

Whether he meant the question for a statement or a challenge I do not know, but without more ado the sultan's steward came forward:

and the sultan's steward told what he took to be a wondrous story: a tale of a rich and handsome man who none the less stole gold for the love of a lady and lost his right hand thereby;

and he was followed by the dinner-man, who told what he took to be a wondrous story: a tale of a doctor of law, who gained entry to the harem of the Caliph Harun-al-Rashid and who married its stewardess, but who lost his thumbs and his big toes because he dared to make love to her while his hands were stained from eating garlic stew;

and he was followed by the doctor, who told what he took to be a wondrous story: a strange tale of love and jealousy, whereby the son of a merchant slept with the sister of his mistress and woke to find her murdered, and how he allowed his hand to be cut off rather than confess to what had happened.

And while all these tales pleased the sultan they seemed to him to be in no way so wondrous as the events concerning the hunchback, and it was left to the tailor to explain how, on the night when the hunchback died, he had first been to a marriage feast for one of his companions, which was attended by the guildsmen of the city: the tailors, the silk-spinners, the carpenters and so on.

Now in the course of the feasting there arrived a young man, of most handsome appearance, except that he was lame in one leg. As he came into the company, so he observed that among the guests there was a certain swarthy barber, and no sooner had he seen him than he turned and made to leave the feast. "For," said he, "I have sworn never to sit in the same place nor tarry in the same town as this black-faced barber of ill omen."

When he was prevailed upon to speak more of this matter it came to light that he had, some time before, been in love with one of the daughters of the great judge in Baghdad. By much contrivance he had arranged to be secretly transported into her chambers while her father was at prayers, but had determined first to be barbered and had therefore sent for the silentest and peaceablest barber who could be found in Baghdad. What should be his torment, however, when a barber came who claimed to be a silent man but who, at his own estimation, was:

an astrologer,
    an alchemist,
        a grammarian,
            a lexicographer,
            a logician,
                a rhetorician,
                    a mathematician,
                        an astronomer,
                        a theologian,
and a Master of the Traditions of the Apostle and the Commentaries of the
Koran. Not only did this Silent Barber talk so much that the young man was
late for his assignation, but he was also so curious about the conduct of the
affair that he caused mayhem round the house of the great judge, with the
result that the young man was tipped out of a window and broke his leg. So
who should wonder that, through losing his lady and losing his limberness, he
should never wish to see the barber again.

For his part, however, the barber gave token of the truth of all that the
young man said, first by telling the assembled company at the marriage feast
of his fame as a Silent Man and then by embarking upon six inconsequential
tales, one for each of his brothers: the Prattler, the Babbler, the Gabbler, the
Long-necked Gugglet, the Whiffler, and the Man of Many Clamours—as a
result of which the tailor and his friends locked the barber in a cupboard and
there let him rest till his tongue should have cooled down.

"In sooth," cried the sultan, "I should like to see this barber," and straightway he was sent for and released from his cupboard and came before the sultan, where were also to be found the tailor and the doctor and the dinner-man and the steward and the corpse of the hunchback. They explained to him how this audience had come into being to hear his adventures, but before he could ever begin, he looked round the faces of them all and then laughed till he fell over backwards.

"Truly," he said, "there is a wonder in every death, but the death of this hunchback is indeed worthy to be written in letters of liquid gold!" And he went over to where the corpse was lying and took from his barber's bag a little pot of ointment, with which he anointed the hunchback's throat, then he drew out the chunk of fish with its bone, all soaked in blood. Thereupon the hunchback sneezed, like one who has eaten raw horse-radish, and jumped up as if nothing had happened.

From that day forth he continued to jest before the sultan, just as the tailor tailored, the doctor doctored, the dinner-man dined, the steward stewed and the barber barbered until there came to them all, each in his turn, the Destroyer of Delights and the Sunderer of Societies.

And when Sheherezade had completed the Tale of the
Hunchback she went on to tell more tales of the kings and
princes of the land. She told too, out of her recollection, fables
of the birds and beasts, among which was:—

## THE FABLE OF THE BIRDS AND THE BEASTS
## AND THE CARPENTER

In times of yore a peacock lived with his wife on a piece of land beside the
sea. But the place was infested with lions and all manner of wild beasts so
the two birds sought for some other abode and eventually happened upon
an island, verdant with trees and fresh with running streams.

Now while the birds were enjoying the fruits and the waters of their new
home there came before them a duck, flapping its wings and crying in terror,
"Beware, and again I say beware, of the Sons of Adam!" But the peacocks
spoke comfortingly to the duck, saying that they would defend her against all
creatures, and that anyway there could be no Sons of Adam upon this island.

"Alhamdohlillah!" cried the duck, "glory to God for your kindness, but
you must know that the Sons of Adam have learned how to traverse the
waters of the sea and that there is none like them for mischief and crafty
cunning." And the duck went on to relate how one day she had been warned
in a dream to flee the Sons of Adam and how in her wanderings she had come
upon the whelp of a lion sitting at the door of a cave.

"Draw near," called the lion, "and tell me thy name and nature."

"My name is Duck, and I am of the bird-kind; and what of thee?"

"My name is Lion. My father hath warned me against those creatures
named the Sons of Adam and I am seeking them across the world that I may
kill them."

So Duck was glad to travel under the protection of Lion, and they had not
gone very far before they saw a cloud of dust approaching them. As it came
near they perceived at its centre a running naked ass, tearing across the land.

"Hark ye, crack-brain!" called Lion. "What is thy name and nature?"

"O Son of the Sultan, I am Ass and I am fleeing a Son of Adam."

"Whyso? Dost thou fear he will kill thee?"

"Nay, O Son of the Sultan, but I fear his cheating ways, for he hath a thing
called a Pack-saddle which he setteth on my back, and a thing called Girths
which he bindeth about my belly, and a thing called a Crupper which he
putteth beneath my tail, and a thing called a Bit which he placeth in my

mouth; and he fashioneth a Goad to drive me to do his bidding and carry his wares. And when I can work no more he will kill me and cast me on the rubbish heap for dogs.''

''Fear not,'' said the lion whelp, ''for Duck and I will defend thee,'' and they continued on their way. They had not gone far before they saw another cloud of dust approaching them across the plain, and this proved to be a black horse with a silver blaze on his forehead.

''Come hither, majestic beast,'' called Lion, ''and tell us thy name and nature.''

''I am Horse of the horse-kind and I am fleeing a Son of Adam.''

''Whyso? How should so mighty a creature as thyself be afraid of a Son of Adam when one such as I is seeking only to meet and slay him? Surely one kick from one of thy hoofs would prevail against him?''

''Nay, O Prince,'' said Horse, ''do not be deluded; for he hath a thing called a Hobble which shall prevent me from doing so, and when he is minded to ride me he hath a Saddle and Girths and a Bit and a Rein with which to make me do

his bidding. Then when I grow old and can no longer run for him he will sell me to the miller to grind corn and the miller, in his turn, will sell me to the knacker, who will cut my throat and flay my hide, and pluck out my tail for the sieve-maker, and boil my fat for tallow candles.''

When the lion whelp heard these words his rage against this Son of Adam increased and he sought directions from Horse where they might find the creature; and before they had gone far they encountered a furious camel, gurgling and pawing the earth with his feet. This mighty beast the lion whelp took to be a Son of Adam, but before he could spring at him and tear him to pieces Duck explained that his name was Camel, and Camel explained that he was himself fleeing from a Son of Adam.

''Whyso? Surely with one kick of thy hoof thou wouldst slay him?''

''Nay, O Prince,'' said Camel, ''for he is a creature of wily ways and he putteth into my nostrils a twine of goat's hair called a Nose-ring, and over my head a thing called a Halter and he delivers me to the least of his children to

lead about the world; and when I am old and good for nothing he selleth me to the knacker who cuts my throat and makes over my hide to the tanners and my flesh to the cooks.''

"Where didst thou leave this Son of Adam?" asked the lion whelp.

"Why, even now he cometh after me and I am away now to the wilds where he will not find me.''

"Nay, O Camel, stay with us and thou wilt see how I shall tear him to pieces and crunch his bones and drink his blood . . ."

And as Lion was speaking there came towards them a little, old, bent, lean man, carrying on his shoulders a basket of carpenter's tools and on his head a branch of a tree and eight planks. When Lion saw him he walked towards him and the man smiled at him and said: "O King, who defendeth these creatures from harm, Allah prosper thy ways and strengthen thee, that thou mayst protect me too!"

"Whyso? What is thy name and nature—for assuredly thou art a beast the like of which I have never seen before and I would wish to aid thee, if only for the eloquence of thy words."

"O Lord of wild beasts, I am a carpenter, and I am journeying to thy father's wazir, the lynx, to make for him a shelter against the Sons of Adam. For he knows the ways of those creatures and he would have a house wherein he might dwell and fend off his enemies."

Now when he heard this the lion whelp grew envious of the lynx and he said to the carpenter, "By my life, I will have you make a house for me with those planks before ever you go to Sir Lynx."

"O Lord of wild beasts," said the carpenter, "that may not be. I will go first to the lynx and then return to thy service and build thee a house."

"By Allah," roared Lion, "thou shalt not leave this place till thou build me a house of planks!" and he sprang at the carpenter so that he fell over and his gear fell to the ground. "Yea; thou mayst in truth fear the Sons of Adam, O Carpenter, for thou art a feeble beast with no force to protect thee."

But the carpenter got up and smiled at Lion, saying, "Well, I will make for thee a house." And he took his planks and nailed together a dwelling in the form of a chest after the measure of a young lion. And he left one end free for a door and he took hammer and nails and said to Lion, "Enter the house through this opening, that I may fit it to thy measure."

So the whelp rejoiced that he had his way and he crept through the opening into the house. Once he was inside, the carpenter whipped the lid on to the opening and nailed it down.

"O Carpenter," cried Lion, "what is this narrow house thou hast made for me? Open the gate and let me out!"

"Alas!" said the carpenter, "I am but feeble and lacking in force and I know not what may befall me if I release you once more among these creatures here. Perhaps I shall send for the lynx, that he may inspect my capacities as a builder of houses."

And with that Ass and Horse and Camel—and even Duck—knew that this was a Son of Adam and they took their ways in haste lest the carpenter should build dwellings for them too.

And after telling that fable Sheherezade went on to tell how there are indeed no limits to greed and betrayal. Firstly she told:—

## THE FABLE OF THE WOLF AND THE FOX

Some time ago a wolf and a fox set up house together. But the wolf was forever tyrannizing the fox, putting him in his place like a servant, buffeting him, and doing down all his offers of friendship. The fox smiled through it all though, but in his heart he said, "There is no help for it; I must encompass the destruction of this wolf."

Now one day the fox came upon a vineyard, and as he walked round it he saw a hole made in part of its wall. But experience had taught him to be wary of such pretty invitations and he crept carefully up to the hole and looked at it closely. And indeed it was a trap, for the owner of the vineyard had dug a deep pit beyond it, lightly covered with a mat of sticks, to catch whatever wild beasts were foolhardy enough to come in to the vineyard through the hole.

So the fox said to himself:

"To refrain
Is to gain—

Praise be to Allah that I was so cautious; but let me see what my friend the wolf thinks of this."

So the fox returned home and said to the wolf, "Allah hath made plain for thee a way into the vineyard."

"How should that be?" said the wolf, "how can such a one as thou know such a thing?"

"Why," said the fox, "I went to the vineyard myself. I saw that the owner was dead (torn to pieces by wolves, so they say) and there was the fruit shining amongst the vines."

The wolf doubted not so precise a report as this and his gluttony was aroused and he set off for the vineyard, with the fox not far behind him.

"There," said the fox, directing him to the fallen wall, "thou mayst enter without the trouble of climbing a ladder," and the wolf jumped and fell straight into the pit.

At this the fox sat back on his haunches and laughed with his chops wide open and his tongue hanging out. But before long he heard the wolf in the pit lamenting and crying, so he, too, put on a sad, tearful face and looked over the

side of the hole. "Why, Friend Fox," said the wolf, "I see that thou, too, art saddened by this dismal fate that has befallen me—but can we not devise a means by which I may escape this pit?"

"Nay, nay, Friend Wolf," said the fox, "do not misunderstand me. I do not weep for thy plight, but for all the long life that has passed, when thou demeaned me and smote me; and I weep that thou didst not fall into this pit months ago." And with that the wolf and the fox fell to arguing over their past life together, and eventually it seemed that the wolf repented. "In truth," he said, "I have woefully wronged thee, but if Allah deliver me from this pit I will assuredly reform my ways, take on the mantle of holiness, and go upon the mountains like a pilgrim praising Him."

At these humble words the fox took pity on the wolf and, coming up to the pit, he turned and dangled his tail over the edge so that the wolf might seize it and drag himself out. But no sooner had he done so than the wolf gave one big tug to his tail and pulled him into the pit as well. "So-ho!" he said, "thou fox of little mercy, once minute thou art up there laughing at me, and the next thou art down here once more under my dominion. Assuredly I will hasten to slay thee before thou seest me slain."

"Aha!" said the fox to himself, "now am I indeed fallen back into the snare of the tyrant and I must use all my craft and cunning to escape this foe." And forthwith he began to argue with the wolf, saying that he had offered help only because the wolf had repented and turned to Allah and that it would do his case no good if they both were to die in the pit, but that they might yet both be saved. "If thou stand up at thy full height," he said, "and I climb on thy back so that I come near the top of the hole, then may I spring and reach the ground and fetch the wherewithal to rescue thee."

The wolf placed no trust in this plan, but he perceived that there might be no other way of getting out of the pit, so he permitted the fox to mount his shoulders, raised himself up to his full height, and the fox jumped out of the pit like a chestnut jumping out of the fire. "O double-deceiver," he cried to the wolf, "make sure of thy repentance and call truly to Allah, for I will never trust thee again."

And at that he climbed on the wall overlooking the vineyard and cried to the men working among the vines that a wolf was fallen into the pit. And as all the men came running with sticks and stones to slay the wolf, the fox walked quietly down to the vineyard and ate up all the grapes.

And then Sheherezade went on to tell:–

## THE FABLE OF THE MONGOOSE AND THE MOUSE

Once upon a time there lived together in the house of an old farmer a mongoose and a mouse, sharing and sharing whatever food they might come by. Now it so happened that the farmer fell sick and the village doctor ordered that he should be given a diet of sesame seeds with the husks taken off. So the farmer's wife sought a measure of sesame from her neighbours and she steeped it in water, took off the husks and spread it out to dry; then she went about her tasks in the fields.

Well, the mongoose observed these goings-on, which seemed to him like the preparation of a banquet for mongooses, and when the farmer's wife went out he came in and began to carry off the husked sesame to his dwelling behind the wall. He laboured at the work all day, and by the evening, when the farmer's wife came back, she found only a few seeds left on the table.

"By Allah!" she said, "there is a thief at work," and she sat down with a cudgel and watched.

After a time the mongoose came out of his hole to bring in all that remained for his feast. However, he perceived the farmer's wife with her cudgel and he said to himself, "So-ho, this lady may be after taking the skins off more than sesame seeds. It behoves me to be prudent," and he straightway returned to his hole and began to carry forth the seeds that he had already collected and lay them back among the rest.

"Forsooth," said the farmer's wife, "this creature cannot be the cause of our loss for he brings the sesame back from the hole of him who stole it. Kindness must surely be the reward of kindness." And she held her hand and continued to sit and watch.

Now the mongoose guessed what she might be thinking and when he saw his companion the mouse, he said, "O my sister, I should not be a good neighbour to you if I did not tell you that our hosts out there, the farmer and his wife, have brought home a feast of sesame. They have eaten their fill of it, and now there are leavings fit for the king and queen of the mice, strewn all over the table."

So, squeaking for joy, the mouse ran from her hole and frisked and frolicked amongst the grain which the mongoose had so diligently returned to the table.

And when the farmer's wife saw this she deduced that here was the culprit and she smote the mouse with her cudgel, bonk!

From that day forth the mongoose lived a life of ease and contentment, cared for by the farmer's wife and not sharing a morsel with anyone.

When these fables were told Sheherezade went on to relate to the Shah Shahryar many extravagant stories of the kings and caliphs of Arabia.

There was, for instance:
The Pathetic Tale of Ali bin Bakkar and Shams al-Nahar and their unrequited love;

The Fantastic Tale of Kamar al-Zaman who chose never to wed mortal woman but changed his mind when the spirits of the air brought to him, as though in a dream, the Princess Budur, who had chosen never to wed a mortal man; and

The Strange Tale of Mohammed bin Ali, the jeweller, who pretended to be the Caliph of Baghdad out of frustrated love for the Lady Dunya, the sister of the Caliph's Wazir.

And after such tales as these Sheherezade told:—

# THE TALE OF THE EBONY HORSE

## *His Coming*

In times gone by there lived a great and generous Emperor of the Persians and he had one son and three daughters—all as radiant as the full moon.

Every year the Emperor was accustomed to hold two festivals, at the time of the New Year and at the Autumn Equinox, when his palace would be open to all who cared to enter and when there would be much rejoicing and giving of gifts. And so it came about that one year three sages came questing to the palace, bringing curious presents by which they hoped to obtain betrothal to the Emperor's three daughters.

The first sage, who was from India, laid before the Emperor the carved figure of a man, inlaid with jewels and bearing a golden trumpet. "What then is the virtue of this gift?" asked the Emperor, and the Indian sage explained that the figure had only to be set up at the gate of the city for it to be guardian over all. "If an enemy approaches," said the sage, "it will blow a blast on this clarion-trumpet and he will be seized of a palsy and drop down dead." So the trumpeter was set up at the gate and the sage was granted the hand of the Emperor's eldest daughter in marriage.

The second sage, who was from Greece, laid before the Emperor a basin of silver in whose midst was fashioned a peacock and twenty-four chicks all of beaten gold. "What then is the virtue of this gift?" asked the Emperor, and the

[ 55 ]

Grecian sage explained that for every hour that passed of the day or night, the peacock would cry and peck one of its twenty-four chicks and flap its wings, and then at the end of the month it would open its beak so that the new crescent moon could be seen inside. And even as he spoke, an hour struck and the peacock cried and pecked and flapped its wings, so the Emperor was well pleased and granted the sage the hand of his second daughter in marriage.

Then there stepped forward the third sage, who was a Persian necromancer, an old man an hundred years old, with white hair and a face like a cobbler's apron: sunken forehead, mangy eyebrows, red goggle eyes, pendulous lips and a nose like a big black aubergine. His gift to the Emperor was a horse, fashioned full-size out of ebony, inlaid with gold and jewels, and harnessed up with saddle, bridle and stirrups. "What then is the virtue of this gift?" asked the Emperor, and the sage replied that one had only to mount the horse and prepare oneself aright, to be able to fly through the air and cover the space of a year in a single day. So the Emperor thanked the Persian magician and granted him the hand of his youngest daughter in marriage.

Now it so happened that the Emperor's daughters had been hiding behind a curtain to watch all these proceedings and when the youngest daughter perceived who her husband was to be, she fled to her chamber and began weeping and wailing and tearing at her hair and her garments. This racket

came to the ears of her brother, Kamar al-Akmar, the Moon of Moons, who had just returned from hunting, and he went up to her room and asked her the cause of her distress. "O my brother," she cried, "know that there has come to court this festival day a dreadful magician, with a face like the Jinni who frightens the poultry in the hen-houses; he has given to our father as a gift a horse made of black wood, to which our father has returned him a

promise that he may have my hand in marriage. Alas, that I should ever have been born."

When her brother heard this, he soothed her as best he could and made his way to the Emperor and said, "Who is this wizard with a face like an ill-made pot who hath bewitched thee into giving away my sister? What is this gift of his that has brought her to such misery?" So the Emperor told him of the visit of the sages and sent servants to fetch the ebony horse and show it to him, little knowing that the Persian wizard had been standing nearby, had heard everything and was filled with mortification and anger.

So when the servants brought the ebony horse and the Prince mounted it to try its virtues, the sage stepped forward as though to instruct him. "Trill this," he said, pointing to a pin on the side of the horse's head, and the Prince had no sooner turned it than the ebony horse seemed to take breath and soared off into the air, with the Prince sitting astride its back.

"Very well," said the Emperor, "but tell me, O sage, how may he turn the horse and how make it descend?"

"Alas, my lord," said the sage, "I can do nothing, and we may never see him again till Resurrection-day, for he was so proud and eager to be off that he did not stay to ask me what mechanism he might use to bring the creature back to the ground." And the magician smiled grimly, for he had so contrived it to be revenged upon the Prince for seeking to thwart his marriage. But the Emperor was himself angry and he ordered that the sorcerer be at once clapped into jail and there bastinadoed on the soles of his feet.

## What Happened to the Prince

When he felt the ebony horse move under him and then rise in the air, the Prince was filled with great joy. Never in his years of hunting had he travelled so fast or seen so far as now. But as the horse made unswervingly towards the sun the Prince became troubled in his mind as to how he might turn the beast round, let alone bring it down. "Verily," he said to himself, "this is a device of the sage to destroy me for championing my sister."

For a huntsman, though, he was not without wit, and he fell to examining the carcass of his horse in the belief that one pin for setting off might be matched by another pin for setting down and, behold! beneath the carved shoulders of the horse he found what seemed to be two ornamental cocks' heads, and as he twisted one, so he was able to steer the horse and as he twisted the other, so he was able to bring it into a gradual descent. Thus he passed over mountains and deserts, oceans and forests, even to the boundaries of China.

By this time the day was waning and he determined to find somewhere he might pass the night, and he saw below him a fine city with, in its centre, the towers and battlements of a majestic castle. "This is a goodly place," he said to himself, and he turned the pin to descend and the horse sank down with him like a weary bird and alighted gently on the terrace roof of the castle:

"Alhamdohlillah," said the Prince, "praise be to Allah for my safe journeying," and since, by now, the night had fallen he set off through the sleeping palace to see if he might find food and water for himself. First he came to a staircase which took him down to a court paved with white marble and alabaster, shining in the light of the moon; then he traversed chambers and passage-ways, all unguarded and empty, until eventually he came upon the entrance to the harem, at whose door slept a giant eunuch as though he were a tribesman of the Jinn, longer than lumber and broader than a bench. Beside him was his sword, whose pommel gleamed in the candle flames, and above his head on a column of granite there hung a leather bag.

Praying again to Allah, the Prince carefully lifted down the bag and found within it a great store of provisions with which he refreshed himself. He then replaced the bag and, taking the eunuch's sword, he crept forward to where Destiny should take him.

Beyond the door of the harem there was a second door, with a curtain
before it. This he raised and beyond it he saw a couch of white ivory, inlaid with
pearls. Slave girls were sleeping at its corners and upon the couch itself there
slept a lady, beautiful as the moon, and robed only in her hair. The Prince was
overcome by her loveliness and, caring nothing for discovery or death, he
went up to her and kissed her on the cheek. At once she awoke, opened her
eyes and said, "Who art thou and whence camest thou?" to which the Prince
replied, "I am thy slave and thy lover."

"But who brought thee hither?"

"My Lord and my fortune."

Now it so happened that only the day before, the lady's father, who was
King of that land, had had audience of the King of Hind who sought to marry
her; but the King of Hind was ugly and uncouth and had been sent away, but
the lady believed that our Prince was he and she deemed it most blameworthy
that she should be denied one so handsome. So she set about shouting with
anguish, at which her slave girls all woke up and before long the palace was in
uproar. The slave girls woke up the eunuch; the eunuch, missing his sword,
believed that bandits had come to the palace and rushed to wake the King; the
King called up his household guard and everyone ran pell-mell to the
Princess's bedroom, where she continued to wail that she had been cheated
of her lover, and where the Prince Kamar al-Akmar was lost in wonder at
all the hubbub.

[ 61 ]

Eventually the eunuch explained to the King that he thought vandals had stolen his sword, and the slave girls explained to the eunuch that he had allowed a man to enter the harem, and the Princess explained to the slave girls that she wanted to marry the Prince, whether he came from Hind or no, and the Prince politely said to all and sundry that he would be glad to sign the marriage-contract as soon as it was indited.

None of this could assuage the wrath of the King, though, who did not care for strangers to make themselves so free with his daughter before ever he had been introduced. "How can we know," he cried, "that thou art an Emperor's son as thou sayst? What Emperor shall save thee if I call upon my slaves and servants to put thee to the vilest of deaths?" To which the Prince replied that he would be pleased to stand in single combat for his honour against the King himself or else stand against the King's whole army to gain his daughter's hand.

Well, the King had no liking for single combat against one so doughty as this strange prince, so it was agreed that next morning he should confront the King's whole army, and that was forty thousand horsemen and a like number of slaves and followers. "This Prince, for his honour," cried the King when all were assembled, "this Prince pretendeth that he can overcome you in combat to gain the hand of my daughter and that, were you an hundred thousand, he would force you to flight, so when he comes upon you, show him that he has chosen a mighty task." Then, turning to the Prince, he said, "Up, my son, and slaughter my army."

But the Prince turned to the King and said, "My Lord, how shall I come against this host without any horse?" To which the King gave answer that he might choose any mount from the King's own stables. "But not one of those horses pleaseth me," said the Prince, "I will ride none other but the horse on which I came."

"Then where is thy horse?" asked the King.

"Atop thy palace," answered the Prince.

"Where in my palace?" asked the King.

"On the roof," answered the Prince—and with those words it seemed to the King that this comely, daring fellow was indeed mad.

"How can a horse be on the roof!" he cried; but he forthwith sent servants back to the palace with instructions to bring back whatever they might find on the roof and before long they returned bearing the ebony horse, which, gallant as it looked (and though it was indeed on the roof), hardly seemed a fit charger to accost the King's whole army. "Is this then thy horse?" asked the King.

"Yes, O King, this is my horse; and if thou wilt bid thy troops retire a bowshot from it then I will mount and charge."

So the troops withdrew and the Prince climbed into the saddle and forthwith trilled the pin of ascent; and as everyone watched to see him charge, the horse began to rock and sway as though it were taking great breaths, and then it rose in the air and flew off over the heads of the waiting troops. "Catch him! Catch him!" cried the King; but his Wazirs and ministers replied, "Oh who can overtake a flying bird?" and as the Prince fled away in the sky, the army was left to return to quarters and the King's daughter relapsed into tears and grief.

"By Allah!" she cried, "I will neither eat nor drink nor sleep till Allah return him to me."

## The Homecoming of the Ebony Horse

Once the Prince had contrived his flight from the King he set his horse's head in the direction of his homeland and before nightfall he was again in the palace of his father. But how changed everything was. For now, instead of the bright traffic of the festival day, all was still and shrouded, with black hangings on the walls and ashes strewn upon the floor; and when he made his way to the Emperor's chamber he found his father and mother and his sisters clad in the black robes of mourning and pale with grief.

When he entered the room though, they started up in surprise for it was his supposed death that they had been mourning, and before long they were clambering over him, hugging and kissing him and shouting for joy. The Emperor ordered a great banquet to be prepared and a holiday was proclaimed throughout the land. Streets and markets were hung with garlands, drums and cymbals were beaten, and a general pardon was given to all who were imprisoned (including, not least, the Persian necromancer, who was rewarded with robes and honour now that the ebony horse had returned, but of whose marriage to the King's youngest daughter nothing more was said).

Amid all the merriment, however, the Prince felt little but sadness and longing for the Princess that he had left behind so far away. He confessed his love to his father, the Emperor, saying that he was determined once more to mount his ebony horse and ride to find her, and his father gave his consent—although privately he wished to make nothing more than a bonfire of the horse and its tricks.

So the Prince rode once more into the sky and made his way to that palace roof where he had alighted so few days ago. He made his way quietly to the harem, finding the eunuch asleep as usual; but when he came to the Princess's chamber there was little need for quietness since she was still wailing and bawling over the loss of the Prince who had flown away. As soon as she saw

him, however, she was struck dumb with wonder, and when he suggested that
she might this time ride back with him to his father's kingdom she was
overwhelmed with joy. She dressed herself in the richest of her dresses,
furnished herself with all manner of gold ornaments and jewels, and the
Prince then carried her up to the terrace roof where the ebony horse patiently
waited. They climbed on its back and the Prince secured the Princess to him
with bonds of silk, twisted the pin to ascend and away they flew over forests
and oceans, deserts and mountains, back to the land of Persia.

When the city of the Emperor came in sight, the Prince determined that he
would take his bride to one of the pavilions in the Emperor's garden where she
might rest awhile, before he summoned his father and the royal court to greet
her. Accordingly, he caused the horse to alight in a secluded corner of the
grounds and there he left the Princess, seated in a summer-house, while he
went to announce their arrival. ''Rest here,'' he said, ''and watch over our
horse, until I, or my messenger, come to thee to bring thee an Emperor's
welcome to this land,'' and he forthwith betook himself to the palace to give
tidings of their coming to his father and his family.

Great was the joy at his return. The Emperor straightway ordered a continuance of the general rejoicing and prepared a great train of courtiers and ministers, members of the royal household, slaves and eunuchs to go to make welcome the Princess. He himself led the procession and to the music of drums and trumpets they made their way across the gardens to the summer-house.

But when they arrived, they discovered with dismay and consternation that no one was there. The Princess and the ebony horse had gone.

## What Happened to the Princess

Now it so chanced that when the Prince brought the ebony horse to rest in his father's demesne he was observed by the Persian necromancer who was in the garden seeking herbs and simples for his cauldron. With great caution, therefore, he slunk over to the pavilion and overheard the last of the Prince's conversation with his bride.

Allowing a suitable amount of time to elapse, the wizard then made his way to the Princess, bowed down before her and kissed the ground between his hands. "And who art thou?" asked the Princess, not a little alarmed at the sudden appearance of a man of such monstrous ugliness.

"O my lady," said the wizard, "I come from the Prince, who hath bidden me to conduct thee to the palace of his father."

"Why came he not himself? And could he not find a messenger more handsome for this joyous occasion?"

"Ah, my lady," said the wizard, "he is even now preparing a royal greeting for thee; while as to myself, is it not fitting that so bright a jewel as thou art, should be set off against so plain an attendant as I?"

"Very well," she said, "then let us go forward to the Prince. But what hast thou brought for me to ride?"

"O my lady, thou mayst ride the horse that thou camest on."

"But I cannot ride it myself."

"Then I must needs accompany thee," said the magician, and he mounted the ebony horse, took the Princess up behind him, and after binding her securely in her seat he trilled the ascent-pin and the horse gathered itself and rose into the air. Away it went, beyond the confines of the palace, beyond the city—over the hills and far away.

"Ho thou," cried the Princess, "where goest thou? Where is the Prince?"

"Allah damn the Prince," cried the magician, "he is a mean, skinflint knave!"

"Then woe to thee, that thou disobeyest thy Lord's commandment!"

[ 66 ]

"He is no Lord of mine, but rather my enemy. For thou must know that I am the creator and master of this horse, which he took from me by a stratagem, and now that I have it again I shall never relinquish it. Thou and I shall fare forward into a new life of power and riches." And he turned the horse's head towards the west and ceased not to ride till they reached the land of the Greeks where he brought them all to rest in a green meadow by a stream.

Now this meadow lay close to the city of a great Grecian king, who at that time was walking nearby in the cool of the evening. When he saw this strange pair with their wooden horse, the rough-visaged Persian and the comely lady, he deemed some mystery was afoot and he sent his slaves to take them and bring them to audience at his royal palace.

"Who art thou?" he asked, "and whence comest thou with thy toy horse?"

"We are of Persia," said the magician, "way-worn travellers, man and wife." But the lady would not hear of such a thing. "O King," she cried, "that is not so. He is naught but a wicked necromancer who has stolen me away by force and fraud . . ." and she prostrated herself before the King.

Well, there seemed little doubt as to the truth of her denunciations, and the Grecian king ordered the sage to be taken to prison and there (again) bastinadoed. The mysterious horse he placed within his treasure-house, and the lady within his harem where she fell to weeping and wailing so that none could come near her.

## And How it All Ended

Now when the Prince Kamar al-Akmar discovered the summer-house empty in the garden, with horse and Princess gone, he realized that their disappearance could only be the work of the Persian necromancer, for he alone knew the secret mechanisms of the horse's flight. So the Prince bade farewell to his father and his family and set out into the world to find the villain.

He travelled through many lands, inquiring if people had heard tell of a strange horse of ebony that flew down out of the sky—but apart from suggestions made about the state of his own wits he was told nothing. Then one day, arriving at a certain khan, he came upon some merchants talking and overheard one of them tell how in such-and-such a city in Greece the King had come upon an ill-assorted couple—a foul-visaged Persian and a beautiful maiden—standing beside a wooden horse which they seemed to have carried to the middle of a field but could carry no further.

At once the Prince besought the merchant for a closer account of what he had heard, and when he had ascertained the name and region of the city he turned his steps towards that part of Greece and did not rest until he was outside its walls. When he arrived, though, it was evening and he was taken into the gatehouse to be questioned and to be held for the night. "Where are you from?" they asked.

"I am a Persian from Persia," he replied, at which the guardsmen fell back with laughter (for in those days the Persians were deemed great liars and the Greeks had a joke about one of them who said, "I am a Persian, but I am not lying now"). "Ho, ho," said the guard, "well let's hope that that is not so great a lie as the ones we have been hearing from that other Persian traveller who even now is taking his ease in our prison." And he went on to tell the story of the King's discovery of the magician and the Princess, how the one kept speaking of a horse that flew through the air and how the other was in a fit of madness, wailing and raving, so that never a doctor could get near to cure her—for the King had fallen madly in love with her and was seeking physicians from all quarters of the earth who might mend her wits.

From these words the Prince gained some notion of how he might proceed in his plan to rescue the Princess, and the next morning, when he was brought before the King, he put out that he was a travelling doctor come to try to cure the Princess's madness. So the King had him taken to the chamber where the Princess was kept and there he found her, not possessed of any evil Jinn, but writhing and wringing her hands that none might approach her.

When the Prince saw her thus he bade her attendants leave the room and he stepped towards her saying, "No harm shall betide thee, O ravishment of the

three worlds"; and when she perceived who spoke she fell down as though in a swoon. Then the Prince went up to her and whispered to her to be calm and patient. She was now to pretend to be cured and was to speak kindly to the King who sought her love, and if Allah willed then they would reach an end of their tribulations.

Then the Prince returned to the King and bade him go in to the woman, for he had taken away her madness. "But beware," he said, "for the completion of her cure it behoveth that thou go forth with all thy guards to the place where thou foundest her, nor shouldst thou forget the beast of black wood which was with her. Therein lies a devil and unless I exorcise him he will return to her and afflict her again."

So the King did as this physician asked. He visited the Princess and was filled with joy at the sweetness of her recovery and he bade his servants bathe her and dress her royally in fine robes and jewels. Then he and the Princess and all the army moved out to the field where first he had seen her and there on the sward they had set up the ebony horse.

"My lord the King," said the Prince, "with thy leave and at thy word I will now proceed to fumigations and conjurations, that we may drive the evil spirit from this horse; but I must first place the damsel upon its back that we may observe whether or no there be a conjunction of spirits." And so, placing the Princess on the horse's back, he jumped into the saddle and urging her to cling to him tightly, he trilled the pin of ascent. The horse shuddered again as though it were drawing breath and forthwith rode up out of the field and over the heads of the King and his army and away across the seas to Persia.

Then was the marriage of the Princess to Prince Kamar al-Akmar indeed celebrated and messages of joy and consolation were despatched to the Princess's father that he might know of his daughter's happiness. As for the Persian magician, for all we know he continued to elaborate his spells in the Greek King's prison till the end of his days, and as for the ebony horse, the Emperor gained his wish and it was burned on a bonfire on the Prince's wedding-night.

When this Tale of the Ebony Horse was finished, Dunyazad pleaded with Sheherezade to tell the Sultan the jests she knew of the pride and foolishness of men, and amongst a score of stories there was none that pleased the Shah Shahryar more than:—

# THE TALE WHICH ALI THE PERSIAN TOLD
# TO AMUSE HARUN AL-RASHID

Know thou, O Commander of the Faithful (said the Persian to Harun), that some years ago I took it into my head to leave Baghdad, and go a-travelling; and I had with me a boy who carried my leather bag.

Now one day, as we were passing through a certain city, a rascally Kurdish man fell upon us, seized the bag and cried out that we had stolen it from him. "How can that be," I said, "seeing that I have brought it with me from Baghdad?" But he would not believe me and there was nothing for it but we must take the matter before the magistrate.

"What brings you here and what is your quarrel?" asked the justice.

"Allah preserve your lordship," said the Kurdish man, "but this Persian vagabond claims to have brought that bag from Baghdad, but the bag is in truth no Baghdad bag at all but my bag, bagging up all my rightful belongings."

"When did you lose it?" asked the justice.

"But yesterday," said the Kurd.

"Well, if it's yours," said the justice, "tell me what is in it."

"Why," said the Kurd, "that bag contains:

two silver brushes for eye-powder and antimony for the eyes,
a handkerchief, wrapping up two gilt cups and two candlesticks,

two tents with two plates, two spoons and a cushion,

two leather rugs, two jugs and a brass tray,

[ 73 ]

two basins, two water-jars and a pot with a ladle,

two sacks, two saddles and a needle,

two sheep, two lambs and a she-goat,

two dogs, two bitches and a she-cat,

two green pavilions with a camel and two she-camels,

a lioness, two lions and a she-bear,

two jackals and a mattress,

[ 74 ]

two sofas and an upper-chamber,

two saloons and a portico, and a whole company of Kurds who will bear witness that this
bag is my bag."

Then the judge turned to me and said, "Well, sir, and what do you say?"
So I came forward in great bewilderment and said:
"Allah preserve your lordship, but in truth there is nothing in this bag save:

a little ruined tenement and a dog-house,

a boys' school with the boys playing dice,

and several tents and tent-ropes,

and an ironsmith's forge          and a fishing-net,

and the cities of Baghdad and Basra, with the palace of Shaddad-bin-Ad
and a thousand citizens who will bear witness that this is my bag.''

So when he heard this the Kurdish man wept and wailed and cried again a
great long list of all the things that were in the bag, to which I could only reply
with a list of equal length.

''Well, then,'' said the justice, ''I can see that you two are little more than
pestilential fellows, come to waste the time of all learned judges and
magistrates. Never yet, from China to Shajarat Umm Ghaylan, or from Persia
to Sudan, or from Wadi Nu'uman to Khorasan, did I hear of a bag so
bottomless as this.'' And he bade his servants open the bag . . . and there was
inside it:

a knob of cheese,   a lemon   and two olives.

So I gave the bag to the Kurdish man and went my way.

 And when Sheherezade had told this tale which Ali the Persian
had told to the Caliph Harun al-Rashid, she went on to relate
little stories of the generosity of the Caliph and of his Wazir,
Ja'afer, and she also told the story of :–

# MA'AN BIN-ZAIDAH, THE DONKEY
# AND THE CUCUMBERS

Now the Emir Ma'an bin-Zaidah was a man of great wealth and
generosity. One day he was out hunting and came upon a herd of
gazelles which he and his men pursued, each one to a different point
of the compass. And Ma'an ran down the gazelle that he was chasing and
slaughtered it, and while he was cutting and dressing it he saw an old man
riding out of the desert on a donkey.

"Greetings," said Ma'an, "and where do you come from on that handsome donkey?"

"My lord," said the old man, "I am from Kuza'ah—a poor outpost in the desert where it is all we can do from one year to the next to raise a few beans. But this year has been a season of plenty and I have raised a fine crop of curly cucumbers which I am carrying to the Emir Ma'an bin-Zaidah, for it is well known that he is a lord of boundless generosity."

"Well," said Ma'an, "and how much do you hope to get from Ma'an bin-Zaidah for this handsome and succulent crop of curly cucumbers?"

"Why," said the old man, "surely a thousand dinars."

"A thousand dinars, eh?" said Ma'an bin-Zaidah, "and what if he says that that is too much?"

"Why then," said the old man, "five hundred."

"And what if he says that that is too much?"

"Why then, three hundred."

And so it went on, with the old man cutting the price from three hundred, to two hundred, to one hundred, to fifty, to thirty . . .

"And what if he says that that is too much?" asked Ma'an.

"Well," said the old man, "I will give him this handsome donkey and these succulent curly cucumbers and I will go home with nothing."

And so they parted, and Ma'an met up again with his company and returned to his palace where he bathed and dressed himself in his robes and sat in his chair of state surrounded by his slaves and his eunuchs and all his other attendants.

Along came the old man with his donkey and his panniers.

"Greetings," said Ma'an bin-Zaidah, "what brings you here, old man of the desert?"

"My lord," said the old man, who could not recognize Ma'an bin-Zaidah amid the trappings of his court, "I come to honour the Emir and to bring him a bounty of curly cucumbers."

"And how much do you want for these curly cucumbers?"

"Why, my lord, surely a thousand dinars."

"Impossible! that is far too much."

"Why, then, my lord, five hundred."

"Scandalous! that is far too much."

"Why, then, my lord, three hundred . . ."

And so they bargained, from three hundred, to two hundred, to one hundred, to fifty, to thirty with Ma'an bin-Zaidah saying all the time, "but that is far too much."

"By Allah," cried the old man, "my meeting in the desert was unlucky and

ill-omened, but I will not take less than thirty dinars.''

And then Ma'an bin-Zaidah laughed and the old man recognized him for the hunter in the desert, and he said, ''Ah, my lord, if you will not give me the thirty dinars then there is my donkey tied to your door-post.''

And Ma'an laughed again and said, ''Give him his thousand dinars, and his five hundred, and his three hundred, and his two hundred, and his one hundred, and his fifty and his thirty—but leave me the donkey at the door-post! I must have the donkey!''

And the old man returned to Kuza'ah rejoicing, loaded down with two thousand, one hundred and eighty dinars, but with never a beast to carry him home.

 At the end of the story of the cucumbers, the night was still dark over the Shah Shahryar's palace and so Dunyazad called upon her sister Sheherezade to tell them :—

# THE STORY OF SINDBAD THE PORTER
# AND SINDBAD THE SAILOR

In the days when Harun al-Rashid was Caliph in Baghdad there dwelt in that city a poor man who was known as Sindbad the Porter, for he made what living he could by carrying baggage on his head for hire.

One day, when the sun was at its hottest and his burden at its heaviest, he found himself beside the gate of a merchant's house. The courtyard beyond the gate was fresh with full-scented flowers, and from the rooms of the house there came the sounds of lutes and zithers and voices more beautiful than song-birds. "Truly, there is no God but Allah," said Sindbad the Porter, "and whom He wishes to raise He exalts and whom He wishes to abase He makes low," and, raising his voice he sang the verses:

> "Thou, Ruler of Heaven, hast placed the rich man
> There in his castle; the poor man at his gate.
> Thou, Ruler of Heaven, teach us Thy patience
> That we rejoice in Thee, whatever be our fate."

Now it so happened that the master of the house was walking in a room overlooking the street where Sindbad was singing, and he forthwith sent a servant to bring the porter before him. Thus it came about that he was led through rooms hung with fine tapestries and adorned with rich furnishings into the presence of the master: a man, grey with age but of resplendent

nobility, sitting among a company of lords at tables garnished with meat and fruits and bowls of wine. Slave girls were playing instruments and singing and it seemed to the porter that he had entered Paradise.

"Welcome," said the master of the house; and he called for food and drink to be placed before his new guest, who, in wonderment, gave praise to Allah, washed his hands, and set to eating as though there might be no more tomorrows in his life. When he had finished the master of the house welcomed him again and asked to know his name and calling.

"My name is Sindbad the Porter," said the man, "and I make my living by carrying other people's goods about the town for hire."

"Now that is passing strange," said the lord, "for my name too is Sindbad—although men call me Sindbad the Sailor—and I too have carried burdens on my back in my time. And when I heard you singing outside my house of the virtues of patience, it brought back to my mind the trials that I too have undergone, and it seemed to me a worthy act that I might offer you my hospitality and set before you the proof that suffering may lead to good cheer, and the way to prosperity may lie through hardship and privation."

 And—as if she had been present at this banquet—Sheherezade began to tell Shah Shahryar of the Seven Voyages of Sindbad the Sailor just as he had told them to the Porter, his namesake.

## THE TALE OF THE VANISHING ISLAND

I should have known from the start (he said) that my engaging to be a mariner was going to be a courtship with calamity. Indeed, if I had behaved myself, I need never have gone to sea at all, for I was born of a wealthy father and only reduced myself to the poverty of one like yourself, O Sindbad the Porter, by too much lavish eating and drinking and by giving myself unrestrained to the delights of youth. So it came about that I had to gather up what remnants of wealth that I had and travel forth with them to trade in different quarters of the world from the Pillars of Hercules in the west to Serendib in the east.

We had not sailed long on my very first voyage before we came to an island that seemed like a little corner of Paradise. Trees and flowers blossomed on its fine soil and birds and small game were there for our eating. Accordingly we cast anchor and landed, and while some went to catch a fresh dinner for us,

others set to lighting great fires for the cooking. Imagine our amazement, therefore, when the ship's master suddenly blew warnings to us on his clarion and summoned us back to the vessel. For this was no island at all that we had camped on, but a huge fish who had lain so long on the surface of the ocean that dust and sand had gathered on his back and nourished the undergrowth through which we hunted. Now the heat from our cooking-fires was so disturbing him that he grew uneasy. With a few quivers, like the first tremors of an earthquake, he flexed the muscles of his back and then suddenly he dived for the cool depths of the sea, leaving those of us who had not got back to the ship floating in an atoll of uprooted trees and bushes.

Only with the utmost difficulty did I escape from this wreckage of my fortune, and only by strange coincidence did I find again the goods and gear that I had left on board the ship; but I did not let this narrow encounter deter me from further voyaging, which led to:—

# THE ADVENTURE OF THE VALLEY OF DIAMONDS

I had taken ship, once more to go trading, and again we hove to at an island (but this time surely too large and mountainous to be a sleeping fish). While my fellows set about exploring and bringing aboard fresh water, I

wandered off on my own to enjoy what I could find of the fruits of the island and to offer prayers and praises to the Omnipotent King.

Later I rested beneath a tree, where I fell asleep, and when I woke it was to find myself alone, for my companions had forgotten me and had sailed without me. Not knowing what to do, I set out to search the shore for help, but could find no trace of human habitation.

On climbing a tree, however, the better to see what lay inland, I observed, glinting in the sunshine, a huge white dome beyond the far side of a forest. So, with great difficulty, I made my way in that direction and eventually arrived at what seemed to be a strange building. It was smooth and pale as alabaster, with its walls curving up to meet the sky, but with no sign of doors or windows through which I might enter.

I set off to walk round it, and I had not gone fifty paces before the day darkened as though the sun had suddenly swept down below the horizon. As I peered westwards though, I saw that I had not been overtaken by a magic sunset, but that a gigantic bird was flying towards me, whose mighty body and widespread wings were hiding the sun from sight.

And in the darkness all suddenly became clear to me. For I remembered seamen's tales of a huge bird called a Rukh that was wont to lay eggs as big as a castle and that fed its young upon elephants. Surely this was just such an one, and surely the dome round which I was walking was none other than the Rukh's egg.

So it proved. The bird circled slowly out of the sun and came to rest on the surface of the dome, covering the shell with its breast and trailing its legs behind, towards the forest; and thus it fell asleep. As it slept though, I bethought me that this might prove an apt means for my escape, and I unwound my turban from my head, twisted it into a rope, and secured myself with it to one of the legs of the Rukh.

There I lay during the night, and in the morning the bird gave a great cry and rose from its nest on its mighty wings and flew with me over the ocean towards land. Eventually it came to rest on top of a high hill and here I speedily untied myself and watched as the bird took off again and swooped on some invisible object in the valley below. As it mounted towards heaven again though, I perceived that it held in its talons a monstrous wriggling serpent that it had plucked from the side of the hill, and as I followed the course that it had taken, I saw that I was lodged in a desert region of rocks and mountains, far less hospitable than the island from which I had flown.

Nevertheless, in search of water, I made my way towards the valley-bottom and discovered as I went that the whole place swarmed with snakes and serpents, each as big as a palm tree. It seemed that they spent much of the day

hiding in holes and caves for fear of being attacked by the Rukhs, and all around their lairs, and spread across the valley floor, there glinted what looked like a pavement of glass. As I got nearer though, I saw that this was a delusion and that the ground was really scattered with diamonds, which lay as thick as the sands by the sea.

As I stood marvelling at all this wealth, lying amongst the serpents, I heard a strange bumping sound and I saw tumbling down the hill towards me a huge piece of meat, as it were the side of an ox; and as it fell, all sticky and bloody as it was, so it gathered to its surface the loose diamonds among which it was rolling. Then I remembered that I had heard tell of the stratagems of diamond-hunters, who proceeded in this way, tossing raw meat amongst the precious stones so that it might be lifted out of the valley by carnivorous birds from whom the diamonds could then be collected.

Trusting to this knowledge, I filled my pockets and my girdle and my turban with as many diamonds as I could and seized hold of the underside of the carcase, all raw and bloody as it was, and awaited events. Sure enough, before long, a great eagle swooped out of the sky and seized the meat in his talons and lifted it—and me—high out of the valley and brought us to ground by its nest on the other side of the mountain. In only a few moments, however, after our landing, there started a great racket of shouting and banging of gongs and from out of hiding came a group of diamond-hunters intent on holding the eagle at bay till they should pluck out whatever riches might be stuck to his dinner.

They were not a little amazed to find a man also entangled with the carcase, but when I told them my adventures and shared with them the stones that I had brought up from the valley, they wished that they might have such surprises every day. And so we returned to their camp and ate and drank until we all cried for Rukhs to come and carry us home.

As it happened though (said Sindbad to Sindbad), this was not the last of my encounters with the Rukh. For after several more years and several more voyages that bird became the direct cause of my adventure with:—

# THE OLD MAN OF THE SEA

I had set sail from Basra with a goodly company, and after several weeks voyaging we found ourselves once again on an island where the Rukhs had chosen to nest. I did not know this when we landed, nor had I ever told my shipmates of my own discovery of the egg, so when some of them saw the white dome rising above the tree-line they had no notion of the dangers that it might portend.

Several of them made their way to examine the object and when (like me) they could find no sign on its smooth walls of what it might be, they began banging it with stones and beating it with fallen branches until suddenly, as all eggs will, it cracked open and they were like to be drowned in the watery fluid that streamed out over them.

As the flood subsided though, they perceived within the egg the body of the young Rukh and forthwith pulled it out and brought it back to the ship to be a handsome augmentation of our stores. But when I heard their story and recognized what they had done, I went straightway to the ship's master and urged him to set sail without delay. ''Vengeance will be upon us otherwise,'' I said.

And I was right. For although the master called his men aboard and stood off from the island as fast as he could, it was not long before the sun was darkened by the wings of the returning birds. When they discovered the destruction wrought upon their egg, they began to utter piercing cries and rose vertically into the air to see who might have done such a thing. Nor did it take even their bird-brains long to determine that we were the culprits and we had barely got a league or two clear of the island before they appeared above us, each carrying in its claws a massive boulder brought from the tops of the mountains.

As soon as the he-Rukh came up with us, he let fall his rock from a great height. But the ship's master saw it coming and put the ship about so that the rock plunged into the sea—but with such violence that we were pitched high on the crest of the wave it made and looked down into the trough to see the bottom of the ocean laid momentarily bare. Then the she-Rukh let fall her boulder, which was bigger than that of her mate, and, as Destiny decreed, it fell straight on to the poop of our ship so that the vessel burst asunder in a thousand pieces and we were all cast into the sea.

[ 85 ]

Such was the tumult of the waves after this battering that there was no hope of us staying together, and before long I found myself separated from my companions and drifting aimlessly astride one of the planks of the broken ship. Through the intercession of Allah, however, I was eventually able to paddle my way towards the shore-line of an unknown coast and there I landed, yearning for food and water to refresh myself.

As I began to explore this new land, however, so it seemed to me that the Divine One had brought me to the edge of His Demesne. For here were fruits and flowers in abundance and clear streams, running with purest water, and all I had to do was to gather and drink my fill to be restored to life. So there I stayed till nightfall, hearing no voice and seeing no other man, and after giving thanks to the Most High and glorifying Him, I lay down and slept till morning.

Next day, following a stream in search of human habitations, I came upon a deep spring, flowing from a well, and there, beside the well, sat a venerable old man dressed in a skirt of palm fronds. I greeted him and he returned my salaam, but never a word he spoke. "Then tell me, nuncle," I said, "why do you sit silent here?" Again he bowed towards me and groaned, signalling with his hand as if to say that he wished to cross the channel from the well but could not do so. So I knelt down, that he might climb on my shoulders, and I stepped into the water and carried him to where he had pointed.

When we reached the other side, I stooped so that he might dismount, but as I did so he wound his legs more tightly round my neck and made no move to be gone. And when I looked at his legs and saw them black and rough like a buffalo's hide I took fright and sought to throw him from me, but to no avail. He clung to me and gripped my neck with his legs till I was nearly choked, and though I fell to the ground and writhed with the pain of it, still he stayed with me. Then he drummed his heels upon me and beat my back with his arms, which were like palm rods, and there was nothing I could do but rise and carry him where it seemed he wanted to go.

From that day forth he stayed as though pinioned upon my back. He drove me among the trees so that he might reach for the sweetest fruits, he lived and slept upon me as though I were there for his domestic comfort, and if ever I refused to do his bidding or loitered about too slowly he would bang me with his arms and feet, so that I was driven nearly mad.

"What reward is this for compassion?" I cried. "By Allah, if I live beyond this time I shall never more do any man service." And so in weariness I wandered on until one day we came to a place where there was an abundance of gourds fallen from their trees and drying in the sun. So I took a large dry gourd, cut it open, and hollowed it out and cleaned it. Then I gathered grapes

which grew on a vine nearby and squeezed them into the gourd till it was full of their juice, and I stopped up its mouth and left it in the sun that it might ferment and become strong wine. In this way I brewed a potion to sustain me through my troubles and bring me some measure of cheerfulness.

One day, as I was unstoppering one of my gourds of wine, the Old Man on my back signed to me that he wished to know what I was drinking. "Ha ha!" I cried, "it is such liquor as makes even porters happy," and I began to dance and reel among the trees with the old man jogging on my shoulders. When he realized how frolicsome the wine appeared to make me, he began drumming on my head and gurgling as much as to say that he, too, wanted a portion. So I passed up a gourd full of the fermented brew and he drained it to the dregs and hurled it into the forest and at once began jigging up and down, mouthing strange noises, which I took to be his kind of singing:

> "yorhorlorlorlor,
> yorhorlorlorlor,
> yorhorlorlorlorkus
> yorhorlorlorlor!"

And as the fumes of the wine rolled round his brain so his side-muscles and his limbs relaxed and I was at last able to tip him off my shoulders on to the ground—yorhorlorlorlor!

There he lay, out of his senses with drunkenness. So I went among the trees and found a great stone and smote him on the head with it, that he might never more be a curse to travellers. Then I took my way back to the sea-coast and dwelt in peace, tending my sores, until I saw the sail of a passing ship and was able to signal to it to put in and rescue me.

When the sailors questioned me as to who I was and how I came to be stranded on this coast, they marvelled to hear of my adventure with the creature that tormented me. "For you should know," they said, "that he is spoken of in these parts as Sheikh a-Bahr, which is to say the Old Man of the Sea, and none but you has ever borne that burden and survived. For those that he traps he marches till they die under him, and then he eats them . . ."

So (said Sindbad the Sailor to Sindbad the Porter), thus may you see how I have done my share of carrying in the world, but such has been my patience under oppression and my perseverance through so many voyages that I came to safe harbour here at last—and since the days are long gone since I swore never to show compassion, and since thou art well-met as a man of my name,

let us render praise to Allah that we live in a world so full of His mercies that we shall all at last come safe to shore.

And Sindbad the Sailor and Sindbad the Porter drank and made merry and were as brothers from that day forth.

"So those were some of the strange adventures of Sindbad the Sailor," said Sheherezade to the Shah Shahryar, "but none was so strange as what I would now tell you of:–

# THE TALE OF THE CITY OF BRASS

## *Of the Jars of Solomon*

Many nights ago (said Sheherezade to the Shah Shahryar) and many stories past, we heard tell of that fisherman who brought up from the depths of the ocean a jar, sealed with the seal of Solomon the King; and you will recall that therein was imprisoned a prince of the Jann upon whom the anger of King Solomon had fallen.

Now it so happens that, in days of ancient time, there dwelt in the city of Damascus a Caliph by the name of Abd al-Malik bin Marwan who loved nothing better than to gather about him his sultans and his grandees to hear tidings of the wide world beyond his own domain. Well, one day there came to him a courtier, one Talib bin Sahl, who was renowned as a man of great learning, even though his study was always to the end of uncovering deep secrets of those places in the world where treasures might be hid.

"Commander of the Faithful," said Talib, "there has come to me news of a strange voyage that was undertaken once by my grandfather who recounted his adventures to my father, through whom they have come down to me." And Talib went on to describe how his grandfather had been carried by storms beyond the great island of Sicily and had made landfall in an unknown country of desert and mountains whose people had no knowledge of the Goodness and Mercy of Allah the Most High. Nevertheless, when the sea-folk of that land went fishing they would often draw up in their nets just such brass jars as those we heard tell of, stamped with the signet of Solomon; and whenever they unstoppered such jars out would come the twisting black smoke of the Jinni, forming itself into a giant whose head was higher than the mountain

tops and who would vanish into the empyrean crying: "I repent, I repent; pardon me O prophet of Allah!" (for the Jinni knew not that Solomon had been dead time out of mind).

The Caliph Abd al-Malik marvelled at Talib's story, for he knew the runes of the All-wise:

'Rise Solomon, and rule Our Land in strength and majesty,
And those who honour not Our Name, subdue for all eternity';

and it came to him that he would like to look upon these brass jars, that they might be a lesson to those who would learn and a warning to those who would be warned. So he consulted with Talib how this might be, and Talib prepared for him a plan whereby a journey might be made under truce through the lands of Egypt and Northern Africa to the mountains where dwelt the fishermen of the jars. "Wise words, O Talib," said the Caliph, "let thee be our messenger and I will give thee letters of passage to our brothers in Egypt and Morocco that they might use thee well, and I will care for thy house and thy family and thy belongings whilst thou art gone."

"With love and gladness, O Commander of the Faithful," said Talib, for he lusted after the possibility of treasure, and he forthwith gathered to him the men and money which the Caliph had assigned, and he rode out to meet whatever fate the Hand of Allah might hold for him.


## Of the Black Castle

Talib with his caravan of footmen and horsemen crossed the desert country between Syria and Egypt, where he was received with high honour by the Emir Musa bin Nusayr, the Caliph's viceroy in all the lands of North-West Africa. And when the Emir had read the Caliph's letter he determined that he too would accompany Talib on his journey, taking with him the Sheikh Abd al-Samad, an ancient man, well-shotten in years and broken down with lapse of days, but yet one who was much travelled in the wastes and wolds where they must go.

"I hear and obey the bidding of the Commander of the Faithful," said Abd al-Samad, when they consulted him on preparations for the journey, "but know, O Emir, that the road we take is long and difficult, a journey of two years going and two years returning, with the ways few and full of terror and of things wonderful and marvellous. It behoves thee, therefore, to appoint a man of wisdom to rule in thy stead, for who knows if we shall ever return."

So the Emir Musa made his son Harun governor during his time of absence, and under the guidance of Abd al-Samad they rode westward with a great train of camels and a thousand water-jars. (For the Sheikh had warned them that in the crossing of the desert of Cyrene they would travel in a silent land, bereft of all water and plagued by the hot winds of the Simoon that would parch their water-skins before ever they were half way across.) And so they travelled, through lands of plenitude and waste lands, for a year's space, until one morning, after they had ridden all night, the Sheikh found himself in a country which he knew not. "Truly, there is no Majesty and no Might save in Allah," he said, "but we have wandered from our road."

"How can that be?" asked the Emir.

"The stars were overclouded and I could not guide myself by them."

"Then where on God's earth are we now?"

"I know not," said Abd al-Samad, "for I never set eyes on this land until this moment, but we can do nothing but fare forward and trust to Allah to guide us."

Thus it was that they journeyed on until they reached a wide land, as it were a calm sea of grass, and away on the horizon there rose some great thing, high and black, in the midst of which a smoke seemed to rise and hang over the confines of the sky. So they rode across the plain, day and night, in the direction of this dark shapelessness, and as they approached it, lo! it became a

[ 93 ]

high castle, built like a mountain, all of black stone, with lowering battlements
and a gate of gleaming China steel that dazzled the eyes and wits of those who
looked upon it. Round about it were a thousand steps, while what had seemed
to be smoke was a vast central dome, built of lead, an hundred cubits high.

"Indeed, there is no God but Allah!" cried the Sheikh Abd al-Samad, "for I
know this to be the Black Castle, and I tell you that from here our way lies
across country to the City of Brass, whence it will be an easy journey along the
sea-coast, past the wells and watering-places of the ancient Emperor Iskander
to the country that you seek. But first let us go and look in yonder palace, for
its marvels are an admonition to those who would be admonished."

So the Emir went up to the castle with Talib and the Sheikh and with his
officers and men and behold, the gate was open and over its lintel there shone
in letters of gold these words:

'Welcome, O traveller, to these halls of stone;
Enter and find that which is only True:
No matter what your gear, your retinue,
You must depart just as you came—alone.'

[ 96 ]

"May Allah comfort us!" said the Emir, and he led his men one by one through the marble portico into the castle. What they found there was a scene of wealth and desolation. Walking from hall to hall, from chamber to chamber, up stairways carved from granite and along passages lined with tapestries, they saw gathered together the riches of a kingdom; but there was no living soul within to take delight in these things, and over every doorway there were words of valediction. At last, under the castle-dome itself, they came upon a pavilion wherein was a long tomb, and on the tomb a tablet of China steel with the inscription that here lay the Prince Kush, the son of Shaddad, son of Ad the Great:

> 'I built this castle and abode here a thousand years, and had
> to wife the daughters of a thousand kings and was blessed
> with a thousand sons as fierce as lions. Here I amassed
> treasures from all quarters of the earth: cisterns of red
> gold and white silver; but there fell upon us the Destroyer
> of delights and the Sunderer of societies, and day by day
> there died two of us till all the company had perished and
> the parcels of our wealth availed us nothing, nor, with all
> our gold, could we ransom for ourselves a single day of life.
> O thou who comest to this place, take warning of that which
> thou seest of the accidents of Time and the vicissitudes of
> Fortune. All, all is vision and dream.'

When he read these words, the Emir Musa wept for the passing of so brave a household, and he would not leave the palace until he had transcribed each and every *memento mori*, that our own generations might learn wisdom.

## Of the Ifrit Dahish

When the Emir Musa had done with his writing and praying, the Sheikh Abd al-Samad led the caravan away from the Black Castle and into the high hills. After three days' journey they espied at the head of a valley what seemed to be a horseman, dressed in glittering armour, staring down upon them. But as they rode towards him he neither moved nor spoke, and when they had climbed up the knoll on which he stood they found him to be a statue made all of brass. On one arm he held a shield, and on the other a couched lance with a broad glittering head, and here they saw graven the words:

'O thou that comest unto me, dost thou seek the City of Brass? If so, touch thou my spear-hand and I will revolve and where my spear points when I come to rest, follow that way. No harm shall befall you if you take that road.'

So the Emir Musa touched the spear-hand of the statue, who spun like dazzled lightning and directed them to a track leading on among the hills.

After days and nights of journeying in the way that the statue had directed they came to a wide tract of open country, in the midst of which they found a gaunt pillar of black stone like a furnace chimney, and sunk to his armpits in the pillar there was a creature the like of which none had seen before. He had two great wings and four limbs, two like human arms and two like lion's paws, with claws of iron. The whole of his body was burned black from the desert sun, his hair hung about him like horses' tails and his eyes blazed like coals, slit upwards in his face, while a third eye in the middle of his forehead gave out sparks of fire.

At the sight of this chimaera the horses became restive and the men of the company turned to flee; but the Emir Musa instructed Abd al-Samad to approach the creature and question him on his condition, "For surely he is hindered from thee, and from us all, by the rock wherein he is placed." So the Sheikh drew near and called upon the monster to make explanation of himself.

"Know then," cried the Wild Thing, "that I am an Ifrit of the Jinn, by name Dahish (which is to say the Amazed One). I am placed here by the judgement of Allah, at the behest of his apostle, Solomon the King, whose rule I flouted. For it occasioned, long years ago, that I was servant to one of the sons of Iblis in his island fastness, remote from all the business of the world. And this King had an idol of red carnelian, of whom I was the guardian, so that when men came to the idol to seek instruction or consolation I would climb into its belly and bid or forbid them.

"Now the King's daughter in this island was a woman accomplished in all beauty, whose fame was such that it eventually came to the knowledge of the Lord Solomon, who at once sent messengers to our land. 'Give me thy daughter to wife,' he claimed of our King, 'and break thine idol of carnelian, in order that thou mayst turn to the One True God and that thou and I may live in amity as father and son. Otherwise I will come upon thee with an irresistible host and make thee as Yesterday, which is gone forever.' But when

himself down into the place.

"By Allah, thou art a dead man!" said the Emir Musa, but at once a companion tribesman came up to him saying, "O Emir, that was a mad fellow, and surely his madness got the better of him with all that climbing of the ladder. Let me go up and open the gate, for I am a man of sense and reason."

"Very well," said Musa, "go up, and may Allah go with thee." So the man mounted after his comrade to the top of the wall. When he got there he, too, stood for a moment surveying all he saw before him with outstretched arms. Then he clapped his hands together, crying, "Splendour of all splendours!" and hurled himself down into the city.

"If such be the act of a man of reason," said the Emir Musa, "then what truly will a madman do? If all our men are as reasonable as this we shall lose everyone, and none shall return from this errand to the Commander of the Faithful. Let us move on." But a third man pleaded to be given his chance to climb the ladder—and a fourth, and a fifth to the number of twelve—all claiming to be men of sense and reason, but all casting themselves to their death as did the first man of all.

Then the Sheikh Abd al-Samad came forward, bent low under his burden of years. "O Emir," he said, "this affair is reserved to none other but myself, for the experienced is not like the inexperienced. I shall climb the ladder."

"Indeed thou shalt not," said the Emir Musa, "for if thou too—experienced or no—perish as these others have perished, we shall be cut off to the last man, for thou art our guide." But the Sheikh would have none of it and crying the name of Allah, the Compassionating, the Compassionate, he mounted the ladder to its topmost rung.

When he reached the parapet he, too, spread wide his arms, so that those watching below clutched themselves and prayed for their own sakes and his, but the Sheikh laughed beyond measure and stayed for an hour upon the wall, reciting the name of Allah the Almighty and repeating the Verses of Safety. Then he rose and cried at the top of his voice to those below, "O Emir, have no fear, for Allah has averted from me all temptation. Know you that I saw here, swimming as it were in a lake below me, ten maidens with hair outflung and with bodies as the full moon, singing and calling me to join them:

'Weialala leia
Wallala leialala.'

So I thought to throw myself down to be with them, but then, by my wisdom, I recalled and saw my twelve companions lying dead at the bottom of the wall, and I restrained myself and called upon Allah to protect me; for surely this was some enchantment devised by the people of the city to defend it against those who might seek to enter."

With these words the Sheikh Abd al-Samad set off along the parapet-walk until he came to the towers of brass, where he saw two gates of gold set close in the tower and without any means for their opening so that he could get down into the tower. Gazing about him, though, he perceived in the middle of one of the gates a further horseman of brass with his hand outstretched as though pointing, and in the palm of his hand were the words:

'O thou who comest to this place, if thou wouldst enter the tower
    turn the pin in my navel twelve times and the gate will open.'

So Abd al-Samad examined the horseman, and there in his navel was a pin of gold which he turned twelve times, whereupon the horseman reared and spun round like lightning and the gate swung open with a noise like thunder.

Abd al-Samad entered the tower and found himself in a long passage which brought him to the steps that led down to the guard-room. There, seated on

benches and fully armed, with swords drawn and bows ready-notched, were the men of the guard, all dead. And beyond the guard-room were the sentries at the gate—dead too—while the gate itself was secured with iron bars and curiously wrought bolts and chains and padlocks. Within the guard-room, however, the Sheikh had spied an old man, seated upon a high wooden bench, whom he took to be the Warder of the Guard, and sure enough when he examined the old man's robe he found therein a great bundle of keys hanging at his girdle. These he took to the gate and one by one undid the locks and bolts until, with a crash like reverberant thunder, the great leaves of the gates flew open and the city was revealed to those who stood outside. "Allaho Akbar; God is Most Great!"

Then the Emir Musa greeted the Sheikh as though they had been parted many years, and making fair disposition for men to guard the gate and for others to bury the fallen bodies of their comrades, he proceeded with Abd al-Samad and Talib bin Sahl to an exploration of the city.

It was a place of mystery and wonder. For as they moved through the streets they found houses and mansions, bazaars and markets, all built from black stone and brass and all peopled with men and women who seemed to be about their daily business, except that they were dead. In the houses, servants waited by the gilded vestibules; in the markets there were traders all in their accustomed places: the silk merchants amongst their silks and brocades, the perfumers surrounded by bladders of musk and ambergris, the money-changers with their shops full of gold and silver coin—but all with their skin dried on their bones, statuesque in the sleep of death.

Then the Emir Musa and his party moved on to the palaces of the great, and they found there pavilions full of rich stuffs, jewels and precious stones, and weapons of tempered steel, while in the courtyards fountains still played and streams flowed in marble channels across the floor.

"Indeed," said Sheherezade to the Shah Shahryar, "I am told that the floors themselves were cunningly made of veined marble, inlaid with precious stones so that they resembled a carpet of flowing water. In this they resembled a floor which the Emperor Solomon had constructed when he was wooing the beautiful Balkis, the Queen who held converse with butterflies. My Lord may remember that it was rumoured that Balkis, whatever her beauty, had legs that were hairy as those on an ass. So the Emperor Solomon called her to meet him in a chamber where he had laid down a pavement of glass over a

[ 106 ]

stream of water with fish swimming in it. Balkis, believing it to be nothing but water, raised her skirts in order to cross and behold! the Emperor could see that the rumours were indeed true. But Balkis was wise as well as beautiful, so he loved her, hairy legs and all.''

In the innermost chamber of the palace, Musa and his comrades found a domed pavilion of stone, gilded with red gold and crowned with a cupola of alabaster, wherein was a ceremonial dais under a canopy of silk. On this dais there lay a lady who seemed to watch them coming. She was more beautiful than a clear pool in a desert oasis, clad in a body-robe of fine gauze

embroidered with pearls and wearing on her breast an amulet filled with musk and ambergris, and about her head a fillet of jewels that were worth more than the empire of the Caesars. "Peace be with thee, O lady," said the Emir Musa; but Talib bin Sahl said to him, "Allah preserve thee, O Emir, but verily this lady is dead, so how shall she return thy greeting? See, she is a corpse, wondrously embalmed, even to the glint and movement in her eyes, and so her servants too." For about the dais there were body-servants of the lady, and on the steps leading up to her couch two statuesque figures of Andalusian copper, the one holding a mace of steel and the other a sword of watered steel which dazzled the eye.

Between these sentries, on the steps to the couch, there lay a golden tablet inscribed with the following words:

'In the name of Allah, Lord of Lords and Causer of Causes!
Behold here Tadmurah, daughter of the Kings of the Amalekites
and queen of this City of Brass. Know ye that I reigned here
in wealth and wisdom as one for whom there would be no end to
the world's glory. But truly it is said:

"The Worldly Hope men set their Hearts upon
    Turns Ashes—or it prospers; and anon,
    Like Snow upon the Desert's dusty Face
    Lighting a little Hour or two—is gone."

For a great famine fell upon us, with seven years of drought,
when no rain fell and no green thing came forth to sustain us,
and though we sent to every quarter of the world with our
treasure, seeking to barter pearls for grain and gold for
meal, ounce against ounce, yet gleaned we nothing. So we
despaired of help and closed the gates of our City upon the
world and committed ourselves forever to the destiny of Allah.
Take warning therefore, ye who follow here, though ye may
gather unto yourselves the riches of my people, they will
avail you nothing; nor may you lay any hand upon me and
mine, for I bide here in the mercy of Allah, an admonishment
to those who would be admonished of the transience of
earthly affairs.'

When the Emir Musa had read this doleful history he commanded that those who heeded the lure of gain more than the prophecy of loss might gather to

them whatever treasures the City should afford, but that the time had now come when they should make ready to seek the final end of their journey.

"But Lord," said Talib bin Sahl, "shall we in truth leave this lady thus? For see, she has about her neck and on her brow a ransom for all the princes of the earth."

"Didst thou not read?" said Musa, "didst thou not apprehend that she makes us free of her City in order that she herself may be unmolested?"

"But Lord," said Talib again, "of what consequence are these things to her now? Behold, she is dead and a single garment of cotton is all her need."

With these words, Talib bin Sahl strode to the dais and set foot upon the steps to the couch to claim her jewels. But as he mounted, he passed between the two slaves and lo! the mace-bearer swept round and smote him on the back with his mace of steel, and the sword-bearer swung his weapon with a single movement and struck off his head, so that he fell dead upon the steps.

## Of the Ending of the Journey

The Emir stayed not to mourn the killing of Talib, saying, "Allah have no mercy on thy resting place, for this is the only end to greed," and calling for the horses and the baggage train, he left the City. And as the last man crossed the threshold of the tower, the great gate crashed to behind him and the place returned to immemorial silence.

Abd al-Samad now led the caravan across the desert past the Wells of Iskander until they came to the fringe of a great sea and here they followed the coast a journey of many days. At last they came within sight of the mountainous shores of the land that they were seeking and in the caves of the mountains there dwelt the tribe of black men who spoke an unknown tongue. Among these they pitched their tents.

They had not long been encamped on the shores of the sea when a huge man, black-skinned from head to toe, came down from the caves and addressed them in their own speech, asking whence they came and whether they were men or Jinn.

"Well, we are men," said Musa, "but you, from your size and majesty, are surely a Jinni."

"That is not so," said the black man, and he went on to relate how he was king of his tribe and how he had long before encountered a prophet on the sea-shore from whom he had learned the worship of Allah, the Most High, and the speech of Mohammed, His Apostle.

"Tell me then," said Musa, "if thou knowest anything of those jars, in

which the Emperor Solomon is said to have sealed half the Devils of Hell and cast them into the sea in such a place as this.''

''With love and gladness,'' replied the chieftain, and he told how the sea-bed below his cliffs was littered with such jars; then, in course of preparing a royal welcome for his guests, he sent divers down to the sea bottom and before his hospitality was at an end they had brought up fifty jars, sealed at the mouth, and impressed with the ring of Solomon.

So after much feasting, and the exchange of many gifts, Musa bin Nusayr and the faithful Sheikh Abd al-Samad turned their caravan towards Damascus. After long months of travel without mishap, they entered at last the great gate of the Caliph's palace and laid before Abd al-Malik bin Marwan the treasures of their journey and the tale of their adventures, even down to the slaughter of Talib bin Sahl.

''Would that I had come with you!'' cried the Caliph; and he rewarded them with riches and high honours for their devotion. And if any man came to his court after that time who spoke slightingly of the Might of Allah and the glory of his prophets, then he would call for one of the jars of Solomon, break the seal, and marvel as the imprisoned spirit spired into the clouds crying repentance to the heavens.

And when she had concluded the Story of the City of Brass, Sheherezade told the Shah Shahryar many tales and anecdotes that she had heard from the men of the desert and from the dwellers in towns. And among these tales there was the tale of:–

# THE MAN WHO STOLE THE DOG'S GOLDEN DISH

There was once a merchant who had fallen upon hard times. His debts grew and his debtors sought to have him imprisoned—so he left his home and his family and wandered at random across the wide world. One day he came to a fine city and met in the main street a company of young men, roistering up and down; so he joined them and followed them to a house of such magnificence that it might have been a royal palace, with domes and turrets reaching to the sky. In went the roisterers and in went our merchant and they walked through corridors and vestibules and saloons until

they came to a great chamber, where sat the Lord of the House, a majestic and dignified man, surrounded by pages and eunuchs and slaves.

Perplexed by the scene, and ashamed of his ragged appearance, the merchant withdrew to a far corner of the room where he watched the feasting and festivities of the crowd. And while he was standing there, behold, a servant came in with four great hounds—each with a silver leash and a collar of gold about its neck. The dogs were fastened to one of the carved pillars of the hall, and the servant went out and returned with four golden dishes, piled with rich meat—one for each of the dogs.

The merchant watched in amazement as the creatures set about taking their dinner, and so hungry was he that he longed to join them and share their meat. And so it occurred that one of the dogs turned to look at him and was inspired by Allah the Almighty to recognize the sadness of his case; and the dog drew back from the dish and signed with his paw to the man to come and eat his meat; and when he had finished the dog pushed the golden dish towards him with his fore-paw, as though telling the man that he should take it, so he did so and left the house and went his way with no one following him.

The merchant journeyed on to another city, where he sold the dish—laying out the money he received on goods which he sold and traded with until once more he became a man of wealth. He returned to his own town, paid off his

debts, and rose to become one of the most prosperous men in those parts.

After some years had gone by he decided that he should return to the city where he had found such good fortune and repay the Lord for the dish that he had stolen. So he furnished himself with money and with suitable presents and journeyed by day and night until he reached the place that he sought for. There was the town, there was the main street where he had met the roistering company—but when he came to the mansion-house he found only ruins. The domes and turrets had fallen in and crows walked amongst the rubble.

"Truly," said the merchant to himself, "there is no constancy and no might save in Allah:

> 'The fretted filigree is turned to rust,
>     Masters and servants now alike are dust!' "

and while he was musing thus he saw a wretched man, dressed only in a ragged gown, poking in the ruins with a stick.

"Ho, thou!" said the merchant, "what has become of this place and of the great Lord who held court here but a few years ago?"

"Here he is," said the beggar-man; "I am he, and this was my mansion—which lies now as a lesson to those who will learn and a warning to those who will be warned that Allah raises up nothing of this world except He cast it down again."

And the man went on to tell of the days of his wealth and how all the world paid him court—until one day he missed a golden platter that was used to feed his hunting-dogs. Such was his rage and frenzy at this loss that his friends gradually moved against him. Fortune turned away from all his dealings, and his future now lay in the broken remnants of his palace.

"In Faith," said the merchant, "do not despair, for I have brought you the recompense of that golden plate and a bountiful token of my gratitude beside." And he told the ragged Lord the story of how the dog offered him the dish and how he used it to regain his affluence and that he was now come to repay his debt of honour.

"Go thy ways," said the Lord; "it was the dog gave thee the dish, and how should I stand debtor to one of my own dogs? I will take nothing from you—not even the parings of your finger nails." And with that he returned to poking in the ruins with his stick.

"But this tale," said Sheherezade, "is not so cheering to the spirit as another that I know, which is:—

# THE TALE OF THE RUINED MAN AND HIS DREAM

There lived once in Baghdad in a house beside a grove of pomegranate trees a great merchant. But, as with the one who got the golden dish, hard times came upon him too and it was all that he could do to earn a poor living by carrying other people's goods about the streets.

Now one night, while he slept, a Speaker came to him in a dream and said, "Behold! your fortune is in Cairo; go there and find it." So he set out for Cairo, and after many days travelling he reached the city, and because it was evening he went in to a mosque to sleep.

He had not been there long before a band of thieves passed through the shrine intent upon robbing the house next door. But the owners heard them at their work and cried aloud for the protection of the law so that the thieves ran off—and when the men-at-arms arrived whom should they find but our merchant sleeping in the mosque. They took him up, beat him with palm rods till he was nearly dead and then threw him in prison, where he lay three days and three nights.

Then came the magistrate: "Who are you and what brought you to Cairo?" he said.

And the merchant answered, "I am an honest merchant from Baghdad, fallen upon evil days. A Speaker came to me in a dream and told me that my fortune was in Cairo and that I should go there to find it—but all the fortune I have found is the bunch of palm rods that you so generously gave me!"

So the magistrate laughed and said, "What a foolish fellow you are to put your trust in shadows. Why, three times now I have myself heard a voice saying to me in a dream, 'Go you to Baghdad and there, under the fountain in the courtyard of such and such a house beside a grove of pomegranate trees you shall find great treasure', but do you think that I am so stupid as to go traipsing so far merely at the behest of a dream?"

So he gave the man money to return home, and the man did so with all speed, for he knew the grove and the house and the courtyard and the fountain for his own. And when he got back he dug beneath the fountain and found there a great store of gold and pearls and rubies, just as the magistrate had foretold; so he lived in peace and contentment all the rest of his days.

 "But this tale," said Sheherezade, "is still not so cheering to the spirit as others which I know," and she proceeded to recount many anecdotes about the fond and the foolish. Among these she told:–

# THE TALE OF THE SIMPLETON AND HIS DONKEY

A simple fellow was walking along the road one day, leading his donkey, when it was his misfortune to pass by two rogues. "I will have that fellow's donkey," said the first rogue.

"Fame and fortune to you if you do," said the second, and he watched while his companion crept along level with the donkey and then, when the simpleton wasn't looking, hooked off the donkey's halter and put it over his own head; and he walked along as though he were the donkey, while his companion made off with the animal itself.

When he saw that they'd got clean away the first rogue stopped stock still. The simpleton pulled the halter, pulled again, and then turned round to see what was the matter. He was amazed to discover that he'd got a man on the end of his rope. "What art thou? Tell me," he said; and the rogue replied,

"Why, I am thy donkey, but first I was a man (as now). Hear my story, and let it be a warning to you to repent of all transgression. For you must know that, in time past, I was a terrible drunkard, and when the wine was hot upon me I used to beat my poor old mother. Well, one day she called upon the Almighty

to avenge her, and Allah turned me into a donkey—but now that my mother's end approaches she must have pleaded to have me restored to my former shape.''

"Truly," cried the simpleton, "there is no majesty and no might save in Allah, the Glorious and Great. May Allah be with thee now, O my brother, and may he acquit me of all injury I may have done thee, riding thee about the land, and beating thee, and so forth." And he let the rogue go (who returned to his comrade) and went home to his wife; and they made offerings and gave alms to atone for their having treated a man as though he were a donkey.

When this time of contrition was over, the simpleton's wife sent him off to the market to get them another donkey so that they might continue their trade. When he got there, though, he was astonished to find his own old donkey among the creatures that were being put up for sale. Privily, when no one was looking, he sidled up to the beast and whispered in its ear, "Woe to thee, thou ne'er do well. Drunk again—and beating thy mother! But by Allah I will not rescue thee this time." And he bought a beast that seemed to him of a more sober constitution.

And, amongst all these anecdotes, Sheherezade also told:—

# THE TALE OF JA'AFAR THE BARMECIDE AND THE AILING BEDOUIN

It came about that one day Harun al-Rashid, the Commander of the Faithful, was walking in the desert with Abu Ya'kub, his Cup-bearer, and Ja'afar, his Wazir, and they encountered an old Bedouin propped up upon his ass.

"Question him," said the Caliph to Ja'afar, "and see if you can bring us some entertainment in this dry desert."

So Ja'afar went up to the Bedouin and asked him where he came from and whither he was going. "I am from Basra," said the old man, "and I am going to Baghdad, there to find a medicine for my eye."

"Well met, then, well met!" cried the Wazir, "for behold! you have encountered the vendors of the finest eyewash in the land. What will you requite us if we prescribe a remedy for your ills?"

"Why," said the Bedouin, "I will seek to pay you exactly what your remedy is worth."

"Here is your prescription then," said Ja'afar. "You must take three ounces of wind, three ounces of sunbeams, three ounces of moonbeams and a small pinch of lamplight. Mix these well together and let them lie in a dark place for three months. Then place them in a mortar without a bottom for another three months, after which you must pound them to a fine powder. After trituration has set in, leave them in the air in a mixing bowl for a further three months, when they shall be ready. Apply the medicine three drams a night while you are asleep and, Inshallah!, you shall be healed and whole in a trice."

Now after the Bedouin had heard this prescription to the end, he stretched himself out on his donkey's back and let fly a terrible fart which resounded across the desert wastes. "Behold!" he cried, "due payment for thy medicine." And the Caliph Harun al-Rashid was so pleased with his answer that he ordered him three thousand silver pieces.

Now on the last night of telling these anecdotes, when Sheherezade was done, she perceived that the dawn was still below the horizon and she told the Shah Shahryar of an unusual event. Some time before, it seems, passing incognito through the market-place on her way to the hammam baths, she had encountered a crowd of people listening to stories from a traveller, recently arrived. He was a stranger from the north, speaking a rustic dialect, but he told stories that he said were famed in his territory; and Sheherezade had attended to the tales that he told. ''Now my Lord,'' she said to the Shah Shahryar, ''from my recollections of this man, let me seek to copy something of his strange speech and recount to you the stories that he told.'' And as the nights passed, Sheherezade told the Shah:–

# THE STORY OF ALI BABA AND THE FORTY THIEVES

## The Cave

One time, many years back, there were two brothers: one a jolly man, round as a sweet apple, who was called Ali Baba; the other thin, and mean as a creaking door, and he was called Kasim. Kasim had married a woman as stingy as himself—the daughter of a merchant down in the market—and when that one took his trade to Heaven, Mr and Mrs Kasim continued in his place and they just got meaner and meaner, and richer and richer.

As for Ali Baba though, he had married a feckless, prodigal lady and they never had a penny to their names. Every day Ali Baba would take three asses into the nearby forest, where he would load them up with brushwood and dry timber to sell round the streets, but whatever he earned he and Mrs Ali Baba would spend, living the good life.

Well, one day he was sitting in the forest, munching a pitta bread sandwich for his dinner, when he heard a jingling of bridles and felt the ground beneath him quiver with the tread of horses' hoofs: many horses, many hoofs. So being a prudent chap—especially when pitta bread sandwiches were on the go—and thinking that this might be a notorious band of forest outlaws, he pushed his asses deep into the undergrowth and shinned up a nearby tree, to be well out of sight when they came along.

And just as well that he did. For this was indeed a bunch of robbers—forty men with horses and baggage and who knows what—and as they got to the tree where Ali Baba was hiding they stopped and their Chief went up to a wall of rock that rose out of the forest floor opposite the tree. The Chief looked at the wall of rock. The wall of rock looked at the Chief. Then the Chief said, "Open, Sesame!"—and straightway, with a noise like a thousand grindstones, part of the rock slid aside to make a great doorway, and the Chief and his men rode inside with their baggage. Then the rock slid closed behind them.

"Allah protect us all," said Ali Baba up in his tree; and he stayed there, not daring to finish his dinner and hoping that his asses wouldn't start braying, for fear he'd be discovered and done away with on the spot. Eventually the rock-door slid open again and the Chief, their captain, rode out, stopping on the threshold to count the men who followed him—one to thirty-nine. When he was sure they were all there he turned to the rock and said, "Shut, Sesame!" and the door slid to and the robbers trotted away.

When he was sure they were all gone, Ali Baba came down from the tree, reckoning to get home as fast as he could. But when he saw the rock-wall, standing there so inviting-like, he couldn't stop himself from saying, "Open, Sesame!" and—squeak, grind, rumble—the door opened for him too.

Well, that could clearly be taken as a sign—from Earth, if not from Heaven—so Ali Baba stepped into the cleft to see what he could see. Sheesh! High up in the ceiling of the rock there had been fashioned cunning air-holes and bullseye windows, and by the light that streamed down Ali Baba could see great bales of embroidered cloths, camel-loads of silks and brocades, mounds of carpets, and bags and sacks full of gold and jewels. Surely not just this band of robbers, but their fathers and grandfathers must have been hiding their loot in this cave for more years than they had donkeys.

Although the rock-door had rumbled shut behind him when he'd got inside the cavern, Ali Baba kept calm, and after he'd looked at all the heaps of treasure he turned and said, "Open, Sesame!" and the door obediently rumbled open. Thereupon he went and found his three asses, brought them to

the cave and loaded them with sacks of gold, hidden by a covering of brushwood and kindling. Then he said, "Shut, Sesame!" and made off back home as fast as his poor tottering animals would let him.

## The Kitchen Scales

When Ali Baba got to the yard by his house he drove in the asses and carefully shut the gate so no one would see what he was up to. Then he began to unload the covering of brushwood so that he could get at the gold. But Mrs Ali Baba, hearing the coins clink and feeling the heavy, knobbly leather bags, straightway thought her man had been up to no good and went to fetch her rolling-pin so that she could talk to him about living an honest life.

Before she could get into the swing of her lecture though, Ali Baba explained what had happened and poured out on the kitchen table some of the golden dinars and sovereigns and asrafis that he had collected from the cave. This caused her to have second thoughts about questions of honesty, and, being of an orderly disposition, she began to count up the coins and stack them according to their values.

"You daft duck," said Ali Baba, "you'll never get through with that all night, and we'll have money piled up to the ceiling. Why don't we just dig a nice hole in the floor and tip it all in; then we can call on it whenever we want a treat."

"Well, you're right," said his wife, "but even so it would be nice to know roughly what we've got. Why don't we weigh it? I'll go round and borrow Mrs Kasim's scales and I'll weigh the stuff while you're digging the hole."

So Mrs Ali Baba went round to her sister-in-law's and asked to borrow her kitchen scales. "Funny," thought Mrs Kasim, "funny. She's never been that wild about cooking before; what's she after with these scales?" and while she pretended to hunt them out from the bottom of a cupboard she secretly smeared some honey over the pan of the balance. "That should tell us something," she said to herself.

Well, the Ali Babas got on with their weighing and their digging, and when they'd finished they carefully stowed all their winnings away under the kitchen floor and Mrs Ali Baba took the scales back to Mrs Kasim—and of course she hadn't bothered to wash them up or anything before she left. So when Mrs Kasim came to inspect them, once Ali Baba's wife had gone home, what should she see stuck to the golden honey but a golden coin. "Asrafis!" she yelled, "asrafis! Those good-for-nothing Ali Babas—they've not just laid hold of some cash somewhere, but they're having to weigh out asrafis on my

scales as though they were corn husks!'' And when old squinty Kasim came back from his shop, she told him what had happened and packed him off round to his brother's to find out what was the beginning and end of it all.

"What's this, then?" said Kasim to Ali Baba. "Just look at you. Holes in your best tunic—and yet you have to borrow my wife's scales to weigh out your gold. What's going on?"

"Don't know what you're talking about," said Ali Baba.

"Look at this then," said Kasim; and he held up the asrafi, still sticky with honey. "Now, what's going on?"

Well, Ali Baba had known his brother and his brother's wife long enough to judge when he could make monkeys out of them and when he couldn't, and this time he saw was a time for plain-dealing. He told Kasim about his adventure in the forest and his discovery of the robbers' gold and how he'd brought back a bag or two to take care of. But that wasn't enough for Kasim.

"If you don't tell me exactly where that place is, and exactly what I have to do to get in, then I'll take you round to the magistrate tomorrow and you can explain to him how you came by so much gold."

*Kasim's Come-uppance*

There was nothing to be done about it. Ali Baba had to tell his brother the exact whereabouts of the cave in the forest, and the exact password for getting into it; and the next day Kasim hired a dozen mules and set off to see what he could see. Everything fitted: track through the forest; clearing; wall of rock; and the magic words. "Open, Sesame!" said Kasim, and the door rolled backwards and in he went with his bags and satchels to collect up whatever winnings he could find.

As was usual, the rock-door had rumbled shut behind Kasim when he'd gone in; but after he'd stuffed all his baggage full of gold and jewels and suchlike he couldn't for the life of him remember how to get it open again. "Open, Barley!" he said—recollecting that the magic had to do with some sort of seed—"Open, Millet! Open, Poppy-head!" (and even, in a reckless effort to be funny, "Open, Cumin!"). But it was all to no avail. The door stayed shut, nor did he have any hope of climbing the smooth walls of the cave up to its high windows. The gold in his sacks glinted at him like grinning teeth.

Then he heard a commotion outside. For the robber band, riding past their
hide-out, were surprised to see a great team of mules browsing around outside
the door—for Kasim had foolishly not bothered to tether them in the
under-brush the way Ali Baba had done. The Captain rode up to the door and
Kasim, wild with anguish, heard him yell the magic words, "Open, Sesame!"
and the rock began to trundle sideways. What could he do? Hoping to gain
something from surprise he rushed out of the cave as soon as there was a gap
wide enough for him to do so, but, alas! he ran full tilt into the Captain, and
before the door had finished its opening the robbers had thrown him to the
ground and chopped him in half.

They were dumbfounded. How could this stranger have found his way into
their lair? How had he known of their riches, that he'd brought all these sacks
to carry them away? Who else might be in the know?

Well, one thing was for sure. If this burglar had got any accomplices then
they'd better look out. So the Captain ordered his men to divide up the two
bits of Kasim's dead body and they hung two quarters of Kasim outside the
door and two quarters inside as a warning to those who would be warned.

## Coping with the Corpse

Back at home, Mrs Kasim was getting more and more worried. By the time it
got dark and her man not back yet, she went round to Ali Baba's to see what

might be done. "Twelve mules," she said, "and all those sacks; we must be able to find him somewhere." And Ali Baba tried to comfort her and promised that he'd start off on a search as soon as it was light.

This he did. He took some of his own asses and made off like he was collecting firewood as usual, and he headed for the robbers' cave. As soon as he got there and saw the bloody bits of Kasim hanging outside the door he settled that his brother wasn't such a bright chap after all and—taking a chance that no one was inside—he called to the door to open.

Well, when he saw the other bits of Kasim, and Kasim's sacks still full of gold in there, he realized what had happened. He straightway bundled as much as he could of his brother and his brother's treasure into his own sacks, covered everything with brushwood, and set off home. He didn't fancy giving the lads a second chance with their cleavers.

When he got home he handed over the sacks of gold to his wife to take care of, and then he took the asses round to Kasim's house to break the bad news to Mrs Kasim. Knock, knock: he tapped at the door. But the door was opened not by Mrs Kasim but by Morgiana, her body slave, who was a pretty bright lass, and as soon as she'd let him in to the courtyard, Ali Baba told her the whole dreadful story.

"Brother of my lady's lord," said Morgiana, "this is thorny brushwood you are tangling with. I have some knowledge of that Captain and his men, and when they find out that someone has called in to collect Kasim and all his gold they won't rest till they have found him. We must act with the greatest circumspection."

By this time Mrs Kasim had also appeared in the courtyard, and when they broke the news to her about the dismemberment of her poor husband, they were hard put to it to stop her going at once into the street and setting up an instant wake. But Ali Baba promised that he would marry her himself, once the time of her mourning was over (for such is the custom of that place), and together they listened to the plan that Morgiana had devised.

This is how it happened. When morning came, Morgiana went down to the druggist's stall in the bazaar, seeking powerful medicine for a dangerous sickness. "Who is so ill that he needs this?" asked the druggist; and Morgiana told him it was her master. The next day she went there again and asked him for a repeat prescription, and the druggist shook his head sagely, as much as to say that no help could be expected when things were in a case like that.

That, of course, was exactly what Morgiana had intended, and it therefore came as no surprise to Kasim's neighbours and to all the merchants in the bazaar when, next day, Morgiana declared that her master was dead and that his wife and his brother and the wife of his brother were prostrate with grief.

To her had fallen the business of preparing the funeral.

Well, those preparations were not exactly conventional. That night Morgiana betook herself to the shop of one Baba Mustafa, a tailor and maker of shrouds and grave-cloths, a man well-shotten in years. Knocking at his door she proffered him a gold piece and asked him if he would accompany her on a secret journey. This he was not inclined to do and it took another asrafi before he allowed her to blindfold his eyes and lead him through streets and byways into the house and into the darkened room where the remains of Kasim were lying.

"Well, master tailor," said Morgiana, "out with your needle and sew me up this body as good as new; then when you've done, take this cloth and make me a shroud for him, for he must be buried tomorrow." So Baba Mustafa set to with his needle and by the time that all was finished he was glad enough to accept a purseful of asrafis and to allow himself once more to be blindfolded and led back through the streets and alley-ways to his tailor's shop.

## Calcification

Meanwhile, there was consternation among the forty thieves. For when they returned to their cave after a day of the usual villainies they found not only that Kasim-outside-the-door, but also Kasim-inside-the-door, had disappeared—and all his sacks of booty too. The secret of the Open Sesame was known, but how could they discover the knower?

"A plan, Captain," said one of the gang, and went on to explain how he might dress up like a foreign merchant and go into the town seeking information about who had died recently and who had fallen upon easy times. That way they might be able to work out who their sneaky visitor had been.

"Very well," said the Captain; so the fellow burrowed about among their bags of garments and turbans and sashes until he had got himself up to look like some wealthy trader from out of town. Then he set off for the bazaar,

getting there first thing in the morning so that he could see as many of the merchants as possible.

Not much was doing when he arrived—most of the shops were still shut up—but there, sitting in the dawn light was Baba Mustafa, sewing away to catch up with the time he'd lost while he'd been attending to Kasim. "Well," said the robber, "what are you up to then? How can you see to sew stitches before it's properly light?"

"Oho," said Baba Mustafa, "it's plain you're not from these parts, I've been known for my sharp eyes longer than you've been born. Why d'y'know, someone even came along the other day to get me to sew up the bits of a dead body in a room without any light at all. And I made the chap's shroud too."

"You're joking," said the robber. "You're a tailor, not a surgeon. How could you do a thing like that?"

"Never you mind," said Baba Mustafa, "it's nowt to do with you."

"Well I do mind," said the robber, clinking a couple of gold pieces in the palm of his hand, "I'd just like to see that place where you did a thing like that."

"Well, that's not easy," said the tailor, "because I never saw it. Whoever wanted the job done put a blindfold on me and took me through the streets as if I were a nervy horse."

"Hmm," said the robber, and he put down his asrafis by the tailor's stool. "Now what about this. If I were to blindfold you too, and start you off from here, why shouldn't someone with your sharp eyes have a sharp memory too, and why shouldn't you be able to remember how the journey went?"

And that's just what occurred. The robber put one of his sashes round the tailor's eyes, and the tailor slowly retraced the steps that he'd made when Morgiana led him; round corners, down alley-ways, right to the front door of Kasim's house. "That's the one," he said, "that's where they live—and very generous they were too—good pay I got for traipsing round here and doing all that work." Which hint was taken by the robber, who gave Baba Mustafa a little bag of dinars and wished him good tailoring for the rest of his days. Then, when Mustafa had left the street, the robber pulled a piece of chalk out of his wallet, chalked a big white cross on Kasim's door and went back to report to his Chief down in the forest.

A few minutes later, out comes Morgiana to do the day's shopping. She couldn't help noticing that someone had lately put a big white cross on the front door, and, having a suspicious turn of mind, it struck her that that someone might be up to no good. So she went back indoors and found a piece of white chalk and she went round the street putting crosses on every-one's doors.

Thus it came about that when the robber came back to the town with the Captain, all ready to show him the house, he found a streetful of chalk-marks and couldn't for the life of him decide which was his and which was not. So the Captain, in a fine fury, hauled him off back to the forest and had his head chopped off for being a pestiferous nuisance, and thereupon sent Robber Number Two to see if he could do any better.

Well the same thing happened to Robber Number Two as to Robber Number One. He found Baba Mustafa, jingled gold pieces at him, got shown the house, and this time, with a touch of genius, he made a red cross immediately next to the original white one. Then he went back to the forest—and Baba Mustafa went back to his shop with a growing belief that golden asrafis were being shovelled up like desert sand.

Unfortunately for Robber Number Two the same sequence of events didn't leave off there. For once again Morgiana spotted the mark on the door and once again she found some chalk to match, so that when the man proudly brought his Chief down the street, he was dismayed to see that red crosses now adorned all the doorways, along with the white ones. The house remained inscrutable and there was nothing for it except a return to the forest and off with his head as well.

## The Captain's Craft

By this time the Captain was starting to have doubts about the intelligence of his troops, so he decided that he would go and find the house for himself (at least he couldn't chop his own head off if he missed it). Thus more tours of the streets were made; more gold pieces slid into the hands of Baba Mustafa; but the Captain took no pains to mark the door but rather marked inside his head the whole placing and appearance of the house so that he would recognize it again. Then he went back to his men and propounded the following plot:

"Comrades: I have no doubt that I have found the house where is lodged the source of all our trouble and I'm going to propose an assault that will settle accounts for good. All forty of us—uh—no—sorry—um—all thirty-eight of us will travel to the town this evening. I shall travel as a sheikh dealing in oil and I shall take with me twenty—er—nineteen mules, each with two jars yoked across its back. One of these jars will indeed be filled with oil, but the other thirty-seven will contain your goodselves, comfortably stowed, and armed with scimitars, cutlasses, daggers or whatever weapons best take your fancy. We will gain admission to the house and in the dark hours of night I shall release you from your jars and we shall rise up and slay the whole household."

So it was. The oil-sheikh and his mule train rode down to the city and by tortuous journeyings made their way to Kasim's house where Ali Baba and Mrs Ali Baba were now living. (They were enjoying themselves as never before, being looked after by Morgiana and Kasim's other servants and helping Mrs Kasim to get accustomed to her grief and to the prospect of becoming another wife for Ali Baba.)

As the Captain and his entourage came up to the house Ali Baba himself was there, strolling to and fro enjoying the evening air after his supper. The Captain salaamed. "My lord," he said, "many and many a time I have come to this town selling my oil, but never before have I arrived so late. I am perplexed as to where I might rest for the night, unburden my mules and give them their fodder. Is it possible that we could tarry here in your courtyard?"

Well, Ali Baba was by nature an hospitable man and liked nothing better than company, so he welcomed the oil-sheikh to his courtyard and gave orders to Morgiana to prepare supper and a guest room for the traveller. (Nor did Ali Baba in any way recognize the sheikh for who he was. The disguise was perfect, and, in any case, he had only seen and heard the Captain before when he'd been perched up in that tree with his teeth rattling and his ears humming.)

The Captain made much ado of feeding his mules and unloading his jars. As

he did so, he whispered to each of his men that he was to wait for a summons in the middle of the night, when they should all rise from out their jars and slaughter the household. Then the Captain went indoors to enjoy his supper.

## The Kitchener's Craft

Now it so happened that, half-way through the evening, while Morgiana was doing the dishes, the lamps began to flicker and fail (it's a well-known characteristic of lamps that when one goes they all go). When Morgiana went to her cruse to replenish the supply she was dismayed to discover that the cruse was empty. A black night threatened.

"What's the worry?" said Abdullah, one of the skivvy-boys, "there's thirty-eight jars of the stuff out there in the courtyard; I'm sure our friend won't miss a ladle or two off the top of one of them." So Morgiana picked up the cruse and went out to where the thirty-eight jars were lined up and began to see if she could find one that would open. Well—you can guess she was a bit startled when, first jar that she came to, she heard a voice whispering out at her, "Is it time now?" (for the chap in the jar thought she was the Captain coming to start things moving). But Morgiana came to her senses pretty quick, realized that this was not a customary thing for oil-jars to say, and replied huskily, "No; the time is not yet." And so it went on. Jar by jar she walked down the courtyard, each time hearing, "Is it time now?" and each time replying, "No; the time is not yet," till she got to the last jar of all, where she found what she'd first come to seek.

"May Allah protect us, the Compassionating, the Compassionate," she said to herself as she filled the cruse. "My lord has given lodging to this sheikh and it seems that this sheikh is going to pay him out with a mule train of bandits"; and when she got back to the kitchen she trimmed her lamps and set a great cauldron to heat on the fire. Then she took Abdullah with her out to the yard, and between them they manhandled the one full jar of oil into the kitchen and tipped it all into the cauldron.

By dint of much stirring and stoking the oil soon began to seethe and bubble in the cauldron. Morgiana then ladled some of its contents into a can, went out to the courtyard and tipped the contents into the first jar, scalding the fellow in it to death. And so, can by can and jar by jar, she went down the line of thirty-seven thieves, making an end of each and every one of them.

Not long after this, the Captain roused himself up, opened his window, and cracked his whip out over the courtyard as a signal that the assault should begin. Nothing happened. He cracked the whip again. Still nothing.

So cursing his men for falling asleep, but fearing to make too much row, he crept out to the yard to take matters into his own hands. When he got out there, though, he was startled by the smell of oil and seething flesh, and when he touched the first jar he found it reeking hot and he realized that his plot was discovered and that of all the forty thieves he was now the last one left. There was nothing for it but to make his escape as quick as he could, so he climbed over the garden wall and made the best of his way back to his cave to think up some new stratagem for revenge.

Next morning, when Ali Baba passed through the courtyard, he was surprised to see the mules still stabled and the jars still waiting to be taken to the market. He sent for Morgiana and asked her to rouse the sheikh who must surely have overslept. "No oil-sheikh he," said Morgiana, "but a bandit-chief, and it's his men who are sleeping." And she took Ali Baba down the line of jars, showing him their contents and telling him all that had happened. They settled between them that, what with the crosses on the doors and the trick with the oil, they were up against the gang of the forty thieves, but what had happened to the Captain and the other two was more than they could tell.

"We may have done for them at the moment," said Morgiana, "but I don't reckon that's the last we'll see of that Captain." With that, she and Ali Baba went down to the tool shed, picked out a couple of shovels, and dug a large pit where they quietly buried their intruders.

## How It Ended

Once again Morgiana was right, of course. The Captain sat in his cave for a few days, brooding on his bad luck, then he gathered up some of his stock of silks and embroidered cloths and took himself off to the town in the guise of a merchant. He rented a pitch in the bazaar and started trading.

Well, as the days and weeks went by he put himself out to be friendly to all his fellow merchants—not least to one Khwajah Hassan, who was the son of our late friend Kasim and who was carrying on with his father's business. The Captain took much pains to cultivate this young man, giving him presents and standing him hot suppers, while for his part Khwajah Hassan was flattered to be taken up by a man who seemed to know so much of the ways of the world.

Now, one day Khwajah Hassan had the idea that he would surprise the Captain with a return treat. He fixed with Morgiana that she would be ready to prepare a fancy dinner for his new friend and then—when the day's trading was over—he suggested to the Captain that they might take a little stroll together. "Let me show you some pretty bits of the Garden District," he said, and he took the Captain down those streets and alley-ways that the Captain had traversed so recently with Baba Mustafa the tailor. "What am I to do about this?" thought he to himself—and privily fingered the dagger that he always kept tucked in his sash.

When they reached Kasim's old house, where Ali Baba was still living comfortably with Mrs Ali Baba, Mrs Kasim, and all Kasim's former servants, Khwajah Hassan stopped. "Well, now," he said, "just see where we've got to. This is my uncle's house; why don't we knock on the door and see if he's in?" The Captain, still puzzled by what was going on, didn't know what to say about that, and while he was still um-ing and er-ing Morgiana opened the door and (as she'd fixed with Khwajah Hassan) straightway asked them both in to supper.

This seemed to the Captain an opportunity for revenge that had been sent direct from Allah, but he set about a canny reply. "I am beholden to the house," he said with great formality, "and to the master of the house for the honour of such hospitality, but alas, I cannot accept; allow me to depart and tarry no longer."

As he'd expected, they wouldn't hear of it, and indeed, Ali Baba himself came to the door to help prevail upon his nephew's new-found friend to give way. "Why," said Ali Baba, "we have heard such reports of your kindness and your wisdom that we would fain entertain you this evening and hear more of your adventures walking up and down in the world."

"Alas again," said the Captain, "I long to accept your gracious invitation,

but you must know that I have for many years suffered an ailment of the belly and I am now ordered by my physician never to eat food with salt in it."

"What matter? What matter?" said Ali Baba, "the meats are not yet cooked. We will prepare dinner without any salt," and he hauled the Captain into the best sitting-room and ordered Morgiana to tell the cook "no salt".

"No salt?" thought Morgiana; "no salt . . . funny . . . now what kind of ailment puts a bar on salt?" and before she left for the kitchen, she looked keenly at Khwajah Hassan's guest and she understood everything. For here surely, under his smooth disguise, was the one-time oil-sheikh, one-time leader of the forty thieves, and by not taking salt with his host he would be under no obligation of custom or of the law of the Prophet, to restrain whatever violent intentions he might harbour. "So-ho!" she thought, "this fellow is up to no good and must be attended to."

As the conversation and the salt-less dinner proceeded therefore, Morgiana took care to observe the company closely, and was not surprised to see the guest of honour fussing and fiddling from time to time with his sash, where, eventually, she perceived what could only be the handle of a hidden poniard. (And, for his part, as he fussed and fiddled, the Captain thought, "How long, how long must I still endure this boring gossip? How soon can we get rid of this tiresome servant girl and her attendants, so that I can get down to the point of the evening?")

Morgiana however, besought Ali Baba that, while they enjoyed the last of their dinner, she might dance for them, the better to show zeal for their guest's entertainment and—to the Captain's great impatience—Ali Baba agreed. So Morgiana left the supper-room and went to her closet where she found a great store of muslins, such as dancers wear. She dressed herself in a transparent veiling, bound a fine turban round her head, and placed within the sash at her waist a dagger rich in filigree and jewellery. Then she found the boy Abdullah, gave him a tambourine, and ordered him to accompany her in her dance.

Thus, with Abdullah rattling the tambourine, Morgiana entered the supper-room, bowed low to the assembled company, and began to cavort round the middle of the floor. She flung veils around, rather like the historic Salome, all the time watching the glinting eyes of the Captain of the forty thieves and she saw a flicker of understanding, and as his hand moved towards his sash, she pulled out her own dagger and lunged at him, thrusting it into his heart.

Uproar! "The girl's gone mad!" cried Ali Baba. "What a way to treat a guest!" cried Khwajah Hassan. "Rattle, rattle," went the tambourine. But Morgiana drew back and bowed to everyone. "Not mad, my lord," she said to

Ali Baba, "but prudent in my master's service;" and she showed him the dagger hidden in the Captain's sash and explained the sure purpose of his refusing to eat salt.

Then Ali Baba did indeed recognize him as the man he had first seen so long ago, down in the forest, crying "Open Sesame!"; the man who had sought his hospitality as oil-sheikh and brought into his courtyard a mule train of thieves. And he blessed Morgiana for her wit and straightway married her to his nephew Khwajah Hassan who, being a son of Kasim, was hardly a match for her beauty or her intelligence. He also gathered together his old train of asses and returned to the robbers' cave to clear it of all its treasure. Then he, and Mrs Ali Baba, and she who had once been Mrs Kasim, and all the rest of them lived (as the saying goes) happily ever after.

 And when Sheherezade had told the story of Ali Baba, which she had got from the stranger from the north, she went on to tell another which she had heard from him:–

## THE STORY OF ALADDIN AND THE SLAVE OF THE LAMP

### The Uncle

Times past, way off in China, in the city of all cities, there was a good-for-nothing fellow called Aladdin. His dad was a tailor, of the Tuanki family, and the idea was that Aladdin would be a tailor too, but he didn't set much store by that for a game of marbles. So instead of learning his trade he hung around street corners with a lot of tykes no better than himself. If they had any money they gambled it away; if they didn't have any they were up to no good till they got some.

Having a son who racketed around like that was bad news for the tailor. He tried all ways to get the boy to shape up, but it was no good, and in the end the chap worried himself into an early grave. There was nothing for it, then, but Aladdin's mum had to sell up the shop, and the best she could do to keep the two of them out of the workhouse was to take up spinning. Not a profitable trade. She had to spin from sun-up to midnight just to pay the rent.

Now it so happened that half-way round the world, in Africa, there lived at this time a Moorish magician. He was a chap who'd spent a lot of time perfecting the arts of geomancy (which is a bit like telling fortunes from tea-leaves, but you do it with sand). Anyway, with his sand and his sand-table he'd discovered that there was a fortune to be found over in China, but that he'd probably need the help of a down-and-out ne'er-do-well called Aladdin to do some of the dirty work.

So the Moorish magician set off for China; and when he got to the city of all cities he set about making a tour of all the back streets till he should come across the Aladdin he was looking for. Well, that wasn't so hard. By this time young Aladdin's reputation as a tear-away was pretty widely known and the magician wasn't long in discovering him with his mates—tying oil-pots to a stray dog's tail, or some such monkey business.

The Moorish magician stood there watching for a bit; then he goes up to the boy, flings his arms round him, hugs him, kisses him and I don't know what-all, and says, "Aladdin! oh, Aladdin! son of my dear old brother; say hello to your long-lost uncle!"

Well—far from saying hello, Aladdin wasn't up to saying anything at all. Nobody'd ever told him that he'd got an uncle, long-lost or otherwise, and he hadn't a clue what to do next. But the uncle had. After a lot more fussing he opened up his purse and took out a handful of golden dinars. "Oh my dear

[ 143 ]

nephew," says he, "take these—take these as a token of all the years that have passed us by—you and me and your dear mother and father (may Allah rest his soul). Go home to your mother and give her my greetings; tell her I'm back from all my wanderings and that tomorrow night, God willing, we'll get together to talk about old times. Here—" (pulling more dinars out of his purse), "make sure you lay on a nice supper; and now just tell me how I get round to your house and we'll meet again tomorrow."

So Aladdin told him where he lived and then rushed off there to give the news to his mum. She was pretty surprised to see him, because he didn't usually come home that early, and she was still more surprised when he told her about his uncle. "What uncle?" she said. "First I've heard of any uncles," and she reckoned it was some fancy excuse to explain how he'd come by all that gold. But Aladdin stuck to his story and made so much to-do about fixing a proper supper the next night that she didn't see she'd much alternative. So she did as he suggested, laid in more steaks and jam-puddings and jars of wine than she'd seen in the last twenty years, and sat back to see what would happen.

Sure enough, next evening, there's a ring at the bell and there stands the magician. "Good evening, Mrs Tuanki," says he, "I know this is a surprise, and I know it's short notice and all that, but now I'm back, I've just got to make amends for being such a hopeless brother-in-law to you . . ." And so he went on; and the end of it all was that she swallowed the lot (including the nice supper), and from that day on Aladdin had an uncle and the Tuanki family had three good meals a day.


## The Cave

The magician worked fast to get Aladdin into a biddable frame of mind. Along with paying the back-rent and suchlike, he said he'd make some inquiries about having the boy apprenticed to the brokers down in the market—and what with promising to set him up in business and buy him some smart clothes, he soon had him trotting around like a tame poodle. They'd go into town, look at all the monuments, eat dinner, and even wander round the public bits of the Sultan's palace, while Aladdin's uncle explained to him all the hierarchies and customs of the state.

So Aladdin wasn't surprised when one day his uncle turned up and suggested a walk in the other direction. "If you'd like to come with me into the country," he said, "I'll show you a sight beside which everything we've seen together so far will be nothing"—a remark pretty well guaranteed to

encourage even a slouch like Aladdin to buckle on his shoes.

Off they went. First of all through gardens at the side of the town, each with its own pretty little pavilion or pagoda, then into open country, and then into a rocky valley that led up to the hills. "What's all this about?" said Aladdin, who'd never set foot out of the city gate before this. "Why do we want to be traipsing about in this rough country when we might be having a picnic or something back in those gardens?"

"Never you mind," said his uncle, "you keep by me and you'll see gardens beyond anything the Kings of the World can manage." And he kept walking into the rocky valley.

Eventually they got to a little flat part covered with small boulders. "Right," said the magician, "now you hunt around here and find me some sticks and stuff to make a fire"—which was a pretty tall order since most of the valley-bottom was all stones. But Aladdin was really keyed-up to know what this uncle of his was up to, so he worked away more than he'd ever done before at finding whatever bits of chippings and brushwood he could. As he brought them along, the magician made him pile them up in a little circle that he'd marked among the boulders, and while Aladdin was fossicking around, he secretly poured on some powder that he'd hidden in a flask underneath his robe.

[ 145 ]

When they'd got a fair pile of tinder together the magician walked round it with his staff, conjuring smoke and fire out of the brushwood, and as the fire took hold he began to mutter cabbalistic words over it. Then, suddenly—whump!—the whole lot exploded with a force that shook the floor of the valley. Aladdin was scared out of his wits and was all for heading back to town as fast as possible, but his uncle caught him a clip round the head that just about knocked his back teeth out and caused him to tumble to the ground.

"Hey—what's that in aid of?" he said, suddenly overcome with serious doubts about how good the intentions of his new relation really were. "All right—all right—easy does it, my dear nephew," said the magician, who didn't want Aladdin running off after all the trouble he'd had to get him there. "Cruel-to-be-kind, you know. If I'm to show you all these marvels then I can't have you clearing off home before we've even started. Now look there where the fire was." And Aladdin looked—and what he saw among the ashes was a big marble slab with a large copper ring sticking out of the middle of it. "Treasure," said the magician; "treasure, buried in your name, such that you are the only one who can redeem it. Do now as I say and you'll become richer than all the Sultans of the East," and he directed Aladdin to pull up the marble slab.

Aladdin took hold of the copper ring and heaved, but the slab wouldn't budge. He heaved again till he almost bust a gut, and the slab still wouldn't budge. "Oh, Aladdin, Aladdin, son of my brother, what did I say," said the magician, "the treasure may be yours to redeem, but you can't just heave away at that slab like a navvy. Pull the ring, and as you pull, recite your name, and your father's name and your mother's name and the stone will come up."

So Aladdin pulled again, saying these names like a prayer, and lo and behold! up came the slab as though it was on oiled bearings, and there below was a dark cave with steps going down. "Bravo!" said the magician, "well done! Now here is what you must manage next:

you must enter that cavern and go down the twelve steps before you;
at the bottom you will find a passage-way of four secret chambers,
and in each chamber you will find four marble tables,
and on each table you will find four golden jars,
and in each jar you will find gold and gems and jewels;

*but* don't put your hands on any of it and don't let your body or your garments or the hem of your robe touch any of it, otherwise you will be turned into a *black stone*. Instead, go carefully through each of the chambers and when you get to the end of the fourth one you will see in front of you a plain door with a copper handle. Take hold of that handle and repeat again the

names of power and you will be able to open the door.

"The other side of the door," said the magician, "is a garden, whose like is not to be found this side of paradise. It is laid out with lawns and pathways, streams and fountains, fruit trees and flowers, of a kind beyond description—but do not be waylaid. You must take a path from the door that winds for fifty cubits until it comes to an open pavilion, and in that pavilion you will see a ladder of thirty rungs, and at the top of that ladder you will see a Lamp suspended from the roof. Climb up and take the Lamp, and once you have it tucked into your robe you shall be free of the garden and of the golden chambers. Wander where you will, take what you like, but be sure to bring the Lamp and everything back to me here at the top of the stairs.

"Go now, and for fear that any harm befalls you before you get to the Lamp take this ring, which will serve as protection so long as you keep to all that I have said," and the magician drew from off his finger his seal-ring and gave it to Aladdin.

Aladdin lowered himself down the hole until his feet reached the top step of the stairs and then he set off to follow all the directions his uncle had given him. Everything was there: the four chambers with their pots of gold, the doorway into the garden, the pathway through the trees, and the Lamp, hanging

over the ladder. So Aladdin climbed
up the thirty rungs, unhooked the
Lamp from its gimbal, stuffed it into
his robe, climbed down the thirty
rungs and set off to explore the
garden.

What his uncle said was true.
There could surely be no other
garden like this one. The grass was
greener and smoother than
anywhere else, the water was bluer
than anywhere else, the flowers
were piled up in colours more
variegated than anywhere else, and
as for the trees—Aladdin more or
less choked. Every tree was not just
more shapely than any tree he'd
ever seen, but every tree also had,
dangling from its branches, great
clusters of glittering fruit of
bewildering brilliance. Now if
Aladdin had spent more time at
study, or working with the
merchants of the bazaar, he would
have realised straightway that this
fruit was not just any sort of glass
bauble and crystal, but was nothing
less than rare gemstones: emeralds
and diamonds, rubies, spinels and
balasses of a size and perfection that
was ridiculous. Such things could
not be possible. But Aladdin was
very taken with them, so he pulled
down as big an assortment of them
as he could and he stuffed them into
his pockets and his turban and every
fold of his clothing that could carry
them, and he made his way back to
the staircase, rattling like a bag of
marbles. He was so weighed down

with the things that there was no hope of him taking any gold from the great jars on the marble tables.

By the time he got back to the top of the stairs his uncle was pretty cross, what with hanging about up there most of the afternoon waiting for Aladdin to finish his fruit-picking. "Come on, then," he said, sharpish, when Aladdin got on to the top step, "give us the Lamp and then I'll help you climb out." Well, it was true that Aladdin needed some help: for one thing it was a big pull up out of the cave, and for another he was so weighed down with all his winnings that he was bothered how he could clamber up on his own, but he didn't see any point in passing the Lamp out first, especially since it was lodged round his belly somewhere, submerged under all the gemstones.

"Oh, no, Uncle, don't worry about that. Just give us a hand and then I'll find it for you."

"Oh, no, Nephew. Lamp first, then I'll give you a hand."

"But that's daft," said Aladdin, and went on arguing the toss until gradually he came to realize that there was more to this Lamp than he thought. His uncle obviously didn't want it just to read in bed with (and that was true, as we shall see). In the end the magician lost his head with fury and frustration. "Damn you to hell!" he cried, "*zambahshalamahzarúska!*" and with that wild and magical imprecation he caused the marble slab to fall back over the hole with a crash, nearly smashing in Aladdin's skull as it did so.

There he was, shut in the dark, while the Moorish magician tramped off down the valley and took his way back to Africa as quick as he could.


## The Lamp

Aladdin was now in a right fix. He tried yelling to see if the man would let him out, but by this time he'd worked out that the wizard fellow was no uncle of his and that he was the victim of some mysterious plot, so he didn't have much hope of seeing daylight soon in that direction. But nor did he have any luck in the other direction either. With the crashing shut of the trapdoor, the doors to all the chambers and the garden crashed shut too, and Aladdin was hemmed in on his staircase in total darkness.

"Truly there is no God but The God," said Aladdin, "He sends us mirth and He sends us misery. Alhamdohlillah; praise to the All-knowing, the Omnipotent, and to his prophet Mohammed." And as he prayed these prayings he lifted his arms into the darkness, lowered them, and brought his hands together in supplication over the gemstones, rattling about in his robe.

Now as he sat there, moving his hands in prayer, it so happened that the

fingers of one hand rubbed against the ring which the magician had given him
when he first set off into the cave. And as he rubbed the ring, so there leapt
forth in a shower of bright sparks an Ifrit from the tribe of the Jann of Solomon
(for Aladdin's ring was one of those blessed with power by the great king). "Speak!"
cried the Jinni. "I am the Slave of the Ring! Speak and tell me your desires!"

Well, Aladdin was flabbergasted; one minute locked in a pitch-black dungeon
for good, the next minute asked to give orders—he didn't well know what to do.
But after goggling for a bit at the Jinni he realized that this was the best chance
he had of getting away, so he said, "Slave of the Ring, get me out of here."

Whoosh! He'd hardly blinked when he found himself sitting on the ground
above the entrance to the cavern, now all tidied over and hidden again. The
Jinni had disappeared and Aladdin decided there was nothing for it but to walk
back home and try to recover his wits a little. So he trudged off down the
valley, and past the gardens, and into the town, with all his treasures still
rattling and rolling round in his pockets and his turban and under his robe.

"Well, what happened to you?" asked his mother when he got home, "and
what's become of Uncle?"

"Don't ask me!" said Aladdin; "don't say a word!" and without more ado
he went off to his room where he unloaded all his pockets and his undergarments into some empty jars, put the Lamp on a table, climbed into bed and
went to sleep.

[ 151 ]

Next morning, first thing, he told his mum what had occurred with his uncle. "Allah protect us!" said Mrs Tuanki, "what are we to do now? No sooner does someone come along to get you out of the gutter, teach you some manners, fix you up in a respectable job, give us some housekeeping-money, than you go and offend him so that he won't come back. That puts me back at my spinning and how we shall make out I just don't know."

"Now stop fashing," said Aladdin, "and we'll sort something out. First off, you may like to know that I brought a few things back from out of that cave, and they should see us through for a while. Look at this old Lamp, for instance," fetching the Lamp out of his room, "we could polish that up for a start and we'd get a bob or two for it down at the market."

Well, that seemed quite a good idea, so his mum fetched out the lamp-cleaning stuff and Aladdin set to work to fettle it up. But no sooner had he started to polish it than there was another great flash and out came a Jinni three times bigger and three times meaner than the last one. "Speak!" he roared, so that poor Mrs Tuanki got all her spinning in a tangle. "I am the Slave of the Lamp and of all who hold the Lamp; command me and all my fellows to whatever you desire!"

This time Aladdin was beginning to get the hang of Jann and he answered, "Breakfast. Breakfast for two—the best you can manage," and in half a shake of a donkey's tail the Jinni was back with a gigantic silver tray. All down both sides of the tray there were twelve golden bowls, steaming with good things, and in the middle there were two silver goblets and two leather bottles full of old wine. "By heck," said Aladdin, "I'm ready for this," and as the Jinni vanished he went and untangled his mother, and the two of them set about their meal.

Now Aladdin's mum was not very keen on tinkering with supernatural forces, and as soon as she'd finished her breakfast she started trying to persuade Aladdin to have no more to do with them. "Take that ring and that Lamp," she said, "and throw them in the river." But Aladdin would have none of it. For one thing he thought he might get breakfasts like that every day of the week, and for another he realized that all the shenanigans with his so-called uncle had been because of the Lamp. If the chap was willing to go through all that plotting to try to get hold of it, then it must be a pretty powerful instrument.

Anyway, to keep his mother happy he decided that he wouldn't call on the Slave more than he had to. Instead he settled to try to get by more comfortably by selling off, one by one, the bowls and the goblets that the Jinni had brought. When the money was used up from selling one he'd sell the next. At first the merchants in the bazaar thought that he was an easy

pushover—probably fencing stolen goods anyway—but he gradually came to see the value of the stuff that he was bargaining with and before long he turned into a shrewd dealer. What's more, when the goods ran out he could always call up the Slave of the Lamp and order some more.

## The Princess

Everything would have gone on nicely from this time forward, except that one day Aladdin was going down to the market when he heard a great racket. The Sultan's men were coming, and with them the Town Crier who was yelling, ''Beware, beware! By order of the Sultan, Lord of the Time and Master of the Age, let all men leave the streets and markets and immure them in their houses; for the daughter of the Sultan, the Princess Badr al-Budur, now comes this way in train for the hammam baths. Let no man be present, upon pain of death, to see the Princess as she passes!''

Well, that was enough for Aladdin. He'd long heard of the beauty and gracefulness of the Princess, and he'd not been shut up in caves and magicked by wizards without reckoning that he could take a look at a Princess if he wanted to. So he went along to the hammam baths and he found a little cranny, at the back of the door, where he could creep in and see the Princess as she came.

Sheesh! For once the newsmongers had got it wrong in the wrong direction. Not all the reports of the Princess's beauty had quite prepared Aladdin for the revelation of her face and form as she passed by his little hidey-hole. His knees went weak with love for her and he almost fell out of concealment—which would have been the worse for him. Anyway, from that day forth there was nothing for it but he must sort out a way to marry her.

What he did was this: first of all he persuaded his mum that she was going to have to make his proposal for him. (She thought he was downright crackers, and decided that they'd both end up getting their heads chopped off, but by this time Aladdin was a pretty determined character and she had learnt to do as he told her.) Then he went into his room and began to sort out some of the fanciest jewels from those that he'd found in the cave. "Now let's have a bowl," he said to his mum, and she hunted around the house, but the best she could come up with was her big baking-bowl out of the kitchen. "That'll do nicely," said Aladdin, and he piled in the jewels, which seemed to glitter and shine all the more brilliantly for their plain setting; and he covered the lot with a blue-check table-cloth.

"Now," says Aladdin, "what I want you to do is to take this lot down to the Sultan's palace and get in the queue for the audience-chamber. They should let you in sometime this morning and you wait in there till someone calls you up to see the Sultan. Then you give him this bowl and say something on the lines of, 'O my Lord, may the blessings of Allah be upon you, my son back home wants to marry your daughter and he's sent this stuff round as a courting-present . . .' and so on, and so forth. That should make him think."

"By gow!" says his mum, "make him think! It'll do more than that. It'll make him send for his Sworder there and then, and they'll have my head rolling on the floor before you can say 'Jack Robinson'!"

"All right, all right," says Aladdin, "I can see that it all looks a bit dodgy—but believe you me, it'll work out all right."

There was nothing she could say any more to persuade him, so she picked up the bowl and made her way down to the palace just as she was, in her moth-eaten widow's weeds.

When she got there, everything happened as Aladdin had predicted—except that she hung around in the audience-chamber all day and nobody took any notice of her. The Sultan did all the Sultan-ish things that he was there for, but the Wazirs and the chamberlains and the vergers paid no heed to the little old woman all in black with her baking-bowl.

The same thing happened the next day, and the next day, and the next, all the same for about a month, till Aladdin began to get a bit vexed. "What're you doing?" he said; "you're not trying. You must just be a bit more pushy."

Equally though, the Sultan was beginning to get more and more curious about this shabby, silent figure who kept turning up day by day. "Who is she?" he asked the Grand Wazir, "what does she want? If she's here tomorrow see that she's called before me."

Accordingly, next day, no one was more surprised, or flustered, than Mrs Tuanki when she was called up to the Sultan first off. "Oh my Lord," she said, kissing the ground in front of him, "Oh my Lord, Allah bless thee, and Allah forgive me, but I have a boon to ask which is for thine ears only. Hear me, and then too grant me forgiveness."

"Very well," said the Sultan, "if it's something that Allah can forgive then I'm sure I can too," and turning to the Grand Wazir he said, "Clear the court!"

Grumbling mightily the folk in the audience-chamber were cleared back to the street; the courtiers went out, and Aladdin's mum was left confronting the Sultan and the Grand Wazir who stayed as his chief adviser. "So what's all the fuss about?" asked the Sultan, and Aladdin's mum entered into the whole story about how Aladdin was wasting away for love of the Sultan's daughter and had sent her along to ask for her hand in marriage.

The Sultan was so astounded by the cheek of this proposal, coming from such a decrepit old woman, that the only thing he could do was laugh. "In the name of Allah," he cried, "we are a noble nation that even a tailor's widow may seek a Princess for a daughter-in-law—and I suppose that's your wedding present in there," pointing to the baking-bowl.

"Well as it happens, my Lord, it is," said Mrs Tuanki, much relieved that the Sultan was taking everything so matily, and she pulled the blue-check cloth off the baking-bowl. Wow! Red, green, blue, silver, gold, the jewels shone out with amazing radiance, turning the audience-chamber into a gallery that danced with colour. Aladdin's mum (who hadn't been expecting anything quite like that) fell over backwards with surprise and the Sultan and his Grand Wazir leapt out of their chairs for fear the whole brilliant vessel might there and then explode.

"Madam," said the Sultan, when he'd come back to his senses, "Madam; allow me to pay mind to this present of yours," and he began to examine the contents of the bowl with some care, picking out gems of especial magnificence and seeing, with a practised eye, that this baking-bowl held more treasure than the treasury of his own palace. Plainly the son of this decrepit widow was a person to be reckoned with, and if he had more jewels where these came from, he would make a match for the Princess Badr al-Budur beyond that of any other suitor.

That was the trouble, though. For before Mrs Tuanki ever appeared on the

scene the Sultan's Grand Wazir had made approaches to his Lord in the interests of his son, and it was all but settled that this young chap was going to marry the Princess—thus keeping all the monkeys together at the top of the tree. But the Wazir's son was not likely to come up with courting-presents like Aladdin's and the Sultan was bothered to know how he could keep his Wazir happy and get his hands on the jewellery.

"Madam," he said again (can't you just hear him!), "we are honoured to be seen as worthy to receive a gift of this ethereal splendour, and honoured that the giver should think so highly of us that he seeks the hand of our daughter in marriage. How could we refuse? But I fear that we cannot accede to your request with absolute spontaneity, for you must know that the Princess Badr al-Budur is just now engaged in a religious retreat, and nothing can be done until her return in three months' time. Pray tell your son, the honourable Messire Aladdin, that we shall convey the treasure of his heart and of his house to our daughter and shall await a prosperous engagement when our daughter shall return."

## Bridegroom Number One

"I don't like it," said Mrs Tuanki when she got back home. "He's given us the brush-off and he's kept all those jewels. What was all that about a religious retreat? First time I ever heard of Princesses doing a thing like that . . ." But Aladdin didn't seem to mind. "You told him," he said; "you gave him the present. He knows what's what. We'll just wait and see what happens." So wait they did.

But although the Sultan had said what he said in order to gain time, he'd reckoned without the persistence of the Grand Wazir. That one wasn't going to see his son lose out to some inconsequential peasant. So he kept on at the Sultan (he was good at keeping on, that was one of the things he was paid for), and so it turned out that the Sultan began to think that the bowlful of jewels was a simple piece of good fortune and that his daughter really ought to marry the Wazir's son. Why not? It had always seemed a good idea. Let's get on with it.

So one day, a couple of months after her audience with the Sultan, Aladdin's mum went down to the town and was startled to see flags flying and bunting in the streets. "What's going on here, then?" she asked; and they told her that the Wazir's son was getting betrothed to the Sultan's daughter. "Where've you been then, missus?" they said. "Haven't you heard about that already?"

Without more ado, Mrs Tuanki went back to Aladdin and told him the news. "I never did trust those folk," he said, "but don't you mind. I've not done with them yet," and he sat quietly at home while everyone in town got drunk. That evening, when they'd all gone to bed, he went into his room and rubbed the Lamp. Flash! there was the Jinni. "I am the Slave of the Lamp!" he roared, "and of all who hold the Lamp; command me and all my fellows to whatever you desire. Speak!" So Aladdin spoke and told him what he was to do: he was to go and fetch the Princess Badr al-Budur and the Wazir's son on their bridal couch, he was to dump the Wazir's son in the bog out back and keep guard over him for the night, then in the morning he was to take them and the couch back to the Sultan's palace.

All this the Jinni accomplished. Aladdin spent the night moonstruck by the sleeping Princess, the Wazir's son spent the night getting cold cramps in the bog, and next day they found themselves back at the palace in time for breakfast. "Well that was a funny dream," said the Princess, and told her mum what had happened; but the Wazir's son sat shivering and said nothing at all.

Next night the same thing happened. The Princess and the Wazir's son had hardly got to bed before the Jinni came again and dumped the boy in the bog and the girl in the room in front of Aladdin's adoring gaze. Then back to the palace for breakfast. This time the Wazir's son spoke up. "I've had enough of this," he said, "if it's someone's idea of a joke they can try it on another muggins in the future," and he went back home and refused to go on with the marriage. The Grand Wazir did all he could to persuade him to change his mind—because, after all, the Princess Badr al-Budur was a pretty good catch—but the lad was so clemmed with the damp-cold and so frightened of the Jinni that he decided the Heavens were against the whole match.

As for the Princess, she still thought that it had all been a dream—but not by any means as offensive as the Wazir's son made out.

## Bridegroom Number Two

With all the excitement over the wedding and everything that happened after, the Sultan had quite forgotten his promise to Aladdin's mother. But of course she'd not forgotten—nor Aladdin neither—and when the three months were up from the day she'd handed over the jewels, she went back to the audience-chamber in the Palace and waited to see the Sultan.

This time though, she didn't have to wait long. No sooner did the Sultan see this little bitty woman in her raggety gown than he remembered what had happened and he called over his Grand Wazir for a hasty confabulation. "Look who's there," he whispered, "you know what she's come for. What are we going to do about that?"

Now the Grand Wazir was still sore about his son backing out of the marriage, and he certainly wasn't keen for anyone else to step in—least of all these people. "Easy, my Lord," he said, "all you have to do is ask for more dowry. Tell her that everything can be arranged but that you'll need—er—hem—um" (counting on his fingers), "forty more bowls of jewellery like the last lot. That should settle her."

So the Sultan called up Mrs Widow Tuanki, who straightway reminded him that this was the end of the three-month interval and hoped that his daughter was now finished with the religious retreat, being as how she should now be set to marry Aladdin. "Indeed, indeed, dear Madam," said the Sultan, "did you think we had forgotten? Why, all is now ready to be set in train—processions, ceremonies, feasts and so forth—and all we need is the rest of the dower-gifts."

"Eh?" said Aladdin's mum, "dower-gifts? That's the first I've heard of those. What does your Excellency have in mind?"

Well, the Sultan got the Grand Wazir to explain about the forty bowls of gemstones, and that gentleman threw in for good measure that they expected delivery to be made by forty white dancing girls, escorted by forty black body slaves, and all by tomorrow afternoon, if you please. What's more, he hoped the weather would keep fine for the wedding.

Aladdin's mum returned home all cast down. She didn't really understand how her boy had come by all those jewels in the first place, and she certainly didn't see how he could get any more—but she gave him the message none the less. "Fine," said Aladdin, "let's get on with it"; and he straightway went off to his room, rubbed the Lamp, and told the Jinni what had happened and what they had to do.

"I hear and obey, Master," said the Jinni, and before Mrs Tuanki could think straight there started up a grand procession from her house to the

Sultan's palace: forty dancing girls, each carrying an earthenware bowl of gems from the Hoard in the Garden, and each protected by a slave, walking beside her with a drawn scimitar. And very lovely they all looked too.

"Go on, Mum," said Aladdin, "go on with them. Give my best respects to the Sultan and tell him that I'll be along to marry the Princess in the morning—while the weather holds."

And so it came about. The Sultan and the Grand Wazir were just finishing the last of the day's business in the audience-chamber when they heard a great racket outside and in walked Aladdin's mum, still in her old robe, followed by the dancing girls with all the trinkets. The hall shone with their brightness, and Mrs Tuanki kneeled before the Sultan and said, "The wedding gifts, my Lord. My son Aladdin will be here tomorrow."

The Sultan was thunderstruck. The Grand Wazir turned green with rage. But there was nothing for it. What they'd asked for, they'd got, and for the second time that season they had to set about fixing a wedding for the Princess Badr al-Budur. (She, of course, didn't have any say in the matter, but she was glad enough to get away from the Wazir's son, whom she'd always thought was a bit of a weed, and she didn't think there could be much wrong with a newcomer who gave her bowlfuls of jewels for a present.)

The flags and the bunting were brought out again, and the next morning Aladdin set out in state to make himself known to his future father-in-law. He had called up the Slave of the Lamp before he left and this was the order of his train:

twenty-four Mamelukes with war-chargers and accoutrements;
Aladdin
on a white stallion, whose saddle and bridle were encrusted with gems;
twelve more Mamelukes with war-chargers and accoutrements;
forty-eight white slaves,
each carrying a bowl in which were a thousand gold pieces;
Aladdin's mum;
twelve handmaids clothed as the daughters of morning,
and all surrounded by a guard of honour,
crying:
"Praise to Allah! Praise to Him who Changeth and is not Changed!"

Admittedly it looked a bit like an army, but Aladdin had various of the Mamelukes and the slaves throw gold pieces in among the crowd as they travelled along the streets, so everybody blessed him for a proper gentleman, just right for their Princess.

When the procession eventually reached the Sultan's palace, Aladdin rode to the front and greeted the King with a pretty speech on the lines of him thanking the Sultan for agreeing to bestow his daughter on so humble a person . . . not being worthy of so precious a jewel . . . tongue-tied by so much honour . . . etc., etc., until the Sultan thought best to interrupt and suggest that they all went indoors for a cup of tea. This they did, and in the course of their further conversation Aladdin happened to remark that he was eager to build a little house or pavilion which might serve as a new home for his bride, and did the Sultan have any thoughts on the matter?

"Well," said the Sultan, "it so happens that there's a stretch of land opposite my palace there which we only use for practising polo on, why don't you build something there?"

"Very well then," said Aladdin, "I'll get that done, and then we can proceed with the wedding and so on," and with much bowing and arm-waving he left the room and took himself off to a quiet place. Here he pulled the Lamp from out of his wedding robes, rubbed it, and out sprang the Slave of the Lamp: "Speak, Lord! Command me and my fellows to whatever you may desire!" and Aladdin thereupon ordered the building of a pavilion that might be one of the wonders of the world:

Its outer stones were of jasper and alabaster, inlaid with marble and mosaic-work; within were chambers within chambers, each furnished to perfection, and containing proper stores of household utensils, and wardrobes of fine robes, and chests full of gold and silverware and caskets of bright gems; and there were kitchens and stables, all serviced with attendants and slaves, and over all there was a great belvedere, looking out over town and country, with twenty-four windows decorated with emeralds and rubies—except at one corner, and there, there was only plain plasterwork—unfinished.

All this Aladdin commanded, and in a trice it was done; whereupon Aladdin asked the Jinni to lay a carpet of gold-inwrought brocade from the door of his pavilion to the entrance of the Sultan's palace. Then he returned to the company and invited them to come and see the little house that he'd put up for his bride.

Well—between you and me—up till now they'd treated Aladdin as a bit of a joke. After all, he'd never tried to hide the fact that he was a tailor's son, and they all thought that he'd struck it lucky somehow or other but that it wouldn't last. When they came to the door of the palace though, and saw that gleaming new building rising up beyond the courtyard they were astounded.

"Wonderful . . . gorgeous . . . majestic," they all said to each other,

but the Grand Wazir said, "Sorcery! We are all at the mercy of the Prince of Darkness!"

"Well, we all know what you mean by that," said the Sultan, "you're still jealous because Aladdin's marrying my daughter instead of your son. Come on, let's go and look at this sorcery."

So with the Sultan in the lead they all trooped along the golden carpet to the door of the pavilion, where Aladdin formally greeted them and bade them welcome. Then he took the Sultan round the rooms of the house, disclosing all their comforts and treasures. Eventually they climbed to the belvedere with its sights across land and sea, and as the Sultan was marvelling at the opulence of it all, so he came to the window set in unadorned plaster. "Ho!" he said, "what of this then? Your builder seems to have missed a bit out."

"Too true," said Aladdin, "too true. But such was the speed that we worked, to please your Highness and the daughter of your Highness, we didn't have time to finish the building before your visit. It shall be done tomorrow."

"There you are then," said the Sultan, looking at the Grand Wazir, "what sort of sorcery is that if it can't finish the job properly? You impugn my son-in-law too readily." And he ordered his own architect and his own builders to complete the work on the window and gave signal for the festivities to begin, to celebrate the marriage of Aladdin to the Princess Badr al-Budur.

## The Wizard

From that day on there seemed to be nothing that could spoil the good fortune and the happiness of Aladdin and his family. The Princess discovered that she liked her new husband even more than she liked the jewels that he kept producing; Aladdin's mum found housekeeping in the royal pavilion a good deal more agreeable than spinning in the back streets; and Aladdin himself struck up a chummy relationship with the Sultan and they used to go hunting and fishing and playing polo together when the Sultan wasn't having to give audiences and suchlike.

But we've forgotten about that Moorish magician who was the cause of all this in the first place (and that's not surprising, because Aladdin had forgotten about him too). Over in Africa though, the magician had not forgotten about Aladdin. He hadn't been home long before he began to be sorry that he'd lost his temper when he shut Aladdin in the cave—especially since he'd shut his Ring of Solomon in there too—and he began to ponder how he might make good some of his losses.

He got out all his sand-tables and stuff and he began to make some prognostications about what might be happening in China—and you can guess his surprise when he discovered that Aladdin was not only still alive but was now Master of the Slaves of the Lamp. He just about had a fit. "Exterminate him; exterminate him!" he yelled, stamping round the room and kicking his apparatus, "I shall not rest till I have encompassed his destruction."

Straightway he began to make his plans, and once again he set off for China. This time he had no need to comb the streets for his victim, because everyone was still talking about the Emir Aladdin, his pavilion of splendour, and his habit of throwing golden dinars around whenever he went for a walk. Indeed, you could see the belvedere of the pavilion, with its (now) twenty-four glittering windows, from every side of the town, and the wizard need only do a few simple spells with his sand-table to discover that the Lamp of Power was kept in the house and not carried about by Aladdin wherever he went.

"That has him," said the magician, and he set about obtaining a stock of

brand-new copper lamps which he carefully packed in baskets for loading on to a donkey. When all was ready he waited till he heard news that Aladdin had gone out hunting, and then he started through the town like any trader in the streets. "New lamps!" he cried. "New lamps for old! Come on, ladies, do yourselves a favour, out with your old lamps; every old lamp gets a new one in exchange! Roll up, roll up! New lamps for old!"

Well, it wasn't long before half the city was following along behind him, pointing their fingers at him and calling everyone else to watch. "He's barmy," they shouted, "look at old barmy-boots! Go fetch your old lamps and get him to give you a new one!"

Before long the wizard made sure that he was in the street going past Aladdin's house, and with all the commotion, the Princess Badr al-Budur couldn't help sending to know if it was bloody revolution or what-all. "Oh, ma'am," said the servant coming back, "it's a mad African, giving away new lamps in exchange for old ones. Everyone's laughing at him. But—come to think of it—the Master's got a dirty old lamp, stuck away in his back room,

let's swap it and give him a surprise." Which is just what they did. They sent a slave down to the street to change Aladdin's old lamp for a new one and as soon as he'd done so the magician discerned that the Lamp of Power was now in his hands. "Take the lot, you idiots! Take the lot!" he cried, and he tipped the donkey-baskets all over the road, and while everyone rushed up to see what they could find he made off into the side streets round the back.

When he'd got clear of the crowds and into a deserted part of the town, the wizard sat down to wait for nightfall, and then he rubbed the Lamp. Shezam! out came the Jinni. "Speak! I am the Slave of the Lamp; command me and all my fellows to whatever you desire!"

"Well, it's good to meet you after all this time," said the wizard, "here's what I want," and he commanded the Slave of the Lamp to uproot Aladdin's pavilion and all that was in it and to carry the lot (with the magician included) back to his estates in Africa. "Hearing and obeying!" said the Jinni, and straightway the whole caboodle was magicked off to Africa, leaving nothing but the polo practice-ground in front of the Sultan's palace.

In the morning, when he woke up, the Sultan did what he usually did and drew the curtains to look across at Aladdin's pavilion. And there it was—gone. He closed his eyes, and opened them again slowly. Still gone. So he sent for the Grand Wazir. "What's happened then?" he asked.

"Wha'd'you mean 'what's happened then?'" asked the Wazir, who'd only just woken up.

"Where is it?" asked the Sultan.

"Where's what?" asked the Wazir.

"That," said the Sultan, and he pointed out of the window.

The Wazir gulped. "Well, it was there last night . . . and . . . and . . . oh! Excellency," (wringing his hands) "isn't that what I've said all along? It's sorcery. We've all been duped by sorcerers!"

This time the Sultan was more inclined to believe his Grand Wazir—especially since he'd now lost his daughter—but it wasn't long before he discovered that Aladdin hadn't been in the pavilion but had gone off hunting. "Very well," he said, "he must be arrested. Guards! . . ." and he called up the captain of the guard and ordered him to go and hunt Aladdin and to bring him back a prisoner. The fellow was a sorcerer and would have his head chopped off.

The captain of the guard was surprised about this because, like everyone else, he'd always found the Emir Aladdin a sociable sort of chap, as unsorcerer-like as they come. But Sultan's orders were Sultan's orders, so he took his men into the forests and before long they'd found Aladdin and taken him back to the palace, a prisoner. He marched up to the Sultan's room:

tramp, tramp, tramp! "Now," said the Sultan, "what's the meaning of this?"
and he pointed out of the window to where Aladdin's pavilion wasn't. Aladdin
looked and, like the Sultan and Wazir before him, looked again. Polo
practice-ground; nothing else.

"Your Highness," said Aladdin, "I don't know. To be sure, everything was
there when I went away, how should I know what's become of it?"

"Well, it's your house," said the Sultan, "you ought to look after it; and
that thing on your neck is your head, and you ought to look after that too. If
you can't find your house and my daughter in the next six months I'll have it
put on a pole by the city gate."

"Six months," cried Aladdin, "six months! Good grief! If I can't find them
all in the next six weeks I'll chop my head off myself and bring it to you as a
present."

So they let Aladdin go and he began to wander round in a disconsolate sort
of way, pondering how a place that size could have vanished and how he could
set about finding it. And as it turned out, his ramblings led him to the
self-same valley where he'd had the adventure with the treasure cave and that
suddenly reminded him about his Ring, blessed with the power of Solomon

himself. So without more ado he rubbed the Ring, there on his finger, and out came the Jinni: "Speak! I am the Slave of the Ring; speak and tell me your desires!"

"Slave of the Ring," said Aladdin, "my house is vanished, my wife is vanished, find them and bring them back to the place of their proper abode."

"Alas!" said the Jinni, "that may not be. These things are beyond my competence, for they are now in the power of the Slave of the Lamp. I dare not attempt it."

"Very well," said Aladdin, "in that case take me to my house."

"I hear and obey," said the Jinni, and in the space of an eye-glance he set Aladdin down beside his pavilion in Africa. There he was, just under the window of the Princess Badr al-Budur.

Hardly had Aladdin staggered to his feet and settled that this was, indeed, his house when the Princess's window opened and the Princess's maidservant put her head out to get some fresh air. She spotted this Chinese-looking chap down below and nearly fell out of the window as she recognized Aladdin. "O my lady! O my lady!" she called back into the room, "here's my Lord Aladdin standing in the garden!" The Princess rushed up to the window, and when she saw that it certainly was Aladdin, she threw down one of her bracelets from her wrist so that he looked up at her. "Round the back!" she called at him in a sort of whisper. "Go through the little door round the back!" and she sent the maidservant down to bring Aladdin to her room.

Apparently the wizard was at that time doing some shopping in an African city down the road, so Aladdin and the Princess Badr al-Budur were able to have a long talk about the peculiar things that had happened. "Tell me," said Aladdin, by way of a start, "have you come across an old copper lamp that I used to keep round at the back of my room?"

"Oh," said the Princess, "don't talk about that. We took it down to the street to a hawker who was swapping old lamps for new ones, and now it's got into the hands of the Maghrabi—the Accursed One—who brought us here, and he treasures it as the source of all Power. He carries it about with him all the time, tucked down the inside of his robe."

When he heard that, Aladdin understood everything, and saw what now had to be done. It seemed that ever since they'd made their instantaneous journey to Africa, the Princess and the magician had been at daggers drawn, because he would keep on trying to persuade her that Aladdin was dead and she'd best marry him and have done with it, while she reckoned she knew different and wasn't going to have any truck with a trickster anyway.

What Aladdin now suggested was that she should appear to change her mind—give up on the idea that her man was still alive and offer a bit of

encouragement to the wizard. Then, if she could inveigle him into having a drink with her, she could spike his liquor and they'd have a fair chance of getting back the Lamp. And Aladdin went off to where his old room used to be, dug around in a cabinet and came back with a couple of white pills. "Crush those up and put them in his glass," he said, "they'll do the trick."

And that's what happened. When the wizard came back from the shops Aladdin hid behind a curtain and the Princess Badr al-Budur got herself up to look all sexy. "Why don't you come up and see me some time this evening?" she said to the magician, "I'm tired of being cooped up here all on my own; I could do with some company."

Well, a nod's as good as a wink to a blind man, so they say, and the wizard was quite taken in by this apparent change of heart. (He'd always had a high opinion of himself, and couldn't see why the Princess hadn't fallen for him first off anyway.) So that evening he smartened himself up and came up to the Princess's apartments for some supper, while the Princess, for her part, made sure that everything was comfy and there was plenty to drink.

Oh dear, you fellows who're listening to this story, let it be a lesson to you all. She waggled her hips at the old chap, in her silken trousers; she flashed her eyes at him over her flimsy veil—and she kept on pouring. From a state of

delight, to a state of euphoria, he went on tipping back his glass until he was eventually almost catatonic and could hardly have got his hands on her if he'd tried. Then it was that she slipped the crushed powder into his drink and he keeled over for good.

Out from behind the curtain came Aladdin, with a dagger in his hand. They fished around inside the wizard's robe till they found where he'd tucked away the Lamp, and when they'd got it out and made sure it was the right one, Aladdin shoved the dagger into his ribs and put an end to his wizardry forever.


## How It Ended

You might think that there's not much more to be said. You might think that all we need to do is to tell how Aladdin once more summoned the Slave of the Lamp, ordered him to take the house back to where it started from, and how the Sultan—waking up next morning—was as surprised to see the pavilion back on the polo-ground as he had been to see it vanished. Obviously he was delighted to have his daughter home again, and was all ready to forgive and forget—so you might think that they all lived happily ever after. But you'd be wrong.

You see the African magician had a brother, who was a pretty good wizard on his own account. They never saw much of each other, but they liked to keep in touch at Christmas, as it were, and the brother began to get a bit agitated when the usual greetings never turned up. So he got his own set of sand-tables and magical instruments and he did a bit of conjuring—and what did he discover but that his brother had been murdered and his body carried off to China, to the city of all cities.

"Vengeance is mine," said Wizard Number Two—or words to that effect—and he straightway set out for China to see what he could do about it. He travelled long weeks and months over the seas and the mountains and finally ended up outside the city in what was called 'the Strangers' Khan', a kind of hostelry for foreigners. Here he began his investigations to find out more about his brother's murderer and ways to get at him, and he had the good fortune one day to hear some dominoes-players in a nearby tavern talking about the Holy Fatimah. Apparently this Holy Fatimah was a saintly hermitess from the mountains, who'd been causing quite a stir lately with various acts of piety and healing, and she was due to be coming to town soon to bless, and be blessed by, the Sultan and his family. So the wizard found out where she lived—up in a little cave above the city—and set off to visit her.

He arrived at the cave, as he'd planned, round about night-time and he

[ 177 ]

waited on guard there till early next morning, when he went inside and found the hermitess just waking up. Before she could say anything he pulled out his dagger and forced her there and then to change clothes with him, or else . . . When he'd done that he made her fetch her staff and her other gear and he got her to show him how she went about her ministrations—and when he'd done that, and got it all off pat, he asked her for a rope for a girdle, and that he used to hang her with. Just like that. He hanged her there in the cave and then threw her body into a nearby pit. So much for wizards. . .

Once he'd got rid of the Holy Fatimah he went down to the city in her cloak, and with her veil covering his beard and his mustachios, and he made for the Sultan's palace. Before he got there though, there was so much commotion, with everybody in the street wanting a benediction or a Touch, that he attracted the attention of the Princess Badr al-Budur, who asked her maid to bring him straight into the house.

This, of course, was just what he wanted. Imitating the Holy Fatimah he behaved all smarmy (said he wouldn't take anything to eat because he was fasting, but really because he was worried about someone seeing his whiskers), and he let her show him around the pavilion. Everywhere they went he gave the right sort of gasps of astonishment, but when at last they got to the belvedere on the roof he allowed himself a sigh of disappointment. "Oh, dear!" he said, "such a beautiful room, but spoiled for want of a last perfection."

"What do you mean?" asked the Princess, "'spoiled for want of a last perfection'; what could possibly make the place more perfect?"

"Ah," said the Fatimah Wizard, "what you need here—right in the middle of the ceiling—is a Rukh's egg. They're not easy to come by. They belong to the largest birds in the world. But a Rukh's egg, hanging there from the middle of the ceiling . . . perfect!"

Well, the Princess Badr al-Badur was pretty upset about this, and after she'd sent Fatimah off to have a rest before meeting the Sultan, she sent for Aladdin. "What's the trouble?" says he.

"Duff!" says she. "A duff job. You set about building the smartest place in the kingdom and you don't finish it off properly. Where's the Rukh's egg that ought to be hanging from the ceiling?" and she explained to him about the visit from Fatimah and what the old girl had said.

"Don't worry!" said Aladdin. "If it wasn't done then it can surely be done now," and he went off to his room, got out the Lamp and rubbed it. Flash! back came the Jinni. "Speak! I am the Slave of the Lamp! Command me and all my fellows to whatever you desire!"

"Well," said Aladdin, "what I want you to do is to fetch me the egg of a bird

called a Rukh and hang it from the dome of my belvedere."

"*Zambahshalamahzarúska!*" roared the Jinni, and Aladdin collapsed on to the floor, "what insolent ingratitude is this? Have not we Slaves of the Lamp done all your biddings? Furnished your processions? Filled your bowls with gold? Built your mansion—and carried it backwards and forwards over the earth? Was that not enough, that you must now ask us to fetch our Mistress of Heaven and hang her up in your pleasure-dome? By Allah, I am minded to turn you to ashes and scatter you to the twelve quarters of the wind. Command me no more such commands." And the Jinni went back into the Lamp.

When Aladdin had recovered a little, and got up off the floor, he began to ponder why the Holy Fatimah should have made this suggestion which had so nearly brought about their downfall. What could she know of Rukhs' eggs? More than that—what could she know of Jann who had this intimate relationship with Rukhs' eggs?

So when he went downstairs he told the Princess, his wife, that he'd like to see the Holy Fatimah because he'd suddenly come over all queer, with a bad headache (which was not too far from the truth). The Princess sent for the hermitess, who should have finished her rest by now, and when the Fatimah Wizard came into the room and saw Aladdin standing there, he realized that all his schemes were moving to success. He went over to Aladdin, feeling in his robe as though to bring out some charm against headaches, but really palming his own dagger. Aladdin watched him with his eyes well open, and as the Holy Lady raised her arm he grabbed it by the wrist, twisted, and, when the dagger fell to the floor . . . picked it up and drove it through the robes and into the heart of the Moorish Wizard.

"Yow!" yelled the Princess; "Screech!" yelled the Princess's servants; but Aladdin stuck his foot on Fatimah's chest, pulled out the dagger, and then tore away the veiling so that everyone could see the Holy Woman's beard and mustachios. "All thanks to Allah and the Rukh's egg," said Aladdin; and now that Wizard One and Wizard Two were both out of the way Aladdin, and Aladdin's wife, and Aladdin's mum, and the Sultan and all the population of the city of cities (except possibly the Grand Wazir), lived happily ever after.

With the ending of this story of Aladdin the first sunbeam touched the minarets of the Sultan's palace and Sheherezade knew that for a thousand nights and one night she had been winning the mind and heart of the Shah Shahryar. Through all this time she had loved him—had borne him three boy-children—and through all this time at the behest of her sister Dunyazad she had told him story upon story. But now, as the dawn broke, she silenced the pleas of Dunyazad, rose to her feet and, kissing the ground before the King, she said: "Lord of the time and of the age, I am thy handmaid. For a thousand nights and one night I have entertained thee with tales and legends, jests and moral instances, and now I crave a boon of thee!"

And the King said, "Ask, O Sheherezade, and it shall be granted unto thee."

Whereupon she cried: "Bring me my children!" And when the nurses and eunuchs had brought the children before the King she said: "O King of the age, these are thy children and I crave that thou release me from the doom of thy judgement, that I may rear them fittingly as they should be reared."

Then the King answered: "O Sheherezade, I pardoned thee before the coming of these children for I found thee to be most candid and most fair. Allah bless thee all thy days and may He witness against me that I exempt thee from aught that can harm thee." And with these words he called for his Wazirs and Emirs and for the Officers of the Crown and decreed that there should be public feasting to celebrate the marriage of the Shah Shahryar to Sheherezade. And in like way his brother, the Shah Zaman, who had ever been attendant upon his actions, besought that he might marry Dunyazad, so thus it came about that, amid rejoicings which no storyteller may describe, the two brothers were united to the two sisters and they dwelt together in all solace and contentment until there came to them the Destroyer of delights, the Sunderer of societies and the Garnerer of graveyards.

[ 182 ]

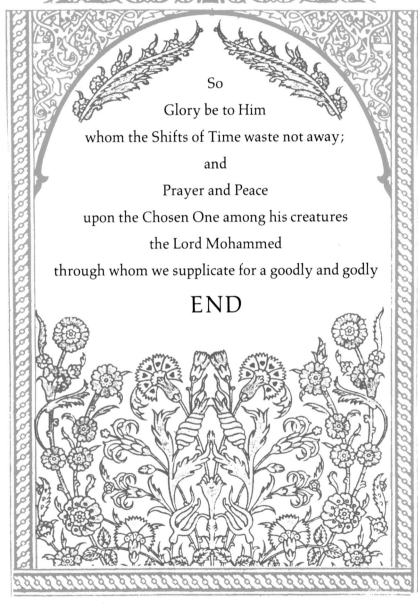

So
Glory be to Him
whom the Shifts of Time waste not away;
and
Prayer and Peace
upon the Chosen One among his creatures
the Lord Mohammed
through whom we supplicate for a goodly and godly

# END

# EDITOR'S REMARKS

To call a book 'The Arabian Nights' is very much to over-simplify a complicated subject. For there is no such thing—neither in Arabic or Persian, nor in French nor English. What we call 'The Arabian Nights' is a huge collection of stories that were set into the framework of the tale of Sheherezade—but if you want to try to settle what exactly those stories were you will need the help of the Slave of the Lamp and the lifetime of a Sage.

The trouble is that these stories, attributed to Sheherezade, are to be found in various ancient manuscripts and that these manuscripts differ from each other both as to the number of stories they include and the versions of the stories that are told. To make matters worse, the real interest in 'The Arabian Nights' as a printed book lay not in Arabia at all, but in Europe, where an explosion of interest occurred once Antoine Galland started to publish his French translation in 1704 (which was quickly translated into English too). These European translations were themselves very different from the Arabian manuscripts—not least because Europeans were coy about printing stories where grown men wet their trousers or where everyone enjoyed making love to everyone else—so that a collection of 'Nights' appeared which did not correspond very closely to that of the original Arabian ones.

(Especially odd is the history of the versions of the two best-known stories in the whole collection: *Ali Baba* and *Aladdin*. Neither of these tales is to be found in the authentic Arabian mss. Both were translated by Galland from a quite separate source, which has never been fully elucidated. He apparently noted the tales while they were being told by a Maronite storyteller in Europe.)

But if we cannot say for sure what 'The Arabian Nights' are, we all have some idea of what they ought to be—exotic tales of magic or passion told over a thousand and one nights by a lady who was anxious not to have her head chopped off. The hope behind this present book is that it will give a satisfying form to that idea: that it will show something of the character and variety of the tales and also preserve the impression of

Sheherezade's storytelling stamina. (That is not altogether easy in a book that is a mere 192 pages long, when the original may be anything up to three thousand.)

In trying to carry out this aim I have worked in cheerful ignorance of all the linguistic and anthropological scholarship that ought to be brought to bear on a proper translation of 'The Arabian Nights', but I have tried always to show respect for the business of storytelling. I have chosen as a base for my adaptation the nineteenth century translation of John Payne, as refurbished and augmented by Sir Richard Burton in the sixteen volumes of his 'Nights' and 'Supplemental Nights' (1885–1888). I have however hacked and hewn at the stories in a manner that would have appalled that fiery gentleman, in order to try to create a consistent, small-scale replica of the original. No doubt many modern Arabists will deplore this reversion to what has been called 'richly upholstered Victorian prose'. I would choose to argue though that, for many English readers, such prose well represents the exoticism that is expected of these Oriental stories and that its formalities and rotundities separate it from the direct colloquialism that we enjoy in European folk tales. Amidst all the 'thee-ing' and 'thou-ing' I have still sought to preserve a prose rhythm which will sound right if the stories are told—as Sheherezade told them—aloud to an audience. Mine be the head that is lopped off if everyone falls asleep.

## The Text

A few notes are given below on the stories that have been re-told in full, although the reader will have noticed that various other stories are mentioned in order to give the impression of the nights going by. The tales are roughly in the sequence in which they appear in Burton, but I have not hesitated to move them around in the interests of giving this book what I hope appears a satisfactory shape.

[ 186 ]

## The Tales: sequence, sources and so on

*The Frame Story:* The practice of using a story as an excuse for telling more stories is of ancient descent, perhaps originating with the Buddhist *Jatakas* of the third century before Christ. Without doubt though the frame story of the two Shahs is the most famous example of the device and, as I have already said, I believe that even a short sequence of the stories should preserve the references to Sheherezade as storyteller.

In this version therefore I have set out fairly fully the events that led up to Sheherezade's marathon endeavour, including the characteristic story-within-a-story when the Shah Shahryar and his brother set off in search of a woman more faithless than their own wretched consorts. (This motif has later parallels in such European comic tales as the Grimms' 'Clever Elsie', or the English 'The Three Sillies', where a wooer will only claim his foolish bride when he finds three people more stupid than she.)

Sheherezade is often left out of abbreviated versions of *The Arabian Nights* or else—as in Galland—the night-by-night sequence is abandoned because it makes for too many interruptions. Nevertheless, despite the extreme variations in the length and complexity of the stories which Sheherezade tells, her submerged presence gives a unifying interest to the collection. She holds its disparate contents together rather as the Baghdad bag was deemed by the Kurdish man to contain so many diverse wonders (see page 73). Furthermore, Sheherezade's presence as originating storyteller helps to emphasize one of the narrative tricks of the *Nights*: the tendency which people within her stories have to introduce additional anecdotes of their own to illustrate a point which they wish to make, so that stories occur within stories like a series of Chinese boxes.

Notable early instances of the appearance of frame-stories in European literature are Boccaccio's *Decameron* (1348–1353), Chaucer's *Canterbury Tales* (1380–1400), and Basile's *Pentamerone* (1634–1636) where the frame surrounds a collection of some fifty folk tales. In these examples the use of the frame probably arises from the author's liking for it as a narrative device rather than from any direct influence from the then-unpublished and far more complex *Arabian Nights*.

[ 187 ]

*The Fisherman and the Jinni* (Burton, Nights 3–6). One of the most ancient stories in the collection, of which only the first half is given here. After the Jinni leaves the Fisherman the narrative swerves off into the barely-related and rather sadistic 'Tale of the Ensorcelled Prince' which has to do with the peculiar nature of the fish which the Fisherman catches. The exemplary tales of the Sage Duban, the Loyal Falcon, and the Faithful Parrot are nice examples of the use of story-within-story but I have changed their sequence in order to move from the darker to the lighter narratives. The parrot story is one of a large number about the bird found all over the world. In England an anecdote slightly similar to the one here was recorded in 1914, when the parrot was deemed a liar because it talked about 'the day it rained beans and bacon' after the cook had thrown the dinner at it.

Although 'The Fisherman and the Jinni' is Oriental to the core, some motifs are also found independently in European folklore: the fisherman who draws up a magic flounder, for instance, in the Grimms' 'Fisherman and his Wife', and the tricking of the Jinni which has an equivalent in the cat's trickery of the ogre in 'Puss-in-Boots'. A story reprinted in Sidney Hartland's *English Fairy and Other Folk Tales* (1890) even has a quick-witted fellow called Tommy persuade a ghost to get into a brandy-bottle which he corks up tight and throws in the river.

*The Tale of the Hunchback* (Burton, Nights 25–34). Another quintessentially Oriental construction which I have abridged by removing a quantity of the interpolated stories. These often lack what a Western reader would regard as point and they seriously delay the hunchback's resurrection.

*The Fable of the Birds and the Beasts and the Carpenter* (Burton, Nights 146–147). This and the following two stories are taken from some of the many short fables which appear in the *Nights*. As might be expected, these are less specific in their setting and in their application than are the longer 'Eastern' stories.

*The Fable of the Wolf and the Fox* (Burton, Nights 148–150). The antagonism between wolf and fox is a standard theme in fable literature; here it has had superimposed upon it a fairly elaborate re-working of the well incident from Aesop's 'Fox and the Goat'. I have omitted a distracting internal story about a falcon and a partridge, and I have supplied a concluding sentence of my own which is intended to round off the fable more pointedly than in the original.

*The Fable of the Mongoose and the Mouse* (Burton, Night 150). In Burton the cunning thief of the fable is an ichneumon. I have replaced him with his more pronounceable relative.

*The Tale of the Ebony Horse* (Burton, Nights 357–371). The story is one of those told to Galland by his Maronite friend, and is thought to be of Persian origin, but I have introduced into it (p. 70) a slanderous remark at the expense of Persians taken from Burton's notes. The theme of aerial flight in pursuit of a princess is re-worked by Hans Christian Andersen in one of his funniest *eventyr*: 'The Flying Trunk'.

*The Tale Told by Ali the Persian* (Burton, Nights 294–295). Along with short fables, *The Arabian Nights* also includes many moral or comic anecdotes, some of which appear in the following sequence of stories. The absurd tale which Ali here tells to Harun Al-Rashid is a piece of Persian nonsense worthy of Edward Lear; I have however curtailed the storyteller's over-zealous listing of possible contents for the bag in the interests of a brisk ending.

*Ma'an Bin-Zaidah, the Donkey and the Cucumbers* (Burton, Night 271). As often happens with these little jokey stories, the Arabian narrator seems more interested in the progression of events than in what Westerners would see as 'a rounded conclusion'. I have therefore tinkered with some of the minor details of this tale in order to give it a slightly sharper edge.

*The Story of Sindbad the Porter and Sindbad the Sailor* (Burton, Nights 536–566). The extensive journeyings of Sindbad the Sailor 'as told to' Sindbad the Porter make up a

frame-story within the larger frame-story of the *Nights*. Its origins however are uncertain and it belongs as much to 'Odyssey' literature, or to the genre of travellers' tales, as it does to Orientalia. (In Sindbad's Third Voyage there is even a ferocious version of the Cyclops story in Homer.) Despite various colourful incidents the full panoply of Sindbad's seven voyages takes on a rather repetitive character when transcribed in full. I have therefore selected three of his most celebrated encounters which I hope will give sufficient indication of the mixture of fantasy and adventure which characterizes his adventures.

As you may guess, 'Sindbad' figures alongside 'Ali Baba' and 'Aladdin' as one of the three most popular stories in the whole of the *Nights*.

*The Tale of the City of Brass* (Burton, Nights 566–578). A story which makes double use of one of the most potent images of *The Arabian Nights*: palaces and cities in the grip of desertion and death. Indeed the family of King Ad did not have much luck in the architectural business, for just as the Black Castle (built by Kush, son of Shaddad, son of Ad) was wasted, so too was the city of many-pillared Iram (built by Shaddad himself) as recounted by Sheherezade during nights 275–279, although it does make a fitful reappearance as part of the Persian's luggage in 'The Tale which Ali the Persian Told' (p. 76).

*The Man Who Stole the Dog's Golden Dish* (Burton, Nights 340–341). An exemplary anecdote whose sober conclusion has no clear parallel in Western fables.

*The Tale of the Ruined Man and his Dream* (Burton, Nights 351–352). Sheherezade here tells a story the like of which is found in a multitude of versions in many parts of the world. In England the best-known retelling is 'The Pedlar of Swaffham'.

*The Tale of the Simpleton and his Donkey* (Burton, Night 388). An example of a 'noodle story', that genre which celebrates the comic behaviour of foolish people in many other places as well as Arabia.

*The Tale of Ja'afar the Barmecide and the Ailing Bedouin* (Burton, Nights 394–395). Another piece of Lear-like nonsense, but with a pay-off that would not have been appreciated by Lear's contemporaries. Breaking wind in times of stress is nonetheless recognized by Sheherezade, or rather by Burton, as a natural human reaction and indeed, in the story 'How Abu Hasan Broke Wind' (Night 410) she perceives its tragic consequences, since Abu Hasan exiled himself for ten years following an embarrassing indiscretion, only to discover that the event had been permanently recorded in his home-town's calendar. (Edward de Vere, Earl of Oxford was not much luckier. According to Aubrey he too was so ashamed of farting before his Queen that—like Abu Hasan—"he went to Travell, 7 years". On his return though "the Queen welcomed him home, and sayd, My Lord, I had forgott the Fart".)

*The Story of Ali Baba and the Forty Thieves* (Burton, Supplemental Nights 625–638). As I have mentioned above, this story, along with 'Aladdin', is notable both for its outstanding popularity and for its obscure origins. Because of the uncertainty surrounding their existence as authentic Arabian tales I have taken the licence to treat Burton's texts more freely and to give a rather more colloquial tang to the retelling of both stories.

I assume that the popularity of 'Ali Baba' led to the adoption of some of the story's motifs into European folk literature. Thus the first part of the tale is replicated in Grimms' 'Simeliberg', while the trick with the scales appears in such stories as the Irish 'Hudden and Dudden and Donald O'Neary' and the cognate Danish tale from which Hans Christian Andersen derived 'Big Claus and Little Claus'.

*The Story of Aladdin and the Slave of the Lamp* (Burton, Supplemental Nights 514–590). See the above note. Aladdin's family name is not given in Burton and I have authenticated it from a source in Drury Lane. As with 'Ali Baba', part of this story has almost certainly found its way into the European tradition through such tales as the Grimms' 'The Blue Light' and Hans Christian Andersen's cognate 'The Tinder Box', both of which also incorporate the door-marking motif from 'Ali Baba'.

Magical Face Relaxer...................... 239
Double-Chin Prevention................. 239
Toweling Off ................................. 239
Chapped Lips................................. 239
Pleasing Tweezing ......................... 240
Fingernail How-to.......................... 240
Matchbook Method ....................... 240
Polish Primer ................................ 240
Manicure Protection...................... 240
General Tips.................................. 240
Paint Remover for Skin ................. 240
Pain-Free Bandage Remover ........... 240
Mirror, Mirror in the Bathroom ...... 240
Perfume Pick-Me-Up...................... 240

**Remedies in a Class by Themselves** .. 243
Kiss of Life................................... 243
Exercise Your Lung Power.............. 243
Yawn All the Way.......................... 243
Confessions...Good for the
   Immune System...................... 244
Success Through Napping............... 244
Practice Preventive Medicine:
   Laugh!.................................... 244
Have a Good Cry........................... 244
Calcium Concern .......................... 245
Give Healing Orders...................... 245
The Ultimate Remedy.................... 245

**Preparation Guide**............................ 249
Barley .......................................... 249
Coconut Milk................................ 249
Eyewash....................................... 249
Garlic Juice .................................. 250
Ginger Tea.................................... 250
Herbal Bath .................................. 250
Herbal Tea.................................... 250
Onions ......................................... 251
Pomanders ................................... 251
Potatoes ....................................... 251
Poultices ...................................... 252
Sauerkraut.................................... 252

**Six Sensational Superfoods** .............. 257
Decisions, Decisions...................... 257

Expand Your Healthy Horizons ....... 258
1. Bee Pollen ............................... 258
2. Flaxseed .................................. 262
3. Garlic ...................................... 266
4. Ginger ..................................... 270
5. Nuts ........................................ 274
6. Yogurt...................................... 280

**Amazing, Super-Duper
Facts and Advice** ............................. 287
Think Positive, Live Longer ........... 287
The Full Moon Boom ..................... 287
The "Rest" of the Story ................. 287
Doctor's Fee ................................. 288
Fever: Friend or Foe?..................... 288
Freshen Up a Sickroom .................. 288
Prescription Reading Made Easy .... 288
How to Take Pills...Really.............. 288
Coming to Your Senses................... 289
Dropper in a Pinch........................ 289
Do-It-Yourself Hot-Water
   Bottle and Ice Pack .................. 289
A Fishy Story ................................ 289
Good Health, Italian-Style.............. 290
Save Vitamins in the Microwave...... 290
Lettuce: Choose Dark Green ........... 290
Moldy Food................................... 290
Herb and Spice Storage ................. 290
Remove Pesticides from
   Fruits and Vegetables .............. 290
Sweet and Salty Substitutes ............ 291
Working with Onions
   Tearlessly...Almost.................... 291
Unhand Those Garlic and
   Onion Odors ........................... 291
Hold on to Your Pantyhose............. 291
Natural Insect Repellents ............... 291
Natural Air Cleaners ...................... 292
Deodorizing Food Jars.................... 292
Salt Rub for Gas Odors................... 292
Stuffed Toys on Ice........................ 293
Cradling Baby................................ 293
Bathing Made Easy ........................ 293

**Sources** ................................................. 297
    Herbal Products and More ............... 297
    Gems, New-Age Products
        and Gifts ................................... 298
    Vitamins, Nutritional Supplements
        and More .................................. 298
    Natural Foods and More ................. 299
    Bee Products and More ................... 299
    Pet Food and Products ................... 299
    Health-Related Products ................. 300
    Health-Related Travel Products
        and More .................................. 300
    Wholesale/Retail Health
        Appliances ................................ 300
    Aromatherapy, Flower Essences
        and More .................................. 300
    Services ......................................... 300

**Health Resources** ................................ 305
    Organizations, Associations and
        Journals .................................... 306
    Online-Only Resources ................... 315
**Recommended Reading List** .............. 319
    Body Power/Brain Power ................. 319
    Food, Healthful Eating and
        Weight Programs ...................... 319
    Herbs ............................................ 319
    Just for Men ................................... 319
    Just for Women .............................. 320
    Just for Pets ................................... 320
    New-Age and Age-Old (Mostly
        Alternative) Therapies ............... 320
    Specific Health Challenges ............. 320
    Vitamins and Other Supplements .... 320
**Recipe Index** ...................................... 321
**Index** ................................................. 323

# Dedication

*Bottom Line's Healing Remedies*
is dedicated to the loving memory of our parents,
Lillian and Jack Wilen.

■

# Acknowledgments

We give a *big thanks* to all the people who offered their loving support, good wishes and—of course—their wonderful healing remedies.

◆ Our *heartfelt thanks* to Ray C. Wunderlich, Jr., MD, PhD, who reviewed every remedy in this book, with your well-being in mind. Many of the "NOTE"s, "WARNING"s and "CAUTION"s found throughout these pages are a reflection of the good doctor's fastidious scrutiny. We feel blessed to know this healer, teacher and the only other person in our time zone who is awake if we call him with a question at 2:00 am.

◆ *Very special thanks* to Marty Edelston—the founder, publisher and resident genius of Boardroom Inc. and its Bottom Line Books division—for being so very special.

We're thrilled to be Boardroom authors and lucky to work with Marty's great Boardroom team, including the incomparable Brian Kurtz, our wonderful editors, Karen Daly and Amy Linkov, and the many people affiliated with Boardroom whose expertise and caring made this book possible. We'll list their names here, and give sincere thanks to each one for his or her contribution.

Marjory Abrams
Tom Dillon
Polly Stewart Fritch
Carolyn Gangi
Terri Kazin
Sandy Krolick
John Niccolls
Rich O'Brien, MD
Paula Parker
Kathi Ramsdell
Ken Sevey
Rebecca Shannonhouse
Jennifer Souder
Carmen Suarez
Melissa Virrill
Alexandra White
Michele Wolk
Phillis Womble

And the brilliant Arthur P. Johnson for working his magic. If there's anyone we inadvertently overlooked—well, we thank you, too! ∎

# A Word from the Authors

Human beings have been consulting healers for thousands of years. Whether it's a medicine man, shaman, naturopath, physician or some other type of health expert, what goes around seems to come around. *Consider this timeline…*

| | |
|---|---|
| | "Doctor, I have a sore throat." |
| 2000 BC | "Here, eat this root." |
| 1000 BC | "That root is heathen. Say this prayer." |
| 1850 AD | "That prayer is superstition. Drink this potion." |
| 1940 AD | "That potion is snake oil. Swallow this pill." |
| 1980 AD | "That pill is artificial and ineffective. Take this antibiotic." |
| 2000 AD | "That antibiotic is artificial, causes side effects and you've built an immunity to it. Take this root!" |

And so we've gone back to our roots. Being city dwellers, we get our roots at herb shops and health food stores. Actually, that's not all we get there. We also take advantage of modern-day technology, and buy vitamins and supplements that are commercially manufactured. You'll notice that, along with the classic folk remedies included in this book, we've added new remedies that may have you going to the health food store!

In this millennium, we've come to realize that we have lots of choices when it comes to health care. It shouldn't be a matter of *alternative medicine* vs. *allopathic medicine. Integrative medicine* combines traditional practices with alternative health treatments. Learn your options and, with the supervision of your health professional, take the best of both.

—Joan & Lydia ■

# Introduction

Our experience with natural remedies goes back to our childhood. When we were growing up in Brooklyn, New York, each winter our mom would crochet little drawstring bags and our dad would make sure they were filled with camphor, which he then insisted we wear around our necks. It wasn't a fashion statement on our dad's part—he believed this would prevent us from catching colds. Of course, we reeked so from the camphor that none of our friends would come near us. And, as a result, we didn't catch their colds. So Daddy was right.

That camphor was our introduction to natural remedies…along with honey and lemon for a sore throat, sugar water for the hiccups, horseradish to clear the sinuses, garlic for a whole bunch of things—and chicken soup for everything else.

Our mom made the world's best chicken soup…when she wasn't crocheting little drawstring bags for the camphor. In fact, her soup recipe is in this book (*see* page 35). We have also included a very potent chicken soup recipe from a doctor (*see* page 36). How potent is it? It's so potent that the dosage is to take only two tablespoons at a time.

When we first started doing research for this book, we went to all our relatives and friends to ask for their home remedies. We heard wonderful "old country" stories about remarkable cures, but the times we live in are so different, and the world has changed dramatically. For example, who could have imagined that extra-virgin coconut oil could be used to treat diabetes? (For more details, *see* page 56.) And we knew we wanted the remedies in this book to be safe and effective, yet practical.

Yes, PRACTICAL! Every fruit, vegetable, herb, vitamin, mineral and liquid—in fact, all the ingredients mentioned in this book—can be found at your local health food store, supermarket, greengrocer or on the Internet—that is, if they aren't already in your home.

Most of the remedies in this book require only a few ingredients, and some require nothing more than your concentration or stimulating an acupressure point. Our directions are easy to follow and specific. However, if an exact amount or measurement is not indicated, then we could not verify it, but we felt that the remedy was effective enough to include.

OK, we've covered the practical aspects of this book...now for EFFECTIVE—do the remedies work? Yes! No one passes along or shares a remedy that doesn't work. Of course, we realize that not every remedy will work for every person. But these remedies are easy to use, inexpensive and have no side effects. In other words, while they may not always help —they certainly wouldn't hurt. *Which brings us to a very important point...*

Several esteemed medical doctors have reviewed each remedy in the book and deemed them SAFE. But you have to do your part for your own well-being—please consult a health professional whom you trust before trying any self-help treatment, including the remedies contained in this book.

Also, if you are pregnant or nursing, have any allergies and/or food sensitivities, or have been diagnosed with any serious illness or chronic condition—please!—talk to your physician, nurse/midwife, dentist, naturopath or other health specialist before trying any of these remedies. And keep in mind that most of these remedies are NOT meant for children. Please see "Healing Remedies for Children" (*see* page 207) for healing suggestions suitable for the wee ones in your life.

Please heed the "NOTE"s, "WARNING"s and "CAUTION"s found throughout the book. They stress the fact that our home-remedy suggestions are scientifically unproven and should not take the place of professional medical evaluation and treatment. Some remedies can be dangerous for people who are taking prescription medication or who suffer from a specific illness or condition.

Effective, proven, traditional health care is available for almost all of the conditions mentioned in this book. You may need to see a physician for certain ailments and/or persistent symptoms. These natural remedies should be used in addition to—but *never* as a substitute for—professional medical help.

One more thing...be sure to check out the "Six Sensational Superfoods" section beginning on page 257. These extraordinary foods have the power to help protect, improve, save and extend people's lives.

To find the most beneficial and tastiest ways to eat these foods, we did a lot of research and experimenting. We soaked, scrubbed, grated, minced, diced, spiced, blended, boiled, whipped, whisked, powdered, peeled, cooked, baked, roasted, toasted and tested...and came up with simple suggestions for incorporating these foods into your daily diet. (However, we have not personally kitchen-tested all of the recipes included in this book. We selected ones that we believed to be simple, healthful and delicious. We hope you enjoy them.)

Please know that we do not have formal medical training and we are not prescribing treatment. We're writers who are reporting what has worked for many generations of people who have shared their remedies with us. For your own safety, please consult your doctor before trying any self-help treatment or natural remedy.

Thank you for reading our book, and— every good wish for your good health!

The Wilen Sisters

Joan & Lydia ■

# Remedies for What Ails You
## A–Z
### (*well*, W)

# Remedies

## ALLERGIES AND HAY FEVER

If you have a runny nose, sore throat and/or itchy eyes, you may be suffering from seasonal allergies. This type of allergy occurs when your body overreacts to pollen from trees or weeds, and sometimes household dust or mold. Hay fever is one variety of this type of allergy.

In addition, there is allergic asthma, conjunctivitis, hives, eczema, dermatitis and sinusitis as well as food allergies, latex allergies, insect-sting allergies and drug allergies. (We feel itchy just reading that list!)

There are almost as many different types of allergies as there are people who have them! Obviously, allergies need to be handled on an individual basis. We found a number of remedies that just may help people who suffer from seasonal allergies or hay fever. But—especially if you have allergies—be sure to check with your doctor first.

## Allergy Relief

▶ It is said that there are chemicals in bananas that repel allergies—that is, unless you're allergic to bananas. If not, eat a banana daily.

▶ Vitamin-rich watercress is said to be an anti-allergen. Eat it in salads, sandwiches and sauces. It's potent stuff, so eat small portions at a time.

## *Allergy Prevention*

▶ We were told that licorice root (the herb, not the candy) helps build up an immunity to allergens. Add 3 ounces of cut licorice root (available at health food stores) to 1 quart of water. Boil it for 10 minutes in an enamel or glass pot, then strain into a bottle.

*Dose:* Take 1 tablespoon before each meal, every other day until you've taken the licorice-root water for six days. By then, we hope, it will make a difference in terms of your resistance to allergies.

**CAUTION:** Do not take licorice root if you have high blood pressure or kidney problems. It can cause renal failure.

3

## Be Careful What You Crave

**W**e met a woman who has a severe, life-threatening almond allergy. Her mother had eaten marzipan on a regular basis throughout her 9-month pregnancy, and marzipan is made of almonds. An allergy specialist later told the woman that it's not uncommon for a child to be allergic to a food that the mother craved and ate lots of for months at a time during her pregnancy.

# Hay Fever Relief

▶ Several studies have shown that bioflavonoids—substances from plants that help maintain cellular health—help the body utilize vitamin C more effectively.

After the morning and evening meals, take one pantothenic acid tablet (50 milligrams [mg]) and one vitamin C tablet (500 mg) along with a bioflavonoid—a grapefruit, orange, a few strawberries, grapes or prunes. If you don't want the whole fruit, take a teaspoon of grated orange or lemon peel sweetened with a little honey. This remedy has been said to have brought relief to many hay fever sufferers.

## Hay Fever Prevention

▶ The US Army tested honeycomb as a desensitizing and antiallergenic substance for hay fever. Their results were very encouraging, especially those from subjects who chewed the honeycomb.

Start this regime about two months before hay fever season. By the time the season rolls around, the honeycomb may have helped you build an immunity to the pollen in your area. (You can also chew a bite-sized chunk of honeycomb at the start of a hay fever attack.)

It's important to find a beekeeper in your vicinity and get local honeycomb. For prevention, chew a 1-inch square of it twice a day. The honey is delicious, and the comb part turns into a ball of wax. Chew the wax for about 10 to 15 minutes, then spit it out.

If you don't have access to a local beekeeper, look for honeycomb at your neighborhood health food store. Hopefully, it's from your neck of the woods.

**CAUTION:** People who are allergic to bee stings or honey should consult a doctor before chewing honeycomb.

▶ Starting three months before hay fever season, drink 1 cup of fenugreek-seed tea each day. The tea is available at health food stores. This remedy goes back to the ancient Egyptians and forward to Armenian mountaineers who drink 1 cup of fenugreek tea before each meal to clear and stimulate their senses of smell and taste.

## ANEMIA

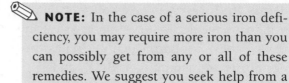

Blood is an extremely complex substance that consists of a variety of liquid and solid elements, including red blood cells, white cells and platelets.

The average adult has between 5 and 6 quarts of blood circulating through his/her body by way of the blood vessels.

Anemia is a condition in which the blood lacks iron, which reduces the blood's ability to carry oxygen. This may make a person feel weak and listless.

To combat anemia, it's important to increase your consumption of iron-rich foods (like beef or spinach) and supplement with B vitamins and minerals like copper.

To help circulation as well as purification of the blood and aid in elimination of iron-deficiency anemia, we offer suggestions *with* the suggestion that you *first* have appropriate professional blood tests performed. And always consult with a physician before embarking on any self-help program.

▶ Grape juice (no sugar or preservatives added) is a wonderful source of iron. Drink 8 ounces every day.

▶ Eat raw spinach salads often. Be sure to wash the spinach thoroughly to reduce the risk of food-borne illness. Combine any of the following in your spinach salad—watercress, radish, kohlrabi, garlic, chives, leek and onion. They're all high in iron.

▶ Every morning after breakfast and every evening after dinner, eat two dried apricots.

▶ Snack on raisins.

**NOTE:** In the case of a serious iron deficiency, you may require more iron than you can possibly get from any or all of these remedies. We suggest you seek help from a health professional.

## Blood Fortifiers

▶ Raw (not canned) sauerkraut is said to do a super job of fortifying the blood. It also helps rejuvenate the body in other ways. Eat 2 to 4 tablespoons a day, right after a meal. (Raw sauerkraut can be found at health food stores, or *see* the "Preparation Guide" on page 252 and learn to make your own sauerkraut.)

▶ **Check with your medical adviser before going on this one-day fast!** Combine 2 tablespoons of lemon, 1 tablespoon of honey and a cup of warm water.

*Dose:* Every two hours, from morning until two hours before bedtime, take 2 tablespoons of the mixture. No food throughout the day, just the lemon/honey/water mixture.

▶ Raw (not cooked or canned) pumpkin pulp and squash are said to have purifying properties. Eat them in salads.

▶ When they're in season, a peach a day helps wash toxins away.

▶ Garlic is said to help thin and fortify the blood. Eat raw garlic and/or take garlic supplements daily.

**CAUTION:** Do not eat garlic or take garlic supplements if you have a bleeding disorder or ulcers, or are taking anticoagulants.

▶ Drink fresh carrot juice as often as once a day if you have access to a juicer, or eat raw carrots. They contain calcium, potassium, phosphorus and vitamins A, B₁, B₂ and C.

## ANIMAL ENCOUNTERS

This section deals with remedies for a variety of animal bites (from spiders, jellyfish, Portuguese man-of-wars, hairy caterpillars, dogs and snakes) as well as insect stings (from bees, wasps, hornets, yellow jackets and mosquitoes).

**CAUTION:** If you have a history of allergies to stinging insects, have a physician-prescribed emergency sting kit on hand at all times!

Everyone knows that to avoid disease from biting insects and animals, you shouldn't bite any insects or animals! If they bite you, try these practical and effective suggestions.

▶ A paste made with water and baking soda can help draw out the heat of a sting, reduce the redness, inhibit the swelling and take the itch out of a bite. Every half-hour, alternate the baking soda paste with ice on the stung or bitten area.

▶ Wheat germ oil also helps soothe a sting. Every half-hour, alternate the wheat germ oil with ice on the stung area.

## Animal Bites

An animal bite—even from your own pet dog, cat, hamster, guinea pig, ferret or parakeet—could be dangerous. If the bite breaks the skin, bacteria in the animal's saliva can cause infection.

First, wash the bitten area thoroughly with soap and water. Then apply pressure to stop the bleeding. Cover the wound loosely with a sterile bandage.

**WARNING:** If an animal bite breaks the skin, doesn't stop bleeding, or if it puffs up or is red and painful, get medical attention immediately. You will need antibiotics and possibly a tetanus shot.

## Insect Stings

When an insect stings, its stinger usually remains in the skin while the insect flies away. However, if the insect stays attached to its stinger in your skin, flick it off with your thumb and forefinger. *Do not squeeze the insect*—not that anyone would want to do that.

Remove the stinger, but *do not* use your fingers or tweezers. Those methods can pump more poison into the skin. Instead, gently and carefully scrape the stinger out with the tip of a sharp knife. You can even use the edge of a credit card.

### Kitchen Cupboard Soothers

▶ To relieve the pain and keep down the swelling of a sting, apply any one of the following for a half-hour, then alternate it with a half-hour of ice around the stung area...

- ◆ A slice of raw onion
- ◆ A slice of raw potato
- ◆ Grated or sliced horseradish root
- ◆ Wet salt
- ◆ Commercial toothpaste
- ◆ Wet, clean mud is one of the oldest and most practical remedies for stings.

If you haven't already removed the stinger, peeling off the dry mud will help draw it out.

♦ Vinegar and lemon juice—equal parts—dabbed on every five minutes until the pain disappears

♦ Diluted ammonia

♦ ⅓ teaspoon of (unseasoned) meat tenderizer dissolved in 1 teaspoon of water. One of the main ingredients in meat tenderizer is papain, an enzyme from papaya that relieves the pain and inflammation of a sting as well as lessens allergic reaction. *Use meat tenderizer only if you are MSG-allergy-free.*

♦ Oil squeezed from a vitamin E capsule

♦ A clump of wet tobacco (but don't tell the US Surgeon General or you'll have to print a warning on your arm)

♦ A drop of honey, preferably honey from the hive of the bee that did the stinging (of course, that's not too likely unless you're a beekeeper)

**CAUTION:** Do not put any foreign substance (mud, tobacco, ammonia, etc.) directly on broken skin. It could cause an infection that is *much* worse than the sting!

## Other Stings

▶ If you are stung by a jellyfish, Portuguese man-of-war or hairy caterpillar, apply olive oil for fast relief…then seek medical attention immediately.

## Mosquito Bites

**WARNING:** Mosquitoes can transmit the West Nile virus and other serious diseases, which can be serious and potentially fatal. Be sure to use mosquito repellent, wear long sleeves and pants when outdoors, eliminate mosquito breeding sites near your house, and repair any broken window and door screens.

▶ Mosquitoes prefer warm over cold, light over dark, dirty over clean, adult over child and male over female.

Once the mosquito bites the hand that feeds it, treat the bite with saliva. *Then apply any of the following…*

♦ Wet soap

♦ Wet tobacco

♦ Wet, clean mud

♦ Diluted ammonia

♦ Mixture of equal parts vinegar and lemon juice

As for the mosquito, after it bites you on one hand, be sure to give it the other hand—palm downward!

### Mosquito and Gnat Bite Prevention

Remember how, when you were a child and got bitten up by mosquitoes, your mother would say, "That's because you're so sweet"? There may be something to it.

Experiments were conducted with people who completely eliminated white sugar and alcoholic beverages from their diets. They were surrounded by mosquitoes and gnats. Not only were those people not bitten, the insects didn't even bother to land on them.

If you're sugar-free, it's so long mosquitoes, and gnuts to gnats!

▶ Mosquitoes have been known to stay away from people whose systems have a high amount of vitamin $B_1$ (thiamine). Before you go to a mosquito-infested area, eat foods that are rich in $B_1$—sunflower seeds, brewer's yeast, Brazil nuts and fish.

Additionally, supplement with 100 mg of vitamin $B_1$ (thiamine) an hour before you reach your destination.

▶ Keep geraniums on porches and other places you like to sit. The potted geraniums keep mosquitoes away.

▶ If you dread mosquito bites more than you mind smelling of garlic, then we've got a remedy for you.

Rub garlic over all your exposed body parts before reaching a mosquito-infested area. Mosquitoes will not come near you. They hate garlic. Garlic is to mosquitoes what kryptonite is to Superman.

One university biologist tested garlic extract on five species of mosquitoes. The garlic got 'em. Not one mosquito survived.

▶ Eucalyptus oil will repel mosquitoes. Rub it over the uncovered areas of your body.

▶ Don't wear the color blue around mosquitoes. They're very attracted to it. They're also attracted to wet clothes. Keep dry!

▶ Rub fresh parsley on the exposed parts of your body to prevent insect bites.

▶ If you have an aloe vera plant, break off one of the stems. Squeeze out the juice and rub it on the uncovered areas of your body for protection against biting insects.

## Snakebites

If you get a snakebite, chances are you're expecting you might get a snakebite. Think that over for a minute. As soon as it makes sense, please read on.

If you're going camping, or are placing yourself in a situation where there's a chance of being bitten by a snake, we recommend that you know the snakes in that area so that you can be prepared for how to handle a bite.

▶ If you get bit, make a poultice (*see* "Preparation Guide" on page 252) from two crushed onions mixed with a few drops of kerosene, and apply it to the bite. After a short time, it should draw out the poison, turning the poultice green.

Get to civilization as soon as possible and see a doctor!

▶ Mix a wad of tobacco with saliva or water. Apply this paste directly on the bite.

As soon as the paste dries, replace it with another wad of the paste and get to a doctor!

### Rattlesnake Bites

▶ Don't get rattled. Wet some salt, put a hunk of it on the bite, then treat the area with a wet-salt poultice (*see* "Preparation Guide" on page 252). But don't stand around reading this. Get to a doctor!

⚡ **CAUTION:** Do not put any foreign substance (tobacco, salt, etc.) directly on broken skin. It could cause an infection that is *much* worse than the bite!

## Spider Bites

There are four types of spiders that have bites that can be serious...

- ◆ *The black widow spider* has a black shiny body and a red or orange hourglass marking on the underside of its abdomen.
- ◆ *The brown recluse spider* is also called the fiddle-back spider because of the violin-shaped marking on its back. It's found mainly in Southern and Midwestern states.
- ◆ *The hobo spider* is brown with a herringbone-like pattern on the top of its abdomen. It's found in the Pacific Northwest.
- ◆ *The yellow sac spider* is light yellow with a slightly darker stripe on the upper middle of its abdomen.

If you think the spider that bit you is any one of these four, try to remain as calm as possible. Call your doctor, a hospital and/or the local Poison Control Center (800-222-1222). If you can collect the spider, or any part of it, do so for identification purposes.

▶ Until you get professional help, apply ice to the bite to help prevent swelling.

▶ After you've been treated by a doctor, take nutrients that have anti-inflammatory action—vitamin C with bioflavonoids, 500 to 1,000 mg every six to eight hours for several days (cut back on the dosage if you get diarrhea)...bromelain, 500 mg three or four times a day on an empty stomach...and/or quercetin, 250 to 300 mg one to three times a day.

## Tick Bites

▶ This is not a pleasant thought, but a remarkable remedy. If a tick has embedded itself in your skin—and it's been there less than 24 hours—take clear fingernail polish and put two drops on the insect. It will release its grasp and back out. Then just wipe it off your skin.

Unfortunately, you won't be able to do a Lyme culture on the tick because of the polish.

If it's still embedded, use tweezers to firmly pull the head of the tick straight out.

Keep a watchful eye on the site where the bug was pulled off—if a bull's-eye mark appears, you should go see your doctor and get tested for Lyme disease.

## Skunk Spray

▶ When you've gotten in the path of a frightened skunk, add a cup of tomato juice to a gallon of water and wash your body with it. Do the same with your clothes.

## ARTHRITIS

One authority in the field feels that *arthritis* is a catchall term that includes *rheumatism* (inflammation or pain in muscles, joints or fibrous tissue), *bursitis* (inflammation of shoulder, elbow or knee joint) and *gout* (joint inflammation caused by an excess of uric acid in the blood). Another specialist believes that arthritis is a form of rheumatism. Still another claims there is no such ailment as rheumatism, that it's a term for several diseases, including arthritis.

No matter what it's called, everyone agrees on two things—the pain...and that all these conditions involve inflammation of connective tissue of one or more joints.

According to the US Centers for Disease Control and Prevention in Atlanta (*see* "Health Resources" on page 314), arthritis is the leading cause of disability in the United States. Approximately 66 million Americans are affected by arthritis—which has over 100 different forms.

## Knowledge Is Power!

Check your local library and the Internet for books on arthritis (and there are lots of them). Also contact the Arthritis Foundation in Atlanta (*see* "Health Resources" on page 309) for more information. Learn about nonchemical treatments and low-acid diets.

### These Veggies Are a Pain

There are foods that have been classified as nightshade foods—white potatoes, eggplants, green peppers and tomatoes are the most common ones—that may contribute to the pain of some arthritis sufferers.

Consider being professionally tested by a nutritionist or allergist for sensitivity to the nightshade foods. Work with a health professional to evaluate your condition and to help you find safe, sensible methods of treatment for relief.

## Natural Remedies

Here are remedies that have been said to be successful for many arthritis sufferers—that is, *former* arthritis sufferers.

 **NOTE:** These remedies are not substitutes for professional medical treatment. Talk to your doctor before trying any natural remedies.

### It's the Cherries

▶ Cherries are said to be effective because they seem to help prevent crystallization of uric acid and to reduce levels of uric acid in the blood. It is also said that cherries help the arthritic bumps on knuckles disappear.

*Eat any kind*—sweet or sour, fresh, canned or frozen, black, Royal Anne or Bing. And drink cherry juice! It is available without preservatives or sugar added, and also in a concentrated form, at health food stores.

One source says to eat cherries and drink the juice throughout the day for four days, then stop for four days and then start all over again. Another source says to eat up to a dozen cherries a day in addition to drinking a glass of cherry juice. Find a happy medium by using your own good judgment. Listen to your body.

You'll know soon enough if the cherries seem to be making you feel better.

**WARNING:** Eating an excess of cherries may cause diarrhea in some individuals.

## Go Green

▶ Eat a portion of fresh string beans every day, or juice the string beans and drink a glassful daily. String beans contain vitamins A, $B_1$, $B_2$ and C and supposedly help relieve the excess-acid conditions that contribute to arthritis. (*See* recipe at right.)

▶ Steep 1 cup of fully packed, washed parsley in 1 quart of boiling water. After 15 minutes, strain the juice and refrigerate.

*Dose:* Drink ½ cup of parsley juice before breakfast, ½ cup before dinner and ½ cup anytime pain is particularly severe.

▶ Celery contains many nourishing salts and organic sulfur. Some modern herbalists believe that celery has the power to help neutralize uric acid and other excess acids in the body. Eat fresh celery daily (be sure to wash it thoroughly). The leaves on top of celery stalks are also good to eat.

If so much roughage is rough on your digestive system, place the tops and tough parts of the stalk in a nonaluminum pan. Cover with water and slowly bring to a boil. Then simmer for 10 to 15 minutes. Strain and pour into a jar.

### ■ Recipe ■

#### *Papaya Salad with String Beans*

1 cup green cabbage, cubed
2 cups green papaya, grated
½ lb string beans, julienned
3 garlic cloves, minced
3 dried red chilies, chopped
1 Tbsp granulated sugar
3 Tbsp soy sauce
3 Tbsp lime juice
3 small tomatoes, cut into wedges
5 Tbsp peanuts, roasted and crushed
4 Tbsp cilantro leaves, chopped

Place green cabbage pieces on a large serving platter and arrange the papaya and beans in layers. In a small bowl, mix together the garlic, chilies, sugar, soy sauce and lime juice.

Just before serving, pour the dressing over the salad and garnish with the tomatoes, peanuts and cilantro. Makes 4 servings.

*Source: www.recipegoldmine.com*

*Dose:* Take 8 ounces three times a day, a half-hour before each meal.

You can vary your celery intake by drinking celery seed tea and/or juiced celery stalks, or do as the Romanians do and cook celery in milk. Remember, celery is a diuretic, so plan your day accordingly.

## Fishy Solution

▶ According to results published in the *Journal of the American Medical Association* (*www.jama.ama-assn.org*), based on experiments by a study team at the Brusch Medical Center in Cambridge, Massachusetts, cod-liver oil in milk helped to reduce cholesterol levels, improve blood chemistry and complexion, increase energy and correct stomach problems, blood sugar balance, blood pressure and tissue inflammation.

Mix 1 tablespoon of cod-liver oil (emulsified Norwegian cod-liver oil is nonfishy) in 6 ounces of milk.

*Dose:* Drink it on an empty stomach, a half-hour before breakfast and a half-hour before dinner.

> **NOTE:** Cod-liver oil is a source of vitamins A and D. If you are taking A and D supplements, check the dosages carefully. The daily recommended dosage of vitamin A is 10,000 international units (IU), for vitamin D, 400 IU. *Do not exceed these amounts.*

Applying cod-liver oil externally is said to help relieve the popping noises of the joints.

► Edgar Cayce, renowned psychic, said in one of his readings, "Those who would take a peanut oil rub each week need never fear arthritis."

# Topical Treatments For Relief

► Garlic has been used to quiet arthritis pain quickly. Rub a freshly cut clove of garlic on painful areas. Also, take a garlic supplement—after breakfast and after dinner.

► Grate 3 tablespoons of horseradish and stir it into ½ cup of boiled milk. Pour the mixture onto a piece of cheesecloth, then apply it to the painful area. By the time the poultice cools, you may have some relief.

### Temporary Relief—for Women Only

Arthritic pains often disappear when a woman is pregnant. This is probably due to hormonal changes, but as soon as researchers find the exact reason, they may also find a permanent cure for arthritis.

### Dig a Potato

► Even if you have a sensitivity to nightshade foods, external potato remedies can be used, as they have been for centuries. Carry a raw potato in your pocket. Don't leave home without it! When it shrivels up after a day or two, replace it with a fresh potato. It supposedly relieves the inflammation that may be causing problems and pain.

► For dealing with the affected areas more directly, dice 2 cups of unpeeled potatoes and put them in a nonaluminum saucepan with 5 cups of water. Boil gently until about half the water is left. While the water is hot, but not scalding, dunk a clean cloth in the potato water, wring it out and apply it to the painful parts of the body. Repeat the procedure for as long as your patience holds out, or until the pain subsides—whichever happens first.

### Get a Rosy Outlook

► When you're feeling twinges in the hinges all over your body, take a bath in rose petals. Take petals from three or four roses that are about to wither and throw them in your bath-water. It should give you a rosy outlook.

### Bitter Makes It Better

Apple cider vinegar has been used in various ways to help arthritis sufferers. See which of the following remedies is most palatable and convenient for you. Have patience—and give it at least three weeks to work.

▶ Every morning and every evening, take 1 teaspoon of honey mixed with 1 teaspoon of apple cider vinegar.

*Or,* before each meal (three times a day), drink a glass of water containing 2 teaspoons of apple cider vinegar.

*Or,* between lunch and dinner, drink a mixture of 2 ounces of apple cider vinegar added to 6 ounces of water. Drink it down slowly.

### Rub Salt on the Wound

▶ Prepare a poultice (*see* "Preparation Guide" on page 252) using coarse (kosher) salt that has been heated in a frying pan. Then apply it to the painful area. To keep the salt comfortably warm, put a hot water bottle on top of it. (Chances are, this old home remedy draws out the pain effectively with nonkosher salt, too.)

You can try more than one remedy at a time. While you're trying these remedies, pay attention to your body and you'll soon learn what makes you feel better.

### Amazing Raisins

Joe Graedon, MS, pharmacologist, adjunct assistant professor at the University of North Carolina, Chapel Hill, is known as "The People's Pharmacist." He

is affiliated with the Research (*www.rti.org*), and they tested Gin-Soaked Raisin Remedy" ( for alcohol content.

*The result:* Less than one drop of alcohol was left in nine raisins. So when people who take the raisins are feeling no pain, it's not because they're drunk, it's because the remedy works.

### ■ Recipe ■

#### The Amazing Gin-Soaked Raisin Remedy

> 1 lb golden raisins
> Gin (approximately 1 pint)
> Glass bowl (Pyrex is good—crystal
>    is bad)
> Glass jar with lid

Spread the golden raisins evenly on the bottom of the glass bowl and pour enough gin over the raisins to completely cover them. Let them stay that way until all the gin is absorbed by the raisins. It takes about five to seven days, depending on the humidity in your area. (You may want to lightly cover the bowl with a paper towel so that dust or insects don't drop in.) To make sure that all of the raisins get their fair share of the gin, occasionally take a spoon and stir the mixture, bringing the bottom layer of raisins to the top of the bowl.

As soon as all the gin has been absorbed, transfer the raisins to the jar, put the lid on and keep it closed. *Do not refrigerate.* Each day, eat nine raisins—exactly and only nine raisins a day. Most people eat them in the morning with breakfast.

Even so, be sure to check with your health professional to make sure that gin-soaked raisins will not conflict with medication you may be taking, or present a problem for any health challenge you may have, particularly an iron-overload condition.

> **☞ WARNING:** Do not give the gin-soaked raisins to children or women who are pregnant or nursing.

We've demonstrated this remedy on national television and the feedback has been incredible. One woman wrote to tell us that she had constant pain and no mobility in her neck.

Her doctor finally told her, "You'll just have to learn to live with the pain." Although that was unacceptable, she didn't know what else to do. And then she saw us on television, talking about a remarkable raisin remedy. We got her letter two weeks after she started "The Amazing Gin-Soaked Raisin Remedy." The woman had no pain and total mobility. She also had all of her friends waiting for their gin to be absorbed by their raisins.

This is one of dozens and dozens of success stories we've received. Some people have dramatic results after eating the raisins for less than a week, while it takes others a month or two to get results. There are some people for whom this remedy does nothing. But it's inexpensive, easy to do, delicious to eat and worth a try. Be consistent—eat the raisins every day. Expect a miracle...but have patience!

## Grapes Are Good, Too

▶ White grape juice is said to absorb the system's acid. Drink one glass in the morning and one glass before dinner.

## Camp Inside

▶ If you have morning stiffness caused by arthritis, try sleeping in a sleeping bag. You can sleep on your bed, but in the zipped-up bag. It's much more effective than an electric blanket because your body heat is evenly distributed and retained. Come morning, there's less pain, making it easier to get going.

▶ Corn-silk tea has been known to reduce acid in the system and lessen pain. Steep a handful of the silky strings that grow beneath the husk of corn in a cup of hot water for 10 minutes.

If it's not fresh-corn season, buy corn-silk extract in a health food store. Add 10 to 15 drops in 1 cup of water and drink. Dried corn silk can also be used. Prepare it as you would prepare an herbal tea. You can get dried corn silk at most places that sell dried herbs and spices (*see* "Sources" starting on page 297).

## Herbal Relief

▶ Each of these herbs is known as a pain reducer—sage, rosemary, nettles and basil. Use any one, two, three or four of them in the form of herbal tea (*see* "Preparation Guide" on page 250). Have 2 cups each day, rotating them until you find the one that makes you feel best.

## Coffee Cure

▶ Our friend's grandfather cleared up an arthritic condition (and lived to be 90) after he used a remedy given to him by a woman who brought it here from Puerto Rico. Squeeze the juice of a large lime into a cup of black coffee and drink it hot first thing each morning.

We're not in favor of drinking coffee, but who are we to argue with success?

▶ An old Native American arthritis remedy is a mixture of mashed yucca root and water. Yucca saponin, a steroid derivative of the yucca plant, is a forerunner of cortisone. The adverse effects of cortisone are too numerous and unpleasant to mention. The positive effects of yucca, according to a double-blind study done at a Southern California arthritis clinic, were relief from headaches as well as from gastrointestinal complaints.

In that study, 60% of the patients taking yucca tablets showed dramatic improvements in their arthritic condition. While it doesn't work for everyone, it works for enough people to make it worth a try.

## Oceanside Resort

▶ For most people, this remedy is not practical—for many, it's not even possible. Then why take up all this space? The results reported to us were so spectacular that we feel if only one person reads this, follows through and is relieved of his/her painful, debilitating condition, it will have been well worth the space on the page.

Starting with the first set of directions, you will see why this is usually considered a "last resort" remedy.

Bring a couple of truckloads of ocean sand to your yard. (What did we tell you?) Select a sheltered spot away from the wind. Dig a hole about 12 feet by 12 feet and about 3 feet deep, then dump the sand in it.

You will, obviously, need help in setting up this arrangement. You will also need help in carrying out the treatment. Incidentally, treatment should take place on hot summer days.

Wear a brief bathing suit, lie on your stomach with your face to the side (so you can breathe, of course), and have your body completely covered with sand, except for your head. Have your assistant put sunscreen on your face. Stay in that position for 15 minutes. Next, turn over on your back and have your body completely covered with sand, except for your head and face. Stay that way for 15 minutes.

Then get out of the sandbath, quickly cover yourself with a warm flannel or woolen robe and head for the shower. Take a hot shower, dry off thoroughly and go to bed for several hours (three to four) and relax. During all of this, make sure there's no exposure to the wind or to any drafts.

According to an Asian saying—"Rheumatism goes out from the body only through sweating."

During the next couple of hours in bed, you may have to change underwear several times because of the profuse sweating. This is good. Be sure to keep rehydrating yourself by drinking lots of water.

One sandbath a day is sufficient. For some people, one week of treatments has been enough to help heal the condition completely.

**NOTE:** The sandbath must have dry sand and be in your yard, in an area that's sheltered from the wind. The beach is too wet, too breezy and usually too far from home.

▶ If you do not have ulcers, drink ⅛ teaspoon of cayenne pepper in a glass of water or fruit juice (cherry juice without sugar or preservatives is best). If the pepper is just too strong for you, buy #1 capsules and fill them with cayenne, or you can buy already-prepared cayenne capsules at the health food store. Take two a day.

### There's the Rub

▶ Combine ½ teaspoon of eucalyptus oil, available at health food stores, with 1 tablespoon of pure olive oil, and massage the mixture onto your painful areas.

▶ You may want to alternate the massage mixture (above) with this one—grate fresh ginger, then squeeze the juice through a piece of cheesecloth. Mix the ginger juice with an equal amount of sesame oil. Massage it on the painful areas. Ginger can be quite strong. If the burning sensation makes you uncomfortable, then tone down the ginger by adding more sesame oil to the mixture.

▶ Aloe vera gel is now being used for many ailments, including arthritis. You can apply the gel externally to the aching joint and you can take it internally—1 tablespoon in the morning before breakfast and 1 tablespoon before dinner.

▶ Vegetable juices are wonderful for everyone. They can be particularly helpful for arthritis sufferers. Use fresh carrot juice as a sweetener with either celery juice or kale juice. (Invest in a juicer or connect with a nearby juice bar.)

### ASTHMA

During an asthma attack, bronchial tubes narrow and secrete an excess of mucus, making it very hard to breathe. It is a serious illness that can often be fatal.

Asthma in certain people may be attributed to exercise, allergies or emotional problems, or possibly a combination of all. (*See also* the "Allergies and Hay Fever" section on page 3.)

Renowned 19th-century British physician Peter Latham said, "You cannot be sure of the success of your remedy, while you are still uncertain of the nature of the disease." And so it is with asthma.

## Worldly "Wisdom"

Folk medicine legends abound with curious asthma remedies from around the world. Although we are not advocating these unorthodox remedies, a few of them may have worked in the days before modern medicine. But be on the safe side and check with your doctor before trying any of them. Asthma is best treated by a health professional.

▶ European and Australian folklore advocates swallowing a handful of spiderwebs rolled into a ball.

▶ Deep in the heart of Texas, they are said to sleep on the uncleaned wool of recently sheared sheep. Legend has it that the asthma is absorbed by the wool.

▶ Another old Texas home remedy requires the asthmatic to get a chihuahua (Mexican hairless dog). The theory is that the asthma goes from the patient to the dog, but the dog does not suffer from it.

▶ According to Kentucky folklore, wearing a string of amber beads around the neck may cure asthma. With the cost of a full strand of amber these days, it would be cheaper to buy a chihuahua, have him get asthma, then buy that tiny dog a strand of amber.

These legendary folk remedies make for good conversation, but in the midst of an asthma attack, who can talk?

**CAUTION:** These remedies are not substitutes for professional medical treatment.

## Natural Remedies

▶ We heard about a man who was able to ease off massive doses of cortisone by using garlic therapy. He started with one clove a day, minced, in a couple ounces of orange juice. He gulped it down without chewing any of the little pieces of garlic. That way, he didn't have garlic on his breath.

As he increased the number of garlic cloves he ate each day, his doctor decreased the amount of cortisone he was taking. After several months, he was eating six to 10 cloves of garlic a day, was completely off cortisone, and was not bothered by asthma.

▶ At the first sign of asthma-type wheezing, take a breath or two from your inhaler. Then saturate two strips of white cloth in white vinegar and wrap them around your wrists, not too tightly. For some people, it stops a full-blown attack from developing.

▶ Generally, dairy products are not good for asthmatics. They're too mucus-forming. We have heard, though, that cheddar cheese might be an exception. It contains *tyramine*, an ingredient that seems to help open up the breathing passages.

### Sweet Solution

▶ Cut a 1-ounce stick of licorice root (the herb, not the candy) into slices and steep the

slices in a quart of just-boiled water for 24 hours. Strain and bottle. At the first sign of heaviness on the chest, drink a cup of the licorice water.

**CAUTION:** Licorice root may cause renal failure in people with kidney conditions or high blood pressure.

**NOTE** (or should we say, **WARNING?**): In France, licorice water is used by women to give them more sexual vitality.

▶ We were on a radio show when a woman called in and shared her asthma remedy—cherry-bark tea. She buys tea bags in a health food store (if teas are alphabetically listed, it may be under "w" for "wild cherry-bark tea") and she drinks a cup before each meal and another cup at bedtime. The woman swore to us that it has changed her life. She hasn't had an asthma attack since she started drinking it five years ago.

▶ This remedy requires a juicer or a nearby juice bar. Drink equal amounts of endive (also called chicory), celery and carrot juice. One glass of the juice a day works wonders for some asthmatics.

▶ Remove the eggs from three eggshells. Then roast the eggshells for two hours at 400° F. The shells will turn light brown. (They'll also smell like rotten eggs.) Pulverize them and mix them into a cup of unsulfured molasses. Take 1 teaspoon before each meal. It just may prevent an asthma condition from acting up.

### See It Disappear

▶Visualization or mental imagery is a potent tool that can be used to help you heal yourself. Gerald N. Epstein, MD, assistant clinical professor of psychiatry, Mount Sinai Medical Center, and director of the American Institute for Mental Imagery (both in New York City), suggests that the following visualization be done to stem an asthma attack. Do it at the onset of an attack, for three to five minutes.

Sit in a comfortable chair and close your eyes. Breathe in and out three times and see yourself in a pine forest. Stand next to a pine tree and breathe in the aromatic fragrance of the pine. As you breathe out, sense this exhalation traveling down through your body and going out through the soles of your feet. See the breath exiting as gray smoke and being buried deep in the earth. Then open your eyes, breathing easily.

✎ **NOTE:** Learn this visualization and practice it when you're feeling fine so that you know exactly what to do and how to do it the second you feel a wheeze coming on.

▶Ray C. Wunderlich, Jr., MD, PhD, director of the Wunderlich Center for Nutritional Medicine in St. Petersburg, Florida, recommends magnesium for helping take away bronchial spasms. Find a dose of a magnesium preparation that is tolerated (if you get diarrhea, you should cut back on the dosage) and use it to relieve asthma. Do not exceed a total dose of 400 mg of elemental magnesium per day, unless prescribed by a physician.

▶Eat three to six apricots a day. They may help promote healing of lung and bronchial conditions.

▶Jerusalem artichokes (*see* recipe below)— also called sunchokes because they're related to sunflowers—may be a real plus for nourishing the lungs of the asthmatic when eaten daily.

▶Put 4 cups of shelled sunflower seeds in 2 quarts of water and boil it down to 1 quart of water. Strain out the little pieces of sunflower seeds, then add one pint of honey and boil it down to a syrupy consistency.

*Dose:* Take 1 teaspoon a half-hour after each meal.

### ■ Recipe ■

#### Sweet Pickled Jerusalem Artichokes

½ cup apple cider vinegar

½ cup water

3 Tbsp evaporated cane juice (available at health food stores)

¼ tsp salt

1½ cups sliced Jerusalem artichokes (½ lb)

1 large carrot, angle-sliced thinly

1 large stalk celery, sliced

Combine first four ingredients in a medium bowl and stir to combine flavors. Add vegetables, stir well and cover with plastic wrap. Store in the refrigerator to marinate for several hours or overnight. Makes about 4 cups.

*Source: www.vegparadise.com*

▶ Similar to, but more potent than, the sunflower-seed syrup is garlic syrup. Separate and peel the cloves of three entire garlic bulbs. Simmer them in a nonaluminum pan with 2 cups of water. When the garlic cloves are soft and there's about a cup of water left in the pan, remove the garlic and put it in a jar. Then, add 1 cup of cider vinegar and ¼ cup of honey to the water that's left in the pan, boiling the mixture until it's syrupy. Pour the syrup over the garlic in the jar. Cover the jar and let it stand overnight.

*Dose:* Swallow one or two cloves of garlic with a teaspoon of syrup every morning on an empty stomach.

☛ **WARNING:** Infants, diabetics and people with honey allergies should not use honey.

### Oldie, But a Goodie

▶ A relative told us that in the "old country," a remedy used at the onset of an asthma attack was to inhale the steam from boiling potatoes that were cut in pieces with the skin left on them. With or without the potatoes, inhaling steam can be beneficial.

*Be careful:* Steam is powerful and can burn the skin.

▶ Mix 1 teaspoon of grated horseradish with 1 teaspoon of honey and take it every night before bedtime.

▶ Slice two large raw onions into a jar. Pour 2 cups of honey over it. Close the jar and let it stand overnight. The next morning you're ready to start taking the "honion" syrup.

*Dose:* Take 1 teaspoon a half-hour after each meal and 1 teaspoon before bed.

▶ Buy either concentrated cranberry juice, sold at health food stores, or unconcentrated cranberry juice, sold at most supermarkets. Read the ingredients on the label and make sure there are no preservatives or sugar added. Or, you can make your own with 1 pound of cranberries in 1 pint of water. Boil until the cranberries are very mushy. Then, pour the mixture into a jar and keep it in the refrigerator.

*Dose:* Drink 2 tablespoons a half-hour before each meal and immediately at the onset of an asthma attack. Be sure to keep your inhaler handy, too.

## ATHEROSCLEROSIS

Atherosclerosis is clogging of the arteries that is caused by deposits of fatty substances, cholesterol, calcium and other matter. This build-up is called *plaque*, and it develops over many years from poor diet, a sedentary lifestyle and smoking. It's important that you work with your doctor to treat this condition. Be sure to consult him/her before trying any natural remedies.

If you are developing atherosclerosis, do something to protect your arteries against the negative effects of improper diet, lack of exercise and bad habits (such as smoking). *These remedies may help...*

## Natural Remedies

▶ Eating a few cloves of garlic each day has been known to help clear arteries. It seems to cleanse the system, and collect and cast out toxic waste.

Mince two cloves and put them in a half glass of orange juice or water and drink it down. There's no need to chew the pieces of garlic. By just swallowing them, the garlic smell doesn't stay on your breath.

In conjunction with a sensible diet, garlic can also help bring down cholesterol levels in the blood. No wonder this beautiful bulb has a fan club, appropriately called "Lovers of the Stinking Rose."

*See* the "Six Sensational Superfoods" on page 266 for more information on garlic.

▶ Rutin is one of the elements of the bioflavonoids. Bioflavonoids (substances from plants that help maintain cellular health) are necessary for the proper absorption of vitamin C. Taking 500 mg of rutin daily, with at least the same amount of vitamin C, is said to increase the strength of capillaries, strengthen the artery walls, help prevent hemorrhaging and help treat atherosclerosis.

▶ According to French folklore, eating rye bread made with baker's yeast supposedly prevents clogging of the arteries.

▶ It is reported that some Russians eat mature, raw potatoes at every meal to prevent atherosclerosis.

▶ Drinking a combination of apple cider boiled with garlic once a day is a Slavic folk remedy. This may not prevent atherosclerosis, but it certainly tastes like it should.

# High Cholesterol Remedies

The US government recently changed the guidelines for what is considered a dangerous level of cholesterol. Previous levels were a maximum of 100 milligrams per deciliter (mg/dL) of low-density lipoprotein (LDL or "bad") cholesterol, and the new recommendation is to have LDLs no higher than 70 mg/dL.

These guidelines are meant for very high-risk people who have heart disease, plus diabetes, high blood pressure and smoke cigarettes. But even people with moderately high risk (for example, those who have already had a heart attack) should keep their LDL levels well below 100 mg/dL.

The only foods that have cholesterol are animal products—meat, poultry, fish, dairy. If you are diagnosed with high cholesterol, start a heart-smart diet immediately by cutting down or cutting out animal products. There are foods that can help lower your LDL and raise your HDL (good cholesterol).

 **NOTE:** Talk to your doctor about any dietary changes you make.

There have been a variety of cholesterol studies conducted over different periods of time with any number of test subjects. Some of the results are impressive, and all of the cholesterol-lowering foods are worth a try.

First—and most important—is to get that heart-smart diet in place, and incorporate the foods that have been shown to help. *According to the studies...*

◆ Eating half an avocado every day may lower cholesterol by 8% to 42%. Yes, avocados are high in fat, but it's monounsaturated fat that does good things for the system. An avocado also contains

13 essential minerals, including iron, copper and magnesium, and is rich in potassium. It tastes great, too.

- ◆ Eating two large apples a day may cause cholesterol levels to drop 16%. Apples are rich in flavonoids and pectin, which may form a gel in the stomach that keeps fats in food from being totally absorbed.

- ◆ Eating two raw carrots a day reduced cholesterol levels by 11%.

- ◆ People who consumed about ¾ cup of fenugreek daily for 20 days cut their LDL ("bad" cholesterol) levels by 33%. Their HDL ("good" cholesterol) stayed the same. Instead of eating tablespoons of ground fenugreek seeds, choose capsules (580 mg), which are available at health food stores. Take one or two with each meal.

- ◆ Eating four cloves of garlic a day can cut total cholesterol by about 7%. (While fresh garlic is best, garlic supplements are fine.)

- ◆ Men and women who started out with low blood levels of vitamin C and then took 1,000 mg of vitamin C every day for eight months had a 7% increase of their HDL (good cholesterol) readings.

- ◆ Kiwi has what it takes to help keep cholesterol down—magnesium, potassium and fiber. It makes a satisfying, energy-boosting afternoon snack.

- ◆ Omega-3 fatty acids have the uncanny ability to break down cholesterol in the lining of blood vessels, and also serve as a solvent for saturated fats in the diet. The end result is less choles-

terol in the body and bloodstream, and a reduced likelihood of cholesterol/heart disease complications in the future.

Omega-3s are healthy polyunsaturated fats found in many foods, including salmon, mackerel and other fatty fish. Flaxseed oil offers the most cost-effective and beneficial method for increasing the intake of omega-3 oils in the diet. (*See* "Six Sensational Superfoods" on page 262 for detailed flaxseed information.)

▶ Ray C. Wunderlich, Jr., MD, PhD, director of the Wunderlich Center for Nutritional Medicine in St. Petersburg, Florida, recommends grape seed oil (available at health food stores) as a reliable increaser of HDL (good cholesterol). Follow the dosage on the label.

▶ Impressive test results build a good case for the effectiveness of lecithin in lowering LDL levels and raising HDL levels.

*Dose:* Take 1 to 2 tablespoons of lecithin granules daily, available at health food stores.

▶ *The American Journal of Clinical Nutrition* (*www.ajcn.org*) mentions that raw carrots not only improve digestive elimination because of their high fiber content, but may also lower cholesterol. Test subjects who ate two carrots for breakfast for three weeks reduced their serum cholesterol level by 11%.

You may want to scrub the carrots you eat instead of peeling them. The peel is rich in $B_1$ (thiamine), $B_2$ (riboflavin) and $B_3$ (niacin). If you can get organically grown carrots, do so.

▶ It seems that very small amounts of chromium are vital for good health. A deficiency in chromium may be linked to coronary artery

## ■ Recipe ■

### *Banana Bread Oatmeal*

3 cups fat-free milk

3 Tbsp firmly packed brown sugar

¾ tsp ground cinnamon

¼ tsp salt (optional)

¼ tsp ground nutmeg

2 cups quick or old-fashioned oats, uncooked

2 medium-size ripe bananas, mashed (about 1 cup)

2 to 3 Tbsp coarsely chopped toasted pecans*

Vanilla nonfat yogurt (optional)

Banana slices (optional)

Pecan halves (optional)

In medium saucepan, bring milk, brown sugar, spices and salt to a gentle boil (watch carefully); stir in oats. Return to a boil, and reduce heat to medium. Cook 1 minute for quick oats, 5 minutes for old-fashioned oats, or until most of liquid is absorbed, stirring occasionally.

Remove oatmeal from heat. Stir in mashed bananas and pecans. Spoon oatmeal into four cereal bowls. Top with yogurt, sliced bananas and pecan halves, if desired. Makes 4 servings.

*To toast pecans, spread evenly in shallow baking pan. Bake at 350° F for 5 to 7 minutes or until light golden brown. Or, spread nuts evenly on microwave-safe plate. Microwave on high for 1 minute, then stir. Continue to microwave, checking every 30 seconds, until nuts are fragrant and brown.

*Source: www.recipegoldmine.com*

disease. Take 1 to 2 tablespoons of brewer's yeast daily (be sure to read labels and select the brewer's yeast with the highest chromium content) or a handful of raw sunflower seeds.

The chromium, like the lecithin, is said to lower the LDL cholesterol level and raise the HDL cholesterol level. If you plan on doing this, get your doctor's approval.

▶ The results of one study conducted at Rutgers University in New Brunswick, New Jersey, showed that oats can bring down blood cholesterol levels. You can reap this benefit by eating oatmeal or any other form of oats two or three times a week. (*See* recipe at left.)

▶ According to James W. Anderson, MD, professor of medicine and clinical nutrition at the University of Kentucky College of Medicine in Lexington, "Including a cup of beans in your diet per day helps to stabilize blood sugars and lower cholesterol." This benefit can be attributed to dry beans, such as navy or pinto, rather than green beans.

▶ Scott Grundy, MD, professor of human nutrition at the University of Texas Health Science Center in Dallas, says that research shows that *mono*unsaturated fatty acid, found in olive oil and peanut oil, is more effective in reducing artery-clogging cholesterol levels than *poly*unsaturated fats, such as corn oil and sunflower oil.

# BACK PAIN

It is estimated that eight out of 10 people have, at some point in their lives, back pain that disables them. Also estimated is the money spent for diagnosis and treatment of back pain—more than $5 billion annually.

> **WARNING:** It's extremely important that any back pain be evaluated by a medical professional to rule out serious illness or injury. If your back pain is chronic, persistent or severe, see a doctor.

We have come across some remedies that are worth trying to relieve minor backaches. At best, they'll help—at least, they'll give you something to talk about the next time someone tells you his/her back went out.

## Healing Position

▶ Thanks to the wise guidance of our cousin Linda, a physical therapist, many people who felt that their backs were on the verge of going out avoided the problem. If you've had back trouble, you know the feeling we're referring to.

When you get that feeling, carefully lie down on the floor, close enough to a sofa or easy chair so that you can bend your knees and rest your legs (knees to feet) on the seat of the sofa or chair. Your thighs should be leaning against the front of the sofa and your tush should be as close as possible, directly in front of it, with the rest of your body flat on the floor.

In position, you're like the start of a staircase. Your body is the lowest step, your thighs are the distance between the steps, and your knees-to-feet are the second step.

Stay in that position for 15 to 30 minutes. It's a restful and healing treatment for the back.

The best and safest way to get up is to lower your legs, roll over on your side, then slowly lift yourself up, letting your arms and shoulders do most of the work.

### For Men Only

Do you have back or hip pain when you sit for any length of time? Is it something you and your doctor(s) can't quite figure out and so you label it "back trouble"?

According to doctors, you may need a "wallet-ectomy."

If you carry around a thick wallet in your hip pocket, it may be putting pressure on the sciatic nerve. Keep your wallet in your jacket pocket instead, and you'll find that sitting can be a pleasurable experience again.

## Natural Remedies

▶ An Asian remedy for the prevention or relief of lower back problems is black beans (also called *frijoles negros*—although not in Asia!), which are available at supermarkets and health food stores.

Soak a cupful of black beans overnight. This softens the beans and is said to remove the gas-producing compounds. Then put them in a pot with 3½ cups of water. Bring to a boil, and let simmer for a half-hour over low heat. During that half-hour, keep removing the grayish foam that forms on top. After a half-hour, cover the pot and let it cook for another two hours. If, by the end of that time, there's still water in the pot, spill it out.

Eat 2 to 3 tablespoons of the black beans each day for one month, then every other day for one month.

Fresh beans should be prepared at least every three or four days.

### Get a Friend

▶ You need to employ the buddy system for this remedy. Put 20 drops of eucalyptus oil in a cup and warm it in the microwave for a few seconds. Then have your buddy gently massage the warm oil on your painful area. The "hands on" are as healing as the oil.

# Sciatica

Sciatica is a painful condition affecting the sciatic nerve, which is the longest nerve in the body. It extends from the lower spine through the pelvis, thighs, down into the legs and ends at the heels. When this nerve gets pinched or pulled (usually because of over-exertion), the resulting back pain can be excruciating.

The home remedies we describe may not cure the condition entirely, but they may help ease the pain.

### Pain-Relieving Juices

▶ The juice from potatoes has been said to help sciatica sufferers. So has celery juice. If you don't have a juicer, a health food store with

a juice bar might be willing to accommodate you. Have them juice a 10-ounce combination of potato and celery juice. Add carrots and/or beets to improve the taste.

In addition to the juice, drink a couple of cups of celery tea throughout the day.

▶ Stimulate the sciatic nerve by applying a fresh minced horseradish poultice to the painful area. Keep it on for one hour at a time.

### Add Some Garlic

▶ Vitamin $B_1$ and garlic may be very beneficial. Eat garlic raw in salads and use it in cooking. Also, take garlic supplements daily, plus 10 mg of vitamin $B_1$ along with a good B-complex vitamin.

**CAUTION:** Do not eat garlic or take garlic supplements if you have a bleeding disorder or ulcers, or are taking anticoagulants.

If you are taking any kind of medication, check with your health professional before taking garlic supplements.

▶ A hot water bag on the painful area may help you make it through the night with less pain and more sleep.

▶ Drink elderberry juice and elderberry tea throughout the day.

▶ Before bedtime, heat olive oil and use it to massage the painful areas.

▶ Eat lots of watercress and parsley every day. (*See* recipe on page 25.)

▶ According to many Germans, eating raw sauerkraut every day prevents sciatica.

## ■ Recipe ■

### Emerald Sauce

2 Tbsp lemon juice

¼ cup chopped parsley

¾ cup lightly packed, rinsed and
      drained watercress sprigs

1 Tbsp chopped tarragon

1 cup sour cream (or half sour cream
      and half plain yogurt)

Salt to taste

In a blender or food processor, combine lemon juice, parsley, watercress, tarragon and sour cream. Whirl until mixture is smoothly puréed, scraping container sides as required. Add salt to taste. Serve over potatoes, fish or chicken.

*Source: www.recipegoldmine.com*

### Be Well-Red

▶ Polish folk healers tell their patients who suffer from sciatica to wear woolen long underwear—red only—and carry a raw beet in their hip pocket.

▶ We heard about a man who went from doctor to doctor seeking help. Nothing worked. As a last resort, the man followed the advice of an alternative medicine practitioner who recommended garlic milk.

The man minced two cloves of garlic, put them in ½ cup of milk and drank it down (without chewing the pieces of garlic). He had the garlic milk each morning and each evening. Within a few days, he felt some relief. Within two weeks, all the pain had completely disappeared.

▶ Water has tremendous therapeutic value for a sciatic condition. It can reduce the pain and improve circulation. Take a long, hot bath or shower and follow it with a short cold shower. If you can't stand the thought of a cold shower, then follow up the hot bath with ice-cold compresses on the painful areas.

## BODY ODOR

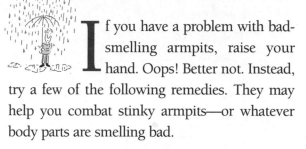

If you have a problem with bad-smelling armpits, raise your hand. Oops! Better not. Instead, try a few of the following remedies. They may help you combat stinky armpits—or whatever body parts are smelling bad.

▶ Take a shower, then prepare turnip juice. Grate a turnip, squeeze the juice through cheesecloth so that you have 2 teaspoons. Now raise your hand and vigorously massage a teaspoon of the turnip juice into each armpit.

## Dietary Remedies

▶ A vegetarian friend's sense of smell is so keen, she can stand next to someone and tell whether that person is a meat eater.

If you are a heavy meat and fowl eater and are troubled by body odor, change your diet. Ease off meat and poultry and force yourself to fill up on green leafy vegetables. There will be a big difference in a short time. You probably won't perspire less, but the smell won't be as strong, and the change of diet will be healthier for you in general. It will also be appreciated by the people in the crowded elevators you ride. (*See* recipe on page 26.)

## ■ Recipe ■

### Organic Garden Salad with Fresh Herbs

Mix of organic leafy greens (arugula, spinach, romaine, endive, etc.)

Organic tomatoes, diced

Sunflower sprouts

Mushrooms, sliced

Yellow peppers, sliced

Basil, minced

Oregano

Mint

Thyme

Parsley

Non-fat Italian dressing

1 Tbsp white balsamic vinegar

Fresh ground pepper, to taste

Mix equal parts of each type of greens in a large salad bowl or platter—adjust quantity based on the number of servings desired. Place the diced tomatoes, sunflower sprouts, sliced mushrooms, sliced yellow peppers and any other organic produce on top of the greens.

Next, sprinkle on the organic fresh herb leaves, minced or whole. Then cover the salad bowl or platter with plastic wrap or aluminum foil and refrigerate.

Just before serving, add 1 Tbsp of white balsamic vinegar to ¼ cup of non-fat Italian dressing. This will thin the dressing and give the characteristic flavor of balsamic vinegar. You could also use red balsamic vinegar or a fresh citrus juice. Add fresh ground pepper (especially red or green peppercorns) to taste.

*Source: www.recipegoldmine.com*

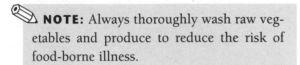 **NOTE:** Always thoroughly wash raw vegetables and produce to reduce the risk of food-borne illness.

### The Grass Is Greener...

▶ In addition to eating green leafy vegetables, take a 500 mg capsule of wheat grass (powdered juice) daily. Or, if your local health food store sells fresh wheat grass juice, have an ounce first thing each morning. Be sure to take it on an empty stomach and drink it down with spring water. The chlorophyll can reduce body odor dramatically or eliminate it completely.

▶ If tension causes you to perspire excessively, which then causes unpleasant body odors, drink sage tea. Use 1½ teaspoons of dried sage, or two tea bags in 1 cup of water. Let the tea steep for 10 minutes. Drink it in small doses throughout the day. The tea should help you to relax, so don't sweat it.

▶ "Think Zinc—Don't Stink!" Credit for that slogan goes to a Pennsylvania man who rid himself of body odor by taking 30 mg of zinc every day. Within two weeks, he was smelling like a rose.

**CAUTION:** Some people get stomachaches from zinc. Also, high amounts of zinc may increase a man's risk of developing prostate cancer.

Consult your doctor for the proper dosage before supplementing with zinc.

## BRUISES AND SKIN DISCOLORATION

Ouch! Bruises generally appear when the skin has undergone some form of trauma (minor or not) that caused little blood vessels to break. This can happen from bumping into the edge of a table or from something more serious like a car accident.

Most minor bruises will go away on their own with time (usually after going through a rainbow of colors), but these remedies may speed up the healing process.

## Bruises

To prevent and heal common, everyday bruises...

▶ Apply a cold pack or ice wrapped in a washcloth as soon as possible after the injury. Hold for 20 minutes. Repeat several times. Cold constricts blood vessels, shortens clotting time and can reduce blood leakage from capillaries.

▶ Elevate the injured area higher than your heart. The longer you can do this, the better. It reduces blood flow to the injury.

▶ Take vitamin C. Vitamin C makes capillaries less fragile. Extra vitamin C is particularly important if you're taking aspirin or corticosteroids, drugs that can strip vitamin C from the body. The amount in a multisupplement, typically 60 to 100 mg, usually is adequate.

*Bonus:* Most multisupplements also contain zinc, a mineral that may reduce capillary leakage.

▶ If you close a door or drawer on your finger, prepare a poultice of grated onion and salt and apply it to the bruised area. The pain will disappear within seconds.

▶ Place ice on a bruise to help prevent the area from turning black and blue, and to reduce the swelling. If ice is not available, immediately press a metal knife (flat side only —we're talking bruises, not amputation) or spoon on the bruise for five to 10 minutes.

### Easy Bruise Erasers

▶ Make a salve by mashing pieces of parsley into a teaspoon of butter. Gently rub the salve on the bruise.

▶ Grate a piece of turnip or a piece of daikon (Japanese radish). Apply the grated root to the bruise and leave it there for 15 to 30 minutes. These two roots have been known to help improve the look of the bruise.

▶ Spread a thin layer of blackstrap molasses on a piece of brown paper (grocery bag) and apply the molasses side to the bruise. Bind it in place and leave it there for a few hours.

▶ Peel a banana and apply the inside of the peel to the bruise. It will lessen the pain, reduce the discoloration and speed healing. Bind the peel in place with a bandage.

▶ Mix 2 tablespoons of cornstarch with 1 tablespoon of castor oil. Dampen a clean white cloth and make a cornstarch/castor oil poultice. (*See* "Preparation Guide" on page 252.) Apply the poultice to the bruise and leave it on until the damp cloth gets dry.

**WARNING:** Most bruises are just evidence of an active life—but if you get a bruise and it doesn't go away or you keep getting bruises, it could be a sign of a dangerous medical condition. Schedule an appointment with your doctor.

## Brown Spots

Large, flat brown spots on your face and hands may be called age spots or liver spots. Many fair-skinned people develop them in middle age from an accumulation of pigment (color) in the skin.

**CAUTION:** Any suspicious mark or skin discoloration should be evaluated by a dermatologist to rule out skin cancer.

The following remedies may not produce instant results. Keep in mind that these brown spots, thought to be caused by sun damage or a nutrition deficiency, took years to form. Give the remedy you use a few months to work. Then, if there's no change, try another remedy. It may take some trial and error to find what works best for you.

▶ Grate an onion and squeeze it through cheesecloth so that you have 1 teaspoon of onion juice. Mix it with 2 teaspoons of vinegar and massage the brown spots with this liquid. Do it daily—twice a day, if possible—until you no longer see spots in front of your eyes.

### Banish Brown Spots with Beans

▶ This Israeli remedy calls for chickpeas. You may know them as garbanzo beans, ceci or arbus. If you don't want to prepare them from scratch, buy canned chickpeas. Mash about ⅓ cup and add a little water. Smear the paste on the brown spots and leave it there until it dries and starts crumbling off. Then wash it off completely. Do this every evening.

### Gimme an E!

▶ Once a day, swallow a vitamin E capsule (check with your doctor for amount). In addi-

tion, at bedtime, puncture an E capsule, squish out the oil and rub it on the brown spots, leaving it on overnight. Wear white cotton gloves to avoid messing up your sheets.

▶ A variation of this remedy is to rub on castor oil and take the vitamin E orally.

## Dark Undereye Circles

▶ If you have access to fresh figs, try cutting one in half and placing the halves under your eyes. You should, of course, lie down and relax for 15 to 30 minutes. Okay, fig face, time to get up and gently rinse the sticky stuff off with tepid water. Dab on some peanut oil.

▶ When figs are not in season, grate an unwaxed cucumber or a small scrubbed (preferably red) potato. Put the gratings on two gauze pads, lie down and put them under your eyes. Rinse thoroughly and dab on some peanut oil.

## Black Eyes

We met a friend who had a shiner. We asked, "Did someone give you a black eye?" He answered, "No. I had to fight for it."

Black eyes are essentially bruises that are located around the eye socket. These remedies should help reduce the swelling and take away some of the color.

### Hawaiian Treat

▶ Eat ripe pineapple and ripe papaya—lots of it—for two or three days, and let the enzymes in those fruits help eliminate the discoloration around the eye. If you can't get fresh pineapple or papaya, try papaya pills (available at health food stores). Take one after every meal. Both fruits are rich in vitamin C, which also promotes healing.

### Steaks Are for Eating

▶ If you were a character in a movie and you got a black eye, in the following scene you would be nursing it with a piece of raw steak.

Cut! The steak may have bacteria that you don't want on your eye, and since the only reason it's being used is because it's cold, retake the scene with a package of frozen vegetables or a cold, wet cloth. Leave it on the bruised area for about 20 minutes, off for 10 minutes, on for 20, off for 10. Get the picture?

▶ Make a poultice (*see* "Preparation Guide" on page 252) by mixing 2 tablespoons of salt with 2 tablespoons of lard or vegetable shortening. Spread the mixture on a cloth and place it over the bruised eye. This poultice may help eliminate the bruised cells around the eye by stimulating the circulation. Be especially careful not to get the salty lard in your eye.

▶ Pour witch hazel on a cotton pad and apply it to the bruised, closed eye. Lie down with your feet slightly higher than your head for a half-hour while the witch hazel stays in place.

▶ Peel and grate a potato (a red potato is best). Make a poultice out of it (*see* "Preparation Guide" on page 252) and keep it on the black eye for 20 minutes. Potassium chloride is one of the most effective healing compounds, and potatoes are the best source of potassium chloride. (This remedy is also beneficial for bloodshot eyes.)

## BURNS

The word "burn" applies to certain types of skin damage—caused by extreme heat or cold, chemicals, large doses of radiation or exposure to the sun.

Burns are classified by degree. In a first-degree burn, the skin is painful and red, but unbroken. In a second-degree burn, the skin is broken and there are painful blisters. A third-degree burn destroys the underlying tissue as well as surface skin. The burn may be painless because nerve endings have also been destroyed.

Second-degree burns that cover an extensive area of skin and all third-degree burns require *immediate medical attention*. Any kind of burn on the face should also receive immediate medical attention as a precaution against swollen breathing passages.

We'll deal mainly with superficial first-degree burns, which occur from things like grabbing a hot pot handle, grasping the iron side of an iron, having the oven door close on your forearm or getting splattered with boiling oil.

⚡ **CAUTION:** Do not use these topical remedies on broken skin due to the risk of infection.

Here are natural remedies using mostly handy household items.

## First-Degree Burns

Apply cold water or cold compresses first! *Then you can...*

▶ Draw out the heat and pain by applying a slice of raw, unpeeled potato, a piece of fresh pumpkin pulp or a slice of raw onion. Leave the potato, pumpkin or onion on the burn for 15 minutes, off for five minutes and then put a fresh piece on for another 15 minutes.

▶ If you have either a vitamin E or garlic oil capsule, puncture one and squeeze the contents directly on the burn.

▶ Keep an aloe vera plant in your home. It's like growing a tube of healing ointment. Break off about a half-inch piece of stem. Squeeze it so that the juice oozes out onto the burned area.

The juice is most effective if the plant is at least two to three years old and the stems have little bumps on the edges.

▶ If you burn yourself while baking and happen to have salt-free unbaked pie crust around, roll it thin and place it on the entire surface of the burn. Let it stay on until it dries up and falls off by itself.

### Good Enough to Eat

▶ Make a poultice (*see* "Preparation Guide" on page 252) of raw sauerkraut and apply it to the burned area. If you don't have sauerkraut, use crushed comfrey root with a little honey. In fact, according to research in India, just plain honey on the burn may ease the pain and help the healing process.

▶ Spread apple butter over the burned area. As it dries, add another coat to it. Keep adding coats for a day or two, until the burn is just about butter—uh, better.

⚡ **CAUTION:** Only put butter or other fatty substances on the most superficial, minor burns due to the risk of infection.

## Second-Degree Burns

For at least 30 minutes, dip the burned area in cold water or apply a soft towel that has been drenched in ice-cold water. *Do not use lard, butter or a salve on the burn, especially if the skin is broken!* Those things are a breeding ground for bacteria. In addition, when you get medical attention, the doctor will have to wipe off the goo to examine the condition of the skin.

If the burn is on an arm or leg, keep the limb raised in the air to help prevent swelling.

## Chemical and Acid Burns

*Call for medical attention immediately.* But until help arrives, put the affected area under the closest running water—a sink faucet, a garden hose or the shower. The running water will help wash the chemicals off the skin. Keep the water running on the burned skin for at least 20 minutes. You can stop when medical help arrives.

# Minor Burns

## *Burnt Tongue*

▶ Keep rinsing your mouth with cold water. A few drops of vanilla extract may relieve the pain, or try sprinkling some white sugar on it.

## *Rope Burns*

▶ Soak your aching hands in salt water.

## *Burnt Throat*

▶ If you've drunk something that was too hot, two teaspoons of olive oil will soothe and coat a burnt throat. A tablespoon of honey may also help.

## *Burning Feet*

▶ For minor foot burns from walking on hot pavement or sand, wrap tomato slices on the soles of the feet (keep them in place with a bandage) and keep them elevated for a half-hour.

▶ Soak your feet in warm potato water (*see* "Preparation Guide" on page 252) for 15 minutes. Dry your feet thoroughly. If you're going right to bed, massage the feet with a small amount of sesame or almond oil. You might want to put on loose-fitting socks to avoid messing up the sheets.

▶ Bavarian mountain climbers, after soaking their feet in potato water, sprinkle hot, roasted salt on a cloth and wrap it around their feet. It not only soothes burning and tired feet, but relieves itchy ones as well.

## *Sunburn*

*See* "Sunburn" on page 172.

# CARPAL TUNNEL SYNDROME (CTS)

This condition results from swollen tendons that compress the median nerve within the carpal tunnel canal in the wrist. It's usually accompanied by odd sensations, numbness, swelling, soreness, stiffness, weakness, tingling, discomfort and pain...a lot of pain. It tends to be caused by continual, rapid use of your fingers, wrists and/or arms.

Many people feel the requirements of their job contribute to the onset of CTS. But people who spend each workday at a computer aren't the only ones doing repetitious work—musicians, supermarket checkers, factory workers, hair stylists, bus drivers, seamstresses, tailors and countless others are plagued by this repetitive motion injury.

Vitamin $B_6$ may help to ease symptoms of CTS. But too much $B_6$ can be toxic and harmful to the nervous system, so work with your health professional to determine a safe dosage of $B_6$ for you.

If your problem is computer-related, visit your local computer store and see what it has in the way of ergonomic products that will support your wrists when you use the computer.

## Sleeping with CTS

The pain may be more severe while sleeping because of the way you fold your wrist. You may find it more comfortable to wear a splint or wrist brace to bed. Now that the problem is so common, you can find a selection of splints and

## Carpal Tunnel Checklist

You may be predisposed to CTS if you are hypothyroid, have diabetes, are pregnant or if you're taking birth control pills. *The following things are situations you can begin to change immediately...*

◆ *Do you smoke?* Smoking worsens the condition because nicotine constricts the blood vessels and carbon monoxide replaces oxygen, reducing the blood flow to your tissues.

◆ *Are you overweight?* Being overweight can reduce the blood flow to your tissues. Also, the more weight, the more the muscles must support to move your hand and arm.

◆ *Do you exercise?* Aerobic exercise—30 minutes, four times a week—can increase the flow of oxygenated blood to your hands, and help remove waste products caused by inflammation.

wrist braces at most drugstores. You may want to wear the splint or brace during the day, too.

## Exercise for CTS Prevention

A team of doctors from the American Academy of Orthopaedic Surgeons in Rosemont, Illinois, has developed special exercises that can help prevent carpal tunnel syndrome. The exercises, which decrease the median nerve pressure responsible for CTS, should be done at the start of each work shift, as a warmup exercise and again after each break.

▶ Stand up straight, feet a foot apart, arms outstretched in front of you, palms down. Then bring your hands and fingers up, pointing toward the sky. Hold for a count of five.

Straighten both wrists and relax the fingers. Make a tight fist with both hands. Then bend both wrists down while keeping the fists. Hold for a count of five. Straighten both wrists and relax the fingers for a count of five. The exercise should be repeated 10 times. Then let your arms hang loosely at your sides and shake them for a couple of seconds. *Don't rush through the exercise.* Let the 10 cycles take about five minutes.

### One Expert's CTS Cure

▶ James A. Duke, PhD, a botanist formerly with the USDA's Agricultural Research Service in Beltsville, Maryland, and one of the world's leading authorities on herbal healing traditions, confesses that he uses a computer as much as 14 hours a day. But he hasn't developed any CTS symptoms. He gives some of the credit to the fact that he's a man.

"Women develop carpal tunnel problems more than men do," explains Dr. Duke, "because the cyclical hormone fluctuations of the menstrual cycle, pregnancy and menopause can contribute to swelling of the tissues that surround the carpal tunnel."

Another reason he thinks he's been spared the discomfort of CTS is hand exercises. "Adopting a Chinese technique that improves flexibility," says Dr. Duke, "I hold two steel balls in one hand and roll them around when I'm not typing. The Chinese balls provide a gentle form of exercise, and the rolling motion massages the tiny muscles and ligaments of the hands and wrists." When he's at the computer, he takes frequent breaks to twirl the Chinese balls in each hand.

Chinese balls are inexpensive and readily available at Chinese markets or on-line. Some health food stores may also carry them.

## If You Use a Computer...

**T**he National Institute for Occupational Safety and Health in Washington, DC, recommends that you...

◆ Position the screen at eye level, about 22 to 26 inches away.

◆ Sit about arm's length from the terminal. At that distance, the electrical field is almost zero.

◆ Face forward and keep your neck relaxed.

◆ Position the keyboard so that your elbows are bent at least 90 degrees and you can work without bending your wrists.

◆ Use a chair that supports your back, lets your feet rest on the floor or on a footrest, and keeps thighs parallel to the floor.

◆ If you can step away from the computer for 15 minutes every hour, it can help prevent eyestrain. Also, frequent blinking will help prevent eye irritation, burning and/or dry eyes.

For more information, go to *www.cdc.gov/niosh/homepage.html.*

## Herbs for CTS

In his book *The Green Pharmacy* (St. Martin's), Dr. Duke reports on quite a few herbs that can help alleviate CTS.

▶ "Willow bark, the original source of aspirin, contains chemicals (salicylates) that both relieve pain and reduce inflammation. You might also try other herbs rich in salicylates, notably meadowsweet and wintergreen."

With any of these herbs, Dr. Duke steeps 1 to 2 teaspoons of dried, powdered bark, or 5 teaspoons of fresh bark, for 10 minutes or so,

■ **Recipe** ■

*Sunrise Salsa*

½ ripe papaya (about ½ pound), seeded, skinned and diced

½ ripe mango, seeded, skinned and diced

½ cup diced fresh pineapple (canned pineapple is fine)

1 medium cucumber, peeled, seeded and diced

1 or 2 jalapeño peppers, stemmed, seeded and minced

4 green onions, trimmed and thinly sliced

2 to 4 Tbsp finely chopped fresh basil or fresh mint

2 Tbsp fresh lime juice

Kosher salt and pepper, to taste

Combine papaya, mango, pineapple, cucumber, jalapeños, green onions, basil or mint and lime juice in a small glass bowl. Toss gently just to combine. Add salt and pepper to taste. Serve immediately or refrigerate, covered, for up to one hour. Makes about 2½ cups.

If making the salsa ahead of time, add the papaya and pineapple just before serving. Otherwise, the salsa will get watery.

*Source: www.recipegoldmine.com*

then strains out the plant material. You can add lemonade to mask the bitter taste. Dr. Duke says to drink 3 cups of tea a day. He cautions that if you're allergic to aspirin, you probably shouldn't take aspirin-like herbs.

▶ Chamomile contains active compounds (bis-abolol, chamazulene and cyclic esters) that also have potent anti-inflammatory action. Dr. Duke says, "If I had CTS, I'd drink several cups of chamomile tea a day."

▶ Ray C. Wunderlich, Jr., MD, PhD, director of the Wunderlich Center for Nutritional Medicine in St. Petersburg, Florida, adds devil's claw and burdock to the list of herbs that often help.

▶ Another option is to try bromelain, the *proteolytic* (protein-dissolving) enzyme found in pineapple. According to Dr. Duke, "Naturopaths suggest taking 250 to 1,500 mg of pure bromelain a day, between meals, to treat inflammatory conditions such as CTS." Bromelain is available at health food stores.

Since ginger and papaya also contain helpful enzymes, Dr. Duke, who favors food sources to store-bought supplements, suggests, "You might enjoy a proteolytic CTS fruit salad composed of pineapple and papaya and spiced with grated ginger." (*See* recipe on left.)

▶ One more suggestion from Dr. Duke— "Also known as cayenne, red pepper contains six pain-relieving compounds and seven that are anti-inflammatory. Especially noteworthy is capsaicin. You might add several teaspoons of powdered cayenne to ¼ cup of skin lotion and rub it on your wrists. Or you could make a capsaicin lotion by steeping 5 to 10 red (hot) peppers in 2 pints of rubbing alcohol for a few days. Just wash your hands thoroughly after using any topical capsaicin treatment, so you don't get it in your eyes. Also, since some people are quite sensitive to this compound, you should test it on a small area of skin before using it on a larger area. If it seems to irritate your skin, discontinue use."

## COLDS AND FLU

Having a cold or flu is nothing to sneeze at! The common cold can wipe you out, and the influenza virus—which is characterized by inflammation of the respiratory tract and fever, chills and muscular pains—can really knock you out.

If you're feeling down for the count with a red, runny nose, chest congestion and that achy-all-over feeling, instead of making much *achoo* about nothing, keep reading for some simple hints to fight back.

## Hot Remedy for a Cold

▶ The first round of ammunition for fighting the cold war is chicken soup (also known as Jewish penicillin). Marvin A. Sackner, MD, retired medical director of the Mount Sinai Medical Center in Miami Beach, Florida, proved that chicken soup can help cure a cold.

Using a bronchofiberscope and cineroentgenograms and measurements of mucus velocity, Dr. Sackner tested the effectiveness of hot chicken soup versus both hot and cold water. *The results…*

Cold water lowered nasal clearance. Hot water improved it, but it was nothing compared with the improvement after hot chicken soup. Then, to negate the effects of the steam from the hot water and hot chicken soup, the fluids were sipped through straws from covered containers. Hot water had very little effect this way. But the hot chicken soup still had some benefit.

## ■ Recipe ■

### Lillian Wilen's Essential Chicken Soup

4 to 5 lbs chicken parts
3 carrots, scrubbed or peeled, cut in thirds
2 parsnips, scrubbed, cut in thirds
2 celery stalks with leaves, cut in thirds
1 large onion, cut in half
1 green pepper, cut in half and cleaned out
10 cups water
1 to 2 tsp salt
2 sprigs dill (optional), or ½ teaspoon dill seeds
4 parsley sprigs
4 cloves garlic, crushed

Add the chicken, carrots, parsnips, celery, onion, green pepper, water and salt to a big pot. Wrap the dill or dill seeds, parsley and garlic in cheesecloth and add that to the pot. Bring it to a boil, clean off the scum from the top of the soup, cover and simmer for 2½ to 3 hours. Remove the chicken and the vegetables. Refrigerate the soup overnight.

The next day, before heating the soup, remove the top layer of fat, skimming the surface with a spoon. Add the chicken and vegetables, heat and eat! Before it gets cold!

### The Proof Is in the Mayo

The respected Mayo Clinic in Rochester, Minnesota, printed the following in its *Health Letter…*

"There is now evidence that our ancestors may have known more about how to treat sniffles than we do. And that should not be surprising. Indeed, scientific study of folk medicines and cures often has proved to be remarkably rewarding.

"Moses Maimonides, a 12th-century Jewish physician and philosopher, reported that chicken soup is an effective medication as well as a tasty food.

"A report published in *Chest*, a medical journal for chest specialists, indicates that hot chicken soup is more effective than other hot liquids in clearing mucus particles from the nose. The cause of this beneficial effect is still not fully understood, but the soup does seem to contain a substance that prompts clearing of nasal mucus. And removal of nasal secretions containing viruses and bacteria is an important part of our body's defense against upper respiratory infections. The study gives scientific respectability to the long-standing contention that chicken soup might help relieve a head cold.

"Chicken soup—particularly the homemade variety—is a safe, effective treatment for many 'self-limiting' illnesses (those not requiring professional attention). It is inexpensive and widely available.

"What does it all add up to? Specifically, this recommendation: Next time you come down with a head cold, try hot homemade chicken soup before heading for the pharmacy. We believe chicken soup can be an excellent treatment for uncomplicated head colds and other viral respiratory infections for which antibiotics ordinarily are not helpful. Soup is less expensive and, most significantly, it carries little, if any, risk of allergic reactions or other undesirable side effects."

## ■ Recipe ■

### Dr. Ziment's Chicken Soup

1 quart homemade chicken broth,
   or 2 cans low-fat, low-sodium
   chicken broth
1 garlic head—about 15 cloves, peeled
5 parsley sprigs, minced
6 cilantro sprigs, minced
1 tsp lemon pepper
1 tsp dried basil, crushed, or
   1 Tbsp chopped fresh basil
1 tsp curry powder
*Optional:* Hot red pepper flakes to taste,
   sliced carrots, a bay leaf or two

Place all ingredients in a pot without a lid. Bring to a boil, then simmer for about 30 minutes. (If the soup is for your own personal use, carefully inhale the fumes during preparation as an additional decongesting treatment.) Remove the solid garlic cloves and herbs and, along with a little broth, purée them in a blender or food processor. Return the purée to the broth and stir. Serve hot.

Visit *www.mayoclinic.com* for more information on the chicken soup study.

### Chicken Soup (The Medicine)

Irwin Ziment, MD, professor emeritus of clinical medicine at the David Geffen School of Medicine, University of California at Los Angeles, is also an authority on pulmonary drugs. Considering the research, experience and expertise it took to earn his credentials, we believe that Dr. Ziment's chicken soup recipe for colds, coughs and chest congestion should be taken seriously and whenever you have a cold. (*See* recipe on page 36.)

![image] **CAUTION:** This chicken soup is a medicine and is not to be eaten as one would eat a portion of soup. Please follow the dosage instructions.

*Dose:* Take 2 tablespoons of Dr. Ziment's Chicken Soup at the beginning of a meal, one to three times a day. (If you feel you want a little more than 2 tablespoons, fine, but do not exceed more than ½ cup at a time.)

# Other Dietary Remedies

▶ In Russia, garlic is known as Russian penicillin. It has been reported that colds have actually disappeared within hours—a day at most—after taking garlic.

Keep a peeled clove of garlic in your mouth, between the cheek and teeth. Do not chew it. Occasionally, release a little garlic juice by digging your teeth into the clove. Replace the clove every three to four hours.

The allicin in garlic is an excellent mucus-thinner and bacteria-killer. It's no wonder many cold remedies include garlic.

▶ If taking garlic by mouth is not for you, then peel and crush six cloves of garlic. Mix them into ½ cup of white lard or vegetable shortening. Spread the mush on the soles of your feet and cover them with a (preferably warmed) towel or flannel cloth. Put plastic wrap under your feet to protect bedding. Garlic is so powerful that even though it's applied to one's feet, it will be on one's breath, too.

Apply a fresh batch of the mixture every five hours until the cold is gone.

## Liquid Measures

▶ Prepare tea by steeping equal parts of cinnamon, sage and bay leaves in hot water. Strain, and before drinking the tea, add 1 tablespoon of lemon juice. If necessary, sweeten with honey.

▶ Keep flushing out your system by drinking lots of nondairy liquids—unsweetened fruit juices, herbal tea and just plain water.

## Contessa Knows Best

▶ When our friend, a Contessa from the Italian hills, has a cold, she makes a mug of very strong, regular tea and adds 1 tablespoon of honey, 1 tablespoon of cognac, 1 teaspoon of butter and ¼ teaspoon of cinnamon. She drinks it as hot as she can and goes to bed between cotton sheets. If she wakes up during the night and is all sweaty, she changes her bedclothes and sheets and goes back to bed. By morning, she feels *"molto bene!"*

▶ People have been known to fake a cold just to take this remedy—combine 4 teaspoons of rum with the juice of one lemon and 3 teaspoons of honey. Then add it to a glass of hot water and drink it before going to bed.

▶ Mix ¼ cup of apple cider vinegar with an equal amount of honey. This elixir is particularly effective for a cold with a sore throat.

*Dose:* Take 1 tablespoon six to eight times a day.

▶ Boil down ½ cup of sunflower seeds (without the shells, of course) in 5 cups of water until there's about 2 cups of liquid left in the pot. Then stir in ¼ cup of honey and ¾ cup of gin. This potion is particularly good for chest colds.

*Dose:* Take 2 teaspoons three times a day at mealtime.

**WARNING:** Infants, diabetics and people with honey allergies should not use honey.

## Soothing Remedy

▶ Take 4 teaspoons of prepared mustard and rub it on the chest. Take a (preferably white) towel and dip it in hot water, then wring it out and place it on top of the mustard already on the chest. As soon as the towel is cool, redip it in hot water, wring it out and put it back on the chest. Reapply the towel four or five times. After the last application of the towel, wash off the chest, dry thoroughly, bundle up and go to bed.

▶ To stimulate appropriate acupuncture points that can help relieve a cold, place an ice cube on the bottom of both big toes. Keep them in place with an elastic bandage or piece of cloth. Place feet in a basin, in two plastic shoe boxes or on plastic to avoid a mess from the melting ice. Do this procedure for no more than 20 minutes at a time…morning, noon and night.

## Mineral or Medicine?

▶ Zinc gluconate—available at health food stores and some pharmacies—works wonders for some people. It either nips the cold in the bud, considerably shortens the duration of the cold or lessens the severity of it.

*For it to be effective, be sure to follow the dosage carefully:* Adults, take two lozenges (23 mg each) at the outset and then one every two hours thereafter, but not more than 12 a day, and for no longer than two days.

Also, do not take them on an empty stomach. Even if you don't feel like eating, consume half a fruit before you take a lozenge. Suck on the lozenge so that it comes in prolonged contact with your mouth and throat. Honey-flavored are the best—lemon are the pits.

Zinc gluconate also comes in 46 mg tablets. If you get them instead of the 23 mg, take one at the outset of your cold and one every four hours, not exceeding six a day, and not for longer than two days.

**CAUTION:** Some people get stomachaches from zinc. Also, high amounts of zinc may increase a man's risk of developing prostate cancer.

Consult your doctor before supplementing with zinc.

For children's dosages, *see* "Healing Remedies for Children" on page 207.

## Flowers to Help You Sniff

▶ Las Vegas–based herbalist Angela Harris (*www.angelaharris.com*) says that the combination of echinacea and goldenseal is effective in either stopping a cold from blossoming, or cutting short the duration and minimizing the severity of a cold.

The secret is to take two droppers of the extract (available at health food stores) in a few ounces of water every hour for the first four hours of the day you feel a cold coming on. After that, take two droppers every four hours.

Do not take echinacea for more than two weeks at a time. (You shouldn't have to.)

## Don't Blow It

▶ Another popular remedy for a head cold is to cut two thin-as-can-be strips of orange rind. Roll them up with the white spongy part (the pith) on the outside, and gently stick one in each nostril. Stay that way until your head cold is better, or you can't stand the rind in your nostrils anymore—whichever comes first. Be sure to leave a bit of orange rind sticking out of your nose so you can dislodge it easily.

▶ The first of our five senses to develop is our sense of smell. Eventually, the average human nose can recognize 10,000 different odors—but not when we have a head cold.

To clear your head and stop a runny nose, begin by cutting the crust off a piece of bread. Plug in your iron and put it on "hot"—wool or cotton setting. Carefully iron the bread crust. When it starts to burn, lift the iron off the crust and *carefully* inhale the smoke through your nostrils for two minutes. Repeat this procedure three times throughout the day. We've been told that the runny nose stops and the head cold clears up in a very short time—one or two days.

▶ The natural sulfur in broccoli and parsley is supposed to help us resist colds. Eat broccoli and/or parsley once a day.

### ■ Recipe ■

### *Jade Green Broccoli*

2 lbs broccoli (1 bunch)
1 Tbsp cornstarch
2 Tbsp soy sauce
½ cup water or vegetable stock
¼ cup oil
⅛ tsp salt
1 clove garlic, minced
2 Tbsp sherry

Clean broccoli. Cut stems on a ⅛" slant. Mix cornstarch, soy sauce and stock or water. Set aside.

Heat a wok or cast-iron pan until it is very hot. Add oil, then salt. Turn heat to medium and add garlic. When golden brown, turn up heat and add broccoli. Stir-fry for 3 minutes. Add sherry and cover the pan quickly. Cook, covered, for 2 minutes. Add cornstarch mixture and stir until thickened.

*Source: www.recipegoldmine.com*

▶ An apple a day…works! A university study showed that the students who ate apples regularly had fewer colds.

▶ Before bedtime, take a ginger bath and sweat away your cold overnight. Put 3 tablespoons of grated ginger in a stocking and knot the stocking closed.

✎ **NOTE:** It's easier to grate frozen ginger than fresh ginger.

Throw the grated-ginger stocking into a hot bath, along with the contents of a 2-ounce container of powdered ginger. Stir the bathwater with a wooden spoon. Then, get in and soak for 10 to 15 minutes.

Once you're out of the tub, dry yourself thoroughly, preferably with a rough towel. Put on warm sleep clothes and cover your head with a towel or woolen scarf, leaving just your face exposed. Get in bed under the covers and go to sleep. If you perspire enough to feel uncomfortably wet, change into dry sleepwear.

### Gem of a Remedy

▶ Talking about "sweating it out," a gem therapist told us that wearing a topaz activates body heat and, therefore, helps cure ailments that may benefit from increased perspiration.

### Healing Power of Onion

The onion is also a popular natural remedy to relieve colds. *Here are some ways in which the onion is used…*

▶ Cut an onion in half and place one half on each side of your bed so you can inhale the scent as you sleep.

▶ Eat a whole onion before bedtime in order to break up the cold overnight.

▶ Dip a slice of raw onion in a glass of hot water. After a few seconds, remove the onion and, when the water cools, start sipping it. Continue to do so throughout the day.

▶ If you like your onions fried, take the hot fried onions, put them in a flannel or woolen cloth and bind them on your chest overnight.

▶ Put slices of raw onion on the soles of your feet, and hold the slices in place with woolen socks. Leave them that way overnight to draw out infection and fever.

 **NOTE:** If you get colds often, your immune system may need a boost. Check out the immune system strengthener in "Remedies in a Class by Themselves" on page 244.

## Fight the Flu

Before flu season starts (in early October), check with your doctor to see if you should get a flu shot. The flu can be deadly, and older people and those with compromised immune systems are especially at risk. *Then, if your doctor approves, try these remedies…*

▶ The second you feel fluish, take 1 tablespoon of liquid lecithin (available at health food stores). Continue to take 1 tablespoon every eight hours for the next two days. Some naturalists believe that these large doses of lecithin may prevent the flu from flourishing.

### Old Family Recipe

▶ This formula was handed down from generation to generation by a family who tells of the many lives it saved in Stuttgart, Germany, during the 1918 flu pandemic. The family claims that this special elixir cleanses the harmful virus from the blood.

**CAUTION:** This remedy is only for people who do not have a problem with alcohol.

Peel and cut ½ pound of garlic into small pieces. Put the garlic and 1 quart of cognac (90 proof) in a dark brown bottle. Seal it airtight with paraffin wax or tape. During the day, keep the bottle in the sun or another light, warm place, like in the kitchen near the oven. At night, move the bottle to a dark, cool place.

After 14 days and nights, open the bottle and strain. Put the strained elixir back in the bottle. It is now ready to be used. The potency of this mixture is said to last one year, so label the bottle with the expiration date accordingly.

If you already have the flu, take 20 drops of the formula with a glass of water, one hour before each meal (three times a day), for five days.

To prevent the flu, take 10 to 15 drops with a glass of water, one hour before each meal, every day during the flu season. Also, be sure to wash your hands frequently and avoid crowds.

▶ The second you've been exposed to someone with the flu, try taking cinnamon oil.

*Dose:* Take 5 drops of cinnamon oil in a tablespoon of water, three times a day.

▶ By drinking raw sauerkraut juice once a day, you should avoid getting the flu. (It's also a good way to avoid constipation.)

▶ Move to the North Pole for the winter. None of the standard cold- and flu-causing microorganisms can survive there. The problem is, you might not be able to either.

## Guggle-Muggle Drink

▶ Philosopher Friedrich Nietzsche once said, "Whatever does not destroy me makes me strong." That's the way we felt about the drink our grandmother (Bubbie) made the second someone in our family came down with a cold.

## ■ Recipe ■

### The Koch Family (for adults only) Guggle-Muggle

1 grapefruit, juiced
1 lemon, juiced
1 orange (preferably Temple), juiced
1 Tbsp honey

Juice the grapefruit, lemon and orange. Combine the juices and put in a saucepan over medium heat. Add the honey. Bring the mixture to a boil while stirring. After it has boiled, take the mixture off the stove and let cool. Then pour it into a glass and add your favorite liquor* (brandy is Ed Koch's).

As with most guggle-muggles, drink it down, then get under the covers and go to sleep. Next morning, no cold!

* Women who are pregnant or nursing should not consume alcohol.

The dreaded drink was called a *guggle-muggle.* We thought it was a cute name that Bubbie made up. Imagine our surprise when Ed Koch, during his last term in office as mayor of New York City, talked about an ancient cure—his family's recipe for a guggle-muggle.

It seems that many Jewish families have their own guggle-muggle recipes—and some are more palatable than others. Our family's is among the worst, but Mr. Koch's is one of the best. As he told us, "It is not only medically superb, it is delicious!"

## Fever Relievers

▶ Bind sliced onions or peeled garlic cloves to the bottoms of your feet. As we mentioned earlier, don't be surprised if it gives you onion or garlic breath. And don't be surprised if it brings down your temperature.

▶ Eat grapes (in season) throughout the day. Also, dilute pure grape juice and sip some of it throughout the day. Drink it at room temperature, never chilled.

▶ Boil 4 cups (1 quart) of water with ½ teaspoon of cayenne pepper. Just before you drink each of these cups (four consumed throughout the day), add to each cup 1 teaspoon of honey and ¼ cup of orange juice. Heat it up just a little and then drink it slowly.

**WARNING:** Do not give honey to infants/ children, diabetics or someone who is allergic to honey.

## Sore Throats

The trouble with sore throats is that each swallow tends to be a painful reminder that you have a sore throat.

Some sore throats are caused by allergies, smoking, postnasal drip, yeast overgrowth and varying severities of bacterial invasion into your throat tissues. Many sore throats are caused by a mild viral infection that attacks when your resistance is low. You may need a health professional to help you determine the cause.

If you have a sore throat right now, think about your schedule. Chances are, you've been

pushing yourself like crazy, running around and keeping later hours than usual.

If you take it easy, get a lot of rest, flush your system by drinking nondairy liquids and stay away from "heavy" foods, the remedies we suggest will be much more effective.

**WARNING:** Chronic or persistent sore throat pain should be checked by a health professional. Severe sore throats need immediate treatment and possibly antibiotics.

### Natural Remedies

▶ Add 2 teaspoons of apple cider vinegar to a cup of warm water.

*Dose:* Gargle a mouthful, spit it out, then swallow a mouthful. Gargle a mouthful, spit it out, then swallow a mouthful. Keep this up until the liquid is all gone. An hour later, start all over.

▶ Mix 1 teaspoon of cream of tartar with ½ cup of pineapple juice and drink it.

*Dose:* Repeat every half-hour until there's a marked improvement.

▶ A singer we know says this works for her every time—steep three nonherbal tea bags in a cup of just-boiled water. Leave them there until the water is as dark as it can get—almost black.

*Dose:* While the water is still quite hot but bearable, gargle with the tea. Do not swallow any of it. (No one needs all that caffeine.) Repeat every hour until you feel relief.

### Salty Soother

▶ Warm ½ cup of kosher (coarse) salt in a frying pan. Then pour the warm salt in a large, clean, white handkerchief and fold it over and over so that none of the salt can ooze out. Wrap

the salted hanky around your neck and wear it that way for an hour.

This was one of our great-aunt's favorite remedies. The only problem was she would get laryngitis explaining to everyone why she was wearing that salty poultice around her neck!

## Be a Sage

▶Next time you wake up with that sore throat feeling, add 1 teaspoon of sage to 1 cup boiling water. Steep for three to five minutes and strain.

*Dose:* Gargle in the morning and at bedtime. It would be wise to swallow the sage tea.

▶Relief from a sore throat can come from inhaling the steam of hot vinegar. Take special care while inhaling vinegar vapors or any other kind for that matter. You don't have to get too close to the source of the steam for it to be effective.

▶What's a sore throat without honey and lemon? Every family has their own variation on the combination. Take the juice of a nice lemon (our family prefaces every noun with the word *nice*) and mix it with 1 nice teaspoon of some nice honey.

*Dose:* Take it every two hours.

▶Add the juice from one lemon to a glass of hot water (our family drinks everything from a glass) and sweeten to taste with honey—about 1½ tablespoons.

*Dose:* Drink one glass every four hours.

▶Grate 1 teaspoon of horseradish and one piece of lemon peel. To that, add ⅛ teaspoon of cayenne pepper and 2 tablespoons of honey.

*Dose:* Take 1 tablespoon every hour.

**WARNING:** Infants, diabetics and people with honey allergies should not use honey.

## Act Like a Brat

▶We came across a beneficial exercise to do when you have a sore throat. Stick out your tongue for 30 seconds, put it back in and relax for a couple of seconds.

Then stick out your tongue again for another 30 seconds. Do it five times in a row and it will increase blood circulation, help the healing process and make you the center of attention at the next executive board meeting.

## Make a Tea Towel

▶Prepare chamomile tea. As soon as it cools enough for you to handle, soak a towel (preferably white) in the tea, wring it out and apply it to the neck. As soon as it gets cold, reheat the tea, redip the towel and reapply it. The chamomile will help draw out the soreness, and the heat will relax some of the tension built up in that area.

▶According to a gem therapist, yellow amber worn around the neck will protect against sore throats. If you already have a sore throat, it is said that the electric powers of this fossilized, golden resin will help cure it.

▶ Prepare a carrot poultice (*see* "Preparation Guide" on page 252) with a large, grated carrot. Put the poultice around your throat. On top of the poultice, apply a washcloth that has been dipped in hot water and wrung out. To keep the heat in, cover it all with a towel or wide elastic bandage. If it seems to soothe your throat, redip the washcloth in hot water as soon as it gets cold.

# Hoarseness/Laryngitis

The trouble with laryngitis is that you have to wait until you don't have it before you can tell anyone you had it.

Rest your vocal cords as much as possible. If you must talk, speak in a normal voice, letting the sound come from your diaphragm instead of your throat. *Don't whisper!* Whispering tightens the muscles of your voice box, and puts more stress on your vocal cords than does talking in your normal voice.

▶ Drink a mixture of 2 teaspoons of onion juice and 1 teaspoon of honey.

*Dose:* Take 3 teaspoons every three hours.

▶ Drink a cup of hot peppermint tea with a teaspoon of honey. After a hard day at the office, it's very relaxing for the entire body as well as the throat.

▶ If your cold seemed to settle in your throat in the form of hoarseness and congestion, peel and mince an entire bulb of garlic. Cover all the little pieces with raw honey and let it stand for two hours. Take a teaspoon of the honey/garlic mixture every hour. Just swallow it down

without chewing the garlic. That way you won't have garlic on your breath.

**WARNING:** Infants, diabetics and people with honey allergies should not use honey.

## Buddhist's Secret

▶ In 1 cup of water, simmer ½ cup of raisins for 20 minutes. Let it cool, then eat it all. This is a Tibetan remedy. It must work because we've never met anyone from Tibet with laryngitis.

▶ Boil 1 pound of black beans in 1 gallon of water for one hour. Strain.

*Dose:* Take 6 ounces of bean water an hour before each meal. The beans can be eaten during mealtime. (If necessary, *see* "Gas/Flatulence" in the "Indigestion" section on page 125.)

▶ When you're hoarse and hungry, eat baked apples. To prepare them, core four apples and peel them about halfway down from the top. Place them in a greased dish with about ½ inch of water. Drop a teaspoon of raisins into each apple core, then drizzle a teaspoon of honey into each core and over the tops of the apples. Cover and bake in a 350° F oven for 40 minutes. Baste a few times with pan juices during the cooking time.

*Dose:* Eat the apples warm or at room temperature. As they say, an apple a day… you know the rest.

▶ *See* the apple cider vinegar remedy on page 42. After seven hours and seven doses of the vinegar and water, plus a good night's sleep, there should be a major improvement.

▶ Grate radishes and squeeze them through cheesecloth to get radish juice. Let a teaspoon of the juice slide down your throat every half-hour.

### Singer's Solution

▶ This is a popular Russian remedy for what they call "singer's sore throat." It promises to restore the singer's voice to normal in a single day. Incidentally, you don't have to be a singer to try this formula.

Take ½ cup of anise seeds and 1 cup of water and boil them slowly for 50 minutes. Strain out the seeds, then stir ¼ cup of raw honey into the anise-seed water and add 1 tablespoon of cognac.

*Dose:* Take 1 tablespoon every half-hour.

> **WARNING:** Infants, diabetics and people with honey allergies should not use honey.

## Strep Throat

This illness is caused by Group A streptococci bacteria. If you have an extremely sore throat, fever, chills and ache all over, then you might have strep.

> **CAUTION:** Strep throat is a serious illness. If left untreated, it can lead to rheumatic fever. See a physician to diagnose and treat this condition.

▶ Do you have a dog or a cat? If you do and you're troubled by frequent bouts of strep throat, have a veterinarian examine the animal for streptococci. Once your pet is free of the bacteria, chances are you will be, too, after treatment by your health professional.

## Tonsillitis

Tonsils are those two little bumps at the back of your throat. They are part of the lymph system and may help fend off respiratory infections. When they swell up for long periods of time—yet you don't feel any better—you probably have tonsillitis.

> **CAUTION:** If you have tonsillitis, your immune system needs to be evaluated and treated by a physician. Be aware that untreated bacterial tonsillitis may have serious consequences, including rheumatic fever, scarlet fever or even kidney disease (nephritis).

Here are some simple remedies to help your tonsils feel less inflamed.

▶ Bake a medium-sized banana in its skin for 30 minutes at 350° F. Peel and mash the juicy banana, adding 1 tablespoon of extra-virgin, cold-pressed olive oil. Spread the mush on a clean white cloth and apply it to the neck. Leave it on for a half-hour in the morning and a half-hour in the evening.

▶ Juice garlic cloves (*see* "Preparation Guide" on page 250) so that you have 1 tablespoon of fresh juice. Add the juice and 2 ounces of dried sage to 1 quart of water in a glass or enamel pot. Cover the pot and bring the mixture to a boil. As soon as it starts to boil, turn off the heat and let it stand until it's lukewarm. Strain the solution.

*Dose:* Drink ½ cup of this sage-garlic tea every two hours. Gargle ½ cup every hour until the condition is better.

> **NOTE:** The holistic health professionals we talked to believe that tonsils should not be removed unless it's absolutely necessary. They function as armed guards, destroying harmful bacteria that enter through the mouth. Asian medicine practitioners believe that when tonsils are unable to fulfill this function, the body's immune system needs to be strengthened—but the tonsils should not be removed.

## CONSTIPATION

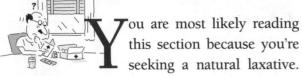

**Y**ou are most likely reading this section because you're seeking a natural laxative. Therefore, you may already know that the commercial chemical laxatives can kill friendly bacteria, can lessen the absorption of nutrients, can stuff up the intestinal walls, can turn users into addicts, can get rid of necessary vitamins and can eventually cause constipation.

We offer easy-to-take, inexpensive, non-chemical constipation relievers that should not present any problem side effects if taken in moderation, using good common sense. In other words, don't try more than one remedy at a time.

**NOTE:** Constipation is a common problem that may be a symptom of disease or lead to more major health problems. It is important to consult a medical professional before starting any self-help treatment.

## Natural Remedies

▶ The most natural time to move your bowels is within the first few hours of the day. Drinking water on an empty stomach stimulates peristalsis by reflex. So, before breakfast, drink the juice of half a lemon in 1 cup of warm water. While it may help cleanse your system, it may also make you pucker a lot. If you find it hard to drink, sweeten it with honey.

If lemon and water is not for you, eat or drink any one of the following at room temperature (not chilled)…

◆ Prune juice or stewed prunes

◆ Papaya

◆ Two peeled apples

◆ Six to eight dried figs. Soak them overnight in a glass of water. In the morning, drink the water, then eat the figs.

▶ The combination of dried apricots and prunes is said to work wonders. Soak six of each overnight. The next morning, eat three of each. Then, in the late afternoon, an hour or two before dinner, eat the remaining three apricots and three prunes.

▶ Eat at least three raw fruits a day. One of them, preferably an apple, should be eaten two hours after dinner.

▶ Take two small beets, scrub them clean and eat them raw in the morning. You should have a bowel movement about 12 hours later.

▶ Flaxseed is a popular folk treatment for constipation. Take 1 to 2 tablespoons with lots of water right after lunch or dinner. (*See* "Six Sensational Superfoods" on page 262.)

▶ Sunflower seeds are filled with health-giving properties and have also been known to promote regularity. Eat a handful of shelled, raw, unsalted seeds every day.

### Sensational Sauerkraut

▶ Raw sauerkraut and its juice have friendly bacteria and may aid digestion. It's also an excellent laxative. Heat destroys the important enzymes in sauerkraut, so make sure you eat it raw. (Raw sauerkraut is available at health food stores, or *see* "Preparation Guide" on page 252 and learn how to prepare your own sauerkraut.)

You can also drink an 8-ounce glass of warm sauerkraut juice and then an 8-ounce glass of grapefruit juice (unsweetened)—one right after the other. It should do the job.

▶ We were told about an acupressure technique that is supposed to encourage a complete evacuation of the bowels in 15 minutes. For three to five minutes, massage the area underneath your lower lip, in the middle of your chin.

## Olive Oil—Olé!

▶ The findings of recent studies say that monounsaturated fatty acid—the kind found in olive oil—is best for lowering cholesterol levels. Olive oil is also a help when a laxative is needed. Take 1 tablespoon of extra-virgin, cold-pressed olive oil in the morning and 1 tablespoon an hour after eating dinner.

▶ For some people, a dose of brewer's yeast does the trick. Take 1 heaping teaspoon of brewer's yeast and 1 heaping teaspoon of wheat germ with each meal. (Both are available at health food stores.)

Start with small amounts of either or both brewer's yeast and wheat germ. Gradually increase your intake and stop when the amount you're taking works for you.

▶ Are persimmons in season? Try one. It's been known to relieve constipation.

▶ For a mild laxative, soak six dates in a glass of hot water. When the water is cool, drink it, then eat the dates. (*Also see* the fig remedy under "Fatigue" on page 83.)

▶ If you have a favorite brand of cereal, add raw, unprocessed bran to it. Start with 1 teaspoon and gradually work your way up to 1 or 2 tablespoons each morning, depending on your reaction to it.

## Exotic, But Effective

▶ Two natural laxatives available at the greengrocer or produce aisle are escarole (eat it raw or boil it in water and drink the water) and Spanish onion (roast it and eat it at bedtime). The cellulose in onions gives intestinal momentum.

▶ Hippocrates (460–377 BC), the Greek physician and father of medicine, recommended eating garlic every day to relieve constipation. Cook with it and eat it raw (in salads) whenever possible.

## Be Convincing

▶ Just as you're falling asleep, when the mind is most open to autohypnotic suggestion, say to yourself, "In the morning, I will have a good bowel movement." Keep repeating the sentence until you doze off. Pleasant dreams!

## For a Gentle Approach

▶ Raw spinach makes a delicious salad, has lots of vitamins and minerals and is a mild laxative, too. Be sure to wash it thoroughly to reduce the risk of food-borne illness.

▶ Aerobic exercise is an excellent laxative. With your doctor's approval, try to move your body for 30 minutes every morning.

▶ One teaspoon of blackstrap molasses in ½ cup of warm water, drunk an hour before lunch, might do the trick.

▶ Soak your feet in cold water, 15 minutes at a time, once in the morning and once before bedtime. Be sure to dry your feet thoroughly.

▶ Okra acts as a mild laxative. Add chicken gumbo soup to your menu from time to time.

## ■ Recipe ■

### *Chicken Soup with Okra*

1 small, cleaned chicken cut into
    serving portions
2 Tbsp flour
1 onion, chopped
2 Tbsp vegetable oil
4 cups okra, chopped
2 cups tomato pulp
½ cup parsley, chopped
4 cups water
Salt and pepper to taste

Coat chicken pieces lightly with flour and sauté with onion in oil. Add okra, tomato, parsley and water as soon as chicken is browned. Season with salt and pepper to taste. Simmer for about 2½ hours, until chicken is tender and okra is well cooked. Be sure to add water as needed during the simmering. Serves 6.

### *Stool Softener*

▶ Every night, before eating dinner, eat a tablespoon of raisins or three prunes that have been soaking in water for a couple of hours.

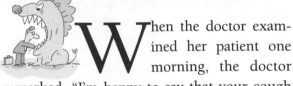

# COUGHS

When the doctor examined her patient one morning, the doctor remarked, "I'm happy to say that your cough sounds much better."

The patient answered, "Well, it should. I had a whole night of practice."

This may be a joke, but it's not funny if you're the one who's coughing, especially at night when coughs seem to act up.

We all have a cough center in our brain. It's generally motivated by an irritation in the respiratory tract. In other words, a cough is nature's way of helping us loosen and get rid of mucus that's congesting our system.

Here are a few natural remedies that may quell the cough and help you sleep better.

 **NOTE:** If cough is chronic or persistent, have it checked by a health professional. Coughs accompanied by a fever or shortness of breath can be serious.

## Natural Remedies

▶ For five minutes, cook the juice of one lemon, 1 cup of honey and ½ cup of olive oil. Then stir vigorously for a couple of minutes.

*Dose:* Take 1 teaspoon every two hours.

▶ Combine ½ cup apple cider vinegar with ½ cup water. Add 1 teaspoon of cayenne pepper and sweeten to taste with honey.

*Dose:* Take 1 tablespoon when the cough starts acting up. Then swallow another tablespoon at bedtime.

**WARNING:** Infants, diabetics and people with honey allergies should not use honey.

## Honion Syrup

▶ Peel and finely chop six medium onions. Put them and ½ cup of honey into the top of a double boiler, or in a pan over a pot of boiling water. Cover the mixture and let it simmer for two hours. Strain this concoction we call "honion syrup," and pour it into a jar with a cover.

*Dose:* Take 1 warm tablespoon every two to three hours.

▶ Grate 1 teaspoon of horseradish and mix it with 2 teaspoons of honey. (Or, one finely chopped clove of garlic can be used in place of horseradish.)

*Dose:* Take 1 teaspoon of the mix every two to three hours.

## Lemony Fresh

▶ For a delicious, thirst-quenching and soothing drink, squeeze the juice of one lemon into a big mug or glass. Add hot water, 2 tablespoons of honey and either three whole cloves or a ½-inch piece of stick cinnamon.

*Dose:* Drink one glass every three hours.

▶ Cook a cup of barley according to the package directions. Then add the juice of one fresh lemon and some water to the barley. Liquefy the mixture in a blender. Drink it slowly.

*Dose:* Drink 1 cup every four hours.

## Holy Rutabagas!

▶ Cut a hole through the middle of a rutabaga or a yellow onion and fill the hole with honey or brown sugar. Leave it overnight. In the morning, drink the juice and it will relieve the cough.

▶ Cut a deep hole in the middle of a large beet and fill the hole with honey or brown sugar. Bake the beet until it's soft. It's a treat to eat the beet…whenever you feel a cough coming on.

## Mull This Over

▶ Adding spices and herbs to wine is called mulling. Into 3 cups of wine, add a 1-inch piece of stick cinnamon, 1 tablespoon of honey, three to six cloves (depending on how much you like the taste of cloves) and a few pieces of well-scrubbed lemon peel. Heat and stir.

*Dose:* Drink 3 cups a day.

Even if this mulled wine doesn't help, you somehow don't mind having the cough as much!

**WARNING:** Do not give honey to infants/children, diabetics or someone who is allergic to honey. Women who are pregnant or nursing should not consume alcohol.

## Ginger Gum

▶ Chew on a bite-sized piece of ginger root, just like you would chew gum. Swallowing the juice should help control a cough. Ginger is strong, and it might take some getting used to.

▶ Take a piece of brown grocery-bag paper, about the size of your chest, and soak it in vinegar. When it stops dripping, sprinkle black pepper on one side of the paper. Then place the peppered side on your bare chest.

To keep it in place overnight, wrap an elastic bandage or cloth around your chest. By morning, there may be a big improvement, particularly with a bronchial cough.

## Oats to the Rescue

▶ Among other ingredients, the polyunsaturated fatty acids found in whole-grain oats have been said to soothe bronchial inflammation and relieve coughing spasms.

▶ Make a mash from the oats by following the directions on the whole-grain oats box, but reduce the amount of water by ¼ cup. Add honey to taste.

*Dose:* Eat 1 cup at a time, four times a day and whenever a coughing spell starts. Be sure the oat mash is eaten warm.

## Turney Syrup?

▶ Peel and slice a large turnip. Spread honey between all the slices and let it stand for several hours while the turnip/honey syrup oozes out and collects at the bottom of the dish. Whenever the cough acts up, take a teaspoon of the syrup.

**WARNING:** Infants, diabetics and people with honey allergies should not use honey.

▶ Add ½ cup of raw, shelled and unsalted sunflower seeds to 5 cups of water and boil in an enamel or glass pot until the water is reduced to about 2 cups. Strain, then stir in ¾ cup of gin and 1½ cups of honey. Mix well and bottle it. Whenever the cough acts up, take 1 to 2 teaspoons, but not more than four times a day.

**WARNING:** People who have problems with alcohol should not try this remedy.

## Love That Licorice!

▶ Licorice root contains saponins, natural substances known to break up and loosen

mucus. When you have a hacking cough, drink a cup of licorice-root tea (*see* "Preparation Guide" on page 250).

 **NOTE:** Do not take licorice root if you have high blood pressure or kidney problems. It can cause renal failure.

## Squeezin' Fights Wheezin'

▶ An acupressure point that has been known to stop a cough is the one near the end of the middle finger. With the fingers of your right hand, squeeze the top joint of the left hand's middle finger. Keep squeezing until you stop wheezing.

## Beany Goodness

▶ This bean purée remedy is for one of those mean, deep-down coughs that nothing seems to reach. Put a cupful of kidney beans in a strainer and rinse them with water. Then put them in water and let them soak overnight (while you probably cough your head off, right?).

The next morning, drain the beans, tie them up in a clean cloth and bruise them—pound them with a blunt object like a rolling pin, frying pan or hammer. Place the bruised beans in an enamel or glass saucepan with three cloves of peeled and minced garlic and 2 cups of water. Bring the mixture to a boil, then simmer for one and a half to two hours, until tender. Add more water if necessary. Take 1 tablespoon of this bean purée whenever your cough acts up.

# Types of Coughs

## Bronchial Coughs

▶ Add 3 drops of oil of fennel and 3 drops of oil of anise to 6 tablespoons of honey. Shake vigorously and bottle it. Take 1 teaspoon when you start to cough.

**WARNING:** Infants, diabetics and people with honey allergies should not use honey.

▶ If you haven't prepared the syrup in advance of your cough and don't have the necessary ingredients, you may want to settle for second best. Do you have the liqueur called anisette? Take 1 teaspoon of anisette in 1 tablespoon of hot water, every three hours.

**CAUTION:** Women who are pregnant or nursing should not consume alcohol.

## Just a Tickle...

▶ Many people are bothered by a tickling type of cough, usually at night in their sleep. Put 2 teaspoons of apple cider vinegar in a glass of water and keep it by your bedside. When the "tickling" wakes you up, swallow one or two mouthfuls of the vinegar water and go back to a restful sleep.

▶ Chew a couple of whole cloves to relieve a throat tickle.

▶ Eat a piece of well-done toast (preferably whole wheat).

## Smoker's Cough

▶ This remedy is updated from the *Universal Cookery Book* (circa 1888). Pour 1 quart of boiling water over 4 tablespoons of whole flaxseed and steep for three hours. Strain, add the juice of two lemons and sweeten with honey (which replaces the crystals of rock candy used in the original remedy). Take a tablespoon whenever the cough acts up.

▶ An even better remedy for smoker's cough—stop smoking! (*See* "Smoking" on page 167.)

## Dry Cough

▶ Take 1 to 2 tablespoons of potato water (*see* "Preparation Guide" on page 252) each time the cough acts up. You may also want to add honey to taste.

## Nighttime Cough

▶ To help loosen phlegm, fry two finely chopped medium onions in lard or vegetable shortening. As soon as it's cool enough to touch, rub the mixture on the cougher's chest and wrap the chest with a clean (preferably white) cloth. Do this procedure in the evening. It may result in a good night's sleep.

▶ Right before bed, add 1 teaspoon of dry mustard powder to a half-filled bathtub of hot water. Prepare a hot drink of your choice—peppermint tea or hot water, honey and lemon. Wear bedclothes that leave the chest accessible.

Have two rough terrycloth towels and a comfortable chair or stool in the bathroom.

Dip your feet in water and keep them there for 15 minutes. (The rest of the body should be seated alongside the tub.) When the water cools, add more hot water. Sip the drink through this entire process.

After 15 minutes of sipping and dipping (no stripping), dunk one of the towels in the bathwater, wring it out and place it on the bare chest. Once the towel cools off, dunk it again, wring it out and place it back on the chest. Repeat this three times, then dry the body thoroughly, bundle up and go to bed.

According to Mark A. Stengler, ND, associate clinical professor at the National College of Naturopathic Medicine in Portland, Oregon, and a naturopathic physician at La Jolla Whole Health Clinic in La Jolla, California, allergies and airborne irritants may cause postnasal drip. Mucous drainage irritates the throat, which can trigger a nighttime cough. Try propping up your pillows to provide more effective drainage. A high-efficiency particulate air (HEPA) filter in your bedroom can help reduce allergens, such as dust or pollen.

You might also try taking vitamin C (1,000 mg twice daily), along with *quercetin* (500 mg twice daily), a relative of vitamin C that acts as a natural antihistamine. Continue until your symptoms subside, typically in two to four days.

### Nervous Cough

▶ We know a theatrical stage manager who wants to make this announcement before the curtain goes up....

"To stop nervous coughs, apply pressure to the area between your lip and your nose. If that doesn't work, press hard on the roof of the mouth. If neither works, please wait until intermission, then go outside and cough."

# DEPRESSION AND STRESS

We all go through periods of depression and stress. Maybe it's because of the weather—you know, a change of season. Or for women, it could be "that time of month." Of course, pressures at the office don't help, nor do tense relationships or problems at home. Then there are additives in foods and side effects from medications that can cause chemical imbalances that may lead to depression and stress.

**CAUTION:** For cases of deep depression, extreme stress and/or chronic fatigue, we suggest you seek professional assistance to help pinpoint the cause and recommend treatment.

Whatever the reason, valid or not, when you're going through a bad time and you reach the point where you say to yourself, "I'm sick and tired of being sick and tired!"—then you're on the road to recovery.

## Basic Solutions

If you are really ready to help yourself, you might start by cutting down on your sugar intake. Excessive sugar can help cause depression, nervous anxiety and spurts of energy followed by extreme fatigue.

Caffeine products (such as coffee, non-herbal tea, cola, chocolate and some medications), cigarettes and alcoholic beverages may also contribute to nervous anxiety, depression and highs and lows of energy. Take them out of your life. They're taking the life out of you.

Be sure to eat a sensible diet of whole grains, steamed green vegetables, lean meat and fish and raw garlic in big salads with onion and lots of celery. Have sunflower seeds, raisins, sauerkraut, whole wheat pasta and beans. What could be bad?

Meanwhile, here are some more anxiety-relieving recommendations that may help…

## Dietary Remedies

▶ Have a pizza with lots of oregano. If you don't have the oregano, forget the pizza. In fact, forget the pizza and just have the oregano. Oregano may ease that depressed, heavyhearted feeling.

▶ If you have a juicer, whip up half a glass of watercress and half a glass of spinach. Throw in some carrots to make the juice sweeter. Then, bottoms up and spirits up.

▶ Eat two ripe bananas a day to chase the blues away. Bananas contain the chemicals serotonin and norepinephrine, which are believed to help prevent depression. (*See* recipe on page 54.)

## Other Mood Lifters

▶ While running a warm bath, prepare a cup of chamomile tea. Add the used tea bag to the

■ **Recipe** ■

### African Banana Fritters

6 well-ripened bananas
1 cup all-purpose flour
¼ cup granulated sugar
¼ cup water
1 tsp nutmeg

Mash bananas with a fork or use blender to make into a pulp. Add flour.

Mix water and sugar to make a syrup. Add syrup and nutmeg to bananas and flour (add more water, if needed, to make batter into pancake consistency.) Mix well. Fry like pancakes in oiled frying pan until golden brown.

Makes 24 small pancakes.

*Source: www.recipegoldmine.com*

bath, along with a new one. If you use loose chamomile, wrap the herb in cheesecloth before putting it in the tub to avoid messy cleanup. Once the bath is ready, take a pen and paper along with your cup of tea and relax in the tub. Make a list of a dozen wishes as you sip your tea. Be careful…the things you wish for may come true.

▶ To lighten a heavy heart, drink saffron tea and/or thyme tea that has been sweetened with honey. (Incidentally, "thyme" was originally called "wild time" because it was thought to be an aphrodisiac.)

▶ Sniffing citrus essential oils every hour you're awake may help you get out of a funk. You can buy lemon or orange oil at a health food store. *Do not* take the essential oils internally. If you have a citrus fruit in your kitchen, you can use a cardboard cutter to carefully make slits in the peel and squeeze it so that the volatile oil seeps out. Then take a whiff hourly.

▶ Cheer yourself up by wearing rose colors—pinks and scarlets. The orange family of colors are also picker-uppers.

▶ Making love can help people overcome feelings of depression—unless, of course, they have no one to make love to and that's why they're depressed.

▶ If you're mildly depressed, simply change your physiology and your emotions will follow suit. In other words, do the physical things you do when you're happy—and you'll feel happy. Smile! Laugh! Jump up and down! Sing! Dance! Get dressed up!

If you believe it will work, it will.

If you're not willing to go along with this suggestion, then you're not willing to let go of your depression. There's nothing wrong with staying in a funk for a brief period…as long as you understand that it is your choice.

## Dietary Stress Relievers

▶ Juices seem to be calming to the nerves. Throughout the day, sip apple, pineapple, prune, grape or cherry juice. Make sure the juice has no added sugar or preservatives, and drink it at room temperature, not chilled.

▶ Chop a large onion into very small tidbits and add a tablespoon of honey. Eat half the

mixture with lunch and the other half with dinner. Onions contain prostaglandin, which is reported to have a stress-relieving effect.

☞ **WARNING:** Infants, diabetics and people with honey allergies should not use honey.

## A Berry Good Idea

▶ If strawberries are in season, eat a few as a dessert after each meal (without the cream and sugar). You may *feel* a difference (you won't be as edgy), and you may *see* a difference (they'll make your teeth whiter).

▶ Acupressure away the pressure of the day by getting a firm grip on your ankle. Using your thumb and third finger, place one just below the inside of the anklebone, and the other finger on the indentation directly below your outer anklebone. Keep steady pressure on the spot as you count down from 100 to one, slowly (taking between one and two minutes in all).

▶ Peppermint tea has a wonderful way of relaxing the system and relieving moodiness. Drink it warm and strong.

## Seeing Green...and Blue

▶ If you are on edge, high-strung and, generally speaking, a nervous wreck, try to surround yourself with calming colors. Green can have a harmonizing effect, since it's the color of nature. Earth colors should make you feel better. Wear quiet blues and gentle grays. Color helps more than we realize.

▶ Sage tea can help relieve the jitters. Steep a sage tea bag or 1 teaspoon of sage in 1 cup of warm water for five minutes. Strain and drink three cups a day.

*Bonus:* Sage tea also helps sharpen one's memory and brain power.

▶ There's a reason why Epsom salt, an ancient natural healer, is still popular—it works! Pour 2 cups of Epsom salt into a warm-water bath. Set aside a half-hour for pure relaxation in the tub—no interruptions—just 30 minutes of stress-free fantasizing.

## Phtheasy for You to Say

▶ According to European folklore, celery helps you forget your troubles from a broken heart and soothes your nerves at the same time. It's probably the *phthalide* in celery, which is known to have sedative properties.

# Nervous Tics

▶ From time to time Joan gets a tic around her eye. She feels like she's winking at everyone. The tic-off switch that works like magic for her is vitamin $B_6$.

⚡ **CAUTION:** Be sure to consult with your naturopathic doctor about the correct dosage for you.

A nervous tic may also be your body's way of telling you that you need more calcium or magnesium—or both. A good supplement can help you get the 1,500 mg of calcium and 750 mg of magnesium you need daily.

## DIABETES

In simplified terms, diabetes is a condition in which the pancreas does not produce an adequate amount of insulin to burn up the body's intake of sugars and starches from food.

You may have this condition if you urinate frequently and are thirsty all the time. The lack of insulin may also deplete your blood sugar, making you feel tired, weak and/or lightheaded. Be sure to consult your doctor if you have any of these symptoms.

## Dietary Controls

Thanks to modern laboratory technology, diabetics can perform urinalysis and blood-sugar tests conveniently in their own homes. While it makes it easy to monitor oneself, remember—*diabetes is a serious condition. Do not embark on any plan of treatment without a doctor's supervision.*

Many cases of diabetes can be completely controlled—controlled, not cured—by a sensible diet. By sticking to a low-calorie, high-carbohydrate with plenty of fiber, and exercising (walking at a normal speed for a half-hour after every meal), many diabetics reduce or eliminate their need for medication and feel better than ever. The importance of controlled weight loss, especially for the obese, cannot be overemphasized.

### Joan's Amazing Blood Sugar Secret

▶ One of our most important remedies requires only one ingredient. As a diabetic, Joan needs to keep her blood sugar level down. When she's eaten something that caused her number to increase (even though she's taken her diabetic medication), she takes 1 to 2 tablespoons of that one special ingredient—organic extra-virgin coconut oil—and within an hour, Joan's blood sugar is dramatically lower.

### Combination Plate

▶ Along with a well-balanced, sugar-free diet, the combination of garlic, watercress and parsley, eaten daily, might help regulate blood-sugar levels for some diabetics.

## Get Choked Up

**S**unchokes, also known as Jerusalem artichokes (although they're not from Jerusalem nor are they artichokes) have been said to help stimulate the production of insulin when eaten daily.

These tubers contain inulin and levulin, carbohydrates that do not convert to sugar in the body. Jerusalem artichokes are similar in texture to potatoes, but taste sweeter. They're great for helping you stick to a weight-loss diet because they satisfy your sweet tooth, and are low in calories and high in vitamins and minerals. Eat them raw as a snack or in salads, boiled in soups or baked in stews. (*See* the recipe on page 18.)

Some greengrocers now carry Jerusalem artichokes. They are easy to grow and worth the effort if you have the space. Ask your local nursery to help you get started.

## DIARRHEA

Diarrhea is a common condition that is often caused by overeating, a bacterial, viral or parasitic infection, mild food poisoning, emotional anxiety or extreme fatigue.

Even a quick and simple bout of diarrhea depletes the system of potassium, magnesium and even sodium, often leaving the sufferer tired, depressed and dehydrated. It's important to keep drinking clear fluids during and after a siege in order to avoid depletion and dehydration.

**CAUTION:** If diarrhea persists, it may be a symptom of a more serious ailment. Get professional medical attention. Bloody diarrhea can be infectious and needs treatment immediately.

## Dietary Remedies

### Milk It

▶ A West Indian remedy for diarrhea is a pinch of allspice in a cup of warm water or milk. A Pennsylvania Dutch remedy is 2 pinches of cinnamon in a cup of warm milk. A Brazilian remedy calls for 2 pinches of cinnamon and 1 pinch of powdered cloves in a cup of warm milk.

---

### A Different Kind of Charcoal

**A**n adsorbent (that's right, *adsorbent*) substance attaches things to its surface instead of absorbing them into itself. Activated charcoal is the most powerful adsorbent known.

Charcoal capsules or tablets can help stop certain types of diarrhea quickly by adsorbing the toxins that may cause the problem. Follow the instructions on the box.

**NOTE:** Be sure to heed the warning and drug interaction precaution—charcoal can interfere with antibiotics. Activated charcoal is not for everyday use, as it adsorbs the vitamins and minerals you need to be healthy.

---

▶ We may as well "milk" this for all it's worth with a Welsh remedy that requires a cup of boiled milk and a redhot fireplace poker.

Carefully place the red-hot poker into the cup of milk. Keep it there for 30 seconds. The poker supposedly charges the milk with iron, which is a homeopathic treatment of diarrhea. Be careful and drink the iron-charged milk slowly—it may be hot!

▶ The combination of cinnamon and cayenne pepper is known to be very effective in tightening the bowels quickly. In fact, it probably takes longer to prepare the tea than for it to work.

Bring 2 cups of water to a boil, then add ¼ teaspoon of cinnamon and ⅛ teaspoon of cayenne pepper. Let the mixture simmer for 20 minutes. As soon as it's cool enough to drink, have ¼ cup every half hour.

▶ Add 1 teaspoon of powdered ginger to 1 cup of just-boiled water. To control diarrhea, drink 3 cups of the mixture throughout the day.

▶ Grate an onion and squeeze it through cheesecloth so you get 2 tablespoons (1 ounce) of onion juice. Take the onion juice every hour, along with 1 cup of peppermint tea.

### Suited to a Tea

▶ Raspberry-leaf tea is a popular folk remedy for children and adults. Combine 1 ounce of dried raspberry leaves with 2 cups of water (a piece of cinnamon stick is optional), and simmer in an enamel or glass saucepan for 25 minutes. Strain, cool and drink throughout the day.

### Hippocratic Oats

▶ According to Hippocrates, the Greek physician and father of medicine, everyone should drink barley water daily to maintain good health. One of the benefits is its effectiveness in treating diarrhea.

Boil 2 ounces of pearled barley in 6 cups of water until there's about half the water—3 cups—left in the pot. Strain. If necessary, add honey and lemon to taste. Not only should you drink the barley water throughout the day, you should also eat the barley.

### Berry Good Berries

▶ Since biblical times, the common blackberry plant has been used to cure diarrhea and dysentery. And so the berry remedy, in one form or another, has been passed down through the generations. Don't be surprised if your neighborhood bartender recommends some blackberry brandy.

*Dose:* Drink 1 shot glass (2 tablespoons) every four hours.

⚡ **CAUTION:** Women who are pregnant or nursing should not consume alcohol.

▶ Blackberry juice or wine will also do fine.

*Dose:* Take 6 ounces blackberry juice every four hours—or 2 ounces (4 tablespoons) blackberry wine every four hours.

### The Big Apple

▶ Scrape a peeled apple with a (preferably nonmetal) spoon and eat the scrapings. In fact, eat no other food but grated apple until the condition greatly subsides.

▶ Boil ½ cup of white rice in 6 cups of water for a half-hour. Strain and save the water, then sweeten with honey to taste.

*Dose:* Drink 1 cup of the rice water every other hour. Do not drink other liquids until the condition disappears.

Eating cooked rice with a dash of cinnamon is also helpful in controlling the problem.

### An A-peeling Remedy

▶ Bananas may help promote the growth of beneficial bacteria in the intestine and replace some of the lost potassium.

*Dose:* Three times a day, eat one ripe banana that has been soaked in milk.

▶ Add 1 teaspoon of garlic (finely chopped) to 1 teaspoon of honey and swallow it down three times a day—two hours after each meal.

▶ Certain drinks are effective in treating diarrhea and help replenish the system's supply of friendly intestinal bacteria. Have 1 to 2 glasses of buttermilk or sauerkraut juice or kefir (found in health food stores).

Or eat a portion or two of yogurt with active cultures, along with pickled beets, pickled cucumbers or raw sauerkraut (*see* "Preparation Guide" on page 253 for sauerkraut recipe).

### Press for Success

▶ The navel is an acupressure point for treating diarrhea. Using your thumb or the heel of your hand, press in and massage the area in a circular motion for about two minutes.

## Chronic Diarrhea

This remedy goes to prove that you can't argue with success. A woman wrote to tell us that eating Archway coconut macaroons—two a day—put an end to her 12-year bout with diarrhea. She suffers from Crohn's disease, which is a chronic inflammation of the intestinal wall. Chronic diarrhea is one of the most common and debilitating symptoms of this condition. The woman asked that we include her remedy, hoping it will help others with this problem.

Upon further investigation, we found that Joe Graedon, MS, pharmacologist, adjunct assistant professor at the University of North Carolina, Chapel Hill, also reported on these cookies and the success many people had with them. One woman couldn't find the Archway cookies, so she made her own coconut macaroons and they, too, worked like magic. While they don't work for everyone, they may be worth a try.

**NOTE:** Take into consideration your dietary needs before trying the coconut macaroon remedy. The cookies are high in fat and contain sweeteners.

## Dysentery

It is common for people traveling in foreign countries to get dysentery. All of the remedies for diarrhea may help treat bacterial dysentery. However, amoebic dysentery (which is caused by amoeba living in the raw green vegetables of some countries) and viral dysentery are more severe forms of dysentery. All types of dysentery should be treated by a health professional.

▶ To help prevent bacterial dysentery, two weeks before you travel to a foreign country, eat a finely chopped raw onion in a cup of yogurt every day.

Before you discard this preventive measure, try it. You may be surprised at how good it tastes. The yogurt somehow makes the onion taste sweet.

## DRINKING PROBLEMS

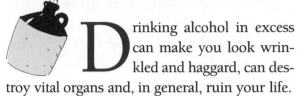

Drinking alcohol in excess can make you look wrinkled and haggard, can destroy vital organs and, in general, ruin your life.

For the problem drinker, we strongly recommend the leading self-help organization for combating alcoholism—Alcoholics Anonymous. Headquartered in New York City, the organization is a support group for people with drinking problems. Go to *www.aa.org* for more information, or check the White Pages of the telephone book for your local chapter.

This section provides natural remedies for the social drinker who, occasionally, has one too many.

## Dietary Remedies

▶ Before you have a drink, sprinkle nutmeg into a glass of milk and sip it slowly. It may help absorb and neutralize the effects of alcoholic beverages.

▶ The Greek philosopher and teacher Aristotle (384–322 BC) advised his followers to eat a big chunk of cabbage before imbibing. Cole slaw—which is made from cabbage and vinegar—is said to be an even more effective intoxication preventive.

▶ The best way to hold your liquor is in the bottle it comes in! One way to help you do that is, when sober, look at a man or woman who is drunk. It's not often a pretty sight.

## Sober Up

The following suggestions are meant for people who have drunk too much alcohol—that is, these remedies may make them more alert and communicative.

However, DO NOT trust or depend on those people's reflexes, especially behind the wheel of a car. It generally takes one hour per 20 milligrams of alcohol consumed to sober up...in other words, wait an hour after each bottle of beer, glass of wine or shot of liquor.

▶ If a drunk person imagines that the room is spinning, have him/her lie down on a bed and put one foot on the floor to stop that feeling.

▶ Honey contains fructose, which promotes the chemical breakdown of alcohol. Start by giving the drunk person 1 or 2 teaspoons of honey. Follow that with 1 teaspoon of honey every half-hour for the next couple of hours.

**WARNING:** Do not give honey to someone who is diabetic or allergic to honey.

▶ To help sober up an intoxicated person, try feeding him cucumber—as much as he is willing to eat. The cuke's enzyme, erepsin, may lessen the effect of alcohol.

▶ Try sobering up someone who's tipsy by massaging the tip of his nose.

**CAUTION:** Stimulation of the tip of the nose can cause vomiting, so don't stand right in front of the person you're sobering up.

▶ This is a Siberian method of sobering up a drunk person. Have him lie flat on his back. Place the palms of your hands on his ears. Next, rub both ears briskly and strongly in a

circular motion. Within minutes, the person should start coming around.

While he may be a lot more sober than before you rubbed his ears, he should NOT be trusted behind the wheel of a car.

## Hangover Help

In simplified terms, a hangover is the disagreeable physical effect—a headache or nausea, for example—caused by drinking too much alcohol. Hangovers can make a fun night turn into a bad morning.

▶ Hangovers can also be caused by an allergy or sensitivity to what you drank. Using homeopathic theory (like fights like), put 1 drop of the alcohol in a glass of water. Take three sips. If the hangover symptoms do not disappear within five minutes, then drink the rest of the glass of water. If you still don't feel better within a few minutes, then your hangover is not allergy-caused.

▶ For the morning after, take ⅛ teaspoon of cayenne pepper in a glass of water.

▶ Evening primrose oil (soft gels are available at health food stores) is said to help replenish the amino acids and gamma-linoleic acid that's lost when you drink alcoholic beverages. Take 1,000 milligrams (mg) with lots of water or orange juice before you go to sleep.

Too late for that? Okay then, take it when you wake up and are desperate for anything that will help you feel human again.

▶ According to the Chinese, a cup of ginger tea (*see* "Preparation Guide" on page 250) will help calm an unsettled stomach caused by a hangover. To relieve eye, ear, mouth, nose and brain pain from the hangover, knead the fleshy part of the hand between the thumb and the index finger on both hands. For a pounding hangover headache, massage each thumb, just below the knuckles.

## Sweet Solution

▶ Take 1 tablespoon of honey every minute for five minutes. Repeat the procedure a half-hour later.

**WARNING:** Do not give honey to someone who is diabetic or allergic to honey.

▶ Rub ¼ lemon on each armpit. That may ease the discomfort of a hangover.

▶ If you insist on drinking, you may be interested to know that a research team from England advises drinkers to guzzle clear alcohols—gin, vodka or white rum—to lessen the chances of that "morning after" feeling. Red wine and whiskey seem to have more hangover-promoting elements.

## Morning-After Breakfast

▶ Bananas and milk is the breakfast of choice of many hangover sufferers. It may be effective due to the fact that alcohol depletes the magnesium in one's body, and bananas and milk replenish the supply.

You may want to add tomato, carrot, celery and/or beet juice to replenish the B and C vitamins along with some trace minerals that alcohol may also deplete.

## Listen to a Wise Old Owl

▶ The famed Roman naturalist Pliny the Elder (who lived from 23–79 AD and wrote a comprehensive encyclopedia called *Natural history*) recommended eating the eggs of an owl.

While owl eggs may be hard to come by, all eggs are a source of cysteine, which helps the body manufacture glutathione, an antioxidant that gets depleted when alcohol is present. So an omelet could be a helpful hangover breakfast.

Pliny may have eased the symptoms of many a hangover with those eggs. Look who was the wise old owl, after all.

▶ Have a hangover? Feel like pulling your hair out? Good idea, but don't go all the way. Just pull your hair, clump by clump, until it hurts a little (don't pull the hair out).

According to a noted reflexologist, hair-pulling is stimulating to the entire body and can help lessen the symptoms of a hangover.

▶ When you have a throbbing hangover headache, eat a raw persimmon for relief. From now on, if you insist on drinking, make sure it's persimmon season.

▶ Hangover sufferers are sometimes advised to just "sleep it off." That's smart advice, since a contributing factor to hangovers is the lack of REM (rapid eye movement) sleep which alcohol seems to suppress. So go ahead and sleep it off!

▶ A Chinese hangover remedy calls for eating 10 strawberries and drinking a glass of fresh tangerine juice. Hmmm—sounds good even if you don't have a hangover.

▶ Hungarian gypsies recommend a bowl of chicken soup with rice. What could be bad?

### Another Chicken Soup Remedy

▶ Cysteine is an amino acid that helps the body manufacture glutathione, an antioxidant that gets depleted when it has the chore of contending with alcohol. According to a study performed at the University of California, San Diego (UCSD), cysteine is present in chicken. Therefore, chicken soup may help replenish the body's needed supply of cysteine, easing hangover symptoms at the same time.

▶ A glass of sauerkraut juice is said to be effective. If the pure juice is hard for you to take, add some tomato juice to it. Or, eat lots of raw cabbage. That's been known to work wonders.

### Gimme a B!

▶ Some of the B-complex vitamins are $B_1$ (thiamine), $B_2$ (riboflavin), nicotinamide and pyridoxine. They are helpful in aiding carbohydrate metabolization, nerve function, the cellular oxidation process and the dilation of blood vessels, all of which are helpful for hangovers. Impressed?

If you have overindulged and are anticipating waking up with a hangover, take a vitamin B-complex supplement with two or three glasses of water before you go to bed. If you pass out before remembering to take the B-complex, take the vitamin as soon as possible after you awaken.

▶ There are some of you who will not be happy until you find a "hair of the dog" hangover remedy. Here's one we were told comes from a voodoo practitioner in New Orleans.

In a blender, add 1 ounce of Pernod, 1 ounce of white crème de cacao and 3 ounces of milk, plus three ice cubes. Blend, drink and good luck!

### Easing the Urge to Drink

▶ A tangy beverage can ease and erase the urge to imbibe. Have a glass of tomato juice with the juice of one lemon added. You might also want to throw in a couple of ice cubes. Stir well. Sip slowly as you would an alcoholic drink.

▶ The supplement glutamine is helpful in easing the urge for alcohol. Take 500 mg three times a day.

## Intoxication Prevention

We're reporting the remedies that supposedly prevent a person from getting drunk, but we ask that you please take full responsibility for your drinking. If you drink, DO NOT trust or test your reflexes—especially behind the wheel of a car—no matter how sober you seem to feel, or which preventive remedies you take. And women who are pregnant or nursing should not consume alcohol.

▶ Native Americans recommend eating raw (not roasted) almonds before drinking. Consume them on an empty stomach.

▶ Healers in West Africa suggest eating peanut butter before imbibing.

▶ Gem therapists tell of the power of amethysts. In Greek, *amethyst* is *ametusios* and means "remedy against drunkenness." Please don't take this to mean that if you carry an amethyst and you drink, you won't get drunk.

It's that carrying an amethyst should give one the strength to refuse a drink and, therefore, prevent intoxication.

### Women, Take Heed

Women who drink right *before* menstruating—when their estrogen level is low—get drunk more easily, usually become more nauseated and experience rougher hangovers than at any other time during their cycle.

## EAR PROBLEMS

"Friends, Romans, country-men, lend me your ears…"—but not if you have an earache! Even Mark Antony (eulogizing Caesar in William Shakespeare's play *Julius Caesar*) would not want ears that are inflamed, painful and runny. Earaches and infections can be serious, but if your ears are burning…just tell people to stop talking about you!

## Earaches

Earaches are generally caused by an infection of the middle ear as a result of a cold or the flu. The pain can be out of proportion to the seriousness of the problem.

> **WARNING:** An earache may be a sign of a serious infection. These remedies should not be considered a substitute for determining the cause of the earache or for getting proper medical treatment.
>
> If an earache persists, don't turn a deaf ear! See a health professional for diagnosis and treatment.

Whenever an ear is draining—discharging thick or thin liquid from the canal—it may be that the eardrum has ruptured, and there could be a potentially serious infection. If that's the case, get medical attention *immediately*. If your ear is draining, do not put anything in it unless medically instructed.

## Natural Remedies

Occasionally, you may have an earache and can determine that medical care is not required at that moment. It is *only* at such times that you should consider the following remedies. And don't try them at all if there's broken skin in or around the ear.

▶ Fill the ear with 3 warm (not too hot) drops of olive oil and loosely plug the ear with a cotton ball. Do this three or four times a day until the earache is gone.

▶ Mix the juice from grated fresh ginger with an equal amount of sesame oil. Drop in 3 drops of the mixture and loosely plug the ear with a cotton ball. It might sting a bit, but try to keep it there for a few hours.

### Please Bite Down

▶ This reflexology remedy requires an object that is sterile and hard to bite down on. The ideal item is one of those cotton cylinders the dentist uses. Or you can wad up a piece of cheesecloth, which works fine.

Place the hard, sterile item in back of the last tooth on the side of the aching ear, and bite down on it for five minutes. This stimulates the pressure point that goes directly to the ear.

Repeat this procedure every two hours until the earache is gone. This process relieves the pain of an earache and has been known to improve hearing as well.

▶ Another effective way of easing the pain of an earache is to place a soothing chamomile poultice (*see* "Preparation Guide" on page 252) over your ear. If you don't have the loose herb, use a couple of tea bags instead.

### Onion Muffs

▶ Cut a large onion in half. Take out the inside of the onion so that the remaining part will fit over your ear. Warm the onion "earmuff" in the oven, then put it over your ear. Be sure it's not too hot. It should help draw out the pain.

▶ Mix ½ cup of unprocessed bran with ½ cup of kosher (coarse) salt and envelop it in a generous piece of folded-over cheesecloth. In other words, bundle it up so it doesn't spill all over the place. Then heat it in a low oven until it's warm but bearable to the touch. Place it over the painful ear and keep it on for an hour.

▶ Put castor oil on a piece of cotton. Sprinkle the oiled cotton with black pepper and apply it to the aching ear—not in the ear canal, but directly on the ear.

### Rye to the Rescue

▶ If you're going to get an earache, try to get it when you're baking rye bread. All you have to do is take 1 ounce of caraway seeds and pummel them. Then add 1 cup of bread crumbs from a soft, hot, newly baked loaf of bread and wrap it all in a piece of cheesecloth. Apply it to the sore ear. If you use already-cooled bread, warm the bread in the oven before applying it.

### Cold, Hot, Tea...Ahh!

▶ Most earache remedies say to put something *warm* on the ear. Las Vegas–based herbalist Angela Harris (*www.angelaharris.com*)

feels that the infection-causing bacteria thrive on warmth, and so her approach is to put *cold* on the ear.

While an ice pack is applied to the infected ear, put your feet in hot water—as hot as you can stand it without burning yourself—and slowly drink a mild laxative herb tea, available at health food stores. Do this cold/hot/tea remedy for about 15 minutes, long enough for the pain to be alleviated.

## Ear Infections

**WARNING:** If your ear infection is painful and persistent, get medical attention. You may have a serious condition that needs professional treatment.

### Inflamed Ear

▶ Mix 1 tablespoon of milk with 1 tablespoon of olive oil or castor oil, then heat the combination in a nonaluminum pan.

*Dose:* Once the mixture has cooled off, put 4 drops into the inflamed ear every hour and gently plug it up with cotton. Be sure the drops are not too hot.

### Runny Ear Infection

▶ You'll need to go to a good, old-fashioned Italian fish store for this remedy. Get the soft, transparent bone from a squid. Bake it until it turns black and crush it into a powder. Taken orally—½ teaspoon before breakfast and another ½ teaspoon before dinner—it is said to help clear up a runny ear infection.

### Swimmer's Ear

Soon after swimming, if you've noticed that it hurts when you touch or move your ear, you may have an infection of the ear canal known as "swimmer's ear." These remedies may bring some relief.

▶ Combine 1 drop of grapefruit extract, 1 drop of tea tree oil and 2 drops of olive oil, then put the mixture in your ear. Gently plug your ear with a cotton ball. This should help clear up the infection.

▶ To prevent infections, add 1 teaspoon of white vinegar to 4 tablespoons (2 ounces) of just-boiled water. Once the liquid is cool, store it in a bottle. Right after swimming, put 2 drops of the vinegar mixture in each ear. Plug each ear with a cotton ball and stay that way for about 10 minutes.

## Ear Pressure

The key to relieving the pressure caused by airplane takeoffs and landings is chewing and swallowing.

▶ The American Academy of Otolaryngology in Alexandria, Virginia, advises that you should chew gum or suck on mints—whatever causes you to swallow more than usual. Stay awake as the plane ascends and descends so that you can consciously increase the amount of times you swallow.

▶ If you're sleepy, that's good. Hopefully, you'll start yawning, which is even better than swallowing because it activates the muscle that opens your eustachian tube. Then air can be forced in and out of your eustachian canal, and that's what relieves the pressure in your ears.

## Other Ear Problems

### Get the Bugs Out

▶ It happens! Not often, but once in a blue moon, an insect will get inside a person's ear. Since insects are attracted to light, if an insect gets in your ear, turn the ear toward the sun. Hopefully, the insect will fly out and away. If it occurs at night, shut off the lights in the room and shine a flashlight in your ear.

▶ If the insect in your ear doesn't respond to the light, pour 1 teaspoon of warm olive oil into your ear and hold it there a minute or two. Then tilt your head the other way so that the oil and the bug come floating out.

If that doesn't work, gently fill your ear with warm water. That should push out the insect and the oil.

If none of this debugs you, get professional medical help to remove the insect.

### Waxy Build-up Begone!

▶ Sprinkle black pepper into 1 tablespoon of warm corn oil, then dip a cotton ball into it and gently put the cotton into your ear. Remove the cotton after five minutes.

▶ In the microwave, warm 1 tablespoon of 3% hydrogen peroxide. Put 10 drops in the ear and let it fizz there for three minutes. Then tilt your head so that the liquid runs out onto a tissue. The wax should be softened. Gently remove the wax with soft cotton. Repeat the procedure with the other ear.

You can also use a solution of half water and half hydrogen peroxide to irrigate and remove wax.

**CAUTION:** Only use cotton balls or swabs on the external part of the ear to prevent puncturing your eardrum.

▶ Warm 2 teaspoons of sesame oil and put 1 teaspoon of oil in each ear. *Be sure the oil is not too hot.* Gently plug the ear with a cotton ball, and allow the oil to float around for a while. Once the sesame oil softens the wax, you can wash out the ears completely. The results—no more oil, no more wax.

## Tinnitus (Ringing in the Ears)

If the bells are ringing…and ringing…and ringing—you may have tinnitus.

 **NOTE:** Although most tinnitus sufferers hear bells, others may hear clicking, hissing, roaring or whistling.

The exact cause of tinnitus is unknown, but may be brought on by noise-induced hearing loss, wax build-up, ear infection, jaw misalignment and even cardiovascular disease.

Ringing in the ears may also be the result of a mild overdose of salicylate, which is found in aspirin and other drugs. If this is what's causing the ringing, it should stop when the drug is discontinued.

▶ If you still hear ringing (and there are no bells nearby)…try onion juice.

*Dose:* Put 2 drops of onion juice in your ears, three times a week, to stop the ringing.

▶ Believe it or not, a heating pad on your feet and one on your hands may ease the ringing in your ears. It all has to do with blood being redistributed, improving circulation and lessening pressure in congested areas.

**WARNING:** If ringing persists, it might be a sign of a more serious illness, in which case you should seek medical attention.

▶ We heard about a woman who had constant ringing in her ears for years. None of the specialists could help her. As a last resort, she started using castor oil. After a month, the ringing subsided considerably. Within three months, it was completely gone.

Try 3 or 4 drops a day in each ear. To get the full benefit from the castor oil, plug the ear with cotton once you've put in the drops, and keep it there overnight.

### Mix It Up

▶ In a blender, combine six large, peeled garlic cloves and 1 cup of almond oil or extra virgin, cold-pressed olive oil. Blend until the garlic is finely minced. Then clean a glass jar by pouring just-boiled water into it.

Once the jar is dry, pour the garlic and oil mixture into the jar, put the cover on and refrigerate it for seven days. Then strain the liquid from the jar into a clean eyedropper bottle.

At bedtime, take the chill out of a small amount of the liquid, then put 3 drops in each ear and plug the ears with cotton balls. Remove the cotton in the morning. Chances are, if the ringing is going to stop at all, it will do so within two weeks.

Always keep this preparation refrigerated, and do not keep it longer than a month.

# Hearing Loss

**NOTE:** Seek professional medical attention for a hearing impairment or any sudden hearing loss.

▶ A loud noise, a head cold or wax build-up can cause partial loss of hearing. In Sicily, where garlic is a cure-all, they stew a few cloves in olive oil, then press it and strain it. On a

daily basis, 3 or 4 drops of the garlic/olive oil juice are placed in the ear(s) and plugged up with cotton. It is said to restore one's hearing.

"Hey, I can hear now."

"Good. I've been wanting to tell you something…you smell of garlic!"

### Improve Your Hearing

Aerobic exercise, including brisk walking or bicycling, can help prevent some age-related deterioration in the ears, as well as damage caused by exposure to loud noises. Exercise also increases the ability to hear faint sounds.

This good news comes from results of studies conducted at Miami University in Oxford, Ohio, which concluded that aerobic exercise improves hearing by circulating blood to inner ear cells and bringing them more oxygen and an increased supply of chemicals that prevent damage to them.

Be sure to check with your doctor before starting any new exercise program.

### Just a Pinch

▶ Pinch the tip of your middle finger four times a day, five minutes each time. Before every meal, pinch the right finger. After every meal, pinch the left finger. When you get up in the morning, pinch the right finger. When you go to bed at night, pinch the left finger.

Your right finger is for your right ear and left finger for left ear, so if you want to improve only one ear, pinch accordingly. Make it easy on yourself and clip on a clothespin.

▶ This potent potion has been said to actually restore hearing—drink 1 ounce of garlic juice with 1 ounce of onion juice once a day. (*See* "Bad Breath" [Halitosis] on page 183 immediately!)

## EMPHYSEMA

Emphysema is an abnormal condition of the lungs, characterized by decreased respiratory function, that is associated with chronic bronchitis, old age or—smoking.

If you've been diagnosed with emphysema and you're still smoking, don't bother reading this anymore. Turn to the "Smoking" section on page 167 and come back to read these remedies when you've stopped smoking.

▶ Now then…combine ½ teaspoon of raw honey with 5 drops of anise oil and take this dosage a half-hour before each meal. We've heard positive reports about this remedy.

▶ When you're having a hard time breathing, call 911 immediately. While you wait for help to arrive, sit down, lean forward and put your elbows on your knees. This position can make breathing easier because it elevates the diaphragm, the most important muscle used for breathing.

*See* "Exercise Your Lung Power" in the "Remedies in a Class by Themselves" section on page 243 and consider learning to play the harmonica.

**WARNING:** Emphysema is a very serious illness that should be treated by a qualified health professional.

## EYE PROBLEMS

How very precious our eyes and vision are to each of us. Agreed? Agreed! Then what have you done for your eyes lately? Do you know there's eye food, eye-strengthening exercises, an acupressure eyestrain reliever, eyewashes to help brighten those baby blues, browns, grays or greens, and natural healing alternatives?

We once noticed a sign in an optometrist's office that said—"If you don't see what you want, you're in the right place."

Likewise. So read the following eye care suggestions, or get someone to read them to you.

### Bloodshot Eyes

▶ If you don't drink in excess and you get enough sleep, but still have bloodshot eyes on a regular basis, you may be bothered by your contacts, allergic to the eye makeup you wear or you may be deficient in vitamin $B_2$ (riboflavin). Take 15 mg of $B_2$ daily. You might also want to have a tablespoon of brewer's yeast every day.

Use any of the eyewashes listed on page 80, and you might want to try the grated potato remedy listed under "Black Eyes" on page 29.

### Cataracts

When the lens of your eye becomes opaque (cloudy)—which occurs from old age, injury or a systemic disease like diabetes—then you have a cataract.

There are revolutionary new methods of removing cataracts, where the patient walks in and out of the doctor's office within a few hours. Cataracts should definitely be treated and removed by a qualified health professional.

## Natural Remedies

While you're checking into today's modern techniques, you might want to try one or more of the following natural remedies to give you some relief until the cataract is professionally removed…

## Mind Your Bs and Cs

▶Research scientists have found that a deficiency of vitamin $B_2$ (riboflavin) can cause cataracts. So it serves to reason that $B_2$ supplements should help to prevent cataracts and may also clear up existing conditions.

Brewer's yeast is the richest source of riboflavin. Take 1 tablespoon a day and/or 15 mg of vitamin $B_2$. Along with a $B_2$ vitamin, take a B-complex vitamin to avoid high urinary losses of B vitamins. Also, eat foods high in vitamin $B_2$—broccoli, salmon, beans, wheat germ, turnip tops and beets.

▶Vitamin C prevents damage in the watery portions of cells, particularly in the cornea and retina. A Tufts University study reported that women who supplemented their diets with 325 mg of vitamin C daily were 77% less likely to develop cataracts than women who did not supplement.

Take 1,000 mg of vitamin C every day or eat foods that contain it, such as broccoli, sweet potatoes, citrus fruits and bell peppers.

▶For five minutes each day, massage the base of the index and middle (second and third)

### ■ Recipe ■

### Beets in Orange Sauce

5 medium beets (1¼ lbs)

6 cups water

1 tsp salt

1 Tbsp packed brown sugar

2 tsp cornstarch

½ tsp salt

Dash of pepper

¾ cup orange juice

2 tsp vinegar

Cut off all but 2 inches of beet tops. Leave beets whole with root ends attached. Heat water and 1 tsp salt to boiling in 3-quart saucepan. Add beets. Heat to boiling, then reduce heat. Cover and cook until tender, 35 to 45 minutes. Drain. Run cold water over beets, then slip off skins and remove root ends. Cut beets into ¼-inch slices.

Mix brown sugar, cornstarch, ½ tsp salt and the pepper in 2-quart saucepan. Stir orange juice gradually into cornstarch mixture, then stir in vinegar. Cook, stirring constantly, until mixture thickens and boils. Boil and stir 1 minute. Stir in beets, and heat until hot. Makes 4 servings.

*Source: www.recipegoldmine.com*

fingers, as well as the webs between those fingers. The right hand helps the right eye and the left hand helps the left eye.

▶The famed 17th-century English physician Nicholas Culpeper was a great believer in the healing effects of chamomile eyewashes to improve a cataract condition. (*See* "Eyewashes" on page 80.)

# Conjunctivitis (Pinkeye)

If your eyes are red, watery and itchy, you may have allergies or just some dust in your eye. But if your eyes are VERY irritated, you may have the serious (and extremely contagious) infection commonly known as pinkeye.

**CAUTION:** Conjunctivitis is a severe and contagious viral, fungal or allergic infection. If the condition doesn't show signs of improvement within a day or two, see a health professional.

▶ Once every day, make a poultice (*see* "Preparation Guide" on page 252) of grated apple or grated raw red potato and place it on your closed eye. Let it stay that way for a half-hour. Within two days—or three at the most—the condition should completely clear up.

▶ Prepare chamomile tea. When it cools, use it as an eyewash (*see* page 79) twice a day until the conjunctivitis is gone.

## The Eyes Have It

▶ The plant eyebright is particularly effective in the treatment of conjunctivitis. Add 3 drops of tincture of eyebright (available at health food stores) to 1 tablespoon of just-boiled water. When cool enough to use, bathe the eye in the mixture.

Since this condition is a very contagious one, wash the eye cup thoroughly after you've washed one eye, then mix a new batch of eyebright with water before you wash the other eye. Do this three or four times a day until the condition clears up. Or, use the eyewashes listed on pages 79–80.

▶ Goat milk yogurt can also help clear up this uncomfortable condition. Apply a yogurt poultice (*see* "Preparation Guide" on page 252) over the infected eye(s) daily.

Also, eat a portion or two of the yogurt each day. The active culture in yogurt can provide you with healthy bacteria in your gastrointestinal tract. Goat's milk yogurt is available at some health food stores and specialty markets or can be ordered on-line.

# Dry Eyes

Tear ducts that do not produce enough fluid to keep the eyes moist can result in an uncomfortable dry eye condition that is characterized by irritation, burning and a gravelly feeling.

## Natural Tears

Check out homeopathic eyedrops for dry eye syndrome. Homeopathic medications are without side effects and are well-tolerated by even the most sensitive system. They work to restore health rather than to suppress symptoms.

 **NOTE:** To get the most benefit from eyedrops, gently pull out your lower lid and let the liquid drop into the eye pocket. Then keep your eyes closed for about two minutes after putting in the drops. This will prevent the blinking process from pumping the drops out of your eyes.

Similasan Eye Drops, known throughout Europe, are available here in the US. For information about these homeopathic drops, go to *www.allaboutvision.com/similasan* or call Similasan at 800-426-1644.

▶ You may be able to eliminate artificial tears completely by adding omega-3 fatty acids to

---

**Dry Eye Don'ts**

There are things you should avoid so that your dry eye condition doesn't become worse…

◆ Don't use a blow dryer on your hair unless you absolutely have to.

◆ Don't go outdoors without sunglasses. The wraparound kind are excellent for keeping the wind out.

◆ Don't dry out your eyes with heating or cooling systems in your home, office, car or even on an airplane. Keep the heat or air-conditioning to a minimum, and be sure the vents are not pointing in your direction. Turn it off completely if it isn't really necessary.

◆ Don't go for any length of time without blinking. People at computers have this problem. Every time you click the mouse, blink. Every time you save a document, blink. Every time you swallow, blink. Do whatever it takes to make yourself conscious of blinking often, especially when you're sitting in front of the computer.

◆ Don't wear contact lenses all the time.

◆ Don't smoke. Smoke exacerbates the burning and other symptoms of dry eyes.

◆ Don't cry about it. It makes the problem worse. Tears brought on by emotion wash away the oils that prevent dry eyes.

---

your diet, which may increase the viscosity of oils made by the body, mostly in the skin and eyes. Omega-3s are found abundantly in cold-water fish and flaxseed oil. This means eating several servings of fish a week—especially all varieties of salmon (except smoked) and canned white tuna—and/or taking flaxseed oil.

We suggest you read about the many benefits of flaxseed oil in the "Six Sensational Superfoods" section on page 262. And *see* the salmon recipe on page 73.

**CAUTION:** If you're on blood-thinning medication, have uncontrolled high blood pressure or bleeding disorders, or are going in for surgery, be sure to check with your doctor before taking flaxseed oil.

▶ Help your eyes do the work they're supposed to do by opening the clogged oil glands in the eyelids. Take a warm, white washcloth and place it on your closed eyelids. Leave it on until it turns cool—five to 10 minutes. Do this a few times a day—obviously, the more the better.

## Eye Irritants

### Chemicals

▶ When chemicals like hair dye get in the eye, immediately wash the eye thoroughly with lots of clean, tepid water. In most cases, you should have a doctor check your eye right after you've washed the damaging substance out.

### Dust

▶ When something gets in your eye, try not to rub the eye. You'll irritate it, then it's hard to tell whether or not the foreign particle is out. Grasp your upper lid lashes firmly between your thumb and index finger. Gently pull the lashes toward the cheek, as far as you can without pulling them out. Hold them there, count to 10, spit three times and let go of the lashes.

Repeat the procedure one more time if necessary. If it still doesn't work, get an onion and try the next remedy.

▶ Mince an onion and let your natural tears wash away the dust in your eye.

Get a tissue ready. With one hand, pull your lashes so that the upper lid is away from your eye. With the other hand, appropriately position the tissue in the center of your face and blow your nose three times.

▶ Warm some pure olive oil in the microwave for a few seconds—long enough to *slightly* warm the oil. Then, using an eyedropper, put 2 drops in the irritated eye.

What? You don't have an eyedropper? Buy one at any health food store or pharmacy and keep it in your medicine chest for just such occasions.

▶ Until you get an eyedropper, you may want to try this—put 1 drop of fresh lemon juice in 1 ounce of warm water and wash your eye with it. It might sting at first, but it should remove the irritant.

▶ If your eyes are irritated from a foreign particle, cooking fumes, cigarette smoke, dust, etc., put 2 drops of castor oil or milk in each eye.

⚡ **CAUTION:** Be careful putting any foreign substance or liquid in the eye. It can be painful and may cause infection.

## Eye Inflammation

▶ Peel and slice an overripe apple. Put the pieces of pulp over your closed eyes, holding

■ **Recipe** ■

### *Champagne-Poached Salmon*

½ cup honey Dijon mustard
1½ tsp fresh tarragon, chopped
4 (6 to 8 oz) salmon steaks or fillets,
    skin and bones removed
Salt and pepper to taste
2 cups champagne
¼ cup fresh lime juice
4 slices red onion
1 Tbsp capers, optional
4 sprigs fresh tarragon

Mix together mustard and chopped tarragon. Set aside.

Season salmon steaks/fillets lightly with salt and pepper. Place in a pan just large enough to hold the salmon in one layer. Add the champagne, lime juice and just enough water to cover the fish. Remove the fish and bring the liquid to a boil.

Return the salmon steaks/fillets to the pan. Top each with an onion slice, capers and tarragon sprig. Reduce heat to a simmer, cover pan with foil and poach at no more than a simmer for 6 to 10 minutes (depending on the thickness of the salmon).

Remove salmon steaks/fillets from the liquid and place on four warm serving plates. Top each piece of fish with 1 ounce of the mustard mixture and serve.

*Source: www.recipegoldmine.com*

the pieces in place with a bandage or strip of cloth. Leave it on at least a half-hour to help alleviate irritation and inflammation.

▶ A poultice of either grated raw potato, fresh mashed papaya pulp or mashed cooked beets is soothing and promotes healing. Apply the poultice for 15 minutes, twice a day.

### Fashion Statement

▶ Reuse steeped tea bags. Make sure they're moist and cool enough to apply to the closed eyelids for 15 minutes. (This remedy is a favorite for fashion models who wake up puffy-eyed.)

▶ Crush a tablespoon of fennel seeds and add it to a pint of just-boiled water. Let it steep for 15 minutes, then dunk cotton pads in the liquid and place them over your eyelids for about 15 minutes.

▶ There's an herb called horsetail that is helpful for inflamed eyes (*see* "Sources" on page 297 for vendors who might sell the herb).

Steep 1 teaspoon of dried horsetail in hot water for 10 minutes. Saturate cotton pads with it and apply the pads to your eyelids for 10 minutes. Redunk the pads in the liquid, then keep them on your eyes for another 10 minutes. Repeat again after a half-hour, and the inflammation should start calming down.

▶ Freshly sliced cucumber placed on eyelids for about 15 minutes is soothing and healing.

▶ Also, use any of the eyewashes on pages 79–80. Try the "palming" remedy, too. It's on page 79.

## Eye Puffiness

We know a man who has so much puffiness under his eyes, it looks like his nose is wearing a saddle.

One reason for puffiness may be an excessive amount of salt in one's diet. Salt causes water retention and water retention causes puffiness. What can be done about it? Stay away from salt. *Here are some more suggestions...*

▶ When you want to look your best, set your clock an hour earlier than usual. Give yourself that extra time to depuff. Either that, or sleep sitting up so the puffs don't get a chance to form under your eyes.

▶ If you already have puffs, wet a couple of chamomile tea bags with tepid water and put them over your closed eyelids. Relax that way for 15 minutes.

## Eyestrain/Tired Eyes

▶ Pinch the ends of your index and middle (second and third) fingers of each hand for 30 seconds on each finger. If your eyestrain isn't relieved after two minutes, do another round of pinching.

▶ Sunflower seeds contain vitamins, iron and calcium that may be extremely beneficial for eyes. Eat about ½ cup of unprocessed (unsalted) shelled seeds every day.

### Put Up Your Feet

▶ If your eyes are strained and tired, chances are the rest of your body is also dragging. Lie down with your feet raised higher than your head. Relax that way for about 15 minutes. This

## ■ Recipe ■

### *Yogurt Fruit Salad with Sunflower Seeds*

2 apples, chopped

2 oranges, chopped

2 bananas, chopped

2 pears, chopped

Handful of blueberries

2 peaches, chopped (can be frozen)

Seedless or seeded grapes, chopped

Canned pineapple chunks, drained

1 cup coconut, grated

½ cup unsalted sunflower seeds

¼ cup honey

1 to 2 cups unflavored yogurt

Combine all the ingredients (you may need to add a little more honey if you like it really sweet). Use your judgment as to how much yogurt to use to make it all stick together. Refrigerate until chilled and serve.

*Source: www.recipegoldmine.com*

gravity-reversing process should make you and your eyes feel refreshed and rarin' to go.

▶ Cut two thin slices of a raw red potato and keep them on your closed eyelids for at least 20 minutes. Red potatoes are said to have strong healing energy, but any other type of potato will work, too.

▶ Steep rosemary in hot water for 10 minutes. Use a rosemary tea bag or 1 teaspoon of the loose herb in a cup of just-boiled water. Saturate a cotton pad with the tea and keep it on your eyes for 15 minutes. Rosemary should help draw out that tired-eye feeling.

Also, *see* the "palming" remedy on page 79 (under "Vision Improvers").

### Eyestrain Prevention

▶ Looking at red ink on white paper for long periods of time can cause eyestrain and headaches. Stay out of the red!

### Eye Twitch

▶ Pressure and tension can cause eyelid twitching. Aside from taking a relaxing two-week vacation, you should try to eat more calcium-rich foods.

According to some nutritionists, adults can (and should) get all the calcium they require through nondairy foods—green vegetables, sesame seeds, whole grains, unrefined cereals, canned salmon and sardines, soy milk and other soy products, including tofu.

## Glaucoma

Glaucoma is a loss of vision that usually occurs suddenly and without symptoms. Vision is impaired when there is damage to the optic nerve, but there may be other factors involved. If you are having trouble seeing, see a qualified eye specialist! Glaucoma may be reversed if treated promptly.

**CAUTION:** Glaucoma is a serious condition. Before using any home remedy, be sure to consult an eye specialist.

▶ Vitamin $B_2$ (riboflavin) deficiency is one of the most common vitamin deficiencies in the US. $B_2$ is also the vitamin that's most beneficial for eye problems like glaucoma. Take 100 mg every day, along with a B-complex supplement.

(The reason for the B-complex supplement is that large doses of any one of the B vitamins can result in urinary losses of other B vitamins.)

▶ Bathe the eyes morning and evening in an eyewash made with fennel seed, chamomile or eyebright. (*See* pages 79–80 for instructions on using these eyewashes.)

**CAUTION:** Be careful putting any foreign substance or liquid in the eye. It can be painful and may cause infection.

## Night Vision

▶ Eat blueberries when they're in season. They can help restore night vision.

▶ You know the old joke about carrots being good for your eyes? Well, you've never seen a rabbit wearing glasses. Eat two or three carrots a day (raw or cooked) and/or drink a glass of fresh carrot juice. It's excellent for alleviating night blindness.

▶ Eat more watercress in salads and/or drink watercress tea.

## Sties

If you have a painful red bump on your eyelid, then the sty's the limit! A sty occurs when the

### ■ Recipe ■

### Chilled Czech Blueberry Soup

> 3 cups blueberries
> 4 cups water
> Pinch of salt
> ¼ tsp cinnamon
> 1 Tbsp granulated sugar
> 1½ cups sour cream
> 6 Tbsp flour

Boil 2 cups of the blueberries in the water. Stir in salt, cinnamon and sugar. Remove from heat.

Whip flour into the sour cream, then whip both into the hot liquid. When well blended, return the pot to the heat and bring to a boil. Reduce heat and stir until thickened.

Remove from heat, stir in another ½ cup of blueberries and refrigerate.

When ready to serve, stir in the remaining ½ cup of blueberries and ladle into bowls.

*Source: www.recipegoldmine.com*

oil glands around the eyelid get infected and inflamed. Some natural remedies may help relieve the discomfort.

▶ Place a handful of fresh parsley in a soup bowl. Pour a cup of boiling water over the parsley and let it steep for 10 minutes. Soak a clean washcloth in the hot parsley water, lie down, put the cloth on your closed lids and relax for 15 minutes. Repeat the procedure before bedtime. Parsley water is also good for eliminating puffiness around the eyes.

▶ Moisten a regular (nonherbal) tea bag, put it on the closed eye with the sty, bandage it in place and leave it there for as long as possible. Hopefully, soon enough it will be "bye-bye sty."

### Go for the Gold

▶ Rub the sty three times with a gold wedding ring. When we started compiling information for this book, we decided not to use any silly-sounding, superstition-based remedies. This remedy for sties, however, comes from so many reputable sources that it must have some credibility.

Fortunately for us, but unfortunately for research purposes, neither of us has had a sty since we began working on this book, so we haven't been able to test the wedding-ring remedy ourselves.

### Banish Sties with Bancha

▶ Roasted-bancha leaves are used to make a popular Japanese tea—these tea bags are available at most US health food stores. Steep a tea bag in hot water for 10 minutes and add 1 teaspoon of sea salt (also available at health food stores as well as supermarkets). Saturate a cotton pad in the lukewarm liquid and apply it to your closed eye, keeping it there for 10 minutes at a time, three times a day.

▶ In addition to—or instead of—the roasted-blancha tea bag remedy, dab on some castor oil several times throughout the day until the sty disappears.

### Sty Prevention

▶ Lydia went to school with a girl named Madeline whose nickname was "Sty." She always seemed to have a sty coming or going.

If you're like Madeline and are prone to sties, prepare a strong cup of burdock-seed tea every morning and take 1 tablespoon before each meal and 1 tablespoon at bedtime.

## Sun Blindness

Sun blindness is caused by exposure to large expanses of snow or ice for a considerable length of time.

▶ **CAUTION:** Sun blindness is a serious condition that can lead to cataracts and retinal damage. It should be prevented by wearing protective sunglasses or goggles.

▶ Skiers find this remedy helpful in coping with large expanses of blinding, white snow. Eat a handful of sunflower seeds every day. (Buy them shelled, raw and unsalted.)

Within no time, the eyes may have a much easier time adjusting to the brightness of the snow, thanks to the sunflower seeds…and a good pair of sunglasses or goggles.

## Eye Strengtheners

▶ Apply cold water on a washcloth to the eyelids, eyebrows and temples each morning, noon and night, five to 10 minutes at a time.

### Get a Rosy Outlook

▶ Throw a handful of rose petals (the petals are more potent as the flower fades) into a pot and cover with water. Put it over a medium flame. When the water boils, take the pot off the flame and let it cool. Then strain the water into a bottle and close it tightly.

When your eyes feel tired and weak and appear red, treat them with the rose petal water. Pour the liquid on a washcloth or cotton pads and keep them on your closed eyes for 15 to 30 minutes. Your outlook might be a lot rosier.

▶ This is an interesting way to end the day. Prepare a candle, a straight-back chair and a five-minute timer. Light the candle and place it 1½ feet from the chair. Then sit in the chair, with your feet uncrossed and flat on the floor. The lit candle should be level with the top of your head.

Set the timer for five minutes. Then, using your index fingers, hold your eyelids open while you stare at the candle without blinking. There will be some tears. Do not wipe them away. Tough out the five minutes every other night for two weeks. Then discontinue the exercise for two weeks. Then start the exercise again, every other night for two weeks.

Once your vision is sufficiently strengthened, blow out the candle for good.

## Vision Improvers

▶ You know all the talk about carrots being good for your eyes? They are! Drink 5 to 6 ounces of fresh carrot juice twice a day for at least two weeks. Obviously, you will need a juicer or access to a juice bar. After the two weeks, ease off to one glass of carrot juice a day…forever!

☛ **WARNING:** If you have a Candida/yeast problem, skip the carrot juice. Its high sugar content can contribute to this condition.

▶ According to the late J.I. Rodale, organic-farming pioneer and founder of *Prevention* magazine, sunflower seeds are a miracle food. We agree. Eat a handful (shelled, raw and unsalted) every day.

## Eye, Eye Matey

▶ We've heard that wearing a gold earring in your left ear improves and preserves one's eyesight, but we thought it was a useless superstition.

Then we read in David Louis's book, *2201 Fascinating Facts* (Greenwich House) that

### ■ Recipe ■

#### Lemon–Parsley Carrots

1 lb carrots sliced ¼-inch thick
(about 3 cups)
2 Tbsp water
2 Tbsp butter or margarine
1 Tbsp granulated sugar
1 Tbsp parsley, freshly chopped
½ tsp lemon peel, grated
2 tsp lemon juice
¼ tsp salt

Place carrots and water in a 2-quart covered glass casserole. Microwave, covered, at 100% power (700 watts) for 8 to 9 minutes until crisp-tender, stirring once after 5 minutes. Drain. Stir in butter, sugar, parsley, lemon peel and juice, and salt. Microwave, covered, at 100% power for 1 to 1½ minutes until heated through.

Makes 4 servings.

*Source: www.recipegoldmine.com*

pirates believed that piercing their ears and wearing earrings improved their eyesight—and the swashbucklers may have been right.

The idea, which had been scoffed at for centuries, has been reevaluated in light of recent acupuncture theory, which holds that the point of the lobe where the ear is pierced is the same acupuncture point that controls the eyes.

Hmmmm. Get out the gold earrings.

### Palm Power

▶ We've thoroughly researched "palming" and no two of our resources agree on the procedure. We'll give you a couple of variations. Test them and see what works for you.

Sit. (They all agree on that.) Rub your hands together until you feel heat. Place your elbows on the table in front of you, then put the heels of your hands over your eyes, blocking out all light. Some feel it's better to keep one's eyes open in the dark while others advocate closed eyes. The length of time to sit this way also ranges—from two minutes to 10 minutes.

"Palming" is beneficial for improving vision, for nearsightedness, tired eyes, astigmatism and inflammation…and it may even help squinters stop squinting.

## Eyeglass Cleaners

▶ To avoid streaks on your eyeglass lenses, clean them with a lint-free cloth and a touch of vinegar or vodka.

## Eyewashes

Commercial eyedrops eliminate the redness because of a decongestant that constricts the blood vessels. Using these drops on a regular basis can worsen the problem. The blood vessels will enlarge again in less and less time. Make your own eyedrops from the following herbs, or just bathe your eyes with these eyewashes.

 **NOTE:** It's important to make sure that all the ingredients are hygienic—boiled and/or sterilized.

### Eyebright

▶ To make an eyebright eyewash, add 1 ounce of the whole dried herb eyebright to 1 pint of boiling-hot water and let it steep for 10 minutes. Strain the mixture thoroughly through a superfine strainer or through unbleached muslin. Wait until it's cool enough to use.

▶ Add 3 drops of tincture of eyebright to a tablespoon of boiled water and wait until it's cool enough to use.

### Chamomile

▶ Add 1 teaspoon of dried chamomile flowers to 1 cup of just-boiled water. Steep for five minutes and strain the mixture thoroughly through a superfine strainer or through unbleached muslin. Wait until it's cool enough to use.

▶ Add 12 drops of tincture of chamomile to 1 cup of boiling-hot water. Wait until it's cool enough to use.

### Fennel Seeds

▶ Add 1 teaspoon of crushed fennel seeds to 1 cup of boiling-hot water. Steep for five minutes and strain the mixture thoroughly through a superfine strainer or through unbleached muslin. Wait until it's cool enough to use.

## Red (Eye) Alert

If you use artificial tears, *do not* use any product that also "gets the red out." When your eyes are red or bloodshot, it's because there's a problem. Your body's way of handling the problem is by enlarging the delicate veins or blood vessels in your eyes. The eye drops that "get the red out" are vasoconstrictors that shrink those veins so that they're not visible. This is not a good thing and is only a temporary masking of the problem.

Also, your eyes can become dependent on those drops and, when you stop using them, the problem will worsen and the blood vessels in your eyes will be more dilated than before.

When you use artificial tears, make sure the box says *preservative-free* or *non-preserved*. Preservatives in artificial tears can be harmful to your eyes.

### Carrots

▶ Carefully wash a bunch of carrots and cut off the tops. Place a handful of the clean carrot tops in a jar of distilled hot water. Let it stand. When it's cool, use the carrot water as an eyewash.

You can also drink the remaining liquid. This drink should help your eyes and also help strengthen your kidneys and bladder. (*See* recipe on page 78.)

▶ Mix 1 drop of lemon juice in 1 ounce of warm distilled water and use it as an eyewash. It's particularly effective when your eyes have been exposed to dust, cigarette smoke, harsh lights and chemical compounds in the air.

### Eyewash Directions

 **NOTE:** Always remove contact lenses before doing an eyewash.

You'll need an eye cup (available at drugstores). Carefully pour boiling water over the cup to sterilize it. Without contaminating the rim or inside surfaces of the cup, fill it half full with whichever eyewash you've selected.

Lean forward, apply the cup tightly to the eye to prevent spillage, then tilt your head backward. Open your eye wide and rotate your eyeball to thoroughly wash the eye.

Lean over again and remove the cup. Clean the cup again, and use the same procedure with the other eye.

# FAINTING

**W**hen you feel dizzy and light-headed as though you're going to faint, lie down. If possible, lie with your feet and torso elevated so that your head is lower than your heart. That's the secret of preventing a faint—getting your head lower than your heart so that blood can rush to your brain.

## Natural Remedies

▶ In India, instead of smelling salts, people take a couple of strong whiffs of half an onion to bring them around.

▶ If you're in a very warm room that's making you feel faint, just run cold tap water over the insides of your wrists. If there are ice cubes around, rub them on your wrists. Relief is almost immediate.

▶ A friend of ours is a paramedic. When one of her patients is about to faint, she pinches the patient's philtrum—the fleshy part between the upper lip and nose. That may help to prevent the faint from happening.

▶ If you're prone to fainting spells—a case of the vapors, perhaps—keep pepper handy. Sniff a grain or two and sneeze. The sneeze stimulates the brain's blood vessels and may help prevent fainting. It's good to remember, since not many households have smelling salts, but just about all have black pepper.

▶ Check your eating habits. Are you eating regularly at mealtimes? Are you eating good, wholesome meals with a sufficient amount of protein, and without an excess of sweets and refined foods? Sometimes low blood sugar or a poor diet can cause a person to faint.

**CAUTION:** If you faint and don't know why, consult a doctor. Fainting can be a symptom of an ailment that needs medical attention.

# FATIGUE

**I**f you're sick and tired of being tired, then you need to figure out the reason for your fatigue. Too many late nights at the office? A crying baby? Poor diet? Check in with your doctor to make sure there's not a medical condition causing your fatigue. Once you get a clean bill of health, try these remedies to help you perk up.

## Natural Remedies

▶ We've read case histories in which, within a few weeks, the intake of bee pollen not only increased a person's physical energy, but restored mental alertness and eliminated lapses of memory and confusion.

*Suggested dosage:* Take 1 teaspoon of granular bee pollen after breakfast, or two 500 mg bee pollen pills after breakfast. (Read more about bee pollen in the "Six Sensational Superfoods" section on page 258.)

Start by taking just a few granules of bee pollen each day to make sure you have no allergic reaction to it. If all is well after three days, increase the amount to ¼ teaspoon every day. Gradually, over the next month or two, work your way up to 3 teaspoons of bee pollen taken throughout the day.

▶ If you're tired the second you wake up in the morning, try this Vermont tonic—in a blender, put 1 cup of warm water, 2 tablespoons of apple cider vinegar and 1 teaspoon of honey. Blend thoroughly, then sip it slowly until it's all gone. Have this tonic every morning before breakfast and, within days, you may feel a difference in your energy level.

> **WARNING:** People who are allergic to bee stings should consult a doctor before taking bee pollen.
> In addition, infants, diabetics and people who are allergic to honey should not use any remedies that contain honey.

▶ A quick picker-upper is ⅛ teaspoon of cayenne pepper in a cup of water. Drink it down and get a second wind.

▶ If you're suffering from mental fatigue, try this Austrian recipe—thoroughly wash an apple, cut it into small pieces, leaving the peel on and place the pieces in a bowl. Pour 2 cups of boiling water over the apple and let it steep for an hour. Then add 1 tablespoon of honey. Drink the apple/honey water and eat the pieces of apple.

## Take Off Your Shoes

▶ If possible, walk barefoot in dewy grass—just watch out for critters! The next best thing is to carefully walk up and back in six inches of cold bathwater. Do it for five to 10 minutes twice a day—in the morning and late afternoon.

▶ If you have a bad case of the drowsies, puncture a garlic pearle (soft gel) or cut a garlic clove in half, and take a few deep whiffs. That ought to wake you up.

# Energy Boosters

▶ A Chinese theory is that "tiredness" collects on the insides of one's elbows and the backs of one's knees. Wake up your body by slap-slap-slapping both those areas.

▶ You don't have to depend on caffeine to stay awake. Mix 1 teaspoon of cayenne pepper to 1 quart of juice—any kind of juice with no sugar or preservatives added. Throughout a long drive, or a night of cramming, as soon as you feel sleep overcoming you, take a cup of the cayenne-laced juice to keep awake and alert.

▶ Tough day at the office? Need to get that second wind? Ready for a drink? Tired of all these questions? Add 1 tablespoon of blackstrap molasses to a glass of milk (regular, skim, soy or rice milk) and bottoms up.

## Reach for the Sky

▶ Call on your imagination for this visualization exercise. Sit up with your arms over your head and your palms facing the ceiling. With your right hand, pluck a fistful of vitality out of the air. Next, let your left hand grab its share. Open both hands, allowing all that energy to flow down your arms to your neck, shoulders and chest.

Start over again. This time, when you open your hands, let the energy flow straight down to your waist, hips, thighs, legs, feet and toes. There! You've revitalized your body. Now stand up feeling refreshed.

### Get Figgy with It

▶ A bunch of grapes can give you a bunch of energy. But grapes may be too perishable for you to carry around. If so, try dried figs. They sure can pack an energy punch! They're delicious, satisfying, have more potassium than bananas, more calcium than milk, have a very high dietary fiber content and no cholesterol, fat or sodium.

Most important, figs have easily digestible, natural, slow-burning sugars that will get you going and keep you going, unlike the quick-fix, fast-crash processed sugar in junk food.

Herbalist Lalitha Thomas, who lists figs as one of the *10 Essential Foods* (in her book of the same name, published by Hohm Press), recommends making a serious effort to get unsulfured figs. Eat a few at a time—but don't overdo it. Figs are also known to help prevent or relieve constipation.

▶ When you just can't keep your eyes open or your head up and you don't know how you'll make it to the end of the workday, run away from it all. Go to the bathroom or a secluded spot and run in place. Run for two minutes—this should help you keep going the rest of the day.

### Three Cheers for Chia

▶ According to a study of American Indians, a pinch of chia seeds helped the braves brave their arduous round-the-clock days of hunting.

Ground chia seeds, available at health food stores, can be sprinkled on salads or in soup for those on-the-go, around-the-clock days when stamina counts.

### Start Your Day the Energy Way

▶ Wake up your metabolism in the morning by squeezing the juice of half a grapefruit into a glass. Fill the rest of the glass with warm water. Drink it slowly, then eat the fruit of the squeezed-out half grapefruit. Now that your thyroid is activated, have a productive day!

⚡ **CAUTION:** Grapefruit can interfere with some prescription medications. Be sure to check with your doctor before trying this remedy.

▶ If, after a full night's sleep, you get up feeling sluggish, it may be due to a tired liver. Stand up. Place your right hand above your waist, on the bottom of your ribs on your right side, with your fingers apart, pointing toward your left side. Place your left hand the same way on your left side. Ready?

You press your right hand in, then bring it back in place. You press your left hand in, then bring it back in place. You do the Hokey-Pokey and you turn your—no! Sorry…we got carried away.

Press your right hand in, then bring it back in place. Press your left hand in, then bring it back in place. Do it a dozen times on each side when you get up each morning. In a couple of weeks, this liver massage may make a big difference in your daily energy level.

▶ Cutting out heavy starches and sweets from your diet can also go a long way in adding to your get-up-and-go.

## FOOT AND LEG PROBLEMS

Our feet carry a lot of weight and are probably the most abused and neglected part of our anatomy. They get cold, they get frostbitten, they get wet, they burn, they blister, they itch and they sweat…as we walk, jog, run, dance, climb, skate, ski, hop, skip and jump. Also, at some time or other, we're all guilty of the Cinderella Stepsister Syndrome—pushing our feet into ill-fitting shoes.

We put our poor, tired tootsies under all kinds of stress and strain. And then we wonder why our feet are "just killing us!" Well, we killed them first.

**CAUTION:** If you have circulation problems or diabetes, do not use any of these remedies without the approval and supervision of your health professional.

Let's get to the bottom of our troubles with some remedies for the feet…

## Aching Feet

▶ During a busy day when your "dogs are barking" and you feel like you're going to have to call it quits, cayenne pepper comes to the rescue! Sprinkle some cayenne into your socks or rub it directly on the soles of your aching feet. Now get going or you'll be late for your next appointment!

▶ After a long day, when your nerves are on edge, your feet hurt and you're tired—too tired to go to sleep—soak your feet in hot water for 10 to 15 minutes. Then (and this is the important part) massage your feet with lemon juice.

After you've done a thorough job of massaging, rinse your feet with cool water. As always, dry your feet completely, then take five deep breaths. You and your pain-free feet should be ready and able to settle down for a good night's sleep.

### Super Soaker

▶ This remedy requires two basins or dishpans or four plastic shoe boxes. Fill one basin (or two shoe boxes) with ½ cup Epsom salts and about 1 gallon of hot (not scalding) water. Fill the other basin (or the other two shoe boxes) with ice cubes. Sit down with a watch or timer. Put your feet in the hot water for one minute and then in the ice cubes for 30 seconds.

Alternate back and forth for about 10 minutes. Your feet will feel better. This procedure also helps regulate high blood pressure and may prevent varicose veins, improve circulation and, if done on a regular basis, relieve chronic "cold feet."

*Modified version:* Stand in the bathtub and first let hot water run on your feet for one minute, then let ice-cold water run on your feet for 30 seconds, alternating the hot/cold water for a total of 10 minutes.

*Do not exceed one minute of hot or cold water on your feet!*

▶ Add 1 cup of apple cider vinegar to a basin (or two plastic shoe boxes) filled halfway with lukewarm water. Then soak your feet for at least 15 minutes. The heat and hurt should be gone by then.

▶ Boil or roast a large turnip until it's soft. Then mash it and spread half of it on a white cotton handkerchief. Spread the other half on another handkerchief. Apply the turnip mush to the bottoms of your bare feet, bandage them in place and sit with your feet elevated for about half an hour. This "sole food" should draw out the pain and tiredness.

## Corns and Calluses

Believe us, this is a type of corn you really don't want to eat!

Corns are hard, thick layers of skin that form on the top or side of a toe—calluses form on the soles of your feet. Neither is a serious condition, but you'll probably be more comfortable if you get rid of the shoes (or whatever else) that are causing the friction that leads to corns and calluses.

These remedies should help, too.

▶ You can soften your calluses by applying any of the following oils—wheat germ oil, castor oil, sesame seed oil or olive oil. Apply the oil as often as possible throughout the day, day after day.

▶ Walking barefoot in the sand, particularly wet sand, is wonderful for your feet. It acts as an abrasive and sloughs off the dead skin that leads to corns and calluses.

▶ If you're not near the beach, add 1 tablespoon of baking soda to a basin or to two plastic shoe boxes filled halfway with lukewarm water…and soak your feet for 15 minutes. Then take a pumice stone (available at health food stores and pharmacies) and carefully file away the tough skin.

### Foot Salad

▶ Cut an onion in half—the size of the onion should be determined by the size of the callused area the onion's surface has to cover. Let the onion halves soak in wine vinegar for four hours, then take the onion halves and apply them to the calluses. Bind them in place with plastic wrap, put on socks and leave them on overnight.

The next morning, you should be able to scrape away the calluses. Be sure to wash and rinse your feet thoroughly to get rid of the onion/vinegar smell.

### Corn Remedies

The difference between an oak tree and a tight shoe is that one makes acorns, the other makes corns ache. *What to do for those aching corns…*

▶ Rub castor oil on the corn twice a day and it will gradually peel off, leaving you with soft, smooth skin.

▶ Every night, put one piece of fresh lemon peel on the corn (the inside of the peel on the outside of the corn). Put a bandage around it to keep it in place. In a matter of days, the corn should be gone.

▶ Make a poultice (*see* "Preparation Guide" on page 252) of one crumbled piece of bread soaked in ¼ cup of vinegar. Let it stand for a half-hour, then apply it to the corn and tape it in place overnight. By morning, the corn should peel off. If it's a particularly stubborn corn, you may have to reapply the bread/vinegar poultice a few nights in a row.

### Fresh Fruit for the Feet

▶ Every day, wrap a strip of fresh pineapple peel around the corn (the inside of the peel taped directly on the corn). Within a week, the corn should disappear, thanks to the enzymes and acid content of the fresh pineapple.

▶ Don't throw away used tea bags. Tape a moist one on the corn for a half-hour each day and the corn should be gone in a week or two.

▶ To ease the pain of a corn, soak the feet in oatmeal water. Bring 5 quarts (20 cups) of water to a boil and add 5 ounces of oatmeal. Keep boiling until the water boils down to about 4 quarts. Then pour off the clear water through a strainer, into a large enough basin for your feet, or into two plastic shoe boxes. Soak your feet for at least 20 minutes.

▶ Make a paste out of 1 teaspoon of brewer's yeast and a few drops of lemon juice. Spread the mixture on a cotton pad and apply it to the corn, binding it in place and leaving it overnight. Change the dressing daily until the corn is gone.

▶ A paste of powdered chalk and water should also take care of the corn.

### Corn Cures from Afar

▶ A Hawaiian medicine man recommends pure papaya juice on a cotton pad, or a piece of papaya pulp directly on the corn. Bind in place and leave it on overnight. Change daily until the corn is gone.

▶ Australian shepherds squeeze the juice from the stems of dandelions and apply it to the corn every day until it disappears, usually within a week or so.

## Cold Feet

▶ If you can't get inside to warm up, then stand on your toes for a couple of minutes, then quickly come back down on your heels. Repeat the toes/heels maneuver several times until your blood tingles through your feet and warms them up.

▶ Before going to bed, walk in cold water in the bathtub for two minutes. Then briskly rub the feet dry with a coarse towel. To give the feet a warm glow, hold each end of the towel and run it back and forth along your feet's arches.

### Spice Up Your Feet

▶ If the thought of putting cold feet into cold water is not appealing to you…add 1 cup of table salt to a bathtub that is filled ankle-high with hot water, and soak your feet for 15 minutes. Dry the feet and then massage them with damp salt.

This will remove dead skin and stimulate circulation. After you've massaged each foot for three to five minutes, rinse them in lukewarm water and dry thoroughly.

▶ Warm your feet by sprinkling black pepper or cayenne pepper into your socks before putting them on. It's an old skier's trick, but you don't have to be an old skier to do it. If you use cayenne, your socks and feet will turn red.

Your feet will be fine, but your socks may never be the same again.

Also, if you're at a restaurant and the meal is too bland, you can always take off a sock and season the food to taste.

## Athlete's Foot

▶ The fungus that causes athlete's foot dies in natural sunlight. So, spend two weeks barefoot in the Bahamas. If that's a bit impractical, then for one hour a day, expose your feet to sunlight. It might eliminate a mild case of athlete's foot.

▶ In between sunbaths, keep the feet well aired by wearing loose-fitting socks.

▶ At night, apply rubbing alcohol (it stings for a couple of seconds), then wait until your feet are completely dry and sprinkle them with talcum powder (the unscented kind is preferable).

▶ Apply one clove of crushed garlic to the affected area. Leave it on for a half-hour, then wash with water. If you do this once a day, within a week, you'll be smelling like a salami, but you may not have athlete's foot.

☞ **WARNING:** When you first apply the garlic, there will be a sensation of warmth. If, after a few minutes, that warm feeling intensifies and the garlic starts to burn, wash the area with cool water. The next day, dilute the garlic juice with plain water and try again.

### Sweet Feet

▶ Every evening, apply cotton or cheesecloth that has been saturated with honey to the infected area. Tape it in place. To avoid a gooey mess (a possibility even with the tape in place), wear socks to bed.

In the morning, wash with water, dry thoroughly and sprinkle them with talcum powder (preferably unscented).

▶ Grate an onion and squeeze it through cheesecloth to get onion juice. Massage the juice into the fungus-infected areas of your foot.

Leave it on for 10 minutes, then rinse your foot in lukewarm water and *dry it thoroughly* (fungi thrive in moist conditions). Repeat this procedure three times a day until the condition clears up.

▶ To avoid reinfecting yourself with athlete's foot, soak your socks and pantyhose in white vinegar. Also wipe out your shoes with vinegar.

The smell of vinegar will vanish after being exposed to the air for about 15 minutes.

## Ingrown Toenails

We were surprised to learn that a tendency toward ingrown toenails is inherited. If the toe is red, swollen and/or painful, see a doctor.

▶ If you have an ingrown toenail, relieve the pain with a footbath. In a plastic shoe box, add ½ ounce of comfrey root to ½ gallon (2 quarts) of warm water. Soak your foot in it for 20 minutes.

Once the nail is softened from soaking, take a piece of absorbent cotton and twist it so that it's like a thick strand of thread. Or twist together a few strands of unwaxed dental floss. Gently wedge the "thread" under the corner of the nail. That should prevent the nail from cutting into the skin. Replace the strands a couple of times a day, every day, until the nail grows out.

Once it grows out, the nail should be cut straight across, not down into the corners, and not shorter than the toe. You might want to have a podiatrist trim the toenail properly. Pay careful attention so you'll be able to take care of your toes yourself and avoid another ingrown nail (and another podiatrist bill).

## Pigeon Toes

▶ If you are slightly pigeon-toed and an orthopedist hasn't helped you...as a last resort, buy a pair of shoes one size larger than you usually take. Wear them to bed every night with the right shoe on the left foot and the left shoe on the right foot. Give it a month to get results.

## Cracked Heels

▶ Before bedtime, wash your feet with warm water and dry them. Liberally apply petroleum jelly on your feet, massaging it into the rough and cracked areas. Wrap each foot with plastic wrap. Put socks on and sleep that way. Repeat the process nightly until your feet are fine. It shouldn't take more than a week...probably less.

## Sweaty Feet

The average pair of feet gives off about ½ pint of perspiration daily. It's amazing we don't all slosh around. *Well, for those of you who feel like you do...*

▶ Put some bran or uncooked oat flakes into your socks. It should absorb the sweat and make you feel more comfortable. Start conservatively, with about 1 tablespoon in each sock. Add more if needed.

## Numb Toes

▶ Daily doses of vitamin $B_6$ and B-complex have been known to eliminate tingling and numbness in toes.

⚡ **CAUTION:** Check the amount of $B_6$ in the B-complex—high doses can be toxic. Check with your naturopathic doctor.

## Varicose Veins

The word *varicose* comes from the Latin word *varix*, which means "twisted." When the little veins in your legs start looking like squiggly worms, you might wish those old Romans had picked another word.

We hope these remedies bring some relief to whatever discomfort or swelling your veins are causing.

▶ Folk medicine practitioners throughout Europe have been known to help shrink varicose veins by recommending the application of apple cider vinegar.

Once every morning and once every evening, soak a cheesecloth bandage in the vinegar and wrap it around the affected area. Lie down, raise your legs and relax that way for at least a half-hour. (This will benefit more than just your varicose vein condition!)

After each vinegar-wrap session, drink 2 teaspoons of the vinegar in a cup of warm water. The practitioners tell us that by the end of one month, the veins shrink enough for there to be a noticeable difference.

## Easy Ways to Ease the Veins

**H**eed these simple suggestions to keep varicose veins from getting worse...

◆ Keep your feet elevated as much as possible. It's ideal to elevate your legs at or above the level of your heart for 20 minutes a few times every day.

◆ Never sit with your legs crossed.

◆ Don't wear knee-high stockings or tight socks.

◆ Wear flats or very low heels, not high heels.

◆ If you're overweight, do your legs a favor and lose those extra pounds.

◆ Exercise. Just walking a half-hour every day will help with circulation.

▶ In between the vinegar wraps, don't forget to sit properly. You may be surprised to know that you can stop varicose veins from getting worse simply by fixing the way you sit.

*Never* sit with your legs crossed. In a relaxed way, keep your knees and ankles together and slightly slant your legs. It's graceful-looking and doesn't add to the congestion that promotes varicose veins.

## Natural Remedies

Here are some suggestions that may help improve the condition of your varicose veins.

▶ Take vitamin C with bioflavonoids daily. Herbs may also be very helpful, particularly butcher's broom, horse chestnut and hawthorn. You can find them in health food stores. Follow the recommended dosage on the label.

▶ Take 1 bilberry capsule (80 mg) and 1 bromelain capsule (500 to 1,000 mg) with each meal. Once a day, take 1 capsule (150 mg) of butcher's broom. All are available at health food stores.

These herbs have many wonderful benefits, including improving your blood circulation and helping the walls of your veins maintain their shape.

▶ Reduce the swelling and constriction of varicose veins by wrapping a cheesecloth bandage soaked in witch hazel around the affected area. Lie down, raise your legs and relax.

▶ At the end of every day, stand in a tub filled with cold water. (The water should be up to your knees.) After two or three minutes, dry your legs thoroughly with a coarse towel, then walk around at a brisk pace for two or three minutes.

▶ Take horse chestnut capsules (which are available at health food stores), 300 mg, once or twice a day.

## Phlebitis

▶ If you know you have superficial varicose vein inflammation (superficial thrombophlebitis), usually in the leg—chances are that you are under a doctor's care and should be.

You probably developed this type of inflammation because you were recovering from childbirth, surgery or were somehow incapacitated and inactive for a long period of time. This inactivity decreased the blood flow in your veins and allowed clots to form. Blood clots are potentially very dangerous.

After the acute care has been medically completed, pay strict attention to optimal diet, optimal bowel function, optimal weight and exercise and meticulous body hygiene—nose, ears, mouth, tongue and gums, fingernails,

## ■ Recipe ■

### Broccoli Slaw

4 broccoli stems, washed and peeled

6" piece of daikon radish, peeled

2 large carrots, peeled

½ bunch green onions, chopped

2 kiwis, peeled and diced

2 Tbsp pine nuts, toasted

2 cloves garlic, minced

1 tsp salt

¼ tsp ground black pepper

2 Tbsp organic canola oil

Black sesame seeds

Coarsely grate the broccoli stems, daikon radish and carrots, and put them into a bowl.

Add green onions, kiwis, pine nuts, garlic, salt, pepper and canola oil to bowl and toss together. Adjust seasoning to taste, and transfer to a serving bowl.

Garnish with a generous sprinkling of black sesame seeds. This slaw tastes best when made 3–4 hours ahead. Use as a side dish.

Makes 6–8 servings.

*Source: www.vegparadise.com*

legs, feet, toes, toenails, scrotum or vulva—to prevent complications and recurrence.

## Natural Remedies

Herbs that assist in vein health include butcher's broom, hawthorn and horse chestnut. All are available at health food stores. Follow the recommended dosage on the label.

And be sure to check with your doctor about the following suggestions.

▶ Apply a comfrey poultice on the outside of the affected area. (*See* "Preparation Guide" on page 252.)

▶ You should be eating a raw vegetable diet. It's important to have leafy greens, plus lots more roughage.

▶ Drink lots of fresh juices.

▶ Take 1 tablespoon of lecithin every day.

▶ Follow your physician's instructions and elevate the affected area for as many hours a day as possible. This will keep the blood circulating properly.

## Weak Ankles

This exercise will promote toe flexibility and strengthen the arches as well as the ankles.

▶ Get a dozen marbles and a plastic cup. Put them all on the floor. Sit down and then pick up each marble with the toes of your right foot—one by one, drop them in the cup. Then do the same with the toes of your left foot.

You may want to add to the fun by timing yourself and seeing if you can keep breaking your previous record. Whatever happens, try not to lose your marbles.

## FROSTBITE/FROSTNIP

Frostbite occurs when the skin of a person's extremities (usually hands, feet and nose) has been exposed to cold temperatures for too long. If the skin is cold, pale or numb, there may be frostbite.

The extent of frostbite varies greatly, depending on the length of time a person has been exposed to the cold…the intensity of the cold, humidity and winds…the kinds and amount of clothing worn…a person's natural resistance to cold…as well as his/her general state of health. The minor chilling of skin is usually considered "frostnip."

**CAUTION:** People with circulation problems, vascular disease, diabetes and other conditions where blood flow is compromised should do everything possible to prevent frostbite. Bundle up and stay dry!

One big problem with frostbite is that it's hard to know you have it until it's already on its way to being serious.

At some ski resorts, the ski patrol does occasional nose-and-cheek checks of skiers. Thanks to those checks, lots of mild frostbite victims are sent indoors to defrost.

**CAUTION:** Seriously frostbitten victims should be placed under a doctor's care and/or hospitalized immediately.

Be sure the frostbite sufferer is in a warm room while waiting for medical help. If the person is conscious, give him or her a warm drink. Do not give alcoholic beverages! They can worsen the condition.

The frozen body parts must be warmed immediately. Be careful, when touching the skin, not to break the frostbite blisters. Cover the frostbitten areas with a blanket. Call 911 and get medical treatment as soon as possible.

For mild cases of frostnip, the following remedies are worth a try…

▶ Get inside to warm up, then steep a teaspoon of sage in a cup of hot water for five minutes and drink it. Sage tea will help improve circulation.

▶ Warm some olive oil and gently dab it on the chilled skin or apply it with a kitchen pastry brush.

▶ If you have an aloe vera plant or bottled aloe vera gel, gently apply it to the chilled area.

▶ Boil and mash potatoes. Add salt and apply the mixture to the chilled areas.

# GALLBLADDER PROBLEMS

The gallbladder is the liver's companion and assistant. Its job is to store bile produced by the liver, then release it to dissolve fats. Your job is to keep the gallbladder healthy and functioning. *These remedies may help…*

**CAUTION:** Pain and/or vomiting can be signs of a serious illness. See a doctor before trying any of these natural remedies.

## Natural Remedies

▶ An inflamed, irritated or clogged gallbladder can be very painful and make you feel sluggish and tired, even when you first wake up in the morning. Take 3 tablespoons of fresh lemon juice in half a glass of warm water, a half-hour before breakfast. Try this for one week and see if there's a difference in your morning energy level. Lemon juice is known to stimulate and cleanse the gallbladder.

▶ The most popular folk remedy for the gallbladder is black radish. Juice the radish either with a juice extractor or by grating the radish and squeezing it through cheesecloth. Take 1 to 2 tablespoons of black radish juice before each meal. Do it for two weeks or more. Your digestion should improve and so should the condition of your gallbladder.

▶ If you have had gallbladder surgery, you may help the healing process by drinking peppermint tea—1 cup one hour after eating each of the two biggest meals of the day. Menthol, the active ingredient in peppermint, gives the liver and gallbladder a workout by stimulating bile secretion.

# GOUT

Isn't it amazing how much pain you can have from one toe? Gout comes on suddenly, but you know it when you have it. Caused by a build-up of uric acid in the joints, it usually settles in a person's big toe. Gout is extremely painful, but also extremely treatable. Be sure to see a doctor for an evaluation and diagnosis. Severe gout conditions can be very serious.

If you have gout, you probably know it's time to change your diet. Once known as "the disease of kings," it's often brought on by a steady diet of rich foods like red meat, wine, cream sauces and sweets. The closer you stick to vegetarian cuisine, the faster the gout will go. You can eat some fish and lean chicken now and then, but stay away from red meat for a while. Also, avoid alcohol and eliminate sugar and white flour from your diet. You may start feeling so good that you'll never want to go back to consuming those things.

## Best Remedy

### It's the Cherries

The one remedy that everyone seems to agree is very effective—cherries! Eat them fresh or frozen. Also, drink cherry juice daily. You can get pure juice (concentrate) at health food stores. (*See* the recipe on page 93.)

## Other Remedies

▶ Soak your gouty foot in comfrey tea (*see* "Preparation Guide" on page 250).

▶ A Russian remedy is raw garlic—two cloves a day. The best way to take raw garlic is to mince the cloves, put them in water (better yet, in cherry juice) and drink them down. Chewing is not necessary. The garlic will not linger on your breath. It may repeat on you— but then, so does a salami sandwich, and this is a lot healthier.

**NOTE:** Eat garlic with a few sprigs of parsley to decrease repeating and smelly breath.

▶ Eating strawberries and very little else for a few days is said to be a possible cure for gout. Strawberries are a powerful alkalizer and contain calcium, iron and an ingredient known as salacin, which soothes inflammatory conditions.

### ■ Recipe ■

#### *Three-Cherry Jam*

2 cups light sweet cherries
2 cups dark sweet cherries
2 cups tart red cherries
6 cups sugar
Juice of 1 lemon

Pit and measure cherries. Grind coarsely. Simmer about 5 minutes to soften skins. Add sugar and juice. Cook until thickened, about 15 to 20 minutes, but no longer than 20 minutes. Skim and pour into hot sterilized jars. Adjust lids at once and process in boiling water bath, 212° F, for 5 minutes. Remove from canner and complete seals, unless closures are self-sealing type.

Makes about 6 pints.

*Source: www.homecooking.about.com*

It worked so well for 18th-century botanist Carl Linnaeus (who developed the modern system for classifying plants) that he referred to strawberries as "a blessing of the gods."

# HAIR PROBLEMS

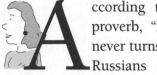

According to a French proverb, "A fool's hair never turns white." The Russians say, "There was never a saint with red hair." According to the German Pennsylvanians, "Pull out a gray hair, and seven will come to its funeral."

The biggest hair worries are having too much or too little. Too much hair, especially in the wrong places, can be permanently removed by electrolysis. It's expensive and painful, but worth every penny and ounce of pain in exchange for a better self-image.

Too little hair, especially in men, is usually hereditary baldness (*alopecia*). If none of the available hair-restoring treatments, including cosmetic surgery (implants and transplants) and the drugs currently on the market are for you, then you may want to try a natural remedy.

People claim that these remedies have stopped the loss of hair as well as restored hair that's already been lost. So they may be worth a try. After all, what do you have to lose—that you aren't already losing?

## Stopping Hair Loss/ Promoting Hair Growth

In an average lifetime, the hair on a person's head grows about 25 feet.

Each of us loses about a hundred hairs a day from our scalp. Mostly, the hairs grow back. When they don't, the hairstyle changes from "parted" or "unparted" to "departed."

Ninety percent of baldness cases can be attributed to hereditary factors. Can something be done to prevent it or overcome it? The people who gave us these remedies say, "Yes!"

▶ An hour before bedtime, slice open a clove of garlic and rub it on the hairless area. An hour later, massage the scalp with olive oil, put on a cap and go to bed. The next morning, shampoo.

Repeat the procedure for a few weeks and, hopefully, hair will have stopped falling out and there will be regrowth showing.

### Fingernail Buffer

▶ Three times a day, five minutes each time, buff your fingernails with your fingernails. Huh? In other words, rub the fingernails of your right hand across the fingernails of your left hand. Not only is it supposed to stop hair loss, it's also supposed to help encourage hair growth and prevent hair from graying.

## Great Hair

Human hair is almost impossible to destroy. Other than its vulnerability to fire, it cannot be destroyed by changes of climate, water or other natural forces. When you think of all the ways some of us abuse our hair—with bleaches, dyes, rubber bands, permanents, mousses, sprays and that greasy kid stuff— you can see how resistant it is to all kinds of corrosive chemicals. No wonder it's always clogging up sinks and drainpipes.

While hair may not be destroyed by this abuse, it may look lifeless and become unmanageable and unhealthy.

One way to tell whether or not hair is healthy is by its stretchability. A strand of adult hair should be able to stretch to 25% of its length without breaking. If it's less elastic than that, it's less than healthy.

▶ Prepare your own hair-growing elixir by combining ¼ cup of onion juice with 1 table-spoon of honey. Massage the scalp with the mixture every day. We heard about a man who had a bottle of this hair tonic. One day, he took the cork out of the bottle with his teeth. The next day, he had a mustache that needed to be trimmed. *But seriously…*

### Russian Hair Restorer

▶ We heard a similar remedy from a man who emigrated to the United States from Russia. He told us that many barbers in the former Soviet Union recommend this to their customers.

Combine 1 tablespoon of honey with 1 jigger of vodka and the juice from a medium-size onion. Rub the mixture into the scalp every night, cover, sleep, awaken, shampoo and rinse.

### Open Sesame

▶ An Asian remedy to stop excessive amounts of hair from falling out is sesame oil. Rub it on your scalp every night. Cover your head with a cap or wrap a dish towel around it. In the morning, wash with an herbal shampoo (available at most stores where shampoo is sold). Your final rinse should be with 1 tablespoon of apple cider vinegar in 1 quart of warm water.

▶ Another version of this nightly/daily treatment calls for equal amounts of olive oil and oil of rosemary. Combine the two in a bottle and shake vigorously. Then massage it into the scalp, cover the head, sleep, awaken, shampoo and rinse.

▶ Yet another version—garlic oil. Puncture a couple of garlic pearles, squish out all the oil and massage it into your scalp. Then follow the routine of covering the head overnight and, in the morning, be sure to shampoo and rinse.

▶ Mix 1 jigger of vodka with ½ teaspoon of cayenne pepper and rub it on the scalp. The blood supply feeds the hair. The vodka and pepper stimulates the blood supply.

▶ And still another version of these massage scalp remedies…take half of a raw onion and massage the scalp with it. It's known to be an effective stimulant. Cover the head overnight, then shampoo and rinse in the morning.

If these remedies don't work, there is a plus side to baldness—it prevents dandruff.

## Natural Remedies
### Dandruff

▶ If you are brunette, wash your hair with a combination of 1 cup of beet juice and 2 cups of water, plus 1 teaspoon of salt. This is an Arabian remedy, and most Arabs have dark hair. Since beets contain a dye, this is not recommended for light-haired people who want to stay that way. To be safe, do a test on a patch of hair.

▶ Squeeze the juice of one large lemon and apply half of it to your hair. Mix the other half with 2 cups of water. Wash your hair with a mild shampoo, then rinse with water. Rinse again with the lemon and water mixture. Repeat these steps every other day until the dandruff disappears.

▶ Massage 4 tablespoons of warm corn oil into your scalp. Wrap a warm, wet towel around your head and leave it there for a half-hour. Shampoo and rinse. Repeat this treatment once a week.

### Good Enough to Eat

▶ Grate a piece of ginger and squeeze it through cheesecloth, collecting the juice. Then mix the ginger juice with an equal amount of sesame oil. Rub the ginger/sesame mixture on the entire scalp, cover the head with a cap or wrap with a dish towel, and sleep with it on.

In the morning, wash with an herbal shampoo (available at most stores where shampoo is sold). The final rinse should be with 1 tablespoon of apple cider vinegar in 1 quart of warm water. Repeat this treatment three or four times a week until the dandruff or other scalp problems vanish.

▶ Prepare chive tea by adding 1 tablespoon of fresh chives to 1 cup of just-boiled water. Cover and let it steep for 20 minutes. Strain and—making sure it's cool—rinse your hair with it right after you shampoo.

### Dry Hair

▶ Shampoo and towel-dry your hair. Then evenly distribute 1 tablespoon of mayonnaise through your hair. (Use more if your hair is long.) Leave the mayonnaise on for an hour, wash hair with a mild shampoo and rinse. The theory is that the flow of oil from the sebaceous glands is encouraged as the natural fatty acids of the mayonnaise help nourish the hair.

### Dull, Permed Hair

▶ After shampooing, rinse with a combination of 1 cup of apple cider vinegar and 2 cups

## Hairy Standing Pose

**D**o not do this exercise if you have high or low blood pressure! Do not do this exercise without your doctor's approval if you are significantly beyond young adulthood!

If you know how to do it properly, stand on your head. If not, then get down on all fours, with your hands about two feet away from your knees. Then carefully lift your rear end in the air so that your legs are straight and your head is between your outstretched arms.

Stay in that position for a minute each day and, after a week, gradually work your way up to five minutes each day. The theory behind this is that you will bring oxygen to the hair follicles, which will rejuvenate the scalp and encourage hair to grow.

of water. Your hair will come alive and shine. This treatment is especially effective on permed hair, but can be used on any lifeless-looking hair.

### Frizzy, Dry Hair

▶ After shampooing, rinse with 1 tablespoon of wheat germ oil, followed by a mixture of ½ cup of apple cider vinegar and 2 cups of water. It will tame the frizzies.

## Remedies for Bad-Hair Days

If your self-esteem is in the cellar and you're feeling less than confident, capable or sociable, it may be because you're having a bad hair day.

The findings of a study conducted at Yale University in New Haven, Connecticut, confirmed the negative effect of a crummy coif on the psyche.

The fascinating aspect of the study was that men were more likely to feel less smart and less capable than women when their hair stuck out, was badly cut or was otherwise a mess.

Here are natural remedies to help you have healthy hair, be the best-tressed person around and boost your self-esteem...

### A Rinse for Shinier Dark Hair

▶ Prepare a rinse in a glass or ceramic bowl. Add 3 tablespoons of either parsley, rosemary or sage (available at health food stores) to 8 cups of just-boiled water. Let it steep until it gets cool. Strain through muslin or a superfine strainer. After shampooing, massage the herb water into your scalp as you rinse with it.

### A Rinse for Shinier Fair Hair

▶ Prepare a rinse in a glass or ceramic bowl. Add 3 tablespoons of either chamomile, calendula or yarrow (available at health food stores) to 8 cups of just-boiled water. Let it steep until it gets cool. Strain through muslin or a superfine strainer. After shampooing, massage the herb water into your scalp as you rinse with it.

### Dry Shampoo

▶ If your home is having plumbing problems, your city is having a water shortage or you just don't feel like washing your hair, you can dry-shampoo it using cornmeal or cornstarch. Sprinkle some on your hair. Then put a piece of cheesecloth or pantyhose on the bristles of a hairbrush and brush your hair with it. The cornmeal/cornstarch will pull out the dust from your hair, and the cloth will absorb the grease.

Shine your hair with a silk scarf, using it as you would a buffing cloth on shoes. After a few minutes of this, if your hair doesn't look clean and shiny, tie the scarf around your head and no one will know the difference.

### Get the Grease Out

▶ Coarse or kosher salt is known to be an effective dry shampoo. Put 1 tablespoon of the salt in aluminum foil and in the oven to warm for five minutes. Using your fingers, work the warm salt into the scalp and throughout the hair.

As soon as you feel that the salt has had a chance to absorb the grease and dislodge the dust, patiently brush it out of your hair. Wash the brush thoroughly, or use a clean brush and brush again to make sure all the salt has been removed.

 **NOTE:** Do not use table salt for a dry shampoo. Not only will you still have dirty hair, but it will look as though you have dandruff, too.

## Hair Revitalizers

▶ This was our mom's favorite hair treatment. (Actually, it was the only hair treatment she ever used.) Slightly warm ½ cup of olive oil. You may want to add a few drops of an extract like vanilla to make it more fragrant. Mom put it in an eyedropper bottle and let it stand in very hot water for a few minutes. Then, using the eyedropper, she'd put the warm oil on the hair and massage it into the scalp. Once the whole head is oiled, shampoo the oil out.

▶ According to reflexology expert Mildred Carter, "To energize the hair roots, grab a handful of hair and yank gently. Do this over the whole head. This is also said to help a hangover, indigestion and other complaints.

"To further stimulate these reflexes in the head, lightly close your hands into loose fists. With a loose wrist action, lightly pound the whole head. This will not only stimulate the hair, but also the brain, bladder and other organs."

An experienced reflexologist, Ms. Carter believes that tapping the reflexes in the head with a wire brush can add even greater electrical stimulation to the hair, as well as other parts of the body.

## Green Hair

▶ Don't you just hate it when you get out of the pool and your blonde hair has a greenish tinge? Next time, take a clean sponge, dip it in red wine and dab it on your hair. The chemicals in a chlorinated pool will be neutralized by the tannic acid in the wine.

▶ Keep a bottle of lemon juice and a box of baking soda near the pool. After your swim, and before you hit the shower, mix ½ cup of the baking soda into a cup of lemon juice. Wet your hair, then rinse it with this bubbly mixture to get the green out. (Maybe blondes *don't* have more fun.)

▶ Dissolve six aspirin tablets in a pint of warm water, massage this into your wet hair and the green will never be seen. Rinse thoroughly with clear water.

## "Natural" Hair Coloring

Herbal or vegetable dyes take time because the color must accumulate. Look at it this way—if you get the gray out gradually, no one will realize you ever had any gray to begin with.

### Brunette Beauty

We have two hair-darkening formulas that use dried sage, which helps to add life to hair and prevents dandruff.

▶ Prepare dark sage tea by adding 4 tablespoons of dried sage to 2 cups of just-boiled water and letting it steep for two hours. Strain. This dark tea alone will darken gray hair—but for an even stronger hair color, add 2 cups of bay rum and 2 tablespoons of glycerine (available at pharmacies). Bottle this mixture and don't forget to label it.

Every night, apply the potion to your hair, starting at the roots and working your way to the ends. Stop the applications when your hair is as dark as you want it to be.

▶ If you're a teetotaler and don't want to use the rum remedy, combine 2 tablespoons of dried sage with 2 tablespoons of black tea and simmer in 1 quart of water for 20 minutes. Let it steep for four hours, then strain and bottle. Massage it into your hair daily until your hair is the color you desire. When you need a touch-up, mix a fresh batch of the teas.

▶ Taking sesame-seed tea internally has been known to darken hair. Crush 2 teaspoons of sesame seeds and bring them to a boil in 1 cup of water. Simmer for 20 minutes. As soon as it's cool enough to drink, drink the potion, seeds and all. Have 2 to 3 cups daily, and keep checking the mirror for darkening hair.

▶ Add a little life to your hair color right after you shampoo by pouring a cool cup of espresso through your hair. Let it stay there for five minutes and rinse.

### Blonde Bombshell

▶ Dried chamomile can help add golden highlights to wishy-washy, bland blonde hair. Add 4 tablespoons of dried chamomile to 2 cups of just-boiled water and let it steep for two hours. Strain and use it as a rinse. Have a basin set up so you can save the chamomile and use it again for the next two or three shampoos.

 **NOTE:** As with most herbal rinses, you mustn't expect dramatic results overnight —if ever. Chamomile tea, no matter how strong you make it, will not cover dark roots.

That reminds us of something we've wondered about for a while. In Sweden, are there brunettes with blonde roots?

▶ Squeeze the juice out of two lemons, strain and dilute with 1 cup of warm water. Comb the juice through your hair. Be very careful not to get any of it on your skin. Why? Because you should sit in the sun for 15 minutes in order to give your hair the glow of a summer day. If your skin has lemon juice on it, it can cause a burn and give your skin mottled stains.

After the sunbath, rinse your hair thoroughly with warm water or, better yet, with chamomile tea.

 **NOTE:** Be sure your skin is properly protected in the sun with sunscreen with a sun protection factor (SPF) of at least 15 (higher is better).

### Ravishing Red

▶ Add radiance to your red hair right after you shampoo by pouring a cup of strong Red Zinger tea (available at health food stores and many supermarkets) through your hair. Let it remain there for five minutes and rinse.

▶ Juice a raw beet (in a juice extractor) and add three times the amount of water as there is juice. Use this as a rinse after shampooing.

 **NOTE:** Since there are many shades of red, we suggest you do a test patch with the beet juice to see how it reacts on your specific color.

### Gray, Gray—Go Away!

▶ Many vitamin therapists have seen proof positive that taking a good B-complex vitamin daily can help change hair back to its original color over a period of two months or more.

▶ In a glass of water, mix 2 tablespoons each of apple cider vinegar, raw unheated honey and blackstrap molasses. Drink this mixture first thing in the morning. Not only should it help you get rid of gray hair, but it should also give you a lot more energy than people who haven't gone gray yet.

 **WARNING:** Do not give honey to someone who is diabetic or allergic to honey.

► According to the Chinese, a combination of fresh gingerroot juice and ground cloves should be massaged into the scalp to prevent gray hair.

## Setting Lotions

If you want your hair to hold its curls, sometimes it's best to use a setting lotion before making waves...

► Don't throw away beer that's gone flat. Instead, dip your comb in it, comb it through your hair and you have a wonderful setting lotion. Incidentally, the smell of beer seems to disappear quickly.

► A friend of ours is a professional fashion model and she knows many tricks of the trade. Her favorite hair-setting lotion is fresh lemon juice. The hair takes longer to dry with the juice on it, but the setting stays in a lot longer. When she runs out of lemons, she uses bottled lemon juice from her fridge and that works well, too.

► If beer or lemon isn't your cup of tea, try milk. Dissolve 4 tablespoons of skim-milk powder in 1 cup of tepid water. Use it as you would any commercial hairsetting lotion. But, unlike most commercial products, the milk helps nourish the scalp and hair.

## Helpful Hair Hints

### Prevent Gray from Yellowing

► By adding a couple of teaspoons of laundry bluing to a quart of warm water and using it as your final rinse after shampooing, you can prevent gray hair from turning that yucky yellow.

### No-No #1—Rubber Bands

► We've always been told not to wear rubber bands in our hair. We just found an explanation for this—the rubber insulates the hair and stops the normal flow of static electricity, so hair elasticity is reduced and the hair breaks more easily.

### No-No #2—Combing Wet Hair

► Combing wet hair stretches it out, causing it to be less elastic and break more easily.

### Gum Remover

► To remove gum from hair, take a glob of peanut butter, put it on the gummed area, then rub the gum and peanut butter between your fingers until the gum is on its way out. Use a comb to finish the job, then get that careless kid (is it you?) under the faucet for a good shampooing.

### A Permanent's Pungent Odor Remover

► The distinctive smell of a permanent has a habit of lingering. Tomato juice to the rescue! Saturate your dry hair with tomato juice. Cover your hair and scalp with a plastic bag and stay that way for 10 minutes. Rinse hair thoroughly, then shampoo and rinse again.

### Hair Spray Remover

► When you are in the middle of shampooing, massage 1 tablespoon of baking soda into your soaped-up hair. Then rinse thoroughly. The baking soda should remove all the nasty hair spray buildup.

### Improvised Setting Rollers

► If you have long hair and want to experiment setting it with big rollers, try used frozen-juice cans, opened at both ends. Be careful not to cut yourself with the open edges.

## Grounding Your Hair

▶ When static electricity makes your hair temporarily unmanageable, you might want to zap it with static spray used on records (that is, if you still have any records!).

*Or,* rub a sheet of fabric softener on your hair as well as on your brush or comb.

## HAND AND NAIL PROBLEMS

Like our feet, hands and fingernails suffer a lot of daily abuse. From washing dishes in hot water to typing on a computer keyboard, our hands and nails seem to touch everything. If your hands and nails are feeling a little rough, dry or brittle, some of these remedies may bring soothing relief.

▶ Chapped hands will be greatly soothed when you massage wheat germ oil into them.

▶ Red, rough and sore hands (feet, too) should be relieved with lemon juice. After you rinse off the lemon juice, massage the hands with olive, coconut or wheat germ oil.

**NOTE:** Give a moisturizer time to work by keeping it on your hands overnight. To maximize the moisturizer's effectiveness, and to protect your bedsheets, put on white cotton gloves after you've applied the moisturizer. If you don't have white cotton gloves, then go to a photographic-supply store and pick up the inexpensive gloves that photographers and film editors wear when handling film.

## Rough Hands

▶ For those chapped hands, try some honey. Wet your hands and shake off the water without actually drying them. Then rub some honey all over your hands. When they're completely honey-coated, let them stay that way for five minutes. (We would recommend you read the paper to pass the time, but turning the pages would definitely present problems.)

Next, rub your hands as you rinse them under tepid water. Then pat your hands dry. Do this every day until you want to clap hands for your unchapped hands.

▶ Tired of being called "lobster claw"? Take 1 teaspoon of granulated sugar in the palm of your hand and add a few drops of castor oil and enough fresh lemon juice to totally moisten the sugar. Vigorously massage your hands together for a few minutes. Rinse with tepid water and pat dry. This hand scrub should leave hands smooth and, in the process, remove stains.

### Hand Cleansers

▶ One simple cleanser consists of scrubbing your hands with a palmful of dry baking soda, then rinsing with tepid water.

▶ For another cleanser, take a palmful of oatmeal, moistened with milk. Rub and rinse.

### Farmer's Friend

▶ This remedy for rough, chapped and soiled hands is a favorite among farmers. In a bowl, combine about ¼ cup of cornmeal, 1 tablespoon of water and enough apple cider vinegar to make the mixture the consistency of a loose paste. Rub this mildly abrasive mixture all over your hands for 10 minutes. Rinse with tepid water and pat dry.

This treatment not only can remove dirt, it can also soften, soothe and heal the hands.

▶ In a jar, combine equal parts of tomato juice, lemon juice and glycerin (available at drugstores). Let one hand massage the other with the mixture. Rinse with tepid water.

▶ The ideal remedy for people with dry hands is having their own sheep as a pet. This is because sheep's wool contains lanolin. By rubbing your hands across the animal's back every so often, you'll keep them in great shape.

## Clammy Hands

▶ In a basin, combine ½ gallon of water with ½ cup of alcohol and put your palms in the mixture. After a few minutes, rinse your hands with cool water and pat dry. This is especially useful for clammy-palmed politicians on the campaign trail.

## Fingernail Remedies

If you're having problems with breaking, splitting and thin nails, you may need to supplement your diet with a B-complex vitamin and zinc sulfate (follow the directions on the bottle for the dosage), along with garlic—raw and/or supplements. Be sure to consult your doctor first!

The following remedies for strengthening fingernails can help if they're used in addition to a well-balanced diet.

▶ Daily, soak your fingers for 10 minutes in any one of these oils…
  ◆ Warm olive oil
  ◆ Warm sesame-seed oil
  ◆ Warm wheat germ oil

As you wipe off the oil, give your nails a mini-massage from top to bottom.

▶ If your nails are very brittle, use a juice extractor to juice parsnip—enough for ½ cup at a time. Drink parsnip juice at least once a day. Be patient for results—give it a couple of weeks or more.

▶ While tapping your nails on a table can be very annoying to people around you, it is very good for your nails. The more you tap, the faster they will grow. Which is good because you may need long nails to defend yourself from those annoyed people around you.

### Stained Nails

Want natural, healthy-looking, pinkish nails? Gaby Nigai, co-owner of Ellegee Nail Salon in New York City, offers some helpful advice.

▶ Stop using colored nail polish directly on the nail. Instead, wear a protein-based coat under nail polish to protect your nails from the polish's color pigments, which cause staining and oxidation.

▶ To get rid of polish stains, toss two denture-cleansing tablets into ¼ cup of water. Soak your fingertips in the solution for about 15 minutes.

If your nails are not as stain-free as you had hoped, gently brush them with a nailbrush. Rinse and dry.

▶ Put tooth-whitening paste on a toothbrush and gently distribute the paste on your nails. Leave it on for about 15 minutes…then brush as you rinse off the paste. Gently dry.

> **NOTE:** It may take several tries, day after day, before the stains are completely gone. But keep working at it—your appearance is worth it!

### Nicotine Nails

▶ If your nails are cigarette stained, we'll tell you how to bleach them back to normal—as long as you promise to stop smoking, okay? (*See* "Smoking" starting on page 167.)

Now then…to remove the stains, rub half a lemon over your nails. Then remove the lemon's pulp and, with the remaining rind, concentrate on one nail at a time, rubbing each one until it looks nice and pink.

>  **NOTE:** If you have citrus juice on your skin and you go in the sun, your skin may become permanently bleached or discolored.
>
> Be sure to completely wash off the lemon juice before you go outdoors.

### Finger Sores (Whitlows)

▶ When you have a painful inflammation around your fingernail, soak it in hot water. Then heat a lemon in the oven, cut a narrow opening in the middle and sprinkle salt in it. Take the infected finger and stick it in the lemon. After an initial sting, the pain should disappear within minutes.

Be sure to discard the lemon and cover your finger—whitlows can be contagious.

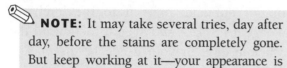

## HEADACHES

Take a holistic approach to your headache. Step back and look at the past 24 hours of your life. Have you eaten sensibly? Did you get a decent night's sleep? Have you moved your bowels since waking up this morning? Are there deadlines you need to meet? Do you have added pressures at home or at work? Is there something you're dreading?

Now that you probably realize the reason for your headache, what should you take for it? Don't refuse any offer.

Studies show that more than 90% of headaches are brought on by nervous tension, so most of our remedies are for the common tension headache. Only a few are for the more serious migraines.

> **WARNING:** In the case of regularly recurring headaches, they can be caused by eyestrain, an allergy or something more serious. Seek professional medical attention, especially if the headache comes on suddenly or is accompanied by nausea, vomiting and/or a fever.

## Natural Remedies

Headaches are such a headache! Use your instincts, common sense and patience to find which one of these remedies works best for you and your headache.

▶ Research scientists tell us that almonds contain salicylates, the pain-relieving ingredient in aspirin. Eat 15 raw almonds to do the work of one aspirin. While it may take a little longer for the headache to vanish, you won't

## Exotic Edibles

**T**he fact that you are reading this book leads us to believe that you're a person who's interested in and open to all kinds of alternatives, variety and new adventures. Usually, when a person is adventurous, it extends to his/her eating habits. And so we would like to introduce you to *daikon*, a Japanese radish (if you aren't already familiar with it). It's delicious eaten raw in salads and wonderful for digestion, especially when eating oily foods.

▶ Grate a piece of daikon and squeeze out the juice through cheesecloth onto a washcloth. Apply the washcloth to your forehead and bandage in place. It should help draw out the headache pain.

While we're talking "exotic edibles" as remedies, you should know about *gomasio*—that's Japanese for sesame salt. You can find it at health food stores. The interesting thing about this seasoning is that the oil from the crushed sesame seeds coats the sea salt so that it doesn't cause an excessive attraction for water. In other words, you can season food with it and it won't make you thirsty like regular table salt.

▶ To get relief from a headache, eat 1 teaspoon of gomasio. Chew it thoroughly before swallowing.

run the risk of side effects. (What the scientists need to find now are fast-acting almonds.)

▶ Get a little bottle of essence of rosemary and rub a small amount of the oil on your forehead and temples, and also behind your ears. Then inhale the fumes from the open bottle four times. If your headache doesn't disappear within a half-hour, repeat the rubbing and inhaling once more.

### Relief from the East

▶ This remedy seems to be a favorite of some Indian gurus. In a small pot, combine 1 teaspoon of dried basil with 1 cup of hot water, and bring it to a boil. Take it off the stove, then add 2 tablespoons of witch hazel. Let it cool, then saturate a washcloth with the mixture, wring it out and apply it to the forehead. Bandage it in place and keep it there until the washcloth dries or your headache disappears, whichever comes first.

▶ This will either work for you—or it won't. Either way you'll find out quickly and easily. Dunk your hands into water that's as hot as you can stand—be careful not to scald yourself! Keep them there for one minute. If you don't start feeling relief within 15 minutes, try another remedy.

▶ If your tension headache seems to stem from the tightness in your neck, use an electric heating pad or a very warm, wet cloth around your neck. The heat should relax you and improve circulation.

### Pass the Mint

▶ A Mexican folk remedy says to paste a fresh mint leaf on the part of the head where the pain is most severe.

▶ In England, the mint leaf is juiced and the juice is used as eardrops to relieve a headache.

### Mr. Potato Head

▶Grate a potato (a red one if possible) or an apple, and make a poultice out of it (*see* "Preparation Guide" on page 252). Apply the poultice to your forehead and bandage it in place, keeping it there for at least an hour.

### Bite Your Tongue—Really!

▶You might want to try some acupressure to get rid of that headache. Stick out your tongue about ½ inch and bite down on it as hard as you can without hurting yourself. Stay that way for *exactly 10 minutes*—not a minute more!

▶Some people rid themselves of headache pain by taking a low dose of vitamin C every hour—just be aware that too much vitamin C can cause diarrhea.

If, after a few hours, you still have a headache, then stop taking vitamin C and try another remedy.

▶Add ½ teaspoon of angelica (available at health food stores) to ¾ cup of hot water and drink. It not only helps ease the pain of a headache, but it is said to give a person a lighter, happier feeling.

▶In Jamaica, a popular headache remedy uses the leaf of an aloe vera plant. Carefully cut it in half the long way, and place the gel side on your forehead and temples. Keep it in place with a handkerchief or bandage and let it stay there until your headache is gone.

## Ask Your Headache to Go Away

**W**e were once told that whatever you fully experience, disappears. The following exercise can help you experience away your headache. *Ask yourself the following questions and answer them honestly…*

◆ *Do I really want to get rid of the headache?* (Don't laugh. A lot of people want to hang on to their headaches. It's a great excuse and cop-out from all kinds of things.)

◆ *What kind of headache do I have?* Be specific. Is it pounding over one eye? Does it throb each time you bend down? Do you have a dull ache at the base of your neck?

Now, either memorize the next questions or have someone read them to you. ("Why?" you wonder.) Close your eyes. ("Aha!" That's why.)

◆ *What size is my headache?* Figure out the exact dimensions of it. Start with the length from the front of your face to the back of your head, the width from ear to ear and the thickness of it from the top of your head down toward your neck.

◆ *What color is my headache?*

◆ *How much water will it hold?* (This is done in your mind through visualization.) Fill a cup with the amount of water needed to fill the area of the headache. Then, pour the water from the cup into the space of your headache. When you've completed that, open your eyes. You should have experienced away your headache.

The first time we used this exercise, our results were quite dramatic. If we hadn't experienced it ourselves, we'd probably think it's as crazy as you're probably thinking we are right now.

## V Is for Vinegar

▶ When our grandmother had a headache, she would dip a large white handkerchief in vinegar, wring it out and tie it tightly around her forehead until the headache disappeared.

A variation of soaking a handkerchief in vinegar is to soak a piece of brown grocery-bag paper in vinegar. Shake off the excess liquid and place it on your forehead. Tie it in place and keep it there for at least 30 minutes.

▶ We used this remedy with great success on the host of a famous TV morning show…he had a monster headache that he'd been suffering with for two days. He tried our "tie a yellow lemon" remedy and felt better by the end of the interview!

Peel the rind off a lemon. Make the pieces as wide as possible. Rub the rind (the inside of the skin should touch your skin) on your forehead and temples. Then place the pieces of rind on the forehead and temples, securing them with a scarf or bandage. Keep it there until the headache goes away, usually within a half-hour.

## Take a Walk

▶ Let ice-cold water accumulate in the bathtub until it's ankle-high. Dress warmly except for your bare feet. Take a leisurely stroll in the tub—from one to three minutes—as long as it takes for your feet to start feeling warm in the ice-cold water. When that happens, get out of the tub, dry your feet and go directly to bed. Cover up, relax and within no time, your headache should be a pain of the past.

▶ Press your thumb against the roof of your mouth for four to five minutes. Every so often, move your thumb to another section of the roof of your mouth. The nerve pressure in your head should be greatly relieved. While this remedy is highly impractical during a speaking engagement, it's worth a try in the privacy of your home.

## Getting Steamy

▶ Mix a cup of water with a cup of apple cider vinegar and bring it to a slow boil in a medium-sized pot. When the fumes begin to rise, turn off the stove and remove the pot. Put a towel over your head and bend over the pot.

Inhale and exhale deeply through your nose about 80 times or for about 10 minutes. Be very careful—steam can burn if you get too close. And make sure you hold the towel so that it catches the vapor for you to inhale, but that it doesn't touch the hot pot or stove.

▶ If strawberries are in season, eat a few. They contain organic salicylates, which are related to the active ingredients in aspirin. (Do not try this remedy if you are allergic to aspirin.)

▶ Vigorously rub the second joint of each thumb—two minutes on the right hand, two minutes on the left hand—until you've done it five times each, or for 10 minutes. Use hand lotion on the thumbs to eliminate friction.

▶ A very old American remedy is to swallow a teaspoon of honey mixed with ½ teaspoon of garlic juice.

☞ **WARNING:** Infants, diabetics and people with honey allergies should not use honey.

▶ Enlist the help of someone who will slowly move his/her thumb down the right side of your back, alongside your shoulder blade and toward your waist. Let that person know when he hits a sore or tender spot. Have your helper exert steady pressure on that spot for a minute. This should bring relief from the headache.

**CAUTION:** See your doctor immediately if your headache is worse or "different" than usual...comes on rapidly and severely...first occurs after age 50...and/or is accompanied by neurological symptoms, such as paralysis, slurred speech or loss of consciousness. These symptoms may indicate an aneurysm, brain tumor, stroke or some other serious problem.

# Migraine Headaches

If you suffer from migraines, sometimes the only thing you can do to relieve the throbbing pain, double vision and nausea is to lie down in a dark, quiet room.

To prevent the onset of an attack, it helps to eat a healthy diet, avoid caffeine and get enough sleep. These remedies may provide some additional relief.

**CAUTION:** Chronic migraine sufferers should seek medical attention. You may need medication to treat your headaches.

▶ Dip a few cabbage leaves in boiling hot water to make them soft. As soon as they're cool enough, place one or two thicknesses on your forehead and on the back of your neck. Secure them in place with a scarf or bandage. Then relax as the cabbage draws out the pain.

▶ Boil two Spanish onions. Eat one and mash the other for a poultice (see "Preparation Guide" on page 252). Then place the poultice on your forehead.

## *Anti-Migraine Massage*

▶ Apply pressure to the palm of one hand with the thumb of the other hand. Then reverse the order. If you feel a tenderness in either palm, concentrate the massage on that area. Keep up the firm pressure and massage for 10 minutes—five minutes on each hand.

▶ We heard about a woman who would eat a tablespoon of honey the second she felt a migraine coming on. If the headache wasn't gone within a half hour, she'd take another tablespoon of honey with three glasses of water and that would do it.

**WARNING:** Infants, diabetics and people with honey allergies should not use honey.

▶ Bathe your feet in a basin or two plastic shoe boxes filled with very strong, warm, black coffee. Some medical professionals recommend drinking a cup or two of coffee as well. Or, for the same effectiveness, but with less caffeine, drink yerba maté, also called Jungle Punch (*see* page 131). It is available at health food stores.

**NOTE:** Be aware that yerba maté contains caffeine, although less than coffee or regular tea.

## *Head to the Salon*

▶ Ready for this one? Sit under a hair dryer. The heat and high-pitched hum of the dryer may relax the tension that brought on the headache.

## ■ Recipe ■

### Apple Salsa with Cinnamon Tortilla Chips

*Apple Salsa*

2 medium tart apples, chopped
      (preferably Granny Smith)
2 tsp lemon juice
1 cup fresh strawberries, chopped
2 medium kiwi fruit, peeled and chopped
1 small orange
2 Tbsp brown sugar, firmly packed
2 Tbsp apple jelly, melted

*Cinnamon Tortilla Chips*

8 eight-inch flour tortillas
Water
¼ cup granulated sugar
2 to 4 tsp ground cinnamon

In a large bowl, toss the chopped apples with the lemon juice to keep them from browning. Add the chopped strawberries and kiwi.

Grate about 1 Tbsp of orange peel (the zest) into the bowl. Then slice the orange in half and squeeze out about 3 Tbsp of the orange juice. Make sure to remove the seeds from the orange so they do not get into your salsa. Stir in the brown sugar and jelly. Set aside.

To prepare the cinnamon tortilla chips, brush both sides of the tortillas with a tiny bit of water (just enough to allow the sugar and cinnamon to stick.)

Blend together the sugar and cinnamon and sprinkle it lightly over the tortillas, turning to cover both sides. If you have an empty spice shaker, it works well to double the mixture and sprinkle it over the tortillas from the shaker. Any leftover sugar and cinnamon is perfect for preparing cinnamon toast, quick and easy.

Cut each tortilla into 8 equal pie-shaped wedges and place the pieces in a single layer on a baking sheet that has been lightly coated with a non-stick cooking spray or a thin brush of butter.

Bake the cinnamon-coated tortillas in a preheated 400° F oven for 6 to 8 minutes or until lightly browned. Cool until crisp, then serve with the apple salsa on the side.

Makes 4 servings.

*Source: www.recipegoldmine.com*

According to one physician, the dryer brings relief to two-thirds of the migraine sufferers who try it. Your local beauty salon will probably be happy to accommodate you as long as you don't have a headache during their busy time.

**WARNING:** If you have chemical sensitivities, stay out of a hair salon. It could make your headache worse.

▶ Open a jar of strong mustard and slowly inhale the fumes several times.

▶ Some people have migraines without having severe headaches. Instead, they are troubled by impaired vision—spots in front of their eyes or seeing double. We heard about a simple remedy for this—chew a handful of raisins. Chew them thoroughly before swallowing.

## Headache Prevention... Sort of

A three-year study conducted at the University of Michigan in Ann Arbor showed that students who ate two apples a day had far fewer headaches than those who didn't eat any apples. The apple eaters also had fewer skin problems, arthritic conditions and colds.

You might want to have an apple for breakfast and one as a late afternoon snack, or one a couple of hours after dinner.

Did we mention that apples contain natural salicylates, substances that are related to the active ingredient in aspirin?

Chances are, eating two apples a day will also prevent constipation, which can be a leading cause of headaches. (*See* recipe on page 108.)

## HEART PROBLEMS

The heart is a four-chambered, hollow muscle and double-acting pump that is located in the chest between the lungs. This hardworking, fist-sized muscle pumps blood through the blood vessels to all parts of the body at the rate of about 4,000 gallons a day. (No wonder so many of us have "tired blood.")

The heart is so complex—and heart trouble is so serious—that the best suggestions we can offer are...

- If you feel as though you're having a heart attack, call for professional medical help IMMEDIATELY!
- If you have a history of heart problems, follow an eating plan that will promote a healthy heart.

- To learn how to help others, take a cardiac pulmonary resuscitation (CPR) course through the local chapter of the American Heart Association or the Red Cross.
- Don't smoke!

## Heart Attack

If you or someone you're with feels as though he/she is having a heart attack, call 911 for professional medical help *immediately*. Symptoms may not seem serious at first, but don't delay.

▶ Unlock your door and, while you're waiting for help to arrive, squeeze the end of the pinky finger on the left hand. Squeeze it HARD! Keep squeezing it. This acupressure procedure has been said to save lives.

▶ If he/she is not allergic or taking blood thinners, have the person having a heart attack chew one full-strength (325 mg) aspirin tablet or four baby aspirin tablets.

**NOTE:** When you receive medical attention, be sure to tell the person treating you about any medication or natural supplements you have taken.

▶ A cup of peppermint tea a day is said to help prevent a heart attack.

**CAUTION:** Beware that peppermint is a powerful herb that can undermine or negate the effectiveness of homeopathic medicine.

## Heart Palpitations

Many healthy people get heart palpitations (*arrhythmia*). You may feel as though your heart has skipped a beat or is beating very fast or strong. The heart is powered by electrical pulses that aren't always perfect. Be sure to see your doctor for an evaluation and diagnosis.

**WARNING:** Seek medical attention if the palpitations persist or are accompanied by dizziness, chest pain or fainting/passing out.

▶ If you are given a clean bill of health, but you experience a minor bout of palpitations (and who hasn't at one time or another?), take a holistic approach to find the cause. Was it the MSG in the Chinese food you had for lunch? The caffeine in the chocolate you pigged out on? Pressure at the office? Cigarette smoke? Sugar? Work on figuring it out so that you learn what not to have next time.

▶ Here's a natural sedative to subdue the thumping. Steep two chamomile tea bags in 2 cups of just-boiled water. Steam a few shredded leaves of cabbage. Then, in a soup bowl, combine the steamed leaves with the chamomile tea. This tea-soup may not taste good, but it can help overcome those skipped heartbeats.

▶ If you have heart palpitations occasionally, drink peppermint tea. Have a mug every day. It seems to have a calming effect on people, especially since it is an herbal tea that does not contain caffeine.

## Heart Helpers

▶ According to the results of a study, orchestra conductors live an average of 7½ years longer than the average person.

To strengthen your heart, tone up your circulatory system and have some fun, go through the motions of conducting an orchestra. Do it for at least 10 minutes a day, or 20 minutes three days a week. Conduct to music that inspires you. If you don't have a baton, use a ruler or a chopstick. Pretend each day of exercise is a command performance. Throw your whole self into it physically and emotionally.

 **NOTE:** If you have a history of heart problems, be sure to check with your doctor before you begin conducting.

### Healing Honey

▶ Two teaspoons of raw honey a day, either in a glass of water or straight off the spoon, is thought by many nutritionists to be the best tonic for strengthening the heart, as well as for general physical repair.

**WARNING:** Infants, diabetics and people with honey allergies should not use honey.

▶ Okay, so you don't want to join a gym. You don't have to. For the best exercise and the perfect body stimulator, just take an old-fashioned walk—make it a *brisk* walk—daily. (Just be sure to check with your doctor before starting a new exercise program.)

Brisk means walking a mile every 20 minutes (three miles an hour). It's slower than running or race-walking, but generally faster than a stroll.

▶ *The New England Journal of Medicine* (*http://content.nejm.org*) recently reported the findings of a long-term study of 72,000 women ages 40 to 65. The heart attack risk was reduced 30% to 40% in the women who did at least three hours of brisk walking a week. The women who walked briskly for five hours or more a week cut their heart attack risk by more than 40%.

In addition to the walking, those who did vigorous exercise for 90 minutes a week cut their risk almost in half. Gardening and housework are considered vigorous exercise. So you can have a clean house, a beautiful garden and a healthy heart.

**CAUTION:** Broccoli and turnip greens are rich in vitamin K, the clot-promoting vitamin. If you take anticlotting medication prescribed by your physician, be aware that eating big portions of these vegetables can counteract the effects of the medicine.

▶ This remedy is recommended for people who have a history of heart problems—right before going to bed, take a 10-minute footbath. Step into calf-high water, as hot as you can take it without scalding yourself. As the minutes pass and the water cools, add more hot water. After 10 minutes, step out of the tub and dry your feet thoroughly, preferably with a rough towel.

Once your feet are dry, give them a one-minute massage, manipulating the toes as well as the entire foot. This footbath/massage may help circulation, remove congestion around the heart and lead you to a peaceful night's sleep.

▶ We recently read a list of supposed benefits of hawthorn berries. We followed up by researching the herb and, as a result, we now take hawthorn supplements daily.

*Benefits:* Normalizes blood pressure by regulating heart action...improves heart valve defects...helps people with a lot of stress...

strengthens weakened heart muscle...and prevents atherosclerosis. (*See* page 19.)

**NOTE:** Check with your health professional for dosage, depending on your size and the state of your heart health.

▶ Omega-3 fatty acids impact many factors linked to cardiovascular disease. They help lower LDL ("bad") cholesterol levels and triglycerides, inhibit excessive platelet aggregation, lower fibrinogen levels and lower both systolic and diastolic blood pressure in individuals with high blood pressure.

Omega-3s are found in many foods, including salmon, mackerel and other fatty fish. Flaxseed oil offers the most cost-effective and beneficial method for increasing the intake of omega-3 oils in the diet. (*See* "Six Sensational Superfoods" on page 262 for detailed flaxseed information.)

▶ For a healthier heart, eat wheat germ every day. You might also want to supplement with vitamin E. It's said to help reduce hardening of the arteries. Be sure to check with your doctor for the amount that is right for you.

▶ Take a garlic supplement every day to protect and strengthen the heart and help thin the blood. Also, use garlic in cooking and eat it raw in salads.

## That's Nothing to Wine About

▶ Moderate consumption of red wine, as reported in the respected British medical journal *The Lancet* (*www.thelancet.com*), is directly associated with lower rates of heart disease.

▶ According to wine therapists, a little champagne sipped daily helps strengthen the heart.

The champagne's tartrate of potassium content supposedly has a positive effect on one's cardiac rhythm.

> ✎ **NOTE:** Please remember—*everything in moderation, especially alcohol!*

▶ We've been told that massaging the pads at the base of the last two fingers of the left hand, or massaging the left foot under the third, fourth and fifth toes, can relieve heart pain within seconds.

### Red Roses for Love

▶ If someone wants to give you an edible treat, instead of candy, suggest red roses. They're said to help strengthen the heart as well as other organs of the body, not to mention what they do for a relationship.

Remove the bitter white part on the bottom of the rose petals and eat the rest of the petals raw, or make rose-petal tea to drink. Be sure the roses are organically grown and haven't been sprayed.

▶ Eat onions once a day. According to Russian scientists, onions are beneficial for all kinds of heart problems.

▶ Every morning, before breakfast, drink the juice of half a lemon in a cup of warm water. It's reputed to be helpful for all kinds of body functions, from proper fluid action in the blood to regularity in the bathroom.

### Rev Up Your Circulation

▶ Once a day, mix ⅛ teaspoon of cayenne pepper in a cup of water and drink it down. It's not easy to take, but it may be beneficial to the circulatory system, since cayenne pepper is reputed to be the purest herbal stimulant.

▶ Japanese medicine recommends ginger footbaths to improve circulation. Add a cup of fresh, minced ginger to a basin with 2 quarts of warm water, or divide the water and ginger into two plastic shoe boxes. Soak your feet in the water until they're rosy red. Then dry thoroughly and notice a more energized feeling.

## HEMORRHOIDS

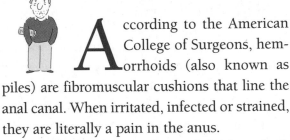

According to the American College of Surgeons, hemorrhoids (also known as piles) are fibromuscular cushions that line the anal canal. When irritated, infected or strained, they are literally a pain in the anus.

Two out of every three adults have had, currently have or will have a case of hemorrhoids. Chances are, if you're reading this, you are one of the two out of the three.

Along with treating your condition with natural, nonchemical remedies, there are ways to speed up the healing process...

◆ Keep the bowels as clear as possible. Drink lots of fruit juices and vegetable juices. Stay away from hard-to-digest, overly processed foods—especially those that contain white flour and sugar—as well as alcoholic beverages.

◆ Eat six or seven servings of fruits and vegetables a day.

112

◆ Do not strain or hold your breath while having a bowel movement. Make an effort to breathe evenly.

◆ Take a brisk walk as often as you can, especially after meals.

# Natural Remedies

Heed these suggestions and, hopefully, in a few days, you'll have this problem behind you.

▶ Apply liquid lecithin directly on the hemorrhoids, once a day, until they disappear.

▶ Eat a large boiled leek every day as an afternoon snack or with dinner.

▶ Eat three raw unprocessed almonds every day. Chew each one about 50 times.

▶ In a blender, finely chop ¼ cup cranberries. Place 1 tablespoon of the blended cranberries in a piece of cheesecloth and place it over the anus. An hour later, remove the cheesecloth and replace it with another tablespoon of cranberries in cheesecloth for another hour. This is a great pain reliever. By the end of two hours, you should feel much better.

## Faster Than a Speeding Bullet

▶ How are you at ice carving? Carefully carve or melt an ice cube down to the size and shape of a bullet. Use it as a suppository. The cold may give you a start, but it may also reduce the swelling and heal the hemorrhoids.

## Witchy Water

▶ Add ¼ cup of witch hazel to a basin of warm water. If it's not irritating, sit in it for at least 15 minutes at a time, at least two times a day.

Complete cures have been reported within three days.

▶ Psychic healer Edgar Cayce recommended this exercise to a hemorrhoid sufferer...

◆ Stand with feet about six inches apart, hands at sides.

◆ Raise your hands up to the ceiling.

◆ Bend forward and bring your hands as close to the floor as you can.

◆ Go back to the first position.

Repeat the entire procedure 36 times. It should take just a few minutes to do. Perform this exercise every day, an hour after breakfast and an hour after dinner, until the hemorrhoids are history.

## Tobacco That's Good for You

▶ Put the tobacco from two cigarettes in a warm pan, add 4 teaspoons of butter and let the mixture simmer for a couple of minutes. (This is a much better use for cigarettes than smoking them!) Next, pour the hot liquid through a strainer onto a sanitary napkin. When it's cool enough, apply it to the hemorrhoid area. Whip up a fresh batch and reapply three times a day.

▶ A consulting physician for the Denver Broncos and Denver Nuggets athletic teams has had success in speeding up the healing process of hemorrhoids with vitamin C baths.

Put 1 cup of ascorbic acid powder to every 5 quarts of cool bath water. Sit in the tub for 15 minutes at a time, two or three times a day.

**NOTE:** Ascorbic acid powder is expensive. If you can fit your tushy into a basin with ½ cup of the powder and 2½ quarts of cool water, you'll save a fortune.

▶ Take advantage of the healing properties of the enzymes in papaya by drenching a wad of sterilized cotton in pure papaya juice. Position it on the hemorrhoid area and secure it in place with a bandage. The juice should help stop the bleeding and bring the irritation under control.

## Hemorrhoid Prevention

To *prevent* hemorrhoids, it's best to increase the fiber and fluids in your diet.

▶ According to psychic healer Edgar Cayce, eating three raw almonds a day will help prevent hemorrhoids.

▶ Since hemorrhoids are a sitter's ailment, it may help to take a long walk every day at a fairly fast pace. A yoga class two or three times a week is also a good preventive measure.

## HERPES

The herpes virus is a common infection that affects the body's nerve cells, making them "break out" in painful sores. *Herpes simplex 1* generally affects the mouth (cold sores and fever blisters) and *simplex 2* affects the genitals. Each type tends to be recurrent (you have an outbreak whenever you are sick or under stress), and each can be contagious during intimate contact—kissing, oral sex or intercourse.

Forty-five million Americans (one out of every five sexually active adults) have genital herpes. Each year, up to one million more get this virus. The best way to prevent transmission of the virus is to abstain from intimate contact during an outbreak.

We spoke with a man who did extensive research and came up with a remedy for overcoming the symptoms of herpes simplex 1. He tested it and had friends test it. The results were impressive.

But first the remedy, next the explanation and then more about the results.

## Dietary Remedy

▶ Do not eat nuts, chocolate or (sorry, Mom!) chicken soup. At the first sign of a herpes flareup, eat 1 pound of steamed flounder. That's it. That's the remedy.

The explanation—in simple terms, as best as we understand it—is that there's a certain balance in the body between two amino acids …arginine and lysine. To contract herpes and to have the symptoms recur, one's body has to have a high level of arginine compared with the level of lysine.

The secret, then, is to reduce the amount of arginine (eliminate nuts, chocolate and chicken soup) and increase the amount of lysine (eat flounder). One pound of flounder has 11,000 mg of lysine. You can take lysine tablets, but you would have to take lots of them, and they contain binders and other things you just don't need. Also, the tablets are not as digestible or as absorbable as the lysine found naturally in flounder.

By steaming the fish, you help to retain the nutrients. An added bonus is that you can add the sauce of your choice to the flounder after it's been steamed. That way, you won't even think of it as medicine!

As for results, the man and his friends have had symptoms disappear overnight after eating flounder and never eating nuts, chocolate and chicken soup.

## Cold Sores and Fever Blisters

▶ Speed up the healing process of a cold sore by cutting a clove of garlic in half and rubbing it on the sore. Not pleasant, but effective.

▶ Combine 1 tablespoon of apple cider vinegar with 3 tablespoons of honey (preferably raw honey) and dab the sore with the mixture in the morning, late afternoon and at night.

⚡ **CAUTION:** Open sores are infectious to hands, eyes and genitalia. They are best left alone to dry and heal. Foreign substances may cause further irritation and infection.

▶ Grind up a few walnuts and mix them with 1 teaspoon of cocoa butter. Apply this "nutty-butter" salve to the sore twice a day. The sore should be gone in three or four days.

▶ Lysine may inhibit the growth of herpes viruses that cause cold sores and fever blisters. Take one L-lysine 500 mg tablet daily with dinner. Or eat flounder for dinner!

▶ This remedy came to us from several people across the country. (If they weren't embarrassed to tell it to us, we won't be embarrassed to tell it to you.) Use earwax (your own, of course) on your cold sore or fever blister.

▶ When a cold sore is on its way, there's often a peculiar tingling sensation. At the first sign of that tingle, take *colorless* nail polish and paint it lightly on the area where the cold sore is about to emerge. The nail polish prevents the sore from blossoming.

Cyndi Antoniak, a producer for MSNBC, got this unique remedy from her dermatologist. Since Cyndi first used this remedy successfully some time ago, she hasn't needed to use it again. Incidentally, the polish peels off naturally within a short time.

## Shingles

Did you have the chicken pox when you were a kid? *Herpes zoster virus* is the chicken pox virus, which is also the shingles virus, revisited. The chicken pox virus stays dormant until your immune system falls down on the job. The resulting painful, blistery flare-up is shingles.

▶ St. John's wort is an antiviral, anti-inflammatory herb that can also strengthen the nervous system. Drink St. John's-wort tea to help you de-stress, and gently massage the tincture directly on the affected area. Both tea and tincture are available at health food stores.

⚡ **CAUTION:** Check with your health professional before taking St. John's wort. It may interfere with some medications.

▶ Aloe vera gel is a soothing, cooling antiseptic. You can buy a bottle at a health food store or you can buy an aloe vera plant. They're inexpensive, easy to grow and they look a lot prettier than a refrigerated bottle.

Look for aloes that have little spikes on the edge of the leaves.

When using the plant, cut off the lowest leaf, then cut that leaf into 2-inch pieces. Slice one of the pieces in half and apply the gel directly to the affected area. Individually wrap the remaining pieces of the leaf in plastic wrap and keep them in the freezer. Every few hours, take a piece of leaf from the freezer and apply the soothing gel.

▶ In order to get a healthy dose of a beneficial amino acid, lysine, eat flounder. (*See* "Dietary Remedy" on page 114.)

**CAUTION:** Shingles that affect the face or forehead—anywhere near the eyes—can lead to cornea damage and/or temporary facial paralysis. Be sure to see your health professional immediately for treatment.

▶ Make a paste of baking soda and water, and apply to the affected area for some relief.

▶ Prepare a paste of Epsom salts and water. Place the paste directly on the affected area. Repeat the procedure as often as possible.

▶ Apply any of the following to relieve the itching and speed the healing—witch hazel (an astringent), apple cider vinegar (an infection fighter), red raspberry tea (particularly good for viral eruptive problems) or aloe vera gel.

▶ According to Frank L. Greenway, MD, medical director, Pennington Biomedical Research Center in Baton Rouge, Louisiana, shingles pain can be eased by geranium oil.

Applied directly on the affected area, 100% geranium oil relieved pain dramatically in 25% of patients whose pain after a case of shingles had lasted for three months or more and was not relieved by standard pain medications. Fifty percent of the patients showed some relief, and 25% did not benefit. Geranium oil is available in health food stores.

## HICCUPS

A hiccup is a spastic contraction of the diaphragm—the large circular muscle that separates the chest from the abdomen.

Hiccups are a great conversation starter. If you're in a room with 30 people, ask each one of them how they get rid of the hiccups and you will probably get 30 different remedies.

According to the *Guinness Book of World Records* (Guinness), the longest recorded attack of hiccups is that which afflicted Charles Osborne of Anthon, Iowa. He was born in 1894 and got the hiccups in 1922, when he was slaughtering a hog.

The hiccups continued but didn't stop him from marrying twice and fathering eight children. (Who knows, maybe they helped.)

In 1983, *Guinness* reported that Charles Osborne had hiccupped—and was still hiccuping—about 420 million times. By the time he died in 1990, the hiccupping had slowed down from 40 times a minute to 20 times a minute. You do the math.

## Natural Remedies

To prevent a case of the hiccups, do not slaughter a hog. To cure a case of the hiccups, try one or more of the following remedies.

▶ Drink a glass of pineapple or orange juice.

▶ Make believe your index finger is a mustache. Place it under your nose and press in hard for 30 seconds.

▶ Drink a glass of water that has a tablespoon in it—the bowl of the spoon being the part that's in the water. As you drink, be sure the metal handle of the spoon is pressed against your left temple.

▶ Swallow a teaspoon of fresh onion juice.

▶ Mix a teaspoon of apple cider vinegar in a cup of warm water and drink it down.

▶ Drink a glass of water from the far side of the glass. You have to bend far forward to do this without dribbling all over yourself.

## Pep It Up

▶ When children between the ages of seven and 14 have the hiccups, promise to double their allowance if they can hiccup once more after you say "Go!" Chances are there will not be one more hiccup after you say "Go!" We don't know why, but it works…most of the time.

▶ Men should place an ice cube right below their Adam's apple and count to 150.

▶ Take a mouthful of water and keep it in your mouth while you stick the middle fingers of each hand into your ears and press fairly firmly. Count to 100, then swallow the water and unplug your ears.

## Do You Know La Bohème?

▶ Pretend you're singing at New York City's Metropolitan Opera House without a microphone, and the foremost opera critic is in the last row of the uppermost tier. One aria and the hiccups should disappear. (Of course, so might your roommate.)

▶ Take seven drinks of water without taking a breath in between swallows. While you're drinking the water, keep turning the glass to the left.

▶ Put a handkerchief over a glass of water and suck the water through it as you would with a straw.

▶ Stick out your tongue as far as possible and keep it out for three minutes. Be careful, one big hiccup and—ouch!

## Sole Solution

▶ The sole of the foot is an acupressure point for curing the hiccups. Massage the center of the sole for as long as it takes for the hiccups to stop.

▶ Mix ½ teaspoon of sugar in ½ glass of water and drink it slowly.

▶ Place a pencil between your teeth so that it sticks out on both sides of your mouth. Chomp down on it while drinking a glass of water. (You might want to wear a bib.)

▶ Locate the area about two to three inches above your navel and between the two sides of your rib cage. Press in with the fingers of both of your hands and stay that way long enough to say to yourself—"One, two, three, four, I don't have the hiccups anymore."

If you still have them, try reciting "The Rime of the Ancient Mariner"—it's a very, very long poem written by Samuel Taylor Coleridge in 1798.

## Bald and Beautiful

▶ Close your eyes, hold your breath and think of 10 bald men. Let us start you off—Sean Connery, Montel Williams, Howie Mandel, Paul Shaffer, Michael Jordan, etc.

▶ Pardon our name-dropping, but…television news journalist Jane Pauley told us that her husband, Garry Trudeau (creator of the "Doonesbury" comic strip), gets painful hiccups. His remedy is to put a teaspoon of salt on half a lemon and then suck the juice out of the lemon.

▶ Our great-aunt Molly used to soak a cube of sugar in fresh lemon juice and then let it dissolve in her mouth. She did it to get rid of the hiccups. She also did it as a shortcut whenever she drank tea.

### Think of Peter Rabbit

▶ Just visualizing a rabbit—its cute little face, quivering nose and white whiskers—has been known to make the hiccups disappear.

▶ One of the most common remedies for hiccups is a teaspoon of granulated sugar. It supposedly irritates the throat, causing an interruption of the vagus nerve impulse pattern that is responsible for triggering the spasms of the diaphragm. (Just reading the previous sentence aloud may help you get rid of the hiccups.)

In Arabia, people have been known to use sand in place of sugar.

▶ Another way you might interrupt the diaphragmatic spasms is by holding your arms above your head and panting like a dog. Well, you might not get rid of the hiccups, but you may end up with some table scraps.

▶ Lay a broom on the floor and jump over it six times. If you want to update this remedy, try jumping over a vacuum cleaner. For all of you rich people, jump over your maid.

▶ Turn yourself into a "T" by spreading out your arms. Then give a big yawn.

▶ Pretend you're chewing gum while sticking your fingers in your ears, gently pressing inward. "What did you say? I can't hear you. My fingers are in my ears."

▶ If nothing else works, take a hot bath. This has helped cure severe cases of hiccups.

### When Someone Else Has Hiccups…

▶ Take something cold that's made of metal—a spoon is good—tie a string around it and lower it down the hiccupper's back.

▶ Suddenly accuse the hiccupper of doing something he/she did not do—"You left the water running in the tub!"…"You borrowed money from me and forgot to pay it back!"…"You skipped the best part!"

## HYPERTENSION

More than 65 million Americans have been diagnosed with hypertension (high blood pressure). If you're one of those people, obviously you're not alone.

We urge you to take a look at your lifestyle and, once and for all, do something to change whatever is causing the blood pressure problem.

The most important dietary recommendation for lowering blood pressure is to increase the consumption of plant foods in the diet, according to Jade Beutler, RRT, RCP, San Diego–based CEO of Lignan Research LLC and a licensed health care practitioner. A primarily vegetarian diet typically contains less saturated fat and refined carbohydrates, and more potassium, complex carbohydrates, fiber, calcium, magnesium, vitamin C and essential fatty acids.

## Basic Solutions

**T**o help combat the effects of hypertension, start with these suggestions—after consulting your doctor.

◆ If you're overweight, diet sensibly (without diet pills).

◆ Eliminate salt (use sea salt in moderation), and cut down on or cut out red meat.

◆ To reduce the stress of your everyday life, try meditation or a self-help program. Ask a health professional for guidance and reputable contacts.

◆ If you smoke, stop! (*See* "Smoking" on page 167.)

◆ If you drink alcohol, stop! Or at least cut down drastically.

Double-blind studies have demonstrated that either fish oil supplements or flaxseed oil, both rich in omega-3 fatty acids, are very effective in lowering blood pressure. (*See* "Six Sensational Superfoods" on page 262 for detailed information on flaxseed.)

When blood pressure is measured, there are two numbers reported. The first and higher number is the systolic. It measures the pressure inside the arteries when the heart beats (constricts). The diastolic is the lower number and measures the pressure in the arteries when the heart is at rest in between beats.

Hypertension is ranked in stages…

|  | Systolic | Diastolic |
|---|---|---|
| **Prehypertension** | 120 to 139 | 80 to 89 |
| **Stage 1** | 140 to 159 | 90 to 99 |
| **Stage 2** | greater than 160 | greater than 100 |

We saw a woman wearing a T-shirt that said—"Anybody with normal blood pressure these days just isn't paying attention."

Read on for more strategies that will help to improve your blood pressure…

## If Your Blood Pressure Is High…

▶ Eat two apples a day. The pectin in apples may help lower high blood pressure.

▶ Eat raw garlic in salads and use it in cooking. Also take garlic supplements daily—one after breakfast and one after dinner.

### Go Fish

▶ According to a university study, blood pressure can be reduced by staring at fish in a fish tank. The relaxation benefits of fish-watching are equal to biofeedback and meditation.

If caring for a tank of fish isn't for you, check the Internet or your local video store for tapes of aquariums and fish swimming in their natural habitats.

▶ Cucumbers are rich in potassium, phosphorus and calcium. They're also a good diuretic and calming agent. To help bring down blood pressure, try eating a cucumber every day. If you have a juicer, drink ½ cup of fresh cucumber juice. You can also include some carrots and parsley, which is another good diuretic.

▶ Drink 2 cups of potato water daily. (*See* "Preparation Guide" on page 252.)

▶ Cayenne pepper is a wonderful blood pressure stabilizer.

## ■ Recipe ■

### Cucumbers in Sour Cream

2 large cucumbers, sliced

1 tsp salt

1 cup sour cream

2 Tbsp vinegar

1 Tbsp chopped chives

1 tsp dill weed

¼ tsp granulated sugar

Dash of pepper

Peel cucumbers and slice thin. Sprinkle with 1 tsp salt and let stand 30 minutes.

Drain well. Combine sour cream, vinegar, chives, dill weed, sugar and pepper. Pour over cucumbers. Taste and add additional salt, if needed. Chill in refrigerator for at least 30 minutes.

*Source: www.recipegoldmine.com*

▶ Add ⅛ teaspoon to a cup of goldenseal tea (*see* "Preparation Guide" on page 250) and drink a cup daily.

### Don't Spit Out the Seeds

▶ In a blender, or by using a mortar and pestle, crush 2 teaspoons of dried watermelon seeds. Put them in a cup of just-boiled water and let them steep for one hour. Stir, strain and drink the watermelon-seed tea a half-hour before a meal.

Repeat the procedure before each meal, three times a day. After taking the tea for a few days, have your pressure checked and see if it has improved. Watermelon-seed tea can be bought at health food stores.

## More Accurate Blood Pressure Readings

**W**hen measuring blood pressure, it's important to make sure your reading is as accurate as possible. One way to ensure you get a proper reading is to keep your arm bent.

According to investigators from the University of California, San Diego (UCSD) School of Medicine and the Medical College of Wisconsin in Milwaukee, blood pressure readings can be 10% higher if a person's arm is held parallel to the body.

So bend that arm! Make sure your elbow is at a right angle to your body with the elbow flexed at a heart level. This should give the most precise reading. And for the record, it doesn't matter if you're sitting, standing or laying down for the test—as long as you're in the same position every time you're tested, results should be accurate.

 **NOTE:** Watermelon seeds are known to strengthen kidney function—and increase urine production. Be prepared to use bathroom facilities often.

▶ How would you like a hot or cold cup of raspberry-leaf tea? It may help bring down your blood pressure. Combine 1 ounce of raspberry leaves to 2 cups of boiling water and simmer for 20 minutes in an enamel or glass saucepan. Drink 1 cup a day, hot or cold (no ice cubes). After a week, check the results by having your blood pressure taken.

▶ The faster you talk, the less oxygen you have coming in. The less oxygen, the harder your heart has to work to maintain the supply of oxygen in your body. The harder the heart has to work, the higher your blood pressure seems to go.

The bottom line here is that if you talk slowly, you should need to take bigger and better breaths, giving you more oxygen and preventing your blood pressure from climbing.

## If Your Blood Pressure Is Low...

Just as there are people with high blood pressure, there are people (not as many) with low blood pressure. These remedies are said to be effective blood pressure regulators and stabilizers.

▶ Scientific studies have shown that five to 10 minutes of laughter first thing in the morning improves blood pressure levels. What's there to laugh at first thing in the morning? Listen to a funny local radio DJ, or go on-line and type in "jokes" at any Internet search engine (Yahoo!, Google, AltaVista, Dogpile, Excite).

▶ We heard from a Russian folk healer who recommends drinking ½ cup of raw beet juice when a person feels that his/her blood pressure may be a little too low. This healer also told us that a person with low blood pressure knows that feeling.

### 7–14–7 Exercise

▶ Deep breathing may help to bring your blood pressure levels up to normal. First thing in the morning and last thing at night, perform this breathing exercise.

Let all the air out of your lungs—exhale, squeezing all the air out—then let the air in through your nostrils slowly, to the count of seven. When no more air will fit in your lungs, hold tight for the count of 14. Next, gently let the air out through your mouth to the count of seven—all the way out. Inhale and exhale this way 10 times.

Even when your blood pressure is normal, continue this breathing exercise for all kinds of physical benefits.

▶ Licorice root, which is available at health food stores, will help raise blood pressure. Take it in the morning and at noon. Ebb off when blood pressure is normal.

**CAUTION:** Do not take licorice root if you have high blood pressure or kidney problems. It can cause renal failure.

# INDIGESTION

The famous actress and comedienne Mae West once said, "Too much of a good thing…is wonderful!" We say, "Too much of a good thing…can cause indigestion!"

There are several different types of indigestion—mild, severe and persistent. Persistent indigestion may be caused by a food allergy. The best course of action is to get professional medical help and have it checked out.

That said, severe indigestion or stomach pain may be something a lot more serious than you think, so it's also important to seek professional help immediately.

**CAUTION:** Never take a laxative when you have severe stomach pain.

Mild indigestion usually produces one or a combination of the following symptoms—stomachache, heartburn, nausea and vomiting, or gas (flatulence). If you are feeling minor tummy troubles, here are some remedies to try.

## Natural Remedies

The first thing a person suffering from a mild case of indigestion usually does is promise never to overindulge again. That takes care of next time. As for now, relief may be just a few paragraphs away.

▶ When you have stomach cramps caused by indigestion, sip some peppermint or ginger tea as your after-dinner drink.

### Roll Some Relief

▶ In the case of acid indigestion, thoroughly chew a teaspoon of dry rolled oats, then swallow them. The oats not only soothe the acid condition, they also neutralize it.

▶ We keep *daikon* in the refrigerator at all times. It's a Japanese radish—white, crisp, delicious and available at your greengrocer or Asian market. It's an effective digestive aid, especially when eating heavy, deep-fried foods.

Either grate 1 to 2 tablespoons or have a couple of slices of the daikon with your meal. It also helps detoxify animal protein and fats.

▶ When you have a white-coated tongue, bad breath and a headache, it's probably due to an upset stomach. A wise choice of herbs would be sage. Sip a cup of herbal sage tea slowly. (*See* "Preparation Guide" on page 250.)

### Red-String Relief

▶ We have come across some strange-sounding remedies for which there seems to be no logical explanation. We've included a few of them, simply because they sometimes work.

This is certainly one of them—when your stomach aches, tie a red string around your waist. (If the pain disappears, fine. If not, try another remedy.)

▶ When you have a sour stomach, chew a few anise seeds, cardamom seeds or caraway seeds. All will sweeten your stomach and your breath as well.

▶ Like rolled oats, raw potato juice also neutralizes acidity. Grate a potato and squeeze it through cheesecloth to get the juice. Dilute 1 tablespoon of potato juice with ½ cup of warm water. Drink it slowly.

## Brush It Off

▶ Take a wire hairbrush or a metal comb and brush or comb the backs of your hands for three to four minutes. It's supposed to relieve that sluggish feeling you get from eating one of those old-fashioned, home-cooked, the-cholesterol-can-kill-ya meals.

▶ This remedy was recommended to us for a nervous stomach. Add ¼ teaspoon of oregano and ½ teaspoon of marjoram to 1 cup of hot water. Let it steep for 10 minutes. Strain and sip slowly. Two hours later, if you still have stomach uneasiness, drink another fresh cup of the mixture.

## International Relations

▶ This remedy from India is recommended for quick relief after a junk-food binge. Crush 1 teaspoon of fenugreek seeds and steep them in 1 cup of just-boiled water for five minutes. Strain and drink slowly. You should feel better in about 10 minutes.

▶ According to a Chinese massage therapist, if you are having stomach discomfort, there will be tender areas at the sides of your knees, just below the kneecaps. As you massage those spots and the tenderness decreases, so should the corresponding stomachache.

▶ Mix 1 tablespoon of honey and 2 teaspoons of apple cider vinegar into a glass of hot water and drink the mixture.

**WARNING:** Diabetics and people with honey allergies should not use honey.

▶ By eating one large radish, all the symptoms and discomfort of indigestion may disappear,

### ■ Recipe ■

#### Papaya Shake

1 ripe papaya, peeled, seeded and cut into chunks
1 tsp vanilla extract
3 Tbsp granulated sugar
⅛ to ¼ tsp ground cinnamon
1 cup milk
12 ice cubes
Fresh mint leaves

Combine the first five ingredients in a blender and process until smooth. Add ice cubes and process until frothy. Garnish with mint leaves, if desired.
Makes 3 cups.

*Source: www.recipegoldmine.com*

unless radishes do not agree with you. In that case, move on to the next remedy.

## Mellow Yellow

▶ Put on a yellow slicker, not because it's raining, but because color therapists claim that the color yellow has rays that can help heal all digestive problems. Eat yellow foods like bananas, lemons, pineapple, squash and grapefruit. Lie down on a yellow sheet and get a massage with some yellow oil. What could be bad?

▶ Chamomile and peppermint teas are very soothing. At the first sign of indigestion, drink a cup of either one.

▶ Eat, drink or take some form of papaya after eating. Fresh papaya (the *yellow* ones are ripe), papaya juice or papaya pills help combat

indigestion, thanks to papain, the potent digestive enzyme they contain. (*See* recipe on page 123.)

► In moderation, drink some white wine *after*—not during—a meal to help overcome indigestion. (Women who are pregnant or nursing should not drink alcohol.)

### Hits the Bullseye

► Arrowroot is a wonderful stomach settler. Combine 1 tablespoon of arrowroot with enough water to make a smooth paste. Boil the mixture. Let it cool, then add 1 tablespoon of lime juice and take it when you have "agita."

► Garlic helps stimulate the secretion of digestive enzymes. If you're plagued by indigestion, take garlic supplements after lunch and after dinner. Use garlic in salads and, whenever possible, in cooking—unless garlic gives you indigestion.

 **NOTE:** Eating garlic with parsley can help prevent the indigestion from garlic.

► Scrub an orange and eat some of the peel five minutes after finishing a meal.

► Boiled or steamed zucchini sprinkled with raw grated almonds is a side dish that will ensure better digestion.

► Cayenne pepper sprinkled sparingly (no more than ¼ teaspoon) on food or in soup will aid digestion.

### Herbal Helper

► Add fresh basil to food while cooking. It will make the food more digestible and also help prevent constipation.

If you really have a taste for basil, add ⅛ to ¼ teaspoon to a glass of white wine and drink it *after*, not during, the meal. (Women who are pregnant or nursing should not drink alcohol.)

## Indigestion Prevention

► If you have trouble digesting raw vegetables, at least three hours before eating, sprinkle the veggies with fresh lemon juice. Somehow the lemon, as wild as this sounds, partly digests the hard-to-digest parts of the greens.

► A doctor we know practices preventive medicine on himself before eating Szechuan or Mexican food or any other "hot" food that would ordinarily give him an upset stomach. He takes 1 tablespoon of extra-virgin, cold-pressed olive oil about 15 minutes before the meal.

### The Quick Kick Test

**A**re you sure it's gas and not your appendix? To test for appendix problems, in a standing position, lift your right leg and then quickly jut it forward as though kicking something. If you have an excruciating, sharp pain anywhere in the abdominal area, it may be your appendix.

If this is the case, seek medical attention immediately. If there is no sharp pain when you kick, it's probably just gas, but you should check with your doctor to be sure.

▶ We've heard that 1 teaspoon of whole white mustard seeds taken before a meal may help prevent stomach distress.

▶ Add 1 cup of bran and 1 cup of oatmeal to a gallon of water. Let it stand for 24 hours, then strain, keeping the liquid. Drink a cup 15 minutes before each meal to prevent indigestion.

▶ To prevent indigestion by aiding digestion, see if this helps—try not to drink any beverages during or after meals. Wait at *least* one hour—preferably two or three hours—after eating to drink any liquids.

## Gas/Flatulence

By now, you probably know which foods give you gas, and which meals may prove lethal. But do you know about food combining? The library has lots of books with information on the subject, and there are simple, inexpensive charts available at health food stores. If you follow proper food combining—for example, wait two hours after eating regular food before eating fruit—you shouldn't ever have a problem with gas. But it's not always convenient to stick to good combinations.

Here are some remedies for when your food combining is less than perfect and, as a result, you're cooking with gas.

### Charcoal, Not Gas

▶ When you know you're eating food that's going to make you and everyone around you

sorry you ate it, take two charcoal tablets or capsules as soon as you finish your meal.

Just be aware that activated charcoal will adsorb medication you may be taking, such as birth-control pills, aspirin and many prescription drugs. (*See* page 57 for more information.)

It's important to take the charcoal quickly because gas forms in the lower intestine and if you wait too long, the charcoal can't get down there fast enough to help.

> **WARNING:** Do not take charcoal capsules or tablets more often than directed. Charcoal is a powerful adsorbent and will rob you of important nutrients you get from food.

▶ A strong cup of peppermint tea will give you relief quickly, especially if you walk around as you drink it.

▶ A hot water compress placed directly on the abdomen can relieve gas pains.

▶ Add 1 teaspoon of anisette liqueur to a cup of warm water. Stir and sip.

### Try the Dagwood Special

▶ An old home remedy for gas and heartburn is a raw onion sandwich. Some people would rather have gas and heartburn than eat a raw onion sandwich, and some people get gas and heartburn from a raw onion sandwich. That said, if onions agree with you, it's worth a try.

▶ Add ½ teaspoon of bay leaves to a cup of boiling water. Let it steep, then strain it and drink it down slowly.

▶ Get rid of a gas condition with mustard seeds and lots of water. The first day, take two seeds, the second day take four and so on until you take 12 seeds on the sixth day. Then work

it down until you're taking two seeds on the eleventh day. By then, you should be fine. Continue to take two seeds a day. Always take the mustard seeds on an empty stomach.

▶ Add 1 cup of bran and 1 cup of oatmeal to a gallon of water. Let it stand for 24 hours, then strain, keeping the liquid. Drink a cup 15 minutes before each meal to prevent indigestion.

## Soothing Seeds

▶ Each one of the following seeds is known to give fast relief from the pain of gas—anise seeds, caraway seeds, dill seeds and fennel seeds (all are available at health food stores).

To release the essential oils, gently crush the seeds and add 1 teaspoon to a cup of just-boiled water. Let it steep for 10 minutes. Strain and drink. If the gas pains don't disappear right away, drink another cup of the seed tea before eating your next meal.

▶ The unripe berries of a pimento evergreen tree are called allspice. It was given its name because it tastes like a combination of spices—cloves, juniper berries, cinnamon and pepper. Allspice is said to be effective in treating flatulent indigestion. Add 1 teaspoon of powdered allspice to a cup of just-boiled water and drink. If you have the dried fruit, chew ½ teaspoon, then swallow.

## Pretzel Logic

▶ This gas-expelling yoga technique should be done in the privacy of your bedroom. Lie on the bed face down with one leg tucked under you. Got the picture? Your knee is under your chest.

Stay that way for three or four minutes, then stretch out that leg and bring the other leg up, with the knee under your chest. Every

three or four minutes, reverse the legs. When you've expelled the gas, you can stop.

▶ If you feel you have a gas pocket, or trapped gas, lie down on the floor or on a bed and slowly bring your knees up to your chest to the count of 10, then back down.

In between this exercise, massage your stomach in a circular motion, with the top half of your fingers, pressing hard to move that gas around and out.

▶ Drink ginger tea after a heavy, gassy meal. Steep ¼ teaspoon of powdered ginger in a cup of hot water for five minutes, or let a few small pieces of fresh gingerroot steep, then drink the tea slowly.

▶ To prevent beans from giving you gas, soak dried beans overnight. In the morning, pour off the water. Add fresh water and an onion, then boil them.

When the liquid comes to a boil, pour off the water and throw away the onion. Then, cook the beans the way you ordinarily cook them—only this time, they may not create gas.

## Belching Relief

▶ This is a Taoist remedy that dates back to the 6th century BC. Scrub a tangerine, then peel it and boil the pieces of peel for five minutes. Strain, let cool and drink the tangerine tea. The tea should stop you from belching. You can also eat the tangerine peel as a digestive aid.

# Heartburn

Certain foods may not agree with you, causing the stomach acid to back up (reflux). That's when you have heartburn (you literally feel like your heart is burning). Our mother used to get heartburn a lot. We remember asking her, "How do you know when you have it?" And our mother would always answer, "You'll know!" She was right.

## Natural Remedies

When you have heartburn, it's best not to lie down. The backflow of stomach acid into the esophagus increases when you lie on your right side, so if you have to lie down, stay on your left side. If that doesn't work, stay on your feet and try one of the following remedies.

▶ Eat six blanched almonds. Chew each one at least 30 times.

▶ Eat a slice of raw potato.

▶ Mix 1 tablespoon of apple cider vinegar and 1 tablespoon of honey into a cup of warm water. Stir and drink.

**WARNING:** Diabetics and people with honey allergies should not use honey.

▶ Grate a raw potato and put it in cheesecloth. Squeeze out the juice in a glass. Add twice the amount of warm water as potato juice and drink it down.

▶ Peel and eat a raw carrot. Chew each bite 30 times.

## Lemon Aid

▶ If you have heartburn from eating something sweet, squeeze the juice from half a lemon into a cup of warm water. Add ½ teaspoon of salt and drink it slowly.

▶ Keep chewable papaya tablets with you and, at the first sign of heartburn or any kind of indigestion, pop papaya pills in your mouth, chew and swallow.

▶ A cup of peppermint tea has been known to relieve the discomfort of heartburn. It helps relieve gas, too.

▶ Eat 1 teaspoon of *gomasio* (sesame seeds and sea salt, available at health food stores). Chew thoroughly before swallowing.

## Be a Flake!

▶ This may not be too appetizing, but it works —swallow a teaspoon or two of uncooked oat flakes, after chewing thoroughly.

▶ The flow of saliva can neutralize the stomach acids that slosh up and cause heartburn.

According to the late Wylie J. Dodds, MD, who was a professor of radiology and medicine at the Medical College of Wisconsin in Milwaukee, chewing gum (we suggest sugarless) can increase the production of saliva eight or nine times, and reduce the damage caused by stomach acids.

## Heartburn Prevention

► Turmeric, a basic ingredient in Indian curry dishes, is also a digestive aid. It stimulates the flow of saliva (saliva neutralizes acid and helps push digestive juices back down to where they belong). If you're about to eat something that typically gives you heartburn, spice up the food with turmeric.

If it's not an appropriate ingredient for the meal, take two or three turmeric capsules, (available at health food stores) before eating.

## Stomach Cramps

► Steep 1 teaspoon of fresh or dried parsley in 1 cup of hot water. After five minutes, strain and slowly drink the parsley tea. Remember that parsley tea also acts as a diuretic, so make sure you plan accordingly, because you may have to "eat and run."

► Slice one medium-sized onion and boil it in 1 cup of milk. Drink this concoction warm. It sounds awful and probably is, but it's an old home remedy that may work.

► American Indians used this one for stomachaches—pour 1 cup of boiling water over 1 teaspoon of cornmeal. Let it sit for five minutes. Add salt to taste and drink slowly.

► Water has amazing healing power. Get in a hot shower and let the water beat down on your stomach for 10 to 15 minutes. By the time you dry off, you should be feeling a lot better.

# **J**ET LAG

**W**hen you travel by air, it generally takes one day to recover for every time zone that you pass through. New York to California—that's three time zones, so three days of jet lag. Actually, going east to west and gaining a few hours is better jet-lag-wise than west to east when you lose a few hours.

In terms of getting that first good night's sleep at your destination, it seems best to plan on arriving in the evening.

England's Royal Air Force School of Aviation Medicine (King's College, London) suggests that when flying east, fly early…when heading west, fly late.

Surely you've heard that alcohol is one of the most powerful dehydrators there is. And you must know that just being in an airplane is dehydrating. But do you know that dehydration makes jet lag worse?

*Conclusion: Do not drink any alcoholic beverages while airborne.* Instead, try to drink lots of water and juice—as much as possible. If you have to keep going to the lavatory, good. Walking up and down the aisles will help refresh and prepare you for your new time zone.

## Natural Remedies

▶ A couple of days before flying, take ginkgo-hawthorn tincture (available at health food stores) and follow the dosage on the label.

▶ It's been reported that taking ½ to 1 mg of melatonin right before boarding the plane has prevented jet lag. If you know that you really suffer from jet lag, ask your doctor about taking melatonin before your upcoming flight. But be careful—some studies in animals suggest that people with high blood pressure or cardiovascular disease should not take melatonin. Again,

---

### **Anti-Jet Lag Diet**

**T**his diet was developed by the US Department of Energy's Argonne National Laboratory in Argonne, Illinois, to help air travelers quickly adjust their bodies' internal clocks to new time zones. Start the program three days before departure day.

*Day 1:* Have a high-protein breakfast and lunch, and a high-carbohydrate (no meat) dinner. No coffee except between 3 pm and 5 pm.

*Day 2:* Have very light meals—salads, light soups, fruit and juices. Coffee only between 3 pm and 5 pm.

*Day 3:* Same as Day 1.

*Day 4:* Departure. If you must have a caffeinated beverage (such as coffee or cola) you can have a cup in the morning when traveling west, or between 6 pm and 11 pm when traveling east. Have fruit or juice until your first meal. To know when to have your first meal, figure out when breakfast time will be at your destination.

If your flight is long enough, sleep until your destination's normal breakfast time, *but no later* (that's important). Wake up and eat a big, high-protein breakfast. Stay awake and active. Continue the day's meals according to mealtimes at your destination, and you'll be in sync when you arrive.

For more information on the diet, go to *www.antijetlagdiet.com.*

always consult with your health professional before taking melatonin.

### Play Make-Believe

▶ As soon as you board the plane, pretend it's whatever time it actually is at your destination. In other words, if you board the plane at 7 pm in New York, and you're headed for London where it's 1 am, pull down your window shade or wear dark glasses and, if possible, go to sleep.

If you board a plane late that night and it's already daylight at your destination, force yourself to stay awake during the flight. Making believe that you're in the new time zone at the very start of your trip should help you acclimate more quickly.

▶ William F. Buckley, famed "conservative intellectual" and founder of the *National Review* magazine, got this remedy from a world traveler friend of a British doctor specializing in jet lag. The theory is that jet lag comes from internal perspiring, which causes a deficiency of salt in the body.

According to Buckley, the doctor said to put a heaping teaspoon of salt in a cup of coffee as soon as you get onto the plane and drink it. Five hours later, drink another cup with salt and you will experience a miracle. The salted coffee will taste like ambrosia. That is your body talking, telling you how grateful it is that you have given it the salt it so badly needs.

**NOTE:** This salty coffee remedy is *not* for anyone who is watching his/her sodium and/or caffeine intake.

## **M**EMORY PROBLEMS

I keep misplacing my house keys, I can't remember anyone's name—I finally told my doctor that my memory has been getting terrible lately."

"What did the doctor do about it?"

"He made me pay in advance."

Sure, it's easy to make jokes, but we know how frustrating it is to feel like your memory is slipping. One remedy for remembering a familiar name, place or fact is to simply relax and forget that you can't remember. When you're not thinking about it, it will pop into your mind.

Neither of us believes a good or not-so-good memory is a matter of age. We think we're all victims of data overload.

The genius scientist and physicist Albert Einstein didn't believe in remembering anything he could look up. While that's not always practical, it is a tension-relieving thought.

Meanwhile, we have some remedies that may help you re-create a wonderful memory.

## Natural Remedies

▶ Choline is used by our brains to make the important chemical acetylcholine, which is required for memory.

At a health food or vitamin store, buy choline chloride or choline hydrochloride—*not* choline bitartrate. (The latter sometimes causes diarrhea.) Taking choline may improve your memory and your ability to learn. You should also notice a keener sense of mental organization.

*Dose:* Take 500 mg of choline twice a day. (Set your alarm clock so you won't forget to take it.)

▶ Here's a memory-improving drink—combine half a glass of carrot juice with half a glass of milk, and drink daily.

▶ Three prunes a day supposedly improves memory. It can also help prevent constipation, and since constipation paralyzes the thinking process, take three prunes a day.

▶ Daily doses of fresh ginger used in cooking and for tea may heighten memory.

▶ Add four cloves to a cup of sage tea. Sage and cloves have been said to strengthen memory. Drink a cup every day.

### *Try This Jungle Punch*

▶ Yerba maté (pronounced *mah-tay*) is considered the national beverage in many South American countries, including Paraguay, Uruguay, Argentina, Chile and Brazil. The herb is cultivated from leaves of a tree that is related to the holly and is grown today mainly in Paraguay and Uruguay.

One of the many positive effects of the herb, according to South American medical authorities, is that it strengthens one's memory. It's also been proven in European studies to boost the body's immunity, make people feel better both physically and mentally, and it can

131

actually help them lose weight. It's no wonder that this amazing drink is guzzled with as much gusto in South America as coffee is in the US. Drink one cup of yerba maté early in the day. It is available at health food stores.

To read more about this near-magical drink, *see* page 195.

> **NOTE:** Be aware that yerba maté contains caffeine, although less than coffee or regular tea.

▶ Take 1 teaspoon of apple cider vinegar in a glass of room-temperature water before each meal. Not only is it said to be an excellent tonic for the memory, but it also curbs the appetite.

▶ Ah, the healing powers of almonds. Eat six raw almonds every day to help improve your memory.

### Eye-Opening Discovery

▶ Our research led us to a Japanese doctor whose records show that he successfully treated more than 500 patients who were having memory problems. How? By recommending they take eyebright, an herb best known for treating eye disorders…until now.

Add ½ ounce of eyebright and 1 tablespoon of clover honey to 1½ cups of just-boiled water. When it's cool, strain the mixture and put it in a bottle. Drink ¾ cup before lunch and ¾ cup before dinner.

▶ Two mustard seeds, taken as you would take pills, first thing every morning, are said to revive one's memory.

▶ Eat a handful of sunflower seeds daily. These seeds are beneficial in many ways, one being memory improvement.

### ■ Recipe ■

#### Cinnamon-Roasted Almonds

1 egg white
1 tsp cold water
4 cups almonds
½ cup granulated sugar
¼ tsp salt
½ tsp ground cinnamon

Preheat oven to 250° F. Lightly grease one 15" x 10" x 1" jellyroll pan.

Lightly beat the egg white, then add water and beat until frothy but not stiff. Add the nuts and stir until well coated.

Sift together the sugar, salt and cinnamon. Sprinkle over the nuts and toss to mix.

Spread on pan and bake for one hour, stirring occasionally.

*Source: www.recipegoldmine.com*

▶ According to a gem therapist, wearing an amethyst helps strengthen one's memory. You just have to remember to wear the amethyst.

### Walk This Way

▶ Walking increases oxygen flow to the brain …and it's never too late! Researchers experimented on adults between the ages of 60 and 75. The group that walked briskly three days a week, starting with 15 minutes each day and working their way up to 45 minutes a day, had a 15% boost in mental functioning. That 15% could mean an end to the frustration of not remembering things…at any age.

▶ What's the most prevalent color in legal pads? In Post-Its? Notice a pattern forming here? According to color therapy research, the color yellow most stimulates the brain. Writing on yellow paper may help you better remember whatever it is you've written.

## The Case for Color

If you don't think that color has an impact on us, think again after you read the following—Alexander Schauss, PhD, president of the Life Sciences Division of the American Institute for Biosocial and Medical Research in Tacoma, Washington, recommended that Blackfriars Bridge in London be painted a particular shade of blue. Called Ertel Blue, the color was supposed to reduce the incidence of suicides off the bridge, the highest of any bridge on the Thames River.

The bridge was painted Ertel Blue and the effect was dramatic. No suicides were reported from that point on.

## MUSCLE ACHES

Muscle strain, a tight, sore neck…leg cramps…an achy body can be such a pain! But most minor muscle aches seem to loosen up quite well when treated to a massage or a nice, hot bath. In addition, these remedies may help ease your aches and pains.

▶ Prepare strong ginger tea with 2 teaspoons of ginger powder or fresh, grated ginger root in 2 cups of water. Let it simmer until the water turns yellowish in color. Add the ginger tea to a bathful of warm water. Relax in the tub for 20 to 30 minutes. This ginger tea bath may relieve muscle stiffness and soreness and is wonderful for one's circulation.

## Charley Horse

▶ When you have sudden muscle stiffness or pain (charley horse), soak in a tub of "old faithful"—Epsom salts. Pour 3 cups into warm water. Stay in the water 20 to 30 minutes and your charley-horse pain may start to ease.

▶ This remedy is said to be particularly effective for a charley horse. Vigorously scrub three small lemons, two small oranges and one small grapefruit. (If you can get organic produce, do so.) Cut up the six fruits and put them into a blender—peel and all. Add 1 teaspoon of cream of tartar and blend. Store the mixture in a covered jar in the refrigerator.

*Dose:* To relieve the stiffness, take 2 tablespoons of the concoction with 2 tablespoons of water twice a day—first thing in the morning and right before bedtime.

## Neck Tension

It's quite common for those of us who are under pressure to have a pain in the neck. People tend to tense up in that area, which is the worst thing to do to yourself. Your neck connects your brain and nervous system to the rest of your body. When you create tension in your neck, you impair the flow of energy throughout your system.

▶ To prevent tension buildup, do neck rolls. Start with your chin on your chest and slowly rotate your head so that your right ear reaches for your right shoulder, then head back, left ear to left shoulder, and back with your chin on your chest. Do these rolls, slowly, six times in one direction and six times in the opposite direction, morning and evening. You may hear lots of crackling, crunching and gravelly noises coming from your neck. As tension is released, the noises will quiet.

▶ If, when you roll your neck around or just turn from side to side, you hear and feel like there's gravel in your neck, eat three or four cloves of raw garlic every day. You may have to work your way up to that amount. (*See* "Six Sensational Superfoods" on page 266 for the easiest way to take raw garlic cloves.)

## Stiff Neck

▶ The medicine men and healers from several Native American tribes prescribe daily neck rubs with fresh lemon juice, as well as drinking the juice of half a lemon first thing in the morning and last thing at night.

▶ According to the ancient principles of reflexology, the base of the big toe affects the neck. Rub your hands together vigorously until you feel heat. Now you're ready to massage your big toes with circular motions. Spend a few minutes massaging the bottom of your feet at the base of the toes and the area surrounding them. As a change of pace, you might want to massage the base of your thumbs, also for a few minutes at a time. Keep at it, at least two times a day, every day.

## Whiplash

Whiplash is the result of neck muscles that were too tense to absorb a sudden thrust (like from a car accident). We've been told by medical professionals that wearing a neck collar is the worst thing you can use for whiplash. It doesn't help realign the neck and it doesn't let the body help realign itself.

Instead, a naturopath, chiropractor or osteopath can realign the neck vertebrae properly. During this uncomfortable time, wear a silk scarf. It has been known to help blood circulation and relieve muscle pain and tension in the neck.

☞ **WARNING:** If you've been in an accident and experience neck pain, get medical attention immediately. You could have a fracture that can result in paralysis if not treated.

## Leg Cramps

We've learned that leg cramps can be caused by certain nutritional deficiencies. For instance, a lack of magnesium, potassium, vitamin E, calcium or protein. Are you eating lots of greens? (And we don't mean having two or three olives in your martini.)

Cut down on fatty meats, sugar and white flour. After a week, see if there's a difference in the incidence of leg-cramping.

### Go Bananas!

▶ If you take a diuretic, you may be losing too much potassium from your system, which may be causing leg cramps. If that's the case, eat a banana or two every day. You might also want to ask your doctor to take you off the chemical diuretic and find a natural one, like cucumber, celery or lettuce.

▶ Drink a glass of tonic water. It may have enough quinine to help you and not enough to harm you.

▶ If you get leg cramps while you sleep, keep a piece of silverware—a spoon seems the safest—on your night table. When the cramp wakes you up, place the spoon on the painful area and the muscle should uncramp. Incidentally, the spoon doesn't have to be silver—stainless steel will work as well.

▶ Cramp bark is an herb that—you guessed it—is good for any sort of cramping. The tincture is available at health food stores. Take 1 to 2 teaspoons, three to five times a day.

▶ Muscular cramps that tend to occur at night may often be relieved within 20 minutes by taking this combination—1 tablespoon of calcium lactate, 1 teaspoon of apple cider vinegar and 1 teaspoon of honey in half a glass of warm water.

▶ The late D.C. Jarvis, MD, suggested taking 2 teaspoons of honey at each meal, or honey combined with 2 teaspoons of apple cider vinegar in a glass of water before each meal, as a way to prevent muscle cramps.

> **WARNING:** Diabetics and people with honey allergies should not use honey.

### Walk on the Wall Side

▶ Before you get out of bed in the morning, turn yourself around so that you can put your feet against the wall, higher than your body. Stay that way for 10 minutes. Do the same thing at night, right before you go to sleep. It will improve blood circulation and may help to prevent muscle cramps. It's also an excellent stretch that in itself may prevent cramps.

▶ *The Lancet*, the prestigious British medical journal (*www.thelancet.com*), reports that vitamin E is helpful in relieving cramps in the legs. Take vitamin E before each meal, daily (check with your doctor for amount). Within a week or two, there should be a positive difference.

▶ Take advantage of the therapeutic value of a rocking chair. Rock whenever you watch television and for at least one hour before bedtime. For those of you who sit most of the time, a rocking chair may prevent varicose veins (*see* pages 88–89) and blood clots. It may also improve circulation as well as relieve you of leg cramps.

▶ Drink 1 cup of red raspberry-leaf tea in the morning and 1 cup at night. Do this every day and you may no longer have leg cramp attacks.

▶ According to one doctor, three weeks after prescribing vitamin $B_6$ to his patients suffering from leg cramps, they were no longer bothered by them. The $B_6$ also took care of numb and tingling toes.

## Pinch It

▶ We were told about a simple acupressure technique called "acupinch." It may help relieve the pain of muscle cramps almost instantly.

The second you get a cramp, use your thumb and your index finger and pinch your philtrum—the skin between your upper lip and your nose. Keep pinching for about 20 seconds. The pain and cramp should disappear.

▶ Try drinking an 8-ounce glass of water before bedtime.

## Jogger's Leg Cramps

▶ After your run, find a cool stream of moving water in which to soak for 15 to 20 minutes.

For those of you who can only dream of that…every night, right before going to bed, walk in about 6 inches of cold water in your bathtub for three minutes.

The feedback from runners who do this has been very convincing—cold water walks prevent leg cramps. Be sure to have those non-slip stick-ons on the floor of the tub.

# NAUSEA AND VOMITING

The conditions nausea and vomiting can both be symptoms of a variety of illnesses. Nausea is an uneasiness in the stomach that may lead to vomiting (throwing up)—but not always. In any case, few things are more uncomfortable than a prolonged bout of nausea and/or vomiting. These remedies may help to settle your stomach and bring relief.

## Natural Remedies

▶ When you have an upset stomach and you're feeling nauseated, take a carbonated drink—seltzer, club soda, Perrier or some ginger ale. If you don't have any of those, and you're not on a sodium-restricted diet, mix 1 teaspoon of baking soda with 8 ounces of cold water and drink slowly. Within a few minutes, you should burp and feel better.

▶ Drink 1 cup of yarrow tea (available at health food stores). This herb is known to stop nausea in next to no time. It's also wonderful for helping tone up the digestive system.

### Gourmet Cure

▶ When the food you ate seems to be lying on your chest—or you have a bad case of stomach overload and you know you'd feel much better if you threw up—reach for the English mustard. It's available at food specialty shops.

*Dose:* Drink 1 teaspoon in a glass of warm water. If you don't vomit in 10 minutes, drink another glass of this mustard water. After

another 10 minutes, if it still hasn't worked, the third time should be the charm.

▶ To help ease a severe bout of vomiting, warm ½ cup of vinegar, saturate a washcloth in it and place the moist cloth on your bare abdomen. Put a hot water bottle on top of the cloth for extra relief.

> ☛ **WARNING:** Severe or prolonged vomiting may be a symptom of a serious illness (and can lead to dangerous dehydration). Consult a doctor for prompt medical treatment.

▶ Drink a cup of chamomile tea to calm your stomach and stop vomiting.

### Spices That Are Nice

▶ A few cloves steeped in boiling water for five minutes may do the trick. If the taste of cloves reminds you too much of the dentist, then steep a piece of cinnamon stick or 1 teaspoon of powdered ginger in boiling water. All of these are fine for stopping nausea and vomiting.

▶ Crack an ice cube and suck on the little pieces. It's worth a try when you have nothing else in the house.

▶ This remedy is the pits—the armpits. Peel a large onion and cut it in half. Place one half under each armpit. As nauseating as it sounds, we've been told it stops vomiting and relieves nausea in no time.

▶ A cup of warm water drunk a half-hour before each meal may prevent nausea.

▶ If you're on the road, feeling nauseated, stop at the nearest luncheonette and ask for a teaspoon of pure cola syrup with a water chaser.

▶ If you're home and have some cola or even root beer, let the soda go flat by stirring it. Once the fizz is gone, drink 2 or 3 ounces to ease the nausea.

**WARNING:** Seek medical attention if your stomach pain is severe or is accompanied by repeated vomiting.

# Motion Sickness

The story is told about the captain of the ship who announced, "There is no hope. We are all doomed. The ship is sinking and we'll all be dead within an hour." One voice was heard after that dire announcement. It was the seasick passenger who cried, "Thank heavens!"

If you have ever been seasick, you probably anticipated that punchline.

## Natural Remedies

Most people think air, land and sea sickness start in the stomach. Wrong! Guess again. Constant jarring of the semicircular canals in the ears cause inner balance problems that produce those awful motion sickness symptoms.

What to do? Go suck a lemon! Really! That's one of the time-tested remedies.

Here are a few more that might help you get through that miserable feeling.

▶ Pull out and pinch the skin in the middle of your inner wrist, about an inch from your palm. Keep pulling and pinching alternate wrists until you feel better.

▶ A cup of peppermint or chamomile tea may calm the stomach and alleviate nausea.

## Make Things Spicy

▶ Mix ⅛ teaspoon of cayenne pepper in a cup of warm water or a cup of soup and force yourself to finish it, even if you think it'll finish you. It won't. But it may stop the nausea.

▶ At the first sign of motion sickness, take a metal comb or wire brush and run the teeth over the backs of your hands, particularly the area from the thumb to the first finger, including the web of skin in between both fingers. You may have relief in five to 10 minutes.

▶ Briskly massage the fourth and fifth fingers of each hand, with particular emphasis on the vicinity of the pinkie's knuckle. You may feel relief within 15 minutes.

▶ During a bout of motion sickness, suck a lemon or drink some fresh-squeezed lemon juice to relieve the queasiness.

▶ To avoid the misery of motion sickness, a doctor at Brigham Young University in Provo, Utah, recommends taking two or three capsules of powdered ginger a half-hour before the expected motion.

Or stir ½ teaspoon of ginger powder into 8 ounces of warm water and drink it about 20 minutes before you travel.

▶ Here's a we-don't-know-why-it-works-but-it-does remedy—tape an *umeboshi* (that's a Japanese pickled plum) directly on your navel, right before you board a bus, train, car, plane or ship, and it should prevent motion sickness. Umeboshi plums are available at health food stores and at Asian markets.

Incidentally, the plums are very rich in calcium and iron. Of course, to reap those benefits, one must eat them, rather than tape them to one's tummy.

### Far-out Idea

▶ On any form of transportation, sit near a window so you can look out. Focus on things that are far away, not on nearby objects that move past you quickly.

▶ On a plane, to assure yourself of the smoothest flight possible, select a seat that's over the wheels, not in the tail. There's a lot more movement in the tail end of a plane.

▶ A Mexican method of preventing motion sickness is to keep a copper penny in the navel. It is supposed to work especially well on crowded bus rides over bumpy roads.

▶ For at least half a day before leaving on a trip, have only liquid foods that are practically sugar-free and salt-free.

▶ This remedy came to us from Hawaii, Afghanistan and Switzerland. Take a big brown paper bag and cut off and discard the bag's bottom. Then slit the bag from top to bottom so that it's no longer round, but instead a long piece of paper. Wrap the paper around your bare chest and secure it in place. Put your regular clothes on top of it and travel that way. It's supposed to prevent motion sickness.

## Seasickness

▶ Marjoram tea is believed to help prevent seasickness. Drink a cup of warm tea before hitting the deck.

▶ Take a teaspoon of *gomasio* (sesame seeds and sea salt, available at health food stores and Asian markets) and keep chewing it as long as you can before swallowing. It should help get rid of that queasy feeling.

## NEURALGIA

The average human body contains 45 miles of nerves. Neuralgia is an inflammation of a nerve—it can result from shingles, fractures or pinched nerves. A neuralgia attack is an excruciating sharp pain in the torso, but can also occur in the face area, usually near the nose, lips, eyes or ears.

Neuralgia is a serious medical condition that should be diagnosed and treated by a physician. But with your doctor's approval, these remedies might help.

## Natural Remedies

▶ To ease the pain of an attack, hard-boil an egg. Take off the shell, cut the egg in half and when it cools enough not to burn you, apply both halves to the trouble spot. By the time the egg cools completely, the pain should be gone.

▶ If you have neuralgic pains in your face, take a shower and let the hot streams of water beat against the problem area. Or, just try a hot water compress if the shower is too much for you to take.

## NOSEBLEEDS

Most people have had a nosebleed. They tend to be minor and can be brought on by allergies, cold weather, sinus infection and other illnesses. When the nasal passages are irritated by rubbing, picking or blowing, the tiny blood vessels break and the nose, it starts a-flowin'!

**CAUTION:** Nasal hemorrhaging—blood flowing from both nostrils—requires immediate medical attention. Rush to the nearest doctor or hospital emergency room.

Also, recurrent nosebleeds may be a symptom of an underlying ailment. Seek appropriate medical attention.

## Natural Remedies

For the *occasional* nosebleed, the first thing to do is to gently blow your nose. It will help rid your nostrils of blood clots that may prevent a blood vessel from sealing. Then try any of the following remedies.

▶ When you have a nosebleed, sit or stand. Do not lie down. Do not put your head back. It will cause you to swallow blood.

▶ The best way to stop a nosebleed is to apply direct pressure. Grasp your nose at the bridge, then move your fingers just above the fleshy part of your nose and squeeze—gently but firmly. Stay this way for 10 to 20 minutes.

If your nose is still bleeding after 20 minutes of direct pressure—get to the hospital.

### Tie Things Up

▶ This is a remedy that came to us from the Caribbean islands—take the pinkie finger of the hand opposite the bleeding nostril and tightly tie a string under the pinkie's fingernail.

▶ We know that cayenne pepper stops the bleeding of a cut or gash. We've been told that drinking ⅛ teaspoon of cayenne in a glass of warm water will help to stop a nosebleed.

▶ Gem therapists say that a nosebleed can be stopped by placing a piece of pure amber on top of the nose.

## ■ Recipe ■

### *Garlicky Greens*

1 bunch kale (about 10 cups)

1 bunch collard greens (about 10 cups)

2 Tbsp olive oil

1 large onion cut into thin half-moons
   (2 cups)

½ cup garlic, minced

½ Tbsp sea salt

1 Tbsp tamari (dark Japanese soy sauce)

De-vein the kale and collard greens. Cut into ½" pieces. In a steamer basket, steam greens for about 2 minutes.

In a large skillet, heat the oil. Add onions, garlic and sea salt.

Sauté for 5 minutes or until the onions are well cooked. Add tamari.

Add the cooked greens. Then toss with the onions and garlic. Sauté for 3 minutes.

Serve immediately.

*Source: www.vegparadise.com*

▶ Vinegar is said to be very helpful in getting a bloody nose under control. Pour some distilled white vinegar on a cloth and wash the neck, nose and temples with it. Also, mix 2 teaspoons in half a glass of warm water and drink it.

## Nosebleed Prevention

▶ If you're prone to minor nosebleeds and you're otherwise in good health, take bioflavonoids. Eat at least one citrus fruit a day, and be sure to include the white rubbery skin under the peel. It's called the "pith" and it's extremely rich in bioflavonoids.

In addition, take a vitamin C supplement with bioflavonoids. And add green leafy vegetables—lots of them—to your diet. They're rich in vitamin K, needed for the production of prothrombin, which is necessary for blood clotting.

**CAUTION:** Broccoli and turnip greens are rich in vitamin K, the clot-promoting vitamin. If you take anticlotting medication prescribed by your doctor, be aware that these vegetables may counteract the effects of the medicine.

# RASHES AND ITCHY SKIN

Dry skin is the most common cause of minor itches…and if you keep scratching it, it might turn into a rash. Other itches are caused by more serious conditions, like eczema or poison ivy.

It's a good idea to keep your nails short and—most important—try not to scratch! (Scratching can lead to infection.) If the itch or rash is persistent, see a doctor.

## Eczema

Eczema is a chronic skin disease that is very uncomfortable, but not contagious. It tends to show up on elbows, knees and wrists, and may be triggered by allergies.

▶ We've been told that eating raw potatoes— at least two a day—has worked miracles in clearing up eczema. Wear gloves, and be sure the potatoes are thoroughly cleaned and scrubbed. If you don't see an improvement after a couple of weeks (or if you start to get sick of eating raw potatoes!), try something else.

**NOTE:** People with eczema should avoid touching raw potatoes with their bare hands. Persistent or chronic eczema is best treated by a health professional.

### Brew Up a Batch

▶ Every morning and night, mix a few tablespoons of brewer's yeast with water, enough to form a paste that will cover the affected area. Gently apply it and leave it on until it dries out and crumbles off.

## Psoriasis

Psoriasis may be caused by a problem with the immune system. Skin cells grow too quickly and build up into hard, itchy, crusty patches.

▶ A cabin at the shore and frequent dips in the surf or a trip to Israel's Dead Sea seems to work wonders for psoriasis sufferers.

The next best thing is to dissolve ½ cup of sea salt in 1 gallon of water. Soak the psoriasis patches in the salty water several times a day—whenever possible.

▶ A leading authority on herbs, James A. Duke, PhD, a botanist formerly with the UDSA's Agricultural Research Service in Beltsville, Maryland, explains in his book, *The Green Pharmacy* (St. Martin's), "Several plant oils are chemically similar to fish oils, which have a reputation for helping to relieve psoriasis. Flaxseed oil contains the beneficial compounds eicosapentaenoic acid and alpha-linolenic acid."

Dr. Duke reviewed studies showing that 10 to 12 grams (5 to 6 teaspoons) of flaxseed oil can help treat psoriasis. (*See* "Six Sensational Superfoods" on page 262 for more details on flaxseed oil and how to take it.)

▶ Every evening, pat garlic oil on the affected area. You can do this by puncturing a garlic pearle (soft gel) and squishing out the oil. It may help clear up the condition.

▶ Add 1 teaspoon of sarsaparilla root (available at health food stores) to 1 cup of just-boiled water and let it steep for 15 minutes. If it's cool enough by then, strain and saturate a white washcloth in the liquid and apply it to the trouble spot.

You may need to use more than one washcloth, depending on the extent of the condition.

If it seems to agree with you, do it morning and night for an entire week and watch for an improvement.

## Pruritis and Hives

Pruritis is the fancy term for itching. This form is usually associated with some type of illness, as opposed to the itch from hives (known as *urticaria*), which is from an allergic reaction or skin sensitivity.

**WARNING:** Any persistent or chronic itch should be examined by a doctor.

*'Tis better than riches to scratch when it itches!* For relief, apply any one of the following to your itchy areas.

- Fresh sliced carrots
- 1 vitamin C tablet dissolved in 1 cup of warm water
- Lemon juice (for genital areas, dilute the juice with water)
- Raw onion slices
- A paste of uncooked oatmeal with a little water
- Apple cider vinegar (for genital areas or areas near the eyes, use diluted apple cider vinegar)

▶ If you're itching to bathe, add 2 cups of apple cider vinegar to the bathwater. Or add 3 tablespoons of baking soda to your bathwater.

Or add a pint of thyme tea to your bathwater. Thyme contains thymol, which is an antiseptic, antibacterial substance that can make your itch disappear.

▶ If you prefer a shower to a bath, take a quick shower under hot water—as hot as you can tolerate without burning yourself. The hot water has been known to stop the itching for hours at a time.

Lydia recently had an itchy patch on her back. The way she found relief was by taking a

### ■ Recipe ■

#### Sweet and Spicy Pumpkin Seeds

1 cup pumpkin seeds (from one 5- to 7-lb pumpkin)
5 Tbsp granulated sugar, divided
¼ tsp coarse salt
¼ tsp ground cumin
¼ tsp ground cinnamon
¼ tsp ground ginger
Pinch cayenne pepper, or to taste
1½ Tbsp peanut oil

Preheat oven to 250° F. Line a baking sheet with parchment paper.

Cut pumpkin open from the bottom, removing seeds with a long-handled spoon. Separate flesh from seeds and discard. Spread seeds on parchment in an even layer. Bake until dry, stirring occasionally, about one hour. Let cool.

In a medium bowl combine 3 Tbsp of the sugar, salt, cumin, cinnamon, ginger and cayenne. Heat peanut oil in a large nonstick skillet over high heat. Add pumpkin seeds and the remaining 2 Tbsp sugar. Cook until the sugar melts and the pumpkin seeds begin to caramelize, about 45 to 60 seconds. Transfer to bowl with spices and stir well to coat. Let cool.

These may be stored in an airtight container for up to one week.

Makes about 1 cup.

*Source: www.recipegoldmine.com*

fast, hot shower and—for a few seconds before ending the shower—letting the c-c-c-c-cold water run on her back. It stopped the itching, and she was able to sleep through the night. See what works best for you.

▶ To stop an itch, wash the itchy part with strong rum. This remedy is from—where else?—Jamaica, mon!

▶ Do you have a drawstring bag made of cotton? You can sew one easily, using a white handkerchief. Fill the bag with 1 pound of uncooked oatmeal and close it tightly. Throw it in your tub as you run the warm bathwater. Then take a bath and, with the oatmeal-filled bag, gently massage the dry, itchy skin. Enjoy staying in the bath for at least 15 minutes.

## *Hives*

You don't have to be a bee to have hives! These pale red bumps usually appear in response to an allergy—from food, medicines, insect stings or sun exposure.

▶ Hives usually disappear almost as fast and as mysteriously as they appear. If yours are hanging on, rub them with buckwheat flour. That ought to teach 'em to hang around!

▶ Combine 3 tablespoons of cornstarch and 1 tablespoon of vinegar. Mix well and apply the paste to the hives.

▶ Form a paste by mixing cream of tartar and water. Apply the paste to the red marks. As soon as the paste gets crumbly dry, apply more paste.

▶ Add 1 cup of baking soda to a bath and soak in it for 20 minutes. Also, drink ¼ to ½ teaspoon of baking soda in a glass of water.

 **NOTE:** None of these remedies offer relief from the Seven-Year Itch.

# Genital Itching

▶ Sprinkle cornstarch all over the area to stop the itching.

▶ Buttermilk is known to stop the itching and help heal the area. Dip a cotton pad in some buttermilk and apply it to the problem spot.

 **NOTE:** Genital and rectal itching may be due to an allergy, yeast overgrowth, poor hygiene or parasites. Go to the doctor and find the cause, then it will be easier to eliminate the problem.

# Rectal Itching

▶ Soak a cotton pad in apple cider vinegar and place it on the itching area. If the area is raw, be prepared for a temporary burning sensation. Leave the soaked cotton pad on overnight. (You can keep it in place with a sanitary napkin.) You should have instant relief. If itching starts again during the day, repeat the procedure—instead of scratching.

▶ Before bedtime, take a shower, then pat dry the itchy area and apply wheat germ oil. To avoid messy bedclothes and sheets, put a sanitary napkin over the oily area.

▶ For years, pumpkin seeds have been used as a folk treatment to control and prevent intestinal parasites (which may result in an itchy bottom). Buy the shelled and unsalted seeds, and eat a handful daily. (*See* also the recipe on page 143.)

## Heat Rash (Prickly Heat)

Heat rash can develop anytime your body overheats—typically in very hot, humid conditions. Stay cool and don't let the heat get to you!

▶ Make a soothing powder by browning ½ cup of regular flour in the oven. Then apply to the rash.

▶ Take a vitamin C supplement regularly. It helps relieve the itch.

▶ Rub the prickly-heated area with the inside of watermelon rind.

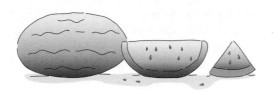

## Shaving Rash

Men, ever get a shaving rash, particularly on your neck? And women, all we need to say are two words—bikini area. These remedies may provide some relief.

▶ Puncture a vitamin E capsule, squish out the contents and mix with a little petroleum jelly. Then gently spread the mixture on the irritated skin.

▶ Cornstarch makes a soothing powder for underarms and other rash-ridden areas.

## Ringworm

Ringworm is a fairly minor fungal infection of the skin's outer layer that is related to athlete's foot, jock itch, nail infections and some forms of diaper rash.

The ringworm rash produces red, scaly patches of blisters, and it can spread quickly.

▶ A woman called us to share her ringworm remedy—mix blue fountain-pen ink with cigar ashes and put the mixture on the fungus-infected area. The woman said she has never seen it fail. Within a few days, the ringworm completely disappears.

But if this remedy is going to get you into the habit of smoking cigars, you may be better off with the ringworm!

▶ Mince or grate garlic, apply it to the trouble spots and cover with gauze. Leave it overnight.

Throughout the day, puncture garlic pearles and rub the oil on the afflicted areas. The garlic should stop the itching and help heal the rash.

**WARNING:** Be careful when putting anything wet on a fungal infection. Fungi thrive in moist conditions.

## Seborrhea

This chronic skin rash occurs most often in babies and teenagers (life stages when the oil glands are active). The rash usually causes red patches of skin and greasy, crusty scales. The itching tends to be mild, but these remedies may provide some relief.

▶ Apply cod-liver oil to blotchy, scaly and itchy skin. Leave it on as long as possible. When you finally wash it off, use cool water. Health food stores should carry Norwegian emulsified cod-liver oil that doesn't smell.

▶ Rub on some liquid lecithin and leave it on the problem areas as long as possible. Use cool water to wash it off. Repeat the procedure as often as possible…several times a day.

## Poison Ivy

At least one of the three poison weeds—ivy, oak and sumac—grows in just about every part of the United States. And these weeds all produce the same sort of uncomfortable reactions. Chances are, if you're allergic to one, you're allergic to all. It's estimated that as many as 10 million Americans are affected by these plants.

**CAUTION:** Poison ivy on the face or any large area of skin is extremely serious and should be treated by a doctor as soon as possible.

### *Poison Ivy Prevention*

The best way to avoid getting poison ivy is to know what the plant looks like and to avoid touching it. It also helps to be able to recognize jewelweed, the natural antidote. Chances are, if you know what jewelweed looks like, then you'll also know what poison ivy looks like and, therefore, you'll have no need for jewelweed.

If you do have occasion to use jewelweed, crush the leaves and stems to get the flower's juice. Apply the juice on the poison ivy rash every hour throughout the day.

▶ If possible, as soon as you think that you may have poison ivy, let cold, running water wash the plant's urushiol oil off the affected

### What to Do with the Poison Ivy Plant

*Never* burn poison ivy. The plant's oil gets in the air and can be inhaled. That can be very dangerous and harmful to lungs. Instead, while wearing gloves, uproot the plants and leave them on the ground to dry out in the sun.

Or kill them with a solution of 3 pounds of salt in a gallon of soapy water. Spray, spray, spray the plants and then spray them some more. Wash your garden tools thoroughly with the same solution.

Once you've gotten rid of the poison ivy and cleaned your tools, carefully take off your gloves, turn them inside out and dispose of them. You may want to dispose of your clothes, too. Poison ivy oil may not wash out completely and can stay active for years.

skin. You have a very short window of opportunity to do this—about three minutes—so just hope the poison ivy patch you stepped in is near a waterfall or a garden hose.

▶ This may be a little *iffy*, but…*if* you know you're going into poison ivy territory, and *if* it's green-tomato season, take some green tomatoes with you.

The second you know that poison ivy sap is on your skin, cut up the green tomato and squeeze the juice on the affected area. It may save you the anguish of the poison ivy itch.

▶ If you have a poison ivy rash, use a mixture made from equal parts of white vinegar and rubbing alcohol. Dab on the solution each time the itching starts. It should relieve the itching and, at the same time, dry up the rash.

▶ Mash a piece of white chalk so that it's powdery. Then mix the powder in a pint of water. With a clean cloth, apply the mixture onto the poisoned parts. Repeat the procedure several times a day. This is an especially convenient cure for schoolteachers.

### Waste Not, Want Not

► Rub the inside part of a banana skin directly on the affected skin, using a fresh banana skin every hour for a full day.

> **NOTE:** Take the leftover bananas, cut them into 2-inch pieces, put them in a plastic bag and freeze them. They're great as an ingredient in a smoothie, along with a couple of strawberries, a dollop of yogurt and 10 ounces of pineapple juice.
>
> Or blend frozen banana pieces in a high-powered blender until the mixture is the consistency of soft ice cream and have it as a delicious, low-calorie dessert.
>
> On a hot day, it's refreshing to munch on plain frozen banana pieces.

► Apply fresh mud to the infected areas. At the end of each day, shower off the mud (not that we have to tell you to do that).

Keep up this daily procedure until the redness caused by the poison ivy disappears.

► Slice one or two lemons and rub them all over your affected areas. It should stop the itching and help clear up the skin.

► Chop four cloves of garlic and boil them in 1 cup of water. After the mixture cools, apply it with a clean cloth to the poison ivy areas.

Repeat often—but that's the way it is with garlic…repeating often.

► Place ice-cold, whole-milk compresses on the affected areas. Once the rash calms down, wash off the milk with cool water. If you don't have whole milk, put ice cubes on your skin.

► Take an oatmeal bath to ease the itching and help dry out the eruptions.

► Put mashed pieces of tofu directly on the itchy areas, and bind them in place with a cloth or bandage. They should help stop the itching and cool off the poison ivy flare-up.

► Don't be a crab, just get one. Cook the whole crab in boiling water, let it cool and then use the water to wash the poison ivy area. Or look inside the crab shell for the green stuff. Apply that green gunk directly on the rash.

► If none of these poison ivy remedies work and you're stuck with the itch—its usual duration is about 10 days—then rub on four-leaf clovers, and have a "rash of good luck!"

### Poison Ivy Test

**T**he white paper test will tell you if that patch of plants you just brushed up against is poison ivy. Take hold of the plant in question with a piece of white paper (DO NOT touch it with your bare hands!). Schmush the leaves, causing liquid from the plant to wet the paper. If it's poison ivy, the juice on the paper will turn black within five minutes.

# SEXUAL PROBLEMS

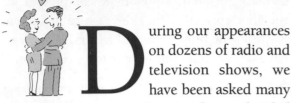

During our appearances on dozens of radio and television shows, we have been asked many sex-related questions. As a result, we decided to give people what they want—more sex! That is, remedies for sexual dysfunctions and some fuel to help rev up the sex drive.

Researchers tell us that about 90% of the cases of decreased sexual ability are psychologically caused. Since a psychological placebo has been known to evoke a prize-winning performance, we're including rituals, recipes, potions, lotions, charms and all kinds of passion-promoting spells.

## Natural Remedies

For history buffs and for history in the buff, we culled the ancient Greek, Egyptian, Indian and Asian sex secrets that are still being used today.

So, if you did but don't...should but won't...can't but want to...or do but don't enjoy it—please read on. Help and newfound fun may be waiting.

### Heighten a Man's Orgasm

Touching a man's testicles before his orgasm is a wonderful way for a woman to greatly excite her lover. It also may hasten—as well as heighten—the orgasm.

**NOTE:** Touching the testicles just after orgasm is a no-no. It may give an unpleasant, almost painful sensation.

## ■ Recipe ■

### Love Elixir

Ancient Teuton brides drank honey-beer for 30 days after their wedding ceremony. It was said to make the bride more sexually responsive. The custom of drinking honey-beer for a month, poetically referred to as a "moon," is the way we got the term "honeymoon."

Rather than go through the bother of preparing honey-beer the way they did way back when, herbalists simplified it to a tea made from hops and honey.

1 oz hops
1 pint water, boiled
1 tsp raw honey

Place the hops (available at health food stores) in a porcelain or Pyrex container. Pour the boiling water over the hops, cover and allow to stand for 15 minutes, then strain. Add the honey to a wineglass of the tea and drink it an hour before each meal. If you prefer warm hops and honey, heat the tea before drinking.

Honey contains aspartic acid and vitamin E. Honey and hops contain traces of hormones. All these ingredients are said to stimulate female sexuality. We'll drink to that!

**WARNING:** Diabetics and people with honey allergies should not use honey.

### Fertili-tea

▶ Add 1 teaspoon of sarsaparilla to 1 cup of just-boiled water and let it steep for five minutes. Strain and drink 2 cups a day.

While sarsaparilla tea may be helpful to a woman who wants to conceive, it should not be given to a man who wants to be potent. Sarsaparilla (available at health food stores) seems to inhibit the formation of sperm.

### Fertility Charm

▶ Hundreds of years ago, witches wore necklaces of acorns to symbolize the fertile powers of nature. In some circles, it is still believed that by carrying an acorn you will promote sexual relations and conception.

### Muscle Strengthener

▶ The ancient Japanese, masters of sensuality, invented Ben Wa Balls. Later, 18th-century French women referred to them as *pommes d'amour* ("love apples"). Doctors throughout the world have recommended them for their therapeutic value.

When these small brass (or sometimes gold-plated steel) balls are placed in the vagina, they create a stimulating sensation upon the vaginal-wall muscles. To keep the balls from falling out, the muscles have to be contracted. This exercise strengthens the vaginal muscles, supposedly giving a woman greater control over her orgasms.

✎ **NOTE:** Make sure Ben Wa Balls have been thoroughly cleaned before inserting them in the vagina.

A strong vaginal muscle is also beneficial to pregnant women. They have more control over their bladders, and it's said to make the birth process a little easier. A strong vaginal muscle also helps prevent incontinence.

You can also do Kegel exercises to strengthen these muscles. Read about Kegels under "Bladder Control" in "Healing Remedies for Women" on page 225.

### It Makes Scents

▶ Have your favorite fragrance linger in the air and help set the mood for romance. Lightly spray your perfume on a lightbulb—one you plan to leave on. In cold weather, spray your radiator, too.

### Time for Love

▶ Testosterone, the hormone that stimulates sexual desire, is at its lowest level in the human body at 11 pm. It's at its highest level at sunrise. (No wonder you may not want to make love during *The Tonight Show*.)

Instead, try getting up with the roosters, and maybe you and your mate will have something to crow about.

### Tea for Two

▶ Turkish women believe fenugreek tea makes them more attractive to men. Besides the sexual energy it may give them, the tea has a way of cleansing the system, sweetening the breath and helping eliminate perspiration odors. (If body odor is affecting your sex life, *see* the remedies on pages 25–26.)

▶Men suffering from lack of desire and/or inability to perform have also turned to fenugreek tea with success.

Many men with sexual problems lack vitamin A. Fenugreek contains an oil that's rich in vitamin A. Trimethylamine, another substance found in fenugreek, and currently being tested on men, acts as a sex hormone in frogs. Fenugreek is available at health food stores.

If you want to do your own testing, add 2 teaspoons of fenugreek seeds to a cup of just-boiled water. Let it steep for five minutes, stir and strain, then add honey and lemon to taste. Drink a cup a day and don't be surprised if you get the urge to make love on a lily pad.

### Sexy Clam Bake

▶Bake the meat of a dozen clams for about two hours at 400° F. When the clam meat is dark and hard, take it out of the oven, let it cool and pulverize it to a powder, either in a blender or with a mortar and pestle. Take ½ teaspoon of the clam powder with water, two hours before bedtime, for one week. This Japanese remedy is supposed to restore sexual vitality.

# Aphrodisiacs

We heard about a married couple whose idea of "sexual compatibility" is for both of them to get a headache at the same time.

They're the ones who asked us to include aphrodisiacs. The word itself means "any form of sexual stimulation." It was derived from the name of Aphrodite, the Greek Goddess of Love, who earned her title by having one husband and five lovers, including that handsome Greek guy Adonis. But enough about her!

After much research, we've come up with a list of foods said to have aphrodisiacal effects. At the top of the list is, believe it or not, celery. Eat it every day.

Of course, we've all heard about eating oysters. Do eat them! But beware of contaminated sources! And always make sure they are thoroughly cooked to reduce the risk of food-borne illness. Oysters contain zinc and, like pumpkin seeds, are said to be wonderful for male genitalia.

The list continues with peaches, honey, parsley, cayenne pepper, bran cereals and truffles. In fact, the 19th-century French general and emperor Napoleon Bonaparte credited truffles for his ability to sire a son.

Here are remedies that you and your mate can try to add new vigor and uninhibited sensuality to your love life.

▶Many Native Americans use ginseng as an aphrodisiac. The Chinese also use ginseng. This herb should be taken sparingly, about ¼ teaspoon twice a month. It is said to stimulate the endocrine system and be a source of male hormones. Ginseng has also been said to help men who have had a sterility problem.

▶Contrary to what we've been led to believe about cold showers, they might help stimulate sexual desire. Every day for about two months, take a cold shower or cold sitz bath and notice a rejuvenated you.

### Sexual Power Pose

▶To improve sexual potency, do this yoga exercise before breakfast and before bedtime—sit on the floor with your back straight, head up and feet crossed in front of you. Tighten all the muscles in the genital area, including the anus. Count to 20, then relax and count to 20 again. Repeat this procedure five times in a row, twice each day.

▶ The English have a commercial preparation called "Tonic for Happy Lovers." The recipe used to make it consists of 1 ounce of licorice root mixed with 2 teaspoons of crushed fennel seeds (both of which you should be able to get at a health food store) and 2 cups of water. Bring the mixture to a boil, lower the heat, cover and simmer slowly for 20 minutes. After it has cooled, strain it and bottle it.

*Dose:* Take 1 to 3 tablespoons twice a day.

**CAUTION:** Do not take licorice root if you have high blood pressure or kidney problems. It can cause renal failure.

## The Curse That Renews Sexual Bliss

**A**ncient mystics used "curses" as a positive way to reverse the negative flow of physical manifestations. In other words, if you're not hot to trot, Curses!

The secret of success lies in the emotional charge behind the incantation as you repeat it morning, noon and right before bedtime. *Here's one to try...*

Eros and Psyche, Cupid and Venus, restore to me passion and vitality.

Mars and Jupiter, Ares and Zeus, instill in me strength and force.

Lusty waters and penetrating winds, renew my vigor, my capacity, my joy.

Cursed be weakness, cursed be shyness,

Cursed be impotence, cursed be frigidity,

Cursed be all that parts me and thee!

### Sensation Stirrer

▶ To get in the mood, prepare a warm bath to which you've added 2 drops of jasmine oil, 2 drops of ylang-ylang oil and 8 drops of sandalwood oil. These essential oils are natural, organic substances that work in harmony with the natural forces of the body. Health food stores carry these "oils of olé"! You might want to save water by bathing together.

### Passion Fruit

▶ Fruits beginning with the letter "p" are said to be especially good for increasing potency in men and enhancing sexual energy in women. The fruits we recommend are peaches, plums, pears, pineapple, papayas, persimmons and bananas—uh, pananas.

### Potion and Chant for Enduring Love

▶ Stir a pinch of ground coriander seeds into a glass of fine red wine while repeating this chant with your partner...

Warm and caring heart

Let us never be apart.

Each of you should sip the wine from the same glass, taking turns. When the wine is all gone, your love should be here to stay.

### Native American Passion Promoter

▶ Add 2 tablespoons of unrefined oatmeal and ½ cup of raisins to 1 quart of water and bring it to a boil. Reduce heat, cover tightly and simmer slowly for 45 minutes. Remove from heat and strain. Add the juice of two lemons and stir in honey to taste. Refrigerate the mixture. Drink 2 cups a day—one before breakfast and another an hour before bedtime.

Oatmeal is rich in vitamin E. Is that where "sow wild oats" comes from?

### A Gem of a Gem

►According to a gem therapist we know, wearing turquoise is supposed to increase the wearer's sexual drive.

### The Honeymoon Picker-Upper

►This is an updated recipe of an ancient Druid formula. Sex therapists who prescribe it believe that taking it on a regular basis can generate a hearty sexual appetite.

Mix the following ingredients in a blender for several seconds—2 level tablespoons of skim milk powder and water (according to the skim milk instructions), ¼ teaspoon of powdered ginger, ⅛ teaspoon of powdered cinnamon, 2 tablespoons of raw honey and a dash of lemon juice, plus any fresh fruit or pure fruit juice you care to add.

Blend and pour into a glass. It's a great drink to have "before the games begin."

►**WARNING:** Diabetics and people with honey allergies should not use honey.

## SINUS PROBLEMS

Ip dor node id stupped up... you probably have sinus problems. Your nose may be runny, stuffy and red from a cold or allergies, and it can really make you feel run down. It may also give you a headache from all the congestion. Keep the tissues handy and try these remedies.

## Natural Remedies

►Slowly, cautiously and gently inhale the vapors of freshly grated horseradish. While you're at it, mix grated horseradish with lemon juice (equal amounts of each).

*Dose:* Eat 1 teaspoon one whole hour before breakfast and at least one hour after dinner. It gives long-lasting relief to some sinus sufferers who are good about taking it every day without fail.

►Crush one clove of garlic into ¼ cup of water. Sip up the garlicky water into an eyedropper. (Make sure no garlic pieces get into the dropper.)

*Dose:* Use 10 drops of clear garlic water per nostril, three times a day for three days. At the end of the three days, there should be a noticeable clearing up of the sinus infection.

►Buy garlic pills and parsley pills.

*Dose:* Take two garlic pills and two parsley pills every four hours while you're awake. (That should add up to four times a day.) After six days, you should be breathing a lot easier.

►To stop sniffling, swallow 1 teaspoon of honey with freshly ground pepper sprinkled on it. Don't inhale the pepper or you'll get rid of the sniffles and start sneezing.

> **WARNING:** Diabetics and people with honey allergies should not use honey.

▶ If you feel a sneeze coming on and you're in a situation where a sneeze would be quite disruptive, put your finger on the tip of your nose and press in.

## Sinus Headaches

▶ Sniff some horseradish juice—the stronger the horseradish, the better. Try to do it slowly.

▶ Prepare poultices of either raw grated onion or horseradish (*see* the "Preparation Guide" on page 256). Apply the poultices to the nape of the neck and the soles of the feet. Leave them on for an hour.

## SKIN PROBLEMS

Skin is the largest organ of the human body. An average-sized adult has about 17 square feet of skin. Thick or thin, it weighs about five pounds.

Five pounds of skin covering 17 square feet of body surface…that's a lot of room for eruptions, cuts, sores, grazes, scrapes, scratches and itches.

Someone named Anonymous once said, "Dermatology is the best specialty. The patient never dies—and never gets well."

We hope these treatments will prove Mr. Anonymous wrong about that last point.

## Acne

When dirt and oil plug up your skin's pores, you can get acne (whiteheads and blackheads). If bacteria gets trapped, then the skin gets red and inflamed—and you get pimples.

Washing your skin regularly with a gentle soap and warm water is the best way to prevent acne break-outs. But for a quick zit-zapper, try one of the following solutions.

### Acne Antidotes

These remedies may not produce dramatic results overnight. Select one and stay with it for at least two weeks. If there's no improvement by then, try another remedy.

▶ Combine 4 ounces of grated horseradish with a pint of 90-proof alcohol. Add a pinch of grated nutmeg and a chopped up bitter orange peel (available at health food stores). With sterilized cotton, dab some of this solution on each pimple every morning and every evening.

▶ This South American remedy was given to us by Las Vegas–based herbalist Angela Harris (*www.angelaharris.com*), who has used it to clear up the faces of many.

Wash with mild soap and hot water. Then apply a thin layer of extra-virgin, cold-pressed olive oil. Do not wash it off. Let the skin completely absorb the olive oil. (Angela emphasized the importance of using "extra-virgin olive oil.")

Do this three times a day. Angela's experience has been that the skin clears up within a week. For maintenance, wash and oil once a day.

▶ Once a day, take ⅓ cup uncooked oats and, in a blender, pulverize them into a powder. Then add water—a little less than ⅓ cup—so that it becomes the consistency of paste. Apply the paste to the pimples. Leave this soothing and healing mush on until it dries up and starts crumbling off. Wash it all off with tepid water.

**NOTE:** Always wash your face with tepid water. Hot water can cause the breaking of capillaries (small veins), as can cold water.

▶ Using a juice extractor, juice one cucumber. With a pastry brush, apply the cucumber juice to the trouble spots. Leave it on for at least 15 minutes, then wash off with tepid water. Do this daily.

▶ Once a day, boil ⅓ cup of buttermilk. While it's hot, add enough honey to give it a thick, creamy consistency. With a pastry brush, brush the cooled mixture on the acne. Leave it on for at least 15 minutes. Wash off with tepid water.

▶ This is an industrial-strength acne remedy taken internally. Before breakfast—or as you eat breakfast—on the first day, start with 2 teaspoons of brewer's yeast, 1 tablespoon of lecithin granules and 1 tablespoon of cold-pressed safflower oil, all mixed in one glass of pure apple juice.

On the second day, add another teaspoon of brewer's yeast and another teaspoon of lecithin granules. Each day, add another teaspoon of brewer's yeast and lecithin granules until you're taking 2 tablespoons (6 teaspoons) of brewer's yeast and almost the same amount of lecithin, along with the 1 tablespoon of safflower oil, all mixed in one glass of apple juice.

As this detoxifies your system and rids you of acne, it should give you added energy and shiny hair.

**NOTE:** It is advisable to do this process only with medical supervision—and if you can stay near a bathroom.

▶ Mix the juice of two garlic cloves with an equal amount of vinegar and dab it on the pimples every evening. The condition may clear up in a couple of weeks.

▶ Simmer one sliced medium onion in ½ cup of honey until the onion is soft. Then mash the mixture into a smooth paste. Make sure it's cool before applying it to blemishes. Leave it on at least one hour, then rinse off with warm water. Repeat the procedure every evening until you can say, "Look Ma, no pimples!"

▶ Eat brown rice regularly. It contains amino acids that are good for skin blemishes.

▶ About four hours before bedtime, steep 1 cup of mashed strawberries in 2 cups (1 pint) of distilled white vinegar. Let it steep until you're ready for bed. Then strain the pulp and seeds. Massage the remaining liquid on your face and have a good night's sleep.

It's not as messy as it sounds. The liquid dries on your face before you touch the pillow. In the morning, wash off the mix with cool water. This is an excellent cleanser and astringent for blemished skin.

## Acne Scars

▶ To help remove acne scars, combine 1 teaspoon of powdered nutmeg with 1 teaspoon of honey and apply it to the scarred area. After 20 minutes, wash it off with cool water.

Do this twice a week, and hopefully within a couple of months you will see an improvement.

## Blackheads

▶ Before going to bed, rub lemon juice over the blackheads. Wait until morning to wash off the juice with cool water. Repeat this procedure several evenings in a row, and you'll see a big improvement in the skin.

## Dead Skin and Enlarged Pores

▶ A friend of ours uses Miracle Whip salad dressing to remove dead skin cells and to tighten her pores. She puts it on her face and leaves it there for about 20 minutes. Then she washes it off with warm water, followed by cold water.

Our friend claims that no other mayonnaise works as well as Miracle Whip. Maybe that's where the "Miracle" comes in.

▶ Papaya contains the enzyme papain, which is said to do wonderful things for the complexion. Wash your face and neck. Remove the meat of the papaya (it makes a delicious lunch) and rub the inside of the papaya skin on your skin. It will dry, forming a see-through mask. After 15 minutes, wash it off with warm water.

Along with removing dead skin and tightening the pores, it may make some light freckles disappear.

▶ To help refine pores, put ⅓ cup of almonds into a blender and pulverize them into a powder. Add enough water to the powder to give it the consistency of paste. Rub the mixture gently across the enlarged pores from your nose outward and upward. Leave it on your face for a half-hour, then rinse it off with tepid water.

As a final rinse, mix ¼ cup of cool water with ¼ cup of apple cider vinegar and splash it on to tighten the pores.

For best results, treat your skin to this almond rub on a regular basis.

### Extra-Large Pores

▶ We're talking *really big* pores here. Every night for one week, or as long as one container of buttermilk lasts, wash your face, then soak a wad of absorbent cotton in buttermilk and dab it all over your face. After 20 minutes, smile. It's a very weird sensation. Wash the dried buttermilk off with cool water.

 **NOTE:** The smile is optional.

# Wounds and Sores

Sores that are open and/or infected are best treated by a medical professional. Keep the wound clean and consult a doctor as soon as possible.

**CAUTION:** If a wound is bleeding profusely, apply direct pressure, preferably with a sterile dressing, and seek medical attention immediately. If a sore doesn't start to heal within a few days, see a doctor.

If a bleeding wound or sore is NOT severe, the following remedies may help. But be aware that there is a risk of infection when applying raw and/or natural substances to an open sore or wound. If an infection persists or a sore does not heal, consult a health professional.

## That's Gotta Sting!

▶ Lemon is an effective disinfectant and also stops a cut from bleeding. Squeeze some juice on the cut and get ready for the sting.

▶ Sprinkle on some cayenne pepper or black pepper to stop the flow of blood from a cut within seconds. Put it directly on the cut. Yes, it will sting.

## Don't Smoke It

▶ A clump of wet tobacco will stop the bleeding. So will wet cigarette paper.

▶ Cobwebs on an open wound can stop the bleeding instantly. In fact, they are so good at clotting a wound that they've been used for years on cows right after they've been dehorned.

However, all kinds of bacteria carried by the cobwebs might infect the open wound. Use cobwebs *only* when there is absolutely nothing else to use—like the next time you get a gash in a haunted house.

▶ The crushed leaves of a geranium plant applied to the cut act as a styptic pencil and help stop the bleeding.

## Weeping Sores

▶ Place a piece of papaya pulp on a weeping sore. Keep it in place with a sterile bandage. Change the dressing every two to three hours until the sore clears up.

▶ Dab on lavender oil throughout the day. It should help heal the sore and also help you feel more relaxed.

▶ Apply a poultice of either raw, grated carrots or cooked, mashed carrots to stop the throbbing and draw out the infection.

▶ A honey poultice is disinfecting and healing. Use raw, unprocessed honey.

 **NOTE:** *See* "Preparation Guide" on page 252 for instructions on preparing poultices.

## Sores and Lesions

▶ Some nonmalignant sores need help healing. Put pure, undiluted Concord grape juice on a sterile cotton ball or gauze pad and apply it to the sore, binding it in place with a sterile bandage.

Do not wash the sore. Just keep the grape juice on it, changing the dressing at least once in the morning and once at night. Be patient.

**WARNING:** Diabetics should see a health professional to receive antibiotic treatment for any infected sores that do not heal.

# Boils

Skin boils usually begin as a red, tender area from an infection deep in the skin. Boils can get large, firm and hard as they fill with pus—which may need to be drained surgically.

⚡ **CAUTION:** If pain gets progressively worse, or if you see a red streak in the boil, get professional medical attention. Don't wait!

If your boil hasn't started to simmer, try these remedies for relief.

▶ Slowly heat 1 cup of milk. Just as slowly, add 3 teaspoons of salt as the milk gets close to boiling. Once the salt has been added, remove the milk from the heat and add flour to thicken the mixture and make a poultice (*see* "Preparation Guide" on page 252). Apply it to the boil. The heat of the poultice will help bring it to a head, but be careful that it's not too hot.

▶ Gently peel off the skin of a hard-boiled egg. Wet that delicate membrane and place it on the boil. It should draw out pus and relieve the inflammation.

▶ Apply several fresh slices of pumpkin to the boil. Replace the slices frequently until the boil comes to a head.

▶ A poultice of cooked, minced garlic or raw, chopped garlic applied to the boil will draw out the infection.

▶ Heat a lemon in the oven, then slice it in half and place the inside part of one half on the boil. Secure it in place for about an hour.

## Fig-get About Boils

▶ "And Isaiah said, 'Take a lump of figs.' And they took and laid it on the boil, and he recovered."—*2 Kings 20:7.*

Roast a fresh fig. Cut it in half and lay the mushy inner part on the boil. Secure it in place for a couple of hours. Then warm the other half of the roasted fig and replace the first half with it. And thou shalt recover when the boil runneth over.

▶ Mix 1 tablespoon of honey with 1 tablespoon of cod-liver oil (Norwegian emulsified cod-liver oil is nonsmelly) and apply it to the boil. Bind it with a sterile bandage. Change the dressing every eight hours.

▶ To draw out the waste material painlessly and quickly, add a little water to about 1 teaspoon of fenugreek powder, making it the consistency of paste. Put it on the boil and cover it with a sterile bandage. Change the dressing twice a day.

## Glop It On

▶ This Irish remedy requires four slices of bread and a cup of milk. Boil the bread and milk together until it's one big, gloppy mush.

As soon as the mush is cool enough to handle, slop a glop on the boil and cover with a sterile bandage. When the glop gets cold, replace it with another warm glop. Keep redressing the boil until you've used up all four slices of bread. By then, the boil should have opened.

## When the Boil Breaks...

▶ The boil is at the brink of breaking when it turns red and the pain increases. When finally does break, pus will be expelled, leaving a big hole in the skin. But almost magically, the pain will disappear.

Boil 1 cup of water and add 2 tablespoons of lemon juice. Let it cool. Clean and disinfect the area thoroughly with the lemon water. Cover with a sterile bandage.

For the next few days, two or three times a day, remove the bandage and apply a warm, wet compress, leaving it on for 15 minutes at a time. Re-dress the area with a fresh sterile bandage.

## Dry Elbows and Knees

▶ Take the skin from half an avocado and rub the inside of it against the rough areas of your elbows and/or knees. Keep rubbing for a few minutes. Don't clean off the area until bedtime.

▶ Rest your elbows in grapefruit halves to get rid of alligator skin. Make yourself as comfortable as possible and keep your elbows in the citrus fruit for at least a half-hour.

▶ Make a paste by combining salt and lemon juice. Rub this abrasive mixture on rough and tough areas such as elbows, feet and knees. Wash the paste off with cool water.

## Freckles

Freckles tend to run in families, but you can also get them if you've spent a lot of time in the sun. Of course, if you get a whole lot of freckles very close together, you'll have a nice suntan and won't have to bother with all this stuff.

▶ If you're determined to do away with your freckles, bottle your own freckle remover. Get four medium-sized dandelion leaves (either pick them yourself, or buy them at the greengrocer), rinse them thoroughly and tear them into small

pieces. Combine the leaves with 5 tablespoons of castor oil in an enamel or glass pan.

Over low heat, let the mixture simmer for 10 minutes. Turn off the heat, cover the pan and let it steep for three hours. Strain the mixture into a bottle. (Don't forget to label the bottle.)

Massage several drops of the oil on the freckled area and leave it on overnight. In the morning, wash your skin with tepid water. Do this daily for at least a week and watch the spots disappear.

▶ Potato water (*see* "Preparation Guide" on page 252) can help fade summer freckles. Dip a washcloth in it, wring it out and apply it to the freckles. Leave it on for 10 minutes daily.

▶ Apply lemon juice, juice of parsley or juice of watercress.

▶ Combine 6 tablespoons of buttermilk with 1 teaspoon of grated horseradish. Since this is a mild skin bleach, coat the skin with a light oil before applying the mixture.

Leave it on for 20 minutes, then wash it off with warm water. Follow up with a skin moisturizer on the bleached area.

▶ If you ever wake up in the morning, look in the mirror and see freckles you never had before, try washing the mirror.

## Cuts and Scrapes

▶ The first thing to do when you get a scratch, small cut or graze is to rinse it with water.

Put honey on the opening and let its healing enzymes go to work.

▶ Put the inside of a banana peel directly on the wound and secure it in place with a bandage. Change the peel every three to four hours. We've seen remarkable and rapid results with banana peels. It might be a good idea to carry bananas when you go camping.

### Paper Cuts

▶ Clean the cut with the juice of a lemon. Then, to ease the pain, wet the cut finger and dip it into powdered cloves. Since cloves act as a mild anesthetic, the pain should be gone in a matter of seconds.

## Scars

▶ According to Las Vegas–based herbalist Angela Harris (*www.angelaharris.com*), you can fade scars by applying a light film of extra-virgin, cold-pressed olive oil every day. Be consistent and be patient. It won't happen overnight.

## Splinters

If you get a tiny piece of wood, metal or glass under your skin, it can really hurt. Remove it carefully to prevent infection. Keep in mind that wood swells when it's wet, so most of these suggestions work best on other types of splinters.

▶ Boil water, then carefully fill a wide-mouthed bottle to within half an inch of the top. Next, place the splintered part of the finger over the top of the bottle and lightly press down. The pressing should allow the heat to draw out the splinter.

▶ If the splintered finger is very sore, tape a slice of raw onion around the area and leave it on overnight. The swelling and the splinter should be gone by morning.

▶ Make a paste of oatmeal, banana and a little water, and apply it to the splintered area. Alternate this with salad oil compresses and, by the end of the day, you should be able to squeeze out the splinter.

▶ Make a poultice from the grated heart of a cabbage. Apply it to the splinter and in an hour or two, it should draw the sliver out.

▶ For real tough splinters, sprinkle salt on the splintered area, then put half a cherry tomato on it. Bind the tomato on the salted skin with a bandage and a plastic covering to keep from messing up the bedsheets.

Oh, we forgot to mention, you're supposed to sleep with the tomato overnight. The next morning, the splinter should come right out.

## Stretch Marks

The skin is very elastic, but it doesn't always recover properly from stretching—such as from pregnancy or weight gain/loss.

▶ After a shower or bath, gently massage sesame oil—about a tablespoon—all over your stretch-marked areas. Eventually, the marks may disappear.

# Wrinkles

It took years to get the folds in your face, and it will take time and persistence to unfold. We know a man who has so many wrinkles in his forehead, he has to screw his hat on. That's a lot of wrinkles!

He can start to smooth them by relaxing more, by staying out of the sun, by not smoking (smokers have far more wrinkles than non-smokers) and by trying one of the following remedies.

▶ Before bedtime, take extra-virgin, cold-pressed olive oil and massage the lined areas of your neck and face. Start in the center of your neck and, using an upward and outward motion, get the oil into those dry areas. Work your way up to and include your forehead. Let the oil stay on overnight.

In the morning, wash with tepid, then cool, water. You may want to add a few drops of your favorite herbal essence to the olive oil, then pretend it costs $60 a bottle.

▶ This is an internal approach to wrinkles. No, it doesn't mean you'll have unlined insides, it means that the nutritional value of brewer's yeast may make a difference in overcoming the external signs of time.

Start with 1 teaspoon a day of brewer's yeast in a pure fruit juice, and gradually work your way up to 2 tablespoons—1 teaspoon at a time.

Some people get a gassy feeling from brewer's yeast. We were told that that means the body really needs it, and the feeling will eventually go away when the body requirements for the nutrients are met. Huh? We're not sure what it all means, but we do know that brewer's yeast contains lots of health-giving properties, and it may help dewrinkle the face. Seems to us it's worth trying.

▶ The most popular wrinkle eraser we found requires 1 teaspoon of honey and 2 tablespoons of heavy whipping cream. Mix them together vigorously. Dip your fingertips in the mixture and, with a gentle massaging action, apply it to the wrinkles, folds, lines, creases, crinkles—whatever.

Leave it on for at least a half-hour—the longer the better. You'll feel it tighten on your face as it becomes a mask. When you're ready, splash it off with tepid water. By making this a daily ritual, you may become wrinkle-free.

## Eye Wrinkles

▶ For those of you who haven't had an eye tuck, applying castor oil on the delicate area around the eyes every night may prevent the need for cosmetic surgery.

## Wrinkle Prevention

▶ To reduce the tendency to wrinkle, mash a ripe banana and add a few drops of peanut oil. Apply it to your face and neck (remember, upward and outward), and leave it on for at least a half-hour. Wash it off with tepid water. If you do this daily—or even every other day—it should make your skin softer and less likely to get lined.

▶ If you eat oatmeal for breakfast, have we got a remedy for you! Separate some of the cooked oatmeal. Add a bit of vegetable oil—enough to make it spreadable—and massage it into your face and neck. Leave this on for a half-hour, then wash it off with tepid water. If you want to be wrinkle-proof, you must repeat the procedure on a regular, daily basis.

▶ Buttermilk is a good wrinkle-preventing facial. Keep it on for about 20 minutes, then splash it off with warm water and pat dry.

### *Au Revoir, Wrinkles!*

▶ This is supposedly the secret formula of a renowned French beauty—combine together and boil 1 cup of milk, 2 teaspoons of lemon juice and 1 tablespoon of brandy. While the mixture is warm, paint it on the face and neck with a pastry brush. When it is thoroughly dry, wash it off with warm water and pat dry.

▶ The best way to prevent wrinkled skin is to avoid excessive sun exposure and always apply sunscreen before going outside.

### *Lip Line Prevention*

▶ The way to prevent those little crinkly lines around the mouth is by exercising the jaw muscle. Luckily, the jaw muscle can work the longest of all the body's muscles without getting tired. So whistle, sing and talk.

Tongue twisters are like aerobics for the mouth, especially ones with "m," "b" and "p" sounds. *Here are a couple to start with…*

- ◆ Pitter-patter, pitter-patter, rather than patter-pitter, patter-pitter.
- ◆ Mother made neither brother mutter to father.

## SLEEP PROBLEMS

*Yaaaawn!* Not getting enough sleep can really make you tired! Most people have trouble sleeping every once in a while—but for others, the problem is chronic. If you have trouble dozing off (or staying dozed off), try these remedies.

## Insomnia

▶ A popular folk remedy for insomnia is counting sheep. We once heard about a garment manufacturer who had trouble sleeping. Not only did he count the sheep, he sheared them, combed the wool, had it spun into yarn, woven into cloth, made into suits, which he distributed in town, watched as they didn't sell, had them returned and lost thousands on the deal. Of course, that's why he had trouble sleeping in the first place.

### *Treating Insomnia*

We have some other remedies to help the garment manufacturer—and you—get a good night's sleep.

▶ In England, it is believed that a good night's sleep will be ensured if you lie in bed with your head to the north and your feet to the south.

▶ Nutmeg can act as a sedative. Steep half of a crushed nutmeg (not more than that) in hot water for 10 minutes, and drink it a half-hour before bedtime. If you don't like the taste of it, you can use nutmeg oil externally. Rub it on your forehead.

▶ Try drinking a glass of pure, warmed grapefruit juice. If you need to have it sweetened, use a bit of raw honey.

**CAUTION:** Grapefruit can interfere with certain medications—check with your doctor before trying this remedy. In addition, diabetics and people with honey allergies should not use honey.

▶ This Silva Method exercise seems to… zzzzzzz. Where were we? Oh yes, once you're in bed, completely relax. Lightly close your eyes. Now picture a blackboard. Take a piece of imaginary chalk and draw a circle. Within the circle, draw a square and put the number 99 in the square. Erase the number 99. Be careful you don't erase the sides of the square. Replace 99 with 98. Then erase 98 and replace it with 97, then 96, 95, 94, etc. You should fall asleep long before you get to zero.

For more information about the Silva Method, go to *www.silvamethod.com.*

▶ Michio Kushi, pioneer of the macrobiotic diet and founder of the Kushi Institute in Becket, Massachusetts, says that when you can't sleep, put a cut, raw onion under your pillow. No, you don't cry yourself to sleep. There's something in the onion that scurries you off to dreamland.

▶ Cut a yellow onion in chunks and place it in a glass jar. Cover the jar, and keep it on your night table. When you can't fall asleep—or when you wake up and can't fall back asleep—open the jar and take a deep whiff of the onion. Close the jar, lie back, think lovely thoughts and within 15 minutes…zzzzzzzz.

▶ A relaxing bath may help you fall asleep. Before you take your bath, prepare a cup of sleep-inducing herb tea to drink as soon as you get out of the tub. Use chamomile, sage or fresh ginger tea. (*See* "Preparation Guide" on page 250.) Then take a bath using any one or a combination of the following herbs—lavender, marigold, passionflower or rosemary. All of these calming herbs should be available at health food stores.

By the time you finish your bath and the tea, you should feel wound down and ready to doze off.

▶ A gem therapist told us about the power of a diamond. Set in a silver ring, it supposedly prevents insomnia. The therapist also said that wearing a diamond—in any setting—protects the wearer from nightmares. Well, there's one of the best arguments for getting engaged!

## Elderberriezzzz…

▶ A glass of elderberry juice, at room temperature, is thought of as a sleep inducer. You can get pure elderberry concentrate at health food stores. Just dilute it, drink it and hit the hay.

▶ According to the record (please don't ask us which one), King George III of England (1738–1820) was plagued with insomnia until a physician prescribed a hop pillow. Hops have been known to have a tranquilizing effect. Lupulin, an active ingredient in hops, has been used to treat a variety of nervous disorders.

Here's how you can use hops to help you sleep better—buy or sew together a little muslin or fine white cotton bag. Fill it with hops and tack it to your pillow. Change the hops once a month.

▶ You may want to try placing a pillow, filled with flaxseed, on your eyes to help you fall asleep. Many health food stores carry them,

## ■ Recipe ■

### *Elderberry Pie*

2½ cups elderberries

3 Tbsp lemon juice

¾ cup granulated sugar

2 Tbsp all-purpose flour

⅛ tsp salt

1 9" double crust pie pastry

Preheat oven to 425° F . Line a 9" pie pan with pastry.

Combine berries and lemon juice. Pour into pie shell.

Mix sugar, flour and salt. Sprinkle over berries. Cover with top crust, then seal and flute edges. Cut a few small steam vents in the top. Bake for 10 minutes, then reduce oven temperature to 350° F and bake 30 minutes longer.

*Source: www.recipegoldmine.com*

and you can find them on-line. The eye pillow applies just enough pressure to the eyes and orbits to help you relax.

### *From Baaa to Zzzz*

► A naturopath we met has had great success in treating patients who suffer from severe insomnia—with goat's milk! He recommends they drink 6 ounces before each meal and 6 ounces before bedtime.

Within a week, he has seen patients go from getting two hours of sleep a night to sleeping eight restful hours night after night. Some supermarkets and most health food stores sell goat's milk.

### *The Rabbit Sleeps Tonight*

► Galen, a Greek physician, writer and philosopher (129–216 AD), was able to cure his own insomnia by eating lots of lettuce in the evening. Lettuce has lactucarium, a calming agent. The problem with eating lots of lettuce is that it's a diuretic. So, while it may help you fall asleep, you may have to get up in the middle of the night to go to the bathroom.

### *Avoid Sleep*

► Worried about not being able to fall asleep? Okay then, don't let yourself go to sleep. That's right—try to stay awake. Sleep specialists call this technique "paradoxical intent." (When we were children and our father used it on us, we precociously called it "reverse psychology.") So, take the worry out of trying to go to sleep, and try hard to stay awake. We bet you'll be asleep in no time.

► Keep the temperature of the room cool and your feet warm. Wear socks to bed, or rest your feet on a hot water bottle.

According to a study done at the Chronobiology and Sleep Laboratory in Basel, Switzerland, sleepiness is caused by a drop in core body temperature. That happens as your body heat slowly dissipates through dilated blood vessels in the feet. Aside from falling asleep faster, warm feet are more comfortable for you and your bedmate.

## Sleep Lives of the Rich and Famous

Renowned British author Charles Dickens (1812–1870) believed it was impossible to sleep if you crossed the magnetic forces between the North and South Poles. As a result, whenever Mr. Dickens traveled, he took a compass with him so he could sleep with his head facing north.

American statesman, inventor and writer Benjamin Franklin (1706–1790) believed in fresh-air baths in the nude as a sleep inducer. During the night, he would move from one bed to another because he also thought that cold sheets had a therapeutic effect on him. (At least, that's what he told his wife!)

Abraham Lincoln (1809–1865), the 16th president of the United States, took a midnight walk to help him sleep.

Celebrated American writer and notorious wit Mark Twain (1835–1910) had a cure for insomnia—"Lie near the edge of the bed and you'll drop off."

According to American journalist and radio personality Franklin P. Adams (1881–1960), "Insomniacs don't sleep because they worry about it and they worry about it because they don't sleep."

► Exercise *during the day*. Get a real workout —take a class or follow an exercise plan from a book or a videotape at home. Do not exercise right before bedtime. And be sure to check with your doctor before starting a new exercise program.

► Try using an extra pillow or two. This works for some people.

► Stay in one position. (Lying on the stomach is more relaxing than on the back.) Tossing and turning acts as a signal to the body that you're ready to get up.

► In a pitch-black room, sit in a comfortable position with your feet and hands uncrossed. Light a candle. Stare at the lit candle while relaxing each part of your body, starting with the toes and working your way up. Include ankles, calves, knees, thighs, pelvis, stomach, waist, midriff, rib cage, chest, fingers, wrists, elbows, arms, shoulders, neck, jaw, lips, cheeks, eyes, eyebrows, forehead and top of the head. Once your entire body is relaxed, take care to extinguish the candle properly and go to sleep.

► Take your mind off having to fall asleep. Give yourself an interesting but unimportant fantasy-type problem to solve. For instance—if you were to write your autobiography, what would be the title?

► Steep 1 teaspoon of chamomile in a cup of boiling water for 10 minutes and sip it right before bedtime.

► Do not go to bed until you're really sleepy, even if it means going to bed very late when you have to get up early the next morning. Nothing will happen to you if you get less than eight, seven, six or even five hours of sleep just one night.

► Get into bed. Before you lie down, breathe deeply six times. Count to 100, then breathe deeply another six times. Good night!

▶ An hour before bedtime, peel and cut up a large onion. Pour 2 cups of boiling water over it and let it steep for 15 minutes. Strain the water, then drink as much of it as you can. Do your evening ablutions (which might include freshening your breath) and go to sleep.

### Tryptophan Toddy

▶ Folk-remedy recipes always include warm milk with ½ teaspoon of nutmeg and 1 or 2 teaspoons of honey before bedtime to promote restful sleep.

The National Institute of Mental Health (*www.nimh.nih.gov*) believes this concoction works because warm milk contains tryptophan. Tryptophan is an essential amino acid (link of protein) that increases the amount of serotonin in the brain. Serotonin is a neurotransmitter that helps to send messages from brain to nerves and vice versa.

The advantage of a tryptophan-induced sleep over sleeping pills is that you awaken at the normal time every day and do not feel sleepy or drugged.

▶ The feet seem to have a lot to do with a good night's sleep. One research book says that before going to bed, put your feet in the refrigerator for 10 minutes. If you're brave (or silly) enough to try this, please proceed with care. Talk about getting cold feet!

▶ Try a little Chinese acupressure. Press the center of the bottoms of your heels with your thumbs. Keep pressing as long as you can—for at least three minutes. (Well, it beats sticking your feet in the fridge.)

▶ If you've reached the point where you're willing to try just about anything, then rub the soles of your feet and the nape of your neck with a peeled clove of garlic. It may help you fall asleep—and it will definitely keep the vampires away.

▶ Prevent sleepless nights by eating salt-free dinners and eliminating all after-dinner snacks. Try it a few nights in a row and see if it makes a difference in your sleep.

▶ It is most advisable, for purposes of good digestion, not to have eaten for two or three hours before bedtime. However, a remedy recommended by many cultures throughout the world as an effective cure for insomnia requires you to eat a finely chopped raw onion before going to bed.

▶ Having an orgasm is a wonderful relaxant and sleep inducer.

That said, totally satisfying sex can help you sleep. But unsatisfying sex can cause frustration that leads to insomnia. So (with apologies to the wonderful English poet, Alfred Lord Tennyson), is it better to have loved and lost sleep than never to have loved at all?

## Nightmares

If you've ever woken up with a start—heart racing and sweating—you may have had a nightmare. These scary dreams can be frightening, but are generally harmless.

▶ Right before going to sleep, soak your feet in warm water for 10 minutes. Then rub them thoroughly with half a lemon. Don't rinse them off, just pat them dry. Take a few deep breaths and have pleasant dreams.

As you're dozing off to sleep, tell yourself that you want to have happy dreams. It works lots of times.

▶ This nightmare-prevention advice comes from Switzerland—eat a small evening meal about two hours before bedtime. When you go to bed, lie on your right side with your right hand under your head. *Then dream of the Alps…*

▶ Before you go to sleep, drink thyme tea and be nightmare-free.

▶ Simmer the outside leaves of a head of lettuce in 2 cups of boiling water for 15 minutes. Strain and drink the lettuce tea right before bedtime. It's supposed to ensure sweet dreams and is also good for cleansing the system.

▶ Lightly sprinkle essence of anise (available at health food stores) on your pillow so that you inhale the scent as soon as you lie down. It is said to give one "happy" dreams, restful sleep—and an oil-stained pillowcase.

## Sleepwalking

▶ A Russian professor who studied sleepwalkers recommended a piece of wet carpeting, placed right by the sleepwalker's bed. In most cases, the sleepwalker awoke the second his or her feet stepped on the wet carpet.

## Snoring/Sleep Apnea

A friend told us he starts to snore as soon as he falls asleep. We asked if it bothers his wife. He said, "It not only bothers my wife, it bothers the whole congregation."

Actually, snoring is not a joking matter. Chronic snoring—that is, snoring every night and loudly—may be the start of a serious condition known as sleep apnea.

*Apnea* is Greek for "without breath." During the night, the windpipe keeps blocking the air as the throat relaxes and closes, making it difficult to breathe. After holding one's breath for an unnatural amount of time (anywhere from 10 seconds to a couple of minutes), the snore occurs as the person gasps for air. The person wakes up slightly each time it happens, and it can happen dozens and dozens of times during the night, without the person realizing it. The interrupted sleep causes that person to be tired all day.

If you have this condition, it is dangerous to drive a car, operate heavy machinery or just cross a street. Aside from the daytime accident aspect, sleep apnea may lead to high blood pressure, heart problems and stroke.

If you think that you may have sleep apnea, ask your doctor to recommend a sleep specialist right away. There are sleep clinics throughout the country.

For bouts of routine snoring, here are some helpful remedies to try…

▶ You may want to sew a tennis ball on the back of the snorer's pajama top or nightgown. This stops the snorer from sleeping on his or her back, which prevents snoring.

▶ Snoring can be caused by very dry air—a lack of humidity—in the bedroom. If you use a radiator in cold weather, place a pan of water on it, or simply use a humidifier.

### Snore Stopper

▶ Lightly tickle the snorer's throat and the snoring should stop. Of course, the laughing may keep you up.

## SMOKING

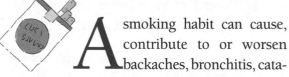

**A** smoking habit can cause, contribute to or worsen backaches, bronchitis, cataracts, emphysema, gum problems, hangovers, infertility, osteoporosis, phlebitis, sleep disorders (including sleep apnea), sore throats, tinnitus, ulcers, varicose veins, endometriosis, heartburn, diverticulosis...and—believe us—that's just for starters.

Smoking has been linked to every serious disease. We'll spare you the statistics from the American Heart Association (*www.americanheart.org*), the American Lung Association (*www.lungusa.org*) and the American Cancer Society (*www.cancer.org*) on the approximate number of Americans who die because of smoking—before they reach retirement age.

All the talk about sickness and premature death doesn't seem to motivate smokers—especially teenagers or young adults—to stop. James A. Duke, PhD, a botanist formerly with the USDA's Agricultural Research Service in Beltsville, Maryland, has a wake-up call. He likes to remind young smokers that the habit hits men in the penis and women in the face.

"Smoking damages the blood vessels that supply the penis, so men who smoke have an increased risk of impotence. Smoking also damages the capillaries in women's faces, which is why women [and men] smokers develop wrinkles years before nonsmokers."

Ready to stop smoking? Hopefully the following suggestions will help make it easier.

## Stop Smoking...Seriously

We are antismoking advocates, so much so that Lydia belongs to an organization that lobbies for nonsmokers' rights. We were happy to find one more reason not to smoke—a condition called "smoker's back."

According to a study conducted at the University of Vermont in Burlington, back pain is more common and more frequent among smokers. Researchers theorize that the effect of nicotine on carbon monoxide levels in the blood causes the smoker to cough. This puts a tremendous strain on the back.

Yup! That's one more good reason to STOP SMOKING!

## Natural Ways to Help You Quit

▶ Make a list of all the reasons you want to quit smoking. You may want to divide the list into "short-term reasons," such as wanting to be more kissable, and "long-term reasons," such as wanting to walk your daughter down the aisle at her wedding. Keep the list handy and refer to it each time you're about to give in and have a smoke.

▶ A professor of behavioral medicine suggests that when a craving comes over you, pick up a pen instead of a cigarette, and write a letter to loved ones, telling them why smoking is more important than they are.

Tell them how you choose to die young and how you'll miss sharing in their happiness. Apologize for having to have someone take care of you when you're no longer well enough to take care of yourself.

Got the picture? These, hopefully, *unfinished* letters may give you the strength to pass up a cigarette one more time, each time, until you no longer feel the horrible craving and want to smoke.

▶ The late Nobel laureate and chemist Linus Pauling, PhD, suggested eating an orange whenever you have the urge to smoke. A research group in Britain conducted experiments with smokers and oranges. The results were impressive.

### ■ Recipe ■

#### Apricot Snowballs

1 8-oz package dried apricots
1½ cups flaked coconut
2 Tbsp confectioners' sugar
2 tsp orange juice
Sugar (optional)

Grind apricots using the medium blade of a food processor.

In a separate small bowl, combine the apricots, coconut, confectioners' sugar and orange juice with your hands. Shape into ½-inch balls. Roll in sugar. Store in a tightly covered container.

Makes 30 snowballs.

*Source: www.recipegoldmine.com*

By the end of three weeks, the orange-eating cigarette smokers smoked 79% fewer cigarettes than they ordinarily would have, and 20% kicked the habit completely. It seems that eating citrus fruit has a kick that's similar to smoking a cigarette.

Incidentally, when you take a piece of orange instead of smoking a cigarette, first suck the juice out and then eat the pulp.

▶ For many smokers, the thought of smoking a cigarette after they've had a citrus drink is unpleasant. If you feel that way—good! Carry a small bottle of citrus juice with you and, whenever you feel like lighting up, take a swig of the juice. And since each cigarette robs your body of between 25 and 100 mg of vitamin C, the juice will help replenish it as well as keep you from smoking.

### Red Clover, Red Clover

▶ To help cleanse your system of nicotine, and to help prevent tumors from forming, take ½ teaspoon of red clover tincture (available at health food stores) three times a day. Drinking a cup of red clover tea once or twice a day may also help.

▶ To help detoxify your liver, drink 2 cups of milk thistle seed tea before every meal. In case you're worried about gaining weight now that you're not going to be smoking, these 6 cups of tea before meals may help you cut down on the amount of food you eat.

▶ Marjoram tea (available at health food stores) makes your throat very dry, so smoking will not be nearly as pleasurable. Marjoram is naturally sweet—nothing needs to be added to it. Have 1 cup of tea when you would ordinarily have your first cigarette of the day. Try ½ cup after that…whenever you have an uncontrollable urge to smoke.

▶ According to some Chinese herbalists, magnolia-bark tea is effective in curbing the desire to light up. You might want to alternate between magnolia-bark and marjoram teas.

▶ If you want to stop or at least cut down on your tobacco habit, after your next cigarette or cigar, replace the nicotine taste in your mouth by sucking on a small clove. After an hour or two, replace the clove with another one. Without that lingering nicotine taste in your mouth, your desire for another smoke should be greatly reduced.

### Bugs Bunny's Secret

▶ James A. Duke, PhD, a botanist formerly with the USDA's Agricultural Research Service in Beltsville, Maryland, smoked three packs of unfiltered, king-sized cigarettes a day—until the day he quit cold turkey. That was close to three decades ago.

According to Dr. Duke, carrots helped him quit. He would munch on raw carrots instead of puffing on a cigarette. "If cigarettes are cancer sticks," says Dr. Duke, "carrots are anticancer sticks."

He explains that carotenoids, the chemical relatives of vitamin A, are abundant in carrots. The carotenoids help prevent cancer, especially if they come from carrots or other whole foods rather than from capsules. Carrots also help lower cholesterol levels.

Buy a bunch of baby carrots and munch on them throughout the day.

▶ Apricots are rich in minerals like beta-carotene, potassium, boron, iron and silica. Not only do they help prevent cancer, they are also good for the heart, for promoting estrogen production in postmenopausal women, for preventing fatigue and infection and for healthy skin, hair and nails. Apricots are especially helpful in minimizing the long-term potential harm caused by nicotine.

Start eating a few dried apricots every day and continue eating them even as a non-smoker. (*See* recipe on page 168.) Buy unsulfured, dried apricots. Sulfur (sulfite) preservatives can produce allergic reactions,

especially in asthmatics. Also, the long-term accumulation of sulfites can cause unhealthy conditions.

▶ In addition to eating carrots and apricots, unsalted, raw sunflower seeds are another wonderful munchie.

Tobacco releases stored sugar (glycogen) from the liver and it perks up one's brain. Sunflower seeds provide that same mental lift.

Tobacco also has a sedative effect that tends to calm a person down. Sunflower seeds stabilize the nerves because they contain oils that are calming and B-complex vitamins that help nourish the nervous system. (Maybe that's why baseball players often eat them during a game.)

Tobacco increases the output of adrenal gland hormones, which reduces the allergic reaction of smokers. Sunflower seeds have the same effect.

Keep in mind that the seeds are fairly high in fat, so don't overdo it. Consider buying sunflower seeds with shells. The shelling process will slow down your consumption of the seeds.

### The Dreadful Withdrawal Time

▶ During the worst time, the dreaded first week or two of withdrawal, push yourself to exercise—walk, swim, bowl, play table tennis, clean your house, do gardening, play with a yo-yo. *Just keep moving.* It will make you feel better. It will help prevent weight gain.

Incidentally, gaining five to 10 pounds because you stopped smoking is worth it when you consider the health risks of smoking. But if you follow these suggestions, and also start eating the foods in the "Six Sensational Superfoods" section (*see* page 257), you may stop smoking and not gain any weight.

◆ *Be kind to yourself and don't place temptation in your face.* Do not frequent bars or other places where people smoke, smoke, smoke. Hang out at places where smoking is not permitted—movie theaters, museums, the library, houses of worship, adult education courses at schools, etc.

◆ *Figure out how much money you'll end up saving each year by not smoking.* Decide on exactly what you want to do with that money—special treat(s) for yourself or your loved ones—and actually put that money away every time you *don't* buy a pack of cigarettes when you ordinarily would have.

## Once You Quit...

**A** nicotine-dependency researcher reported that nicotine causes smokers to process caffeine two and a half times faster than non-smokers.

So, once you quit smoking and the nicotine is washed out of your system, you'll need only about a third as much coffee to get the same buzz you got from drinking coffee while still smoking.

The same goes for alcoholic beverages. Take into consideration that you'll get drunk faster without nicotine in your body.

Think of the additional money you'll be saving on coffee and booze!

## Clearing the Air

▶ If cigarette smokers are at your home and you don't want to ask them not to smoke, place little saucers of vinegar around the room in inconspicuous spots. The vinegar absorbs the smell of tobacco smoke.

▶ Lit candles add atmosphere to a room and absorb cigarette smoke at the same time. Scented candles emit a lovely aroma that can mask the tobacco stench.

## SPRAINS AND STRAINS

**Y**ou may have sprained an ankle playing sports or running to catch a bus. Any sudden twist to a ligament causes a sprain. Strains are more minor injuries that affect tendons and muscles.

According to Ray C. Wunderlich, Jr., MD, PhD, director of the Wunderlich Center for Nutritional Medicine in St. Petersburg, Florida, as soon as you get a sprain, take large amounts of enzymes hourly, in the form of fresh vegetable juices and/or bromelain, papaya and pancreatic supplements (available at health food stores). The sooner you start taking enzymes, the better! Then read on to decide what to do next.

## Treating Sprains

We questioned a number of medical professionals about what works best for a sprain, and here is the consensus...

▶ Don't use the injured joint, and treat it with the RICE method (Rest, Ice, Compression, Elevation). During the first 12 hours after the injury, starting as soon as possible, apply an ice-cold water compress to the hurt area. This will reduce the swelling.

Leave the compress on for 20 minutes, then take it off for 20 minutes. Extend the 12 hours of cold compresses to 24 hours if it seems necessary.

**WARNING:** Seek medical attention as soon as possible to make sure the sprain is just a sprain and not a fractured, chipped or dislocated bone.

## Natural Remedies

We've also heard about other remedies that have worked wonderfully well. *For example...*

▶ Put the sprained area in a basin of ice-cold water, and keep it there for five minutes. Then bind the area with a wet bandage and cover the wet one with a dry bandage.

▶ Warm a cupful of apple cider vinegar, saturate a washcloth with it and apply the cloth to the sprain for five minutes every hour.

▶ Take the peel of an orange and apply it to the sprained area—put the white spongy side on the skin—and bind it in place with a bandage. It should reduce the swelling of a sprain.

▶ Add 1 tablespoon of cayenne pepper to 2 cups of apple cider vinegar and bring it to a slow boil in an enamel or glass saucepan. Bottle the liquid and use it on sprains, pains and sore muscles.

▶ Grate ginger (frozen ginger is easier to grate) and squeeze the grated ginger through cheesecloth, getting as much juice as you can. Measure the amount of ginger juice and add an equal amount of sesame oil. Mix it thoroughly, and massage it on your painful parts.

▶ Add 1 teaspoon of catnip to 1 cup of just-boiled water and steep it for five minutes. Saturate a washcloth with the catnip tea and apply it to the sprained area to reduce swelling. When the washcloth gets to be room temperature, resaturate the cloth in the heated liquid and reapply it.

Catnip is available at most health food stores—and pet stores.

## Comfrey Comfort

▶ Comfrey is popular among professional athletes and their smart coaches. This herb helps speed up the healing process and relieve the pain of pulled tendons and ligaments, strains, sprains, broken bones and tennis elbow.

Use a comfrey poultice (*see* "Preparation Guide" on page 252) on the sprained area, changing it every two to three hours. Comfrey is safe to use topically, if there is no open wound. It's always best to consult with your naturopathic doctor, of course.

## Leek-y Relief

▶ To help relieve the pain from a severe sprain, rub on leek liniment. To prepare the liniment, simmer 4 leeks in boiling water until they're mushy. Pour off the water and mash 4 tablespoons of coconut butter into the leek. As soon as it's cool, massage it into the sprained area. Keep the remaining liniment in a covered container. It can also be used for most muscle aches and pains.

## Recurrent-Sprain Prevention

▶ This applies mostly to athletes and dancers who keep spraining the same weakened parts of their bodies.

Before a warm-up session, saturate a washcloth with hot water and apply it to your vulnerable area for about 10 to 15 minutes. In other words, preheat the trouble spot before you work out.

## Tennis Elbow

▶ *See* the comfrey remedy on this page.

## SUNBURN

I t's important to protect your skin from the ultraviolet (UV) rays of the sun. Use sunscreen with a sun protection factor (SPF) of at least 15—more is better. Use it all year long, not just in the summer. In fact, during the day, don't leave home without it!

For optimal effectiveness, apply sunscreen a half-hour before going outside, to give it time to soak in. While you're enjoying the sunny outdoors, reapply sunscreen often, especially if you perspire and/or go swimming. Don't hesitate to slather it on. One ounce of sunscreen should cover the exposed skin of an average-sized adult wearing a swimsuit. It's worth it, especially when you consider the cost of skin problems down the road.

**WARNING:** If you're on any kind of medication, ask your doctor or pharmacist about interactions with sunscreen.

▶ Do *not* use sunscreen on infants six months or younger. The chemicals in it may be too harsh for their delicate skin. Babies that young should never be exposed to the sun for any length of time. The melanin in their skin will not offer them proper protection. When you take a baby out, dress him/her in a tightly woven long-sleeved shirt, long pants and a wide-brimmed hat.

## Soothing the Burn

▶ When you've gotten more than you've basked for, fill a quart jar with equal parts of milk and ice and 2 tablespoons of salt. Soak a washcloth in the mixture and place it on the sunburned area. Leave it on for about 15 minutes. Repeat the procedure three to four times throughout the day. This cooling compress can be very soothing.

▶ Empty a package of powdered nonfat milk or a quart of regular low-fat milk into a tub of warm water, and spend the next half-hour soaking in it.

**⚡ CAUTION:** Severe sunburns can be second-degree burns (*see* "Burns" starting on page 29). If the skin is broken or blistering, treatment should include cold water followed by a dry and sterile dressing. See a doctor as soon as possible.

### The Shadow Knows

If you have any question about whether or not you are at risk for being sunburned, look at your shadow. If your shadow is shorter than your height, you can get sunburned.

Don't be surprised to see that your shadow can be shorter than your height as late in the day as 4 pm. The sun is strongest at about 1 pm (daylight savings time). If you're going outdoors, be sure to use sunscreen starting at least three hours before and until three hours after 1 pm.

▶ Steep six regular (nonherbal) tea bags in 1 quart of hot water. When the tea is strong and cool, drench a washcloth in the liquid and apply it to the sunburned area. Repeat the procedure until you get relief.

▶ Spread sour cream over the sunburned area, particularly the face. Leave it on for 20 minutes, then rinse off with lukewarm water. The sour cream is said to take the heat out of the sunburn and tighten pores, too.

**⚡ CAUTION:** Do not put sour cream on broken skin. It can cause an infection.

▶ Apply cool raw slices of cucumber, apple or potato skin.

▶ Use aloe vera, either in commercial gel form or squeezed fresh from a plant.

### Preventing the Pain

One way to prevent a sunburn from hurting is by taking a hot—yes, hot—shower right after sunbathing. According to homeopathic principle, the hot water desensitizes the skin.

## Sunburned Eyes and Eyelids

▶ Make a poultice (*see* "Preparation Guide" on page 252) of grated apples and rest it over your closed eyelids for a relaxing hour.

▶ Take vitamin C—500 mg—twice a day to help take out the burn.

▶ Soothe burned eyelids with tea bags soaked in cool water.

▶ To make a compress for inflamed skin, soak a clean washcloth in apple cider vinegar, witch hazel or a mixture of one part skim milk to four parts water and wring halfway. Apply the cloth for five to 10 minutes.

**CAUTION:** If blisters develop, do not treat the sunburn yourself—see a doctor.

### Sun-Abused Skin

▶ Soften that leathery look with this centuries-old beauty mask formula. Mix 2 tablespoons of raw honey with 2 tablespoons of flour. Add enough milk (2 to 3 tablespoons) to make it the consistency of toothpaste.

Be sure your face and neck are clean and your hair is out of the way. Smooth the paste on the face and neck. Stay clear of the delicate skin around the eyes. Leave the paste on for a half-hour, rinse it off with tepid water and pat dry.

▶ Now you need a toner. May we make a suggestion? In a juice extractor, juice two cucumbers, then heat the juice until it's boiling, skim off the froth (if any), bottle the juice and refrigerate it.

*Dose:* Twice daily, use 1 teaspoon of juice combined with 2 teaspoons of water. Gently dab it on your face and neck and let it dry.

▶ Now you need a moisturizer. Consider using a light film of extra-virgin, cold-pressed olive oil or castor oil.

# TENSION AND ANXIETY

Sweaty palms, indigestion, a stiff neck, hyperventilating, an ulcer, a dry mouth, a tic—yes, even a canker sore —all of these conditions can be caused by nervous tension, anxiety and stress.

There are as many symptoms and outward manifestations of anxiety as there are reasons for it. Throughout this book, we generally address ourselves to the problem at hand, like sweaty palms. In this section, we address the problem that may have caused the symptom—nervous tension and anxiety.

Psychologist Joyce Brothers, PhD, unwinds by doing heavy gardening on her farm. Sailing is a great release for former CBS News anchor Walter Cronkite. Actor John Travolta pilots his own plane for relaxation.

## Natural Remedies

While not all of us have a plane, a sailboat or a farm, most of us have a kitchen, a neighborhood health food store—and the following tension-relieving remedies.

▶ A good first step would be to cut out caffeine. Substitute herbal teas for regular tea and coffee. If you're a chocoholic, check out carob bars when you get a craving for chocolate. Health food stores have a big selection of carob treats that contain no caffeine. The taste and texture of some carob brands are similar to chocolate.

▶ Harried homeowners, do not paint your kitchens yellow to cheer you up. According to color therapist Carlton Wagner, founder of the Wagner Institute for Color Research in Santa Barbara, California, a yellow room contributes to stress and adds to feelings of anxiety.

### Pressure Relieves Pressure

▶ Here's a little acupressure to relieve life's pressure. For at least five minutes a day, massage the webbed area between your thumb and index finger of your left hand. Really get in there and knead it. It may hurt. That's all the more reason to keep at it.

Gradually, the pain will decrease, and so should the tightness in your chest and shoulders. Eventually, you should have no pain at all, and you may notice a difference in your general relaxed state of well-being.

▶ For a burst of energy without the tension that's usually attached to it, add ⅛ teaspoon of cayenne pepper to a cup of warm water and drink it down.

It's strong stuff and may take a while to get used to, but cayenne is so beneficial, it's worth it. Once you get used to it, increase the amount to ¼ teaspoon, then to ½ teaspoon.

▶ Make two poultices out of a large, raw, grated onion. (*See* "Preparation Guide" on page 252.) Place a poultice on each of your calves and leave them there for a half-hour. We know, it's hard to believe that onions on your legs can eliminate nervous anxiety, but don't knock it until you try it.

▶ If all of your tension is preventing you from falling asleep, try the tranquilizing effect of a hop pillow. (*See* "Sleep Problems" on page 162 for details.)

▶ Let's talk about something some of you may already know about—Valium (brand name *diazapam*). Often prescribed to relieve tension, it can have side effects. But there is an alternative that is said to have no side effects. It's called valerian root, and it's the natural forerunner to Valium. Capsules and tablets are available at health food stores. Follow the dosage on the label.

Cut and powdered valerian root is available, but the smell is so vile, we can't imagine anyone wanting to make their own tea with it.

▶ Did you know there's a Center for the Interaction of Animals and Society? Well, there is, and it's at the University of Pennsylvania School of Veterinary Medicine in Philadelphia. Results of a study conducted at the Center showed that looking at fish in a home aquarium is as beneficial as biofeedback and meditation, in terms of relaxation techniques. Yup, just sitting in front of a medium-sized fish tank—watching ordinary, nonexotic little fish—relaxed people to the point of considerably improving their blood pressure.

Get a few guppies and pull up a chair! Or, if you have a VCR or DVD player, there are videos of fish in aquariums and in the ocean. Go to *www2.vet.upenn.edu/research/centers/cias* for more information on the Center.

▶ Chia seeds are a calmative. Drink a cup of chia-seed tea before each meal. You can also sprinkle the seeds on salads.

### *Switch Nostrils to Relax*

▶ Alternate-nostril breathing is a well-known yoga technique that is used to put people in a relaxed state with a feeling of inner peace.

Pay attention—it sounds more complex than it is.

- Place your right thumb against your right nostril.
- Place your right ring finger and right pinkie against your left nostril. (This is not an exercise for anyone with a stuffed nose.)
- Inhale and slowly exhale through both nostrils.
- Now press your right nostril closed and slowly inhale deeply through your left nostril to the count of five.
- While your right nostril is still closed, press your left nostril closed.
- Holding the air in your lungs, count to five.
- Open your right nostril and exhale to the count of five. Inhale through your right nostril to the count of five.
- Close both nostrils and count to five. Exhale through the left nostril to the count of five.

Keep repeating this pattern for—you guessed it—five minutes. Do it in the morning when you start your day and again at day's end.

▶ *Kombu* is a type of seaweed. Kombu tea can be a potent nerve tonic. Add a 3-inch strip of kombu to a quart of water and boil it for 10 minutes. Drink ½ cup at a time throughout the day. Kombu is available at health food stores and Asian markets.

### Pin Up Your Hands

▶ Do you have some clothespins hanging around? Take a handful of them and clip them to the tips of your fingers, at the start of your nails of your left hand. Keep them there for seven minutes. Then put those clothespins on the fingers of your right hand for another seven minutes. Pressure exerted on nerve endings is known to relax the entire nervous system.

Do this clothespin bit first thing in the morning, and before, during or right after a particularly tense situation.

### Relax—From Head to Toe

▶ Here's a visualization exercise used by hypnotherapists and at many self-help seminars. Make sure you're not going to be disturbed by telephones, pagers, cell phones, doorbells, dogs, whistling teapots, etc.

Sit in a comfortable chair. Close your eyes and…wait! Read these directions first, then close your eyes. Once your eyes are closed, put all your awareness in your toes. Concentrate on feeling as though nothing else exists but your toes. Completely relax the muscles in your toes. Slowly move up from your toes to your feet, ankles, calves, knees, thighs, pelvis, hips, back, stomach, chest, shoulders, arms, hands, neck, jaw, mouth, cheeks, ears, eyes and brow. Yes, even relax the muscles of your scalp. Now that you're relaxed, take three slow, deep breaths, then slowly open your eyes.

## Stage Fright

Most of us get nervous when we have to do any kind of public speaking. In fact, lots of professional performers get a bad case of butterflies before the curtain goes up.

Here are a couple of exercises that can make nervousness a thing of the past…

▶ Before "showtime," stand squarely in front of an immovable wall. Put both your palms on the wall, elbows bent slightly. With your right foot a step in front of the left one, bend both legs at the knees and push, push, push! Be sure to tighten your abdominal muscles. This flexing of your diaphragm somehow dispels the butterflies.

One time, Lydia thought a TV studio wall was immovable and it turned out to be part of a set that was quite movable. (That's one show to which we probably won't be invited back.)

▶ A minute before "You're on!" slowly take a deep breath. When no more air will fit into your lungs, hold it for two seconds, then let the air out very fast, in one big "whoosh." Do this two times in a row, and you should be ready to go out there in complete control.

### Dry Mouth

▶ When it's time to make that all-important speech—or pop that critical question—you want to seem calm and sound confident. That's hard to do when your mouth is dry.

When this happens, do not drink cold beverages. Doing so may help your dry mouth, but it will tighten up your already-tense throat.

Also, stay away from drinks with milk or cream. They can create phlegm and more problems talking. Warm tea is your best bet.

If there's none available, gently chew on your tongue. In less than 20 seconds, you'll manufacture all the saliva you'll need to end your dry mouth condition.

▶ Mix 1 tablespoon of honey with ½ cup of warm water, and swish and gargle with the mixture for about three to five minutes. Then rinse away the sweetness with water. The levulose in honey increases the secretion of saliva, relieving dryness of the mouth and making it easier to swallow.

**WARNING:** Diabetics and people with honey allergies should not use honey.

## TOOTH AND MOUTH PROBLEMS

**B**e true to your teeth or they will become false to you! Irish dramatist and Nobel prize–winner George Bernard Shaw (1856–1950) once said, "The man with toothache thinks everyone happy whose teeth are sound."

Natural remedies can help ease the pain of a toothache and, in some cases, alleviate problems caused by nervous tension and low-grade infections.

Since it is difficult to know what is causing a toothache, make an appointment to see

your dentist as soon as possible. More important, have the dentist see your teeth.

## Tooth Problems

▶ If your teeth are loose, strengthen them with parsley. Pour 1 quart of boiling water over 1 cup of parsley. Let it stand for 15 minutes, then strain and refrigerate the parsley water.

*Dose:* Drink 3 cups a day.

### Toothache

Until you get to the dentist for the drilling, filling and billing, try one of these remedies to ease the toothache pain.

▶ Prepare a cup of chamomile tea and saturate a white washcloth in it. Wring it out, then apply it to your cheek or jaw—the outside area of your toothache. As soon as the cloth gets cold, redip it and reapply it. This chamomile compress should draw out the pain before it's time to reheat the tea.

▶ Soak your feet in hot water. Dry them thoroughly, then rub them vigorously with bran.

No, this didn't get mixed into the wrong category. We were told this is a Cherokee Indian remedy for a toothache.

### Papa Wilen's Pig Fat Story

▶ Whenever the subject of toothaches came up in our home, we would prompt our dad to tell the "pig fat" story.

He would begin by telling us that one time, when he was a teenager, he had dental work done on a Thursday. Late that night, there was swelling and pain from the work the dentist did. In those days, dentists were not in their offices on Friday, and the thought of waiting until Monday was out of the question because the pain was so severe.

Friday morning, our grandmother went to the nonkosher butcher in the neighborhood and bought a piece of pig fat. She brought it into the house (something she had never done before, since she kept a strictly kosher home), heated it up and put the melted fat on a white handkerchief, which she then placed on top of Daddy's cheek. Within a few minutes, the swelling went down and his pain vanished.

At this point in the telling of the story, our father would get up and demonstrate how he danced around the room, celebrating his freedom from pain.

Recently, we've come across another version of that same remedy (we promise, no more stories). Take a tiny slice of pork fat and place it between the gum and cheek, directly on the sore area.

Keep it there for 15 minutes, or however long it takes for the pain to subside. (The dance afterward is optional.)

▶ Make a cup of stronger-than-usual sage tea. If your teeth are not sensitive to "hot," hold the hot tea in your mouth for half a minute, then swallow and take another mouthful. Keep doing this until you finish the cup of tea and, hopefully, have no more pain.

▶ Grate horseradish root and place a poultice of it behind the ear closest to the aching tooth. To ensure relief, also apply some of the grated horseradish to the gum area closest to the aching tooth.

▶ Pack powdered milk in a painful cavity for temporary relief. But see a dentist pronto!

### Let Your Fingers Do the Healing

▶ Acupressure works like magic for some people—hopefully, you're one of them. If your toothache is on the right side, squeeze the index finger on your right hand (the one next to your thumb), on each side of your fingernail. As you're squeezing your finger, rotate it clockwise a few times, giving that index finger a rapid little massage.

▶ Apply just a few grains of cayenne pepper to the affected tooth and gum. At first it will add to the pain, but as soon as the smarting stops (within seconds), so should the toothache.

▶ Soak a cheek-sized piece of brown paper (grocery bag) in vinegar, then sprinkle one side with black pepper. Place the peppered side on the outside of the face next to the toothache. Secure it in place with a bandage and keep it there at least an hour.

▶ Split open one fresh, ripe fig. Squeeze out the juice of the fruit onto your aching tooth. Put more fig juice on the tooth in 15-minute intervals, until the pain stops or until you run out of fig juice.

This is an ancient Hindu remedy. And it must really work well…because when was the last time you saw an ancient Hindu with a toothache?

▶ Roast half an onion. When it is comfortably hot, place it on the pulse of your wrist, on the side opposite your troublesome tooth. By the time the onion cools down completely, the pain should be gone.

### Sweet Relief from Cloves

▶ An old standard painkiller is cloves. You can buy oil of cloves or whole cloves. The oil should be soaked in a wad of cotton and placed directly on the aching tooth. The whole clove should be dipped in warm honey.

Then chew the clove slowly, rolling it around the aching tooth. That will release the essential oil and ease the pain.

**WARNING:** Diabetics and people with honey allergies should not use honey.

▶ Saturate a slice of toast with alcohol, then sprinkle on some pepper. The peppered side should be applied externally to the toothache side of the face.

▶ If you love garlic, this one's for you. Place one just-peeled clove of garlic directly on the aching tooth. Keep it there for a minimum of one hour. (Follow up with "Bad Breath" remedies on pages 183–185.)

▶ If you are scheduled to go to the dentist, take 10 mg of vitamin $B_1$ (thiamine) every day, starting a week before your dental appointment. You may find that the pain during and after dental procedures will be greatly reduced.

It is thought that the body's lack of thiamine might be what lets the pain become severe in the first place.

## Preparing for Dental Work

▶ As soon as you know you're going to the dentist to have work done, start eating pineapple. Have fresh pineapple or a cup of canned pineapple in its own juice, and drink a cup of 100% pineapple juice every day.

Continue the pineapple regimen for a few days after the dental work is completed. The enzymes in pineapple should help reduce pain and discomfort. They can also help speed the healing process.

## Tooth Extractions
### To Stop Bleeding

▶ Dip a tea bag in boiling water, squeeze out the water, and allow it to cool. Then pack the tea bag down on the tooth socket and keep it there for 15 to 30 minutes.

### To Stop Pain

▶ Mix 1 teaspoon of Epsom salts with 1 cup of hot water. Swish the mixture around in your mouth and spit it out. (Do not swallow it—unless you need a laxative.) One cup should do the trick. But if the pain recurs, get the Epsom salts and start swishing again.

▶ Wrap an ice cube in gauze or cheesecloth. (Hopefully you'll figure out this remedy before the ice melts.)

When your thumb is up against the index finger, a meaty little tuft is formed where the fingers are joined. Acupuncturists call it the "hoku point."

Spread your fingers and, with the ice cube, massage that tuft for seven minutes.

If your hand starts to feel numb, stop massaging with the ice and continue with just a finger massage. It should give you from 15 to 30 minutes of "no pain."

This is also effective when you have pain after root canal work.

## Gum Problems

▶ It's helpful to brush your teeth and massage the gums with goldenseal tea (available at health food stores).

▶ Myrrh (yes, one of the gifts brought by the wise men) is a shrub, and the gum from that shrub is an antiseptic and astringent used on bleeding or swollen gums to heal the infection that's causing the problem.

Myrrh oil can be massaged directly on gums, or use myrrh powder on a soft-bristled toothbrush and gently brush your teeth at the gum line. Do this several times throughout the day for relief.

### Pyorrhea

Pyorrhea is a degeneration of the gums and tissues that surround the teeth. This disease is marked by severe inflammation, bleeding gums and a discharge of pus. As pyorrhea advances, the gums may recede altogether.

Pyorrhea is a serious condition that should be treated by a dentist. But the following remedies may provide some temporary relief for those aching gums.

▶ In parts of Mexico, pyorrhea is treated by rubbing gums with the rattle from a rattlesnake. (We'd hate to think of how they do root canals.)

▶ Make your own toothpaste by combining baking soda with a drop or two of hydrogen peroxide. Brush your teeth and massage your gums with it, using a soft, thin-bristled brush.

▶ Take Coenzyme Q-10—15 mg twice a day. Also, open a CoQ-10 capsule and use the powder to brush your teeth and massage your gums.

Each time you take a CoQ-10, also take 500 mg of vitamin C with bioflavonoids.

▶ Brian R. Clement, director of the Hippocrates Health Institute in West Palm Beach, Florida, reports that garlic is the first and foremost remedy for clearing up gum problems.

He also warns that raw garlic can burn sensitive gums. It is for that reason the Institute's professional staff mixes pectin with garlic before impacting the gums with it. The garlic heals the infection while the pectin keeps it from burning the gums. Suggest this line of defense to a (new age or holistic) periodontist.

## Bleeding Gums

▶ Bleeding gums may be your body's way of saying you do not have a well-balanced diet. After checking with your dentist, consider seeking professional help from a vitamin therapist or nutritionist, who can help you supplement your food intake with the vitamins and minerals you're lacking. Meanwhile, take 500 mg of vitamin C twice a day.

 **NOTE:** Persistent bleeding gums should be checked by a health professional.

## Cleaning Teeth and Gums

▶ Cut one fresh strawberry in half and rub your teeth and gums with it. It may help remove stains, discoloration and tartar without harming the teeth's enamel. It may also strengthen and heal sore gums.

Leave the crushed strawberry and juice on the teeth and gums as long as possible—at least 15 minutes. Then rinse with warm water. Use only fresh strawberries which are kept at room temperature.

▶ If you can't brush after every meal, kiss someone. Really—kiss someone! It starts the saliva flowing and helps prevent tooth decay.

▶ Actually, the best way to clean your teeth is the way you do it right before leaving for your dental appointment.

## Cavity Prevention

▶ To avoid being "bored" to tears by the dentist, eat a little cube of cheddar, Monterey Jack or Swiss cheese right after eating sugary, cavity-causing foods. It seems that cheese reduces bacterial acid production, which causes decay.

### ■ Recipe ■

#### Peanut Slaw

3½ cups cabbage, shredded
¾ cup celery, chopped
½ cup cucumber, peeled and chopped
½ cup cocktail peanuts, chopped
3 Tbsp onion, diced
½ cup mayonnaise
½ cup sour cream
¾ tsp prepared horseradish
¼ tsp honey mustard
Salt and pepper to taste

Combine cabbage, celery, cucumber, peanuts and onion in a large bowl. Set aside. Combine remaining ingredients and mix well. Add to cabbage mixture, then toss well. Cover and chill.

Makes 6 servings.

*Source: www.freerecipe.org*

▶ Peanuts also help prevent tooth decay. They can be eaten at the end of the meal, instead of right after each cavity-causing food.

▶ Tea is rich in fluoride, which resists tooth decay. Some Japanese tea drinkers believe it helps fight plaque. Take some tea and see. You may want to try Kukicha tea. It's tasty, relaxing, caffeine-free and available at health food stores or Asian markets. Incidentally, you can use the same Kukicha tea bag three or four times.

▶ Blackstrap molasses contains an ingredient that seems to inhibit tooth decay. Sunflower seeds are also supposed to inhibit tooth decay. Have a tablespoon of molasses in water and/or a handful of shelled, raw, unsalted sunflower seeds every day. Be sure to rinse thoroughly with water after consuming the molasses.

### Clean Your Toothbrush

▶ Dissolve a tablespoon of baking soda in a glass of warm water and soak your toothbrush overnight. Rinse it in the morning and notice how clean it looks and feels.

### Throw Away Your Toothbrush

▶ Bacteria from your mouth settle in the bristles of your toothbrush and can reinfect you with whatever you have—a cold sore, a cold, the flu or a sore throat.

As soon as symptoms appear, throw away your toothbrush. Use a new one for a few days, then throw that one away and use another new one. If you want to be super-cautious, use a new toothbrush as soon as you're all better.

### Plaque Remover

▶ Dampen your dental floss and dip it in baking soda, then floss with it. It may help remove some of the plaque buildup.

### Tartar Remover

▶ Mix equal parts of cream of tartar and salt. Brush your teeth and massage your gums with the mixture, then rinse very thoroughly.

### Teeth Whitener

▶ Burn a piece of toast—really char it. (For some of us, that's part of our everyday routine.) Then pulverize the charred bread, mix it with about ½ teaspoon of honey and brush your teeth with it. Rinse thoroughly. Put on a pair of sunglasses, look in the mirror and smile!

**WARNING:** Diabetics and people with honey allergies should not use honey.

## Halitosis (Bad Breath)

Most people have bad breath at some point every day (like when you wake up—*yeeech!*). This is basically caused by tiny bits of food that decay in the mouth. Proper to othbrushing can tackle most cases of the stinkies, but chronic bad breath may be caused by an underlying illness.

**NOTE:** It's important to find the cause of bad breath. Get checked for chronic sinusitis or indigestion, and see a dentist.

While no one ever dies from bad breath, it sure can kill a relationship. Here are some refreshing remedies that are worth a try.

▶ Suck on a piece of cinnamon bark to sweeten your breath. Cinnamon sticks come in jars or can be bought loose at some food specialty shops. They can also satisfy the craving for a sweet treat or cigarettes.

▶ Bad breath is sometimes due to food particles decaying between one's teeth. If that's the case, use dental floss and brush after every meal.

▶ Take a piece of 100% pure wool—preferably white and not dyed—put ½ teaspoon of raw honey on it and massage your upper gums. Put another ½ teaspoon of raw honey on the wool and massage the lower gums.

**WARNING:** Diabetics and people with honey allergies should not use honey.

Did you say that sounds crazy? We can't argue with you there, but it's worth a try. Rinse your mouth thoroughly with water after using honey—it can contribute to tooth decay.

▶ If your tongue looks coated, it may need to be scraped, which will help combat bad breath. Use your toothbrush or a tongue scraper (available at health food stores-and pharmacies) to scrape your tongue after breakfast and at bedtime.

## Herbal Rinse

▶ Stock up on mint, rosemary and fennel seeds (available at health food stores) and prepare an effective mouthwash for yourself.

For a daily portion, use ⅓ teaspoon of each of the three dried herbs. Pour 1 cup of just-boiled water over the mint, rosemary and fennel seeds, cover the cup, and let the mixture steep for 10 minutes. Then strain it.

At that point, it should be cool enough for you to rinse with. You might also want to swallow a little. It's wonderful for digestion (which may be causing the bad breath).

▶ At bedtime, take a piece of myrrh the size of a pea and let it dissolve in your mouth. Since myrrh is an antiseptic and can destroy the germs that may cause the problem, hopefully you can say "bye-bye" to dragon breath.

▶ When leaving an Indian restaurant, you may have noticed a bowl filled with seeds near the door. They are most likely anise. Suck on a few of those licorice-tasting seeds to help sweeten your breath.

You may want to have a bowl of anise at your next dinner party.

## Garlic or Onion Breath

▶ Mix ½ teaspoon of baking soda into a cup of water, then swish it—one gulp at a time—around your mouth. Spit out. Be careful not to swallow this mouthwash. By the time you've rinsed your mouth with the entire cup, your breath should be fresh.

▶ Chew sprigs of parsley—yes, especially after eating garlic. Take your choice—garlic breath or little pieces of green stuff between your teeth.

▶ If you're a coffee drinker, drink a strong cup of coffee to remove all traces of onion from your breath.

Of course, then you have coffee breath, which, to some people, is just as objectionable as the onion breath. So eat an apple. That will get rid of the coffee breath. In fact, forget the coffee and just eat an apple.

▶ Chew a whole clove to sweeten your breath. People have been doing that for over 5,000 years to freshen their breath.

▶ Suck a lemon! It should make your onion or garlic breath disappear. Some people get better results when they add salt to the lemon, then suck it. (That's also a good remedy for getting rid of hiccups.)

▶ **CAUTION:** Do not suck lemons often. Do this only in an emergency social situation. With repeated use, the strongly acidic lemon juice can wear away tooth enamel.

### Mouthwash

▶Prepare your own mouthwash by combining ¼ cup of apple cider vinegar with 2 cups of just-boiled water. Let it cool and store it in a jar in your medicine cabinet.

Swish a mouthful of this antiseptic solution as you would commercial mouthwash, for about one minute, and spit it out. Then, be sure to rinse with water to remove the acid stains.

## Canker Sores

Canker sores are painful, annoying little sores that develop on the gums, cheeks and tongue, which can last for weeks. They are believed to be brought on by stress.

▶Get an ear of corn, discard the kernels and burn a little piece of cob at a time. Apply the cob ashes to the canker sore three to five times a day. (Too bad this isn't a remedy for the toes—we'd have "cob on the corn.")

▶Several times throughout the day, keep a glob of blackstrap molasses in your mouth on the canker sore. Molasses has extraordinary healing properties. Be sure to rinse thoroughly with water after using molasses.

▶According to psychic healer Edgar Cayce, castor oil is soothing and promotes healing of canker sores. Dab the sore with it each time the pain reminds you it's there.

### Bacterial Cure

▶Yogurt with active cultures (make sure the container specifies "living" or "active" cultures) may ease the condition faster than you can say *Lactobacillus acidophilus*. In fact, lactobacillus tablets may be an effective treatment for canker sores.

Again, make sure the tablets have living organisms. Start by taking two tablets at each meal, then decrease the dosage as the condition clears up.

▶Until you get the *Lactobacillus acidophilus*, dip one regular (nonherbal) tea bag in boiling water. Squeeze out most of the water. When it's cool to the touch, apply it to the canker sore for three minutes.

▶Take a mouthful of sauerkraut juice (use fresh from the barrel or in a jar found at health food stores, rather than the cans found in supermarkets) and swish it over the canker sore for about a minute. Then either swallow the juice or spit it out.

Do this throughout the day, four to six times every day, until the sore is gone. It should disappear in a day or two.

If you're like us, you'll come to love the juice. You may even want to try making your own sauerkraut. (*See* "Preparation Guide" on page 252.)

# ULCERS

There is a small percentage of people who develop ulcers (sores on the lining of the stomach or small intestine) from continual use of aspirin and other painkillers. If that doesn't apply to you, keep reading.

A recent incredible discovery was made about the main cause of ulcers. About 80% of all ulcers can be blamed on *Helicobacter pylori,* bacteria that are more commonly referred to as H. pylori. It is estimated that half of the American adult population has H. pylori present but dormant in their stomachs.

Why do some people develop ulcers and others don't? Our commonsense guess is that emotional upsets, fatigue, nervous anxiety, chronic tension and/or the inability to healthfully handle a high-pressure job or situation may devitalize the immune system, lowering one's resistance to the H. pylori.

If you're a member of this "fret set," we can suggest remedies for the ulcer, but you have to remedy the cause first. Change jobs, meditate, look into self-help seminars or do whatever is appropriate to transform your specific problem into something that is positive and manageable.

And now, we're asking you nicely—please don't try any of these remedies without your doctor's blessing, okay?

## Dietary Remedies

▶ According to a report that was published in the medical journal *Practical Gastroenterology* (*www.practicalgastro.com*), "Aside from its failure to promote healing of gastric ulceration, the bland diet has other shortcomings—it is not palatable, and it is too high in fat and too low in roughage." So jazz up your food with some spices!

▶ We learned that milk may not be the cure-all we thought it was. It may neutralize stomach acid at first, but because of its calcium content, gastrin is secreted. Gastrin is a hormone that encourages the release of more acid. Steer clear of milk.

### High-Fiber Healing

▶ A high-fiber diet is believed to be best for treatment of ulcers and prevention of relapses.

▶ If your doctor approves, take 1 tablespoon of extra-virgin, cold-pressed olive oil in the morning and 1 tablespoon in the evening. It may help to soothe and heal the mucous membrane that lines the stomach.

▶ Barley and barley water are soothing and help rebuild the stomach lining. Boil 2 ounces of pearled barley in 6 cups of water until there's about half the water—3 cups—left in the pot. Strain. If necessary, add honey and lemon to taste. Drink it throughout the day. Eat the barley in soup, stew or by itself.

*See* the "Barley Water" information on page 249 of "Preparation Guide."

▶ Recent research has substantiated the effectiveness of cabbage juice, a centuries-old folk remedy for relief of ulcers. While today's pressured lifestyle is quite conducive to developing ulcers, we, at least, have modern machinery to help with the cure—a juice extractor.

Juice a cabbage and drink a cup of the juice right before each meal, then another cup before bedtime. Make sure the cabbage is fresh, not wilted. Also, drink the juice as soon as you prepare it. In other words, don't prepare it ahead of time and refrigerate it. It loses a lot of value that way.

According to reports on test groups, pain, symptoms and ulcers disappeared within two to three weeks after starting the cabbage-juice regimen.

People often ask, "Why cabbage?" *We researched and found two reasons...*

◆ Cabbage is rich in the nonessential amino acid glutamine. Glutamine helps the healthy stomach cells regenerate and stimulates the production of mucin, a mucoprotein that protects the stomach lining.

◆ Cabbage contains gefarnate, a substance that helps strengthen the stomach lining and replace cells. (It's also used in anti-ulcer drugs.)

Gentlemen, start your juicers! Raw cabbage is also good in sauerkraut, cole slaw and the Korean dish *kim chee.*

▶ For the acute distress of ulcers (and gastritis), Ray C. Wunderlich, Jr., MD, PhD, director of the Wunderlich Center for Nutritional Medicine in St. Petersburg, Florida, recommends lecithin granules—1 heaping tablespoon as needed. Lecithin capsules will also suffice. Both are available at health food stores.

# URINARY PROBLEMS

The urinary system includes the kidneys, ureters, bladder and urethra.

Many of the remedies in this section are helpful for more than one condition. Therefore, most of the bladder and kidney ailments (infections, stones, inflammation, etc.) are bunched together. We suggest you read them all in order to determine the most appropriate one(s) for your specific problem.

**CAUTION:** Urinary infections, kidney stones and inflammation of the bladder and kidneys are serious conditions that should be evaluated by a health professional.

## Natural Remedies

With your doctor's approval, here are some worth-a-try remedies that may help to ease your condition.

▶ Drink plenty of fluids, including parsley tea—3 to 4 cups a day. If you have a juicer, one or two glasses of parsley juice drunk each day, should prove quite beneficial.

Also, sprinkle fresh parsley on the foods you eat. You may start to see improvements in a mere three days or up to three weeks.

▶ Onions are a diuretic and will help to cleanse your system. So eat fresh onions often. Also, for kidney stimulation, apply a poultice of grated or finely chopped onions externally to the kidney area—on your back, just under the rib cage.

▶ Pure cranberry juice (no sugar or preservatives added) has been known to help relieve kidney and bladder infections.

*Dose:* Drink 6 ounces of room-temperature cranberry juice three times a day.

### It's the Tops!

▶ Carrot tops and celery tops are tops in strengthening the kidneys and bladder. In the morning, cover a bunch of scrubbed carrot tops with 12 ounces of boiled water and let them steep. Drink 4 ounces of the carrot-top water before each meal. After each meal, eat a handful of scrubbed celery tops.

Within five weeks, there should be a noticeable and positive difference in the kidneys and bladder.

▶ Pumpkin seeds are high in zinc and good for strengthening the bladder muscle.

*Dose:* Eat one palmful (about 1 ounce) of unprocessed (unsalted) shelled pumpkin seeds three times a day.

▶ According to some Native Americans, corn silk (the silky strands beneath the husk of corn) is a cure-all for urinary problems. The most desirable corn silk is from young corns, gathered before the silk turns brown.

Take a handful of corn silk and steep it in 3 cups of boiled water for five minutes. Strain and drink the 3 cups throughout the day. Corn silk can be stored in a glass jar, not refrigerated.

If you can't get corn silk, use corn silk extract, available at most health food stores. Add 10 to 15 drops of the extract to a cup of water.

## Bed-Wetting and Nighttime Urination

Frequent nighttime urination, known as nocturia, is a common but often-overlooked medical problem. To most people, a mild case—waking a few times a night—is bothersome, but not a reason to see a doctor.

But ignoring even mild nocturia is a mistake. Our kidneys and bladder are designed to retain urine during an 8-hour sleep. If you wake to urinate more than twice a night, consider these suggestions...

☞ **WARNING:** Hypertension, diabetes, prostate problems, stroke, kidney disease and, in some cases, a tumor in the bladder can cause nocturia. Get a thorough physical, including a urinalysis to check for a bladder infection.

▶ Cut back on beverages. Certain beverages have a diuretic effect that can lead to nighttime urination—coffee, black or green tea, alcohol, caffeinated soda and herbal teas containing dandelion, burdock, linden, nettle or parsley. Abstain from these beverages after 6 pm, and limit your total fluid intake after dinner to 12 ounces of water or a nondiuretic, non-caffeinated tea, such as chamomile or peppermint.

▶ In people with allergies or certain medical conditions, including benign prostatic hyperplasia and interstitial cystitis, inflammation is the cause of nocturia. Quercetin, a strong antioxidant, decreases inflammation and inhibits cell damage in the kidneys. Cranberries and other dark red or purple berries, such as blueberries and raspberries, contain a good amount of quercetin. Eat one cup of fresh berries every day, or take a 500-mg quercetin supplement twice daily with meals.

▶ Get tested for food allergies. Food allergens act as irritants, so your body tries to eliminate them quickly through a variety of mechanisms, including urination.

▶ Just when you may have thought that nothing could help, heeeeeere's uva ursi! This herb is said to help strengthen the urinary tract and, taken in small doses, has been known to end bed-wetting.

Add 1 tablespoon of dried uva ursi leaves or one tea bag to 1 cup of just-boiled water and steep for five minutes. Strain into a jar.

*Dose:* Take 1 tablespoon before each meal every day for six weeks. (Uva ursi is available at health food stores.)

**NOTE:** Arbutin, the main component of the herb uva ursi, may cause the urine to turn brownish in color. It's absolutely nothing to worry about.

**WARNING:** We do not list this as a children's bed-wetting remedy because none of our sources mentioned it for use by children. Uva ursi may be too strong for their delicate systems.

### Diuretics

To stimulate urination, try any of the following foods in moderation, using good common sense and listening to your body...

◆ *Celery:* Cooked in chicken soup or raw in salads.

◆ *Watercress:* Soup or salads.

◆ *Leek:* A mild diuretic in soup, it's much stronger when eaten raw, and a perfect opening for a cheap joke about urination.

◆ *Parsley:* Used in soups, salads, juices or as a tea.

◆ *Asparagus:* Raw or cooked, or as a tea.

◆ *Cucumber:* Raw.

◆ *Corn silk:* Tea.

◆ *Onions:* Raw in salads and/or sliced to rub on your loins. (Yes, you read that correctly.)

◆ *Horseradish:* Grate ½ cup of horseradish and boil it with ½ cup of beer. Drink this concoction three times a day.

◆ *Watermelon:* Eat a piece first thing in the morning and do not eat any other foods for at least two hours.

## Incontinence

Any problems with incontinence should be evaluated by a health professional. But, until you get treated, these remedies may help.

▶ Direct the stream of water from an ordinary garden hose onto the soles of the feet for up to two minutes. It has been known to reduce urinary incontinence, particularly in older people. It also helps circulation in the feet.

### Bully for Buchu

▶ This remedy comes from the Hottentot tribe of South Africa, where buchu shrubs grow. Steep 1 tablespoon of buchu leaves (available at health food stores) in 1 cup of just-boiled water for a half-hour.

*Dose:* Take 3 to 4 tablespoons, three to four times a day. Buchu leaves are known to be helpful for many urinary problems, including inflammation of the bladder and painful urination, as well as incontinence.

### Frequent Urination

▶ Cherry juice or cranberry juice (no sugar or preservatives added) has been said to help regulate the problem of constantly having to urinate.

*Dose:* Drink 3 to 4 glasses of cherry or cranberry juice throughout the day. Be sure it's room temperature, not chilled.

**NOTE:** Persistent frequent urination may be a sign of a urinary tract infection or diabetes and should be checked by a health professional.

## Kidney Problems

▶ Lots of folk remedies include the use of apple cider vinegar to help flush the kidneys and to provide a natural acid. Dosage varies from source to source.

We think it makes the most sense to take 1 teaspoon of apple cider vinegar for every 50 pounds you weigh, and add it to 6 ounces of drinking water.

In other words, if you weigh 150 pounds, the dosage would be 3 teaspoons of vinegar in 6 ounces of water. Drink this twice a day, before breakfast and before dinner. Keep it up for two days, then stop for four days. Continue this two-days-on/four-days-off cycle as long as you feel you need it.

### Aduki Dukes It Out

▶ Aduki (or azuki) beans, which can be found in health food stores, are used in the Orient as food and medicine. They're excellent for treating kidney problems.

Rinse a cupful of aduki beans. Combine the cup of beans with 5 cups of water and boil them together for one hour. Strain the aduki-bean water into a jar. Drink ½ cup of aduki water at least a half-hour before meals. Do this for two days—six meals.

To prevent the aduki water from spoiling, keep the jar in the refrigerator, then warm the water before drinking.

▶ Our gem therapist friend recommends wearing jade against the skin to help heal kidney problems. If your mate reads this and surprises you with a piece of jade jewelry, chances are you'll start to feel better immediately.

### Kidney Stones

▶ According to a good old medical book called *The Elements of Materia Medica* (edited in 1854), asparagus was a popular remedy for kidney stones. It is said that asparagus acts to increase cellular activity in the kidneys and helps break up oxalic acid crystals.

*Dose:* Eat ½ cup of cooked and blended or puréed asparagus before breakfast and before dinner, or boil 1 cup of asparagus in 2 quarts of water and drink a cup of the aspara-gus water four times a day.

✎ **NOTE:** After eating asparagus, you may notice that your urine has an unusual smell. There are a few scientific theories as to what causes that specific smell.

In 1891, the experiments of Polish doc-tor and chemist Marceli Nencki led him to conclude that the scent is due to a metabo-lite called *methanethiol*. This odoriferous chemical is said to be produced as the body metabolizes asparagus. Some say that the smell is a sign of kidney-bladder cleans-ing—others believe it indicates faulty secre-tion of gastric hydrochloric acid (HCL).

▶ A respected French herbalist recommends eating almost nothing but strawberries for three to five days. This is believed to relieve the pain of kidney stones.

▶ A high level of oxalate in the urine con-tributes to the formation of most (calcium) kidney stones. If this problem runs in your family, or if you've already gone through the agony of a kidney stone, chances are you'll need to take every precaution to help prevent it from happening to you once…or again.

Completely eliminate, or at least limit, your intake of the foods and beverages that are high in oxalates or that can produce oxal-ic acid. These include caffeine—coffee, black tea (including orange pekoe), cocoa, choc-olate—spinach, sorrel, beets, Swiss chard, parsley, dried figs, poppy seeds, rhubarb, lamb's-quarters, purslane, nuts and pepper.

▶ Eat foods that are rich in vitamin A, the vita-min that can help discourage the formation of stones. These include apricots, pumpkin, sweet potatoes, squash, carrots and cantaloupe.

⚡ **CAUTION:** Any sudden or dramatic change of diet should be supervised by a health profes-sional. And always thoroughly wash produce to reduce the risk of food-borne illness.

▶ Start your day by drinking a glass of (dis-tilled, if possible) water in which you squeezed the juice of a lemon. The citric acid and mag-nesium in the lemon may also help prevent the formation of kidney stones.

Most important is that you drink a lot of water daily. Distilled water is ideal.

# WARTS

No matter how you feel about warts, they seem to have a way of growing on you.

*Verruca vulgaris* is the medical term for the common wart. (Don't you think a wart looks like a *Verruca vulgaris*?)

Warts usually appear on the hands, feet and face, and are believed to be caused by some type of virus.

The "quantity" award for home remedies goes to warts. We got a million of 'em—remedies, that is…not warts.

We tried to get warts for research purposes. We kept touching frogs. But it's a fallacy. You do not get warts from touching frogs. (Incidentally, you do not get a prince from kissing them either.)

## Natural Remedies

If you have a wart, there are a wide variety of remedies to try in order to find the one that works for you.

▶ Crush a fresh fig until it has a mushy consistency and put it on the wart for a half-hour each day. Continue doing that until the wart disappears.

▶ First thing each morning, dab some of your own spittle on the wart.

▶ Pick some dandelions. Break the stems and put the juice that oozes out of the stems directly on the wart—once in the morning and once in the evening, five days in a row.

▶ Apply a used tea bag to the wart for 15 minutes a day. Within a week to 10 days you should be wartless.

▶ Warts on the genitals? Gently rub the inside part of pineapple skin on the affected area. Repeat every morning and evening until the warts are gone or the pineapple's gone.

**NOTE:** Genital warts are a serious sexually transmitted disease. They are highly contagious and should be treated by a medical professional as soon as possible.

### Get the Lime Out

▶ If you have warts on your body, you may have too much lime in your system. One way to neutralize the excess lime is to drink a cup of chamomile tea two or three times a day.

▶ Grate carrots and combine them with a teaspoon of olive oil. Put the mixture on the wart for a half-hour twice a day.

▶ Dab lemon juice on the wart, immediately followed by a raw chopped onion. Do that twice a day for 15 minutes each time.

### Potato Popper

▶ Put a fresh slice of raw potato on the wart and keep it in place with a bandage. Leave it on overnight. Take it off in the morning. Then repeat the procedure again at night. If you don't get rid of the wart in a week, replace the potato with a clove of garlic.

▶ Every morning, squish out the contents of a vitamin E capsule and rub it vigorously on the wart. This remedy is slow (it may take more than a month), but what's the rush?

► Dab on the healing juice of the aloe vera plant every day until the wart disappears.

► Every day, apply a poultice of blackstrap molasses (*see* "Preparation Guide" on page 252) and keep it on the wart as long as possible. You should also eat a tablespoon of molasses daily (be sure to rinse your mouth with water after eating molasses).

   In about two weeks, the wart should drop off without leaving a trace.

### Chalk It Up to Experience

► We heard about a young woman who used an old remedy. She applied regular white chalk to the wart every night. On the sixth night, the wart fell off.

► In the morning and in the evening, rub the wart with one of the following—a radish, juice of marigold, flowers, bacon rind, oil of cinnamon, wheat germ oil or a thick paste of buttermilk and baking soda.

### Egg Water

► Boil eggs and save the water. As soon as the water is cool, soak your warted hand(s) for 10 minutes. Do this daily until the wart(s) disappear.

► If you don't have the patience to tend to the wart on a daily basis, consider finding a competent, professional hypnotist. Warts may actually be hypnotized away.

## Plantar Warts

► Plantar warts are the kind you find on the soles of the feet, usually in clusters. The wart starts as a little black dot. Don't pick it—you'll only make it spread. Instead, rub castor oil on it every night until it's history.

► At bedtime, puncture one or two garlic pearles (soft gels) and squeeze out the oil onto the plantar warts. Massage the oil on the entire area for a few minutes. Put a clean white sock on each foot and leave it on while you sleep.

   Do this every night for a week or two, until the little black roots come out and fall off.

## WEIGHT PROBLEMS

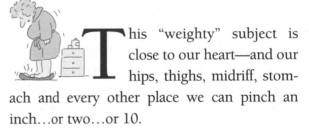

This "weighty" subject is close to our heart—and our hips, thighs, midriff, stomach and every other place we can pinch an inch...or two...or 10.

   As hundreds of books and articles tell us, losing weight is hard—keeping it off is harder.

   Most people go on a diet, living for the moment they can go *off* the diet.

   The answer, then, is *not* to go on a diet. If you're not on a diet to begin with, you can't go off it, right?

   We found some remedies that may help you lose weight without a temporary, "I-can't-wait-to-go-off-it" diet.

So, put some motivational reminders on your refrigerator—*Nothing stretches slacks like snacks! To indulge is to bulge! Those who love rich food and cook it, look it!*—and start to practice "girth control."

 **NOTE:** As for diet pills, they can be very helpful. Twice a day, spill them on the floor and pick them up one at a time. It's great exercise, especially for the waistline.

## Weight Control Tips

Whether you've spent years yo-yoing your way through one diet after another and are heavier than ever, or you just need to lose a few pounds to look better in that bathing suit, here are suggestions to healthfully help you shed those unwanted pounds.

### Common-Sense Reducing Principles

▶ Try eating your larger meals early rather than late in the day. This gives your body lots of time to digest and burn off the calories.

We've come across an appropriate saying—"Eat like a king in the morning, a prince at noon and a pauper in the evening." While it's not always practical to have a four-course breakfast, you may want to eat a big lunch and a small dinner whenever possible.

## Ancient Slimming Herbs

Each of these herbs has several wonderful properties—but the one component they all have in common is the ability to help you to be a weight loser. However, please try the herbs one at a time—not all at once.

 **NOTE:** Using these herbs does not give you license to start eating as though there's no tomorrow. They are tools that may help decrease the appetite and/or metabolize fat quickly, but they should be used in conjunction with a well-balanced eating and exercise plan.

Check with your doctor before taking any herbs or natural supplements as part of a weight-loss plan.

It probably took you a while to reach your current weight. And it will take you a while to lose it. Be patient with yourself and give the herbs time to do their stuff. You can help the process along by eliminating or at least cutting down on foods with sugar, salt and white flour.

Within a couple of months, you should be ready for the "Nobelly Prize"!

You may want to taste each herb before deciding on one to stick with for at least a month. All of the herbs mentioned here are available in tea bags or loose at most health food stores.

### Herb Preparation

To prepare, add 1 teaspoon of the dried, loose herb (or one tea bag) to a cup of just-boiled water. Cover and let steep for 10 minutes. Strain and enjoy.

Drink 1 cup about a half-hour before each meal and 1 cup at bedtime. It may take a

month or two before you see results, especially if you hardly change your eating habits at all.

## Fennel Seeds

The Greek name for fennel is *marathron*, from *mariano*, which means "to grow thin." Fennel is known to metabolize and throw off fatty substances through the urine. Fennel is rich in vitamin A and is wonderful for the eyes. It also aids digestion.

## Cleavers

Like fennel seeds, cleavers is not known to lessen the appetite, but rather to somehow accelerate fat metabolism. It's also a natural diuretic and can help relieve constipation. You may want to combine cleavers with fennel seeds for your daily drink.

## Raspberry Leaves

As well as having a reputation as a weight-loss aid, raspberry-leaf tea is said to help control diarrhea and nausea, help eliminate canker sores and make pregnancy, delivery and post-delivery easier for the mother.

## Yerba Maté (Jungle Punch)

We've heard that South American medical authorities who have studied yerba maté concluded that this popular beverage can improve one's memory, nourish the smooth tissues of the intestines, increase respiratory power, help prevent infection and is a tonic to the brain, nerves and spine as well as an appetite depressant and a digestive aid. (*See* page 131 for more information on this powerful beverage.)

### ■ Recipe ■

### Mexican Eggplant with Fennel Seeds

> 2 large or 3 medium eggplants
> 2 Tbsp olive oil
> 1 tsp cumin seeds
> 1 tsp fennel seeds
> 1 lb fresh tomatoes, pared and chopped
> 1" fresh ginger, grated
> 4 cloves garlic, crushed
> 1 tsp ground coriander
> 1 cup water
> Salt and pepper
> 2 to 4 serrano or jalapeño peppers, thinly sliced
> Sprigs of fresh parsley

Wash eggplant, remove stalks and cut into bite-size pieces. Fry cubes in oil for approximately 5 minutes or until brown. Drain on paper towels.

Fry cumin and fennel seeds for about 2 minutes, stirring constantly, until they turn a shade darker. Mix in chopped tomatoes, grated ginger, crushed garlic, peppers, coriander and water. Simmer for about 20 minutes until the mixture becomes thick.

Add the fried eggplant cubes to the mixture and heat through. Garnish with the sprigs of parsley and serve.

*Source: www.recipegoldmine.com*

**NOTE:** Yerba maté contains caffeine (although not as much as coffee). We were told that, while it may act as a stimulant, it should not interfere with sleep.

### Horehound

This Old World herb is a diuretic and is used in cases of indigestion, colds, coughs and asthma. It is also reported to be an effective aid for weight reduction.

### Spirulina

This blue-green algae is an ancient Aztec food that's user-friendly. It's easily digestible and is reported to enhance the immune system, help detoxify the body and boost one's energy. Spirulina, taken daily, can help lift your spirits because of its high L-tryptophan content.

As for helping you lose weight, take spirulina about 20 minutes before mealtime, and it may give you that full feeling, like you've already eaten a meal and hardly have room for more. Spirulina comes in several forms—powder, tablets, capsules and freeze-dried. Look for it at your health food store.

## Other Slimming Remedies

▶ We have a friend who's a light eater—as soon as it gets light, she eats. We told her about the grape juice remedy recommended by psychic healer Edgar Cayce. Since starting this grape juice regimen, our friend's craving for desserts has almost disappeared, her eating patterns are gradually changing for the better and she's fitting into clothes she hasn't worn in years.

Drink 3 ounces of pure grape juice (no sugar, additives or preservatives) that is mixed with 1 ounce of water a half-hour before each meal and at bedtime. Drink the mixture slowly, taking from five to 10 minutes for each glass.

▶ This Chinese acupressure technique is said to diminish one's appetite. Whenever you're feeling hungry, squeeze your earlobes for one minute. If you can stand the pressure, clamp clothespins on your lobes and leave them there for 60 seconds.

We wonder if women who wear clip-on earrings are generally slimmer than women without them. *Hmmmmm…*

### Apple Cider Solution

▶ A woman we know dieted religiously (that means she wouldn't eat anything when she was in church). Out of control, desperate and tired of all the fad diets, she came to us, looked in our "overweight" remedy file and decided to follow the apple cider vinegar plan.

First thing in the morning, drink 2 teaspoons of apple cider vinegar in a glass of water. Drink the same mixture before lunch and dinner, making it three glasses of apple cider vinegar and water a day.

Within three months, the woman was no longer out of control or desperate. She felt that her days of binges were over and, thanks to the apple cider vinegar, she had the strength and willpower to stick to a well-balanced eating plan as the pounds slowly came off.

## Fat's Where It's At

**A**n unlikely hero in the battle of the bulge is, in fact, classified as a fat," says Jade Beutler, RRT, RCP, San Diego–based CEO of Lignan Research LLC, a licensed health care practitioner and a foremost authority of the benefits of flaxseed oil. *According to Beutler's research findings, flaxseed oil can help...*

◆ Decrease cravings for fatty foods and sweets
◆ Stoke metabolic rate
◆ Create satiation (feeling of fullness and satisfaction following a meal)
◆ Regulate blood sugar levels
◆ Regulate insulin levels
◆ Increase oxygen consumption

The ideal method of taking flaxseed oil for purposes of weight loss or maintenance is 1 to 2 tablespoons daily, in divided doses taken with each meal.

Read more about flaxseed oil in the "Six Sensational Superfoods" section on page 262.

▶ Lecithin is said to help break up and burn fatty deposits from stubborn bulges. It can also give you a full feeling even when you've eaten less than usual. The recommended daily dosage is 1 to 2 tablespoons of lecithin granules.

### Doggy Bags

▶ As soon as you're served food at a restaurant, separate half the meal and ask for a doggy bag. Explain that you're into "portion control," and don't want to tempt yourself to finish everything on the plate.

### High-Protein Lunch

▶ If you eat a high-protein lunch—filled with fish, soy products, yogurt, meat or chicken—you may find yourself eating fewer calories for dinner. Protein—just 2 or 3 ounces—is said to trigger a hormone that cuts your appetite and leaves you feeling satisfied. Give it a try.

Avoid high-carbohydrate lunches—ones that are heavy in pasta, rice and potatoes—and see if a higher portion of protein (along with veggies or salad—the good stuff) helps reduce your calorie intake at dinner.

### Filling Foods

▶ Plan on eating foods that have a high water content. Prepare meals with fruits and vegetables—soups, stews and smoothies. An apple is 84% water, which is almost 4 ounces of water. A ½ cup of cooked broccoli is 91% water, giving you 2.4 ounces of water. Look how much water it takes to make rice (spaghetti, too). High water-content foods will fill you up and hydrate you at the same time.

### Soup's On!

▶ In a study of 147 men and women who ate a reduced-calorie diet for a year, those who consumed 10.5 fluid ounces of low-fat, low-calorie soup twice a day lost 50% more weight than those who ate healthful but carbohydrate-rich snacks, such as baked chips or pretzels.

Although the soup had the same calories as the other snacks, the soup's greater weight and volume made study participants feel full enough to eat less for the rest of the day.

Consume one large mugful of a broth-based, low-fat, low-calorie and low-sodium soup that's rich in vegetables and/or beans as a first course twice daily.

### The Salad Trick

▶ Large salads help you consume fewer calories. A recent study found that diners who have a large low-calorie salad before the main course of their meal consume 12% fewer total calories at the meal than those who have nothing before the main course at all.

Salad takes the edge off your appetite and helps fill you up.

### Laugh Away the Pounds

▶ A recent study of students who watched comedy clips found that laughing for 10 to 15 minutes can burn 10 to 40 calories.

This means that 10 to 15 minutes of laughing daily could result in weight loss of about 4 pounds a year.

### Mirror, Mirror on the Kitchen Wall

▶ Studies were done with more than 1,000 people who were divided into two groups—those who ate in front of mirrors and those who ate without seeing themselves in mirrors. The subjects who watched themselves chow down ate considerably less fat than those who were mirrorless.

Hanging a mirror in your kitchen may be the reminder you need each time to help you decide what to eat.

## Healthy Snacks

▶ Fruit is a great, easy-to-prepare, fibrous, health-giving, sweet treat. We could fill a book

naming each fruit, its nutritional value and ways to prepare it.

Instead, we suggest that you be adventurous and creative. Go to your greengrocer or any ethnic market and find exotic fruit to add to your repertoire.

 **NOTE:** Be sure to wash produce thoroughly before you eat it in order to reduce the risk of food-borne illness.

### Yam It Up!

▶ Ever think of having a sweet potato or a yam as a snack? "Yam" is from the Guinean word for "something to eat." And it's something *wonderful* to eat!

Yams are rich in potassium. Sweet potatoes are rich in vitamin A. Both are good sources of folate (the heart-protective vitamin B) and vitamin C. Both are filling, easy to prepare, fat-free and worth the 100 to 140 satisfying calories.

▶ When you crave something crunchy, get out the finger vegetables. Chomp on baby carrots,

## Remove Pesticides and Wax From Fruits and Vegetables

In a bowl or a basin, mix 4 tablespoons of table salt, 4 teaspoons of lemon juice and 1 quart of cool water. Soak fruits and vegetables in this mixture for five to 10 minutes.

*Exceptions:* Soak leafy greens for two to three minutes…berries, one to two minutes.

After soaking, rinse produce in plain cold water and dry.

An alternative is Veggie Wash. Made of 100% natural ingredients, it is available at supermarkets, health food store and on-line at *www.veggie-wash.com* (800-451-7096).

jicama and fennel sticks, strips of yellow or red bell pepper and the old standby, celery.

On a weekend morning, prepare a bowl of cut-up vegetables. Keep them in ice water in your refrigerator, and reach for the bowl whenever you need to nibble.

### *The Diet "Blues"*

▶ Color therapist Carlton Wagner, founder of the Wagner Institute for Color Research in Santa Barbara, California, claims that blue food is unappetizing. Put a blue lightbulb in the refrigerator and a blue light in your dining area. Wagner points out that restaurants know all about people's responses to the color blue when it comes to food. When serving food on blue plates, customers eat less, saving the restaurants money on their all-you-can-eat "Blue Plate" specials.

## Slowly, But Surely

▶ Change your lifestyle habits gradually. The key word is "gradually." *Gradually,* day by day, replace a couple of fattening foods with healthier choices. In doing so, you become super-aware of what you're eating. That's a major step in improving your daily food intake.

▶ Also, *gradually* start exercising. Check with your doctor before starting an exercise program, and start walking briskly for 10 minutes the first few days, then 12 minutes, then 15. Keep going until you work your way up to doing a supervised exercise routine that's appropriate for you.

Be happy if you lose one or two pounds each week. In terms of keeping the weight off permanently, losing no more than two pounds a week makes sense. If you lose more, your body thinks you're going to starve and, in an effort to protect you from dying of hunger, it will slow down your metabolism. A loss of one or two pounds a week adds up to a big difference in a matter of months. And that's weight that will most likely *stay off.*

### *Calories Per Hour*

▶ Calories burned per hour—for a 155-pound person...

- ◆ *281 calories:* Raking the lawn, sweeping the sidewalk, leisure walking.
- ◆ *387 calories:* Scrubbing floors on hands and knees, mowing the lawn, light stationary biking, dancing—such as jazz, ballet or tango.
- ◆ *422 calories:* Moving furniture, cross-country skiing, shoveling snow.
- ◆ *493 calories:* Jogging, carrying boxes.
- ◆ *598 calories:* Vigorous stationary biking, mountain biking.
- ◆ *705 calories:* Moderate jumping rope, swimming, judo or karate, kick-boxing, running six miles per hour.

### *Yoga May Slow Midlife Weight Gain*

▶ In a recent finding, people in their 50s who regularly practiced yoga lost about five pounds over 10 years, while those who did not practice yoga gained about 13 pounds.

Most yoga exercises do not burn enough calories to account for the weight loss, but some practitioners believe that yoga keeps people aware of their bodies and eating habits.

## Cellulite Eliminator

▶ Former fashion model Maureen Klimt was determined to get rid of cellulite, so she started taking omega-3 fatty acids—in the form of flaxseed. Maureen grinds the seeds in a little coffee grinder, sprinkles 1 to 2 tablespoons on her oatmeal every morning and then adds a touch of maple syrup.

After eating the flaxseeded oatmeal daily for months, she reports that the cellulite is no longer there. Although Maureen eats healthfully and exercises, she credits the flaxseed for the loss of her cellulite.

Read more about flaxseed in the "Six Sensational Superfoods" section on page 262.

### Firm Thighs

▶ The Fairmont Sonoma Mission Inn & Spa in Sonoma, California (*www.fairmont.com/sonoma*), shared with us its once-secret treatment for jiggly thighs.

Rosemary is the key ingredient. (No, that's not a physical trainer who gives you a tough workout!) Rosemary is an herb that stimulates circulation and drains impurities, leaving skin firmer and tighter.

Mix 1 tablespoon of crushed dried rosemary (available at herb and health food stores) with 2 tablespoons of extra-virgin olive oil. Smooth the mixture over thighs, wrap in plastic wrap and leave on for 10 minutes. Then rinse. Do this treatment at least once a week.

### Leg Slimming

▶ Every night, while lying on the floor or in bed, rest your feet as high on a wall as is comfortable. Stay that way for about an hour. At most, your legs will slim down. At least, it will be good for your circulation.

## Rev Up Your Metabolism

▶ Kelp is seaweed that's rich in minerals and vitamins, especially the B family. Its high iodine content can help activate a sluggish thyroid. Dried kelp can be eaten raw, or crumbled into soups and on salads. Powdered kelp can also be used in place of salt. It has a salty, fishy taste that may take getting used to. If you really don't like the taste, there are kelp pills. Follow the recommended dosage on the label.

One of the good side effects of kelp is that it may make your hair shinier. But if you eat too much kelp, it can have a laxative effect.

### Hot Stuff

▶ One British study showed that adding 1 teaspoon of hot-pepper sauce (something with cayenne pepper, like Tabasco sauce) and 1 teaspoon of mustard to every meal raised one's metabolic rate by as much as 25%.

▶ Before you eat dinner, exercise for 20 to 30 minutes. Just brisk walking will do. Exercise boosts your metabolic rate and it lasts through dinner, helping you digest and burn off the evening meal. For many, that before-dinner walk seems to reduce the urge for late-night snacks.

▶ Do not eat within three hours of bedtime. The body seems to store fat more easily at night, when the metabolism slows down.

### Vitamin C Helps You Burn More Fat

▶ *In a recent study,* people who took 500 mg of vitamin C daily burned 39% more fat while exercising than people who took less. Since it is difficult to get enough vitamin C just from fruits and vegetables, take a vitamin C supplement to be sure you get at least 500 mg per day.

### Why Juice or Water?

▶ The results of a study that was reported in the *American Journal of Clinical Nutrition* (*www.ajcn.org*) shows that drinking water or juice before a meal—rather than beer, wine or a cocktail—goes a long way with weight control.

The imbibers consumed an average of 240 calories in their alcoholic beverage and wolfed down about 200 more calories in their meals. They also ate faster. It took them longer to feel full, but that didn't stop them. They continued eating *past* the point of feeling full. And

all because they had an alcoholic drink before their meal. Waiter, just water for me, please!

### Why Not Soda?

▶ It's been reported that people who are frequent soda drinkers (either diet or regular) have higher hunger ratings than people who drink unsweetened or naturally sweet beverages. Experiment by going off soda for a week to see if your desire for food decreases.

## Holiday Challenges

▶ Forget about losing weight during the holidays. Settle for not *gaining* weight. Fill up on sweet potatoes, fruits, vegetables, white-meat turkey, whole-grain bread and an *occasional, tiny* portion of an obscenely fattening dessert.

▶ Eat a portion of healthy, nonfattening food right before you go to a holiday party.

▶ At a holiday event, drink designer water or sparkling water with a twist of lemon. A little wine is okay, but stay away from mixed drinks and liqueurs.

▶ According to Alan Hirsch, MD, director of the Smell & Taste Treatment and Research Foundation in Chicago, "People who are exposed to smells of food during the day eat less at night."

Proof that this may be so is evident during Ramadan, the Muslim holiday during which daytime fasting is followed by nighttime feasting. Muslim women's hunger ratings dropped, but men's hunger stayed the same throughout the month-long holiday.

Why? The women prepared food all day and, by mealtime, their hunger had abated. The food simply wasn't as appealing to them.

### Use Smell to Lose Weight

In a recent study, participants who sprinkled powders that smelled like cheddar cheese, banana and raspberry on their food lost an average of 5.6 pounds per month over a six-month period.

Added scents fool the brain into thinking you have eaten enough. Smell every food before you eat it.

### The Great Outdoors

A day without sunshine is like a day without serotonin, a brain chemical that can allay hunger. Your body needs sunlight to make serotonin, so get out there every chance you get. While you're outdoors, you may as well get a little exercise, too. Walk. Play. Skip. Enjoy yourself! And don't forget the sunscreen.

## Determining Your Weight/ Health Profile

Body Mass Index (BMI) is one of the most accurate ways to determine when extra pounds translate into health risks. BMI is a measure that takes into account a person's weight and height to gauge total body fat in adults.

According to guidelines set by the National Institutes of Health, the definition of a healthy weight is a BMI of 24 or less. For both men and women, a BMI of 25 to 29.9 is considered overweight. Individuals who fall into the BMI range of 25 to 34.9 and have a waist size of more than 40 inches (for men) or 35 inches (for women) are considered to be at especially high risk for health problems.

BMI is reliable for most people between 19 and 70 years of age except women who are pregnant or breastfeeding, and people who are competitive athletes, body builders or chronically ill.

To use the table on page 203, find the appropriate height in the column on the left. Move across to a given weight. The number at the top of the column is the BMI for that height and weight. Pounds have been rounded off. ■

# BODY MASS INDEX CHART

| HEIGHT (in inches) | 19 | 20 | 21 | 22 | 23 | 24 | 25 | 26 | 27 | 28 | 29 | 30 | 31 | 32 | 33 | 34 | 35 |
|---|---|---|---|---|---|---|---|---|---|---|---|---|---|---|---|---|---|
| | | | | | | BODY WEIGHT (in pounds) | | | | | | | | | | | |
| 58 | 91 | 96 | 100 | 105 | 110 | 115 | 119 | 124 | 129 | 134 | 138 | 143 | 148 | 153 | 158 | 162 | 167 |
| 59 | 94 | 99 | 104 | 109 | 114 | 119 | 124 | 128 | 133 | 138 | 143 | 148 | 153 | 158 | 163 | 168 | 173 |
| 60 | 97 | 102 | 107 | 112 | 118 | 123 | 128 | 133 | 138 | 143 | 148 | 153 | 158 | 163 | 168 | 174 | 179 |
| 61 | 100 | 106 | 111 | 116 | 122 | 127 | 132 | 137 | 143 | 148 | 153 | 158 | 164 | 169 | 174 | 180 | 185 |
| 62 | 104 | 109 | 115 | 120 | 126 | 131 | 136 | 142 | 147 | 153 | 158 | 164 | 169 | 175 | 180 | 186 | 191 |
| 63 | 107 | 113 | 118 | 124 | 130 | 135 | 141 | 146 | 152 | 158 | 163 | 169 | 175 | 180 | 186 | 191 | 197 |
| 64 | 110 | 116 | 122 | 128 | 134 | 140 | 145 | 151 | 157 | 163 | 169 | 174 | 180 | 186 | 192 | 197 | 204 |
| 65 | 114 | 120 | 126 | 132 | 138 | 144 | 150 | 156 | 162 | 168 | 174 | 180 | 186 | 192 | 198 | 204 | 210 |
| 66 | 118 | 124 | 130 | 136 | 142 | 148 | 155 | 161 | 167 | 173 | 179 | 186 | 192 | 198 | 204 | 210 | 216 |
| 67 | 121 | 127 | 134 | 140 | 146 | 153 | 159 | 166 | 172 | 178 | 185 | 191 | 198 | 204 | 211 | 217 | 223 |
| 68 | 125 | 131 | 138 | 144 | 151 | 158 | 164 | 171 | 177 | 184 | 190 | 197 | 203 | 210 | 216 | 223 | 230 |
| 69 | 128 | 135 | 142 | 149 | 155 | 162 | 169 | 176 | 182 | 189 | 196 | 203 | 209 | 216 | 223 | 230 | 236 |
| 70 | 132 | 139 | 146 | 153 | 160 | 167 | 174 | 181 | 188 | 195 | 202 | 209 | 216 | 222 | 229 | 236 | 243 |
| 71 | 136 | 143 | 150 | 157 | 165 | 172 | 179 | 186 | 193 | 200 | 208 | 215 | 222 | 229 | 236 | 243 | 250 |
| 72 | 140 | 147 | 154 | 162 | 169 | 177 | 184 | 191 | 199 | 206 | 213 | 221 | 228 | 235 | 242 | 250 | 258 |
| 73 | 144 | 151 | 159 | 166 | 174 | 182 | 189 | 197 | 204 | 212 | 219 | 227 | 235 | 242 | 250 | 257 | 265 |
| 74 | 148 | 155 | 163 | 171 | 179 | 186 | 194 | 202 | 210 | 218 | 225 | 233 | 241 | 249 | 256 | 264 | 272 |
| 75 | 152 | 160 | 168 | 176 | 184 | 192 | 200 | 208 | 216 | 224 | 232 | 240 | 248 | 256 | 264 | 272 | 279 |
| 76 | 156 | 164 | 172 | 180 | 189 | 197 | 205 | 213 | 221 | 230 | 238 | 246 | 254 | 263 | 271 | 279 | 287 |

*Source:* National Heart, Lung and Blood Institute. For more information, go to *www.nhlbisupport.com/bmi/bmicalc.htm*.

# Healing Remedies
# for Children

# Healing Remedies
# for Children

## Safety First

Every baby-care book tells you to "childproof" your home. Make a crawling tour of each room in order to see things from a child's-eye view. Once you recognize the danger zones, you can eliminate problems by covering wires, nailing down furniture, etc. Do this every four to six months as your child grows.

Still, no matter how childproof a place is, a mishap can happen. We suggest that parents have a first aid book handy and/or take a first aid course through a local chapter of the American Red Cross (*www.redcross.org*).

It's also very important to keep a list of emergency numbers near every telephone in the house. *The list should include...*

- Pediatrician
- Poison Control Center (800-222-1222)
- Police
- Fire department
- Hospital
- Pharmacy
- Dentist
- Neighbors (with cars)

In terms of home remedies for common conditions, we caution you that children's systems are much more delicate than adults'. So, while many remedies in the book can be used for youngsters, common sense must be applied in estimating doses and strengths.

In all cases, check with your child's pediatrician first.

**ONE MAJOR CAUTION:** Never give raw honey to a child under one year of age! Spores found in honey have been linked to botulism in babies.

Here are natural remedies that are specifically meant for children's ailments. They should help you—as well as your child—get through those tough times.

## Acne

▶ It's common to see infants with an outbreak of pimples. According to a folk remedy from the 17th century, gently dab the acne with some of the mother's milk.

If you're not nursing, use a few drops of whole milk (not skim milk).

## Attention Deficit/ Hyperactivity Disorder (ADHD)

This common disorder is a neurobehavioral condition that affects many school-age children (and some adults). It is characterized by inappropriate and distracting impulsivity, inability to focus (pay attention) and, in some cases, hyperactivity.

If your child has been diagnosed with ADHD, chances are you are looking for an answer so that your child doesn't have to take Ritalin or another prescribed medication.

Before trying any natural remedies, you should rule out other things that could be contributing to your child's behavior. *For example...*

◆ Toxic-metal excess

◆ Pesticides in the home

◆ Behavioral issues in the home and at school

◆ Malnutrition

◆ Allergies (including those to sweets, milk and cheese)

◆ Gluten intolerance

Your child's diet may play a major part in causing and overcoming this condition. But you may not know that several studies point to a connection between children with ADHD and an omega-3 fatty acid deficiency.

According to a paper published in *Physiology & Behavior* (*www.ibnshomepage. org,* then click on "Other Links") by a research team from the Department of Foods and Nutrition at Purdue University in West Lafayette, Indiana, boys with lower levels of omega-3 fatty acids in their blood showed more problems with behavior, learning and health than those with higher total levels of omega-3 fatty acids.

You may want to find out more about this and then consider adding flaxseed oil—the richest source of omega-3 essential fatty acids—to your child's daily diet. For more flaxseed information, *see* the "Six Sensational Superfoods" section on page 262.

## Bed-Wetting

Wetting the bed may happen frequently as a child learns to control his/her bladder overnight. Be patient during this time, but if your child doesn't show improvement, consult his pediatrician.

### Cinnamon Solution

▶ Give the child a few pieces of cinnamon bark to chew on throughout the day. For some unknown reason, it seems to control bedwetting for some kids.

▶ Prepare a cup of corn silk tea by adding 10 to 15 drops of corn silk extract to a cup of boiled water. Stir, let cool and have the child slowly sip the tea right before bedtime.

### The Back Is Best

▶ If all else fails, try this—at bedtime, tie a towel around the child's pelvis, making sure the knot is in front. This teaches the child to sleep on his/her back, which seems to lessen bedwetting urges.

 **NOTE:** Chronic bedwetters should be treated by a health professional.

▶ This exercise strengthens the muscles that control urination. Starting with the first urination of the day, have the child start and stop urinating as many times as possible until he/she has finished.

If you make it into a game, counting the number of starts and stops, the child might look forward to breaking his own record each time. It's important, however, not to make the child feel inadequate if he finds this exercise difficult.

# Chicken Pox

When we were children, it seemed like everyone had chicken pox—and if someone had it, he was expected to give it to the rest of us. This virus is more uncommon now that kids receive childhood vaccinations, but it's still extremely contagious and spreads through coughs and sneezes. A child with chicken pox should be in bed, kept warm and on a light diet, including lots of pure fruit juices.

▶ According to herbalists, yarrow tea helps children's eruptive ailments. Add 1 tablespoon of dried yarrow (available at health food stores) to 2 cups of just-boiled water and let it steep for 10 minutes. Strain, then add 1 tablespoon of raw honey (if the child is older than one year). Give the child ¹⁄₁₆ cup three or four times a day.

# Eye Irritants

*See* adult "Eye Irritants" on pages 72–73.

▶ Irrigate eye with water.

▶ Peel an onion near the child so that his natural tears wash away the irritant.

**WARNING:** If chemicals or another toxic substance have gotten into the child's eye, call 911 or the Poison Control Center (800-222-1222) immediately.

# Colds and Flu

▶ According to a study published by two doctors in a respected scientific journal, zinc gluconate lozenges can dramatically shorten the duration of a cold.

The lozenges (honey-flavored are the best…lemon are the pits) should not be taken on an empty stomach. Even if the child is not eating much because of the cold, have him/her eat half a fruit before sucking a lozenge.

*Dose:* If a child weighs less than 60 pounds, he/she should take one to three zinc lozenges—as tolerated—23 mg each, per day. For teenagers, the maximum dose is three to six lozenges—as tolerated—23 mg each, per day.

*Important:* Do not give a child zinc lozenges for more than two days in a row.

# Coughs

▶ When a child has a bad, hacking cough, spray his/her pillow with wine vinegar. Both you and the child may sleep better for it.

▶ Add ½ teaspoon of anise seeds and ½ teaspoon of thyme to 1 cup of just-boiled water. Let it steep for 10 minutes. Stir it, strain and let cool. Then add a teaspoon of honey.

*Dose:* Give 1 tablespoon to the child every half-hour. This remedy is for children who are over two years of age.

## Black Thread at Night

▶ A woman from Oklahoma told us that whenever her child gets a cough that acts up at night, she loosely ties a black cotton thread around the child's neck. *The thread must be black.* This woman said she tried other colors and nothing but the black works.

We were intrigued with the remedy and tested it on our friend's child. It worked like magic. We researched it and found a printed source that credited this remedy to shamans (spiritual practitioners) in ancient Egypt.

## Croup

Oh, the barking! Oh, the hacking! If your child sounds like a seal from Sea World, he/she probably has the croup. Young children often develop this terrible cough when they have a cold.

▶ Scottish folk healers treat the croup by wrapping a piece of raw bacon around the child's neck, bundling him up in a blanket and taking him into a steamy bathroom for a few minutes.

**WARNING:** Do not put raw meat on broken skin. It can cause an infection.

## Diarrhea

▶ Give the baby pure blackberry juice, 2 or 3 tablespoons, four times a day.

### Soupy Soother

▶ Carrot soup (*see* recipe at right) not only soothes the inflamed small bowel, it also replaces lost body fluids and minerals. Carrots also contain an antidiarrheal substance called pectin.

You can also prepare the soup by mixing a jar of strained-carrots baby food with a jar of water. Feed the child carrot soup until the diarrhea abates.

▶ Another way of treating diarrhea in infants is to give them barley water throughout the day.

### ■ Recipe ■

### Carrot Soup

1 lb carrots
½ oz onions
1 oz butter
1 pint boiling water
½ oz flour
1 pint milk
Salt and pepper to taste

Cut the carrots and onions into small pieces, and cook them in the butter for five minutes. Add the water and cook until the vegetables are tender. Rub through a sieve. Return to the saucepan.

In a small bowl, mix the flour smoothly with a little bit of the milk. Set aside.

Add the remainder of the milk to the main mixture and bring to a boil. When boiling, add the flour mixture. Cook for 10 minutes. Season and serve.

*Source: www.freerecipe.org*

(*See* "Preparation Guide" on page 249 for the barley water recipe.)

### Dutch Treat

▶ This children's remedy for diarrhea comes from the Pennsylvanian Dutch. In a warmed cup of milk, add $\frac{1}{16}$ teaspoon of cinnamon. The child should drink as much as possible.

▶ Raspberry-leaf tea is excellent for treating diarrhea. Combine ½ ounce of dried raspberry leaves with 1 cup of water and simmer in an enamel or glass saucepan for 25 minutes. Strain and let the liquid cool to room temperature.

*Dose:* For a baby under one year of age, give ½ teaspoon four times a day...for a child over one year, give 1 teaspoon four times a day.

> ☛ **WARNING:** Seek medical attention if the child's digestive problem is painful, persistent or accompanied by repeated vomiting.

## Fever

▶ To help bring down a child's fever, put sliced, raw potatoes on the soles of his/her feet and bandage in place. Let the novelty of this remedy provide a few laughs for you and your child. Isn't laughter the best medicine?

▶ Give your child a long, soothing bath in tepid water. Then, when you tuck your child in, be sure the blanket is not tucked in too tight. Leave it loose so that heat can escape.

> ☛ **WARNING:** If a fever persists for more than three days, seek medical attention.

## Foreign Substance In the Nose

Lots of kids stick things up their noses. Lydia put a yankee bean in her nostril when she was three years old, and it began to take root. Luckily, our father noticed that she was sitting still for more than 30 seconds at a time, so he realized something was wrong.

▶ Before you take a child to the doctor to perform a yankee-beanectomy, hold the unclogged nostril closed, open the child's mouth (make sure it's empty), place your mouth over it and briskly blow once. Your gust of breath may dislodge the object from the child's nostril. If it doesn't, seek medical attention.

## Head Lice

It's estimated that at any given time, 10 million Americans have head lice. Lice can be transmitted from child to child via a common headrest, like a mat in the school gymnasium or from a seat at the movies. Just about the only way you can prevent a child from ever being exposed to lice is by keeping that child in a bubble.

Since the bubble is not an option, if your child has lice, there are over-the-counter shampoos that are safe and effective, unlike the prescription shampoos that can be dangerous to young children, pregnant or nursing women and anyone with a cut on his hand or arm. A friend tried several over-the-counter shampoos and found that the safest one that also worked best was RID.

For the shampoo to be effective, leave it on the child's head for at least five minutes—10 minutes is even better.

### Nit-Picking

▶ After you shampoo and kill the lice, make sure you get rid of any remaining nits (eggs or young lice) by thoroughly rinsing the child's scalp with equal parts of white vinegar and water. Or first you can comb tea tree oil (available at health food stores) through the hair, and then rinse with vinegar and water.

> ⚡ **CAUTION:** Do not use your fingers to hunt down these critters. They can burrow their way under your fingernails. Yuck!

211

### Eyelash Nits

▶ If the nits move down to the eyelashes, DO NOT use tea tree oil. It's much too strong and dangerous near the eyes.

Instead, before breakfast and after supper, carefully put a thin layer of petroleum jelly on the lashes. Do this for eight days. By then, the jelly will have smothered the nits and you will be able to simply remove them.

## Indigestion, Colic and Gas

If your child has indigestion or gas, he/she might get very cranky from the tummy ache. If your baby has colic, he might cry for hours without stopping—and you'd try anything in the world to make him feel better. Doctors aren't sure what causes colic (allergy, indigestion or just disposition), but these remedies are worth a try.

👉 **WARNING:** Seek medical attention if the child's digestive problem is painful, persistent or accompanied by repeated vomiting.

### Indigestion

▶ If a baby can't seem to keep his food down, you may want to try putting a teaspoon of carob powder (available at most health food stores) in the baby's milk. In some cases, it may make a big difference.

▶ Mild chamomile tea will soothe an upset stomach and calm tummy troubles. That is, if you can calm the kid long enough to drink the chamomile tea.

▶ Give your infant mild ginger tea. It's wonderful for digestion and gas problems.

▶ If your child seems to have a minor digestion problem, try 2 teaspoons of apple juice concentrate in half a glass of water before meals. Make sure the liquid mixture is room temperature, not chilled.

### Colic

▶ A popular European colic calmer is fennel tea. Add ½ teaspoon of fennel seeds to 1 cup of just-boiled water and let it steep for 10 minutes. Strain the liquid tea into a baby's bottle. When it's cool enough to drink, give it to the baby. If he/she is not thrilled with the taste of fennel, try dill seeds instead.

▶ For 15 minutes, boil a cup of water with ⅓ of a bay leaf. Let it cool, remove the bay leaf, then pour the water into the baby's bottle and let the baby drink it. This old Sicilian remedy has cured many colicky bambinos.

▶ Caraway seeds are said to bring relief to colicky kids (and parents and neighbors). Add 1 tablespoon of bruised caraway seeds to 1 cup of just-boiled water. Let it steep for 10 minutes. Strain and put 2 teaspoons of the tea into a baby's bottle. When it's cool enough to drink, give it to the baby.

### Go Cow-Free

▶ If you are breast-feeding your baby and he/she is colicky, try eliminating cow's milk from your diet. There's a 50/50 chance that if you no longer drink milk, the baby will no longer have colic.

Be sure, however, that you eat more calcium-rich foods, such as canned salmon, canned sardines, sunflower and sesame seeds, almonds, whole grains, green leafy vegetables, soy products (including tofu) and molasses.

▶ Milk isn't the only thing to eliminate from your diet if you are breast-feeding. You should also avoid whatever may be hard for you and/or your baby to digest, including bell (green) peppers, beans, cucumbers, eggs, chocolate, onions, leeks, garlic, eggplant, lentils, zucchini, tomatoes, sugar, coffee and alcoholic beverages. Also, go easy on the amount of fruit you eat.

Remember, it's not forever—either the diet restrictions or the colic!

▶ When baby is teething or has mild colic— or is just irritable because of indigestion or disturbed sleep—steep a chamomile tea bag in a cup of hot water. If the problem is indigestion, throw in a small piece of fresh ginger.

After steeping for about 10 minutes, take out the tea bag and the ginger. Give the baby a teaspoon of the tea every 15 minutes until he/she seems better.

### Just Peachy

▶ Warm up a little of the heavy syrup from a can of peaches and give the syrup to your baby to stop nausea.

## Picky Eaters

▶ Prepare a cup of chamomile tea and add ¹⁄₁₆ teaspoon of ground ginger. An herbalist recommends giving 1 teaspoon of the warm tea a half-hour before meals to help stimulate a child's appetite.

## Rashes

▶ If the rash is minor (and not on the face), gently rub the afflicted area with the red side of a piece of watermelon rind. It should stop the itching and help dry out the rash.

### Diaper Rash

▶ Let the baby's bottom be exposed to the air. If weather permits, the sun (10 to 15 minutes at a time) can do wonders for clearing up diaper rash. Be sure to apply sunscreen to all of the exposed skin first.

**CAUTION:** Babies six months of age or younger should not be exposed to the sun.

## Splinters

▶ To pinpoint the exact location of a wood splinter, pat some iodine on the area and the sliver of wood will absorb it and turn dark. Wait until the area is dry before trying to remove the splinter.

▶ If the child has a glass splinter, numb the area with an ice cube or some teething lotion before you start squeezing and scraping. But don't dig! If a splinter does not come out easily, see a doctor for treatment.

# Teething

▶ When teething children are being fed, they often cry as if they do not want the food. But they may be crying because of the pain caused by a metal spoon. Feed the teething tot with an ivory, wood or bone spoon and make sure the edges are nice and smooth.

▶ Rub sore little gums with olive oil to help relieve the pain.

# Tonsillitis

Most cases of tonsillitis are caused by infection and should be treated with antibiotics. In some cases, however, swollen tonsils may occur because of an intolerance for cow's milk. That's easy enough to test. Simply eliminate milk from the child's diet and see if he/she improves within a day or two.

If the child does not assimilate and digest cow's milk properly, there are many other wonderful sources of calcium and it is no big deal for a child not to have milk. Sunflower seeds and sesame seeds are rich in calcium. So are almonds, green leafy vegetables, canned salmon, sardines, molasses and whole grains.

There are also supplements, such as bonemeal, dolomite and calcium lactate. Check with your child's pediatrician before changing your child's diet or giving him/her supplements. ■

# Healing Remedies
# for Men

# Healing Remedies for Men

## Prostate Enlargement

It is estimated that one out of every three men over the age of 60 has some kind of prostate problem, such as inflammation (prostatitis), enlargement (benign prostatic hyperplasia) or prostate cancer.

**WARNING:** Consult a physician before trying any of these prostate remedies. Some are not appropriate for men who have been diagnosed with prostate cancer.

▶ To ease prostate tension, stimulate circulation and generally soothe the male organs, massage the area behind the leg in back of the ankle, about one or two inches higher than the shoe line of each foot.

### Powerful Pumpkin

The prostate gland contains 10 times more zinc than most other organs in the body. Pumpkin seeds have a very high zinc content. That may account for the normalizing effect the seeds have on prostate disorders.

Eating pumpkin seeds may also be beneficial because of their content of iron, phosphorus, vitamins A and $B_1$, protein, calcium and unsaturated fatty acid.

▶ Eat ½ cup of unprocessed (unsalted) shelled pumpkin seeds daily. If you can't get pumpkin seeds, sunflower seeds are next best.

Or take zinc tablets—15 mg, two times a day. For chronic prostate trouble, take 50 mg a day for six months, then reduce the dosage to 30 mg a day.

**WARNING:** If you are suffering with pain, burning urination, testicular or scrotal swelling, have your condition evaluated by a health professional.

▶ Bee pollen is said to be effective in reducing swelling of the prostate. Pollen contains the hormone testosterone and traces of other male hormones. It seems to give the prostate a boost so that it may heal itself.

*Dose:* Take a total of five pollen pills daily —two in the morning, two in the afternoon and one in the evening (or take the equivalent in bee pollen granules).

**CAUTION:** People who are allergic to bee stings or honey should consult a doctor before taking bee pollen.

For more information on bee pollen, *see* the "Six Sensational Superfoods" section on page 258.

▶ Drink 2 to 4 ounces of coconut milk every day to strengthen the prostate gland. The milk is pure and uncontaminated and loaded with minerals. It's also a soothing digestive aid. (*See* "Preparation Guide" on page 249 for instructions on milking a coconut.)

## Circle Massage

▶ To relieve prostate pain, in a circular motion, massage the area above the heel and just below the inner ankle of each foot and/or the inside of the wrists, above the palm of each hand. Keep massaging until the pain and soreness disappear.

▶ Prepare parsley tea by steeping a handful of fresh parsley in a cup of hot water for 10 minutes. Drink a few cups of the parsley tea throughout the day.

## Sitz on This

▶ Take hot sitz baths—two a day. Sit in six inches of comfortably hot water for about 15 minutes each time. Within a week, inflammation and swelling should be greatly reduced.

▶ Corn silk tea has been a popular folk remedy for prostate problems. Steep a handful of the silky strings that grow around ears of corn in a cup of hot water for 10 minutes. Drink a few cups throughout the day.

If it's not fresh corn season, buy corn silk extract from a health food store, then add 10 to 15 drops in 1 cup of water and drink.

▶ For an enlarged prostate, grate part of a yellow onion and squeeze it through cheesecloth —enough for 1 tablespoon of onion juice. Take 1 tablespoon of onion juice twice a day.

## Slip-Sliding Away

▶ In extremely painful cases, get slippery-elm capsules at a health food or vitamin store. Take the capsules apart—enough for ½ teaspoon of the slippery-elm powder—and mix the powder with 6 ounces of (preferably distilled) water. Drink the mixture before breakfast and a couple of hours after dinner.

▶ Asparagine, a health-giving alkaloid found in fresh asparagus, is said to be a healing element for prostate conditions. Use a juicer and juice equal amounts of fresh asparagus, carrots and cucumber—enough for an 8-ounce glass of juice. Drink a glass of the juice daily.

**NOTE:** Organic vegetables are always preferable. If they're not available, wash the asparagus thoroughly, scrub the carrots and peel the cucumber.

▶ A teaspoon of unrefined sesame oil taken every day for one month has been known to reduce an enlarged prostate back to normal.

▶ Lecithin (available at health food stores) comes highly recommended from many sources. Take one lecithin capsule—1,200 mg each—three times a day, after each meal, or 1 to 2 tablespoons of lecithin granules daily.

▶ If your doctor hasn't already told you, eliminating all coffee and alcoholic beverages from your diet can help prostate problems.

▶ And now for a self-help prostate massage—lie down on the floor on your back. Put the sole of one foot against the sole of the other foot so that you're at your bowlegged best. While keeping the soles of your feet together, extend your legs as far as possible and then bring them in as close as possible to your chest. Do this "extend and bring in" exercise 10 times in the morning and 10 times at night.

▶ Ray C. Wunderlich, Jr., MD, PhD, director of the Wunderlich Center for Nutritional Medicine in St. Petersburg, Florida, recommends that you empty the gland by having ejaculations as frequently as you can tolerate. It may improve your urinary stream.

# Impotence (Erectile Dysfunction)

Most men at some time during their lives experience the dreaded inability to have an erection. That's the bad news. The good news is that it is usually a temporary condition commonly caused by prescription drugs or by some kind of psychological trauma and emotional tension. While the psyche is being treated with professional help, physical steps can be taken to improve one's sexual energy.

You might want to read through these health hints whether or not anything is bothering you. Chances are you'll find some information you can use to help you maintain your health and sexual potency.

**WARNING:** Men who are experiencing erectile dysfunction should see a doctor for a complete physical evaluation.

## Time for Love

▶ According to the teachings of the late Yogi Bhajan, PhD, counselor and yoga master, a man should never have sexual intercourse within 2½ hours after eating a meal, the length of time it takes to digest food.

The sex act is strenuous and requires your mind, your entire nervous system and all of the muscles needed for the digestion process. Yogi Bhajan felt that lovemaking right after eating could ruin your stomach and, if done often, could eventually result in premature ejaculation.

While the Yogi believed that four hours between eating and sex is adequate, he recommended that, for optimal sexual function, a man should have nothing but liquids and juices 24 hours before making love.

## Giddyup with Garlic

▶ Garlic is said to stimulate sexual desire and the production of semen. Eat raw garlic in salads, use it in cooking and take two garlic pills a day. Then find a companion who doesn't mind the smell of garlic.

By the way, we wonder if it is a coincidence that the French and Italians have a diet that includes lots of garlic and are said to be incredible lovers?

▶ Mint is supposed to restore sexual desire. Eat mint leaves and drink mint tea. It's also good for combating garlic breath.

## ■ Recipe ■

### 40-Clove Garlic Chicken

    8 pieces of chicken, skinned
    2 Tbsp extra-virgin olive oil
    1 cup onion, minced
    2 cups celery, diced
    2 Tbsp fresh parsley, minced
    1 tsp dried tarragon
    ½ cup dry white vermouth
    ½ tsp salt
    ½ tsp ground pepper
    ½ tsp nutmeg
    40 cloves garlic, separated but not
        peeled (about 3 bulbs)

Preheat the oven to 325° F. Brush chicken pieces on all sides with olive oil. In a Dutch oven or large casserole dish, combine the onion, celery, parsley and tarragon. Arrange the chicken pieces on top and pour the vermouth over the chicken. Sprinkle with salt, pepper and nutmeg. Distribute the unpeeled garlic cloves throughout the casserole, tucking them under and around the chicken.

Tightly cover the casserole or pan with aluminum foil, and bake for 1½ hours. When done, serve the chicken over rice, barley or millet, along with the garlic.

*Source: Garlic: Nature's Super Healer*

## "Stamp Out" Impotence—Is It Organic Or Psychological?

Most men have about five erections while they're asleep. No matter how uptight they might be—and no matter what trouble they might be having with erections while they're awake—men who suffer from psychological impotency will have firm erections every night in their sleep.

To test for these erections, get an old-fashioned roll of need-to-be-licked postage stamps (any denomination) and gently wrap it once around the shaft of the penis. Tear off the excess stamps, then tape the two ends (the first and the last stamps) around the penis, firmly but not too tight. Sweet dreams!

When a nighttime erection occurs, the increased diameter of the penis should break the stamps along the line of one of the perforations. If impotency is organically caused, you will not have nightly erections and the stamps will be intact in the morning.

The "stamp act" should be repeated every night for two to three weeks. If, each morning, the stamps are broken along a perforation, chances are that you have a normal capability for erections, and impotency is psychologically caused. Sometimes just knowing that everything is working well physiologically will give you the confidence and assurance you need to help you "rise to the occasion."

## The Fear of Failure

▶ In the Mexican pharmacopoeia, *damiana* is classified as an aphrodisiac and a tonic for the nervous system. It's been known to be an effective remedy for "performance anxiety."

Add a teaspoon of damiana leaves (available at health food stores) to a cup of just-boiled water. Let it steep for 10 minutes. Strain and drink before breakfast, on a daily basis.

▶ El Indio Amazonico, a Bogotá *botánico* (medicine man), advises his impotent patients to not even try to have sex for 30 days. During that time, he suggests they eat goat meat every

## ■ Recipe ■

### Sexual-Stamina Eggplant

Hindi records, circa 10th century, tell about men who went to view the famous Temple of Khajuraho in India to study its pornographic stone carvings, depicting every known position of love. In order to have the stamina to test the positions, they were fed this dish.

> 1 eggplant
> Butter
> Chives, minced
> Curry sauce

Slice the eggplant and cover with butter and minced chives on both sides. Brown the slices and cover with a spicy curry sauce.

The recipe (unspecific as it is) has been passed down from generation to generation—along with its reputation for making old men young again.

day, in addition to bulls' testicles ("mountain oysters"). He also recommends drinking tea made of cinnamon sticks and cups of cocoa.

When the abstention period is over, El Indio instructs his patients to rub a small amount of petroleum jelly mixed with a bit of lemon juice around—but not on—the scrotum. Then the patients are on their own.

### Love Longer

▶ Eat a handful of raw, hulled pumpkin seeds every day. (The cooking process may destroy some of the special values of the seeds, so steer clear of the roasted ones.) Pumpkin seeds contain large amounts of zinc, magnesium, iron, phosphorus, calcium, vitamin A and the B vitamins.

According to a German medical researcher, there are one or more substances not yet isolated that have vitalizing and regenerative effects and actually cause additional sex hormones to be produced. Many health authorities agree that a handful of pumpkin seeds a day may help prevent prostate problems and impotence. Pass the pumpkin seeds!

▶ It is said that the higher a man's voice, the lower his masculine vitality. The theory is based on the fact that the vortex at the base of the neck and the vortex in the sex center are directly connected and affected by each other. So lower your voice and you'll increase the speed of vibration in these vortexes, which, in turn, may increase your sexual energy.

### Stay Out of Hot Water

▶ Fast cold showers do not cool or dampen one's sexual desire. *Au contraire!* Short applications of cold water, particularly on the nape of the neck, can be sexually stimulating.

### Stronger Erection

▶ Most men get a stronger erection and feel more of a sensation when their bladder is full. However, some sexual positions may be uncomfortable if the bladder is very full.

> **WARNING:** Men with prostate problems should not practice this full-bladder erection technique.

## Premature Ejaculation

▶ According to sex therapists, premature ejaculation seems to be one of the easiest conditions to cure, simply by behavior modification.

The late William H. Masters, MD, and Virginia E. Johnson—the pioneering sex therapists and researchers—developed this conditioning treatment. First, enlist the assistance of your mate. Lie on your back with your partner straddling your legs. Have her stimulate your penis until you feel that orgasm is just around the corner. At that second, give her a prearranged signal.

In response to the signal, she should stop stimulating and start squeezing the penis just below the tip. She should squeeze it firmly enough to cause you to lose your erection, but not to cause you pain. When the feeling that you are about to ejaculate leaves you, have her stimulate you again.

As before, signal her when orgasm is imminent and, once again, she should stop stimulating and start squeezing the penis. The erection should go down and you will not ejaculate.

Keep this up (and down) for a while and soon you will be able to control ejaculation.

The next step is intercourse. As soon as you feel like you are about to climax, signal your partner, withdraw from her and have her squeeze your penis until you lose the erection.

Remember—practice makes perfect! Masters and Johnson reported that in just two weeks of using this behavior modification program, 98% of men with premature ejaculation were cured.

## The Heart and the Heat of Passion

It's a myth that sex is dangerous to the heart, according to Richard A. Stein, MD, director of preventive cardiology, Beth Israel Medical Center in New York City and spokesperson for the American Heart Association (*www.americanheart.org*).

The stress to the heart is really very mild. The average heart rate increases up to 115 to 120 beats per minute during intercourse—a muscle workload equal to walking up two flights of stairs.

**WARNING:** If a man is cheating on his mate, the heart rate and risk tend to rise with the excitement and danger of being caught.

# Healing Remedies
# for Women

# Healing Remedies for Women

 **W**e've come a long way, baby!" That old sentiment has never been more appropriate than it is now.

Today, we talk openly about menstruation, pregnancy and menopause, not as sicknesses, but as natural stages of life. We also recognize and deal with premenstrual tension and menopausal irregularities.

We are finally learning to question the male-dominated medical profession after hearing countless stories about hysterectomies, radical mastectomies and other surgeries that are sometimes performed—whether or not a woman needs the procedure.

Knowledge is power. Daytime talk shows, bookstores, local libraries and the Internet are filled with women's health information. Take advantage of these sources so that you can take responsibility for your own body and good health by intelligently choosing the most appropriate medical care and caregivers.

Meanwhile, here are several natural remedies that are time-tested, whispered down from generation to generation...

▶ As a general remedy, gently but firmly massage the back of your leg, around the ankle. Massaging that area can relax tension, stimulate circulation and soothe the female organs.

## Bladder Control

▶ The Kegel (or pubococcygeus) exercises can help you gain control over your bladder, strengthen your abdominal muscles and tighten muscles that can enhance sexual activity.

Each time you urinate, start and stop as many times as possible. While squeezing the muscle that stops the flow of urine, pull in on the muscles of the abdomen. You can also do this exercise when not urinating. Sit at your desk, in your car, at the movies—anyplace— and flex…release…flex…release.

## Cystitis

This chronic pain disorder can make life complicated, with frequent trips to the bathroom and constant discomfort in the pelvic region. Some of these remedies may provide relief.

▶ Pour a small box of baking soda into a bath of warm water and soak in it for at least a half-hour. Afterward, rinse under the shower.

▶ Even some physicians suggest cranberry juice for cystitis. You can get juice that's sugarless with no added preservatives at most supermarkets, or you can buy cranberry concentrate (which needs to be diluted) at health food stores, or use cranberry capsules and follow the dosage on the label.

*Juice dose:* Drink one 8-ounce glass of juice in the morning, before breakfast, and one glass in the late afternoon. Make sure it's at room temperature, not chilled.

▶ Take two garlic capsules a day and, if you don't mind smelling like a salami, drink garlic tea throughout the day. Mash a couple of garlic cloves into hot water and let them steep for five minutes. You can also make garlic tea with 1 teaspoon of garlic powder in hot water.

✎ **NOTE:** Persistent cystitis may require antibiotics prescribed by a doctor. If that is the case, be sure to eat yogurt that contains live or active cultures, during and after taking the antibiotics.

### Silky Solution

▶ According to Native Americans, corn silk (the silky strands beneath the husk of corn) can be a cure-all for urinary problems. The most desirable corn silk is from young corns, gathered before the silk turns brown. Take a handful of corn silk and steep it in 3 cups of boiled water for five minutes. Strain and drink the 3 cups throughout the day.

Corn silk should be stored in a glass jar, not refrigerated. If you can't get corn silk, use corn silk extract, available at health food stores.

Add 10 to 15 drops of the extract to a cup of hot water. Dried corn silk is also available.

### Cystitis Prevention

▶ Women who frequently get cystitis should empty their bladders, if passion allows, *before* intercourse. It's also possible to lessen the number of attacks or stop them forever by urinating immediately *after* the act of intercourse. Forgo receiving oral sex.

▶ We've heard folk remedies requiring the cystitis sufferer to take baths. Recently, we were told by a research scientist that baths may cause the recurrence of the condition. If you are a bath-taker and have recurring cystitis, refrain from taking a bath for at least a month, and shower instead. You just may find you aren't troubled with cystitis anymore.

## Lack of Desire

A lack of interest in sex (sometimes diagnosed as sexual arousal disorder or sexual dysfunction) often stems from poor communication between a woman and her partner. Sex counseling may be the only remedy that works.

Otherwise, here are some helpful natural remedies to try…

▶ As for the "Not tonight, honey" syndrome, eating a piece of halvah may awaken a woman's sexual desires. This Middle Eastern treat is made of sesame seeds and honey. The sesame seeds are high in magnesium and potassium. Honey contains aspartic acid. All three substances have been said to help women overcome lack of interest in sex.

▶ Licorice (the herb, not the candy) can do wonders for your love life. It is known to have a positive effect on one's libido. In France, it is not uncommon to see women drink licorice water, believing it may help to improve their love life.

Powdered licorice root is available at health food stores. Drink 1 teaspoon in a cup of water and get out the sexy lingerie. However, if you have high blood pressure, use the lingerie, but *NOT* the licorice.

**CAUTION:** Do not take licorice root if you have high blood pressure or kidney problems. It can cause renal failure.

### A Bubbly Mix

▶ In ancient Greek mythology, Anaxarete was cold to her suitors. How cold was she? She was so cold that Aphrodite, the Goddess of Love, turned her into a marble statue. That's cold!

Here is an "antifreeze" that might work even for Anaxarete—boil 1 cup of finely minced chive leaves and roots (available at a greengrocer) with 2 cups of champagne. Then simmer until reduced to a thick cupful. Drink it unstrained.

It's no wonder this syrup may work. Centuries later, we learned it's rich in vitamin E (the love vitamin). Also, champagne has always been known to provoke passion. The legendary Italian lover Giacomo Casanova (1725–1798) used it continually in his erotic cookery.

## Vaginitis (Vaginal Infections)

If you've got itching, swelling and burning "down there," you probably have this common infection, caused by bacteria or fungus.

▶ Wear cotton panties to absorb moisture, since moisture encourages the growth of fungus and bacteria. For that reason, stay away from moisture-inducing garments like pantyhose, girdles, leotards, tights, spandex, etc.

▶ Take showers instead of baths. Baths can add to your problems when the vaginal area is exposed to bathwater impurities.

▶ Do not use any chemical products, such as feminine hygiene sprays. Also, avoid tampons and colored or scented toilet tissue.

▶ Do not launder panties along with socks, stockings or other undergarments. Wash your panties separately with a mild soap or detergent, and rinse them thoroughly.

## Menstruation

 **NOTE:** None of these remedies will work if you are pregnant or have undergone a hysterectomy.

### Bringing on Menstruation

▶ To help bring on and regulate menstruation, eat and drink fresh beets and beet juice. Have about 3 cups of beets and juice each day past your period-date until the flow begins.

▶ A footbath in hot water has been said to help start a late menstrual period.

▶ Add 1 tablespoon of basil to a cup of boiling water. Let it steep for five minutes. Strain and drink.

▶ In a circular motion, massage below the outer and inner ankle of each foot, as well as the outer and inner wrist of each hand. If there is tenderness when you rub those areas, you're in the right place. Keep massaging until the tenderness is gone. Chances are your problem will also soon be gone. Within a day or two, your period should start.

▶ Ginger tea can stimulate the onset of menstruation. Put four or five quarter-sized pieces of fresh ginger in a cup of boiling-hot water and let it steep for 10 minutes. Drink 3 or 4 cups of the tea throughout the day. It also helps ease menstrual cramps.

## Excessive Menstrual Flow

If your menstrual flow is excessive, the following remedies have been said to help. We also suggest you have a medical checkup.

**CAUTION:** Hemorrhaging requires immediate medical attention! If you are not sure about the difference between hemorrhaging and excessive menstrual flow, do not take a chance—if you are bleeding profusely, call 911 and get medical attention quickly.

▶ Mix the juice of ½ lemon into a cup of warm water. Drink it down slowly an hour before breakfast and an hour before dinner.

▶ Throughout the day, sip cinnamon tea made with a piece of cinnamon stick steeped in hot water. Or put 4 drops of cinnamon bark tincture in a cup of warm water.

▶ When bleeding excessively, stay away from alcoholic beverages and hot, spicy foods— except for cayenne pepper because…

▶ Cayenne pepper is a powerful bleeding regulator. Add ⅛ of a teaspoon of cayenne pepper to a cup of warm water or your favorite herbal tea and drink it.

▶ To help control profuse menstrual flow, it's time for thyme tea. Steep 2 tablespoons of fresh thyme in 2 cups of hot water. Let it stand for 10 minutes. Strain out the thyme and drink 1 cup. Add an ice cube to the other cup of tea, then soak a washcloth in it and use it as a cold compress on the pelvic area.

▶ Drink yarrow tea—2 to 3 cups a day until the period is over. To prepare the tea, add 1 or 2 teaspoons of dried yarrow (depending on how strong you want the tea to be) to 1 cup of just-boiled water. Let it steep for 10 minutes. Strain and drink. You may not like the taste of the tea, but drink it as long as you get results.

## Menstrual Cramps

▶ When it comes to menstrual cramps, how do naturalists spell relief? L-E-A-F-Y G-R-E-E-N-S. Eat lots of lettuce, cabbage and parsley before and during your period. To get the full benefit of all vegetables, eat them raw or steamed. Aside from helping reduce cramps, leafy greens are diuretics and will relieve you of some bloat.

 **NOTE:** Be sure to thoroughly wash all raw produce to reduce the risk of food-borne illness.

## Break Out the Tonic Water

▶ When your menstrual pains drive you to drink, head for the liquor cabinet and mix yourself a small gin and tonic. The quinine in the tonic will relax your muscles and believe us, the gin won't hurt either. Gin is prepared from a mash consisting of 85% corn, 12% malt and 3% rye, and is distilled in the presence of juniper berries, coriander seeds, etc. But go easy on it. You may get rid of the cramps, but you don't want to have to deal with a hangover.

**NOTE:** Don't try the gin remedy if you have a problem or a past history of problems with alcohol. And if you do try this remedy, don't drive!

## Menstrual Irregularities

▶ On a daily basis, thoroughly chew and then swallow 1 tablespoon of sesame seeds. Or you can grind flaxseed and sprinkle a tablespoon on your cereal, soup or salad. Both types of seed have been known to help regulate the menstrual cycle.

## Premenstrual Relief

▶ Chamomile tea is a superb tension reliever and nerve relaxer. As soon as menstrual cramps start, prepare chamomile tea and sip it throughout the day.

▶ Premenstrual tension as well as menstrual cramps may be relieved by increasing calcium intake. Menopausal symptoms may also be prevented by adding calcium to the diet. On a daily basis, it is a good idea to eat at least one portion of two or three of these calcium-rich foods—leafy green vegetables (collard greens, dandelion greens, kale, mustard greens, broccoli, turnip greens, watercress, parsley, endive) as well as canned salmon, sardines and anchovies, figs and yogurt.

 **NOTE:** Be sure to thoroughly wash all raw produce to reduce the risk of food-borne illness.

▶ Minimize or completely eliminate caffeine and alcoholic beverages. Both increase the amount of calcium lost in the urine.

## ■ Recipe ■

### Country Cole Slaw

½ large head green cabbage, shredded
1 cup red cabbage, shredded
2 medium carrots, shredded
1 large apple, chopped
½ cup raisins, plumped in hot water to cover
3 or 4 dates, chopped
½ cup of any chopped nuts

*Dressing*
½ cup soy mayonnaise
2 to 4 Tbsp lemon juice
1 Tbsp white miso
Freshly ground black pepper
1 tsp caraway seeds (optional)

Combine the cabbage, carrots, apple, raisins, dates and nuts in a large bowl and toss to distribute ingredients evenly.

Combine dressing ingredients in a small bowl, pour over the slaw and mix well. Makes about 4 to 6 servings.

*Source: www.vegparadise.com*

**WARNING:** Check with a health professional before taking a calcium supplement. These supplements have been known to cause kidney stones in some people.

## Peppermint Power

▶ Peppermint tea is soothing. It also helps digestion and rids you of that bloated feeling. Drink a cup of peppermint tea *after* (not during) your meal.

▶ For premenstrual relief for everything from the blues to breast tenderness, take two garlic supplements daily.

# Pregnancy

Be sure to consult your obstetrician or midwife before trying any natural remedies or supplements.

### During and After

*Morning sickness:* If you are troubled by morning sickness, check with your obstetrician about supplementing with 50 mg of vitamin $B_6$ and 50 mg of vitamin $B_1$ daily. Since garlic greatly increases the body's absorption of $B_1$, make an effort to eat garlic raw in salads and to cook with it.

**CAUTION:** Do not eat raw garlic or take garlic supplements if you have a bleeding disorder or ulcers, or are taking anticoagulants.

▶ A doctor at Brigham Young University in Provo, Utah, recommends taking 2 or 3 capsules of powdered ginger first thing in the morning to avoid morning sickness.

▶ Mix ⅓ cup of lime juice and ⅛ teaspoon of cinnamon in ½ cup of warm water. (Ugh—it sounds like it could bring on morning sickness!) Drink it as soon as you awaken. It's known to be quite effective.

*Constipation during pregnancy:* Keep a chair, stool or carton in the bathroom so that you can rest your feet on it when you're sitting on the toilet. Once your feet are on the same level as the seat, lean back and relax. To avoid hemorrhoids and varicose veins, do not strain and do not hold your breath and squeeze.

*Increase milk production after pregnancy:* Bring to a boil 1 teaspoon of caraway seeds in 8 ounces of water. Then simmer for five minutes. Let the tea cool and drink. Several cups of caraway seed tea each day may increase mother's milk supply.

▶ Brewer's yeast (available at health food stores) may also help to replenish milk.

### Labor and Delivery

▶ Many sources agree on raspberry tea for the mother-to-be. What our sources don't agree on is the best time to start drinking the tea. Some say right after conception…others say three months before delivery…and still others say six weeks before your due date.

The consensus is that pregnant women should drink 2 to 3 cups of raspberry tea every day, starting at least six weeks before their due date. Ask your obstetrician or midwife about it.

To make the tea, add 1 teaspoon of dried raspberry leaves to 1 cup of just-boiled water. Let it steep for five minutes, strain and drink.

### Breast-Feeding

▶ Add lentil soup to your diet. Lentils are very rich in calcium and other nutrients necessary for nursing mothers (*see* recipe on page 231).

▶ To stimulate milk secretion, drink a mixture of fennel seeds and barley water. Crush 2 tablespoons of fennel seeds and simmer them in a quart of barley water (*see* "Preparation Guide" on page 249) for 20 minutes. Let it cool and drink it throughout the day.

▶ Peppermint tea is said to increase the supply of mother's milk and it's also known to relieve nervous tension and improve digestion. Drink 2 to 3 cups a day.

### Cracked and/or Sore Nipples

▶ When Las Vegas–based herbalist Angela Harris (*www.angelaharris.com*) was nursing each of her eight children, between nursings, she would moisten a black tea bag (usually Lipton's Orange Pekoe) and apply it to her cracked or sore nipple. It relieved the pain and helped heal the cracking.

## Menopause

If you are getting hot flashes, it could mean one of two things—either the paparazzi are following you, or you're going through menopause. We have no remedy for the paparazzi, but we can provide recommendations that may relieve some of the menopausal chaos.

▶ A Viennese gynecologist has reported positive results among his female patients treated with bee pollen. Bee pollen contains a combination of male and female hormones. It has been known to help some women do away with or minimize hot flashes.

---

### ■ Recipe ■

#### Lentil Vegetable Soup

If you prefer thick soups, reduce the lentil cooking water to 6 cups and the vegetable cooking water to 1½ cups.

1 cup dried lentils
1 bay leaf
1 small onion, chopped
7 cups water
2 whole cloves
1 stick cinnamon
2 pinches fennel seeds
3 pods cardamom seeds, cracked
1 small onion, chopped
2 medium carrots, sliced
2 stalks celery, diced
1 large zucchini, cut into bite-sized
    pieces
1 yellow crookneck squash, cut into
    bite-sized pieces
1 small turnip, diced
2 cups water
Juice of one lemon
Salt and pepper to taste

Combine lentils, bay leaf, onion and 7 cups water in a large stock pot.

In a piece of cheesecloth, tie together the cloves, cinnamon stick, fennel seeds, and cardamom seeds and add to stockpot.

Bring to a boil, uncovered. Turn heat down to medium and simmer 45 minutes.

Combine onion, carrots, celery, squashes, turnip and water in a large wok or skillet, and cook over high heat just until tender, stirring frequently, about 6 to 8 minutes.

Add vegetables to cooked lentils and stir to distribute evenly.

Season to taste with lemon juice, salt and pepper. Makes 6 servings.

*Dose:* Take 3 bee pollen pills (500 mg) a day, or the granule equivalent.

For more information about bee pollen, *see* page 258 of the "Six Sensational Superfoods" section.

**CAUTION:** People who are allergic to bee stings or honey should consult a doctor before taking bee pollen.

▶ The estrogenic substances in black cohosh may relieve menopause symptoms, such as hot flashes and vaginal dryness. You'll find the herb in tincture form at health food stores. Follow the recommended dosage on the label.

### Rummy Remedy

▶ If you have excessive menstrual flow during menopause, mix 1 ounce of grated nutmeg in 1 pint of Jamaican rum.

*Dose:* Take 1 teaspoon three times a day for the duration of your period.

**WARNING:** Do not take this remedy before driving or operating heavy machinery.

▶ Eat a cucumber every day. Cukes are said to contain beneficial hormones.

▶ Step into a tub that has six inches of cold water in it. Carefully walk back and forth for about three minutes. (Be sure to have nonslip stick-ons on the floor of the tub.)

Step out, dry your feet thoroughly and put on a pair of walking shoes (socks are optional). Then take a walk—even if it's just around your room—for another three minutes.

▶ Naturalists call pure licorice and sarsaparilla "hormone foods." These herbs are available at health food stores. Use each of them as teas and drink them often (*see* "Preparation Guide" on page 250).

**WARNING:** If you're on medication, do not take any herbs or supplements until you check with your health professional.

# Remedies for
# Natural Beauty

# Remedies for Natural Beauty

## SKIN CARE

**M**irror, mirror on the wall…who's the fairest one of all?" Even Snow White had to take care of her complexion! Most people have skin problems at one time or another (*see* "Acne" starting on page 153), but one of the best ways to ensure you put your "best face" forward every day is to cleanse it properly, according to your skin type. Here are some good general cleansing recommendations.

## Basic Skin Care

▶ Always use an upward and outward motion when doing anything to your face—whether you're washing it, doing a facial, applying makeup or removing makeup.

▶ When you wash your face, use tepid water. Either very hot or very cold water could break the small capillaries—those little red squiggly veins—in your face.

### What's Your Type?

**F**irst, ask yourself, "What kind of skin do I have—dry, oily, combination or normal?" Once you know what kind of skin you have, you can learn how to take care of it. If you're not sure, Heloise (the helpful hints lady) developed a test you can take.

"Wash your face with [plain, non-gel] shaving cream. Rinse. Wait about three hours so that your skin can revert to its regular self. Then take cigarette papers or any other thin tissue paper and press pieces of it on your face.

"If it sticks, leaving an oily spot that's visible when you hold it up to the light, you've got oily skin. If it doesn't stick, your skin is dry. If it sticks, but doesn't leave oily spots, you've got normal skin. If the paper sticks on some areas, leaving oily spots, and doesn't stick on other areas, you have combination skin."

▶ It's important to wash your face twice a day. Washing removes dead skin, and keeps pores clean and skin texture good.

The morning cleansing is necessary because of metabolic activity during the night.

The night washup is necessary because of all the dirt that piles up during the day. Wash with a mild soap and a washcloth or cosmetic sponge, upward and outward. *Now, onward…*

> ✎ **NOTE:** We have included masks to treat oily, dry, normal and combination skin. But no matter what type of skin, the best time to apply a mask is before going to sleep, when you don't have to wear makeup for at least six to eight hours.
> Also, try to apply the mask after you've taken a bath or shower, or after you've gently steamed your face, so that the pores are open.

## Firming Facial

▶ Chocolate is rich in copper, an essential nutrient for the skin-firming connective tissues.

Mix 1 heaping tablespoon of unsweetened cocoa powder with enough heavy cream to form a paste. Apply it to your clean, dry skin and leave it there for 15 minutes. Then lick it off…*just kidding*! Rinse it off with a washcloth and lukewarm water, then pat dry.

## Make Your Own Beauty Mask

▶ In a blender, purée 1 cup of fresh pineapple and ½ cup of fresh (slightly green) papaya. Put the puréed fruit in a bowl and mix in 2 tablespoons of honey. Apply it to your just-washed face and neck, but NOT on the delicate area around your eyes. Leave it on for five minutes—not more—and rinse with cool water.

This once-a-week alpha hydroxy facial can boost the production of collagen (making your face firmer), slough off dead skin cells, even out skin tone and make tiny lines less noticeable. The enzymes in pineapple (brome-lain) and papaya (papain) do most of the work as the honey hydrates the skin.

## Skin-Awakener Formula

One source described this treatment as "the cleansing acid that cuts through residue film and clears the way for a healthful complexion." Another source said, "This treatment will restore the acid covering your skin needs for protection." And still another said, "This formula is, by far, the simplest natural healer for tired skin. It gives you the glow of fresh-faced youth." With endorsements like that, what are you waiting for?

▶ Mix 1 tablespoon of apple cider vinegar with 1 tablespoon of just-boiled water. As soon as the liquid is cool enough, apply it to the face with cotton balls. Do NOT get it near the eyes.

Lydia tried this treatment. It made her skin feel smooth and tight. Her eyes were a little teary from the strong fumes of the diluted vinegar and, for about 10 minutes, she smelled like coleslaw.

Use this treatment to freshen you skin at least every other day—or whenever you have a craving for coleslaw.

▶ After a shower or bath, some people spray their bodies with a plastic plant mister filled with equal amounts of apple cider vinegar and water. It not only restores the acid mantle (pH balance) in the skin, it removes soap residue and hard water deposits, too.

## Skin Toner

▶ In a blender, purée 4 medium-sized, well-washed strawberries, 2 dollops of plain yogurt and 1 tablespoon of fresh lemon juice.

Distribute the strawberry purée all over your face and neck, avoiding the delicate eye area. Leave it on for about 20 minutes, then rinse with tepid water.

Doing this skin-toning treatment twice a week is said to help prevent little age lines.

# Caring for Oily Skin

## The Basics

▶ Many folk healers suggest drinking a strong cup of yarrow tea, which is an astringent, to cut down on skin oiliness. Use 2 teaspoons of dried yarrow (available at health food stores) in a cup of just-boiled water. Let it steep for 10 minutes. Strain and drink every day.

▶ In a blender, blend ¼ of a small eggplant (skin and all) with 1 cup of plain yogurt. Smear the mush on your face and neck (but not on the delicate skin around your eyes) and leave it there for 20 minutes. Rinse with tepid water.

Finish this treatment with a toner—a nonalcoholic astringent like the yarrow tea (above) is ideal. Also, fill a plastic plant mister with a cup of the tea (chamomile is an astringent and can be used) and spray your face with it. Keep the mister in the refrigerator so you can use it to set your makeup or to freshen up.

## Makeup Remover

▶ Cleansers seem to be a problem for oily skin because of the high alcohol content of most makeup-removing astringents. They're usually too harsh to be used on a regular basis.

Instead, use 1 teaspoon of powdered milk with enough warm water to give it a milky consistency. With cotton balls, apply the liquid to your face and neck (avoiding the delicate eye area), gently rubbing it on. Once you have

covered your entire face and neck, remove the makeup and dirt with a tissue…again, gently. Pat dry.

## Mask

▶ Kitty litter has great absorbency and can be used for lots of things, including the *purr-fect* facial for oily skin. Be sure to get a natural litter that's 100% clay, no chemicals added.

Mash 2 tablespoons of the litter with enough water—about an ounce—to make a paste. Apply it to your just-washed face, but NOT to the delicate area around your eyes. Leave it on for about 15 minutes. Then rinse with tepid water.

# Caring for Dry Skin

A leading cause of dry skin is towels. (Just checking to see if you're paying attention!)

## The Basics

▶ Avocado is highly recommended for dry skin. Take the inside of an avocado skin and massage your just-washed face and neck with it.

Or, mix equal amounts of avocado (about ¼ cup) with sour cream. Gently rub it on the face and neck (but not on the delicate skin around the eyes) and leave it there for at least 15 minutes. Rinse with tepid water.

When you can no longer see a trace of the mixture, use your fingertips to work the invisible oil into your skin with an upward and outward sweep…again, gently.

## Makeup Remover

▶ Instead of using soap and water, clean your face with whole milk. Warm 2 to 3 tablespoons of milk, add ½ teaspoon of castor oil and shake well. Dunk a cotton ball (not a tissue) into the mixture and start cleaning, using upward and outward strokes. Avoid the delicate eye area.

This combination of milk and oil is said to take off more makeup and city dirt than the most expensive professional cleansing products ever could. And it does it naturally, not chemically.

Complete the treatment by sealing in moisture with a thin layer of castor oil applied to the face.

### Mask

▶ Scrub 2 to 3 medium-sized carrots, then cut each carrot into 1-inch pieces and put them in a pot with a few cups of water. Cook the carrots until they are slightly softened. Transfer the carrots to a blender or food processor and purée.

Massage the carrot purée all over your just-washed face and neck, avoiding the delicate eye area. Keep it there for about 20 minutes, then rinse with tepid water.

This mask is popular in European spas, where regular use is said to improve elasticity as well as smooth out wrinkles.

## Caring for Combination Skin

Using different treatments for the dry and oily parts of your face can become a real nuisance. Instead, you may want to try these treatments, which are good for all types of skin.

### The Basics

▶ This papaya facial helps remove dead skin cells and allows the new skin to breathe freely. Papaya accomplishes naturally what most commercial products do chemically.

In a blender, purée a ripe, peeled papaya. Spread the fruit on your face and neck and keep it there for 20 minutes. Rinse off with tepid water.

It would be most beneficial to have this facial once or twice a month, but since it's not always possible to get a ripe papaya, do it whenever you can.

### Makeup Remover

▶ No makeup remover? Use whipped sweet butter or vegetable shortening instead. (Doesn't this sound like it's from a *Cosmopolitan* magazine list of "sleep-over" suggestions?)

Whatever makeup remover you use, keep it on your eyes and face for at least 30 seconds so that it has a chance to sink in and make it easier to gently rub off the makeup.

### Mask

▶ This mask is for everyone, year-round. It's a honey of a honey mask. Folk practitioners claim that it helps rid the face of blemishes and blackheads…leaves a person feeling refreshed and invigorated…restores weather-beaten skin …prevents skin from aging by helping it maintain a normal proportion of moisture. The longer we go on, the more the skin is aging!

Here's how to apply the mask—start with a clean face and neck and pull your hair out of the way. Dip your fingertips in raw, unheated honey and gently spread it on your face and neck in an upward and outward motion. Make sure to avoid the eye area. Leave this on for 20 minutes, then rinse with tepid water. It's sweet and simple…and sticky.

### Moisturizer

▶ Wet your clean face and rub on a glob of petroleum jelly. Keep adding water as you thin out the layer of jelly all over your face and neck until it's no longer greasy.

This inexpensive treatment is used at expensive spas because it's very effective.

## Exfoliation Scrub

▶ Mix 1 teaspoon of sugar with a few drops of champagne—enough to form a paste. In circular motions, apply the mixture to your face and neck, then rinse it off with lukewarm water and pat dry.

The enzymes that are in champagne's tartaric acid, along with the abrasive quality of the sugar, should do a very thorough job of exfoliating your skin.

## Make Your Own Body Scrub

▶ Create a paste by mixing together ¼ cup of freshly squeezed lemon juice and ¼ cup extravirgin olive oil along with ½ cup of kosher (coarse) salt.

Massage the paste onto the parts of your body that need exfoliating. Then rinse off the mixture and feel how smooth it leaves your skin.

☞ **WARNING:** Never use this scrub on your face. It's too strong and coarse for delicate facial skin.

## GROOMING

## Enrich Your Night Cream

▶ According to the legendary cosmetics expert Adrien Arpel, "To transform a skimpy night cream into an enriched vitamin skin treat, add ⅛ teaspoon of liquid vitamin C and the contents of a 100 IU vitamin E capsule to 4 ounces of ordinary night cream."

## Magical Face Relaxer

Before applying your makeup for an evening out, take time to get the day's tension out of your face. *Here's how...*

▶ Lie down with your feet up. Take the cork from a wine bottle and put it between your teeth. Don't bite down on it—encircle it with your lips. Stay that way for 10 minutes—breathe easily and think lovely thoughts.

After the 10 minutes have flown by, your face should be smoother and more receptive to makeup. And you should be refreshed and more receptive to having a fun evening.

## Double-Chin Prevention

▶ A simple yoga exercise called "the lion" firms the throat muscles under the chin.

The entire exercise consists of sticking your tongue out and down as far as it will go. Do this dozens of times throughout the day—in your car, watching TV, while doing the dishes or waiting for your computer to start up.

It's possible you'll see an improvement in your chin line within a few days.

## Toweling Off

▶ Towels made of 100% cotton will dry you faster and more thoroughly than towels made of blended fibers.

## Chapped Lips

▶ Apply a thin film of glycerin (available at drugstores) to soften and protect your lips.

## Pleasing Tweezing

▶ If you can't stand the pain of tweezing your eyebrows, numb the area first by putting an ice cube on for a few seconds.

▶ If you don't need to go so far as to numb the area, but just want to have an easy time of it, tweeze right after a warm shower. The hairs come out more willingly then.

## FINGERNAIL HOW-TO

## Matchbook Method

▶ When you need an emery board and can't find one, look for a matchbook. File down a jagged-edged fingernail with the rough, striking part of the matchbook.

## Polish Primer

▶ Wipe your unpolished fingernails with white vinegar to clean and prime the surfaces for nail polish. Once the vinegar dries, this treatment will help the polish stay on longer.

## Manicure Protection

▶ Use a toothbrush and toothpaste to clean office-type stains (carbon, ink, etc.) off your fingertips without damaging your manicure.

## GENERAL TIPS

## Paint Remover for Skin

▶ If you've been painting walls or canvas, a little vegetable oil should clean off your paint-bespeckled face and arms—without torturing your skin.

## Pain-Free Bandage Remover

▶ When you're wearing a bandage that's not "ouchless," saturate it with vegetable oil so that you can remove it painlessly.

## Mirror, Mirror in the Bathroom

▶ Clean the bathroom mirror with plain, non-gel shaving cream, which will prevent it from fogging up for several weeks.

▶ After a shower or bath, use a hair dryer to unfog the steamed-up mirror.

## Perfume Pick-Me-Up

▶ Douse a small natural sponge with your favorite perfume and put it in a plastic sandwich bag in your purse.

During or after a hard day at the office, moisten the sponge with some cold water and dab it behind your ears and knees, in your elbows and on your wrists to give you a refreshed feeling. ■

# Remedies in a Class
# By Themselves

# Remedies in a Class By Themselves

## Kiss of Life

There is a research center in Germany where scientists are studying the act of kissing. One of their findings is that the morning "Good-bye, dear" kiss is the most important one of the day. This particular kiss helps start the day with a positive attitude that leads to better work performance and an easier time coping with stress.

According to the researchers, that morning send-off kiss given on a daily basis can add up to earning more money and living a longer, healthier life.

Hey, what about us single people? We don't know about you, but we're going to make a deal with our doorman.

▶ According to a doctor quoted in a Roman newspaper, "Kissing is good for your health and will make you live longer." We certainly like that idea—tell us more!

The doctor explains, "Kissing stimulates the heart, which gives more oxygen to the body's cells, keeping the cells young and vibrant." He also found that kissing produces antibodies in the human body that, in the long run, can provide protection against certain infections.

## Exercise Your Lung Power

▶ This remedy requires an investment of some money and time. But if you want to increase your lung power and breath control, try taking up a musical instrument—the harmonica. It's fun! Get the "Marine Band" style, made by Hohner. It's a good beginner's harmonica, and it's inexpensive.

Hohner also publishes books that teach you to play the harmonica while you strengthen your lungs. Playing the harmonica has even been known to alleviate symptoms of emphysema. Who knows—it may start you on a whole new career. Visit *www.hohnerusa.com* for more information.

## Yawn All the Way

▶ Do not stifle a yawn. Yawning restores the equilibrium between the air pressure in the middle ear and that of the outside atmosphere, giving you a feeling of relief. (And you thought you were just bored!)

## Confessions...Good for the Immune System

▶ We've all heard that "confession is good for the soul." According to James W. Pennebaker, PhD, professor of psychology at the University of Texas in Austin, "When we inhibit feelings and thoughts, our breathing and heartbeat speed up, putting an extra strain on our autonomic nervous system."

By writing about the stresses in your life, you release pent-up emotions, freeing the immune system to do its real job, that of guarding the body against unwanted invaders.

After following Dr. Pennebaker's formula exactly as directed, you should feel lighter, happier and may experience better health during the next six months.

### Dr. Pennebaker's Process

◆ Find a quiet place where you can be alone for 20 minutes.

◆ Write down a confession of what's bothering you. Be as specific as you can.

◆ Don't worry about spelling or grammar. Just write continuously for the entire 20 minutes.

◆ Keep going, even if it feels awkward. Letting go takes practice. If you reach a mental block, repeat your words.

◆ For four days in a row, write for 20 minutes a day. After four days of writing, you should be ready to throw the paper away and enjoy your newly recharged immune system.

Feel free to repeat this exercise anytime something stressful comes up. Regular release will keep your immune system strong.

## Success Through Napping

▶ It is said that a nap during the day can do wonders for balancing emotions and attitudes and, in general, harmonizing one's system without interference from the conscious mind.

US presidents Harry S Truman, John F. Kennedy and Lyndon B. Johnson were well-known nappers. Other prestigious, productive people who caught some shut-eye on a daily basis include inventor Thomas A. Edison, politician and statesman Winston Churchill and, appropriately, French general and emperor Napoleon Bonaparte.

## Practice Preventive Medicine: Laugh!

▶ The late writer and magazine editor Norman Cousins turned to laughter as a medicine to help overcome his doctor-diagnosed "incurable" disease (tuberculosis), for which he was incorrectly hospitalized as a child.

According to Cousins, who referred to laughter as "inner jogging," there's scientific proof that it oxygenates the blood, improves respiration, stimulates the body's immune system and helps release substances described as "the body's anesthesia and a relaxant that helps human beings to sustain pain."

Log on to any Internet search engine, enter "jokes" or "humor," and laugh it up!

## Have a Good Cry

▶ Emotional tears have a higher protein content than onion-produced tears. A researcher at the St. Paul-Ramsey Medical Center (now called Regions Hospital) in St. Paul, Minnesota, accounted for that difference as nature's way of releasing chemical substances (the protein) created during an emotional or stressful situation. In turn, the release of those chemical substances lets the negative feelings flow out, allowing a sense of well-being to return.

According to Margaret T. Crepeau, PhD, professor of nursing at Marquette University in Milwaukee, Wisconsin, people who suppress tears are more vulnerable to disease. In fact, suppressing any kind of feeling seems to take its toll on one's system. Face your feelings and let 'em out!

## Calcium Concern

The mineral calcium helps your body build strong bones and teeth—and to keep them strong, you need to get adequate amounts of calcium in your diet.

We should all—particularly women—eat foods rich in calcium. These include canned sardines, canned salmon, soybean products (including tofu), dark-green leafy vegetables, asparagus, blackstrap molasses, sunflower seeds, sesame seeds, walnuts, almonds, peanuts, dried beans, corn tortillas and dairy products.

The body is depleted of calcium when there is a high consumption of caffeine, colas and other soft drinks. Also, calcium absorption is compromised in people who smoke, take antacids that are high in aluminum or are on a low-sodium and/or a high-protein diet.

## Give Healing Orders

A survey conducted at Johns Hopkins Hospital in Baltimore concluded that three out of four ailments stemmed from emotional factors. It makes sense. Crises in our lives cause emotional reactions which cause biochemical changes that disrupt the body's harmony, weaken immunity and upset hormone production.

We do it to ourselves—therefore, we can undo it!

▶ Relax every part of your body (follow the visualization exercise in the "Tension and Anxiety" section—it's on page 177).

Once you're completely relaxed, order your body to heal itself. Actually give your body this command out loud. Be direct, clear and positive. Picture your specific problem. (There's no right or wrong—it's all up to your own imagination.)

Once you have a clear picture of your problem, see it healing. Envision pain flying out of your pores…picture the condition breaking up and disintegrating. Say and see whatever seems appropriate for your particular case.

End this daily session by looking in the mirror and repeating a dozen times, "Wellness is mine"—and mean it!

## The Ultimate Remedy

According to retired professor emeritus Sidney B. Simon of the University of Massachusetts in Amherst, "Everyone needs at least three hugs a day in order to be healthy."

And the oft-quoted St. Aelred, abbot of Rievaulx (1110–1167), said, "No medicine is more valuable, none more efficacious, none better suited to the cure of all our temporal ills than a friend."

Keeping those thoughts in mind, we figured out The Ultimate Remedy—hug three friends once a day…or hug one friend three times a day! Either way, it will make you (and your friends) feel great. ■

# Preparation Guide

# Preparation Guide

## Barley

**H**ippocrates, the Greek physician and father of medicine (460–377 BC), believed that everyone should drink barley water every day to maintain good health. Barley is rich in iron and vitamin B. It is said to help prevent tooth decay and hair loss, improve the strength of fingernails and toenails, and help heal ulcers, diarrhea and bronchial spasms.

Pearl or pearled barley has been milled. During the milling process, the double outer husk is removed—along with its nutrients. A less refined version is pot or Scotch barley. Once it's gone through a less severe milling process, part of the bran layer remains, along with some of the nutrients.

Hulled barley, with only the outer, inedible hull removed, is a rich source of dietary fiber, and has more iron, trace minerals and four times the amount of thiamine (vitamin $B_1$) of pearled barley. It's available at some health food stores, as is Scotch barley. If you can't get either, you should be able to find pearled barley at the supermarket.

### Barley Water

Boil 2 ounces of barley in 6 cups of water (distilled water, if possible) until there's about half the water—3 cups—left in the pot. Strain. If necessary, add honey and lemon to taste.

## Coconut Milk

To get the milk in the easiest way possible, you need an ice pick or a screwdriver (Phillips head, if possible) and a hammer. The coconut has three little, black, eye-like bald spots on it. Place the ice pick or screwdriver in the middle of one black spot, then hammer the end of it so that it pierces the coconut.

Repeat the procedure with the other two black spots and then pour out the coconut milk. The hammer alone should then do the trick on the rest of the coconut. Watch your fingers! (Also watch your figure. Coconut meat is high in saturated fat.)

## Eyewash

You'll need an eye cup (available at drugstores). Carefully pour just-boiled water over the cup to sterilize it. Then, without contaminating the rim or inside surfaces of the cup, fill it half full with whichever eyewash you've selected (*see* "Eyewashes" on pages 79–80). Lean forward, apply the cup tightly to the eye to prevent spillage, then tilt your head back. Open your eye wide and rotate your eyeball to thoroughly wash the eye. Lean forward and discard the eyewash contents. Use the same procedure with the other eye, if necessary.

 **NOTE:** Always remove contact lenses before doing an eyewash.

# Garlic Juice

When a remedy calls for garlic juice, peel a clove or two of garlic, mince it finely onto a piece of cheesecloth, then squeeze out the juice. A garlic press will make the job even easier.

# Ginger Tea

Peel or scrub a nub of fresh ginger and cut it into three to five quarter-sized pieces. In a cup or mug, pour just-boiled water over the pieces and steep for five to 10 minutes.

If you want strong ginger tea, *grate* a piece of ginger, then steep it, strain it and drink it. Television personality and chef Ainsley Harriott told us that he freezes fresh ginger, which makes it easier to grate.

# Herbal Bath

Besides offering a good relaxing time, an herbal bath can be extremely healing. The volatile oils of the herbs are activated by the heat of the water, which also opens your pores, allowing for absorption of the herbs.

As you enjoy the bath, you're inhaling the herbs (aromatherapy), which pass through the nervous system to the brain, benefiting both mind and body.

## *Herbal Bath Directions*

Simply take a handful of one or a combination of dried or fresh herbs and place them in the center of a white handkerchief. Secure the herbs in the handkerchief by tying a knot and turning it into a little knapsack. Toss the herb-filled knapsack into the tub and let the hot water run until it reaches the level you want. When the water cools enough for you to sit comfortably, do so. Enjoy the scented soak.

After your bath, open the handkerchief and spread out the herbs to dry. You can use them a couple more times.

Instead of using dried or fresh herbs, you can also use herbal essential oils. Be careful—oils will cause the tub to be slippery. Take it easy getting out of the tub, and be sure to clean the tub thoroughly after you've drained the bath.

# Herbal Tea

Place a teaspoon of the herb (or the herbal tea bag) in a glass or ceramic cup and pour just-boiled water over it.

 **NOTE:** The average water-to-herb ratio is 6 to 8 ounces of water to 1 round teaspoon of herb. There are exceptions, so be sure to read the directions on the tea package.

According to the herbal tea company Lion Cross, never use water that has already been boiled. The first boiling releases oxygen, so the second boiling results in "flat," lifeless tea.

Cover the cup and let the tea steep according to the package directions. The general rule of thumb is to steep approximately three minutes for flowers and soft leaves…about five minutes for seeds and leaves…and about 10 minutes for hard seeds, roots and barks. (Of course, the longer the tea steeps, the stronger it will get.)

Strain the tea or remove the tea bag. If you need to sweeten it, use a bit of raw honey (never use sugar because it is said to negate the value of most herbs), and when it's cool enough, drink the tea slowly.

## Onions

The onion belongs to the same plant family (*Liliaceae*) as garlic—and is almost as versatile. The ancient Egyptians looked at the onion as the symbol of the universe. It has long been regarded as a universal healing food, used to treat earaches, colds, fever, wounds, diarrhea, insomnia, warts…and the list goes on.

It is believed that a cut onion in a sickroom disinfects the air, as it absorbs the germs in that room. And half an onion will help absorb the smell of a just-painted room. With that in mind, you may not want to use a cut piece of onion that has been in the kitchen for more than a day, unless you put it in plastic wrap and refrigerate it.

### Onion Juice

When a remedy calls for onion juice, grate an onion, put the gratings in a piece of cheesecloth and squeeze out the juice. A garlic press should also work.

## Pomanders

To make an orange-spice pomander, you will need…

    1 thin-skinned orange
    1 box of whole cloves
    1 oz orrisroot
    1 oz cinnamon
    ½ oz nutmeg
    2 ft of ¼"–½"-wide ribbon

Tie the ribbon around the orange and knot it, leaving two long ends of ribbon. Stick the cloves all over the orange, but not through the ribbon. Mix the three herbs together in a bowl, then place the orange in the bowl. Let it stay there for four or five days, turning the orange occasionally. When it's ready, hang the orange-spice pomander in a closet.

## Potatoes

Raw, peeled, boiled, grated and mashed potatoes…potato water…and potato poultices all help heal, according to American, English and Irish folk medicine. In fact, a popular 19th-century Irish saying was, "Only two things in this world are too serious to be jested on—potatoes and matrimony."

The skin or peel of the potato is richer in fiber, iron, potassium, calcium, phosphorus, zinc and vitamins C and B than the inside of the potato. Always leave the skin on when preparing potato water, but scrub it well first.

*Do not use potatoes that have a green tinge.* The greenish coloring is a warning that there may be a high concentration of solanine, a toxic alkaloid that can affect nerve impulses and cause vomiting, cramps and diarrhea. The same goes for potatoes that have started to sprout. They're a no-no.

### Potato Water

Scrub two medium-sized potatoes (use organic, if possible) and cut them in half. Put the four halves in a pot with 4 cups of water (filtered, spring or distilled, if possible) and bring to a boil. Lower the flame a little and let the potatoes cook for 30 minutes.

When they're done, take out the potatoes (eating them is optional) and save the water. Most remedies suggest that you drink 2 cups of potato water. Refrigerate the leftover water for the next time.

 **NOTE:** People with eczema should avoid touching raw potatoes with their bare hands. Persistent or chronic eczema is best treated by a health professional.

## Poultices

Poultices are usually made with vegetables, fruit or herbs that are either minced, chopped, grated, crushed or mashed, and sometimes cooked. These ingredients are then wrapped in clean fabric—such as cheesecloth, white cotton or unbleached muslin—and applied externally to the affected area.

A poultice is most effective when moist. When the poultice dries out, it should be changed—the cloth as well as the ingredients.

Whenever possible, use fresh fruits, vegetables or herbs. If these are unavailable, use dried herbs. To soften dried herbs, pour hot water over them. Do not let herbs steep in water that's still boiling, unless the remedy specifies to do this. For the most part, boiling herbs will diminish their healing powers.

Let's use comfrey as an example of a typical poultice. Cut a piece of cloth twice the size of the area it needs to cover. If you're using a fresh leaf, wash it with cool water, then crush it in your hand. Place the leaf on one half of the cloth and fold over the other half.

If you are using dried comfrey root and leaves, pour hot water over the herb, then place the softened herb down the length of the cloth, about two inches from the edge.

Roll the cloth around the herb so that it won't spill out, and place it on the affected body part. Gently wrap an elastic bandage or another piece of cloth around the poultice to hold it in place and to keep in the moisture.

## Sauerkraut

Sauerkraut, which is fermented cabbage, has been a popular folk medicine throughout the world for centuries. The lactic acid in sauerkraut is said to encourage the growth of friendly bacteria and help destroy enemy bacteria in the large intestine (where many people believe disease begins) and in other parts of the digestive tract.

Sauerkraut is rich in vitamin $B_6$, which is important for brain and nervous system functions, and high in calcium—for healthy teeth and bones. In fact, in the hills of western Germany, it is reported that sauerkraut is given to children as a snack to help prevent tooth decay and heal bad skin conditions.

The sauerkraut that comes in cans has been processed, and this may destroy its valuable health-giving properties. It is for that reason you should eat fresh sauerkraut cold (straight from the refrigerator), at room temperature or after it's been warmed over a low flame. Overheating sauerkraut may destroy the lactic acid and beneficial enzymes.

You can buy raw sauerkraut in jars at the health food market or out of barrels at some ethnic stores. You can also make your own sauerkraut, which is what we recommend. *Here's how to do it...*

## Ingredients and Supplies

> 1 large head of white cabbage (about 8 cups when shredded)
>
> 8 tsp sea salt
>
> 1 Tbsp caraway seeds or fresh or dried dill (optional)
>
> 1 large container (earthenware crock, glass bowl or stainless steel cookware)
>
> A cover or plate that fits snugly inside the above container
>
> A brick, a few stones or any 10-lb weight that's clean
>
> A cloth or towel that will fit over the container

## Preparation

Remove the large, loose outer leaves of the cabbage, rinse them and set aside for later. Core and finely shred the rest of the cabbage. Spread a layer of shredded cabbage (about 1 cup) on the bottom of the container. Sprinkle the layer with a teaspoon of sea salt and a few caraway seeds or dill. Repeat layering with shredded cabbage, salt and seeds, ending with a layer of salt. Place those loose outer leaves of cabbage over the top layer of salt.

Then, press the cabbage down with the plate or cover and place the 10-pound weight on top of it. Cover the entire container with a cloth or towel and set it aside in a warm place for seven to 12 days, depending on how strong you like your sauerkraut.

When it's ready, remove the weight and the plate. Throw away the leaves on top and skim off the yucky-looking mold. Transfer the sauerkraut to smaller glass jars with tight lids, and refrigerate them. The sauerkraut should keep this way for about a month. ■

# Six Sensational Superfoods

# Six Sensational Superfoods

H ippocrates, the famed Greek physician who is considered to be the father of medicine, said, "Let food be your medicine." Those wise words were considered revolutionary back in 400 BC. But today, those same words are being repeated by many health professionals.

After years of study and research, the scientific community now recognizes the great value of food that can be used for the prevention and treatment of just about every ailment. (Lots of examples are listed throughout the main "Remedies" section of this book.)

Supplement companies certainly realize the healing power of food—they've been extracting and processing beneficial food substances for years. These foods have been packaged as pills, pearles, capsules, powders, teas, tinctures, creams, gels and more.

With all due respect to the esteemed Dr. Hippocrates, we would like to paraphrase his timeless words of wisdom—to make them even more appropriate for the information contained in this section—"Let food help *prevent* your need for medicine."

## Decisions, Decisions

We considered several criteria for choosing the Six Sensational Superfoods. First and foremost, we decided that each one had to be extremely health-giving in many ways, readily available and—very important—affordable.

Then we narrowed down our list by selecting foods that most people eat, or at least are familiar with, but might not know how very healthful they are. That's how garlic, ginger, nuts and yogurt made our list. Four down and two to go.

We then thought of including foods that may need an introduction. In other words, if not for reading about them here, you might not have known about the big difference they can make in the way you eat and feel. That's how we decided to include flaxseed and bee pollen, which round out our Six Sensational Superfoods.

Eating these superfoods regularly can go a long way toward alleviating certain health conditions, preventing others and, in general, helping you overcome the shortcomings of your gene pool.

# Expand Your Healthy Horizons

Read about our Six Sensational Superfoods and consider working them into your daily diet. So as not to overwhelm yourself, add one or two of these foods each week, replacing one or two less health-giving foods. Try to be creative. Experiment with different ways to prepare the foods, try different brands and different varieties. Approach it as a rewarding adventure. It will be.

Hearty appetite!

# 1. Bee Pollen

The bee is awesome. Any engineer knows that, when you consider the size and shape of this creature, there is no way it should be able to fly. Honeybees are frequent flyers. Their flights from flower to flower are responsible for cross-pollination.

In case you don't remember learning about it in school, here's a quick refresher course—every flower produces pollen, which is the male reproductive element that is transferred by wind or insects (mostly bees) to fertilize the ovule of another flower. Each tiny grain of pollen (it takes tens of millions to fill a spoon) has the power to produce the seed that can eventually become a flower, a bush or a tree. The pollen that honeybees collect is called, appropriately, bee pollen.

## Quality, Color, Taste and What-for

"The honeybee instinctively collects only the freshest and most potent pollen from what's available," says James Hagemeyer, a beekeeper who works with Health from the Hive in Madisonville, Tennessee. "There are numerous varieties of flowers in bloom at any given time, so the pollen collection varies with the season, resulting in all colors of pollen (from white to black and every color in between) with differing and distinctive tastes—some sweet and some bitter. The overall taste of most pollen is slightly bitter."

Mr. Hagemeyer, or "Mr. Bee Pollen" as he is known in the beekeeping community, tells everyone who he encounters—"Although pollen is a food, not a drug, it shouldn't be eaten just because it tastes good—it should be eaten because it's good for you!"

## Nature's Perfect Food

Referred to as the most complete food in nature, bee pollen has all of the necessary nutrients needed for human survival—at least 18 of the 22 amino acids…more than a dozen vitamins—it's especially rich in B-complex, A, C, D and E…almost all known minerals…trace elements…11 enzymes or co-enzymes…and 14 beneficial fatty acids. Bee pollen contains the essence of every plant the bees visit, combined with digestive enzymes from the bees.

It's 35% proteins, 55% carbohydrates, 2% fatty acids, and 3% vitamins and minerals. That leaves 5% unaccounted for. That 5%, which science has not yet been able to isolate and identify, may be what's alluded to in whispers—"the magic of the bee" that makes bee pollen so powerful. (Unfortunately, there are no recipes that use bee pollen. But we have included a few honey recipes instead.)

## Pollen Power

According to Steve Schechter, ND, HHP, director of the Natural Healing Institute in Encinitas, California, more than 40 research studies document the therapeutic efficacy and safety of bee pollen. Clinical tests show that orally ingested bee pollen particles are rapidly and easily absorbed—they pass directly from the stomach into the blood stream.

Dr. Schechter's overview is that "Bee pollen rejuvenates your body, stimulates organs and glands, enhances vitality and brings about a longer life span."

**CAUTION:** People who have had an allergic reaction to bee stings or honey should consult their doctor before taking bee pollen.

Here are some specifics…

◆ *Bee pollen offers relief from allergies.* The pollen reduces the production of histamine, which can cause problems like hay fever. The pollen's protein can help the body build a natural defense against allergic reactions. To desensitize yourself, start taking bee pollen daily, a month or two before the start of hay fever season.

Do not confuse the pollen that the wind blows around, which is a cause of allergies, with bee pollen. The pollen collected by bees is heavier and stickier and, even though it will rarely cause allergy symptoms, it is best to begin taking it in very small amounts.

Start with just one or two granules the first day, and increase the amount daily until you reach your target dose.

◆ *If, at any time, you have an allergic reaction,* such as a rash, hives, wheezing or swollen lips, take ¼ to ½ teaspoon of baking soda in water along with an antihistamine, then seek medical attention immediately. Needless to say, discontinue taking bee pollen.

◆ *Bee pollen is used by many athletes to help increase their strength,* endurance, energy and speed. Pollen is said to help the body recover from exercise, bringing the breathing and heart rate back to normal more quickly.

◆ *Bee pollen can alleviate mental fatigue and improve alertness and concentration,* helping you remain focused for longer periods of time. It's reported that bee pollen improves the mental as well as the physical reactions of athletes.

◆ *Bee pollen has been known to promote fertility as well as sexual vitality.* Noel Johnson—a San Diego–based marathon runner who is in his 90s—credits bee pollen as one of the reasons for writing his autobiography, *A Dud at 70…A Stud at 80!*

◆ *"The skin becomes younger-looking,* less vulnerable to wrinkles, smoother and healthier with the use of honeybee pollen," according to dermatologist Lars-Erik Essen, MD, of Halsingborg, Sweden, who pioneered the use of bee products in treating skin conditions.

◆ *Studies show that food consumption is decreased by 15% to 20%* when bee pollen is taken daily with a glass of water (about 15 to 30 minutes before meals). Bee pollen is said to help correct an imbalance in the body's metabolism that may contribute to weight gain. It is thought that the lecithin in pollen speeds up the burning of calories. It also may assist in the digestive process and the assimilation of nutrients.

## ■ Recipe ■

### Honey Lemon Basil Chicken

½ cup honey

¼ cup lemon juice

4 boneless, skinless chicken breast
    halves

¼ cup diced basil leaves

1 tsp garlic powder

½ tsp salt

2 Tbsp lemon zest

Mix together all ingredients (except chicken) in a plastic bag. Add chicken and let marinate for at least two hours, refrigerated. Grill or bake at 350° F for 35 to 45 minutes or until juices run clear. Do not overcook. Makes 4 servings.

*Source:* Sue Bee Honey, a trademark of the Sioux Honey Association

◆ *Bee pollen protects against radiation's adverse effects,* and helps strengthen the immune system. In our environment, humans are exposed to radiation (radioactive toxins) and chemical pollutants, which are known to cumulatively stress our immune systems. According to Dr. Schechter's research, several nutrients in bee pollen—such as proteins, beneficial fats, vitamins B, C, D and E, as well as beta-carotene, calcium, magnesium, selenium, nucleic acids, lecithin and cysteine—have been scientifically proven to strengthen immunity, counteract the effects of radiation and chemical toxins and generate optimal health and vitality.

▶ In one research study, bee pollen significantly reduced the usual side effects of both radium and cobalt-60 radiotherapy in 25 women who had been treated for cancer. The women who took the pollen were considerably healthier, had stronger immune responses and reported feeling an improved sense of well-being. The dosage of bee pollen prescribed for these women was approximately 2 teaspoons taken three times per day.

☛ **WARNING:** This dosage should only be taken under the supervision of your health professional.

### Forms and Dosage

Bee pollen is available in gelatin caps, tablets and granules. We suggest the granules. We feel that the body absorbs the granules more efficiently, and they're less processed.

We like to take 1 teaspoon with water before each meal. If we need an extra boost in energy, we take another teaspoon during the day.

▶ Dr. Schechter reports that, for preventive purposes, a common adult dosage of bee pollen granules is initially ⅛ to ½ teaspoon once per day. The dosage is gradually increased to 1 to 2 teaspoons, taken one to three times per day.

⚡ **CAUTION:** Adults suffering from allergies are best advised to start off with 1 to 3 granules daily, and then gradually increase to higher doses, usually over a period of one month or more.

▶ If you prefer to take bee pollen capsules for preventive purposes, the suggested amount is two 450 to 580 mg capsules, taken three to four times daily. A short-term, therapeutic amount of bee pollen is about three times the preventive amount and should be taken only under the supervision of your health professional.

✎ **NOTE:** Be sure to buy bee pollen that comes from the US. Foreign pollens may be fumigated and baked.

▶ Bee pollen should not be heated in any way. It's best to keep it in the refrigerator. If, for economical reasons, you buy a large quantity, you can keep what you're not using in the freezer. James Hagemeyer told us that viable bee pollen was found in 5,000-year-old Egyptian tombs. If it kept that long in tombs, it should keep at least 1,000 years in your freezer!

### Bee Pollen for Animals

Have you noticed that some dogs seem to suffer from the same health challenges as humans? According to Janet Lipa, breeder of golden retrievers and owner of Golden Tails, a holistic food company for animals in Bowmanville, New York (*see* "Sources" on page 299), overvaccinating pets, particularly purebred dogs, may be responsible for the animals' health problems. Those annual inoculations may cause a buildup of toxins in the liver, compromising the immune system and making the animal more susceptible to illness.

Bee pollen can help boost an animal's immune system and help your pet get rid of allergies. Be sure to check with your veterinarian before giving your animal bee pollen or any natural supplement.

▶ For a 1,000-pound horse, mix 1 heaping tablespoon of bee pollen into the morning feeding, and repeat with the afternoon feeding.

■ **Recipe** ■

### Four-Bean Bake

    1 can baked beans
    1 can butter beans
    1 can lima beans
    1 can kidney beans
    1 small onion, chopped
    ½ lb bacon, cooked and cut up
    ½ lb browned hamburger
    ½ cup brown sugar
    1 cup honey
    1 cup ketchup
    2 Tbsp chili powder
    1 tsp dry mustard

Mix all ingredients in large saucepan and bring to a boil. Simmer on the stovetop, about 30 minutes. The mixture can also be baked at 350° F for 1 hour in a 9" x 13" pan instead.

*Source:* Sue Bee Honey, a trademark of the Sioux Honey Association

▶ For other animals, use ⅛ teaspoon per 15 pounds of body weight. Mix the bee pollen in with their food in the morning, and repeat with the afternoon feeding. Allow approximately 30 to 60 days to see results.

### Make a Beeline...

Your local beekeeper or health food store should sell bee pollen or have information on how you can obtain it. The "Sources" section on page 299 can also point you in the right direction, so that you can *bee all that you can bee.*

## ASSOCIATIONS

### American Apitherapy Society

This non-profit association is committed to encouraging the use of bee products for healthy living and researching the various restorative benefits of bee products.

> 5535 Balboa Blvd., Suite 225
> Encino, CA 91316
> Phone: 818-501-0446
> Fax: 818-995-9334
> *www.apitherapy.org*

### International Bee Research Association

Contact this non-profit organization to learn more about the vital roles bees play in our environment and in all our lives.

> 18 North Rd.
> Cardiff, Wales
> CF10 3DT United Kingdom
> Phone: +44-0-29-2037-2409
> Fax: +44-0-29-2066-5522
> *www.ibra.org.uk*

### The Honey Association

This organization provides a multitude of information on the beneficial qualities and uses of honey. The information is enhanced with recipes, honey facts and includes beauty and health uses for this nourishing food.

> c/o Grayling Group
> 1 Bedford Ave.
> London, England
> WC1B 3AU United Kingdom
> Phone: +44-0-20-7255-1100
> Fax: +44-0-20-7255-5454
> *www.honeyassociation.com*

## BOOKS

*Bee Pollen, Royal Jelly, Propolis, and Honey: An Extraordinary Energy and Health Promoting Ensemble,* by Rita Elkins. Woodland Publishing.

*Bee Well, Bee Wise: With Bee Pollen, Propolis and Royal Jelly,* by Bernard Jensen, PhD. Bernard Jensen Publishing.

*Bee Pollen,* by Jack Scagnetti, Lynda Lyngheim. Wilshire Book Company.

# 2. Flaxseed

People have been eating flaxseed for thousands of years. In the south—that is, southern Mesopotamia, circa 5,200 to 4,000 BC—records show that irrigation was used to grow flax. The Babylonians cultivated flaxseed as early as 3,000 BC and—wouldn't you know it—Hippocrates, the great Greek physician of the ancient world, used flaxseed for the relief of intestinal discomfort. He might have told his patients, "Take two tablespoons of flaxseed and call me in the morning."

Stephan Cunnane, PhD, a leading nutrition and brain-metabolism specialist at the Research Centre on Aging in Sherbrooke, Canada, said, "Flaxseed will be the nutraceutical food of the 21st century because of its multiple health benefits." *That makes sense to us, and here's why…*

## What's So Great About Flax?

Flax oil, which is processed from flaxseed, contains the highest concentration of *essential* omega-3 fatty acids of any source on the planet. A deficiency of omega-3 has been positively correlated with more than 60 illnesses, including arthritis, atherosclerosis, cancer, diabetes, hypertension (high blood pressure), immune disorders, menopausal discomfort and stroke. And so, adding omega-3 to your daily diet may go a long way in helping to prevent, improve or reverse those unhealthy conditions.

## ■ Recipe ■

### Pancake or Waffle Mix

1½ cups whole wheat flour, semolina grind

½ cup ground flaxseed

1½ cup pancake mix or all-purpose flour

¼ tsp baking powder (double if you use flour, not mix)

¼ tsp baking soda (double if you use flour, not mix)

1 Tbsp sugar

¼ tsp salt

2 Tbsp olive or canola oil

1 whole egg (or 2 egg whites)

3–4 cups (approx.) buttermilk to preferred consistency

Mix all ingredients. Pour pancakes on griddle or electric skillet at 375° F to 400° F, or cook waffles on waffle iron.

*Source:* Flax Institute of the United States

Flaxseed contains phytonutrients called lignans. Lignans are reported to have the following attributes—an estrogen-mimicking effect without the risks associated with estrogen therapy…powerful antioxidant capabilities…antiviral properties…antibacterial properties…and antifungal properties.

Studies suggest that lignans may help prevent many health problems, including breast and colon cancer, and can help lower cholesterol, regulate women's menstrual cycles and reduce or eliminate menopausal symptoms.

### Forms and Dosage

If you're thinking that flaxseed, in some form, should be part of your daily diet, we think it's a wise decision.

To help you decide which form(s) to take, you should know…

▶ Flaxseeds have hard outer shells. You can eat them as is after you've soaked the seeds in water overnight. Or, the most popular way to eat flaxseeds is to grind them in a spice or coffee grinder. Then sprinkle a tablespoon of the ground flax on your cereal, add it to a smoothie or mix it into a portion of fat-free yogurt or fat-free cottage cheese. When baking, you can replace a few tablespoons of your regular flour with this ground-flax flour.

▶ To make sure we get our daily dose of the omega-3 oils and lignans, we find it most convenient to take flax oil. We were advised to start with 2 tablespoons a day—one in the morning and one either in the afternoon or evening. Then, after a couple of months, regulate the daily dosage to 1 tablespoon of flax oil per every 100 pounds of body weight.

### Smooth Operator

▶ We also add the flax oil to a smoothie—it doesn't change the taste of the smoothie, it just keeps it from getting overly aerated, which is a good thing—or we mix flax oil into fat-free yogurt, along with a minced clove of garlic. It's delicious! We also use flax oil in a homemade salad dressing. There are lots of recipes using flax oil. (*See* the "Recommended Reading List" on page 319 for a flax oil cookbook.)

▶ When we first started looking for flax oil, we went to the refrigerated section of our local health food store and found Barlean's Flax Oil. (*See* "Natural Foods and More" listed in the "Sources" section on page 299.) It had all of the qualities we were looking for, including and especially "lignan rich." (Typically, lignans—the important phytoestrogens that may help prevent cancer—are not present in appreciable amounts in most flaxseed oils.)

Also, due to flaxseed oil's limited shelf life—it's an oil that can become rancid and should be kept refrigerated—we checked the "pressing date" and the "best before date," making sure they didn't exceed a four-month timespan.

## Your Life in the Balance

For those of you who want more of the whole picture of essential fatty acids in our body, Jade Beutler, RRT, RCP, San Diego–based CEO of Lignan Research LLC, and a licensed health-care practitioner, agreed to share some information with us.

Health, life and longevity critically rely on a delicate balance of two *essential* nutrients. The imbalance of these two vital nutrients is credited as possibly the leading cause of death and disability in America today.

Both omega-3, found abundantly in flax oil, and omega-6, found in a plethora of processed oils (including corn, safflower and sunflower), have been deemed as essential nutrients by the World Health Organization, headquartered in Geneva, Switzerland. As *essential* nutrients, we must get these essential fatty acids (EFAs) directly in the foods we eat or through nutritional supplementation. The body cannot manufacture them from other nutrients.

According to Artemis P. Simopoulos, MD, president of the Center for Genetics, Nutrition and Health in Washington, DC, "Throughout human history, omega-3 and omega-6 fatty acids have been ingested in near-perfect proportion. That is to say, roughly a 50/50 concentration.

"For millions of years, the equal ingestion of these two EFAs has created a delicate check-and-balance system within the body that is in control of, literally, thousands of metabolic functions. That means everything including immune function, cellular communication, insulin sensitivity and inflammatory response to hormone and steroid production. It is impossible for optimal health to be attained with a tissue imbalance of omega-3 to omega-6 fatty acids."

## Fooling Mother Nature?

"Within the last 100 years, coinciding with the industrial revolution, has come the processing of seeds that are dominant in omega-6 oils," explains Mr. Beutler.

These oils, once ingested moderately in the diet, are now ingested disproportionately as vegetable oil and in the fried and processed foods that contain them.

Removing natural omega-3 fatty acids from the food chain has compounded the problem. Food manufacturers were quick to find out that omega-3 fatty acids greatly diminished the desired shelf life of one to two years. Therefore, omega-3s are either removed from the food or avoided entirely.

Modern methods of animal husbandry call on the predominant use of omega-6 dominant seeds and oils to *fatten up* the livestock for slaughter. As a result, animal meats that once provided a concentrated source of omega-3 are

## ■ Recipe ■

### Flax Cookies

1 cup buttermilk

½ cup applesauce

½ cup canola or olive oil

2 whole eggs (or 4 egg whites)

1 tsp vanilla extract

1 cup brown sugar

½ cup granulated sugar

½ tsp salt

1 tsp baking soda

1 tsp cinnamon

1 cup raisins and chocolate chips
    (combined)

1½ cups all-purpose flour

1 cup ground flaxseed

3 cups quick Quaker Oats

Preheat oven to 350° F. Mix and beat all wet ingredients with sugar, salt, soda and cinnamon. Add raisins and chips, then add flour, flaxseed and quick oats. If necessary, gradually add more milk or water to get a "flowing" dough. Drop by teaspoons onto a cookie sheet and bake for 15 to 18 minutes.

*Source:* Flax Institute of the United States

now nearly completely devoid of it, although they teem with omega-6.

## Consequences and Conclusions

Beutler's research has led him to the realization that, "The mass ingestion of omega-6 at the expense of omega-3 has created a drastic shift in human biophysiology."

In addition, Japanese researchers, after reviewing more than 500 studies, concluded, "The evidence indicates that increased dietary linoleic acid (omega-6) and relative omega-3 deficiency are major risk factors for Western-type cancers, cardiovascular and cerebrovascular diseases, and also for allergic hyper-reactivity. We also raise the possibility that a relative omega-3 deficiency may be affecting the behavioral patterns of a proportion of the young generations in industrialized countries."

## Getting Back to Balance

Dr. Simopoulos believes that it would take the human body one million years to adapt to the drastic shift in ingestion of omega-3 to omega-6 fatty acids that has occurred in only the last 100 years.

"The implication is clear," says Mr. Beutler. "And so is the solution. We must consciously shift the omega-3/omega-6 balance by supplementing our diet with omega-3 to avert otherwise certain degenerative disease."

As mentioned before—flax oil contains the highest concentration of essential omega-3 fatty acids of any source on the planet.

### ASSOCIATIONS
#### AmeriFlax

This association promotes healthy living through flaxseed products. The site is a treasure trove of flaxseed information—it describes the benefits of flaxseed, offers recipes, gives locations where flaxseed products are available, provides nutrition information and more.

3015 Highway 25
Mandan, ND 58554
Phone: 701-663-9799
Fax: 701-663-6574
*www.ameriflax.com*

**Flax Institute of the United States**

The Web site for the Institute offers contacts for obtaining flaxseed, recipes that use this nutritional food, information on the Institute's work and more.

Department of Plant Sciences
North Dakota State University
Box 5051
Fargo, ND 58105
Phone: 701-231-7973
*www.ndsu.nodak.edu/flaxinst/*

**Flax Council of Canada**

Provides fun flaxseed facts for consumers, as well as more specialized information for nutritionists, dietitians, food producers, manufacturers and flax growers.

465-167 Lombard Ave.
Winnipeg, Manitoba
Canada, R3B 0T6
Phone: 204-982-2115
Fax: 204-942-1841
*www.flaxcouncil.ca*

**BOOKS**

*Flaxseed Oil: The Premiere Source of Omega-3 Fatty Acids,* by Rita Elkins, Kate Gilbert Udal. Woodland Publishing.

*Flaxseed (Linseed) Oil and the Power of Omega-3,* by Ingeborg Johnston, James R. Johnston. McGraw-Hill.

*The Flax Cookbook: Recipes and Strategies for Getting the Most from the Most Powerful Plant on the Planet,* by Elaine Magee. Marlowe & Company.

# 3. Garlic

When it comes to garlic, we wrote the book. No, we really did! This comprehensive tome is appropriately titled *Garlic: Nature's Super Healer* (Prentice Hall). In the book, we talk about how you can use the healing power of garlic for more than 90 ailments.

Garlic is a natural antibiotic with antiviral, antifungal, anticoagulant and antiseptic properties. It can act as an expectorant and decongestant, antioxidant, germicide, anti-inflammatory agent, diuretic and sedative, and it is believed to contain cancer-preventive chemicals. It's also said to be an aphrodisiac, but you must find a partner who likes garlic.

**CAUTION:** Do not eat raw garlic or take garlic supplements if you have a bleeding disorder or ulcers, or are taking anticoagulants.

## Why the Smell?

Once a garlic clove is bruised in any way (cut, crushed, mashed, pressed, diced, sliced or minced), there is a highly complex conversion process that occurs in which allicin is formed and spontaneously decomposes into a group of odoriferous compounds. This is also what provides much of garlic's medicinal punch.

## How to Eat Raw Garlic

Using garlic in cooking is fine, but when garlic is heated, it loses some of its health-giving power. Garlic gurus agree that *raw* garlic does the most good as an antibiotic and as preventive medicine.

**CAUTION:** Eating too much raw garlic can cause headaches, diarrhea, gas, fever and, in extreme cases, gastric bleeding. This garlic is strong stuff! Do not overdo it.

## The Power of Two

▶ The most delicious and soothing way to eat raw garlic is to mix a minced clove into a dollop of plain, nonfat yogurt or fat-free cottage cheese. Yes, it tastes good!

After reading the information on flax, you may also want to mix in a tablespoon of flax oil, making it an extremely healthy snack.

Anna Maria Clement, co-director and chief health administrator of the Hippocrates Health Institute in West Palm Beach, Florida, recommends a variation. She says to put a tablespoon of ground flaxseed in a glass of water and leave it overnight. In the morning, the flaxseed water will have a viscous consistency. Stir it and drink up. It will protect your stomach so that you can eat a clove or two of raw garlic.

## Raw Garlic Made Easy

▶ The more we research and write about the benefits of garlic, the more garlic we want to eat! And we found a way to eat it so that we

### Shopping for Garlic

- ◆ Buy bulbs that are sold loose rather than packaged so that you can see and feel them.
- ◆ The papery, outer skin should be taut and unbroken.
- ◆ Beware of sprouting green shoots, discoloration, mold, rot (feel for soft spots) or shriveling. When garlic gets old, it dries out, its flavor dissipates and it becomes bitter.
- ◆ Look for garlic bulbs that are plump, solid and heavy for their size.
- ◆ A bulb has anywhere from eight to 40 cloves. The average is about 15 cloves. Look for bulbs that have large cloves so you can cut down on peeling time.

don't walk around with garlic breath. We mince the garlic cloves and drink them down in some water or orange juice. As long as we don't chew the little pieces of garlic, the smell doesn't linger on our breath. Chewing a sprig of fresh parsley also helps.

And you can put a minced clove of garlic in applesauce, yogurt or sour cream. It's delicious that way, and no one will know that you just ate raw garlic.

▶ Brian Clement, director of the Hippocrates Health Institute in West Palm Beach, Florida, says to take a big bite of an apple (organic, of course). Make sure to chew it thoroughly, letting the apple's pectin get around your mouth before swallowing. Then pop a raw garlic clove. There shouldn't be any burning, thanks to the enzymes and pectin in the apple.

▶ Minced garlic in applesauce is a tasty, painless way to eat raw garlic.

### ■ Recipe ■

### Roasted Garlic

Peel outer skin layer from head of fresh garlic, leaving cloves and head intact. Place head on double thickness of aluminum foil. Top with 1 teaspoon butter and a sprig of fresh rosemary or oregano (or ¼ teaspoon dried). Fold up and seal. Bake in a 375° F oven for 55 to 60 minutes. Squeeze cloves from skins and discard skins. Spread the garlic on crusty bread.

*Source:* The Gutsy Gourmet

## ■ Recipe ■

### *Mashed Sweet Potatoes with Garlic*

5 lbs sweet potatoes/yams (about 8), roasted

2 heads garlic, roasted (*see* recipe, page 267)

1 tsp olive oil

1 cup soy margarine

1 cup milk

3 cups vegetarian chicken broth (available at health food stores)

Salt and pepper to taste

Cut the sweet potatoes in half and, into a bowl, scoop out the potato from the skins. Squeeze the roasted garlic pulp into the bowl and mash with olive oil. Add margarine, milk and enough broth to give the mixture a light consistency. Season with salt and pepper, and serve. Makes 6 servings.

*Source: Garlic: Nature's Super Healer*

▶ A fast and easy way to peel a clove of garlic is to pound the clove with a blunt object—the side of a heavy knife, a rolling pin or the bottom of a jar.

▶ You can also sprinkle raw, minced garlic on a salad, or prepare dressing with it.

### *Storing Garlic*

Store garlic bulbs away from any heat source like a stove or the sun. A cool, dry, dark place is ideal, and in an open container, a crock with ventilation holes or a net bag that allows air to circulate around them.

## ■ Recipe ■

### *Pasta with Zucchini and Roasted Garlic*

1 lb pasta (rotini, twists or spirals), uncooked

8 medium cloves of garlic, peeled

½ tsp dried thyme

½ tsp dried rosemary, crushed

2 Tbsp vegetable oil

3 medium zucchini, coarsely grated (about 5–6 cups)

Salt and ground pepper to taste

Preheat oven or toaster oven to 450° F. Lay a 12"-square piece of tinfoil on the counter, and put the garlic on it. Sprinkle the thyme and rosemary over the garlic. Then pour the vegetable oil over the garlic and herbs. Draw up the edges of the foil and make a sealed package, and bake for 20 minutes.

While the garlic is baking, cook the pasta according to package directions. Two minutes before the pasta is done, add the grated zucchini to the pasta's cooking water. Cook for 2 minutes, then drain the zucchini and pasta.

When the garlic is ready, open the foil package, and mash the garlic and herbs lightly with a spoon. Toss mixture into the pasta and zucchini, then season with salt and pepper to taste. Makes 4 servings.

*Source: Garlic: Nature's Super Healer*

Do not freeze uncooked garlic. Its consistency will break down and it will emit an awful, ungarlicky smell.

Homemade preparations containing garlic-in-oil must be refrigerated. Put a date on the label. Do not keep it longer than two weeks! Rancid oil can be dangerous.

## Garlic Supplements

Commercial supplements should not be chosen by impressive advertising campaigns, and expensive pills are not necessarily better.

"Basically, it's a consumer-beware market for garlic supplements," believes Elizabeth Somer, MA, RD, a nationally recognized dietician and nutritionist. "Some garlic products have 33 times more of certain compounds than other garlic products. Unless the label lists specific amounts (per capsule or tablet) of the active ingredients, such as allicin, S-allyl-cysteine, ajoene, dialyl sulfides or at least total sulfur content, then assume the product is 'condiment grade' and no better or worse than garlic powder seasoning—just a lot more expensive." We think it's important that the label says "allicin" or "allicin potential" and lists one or more of the other active ingredients.

The late Varro E. Tyler, dean emeritus of the School of Pharmacy and professor of pharmacognosy (drugs made from natural sources) at Purdue University in West Layfayette, Indiana, told us that *enteric-coated* garlic supplements are recommended for the maximum absorption of allicin. A supplement that is enteric-coated resists the effects of stomach acid and allows the intestinal enzymes to dissolve it so that the full benefit of the supplement is obtained. Check labels for the words "enteric-coated" as well as "allicin."

### ■ Recipe ■

### Garlic Soup

3 cups vegetable broth
1 head garlic, peeled
2 potatoes, cubed
1½ cups carrots, chopped
½ cup evaporated milk plus ½ cup water (combined)
Ground pepper and hot sauce to taste

Simmer the broth, garlic, potatoes and carrots in a covered pot for 20 minutes. Purée in a food processor when cool. Season with ground pepper and hot sauce, then add enough of the milk/water mixture to reach your idea of the perfect soup consistency. Heat and serve with croutons.

*Source: Garlic: Nature's Super Healer*

## ASSOCIATIONS

### The Garlic Seed Foundation

This is an association for people who love garlic—growing it, marketing it and testing its durability as a crop. The Foundation's Web site provides the dates and locations for garlic festivals around the country, publishes a newsletter for garlic fans and more.

c/o Rose Valley Farm
Rose, NY 14542-0149
Phone: 315-587-9787
*www.garlicseedfoundation.info*

### Gilroy Garlic Festival Association, Inc.

Located in California, the leader of the garlic-growing states, the Gilroy Garlic Festival uses its annual celebratory garlic festival to benefit local charities.

Box 2311
7473 Monterey St.
Gilroy, CA 95020
Phone: 408-842-1625
*www.gilroygarlicfestival.com*

### American Botanical Council

As a distinguished international research organization, the American Botanical Council uses
education to promote the safe and beneficial
use of herbal medicine. A great informational
resource!

6200 Manor Rd.
Austin, TX 78723
Phone: 512-926-4900
Fax: 512-926-2345
*www.herbalgram.org*

### Herb Research Foundation

The HRF is the world's first and foremost
source of accurate, scientific data on the health
benefits and safety of herbs—including garlic.

4140 15th St.
Boulder, CO 80304
Phone: 303-449-2265
Voicemail: 800-748-2617
Fax: 303-449-7849
*www.herbs.org*

### Gourmet Garlic Gardens

For anyone interested in learning more about
garlic, this site contains articles on everything
from tips on growing garlic to how garlic works
in the human body. There are several links
where consumers can order different varieties
of garlic as well as other garlic-related products.

12300 FM 1176
Bangs, TX 76823
Phone: 325-348-3049
*www.gourmetgarlicgardens.com*

### BOOKS

*The Garlic Cure,* by James F. Scheer, Lynn Allison,
Charlie Fox. McCleery and Sons Publishing.

*Garlic, Garlic, Garlic: Exceptional Recipes for the
World's Most Indispensable Ingredient,* by Linda
Griffith, Fred Griffith. Houghton Mifflin Co.

*Honey, Garlic & Vinegar: Home Remedies &
Recipes: The People's Guide to Nature's Wonder
Medicines,* by Patrick Quillin. Leader Company.

*Garlic: Nature's Super Healer,* by Joan Wilen,
Lydia Wilen. Prentice Hall.

## 4. Ginger

What are friends for? To share their expertise
with you and your readers—that is, if you're
lucky enough to be friends with someone like
Paul Schulick, master herbalist, founder and
CEO of NewChapter (*www.new-chapter.com*)
in Brattleboro, Vermont, and a leading authority on ginger, one of our Six Sensational
Superfoods. *He told us the following story…*

"Doctor," said the imaginary patient, "I
have a host of serious problems." The doctor
listened very carefully and compassionately
(remember, this is make-believe) as the patient
recounted his ailments.

"Doctor, I think I have parasites, and they
make me nauseated all the time. In addition,
my family has a history of colon cancer, and I
have some blood in my stool. And I suppose I
could handle that, but I feel feverish, and my
joints constantly ache. I started out this year at
5' 7", and I think I must be shrinking. Also, my
cholesterol is elevated, and I was taking aspirin
to avoid blood clotting, but it tore my stomach
up. I think I now have ulcers! Doctor, what
should I take? And don't prescribe too much,
because my memory is not what it used to be."

## ■ Recipe ■

### Ginger Cookies

1 tsp baking soda

½ cup boiling water

1 cup granulated sugar

1 cup melted butter

½ tsp salt

1 cup dark molasses

½ tsp ginger

½ tsp cloves

1 tsp cinnamon

1 egg

3 cups flour

Dissolve baking soda in the boiling water. Mix all other ingredients together. Roll thin. Cut dough with cookie cutter. Bake at 325° F until light brown. Watch carefully, though...these cookies brown very quickly.

*Source: www.recipegoldmine.com*

## Did You Know?

**G**inger *potentiates* or increases the power of other herbs, so it is valuable to use with green tea, echinacea, ginseng and kava.

Most recently, a new extract of ginger called a "Supercritical Extract" has become available, which allows you to take a powerful and pure concentrate (up to 250:1) of the healing, pungent compounds.

*See* page 274 for more information on forms and dosage.

The doctor listened to this patient and then told him about the medicinal power of one herb that might just be the answer for all his problems. The doctor told the story of *Zingiber officinale*, commonly known as "ginger." This common herb, really a rhizome (edible root), has some profound and scientifically well-documented healing properties. The doctor told the patient to listen, but not to worry about memorizing the features. *They are...*

- ◆ Antiparasitic (against schistosoma mansoni, anisakis and dirofilaria immitis).

- ◆ Antibacterial (against staph, E. coli, salmonella and strep) and antiviral.

- ◆ Anti-emetic (for relief from nausea) that is more effective than the prescription drug metoclopramide.

- ◆ Antimutagenic (cancer preventative) against COX-2 related cancers (such as colon, pancreas, skin, esophageal), leukemia and multiple tumor growth factors.

- ◆ Balances and modulates inflammatory hormones associated with arthritis.

- ◆ Balances and modulates the enzyme 5-lipoxygenase, which is associated with prostate and breast cancers, bone resorption (osteoporosis) and conditions of inflammation. (There are 22 identified 5-lipoxygenase inhibitors.)

- ◆ Inhibits the COX-2 enzyme associated with brain inflammation and with the neuronal death in Alzheimer's disease. (There are three known COX-2 inhibitors—melatonin, kaempferol and curcumin.)

## ■ Recipe ■

### *Ginger–Onion Vinaigrette*

¼ cup extra-virgin olive oil

1 cup very fine strips of white leeks

1 small red onion, finely chopped

12 whole fresh green onions, thinly
sliced

1 tsp finely chopped fresh garlic in oil

2 medium shallots, skinned and finely
chopped

1 cup red wine vinegar

1 cup chicken stock or broth

1 tsp fresh ginger, peeled and finely
grated

1 tsp finely chopped crystallized
ginger

2 cups mayonnaise

Kosher salt to taste

Dash of cracked black pepper

Heat olive oil in a large sauté pan.
When the oil is hot, sauté the leeks, red and
green onion, garlic and shallots until they
are about half done. Remove from the heat,
then add the red wine vinegar. Return to
the heat. This will help de-glaze the pan.
Add chicken stock, fresh and crystallized
ginger and bring the mixture to a boil.
Cook until the liquid has been reduced by
half. Remove from heat and let cool at room
temperature for at least 15 minutes.

In a large bowl, combine cooked
mixture and all other ingredients. Taste. If it
is too vinegary, add just a touch of sugar.
Additional salt and pepper may also be
added to your taste.

*Source: www.recipegoldmine.com*

◆ Powerful antioxidant that enhances
the potency of other antioxidants.
Contains at least 12 known anti-aging
constituents that deactivate destructive free radicals.

◆ Wound healing and anti-ulcerative.
Contains more wound-healing compounds than any other botanical.

◆ Aphrodisiac.

◆ Antihistamine.

◆ Powerful digestive enzyme—ginger
has 180 times the protein-digesting
power of papaya.

◆ Supports the growth of beneficial bacteria in the large intestine, specifically
Lactobacillus plantarum, by a factor
of five.

◆ Modulates thromboxane, the hormone
responsible for blood platelet aggregation and blood clotting, thus protecting
against heart attack and stroke. More
effective in this respect than garlic.

◆ Reverses the inflammation associated
with rheumatoid arthritis more effectively than prescription drugs, according to international medical research.

◆ Increases bile secretion for better fat
metabolism.

◆ Lowers serum cholesterol.

◆ Contains 11 sedative compounds,
more than any other spice.

The patient listened with astonishment.
"Do you mean to tell me that *one drug* can do
all that?"

The doctor replied, "No, I am not talking
about a drug. Remember, I am that rare MD
who is open to the phytomedicinal power of

## ■ Recipe ■

### Sautéed Tofu with Ginger Sauce

*Ginger Sauce*

6 Tbsp rice vinegar

6 Tbsp granulated sugar

¾ cup plus 1 Tbsp water

2 Tbsp soy sauce

1 tsp cornstarch

1 Tbsp finely minced gingerroot

In small saucepan, combine vinegar, sugar, ¾ cup water and soy sauce. Bring to a boil, reduce heat and simmer, stirring occasionally, for 5 minutes.

Meanwhile, in a small bowl, combine cornstarch and 1 tablespoon water—then stir into sauce. Cook mixture, stirring, until clear and thickened. Remove pan from heat, and stir in ginger. Makes 1 cup of sauce.

*Tofu*

½ lb firm tofu

½ cup unbleached flour

2 Tbsp toasted wheat germ

½ tsp thyme

¼ tsp dill weed

¼ tsp garlic powder

¼ tsp paprika

¼ tsp black pepper

1 whole egg (or 2 egg whites)

1 Tbsp milk

3 drops hot pepper sauce

2 Tbsp safflower oil

While ginger sauce is simmering, cut tofu into 1" squares about ¼" thick. Set aside. In a medium bowl, combine flour, wheat germ and seasonings.

In a separate bowl, lightly beat egg. Add milk and hot pepper sauce. In a large skillet, heat oil. Piece by piece, dip tofu in flour, then in egg mixture and again in flour. Sauté until lightly browned, about 3 minutes on each side.

Serve warm, arranged on a platter with cocktail forks and a bowl of ginger sauce. Surround platter with curly lettuce leaves or large sprigs of parsley. Makes 4 to 6 servings.

*Source: www.recipegoldmine.com*

healing botanicals. I am talking about 'ginger,' which is absolutely NOT a drug. A drug has one synthetic molecule, and ginger has at least 477 natural compounds, all working together to promote safe and balanced healing."

This conversation may never have occurred in any MD's office that you have visited, but people are talking about ginger. Its popularity is long overdue. For thousands of years, ginger has been known in Ayurvedic medicine as *vishwabhesaj*, the Universal Medicine. It is said

that legendary Chinese sage and philosopher Confucius (551–479 BC) considered no meal complete without ginger…it was considered to be the Alka-Seltzer of the Roman Empire…and it was so valuable to Arab traders that purchasers were told that ginger came from the mythical kingdom of Xanadu so as to hide its true origins. And to top it all off, its invigorating taste has stimulated palates and calmed stomachs for thousands of years. High-quality ginger remains a prized commodity.

## Forms and Dosage

There are several ways to enjoy the benefits of ginger. Fresh ginger is delightful, but it is important to use organic ginger, because *conventional* (often better described as *chemically grown*) ginger is often heavily fumigated.

▶ Ginger can be purchased both dried and ground, which is an excellent way to obtain the intestinal and protein-digesting benefits of this whole-fiber herb. Extracts are available of the fresh ginger juice, which can be used to make hot or cold teas or ginger ales.

But most important, organic ginger belongs in your daily life, for it is simply one of the finest (if not the finest) daily tonics available from the botanical world.

## ASSOCIATIONS
### American Botanical Council

As a distinguished international research organization, the American Botanical Council uses education to promote the safe and beneficial use of herbal medicine. A great informational resource!

6200 Manor Rd.
Austin, TX 78723
Phone: 512-926-4900
Fax: 512-926-2345
*www.herbalgram.org*

### Herb Research Foundation

The HRF is the world's first and foremost source of accurate, scientific data on the health benefits and safety of herbs—including ginger.

4140 15th St.
Boulder, CO 80304
Phone: 303-449-2265
Voicemail: 800-748-2617
Fax: 303-449-7849
*www.herbs.org*

### The Ginger People

This Web site was created by Royal Pacific, an innovative, quality-oriented and environmentally conscious ginger producer. Learn about all things ginger and get ginger-related information, recipes, products, tips and more.

2700 Garden Rd., Suite G
Monterey, CA 93940
Phone: 800-551-5284
Fax: 831-645-1094
*www.gingerpeople.com*

## BOOKS

*Ginger: Common Spice and Wonder Drug,* by Paul Schulick. Hohm Press.

*A Spoonful of Ginger: Irresistible Health-Giving Recipes from Asian Kitchens,* by Nina Simonds. Knopf.

# 5. Nuts

Nuts! For years, neither of us ate nuts. We love nuts, but they're very high in fat. And then, one day in the mid-1990s, we read an article extolling the health-giving properties of nuts—fat and all. What a wonderful surprise! The article reported the findings of a research team at Loma Linda University's School of Public Health in Loma Linda, California. The research team was headed by Joan Sabaté, MD, DrPH, professor and chair of the School's department of nutrition.

We immediately called the university and got another surprise. Dr. Joan Sabaté is a man—"Joan" being a man's name in Spain and Portugal—and, lucky for us, one who was willing to share his research.

### Results of the Studies

Starting in the mid-1970s, a team of epidemiologists at Loma Linda followed the eating habits of more than 25,000 Seventh Day Adventists. At the end of 10 years, the researchers found that there was only one common food linked to good health—nuts.

Dr. Sabaté said, "The results couldn't have been more striking. People who ate nuts often—five or more times a week—were half as likely to have a heart attack or die of heart disease as people who rarely or never ate them. Eating nuts just one to four times a week cuts the heart risk by 25%." The doctor said it did not matter if people were slim or fat, young or old, active or sedentary.

Dr. Sabaté conducted his own study with two groups of people. Both groups ate a typical cholesterol-lowering diet from the American Heart Association (*www.americanheart.com*)—the kind that doctors would recommend.

In addition to the food that was allowed on the diet, one group ate 2 to 3 ounces of walnuts daily and the other group ate no walnuts. The cholesterol levels went down in both groups, but more so among the walnut eaters. Their blood cholesterol levels dropped 22 points in just a few weeks.

Many studies of the effects of nuts have been done—an almond study at the Health Research and Studies Center in Los Altos, California…a walnut study at the University of California at San Francisco…a Harvard Nurses' Study conducted by the Harvard School of Public Health in Boston, Massachusetts, that tracked 86,000 nurses…a Harvard Physicians' Health study with 22,000 doctors…another study with 31,000 vegetarians…and still another with 40,000 postmenopausal women.

The results all point to the same conclusion—nuts are a health-giving superfood!

### Health Benefits—in a Nutshell

All nuts contain flavonoids, which are potent antioxidants that help protect the body against cancer and heart disease.

Nuts are one of the best sources of vitamin E. They also have B vitamins—thiamine, niacin, folic acid and riboflavin. Most nuts are rich in potassium, which is needed to help regulate blood pressure and heart rate. Nuts are also a good source of the fatigue- and stress-fighting minerals iron, magnesium and zinc. (Almonds and pecans are particularly rich in magnesium…cashews and pecans are rich in zinc.)

Nuts are packed with the antioxidants selenium and copper. (Brazil nuts are particularly rich in selenium…cashews, filberts and walnuts are rich in copper.)

In the 16th and 17th centuries, it was thought that various foods helped heal the body parts that they resembled. And so, our ancestors believed that walnuts helped the head and brain. They may have been right. Copper, an essential mineral for maintenance of the nervous system *and* brain activity, is found in many types of nuts.

Most nuts also have some calcium, but almonds have more than any other nut. Brazil nuts and filberts also have substantial amounts of calcium.

One ounce of nuts gives you as much fiber as two slices of whole wheat bread. Almonds have the highest dietary fiber content of any nut.

Nut protein is loaded with the amino acid arginine, known to protect arteries from injury and to stop blood clots from forming.

### ■ Recipe ■

## Walnut Macaroni Casserole

1 Tbsp salt

8 oz elbow macaroni

2 cups (one 16-oz can) canned
tomatoes

½ tsp low-sodium baking soda

1 cup (one 8-oz can) tomato sauce

1¼ cups low-fat cottage cheese

¼ cup grated parmesan cheese

1 (10-oz) package frozen chopped
spinach, thawed and squeezed dry

1½ cups frozen peas, thawed

1 tsp dried basil

½ tsp pepper

¾ cup toasted* walnuts, chopped

2 Tbsp parsley, chopped

Salt to taste

Preheat the oven to 350° F. Bring about 6 quarts of water to a boil with 1 tablespoon salt. Add the macaroni and cook, stirring occasionally, for about 8 minutes or until done.

While the macaroni is cooking, place the tomatoes and their juice into a large bowl. Add the baking soda and, with a fork or your fingers, break the tomatoes into small chunks. Stir in the tomato sauce. Add the cottage cheese, parmesan cheese, spinach, peas, basil and pepper, and toss to combine—set aside.

When the macaroni is done, drain well in a colander. Add to the cheese mixture, toss to mix thoroughly, then pour into an oiled 2¼-quart baking dish.

Cover the baking dish with aluminum foil and bake the casserole for 20 minutes. Then uncover and bake 10 minutes longer. Stir in the walnuts and sprinkle with parsley. Makes 6 servings.

*Toasting walnuts is optional

*Source:* Walnut Marketing Board

Nuts contain phytochemicals (plant sterols or phytosterols, which help lower cholesterol and are thought to protect against colon cancer)…antioxidants (which help to protect against heart disease and cancer)… saponins (which help lower cholesterol and also show evidence of having anticancer properties) …and phytic acid or phytate (which has been found to be protective against colon cancer).

Here are some nutty facts (in case you're ever on a TV game show)…

◆ The oldest food tree known to humankind is the walnut tree. It dates back to 7,000 BC.

◆ The nut with the highest fat content (over 70%) is the pecan.

◆ Cashew shells are thick, leathery and have a blackish-brown oil that causes human skin to blister in a way similar to poison ivy.

◆ You may know that filberts are also called hazelnuts, but do you know another name for them? Cobnuts.

◆ Brazil nuts have the hardest shell of all nuts. Before cracking them—or any hard-shell nut—put them in the freezer for six hours. The deep-freeze makes the shells much easier to crack.

## ■ Recipe ■

### New West Crab Cakes

1 lb crabmeat, picked over

2 egg whites

1 egg yolk

¾ lb mashed potatoes (instant may be used)

⅓ cup chopped red onions or chives

Pinch of salt

½ cup walnuts, chopped

1 cup bread crumbs

Combine crabmeat, egg whites, egg yolk, potatoes, onions, salt, ¼ cup chopped walnuts and ½ cup bread crumbs in a bowl. Form mixture into 8 flat patties. Mix together remaining ½ cup of bread crumbs and finely chopped walnuts. Coat crab patties with bread crumb mixture. Cook over medium heat in skillet with brushed oil.

Serve with lemon wedges or fresh tomato relish made with chopped green and yellow peppers, red onion and diced, seeded tomatoes, seasoned to taste (or you may substitute already prepared salsa).

*Source:* Walnut Marketing Board

---

◆ Peanuts are really legumes (related to beans and peas), but are nutritionally similar to nuts.

◆ Nuts in their shells stay fresh twice as long as shelled nuts. If kept in a cool, dry place, raw, unshelled nuts can keep for six months to a year. But why would you want to keep them that long? Eat 'em now!

## Dosage

Nuts have helped us change the way we think of fats. We now know that there are good fats—the unsaturated fats—which are found in flaxseed, cold-water fish, avocado and, of course, in nuts.

Dr. Sabaté told us that 1 to 2 ounces of either almonds, cashews, pistachios, walnuts or even peanuts five times a week is a heart-healthy amount to eat.

## How to Eat Nuts

▶ Be sure the nuts are raw, except for peanuts. (Most of the recipes included here contain nuts that are cooked or roasted…these treats should be consumed in moderation.) Organically grown nuts are always preferred. Stay away from the red-dyed (how and why did *that* get started?) and salted pistachios.

If you want peanut butter, the best is the natural kind you grind yourself or that you can get from a health food store. Avoid commercially prepared peanut butter with all its additives and preservatives.

▶ For optimum health, don't just add nuts to your diet. Let nuts take the place of saturated, unhealthy fat. Cut back on meat, cheese and deep-fried foods. Keep working your way toward a predominantly plant-based diet.

▶ The late Gene Spiller, PhD, director of the Health Research and Studies Center in Los

## ■ Recipe ■

### Pecan Four-Cheese Pizza

1 12" prepared pizza crust
1 Tbsp olive oil
2 large onions, sliced
3 Tbsp goat cheese, softened
3 Tbsp cream cheese, softened
½ cup feta cheese, crumbled
1 cup shredded mozzarella cheese
⅔ cup pecans, coarsely chopped
Chopped parsley for garnish

Preheat oven to 450° F. Place pizza crust on cookie sheet. In frying pan, heat oil. Add onions and cook slowly until caramelized, about 20 minutes. Cool slightly. Mix the goat cheese and cream cheese together and spread on crust, then spread the cooked onions over the cheese. Sprinkle the feta and mozzarella cheeses over the onions, and top with the pecan pieces. Bake for about 5 minutes or until cheeses melt.

Sprinkle parsley over top before serving. Cut into 6 wedges to serve. Makes 2 to 3 servings.

*Source:* National Pecan Shellers Association

## ■ Recipe ■

### Hazelnut Corn Bran Muffins

1 cup milk
½ cup bran flakes
¼ cup (½ stick) butter
3 Tbsp brown sugar
1 egg, room temperature
1 tsp oil
1 cup white flour
½ cup cornmeal
½ cup hazelnuts, roasted and chopped
2 tsp baking powder
½ tsp salt

Combine milk and bran flakes in medium bowl and let stand at room temperature 8 hours or overnight. Preheat oven to 400° F. Grease 12 2½" muffin tins. Cream butter with sugar in large bowl. Stir in egg and oil, blending well. Fold in flour, cornmeal, hazelnuts, baking powder, salt and bran mixture until dry ingredients are just moist. Divide batter in muffin tins. Bake about 20 to 25 minutes or until tester comes out clean. Cool 7 minutes. Makes 12 muffins.

*Source:* Oregon Hazelnut Industry

Altos, California, believed that nuts are so nutrient-rich that they quell hunger pangs. It's possible that by eating a few nuts, you won't want to eat as much of everything else.

▶ A nutritionist/spokesperson for Weight Watchers (*www.weightwatchers.com*) said that the problem with nuts is that once you start eating them…too much of a good thing is no longer a good thing. So the bottom line is—try not to go nuts!

## ASSOCIATIONS

### Northern Nut Growers Association

The NNGA is a great resource for information on nut tree–growing. This national non-profit organization has a library that contains many articles and research papers on nuts and how

### ■ Recipe ■

#### *Cashew Shrimp*

1 lb medium shrimp
1 Tbsp plus 1 tsp cornstarch
¼ tsp granulated sugar
¼ tsp baking soda
¼ tsp salt
⅛ tsp pepper
½ cup vegetable oil
½ cup onions, chopped
¼ cup red peppers, chopped
1 clove garlic
1 cup unpeeled zucchini, chopped
3½ cups cooked rice
¾ cup cashews
Sweet red pepper rings

Cut shrimp in half lengthwise. Combine cornstarch, sugar, baking soda, salt and pepper. Mix well. Add shrimp and toss gently to coat. Let stand 15 minutes.

Heat oil in a large skillet over medium heat. Add shrimp. Cook, stirring constantly, 3 to 5 minutes. Remove shrimp and set aside. Drain off drippings, leaving 2 tablespoons in the skillet. Sauté onions, chopped red peppers and garlic until tender. Add zucchini and sauté 2 minutes. Stir in shrimp, rice and cashews. Cook over low heat, stirring constantly, until thoroughly heated.

Spoon into serving dish. Garnish with red pepper rings.

*Source: www.recipegoldmine.com*

to cultivate them. The Web site provides links to other nut-growing associations as well as recipes and expert advice on nut growing.

Box 550
648 Oak Hill School Rd.
Townsend, DE 19734
Phone: 302-659-1731
*www.northernnutgrowers.org*

### Almond Board of California

Almonds are California's largest tree crop. The ABC devotes itself to expanding the market for almonds through public relations, advertising and nutrition research. The Board also tracks and publishes industry statistics on almonds in the *Almond Almanac*.

1150 Ninth St., Suite 1500
Modesto, CA 95354
Phone: 209-549-8262
US Info Line: 800-610-5388
Fax: 209-549-8267
*www.almondboard.com*

### Walnut Marketing Board

Representing the walnut growers and handlers of California, the Walnut Marketing Board seeks to encourage the consumption of walnuts by publishing healthy recipes and facts.

1540 River Park Dr., Suite 203
Sacramento, CA 95815
Phone: 916-922-5888
Fax: 916-923-2548
*www.walnut.org*

### National Pecan Shellers Association

This trade association is committed to educating everyone about the nutritional benefits, various uses and great taste of pecans.

1100 Johnson Ferry Rd., Suite 300
Atlanta, GA 30342
Phone: 404-252-3663
*www.ilovepecans.org*

## ■ Recipe ■

### Peanut Ice Cream (circa 1925)

1 pint peanuts

2 cups sugar

2 quarts milk

1 pint cream

2 tsp vanilla

Roast, shell and roll the peanuts until they are quite fine. Brown one cup of sugar and add to the milk. Then add the remainder of the sugar, cream, vanilla and, lastly, the peanuts. Freeze.

*Source:* George Washington Carver (Tuskegee Institute National Historic Site)

### National Peanut Board

This organization represents all US peanut farmers and their families. It works to increase peanut production while advancing the great taste, nutritional value and versatility of US-grown peanuts.

2839 Paces Ferry Rd., Suite 210
Atlanta, GA 30339
Phone: 866-825-7946
678-424-5750
Fax: 678-424-5751
*www.nationalpeanutboard.org*

### BOOKS

*Nuts: Sweet and Savory Recipes from Diamond California,* by Tina Salter, Holly Stewart. Ten Speed Press.

*The Totally Nuts Cookbook (Totally Cookbooks),* by Helene Siegel, Caroline Vibbert. Celestial Arts.

## ■ Recipe ■

### Tropical Fruit Salad with Ginger and Peanuts

2 Tbsp honey

2 Tbsp tangerine or juice concentrate

1 tsp fresh lime or lemon juice

5 cups mixed fresh fruit chunks, such as papaya, mango, Asian pear, pineapple, kiwi fruit and/or banana

½ cup dry-roasted peanuts

2 Tbsp crystallized ginger, chopped

In a small bowl, stir together honey, juice concentrate and the lime or lemon juice. Combine the fruit in 1½- to 2-quart bowl. Gently toss with juice mixture, peanuts and ginger. Serve promptly, or cover and chill for about an hour. If prepared more than 1 hour ahead, stir in peanuts and ginger just before serving. Makes 4 1-cup servings.

*Source:* National Peanut Board

# 6. Yogurt

In Egypt, it's called *benraid.* The Armenians call it *mayzoom.* The Persian word is *kast.* In Turkey, it's known as *yogurut,* from which our word "yogurt" is derived.

Although people have been making and eating yogurt for more than 4,000 years, it took the research of Nobel Prize–winning scientist Ilya Mechnikov in the beginning of the 20th century to stir up European interest in yogurt, which eventually made its way to America around 1940. In the 1950s, yogurt's reputation as a healthy, nutritional food started to spread across the country. Now, yogurt production is a major industry.

## The Culture Club

Yogurt is most often made with the milk of cows. But it can also be made with milk from goats, sheep and buffalo, or with soymilk. Once the milk gets pasteurized, many commercial yogurt producers enrich it with powdered milk. So when ads say that the yogurt has more protein and calcium than dairy milk, it's true.

To meet the legal definition of yogurt, it is required that two cultures be added to the mixture. These cultures break down the lactose (milk sugar), producing lactic acid and giving yogurt its unique taste. The live, active cultures are primarily what make yogurt a health-giving superfood.

## Health Benefits

Thanks to the live cultures, yogurt is a soothing and easily digested food, even for people who are lactose intolerant. In fact, yogurt helps digestion and, as a result, may clear up bad breath caused by stomach-acid imbalances.

As an added bonus, a daily dose of yogurt may completely eliminate gas problems.

▶ Yogurt is not only a good source of calcium, but the lactose helps improve calcium absorption. People at risk for osteoporosis should consider including a portion in their daily diet.

▶ Yogurt contains $B_{12}$, riboflavin, potassium, magnesium and zinc. It's also a wonderful source of protein. In fact, the US Department of Agriculture (*www.usda.gov*) recommends yogurt as a meat alternative in school lunches.

▶ Studies show that eating a daily 8-ounce serving of yogurt with active bacterial cultures restores and maintains a healthy bacterial environment that can help prevent both bladder infections and vaginal yeast infections.

▶ A daily serving of yogurt with "live cultures" seems to increase immune-enhancing chemicals, according to the results of experiments performed by George Halpern, MD, professor emeritus of the department of internal medicine at the University of California, Davis, School of Medicine. Dr. Halpern emphasizes the need for the yogurt to contain "live" or "active" cultures.

## Friendly Acidophilus

Antibiotics have no discretion. They destroy the good as well as the bad bacteria found naturally in your digestive system. Replace the beneficial bacteria with *Lactobacillus acidophilus*. You can do that by eating yogurt—make sure the container says *Live* or *Active Culture with L. acidophilus*—or drinking acidophilus milk, or by taking an acidophilus supplement, available at health food stores.

▶ Whether you take a supplement, drink milk or eat yogurt (fat-free is fine as long as it says it contains *L. acidophilus*), do it two hours *after* taking an antibiotic, making sure that it's also at least two hours *before* you have to take another dose of the antibiotic. Allow that amount of time before and after the antibiotic so that the acidophilus doesn't interfere with the work of the antibiotic.

Keep consuming acidophilus in some form for at least a couple of weeks after you stop taking an antibiotic. It will help normalize the bacterial balance in the intestines, getting your digestive system working properly again.

## ■ Recipe ■

### Eggplant–Yogurt Dip

3 large eggplants, whole with skin on

1 large head garlic, roasted (*see* recipe
    on page 267)

1 cup thick yogurt (plain)

2 Tbsp olive oil

1 medium Vidalia, red or other sweet
    onion, chopped

½ cup fresh Italian parsley, chopped

1 Tbsp fresh basil, chopped (optional)

¼ tsp Tabasco sauce (optional)

Salt and pepper to taste

On a gas or preferably charcoal barbecue, roast the whole eggplant evenly on all sides until the skin is charred or the eggplant is soft. Set aside and let cool. When cool, peel off the charred skin or scoop out the soft insides of the eggplant. Place in a large bowl.

Add garlic, yogurt, olive oil, onion, parsley, basil, Tabasco sauce, salt and pepper to taste. Mix well.

Serve along with Armenian cracker bread, as a vegetable dip or as a vegetable side dish. Can be served hot or cold.

*Source:* The Gutsy Gourmet

▶ After a bout of diarrhea, yogurt can help reestablish bacterial balance. Studies show that yogurt can decrease the duration of an attack of diarrhea in infants and children.

▶ Studies also indicate that *Lactobacillus acidophilus* in yogurt helps lower cholesterol levels by interfering with cholesterol reabsorption in the intestine.

▶ All of the live cultures of bacteria in yogurt can enhance immunity, kill off certain unwanted strains of unhealthy bacteria and increase production of antibodies (the natural killers of disease organisms) in your blood.

What's great is that those beneficial bacteria stay in your system and continue to help long after the yogurt is gone.

### Whey to Go

You know that watery part that you spill off before spooning out a portion of yogurt? That's the whey, and it has B vitamins and minerals, and little, if any, fat. Stir the whey into the yogurt so that it's part of your portion.

### What to Look for

First and foremost, whether you want regular, low-fat or fat-free yogurt, be sure that the label says it contains "live" or "active" cultures. Most yogurt manufacturers list their specific

## ■ Recipe ■

### Curried Turkey

2 cups cooked turkey breast, diced

¼ cup raisins

1½ stalks celery, chopped

¼ cup peanuts, finely chopped

½ cup plain nonfat yogurt

2 Tbsp light mayonnaise

½ tsp curry powder

Fresh-ground black pepper to taste

Combine ingredients and serve. Makes 4 servings.

*Source:* National Yogurt Association

live cultures. Look for and expect to find at least one, maybe two or three (more is better) types of friendly and helpful bacteria. *Try to get…*

- ◆ Lactobacillus acidophilus
- ◆ Lactobacillus bulgaricus
- ◆ Lactobacillus casei
- ◆ Lactobacillus reuteri
- ◆ Streptococcus thermophilus
- ◆ Bifidobacteria

► If fruit is mixed through yogurt, there's not much chance of there being live or active cultures in it. Buy plain yogurt and add a banana, berries, peaches or pineapple—this can be one of your five daily cancer-risk-reducing servings of fresh fruit. Plain yogurt also tastes great with a little honey mixed in.

► See what other ingredients are listed on the label. You do not want yogurt to contain any additives or artificial sweeteners.

► Before buying yogurt, check the expiration date and be sure the container's contents have not exceeded that date—or even come close.

► If you really get into yogurt, you may want to try making your own (*see* recipe on page 284). Kits are available in some health food stores. You'll need to use yogurt as a starter to make more yogurt. And that's one way to test the store-bought product for active live cultures. If the cultures are alive and well, they will help produce more yogurt.

► Sorry, but none of the health benefits of yogurt apply to frozen yogurt. Freezing tends to destroy the good stuff.

There is also the unwanted presence of sugar or aspartame and lots more ingredients on the less-than-healthy list.

## ■ Recipe ■

### Yogurt Cereal Bars

2 cups corn flakes
¾ cup flour
¼ cup firmly packed brown sugar
½ tsp ground cinnamon
½ cup margarine
1 cup lowfat vanilla yogurt
1 egg, slightly beaten
2 Tbsp flour

Preheat oven to 350° F. Combine cereal, ¾ cup flour, sugar and cinnamon in a small bowl. Cut in margarine until coarse crumbs form. In the bottom of a greased 8" square pan, press half the mixture firmly. Mix yogurt, egg and 2 tablespoons flour in another small bowl. Spread over cereal mixture in pan, and sprinkle with remaining cereal mixture. Bake 30 minutes or until golden brown. Cool in pan on wire rack. Cut into bars, and store in an airtight canister. Makes 16 servings.

*Source:* Stonyfield Farm Yogurt

## The Last Word on Yogurt

In several ancient Middle Eastern languages, the word for yogurt was synonymous with *life*.

### ASSOCIATIONS
#### National Yogurt Association
The NYA is the national trade association representing manufacturers of refrigerated cup and frozen yogurt products that contain live and active cultures. Products that meet the NYA's standards will have a "Live and Active

## ■ Recipe ■

### *Make Your Own Yogurt*

½ gallon whole milk (you can also use low-fat or skim milk)

½ cup mahdzoon or yogurt starter (available at specialty and health food stores, or you may use plain yogurt from the supermarket)

Bring milk to just a boil and then set aside to cool—just cool enough not to bite the finger to touch (about 120° F). Pour warm milk into a glass or Pyrex bowl, and add the mahdzoon starter. Mix well by stirring in the starter slowly. Completely cover the bowl with towels top and bottom to maintain an even temperature. Keep covered at room temperature until mahdzoon has set, about 3 to 4 hours. Refrigerate for 8 hours before serving. Serves 6 to 8.

To store, keep in the refrigerator. This will keep well for a week or more.

*Source:* The Gutsy Gourmet

Cultures" seal on the side of the container. This will assure that the product has met standards for cultures used in production.

The NYA sponsors scientific research regarding the health benefits of eating yogurt, and serves as a source of information about these benefits. The NYA also acts as a resource for both the media and the general public on subjects related to yogurt that contains live and active cultures.

2000 Corporate Ridge, Suite 1000
McLean, VA 22102
Phone: 703-821-0770
*www.aboutyogurt.com*

### The National Dairy Council

The NDC, a division of Dairy Management Inc., strives to provide timely scientific data on the amazing health benefits of dairy products. The Council is also involved in dairy nutrition research, education and communication.

10255 West Higgins Rd., Suite 900
Rosemont, IL 60018
Phone: 800-426-8271
847-803-2000
Fax: 847-803-2077
*www.nationaldairycouncil.org*

### BOOKS

*Cooking with Yogurt: The Complete Cookbook for Indulging with the World's Healthiest Food,* by Judith Choate. Atlantic Monthly Press.

*The Book of Yogurt,* by Sonia Uvezian. Ecco Publishing.

*Yogurt, Yoghurt, Youghourt: An International Cookbook,* by Linda K. Fuller. Food Products Printing. ■

# Amazing, Super-Duper
# Facts and Advice

# Amazing, Super-Duper Facts and Advice

## Think Positive, Live Longer

**H**aving an optimistic outlook may actually prolong your life span, according to a study conducted at the Mayo Clinic in Rochester, Minnesota. Researchers studied patients for more than 30 years and concluded that the pessimistic participants ran a 19% greater risk of death compared with the more optimistic ones.

It's difficult to put much credence in this study since so many variables come into play. But we hope you can see that being optimistic is a happier way to go through life than being pessimistic—and it's certainly much more pleasant for everyone around you.

## The Full Moon Boom

Research that was conducted at the University of Illinois Medical Center in Chicago concluded that some health problems may act up—and can possibly become more severe—when there's a full moon. (Are there any werewolves reading this?)

## The "Rest" of the Story

Everyone—from your mother and mate to your doctor—at one time or another probably suggested or insisted on "bed rest" to recuperate from an illness.

A study done by researchers at Michigan State University in East Lansing said, "Rest, not bed rest." The difference between the two is important.

When you *rest*, you slow down but keep moving. *Bed rest* implies staying still (in bed) for a long period. This can lead to muscle fatigue and even overall weakness. The researchers based their findings on close to 6,000 patients with 17 different medical conditions.

*Conclusion:* It's good to get sick people out of bed as soon as possible. Although you may get out of bed, you may still need rest. It's important to find the proper balance. As your mother, mate or doctor will tell you, "Don't overdo it!"

> ✎ **NOTE:** Equal time is demanded by one of our medical advisors, who reminds us that, in some cases, "Don't underdo it!"

## Doctor's Fee

In ancient China, doctors were paid when they kept their patients well. Believing it was their job to prevent illness, the doctors often paid patients who got sick.

*Those* certainly were the good old days!

## Fever: Friend or Foe?

Thomas Sydenham, a 17th-century English physician—who was one of the principal founders of epidemiology—once famously said, "Fever is Nature's engine which she brings into the field to remove her enemy."

It looks like research scientists agree with Dr. Sydenham when it comes to fevers that are below 104° F.

Matthew J. Kluger, PhD, is vice president for research and economic development at George Mason University in Fairfax, Virginia. As one of the leading researchers of fever therapy, Dr. Kluger recommends that fever be allowed to run its course and believes that it may actually shorten the duration of an illness. Studies done at the University of Texas Southwestern Medical Center in Dallas showed that fever supports antibiotic therapy. And researchers at Yale University School of Medicine in New Haven, Connecticut, proved that patients with fever are less contagious than those with the same infection but who have suppressed their fever with medication.

Ray C. Wunderlich, Jr., MD, PhD, director of the Wunderlich Center for Nutritional Medicine in St. Petersburg, Florida, says, "Mothers whose babies get hot in the middle of the night know that high fever paralyzes the household and may create extreme stress. Be sure the baby is not excessively clothed and blanketed. A 20- to 30-minute tepid bath may help the baby feel better and even feel like ingesting fluids or food."

## Freshen Up a Sickroom

▶ Dip a cotton ball into eucalyptus oil (available at health food stores), put it on a little dish and place it on a surface—not near an open window or a draft—in the room where someone is recovering. Eucalyptus oil is said to generate ozone. It's also a strong antiseptic. The oil has a powerful scent, so before you do this, be sure the sick person agrees to having it there.

## Prescription Reading Made Easy

These are some of the Latin terms commonly used on prescription medication...

| Term | Abbreviation | Meaning |
| --- | --- | --- |
| ante cibum | ac | before food |
| bis in die | bid | twice a day |
| gutta | gt | drop |
| hora somni | hs | at bedtime |
| oculus dexter | od | right eye |
| oculus sinister | os | left eye |
| per os | po | by mouth |
| post cibum | pc | after food |
| pro re nata | prn | as needed |
| quaque 3 hora | q3h | every 3 hours |
| quaque die | qd | every day |
| quattuor in die | qid | 4 times a day |
| ter in die | tid | 3 times a day |

## How to Take Pills...Really

▶ Take pills standing up and keep standing for about two minutes afterward. Swallowing them with at least a half cup of water and while standing will give the pills a chance to move swiftly along, instead of staying in your esophagus where they may disintegrate and cause nausea or heartburn.

▶ According to Stephen H. Paul, PhD, professor of pharmaceutical economics and health care delivery at Temple University's School of Pharmacy in Philadelphia, a multivitamin and fat-soluble vitamins A, D and E should be taken with the largest meal of the day. That's when the most fat is present in the stomach to aid in the absorption of the vitamins.

▶ The water-soluble vitamins—C and B-complex—should be taken while eating a meal or a half-hour before the meal. The vitamins help start the biochemical process that breaks down food, making it available to use for energy and tissue building.

▶ If you take large doses of vitamin C, take it in small amounts throughout the day. Your body will use more of it that way, and you will help prevent urinary-tract irritation.

**CAUTION:** Never take megadoses of any vitamins, minerals or herbs unless you do so under the supervision of a health professional.

## Coming to Your Senses

The average pair of eyes can distinguish nearly 8 million differences in color.

The average pair of ears can discriminate among more than 300,000 tones.

The average nose can recognize 10,000 different odors.

There are 1,300 nerve endings per square inch in each average fingertip. The only parts of the body more sensitive to touch are the lips, the tongue and the tip of the nose.

That covers four of our five senses. As for the fifth sense, well—everyone knows, there's no accounting for taste!

## Dropper in a Pinch

▶ If you need a dropper *now* for any of your orifices and don't have one (a dropper, that is), you may be able to improvise with a drinking straw. A 3-inch piece of plastic straw will yield about 15 drops of liquid. Of course, that means you have to have a straw *now*.

## Do-It-Yourself Hot-Water Bottle and Ice Pack

▶ Don't throw away empty plastic containers made for laundry detergent. The next time you need a hot-water bottle, fill one of those containers. Just be sure the cap is tight-fitting.

▶ You know the plastic bottle with the tight-fitting cap that you just used for a hot-water bottle? You can also fill it with ice and cold water for an instant ice pack.

▶ You can make a flexible ice pack with a towel. Dunk a towel in cold water, wring it out and place it on aluminum foil in the freezer. Before it freezes stiff, take it out and mold it around the bruised or injured body part.

## A Fishy Story

Do you have any idea how the custom of serving a slice of lemon with fish first started? It wasn't to cut the fishy taste or to heighten the flavor.

A long time ago, lemon was thought to be more medicine than food. If someone swallowed a fish bone, the thinking was that the lemon juice was so strong that it would dissolve the bone.

## Good Health, Italian-Style

It's unusual to find older Italians who have asthma, tuberculosis or gallbladder trouble, thanks to the garlic and olive oil they consume in two of their three daily meals.

## Save Vitamins in the Microwave

Fewer vitamins are destroyed during the cooking process when you prepare food in a microwave. Prevent food from burning by adding water—just a little will help to retain as many of the food's nutrients as possible. Also, cover foods while microwaving them in order to reduce the zapping time and keep in more of the nutrients.

## Lettuce: Choose Dark Green

The darkest-green salad greens are the best. Compared to iceberg lettuce, romaine lettuce has two times as much folic acid, six times as much vitamin C and eight times as much beta-carotene. Spinach? Dark green. Watercress? Dark green. Collard greens, mustard greens—both dark green.

While you're at it, you may want to include parsley as a salad green, not just as a garnish. Parsley is rich in beta-carotene and vitamin C. It tastes good, too.

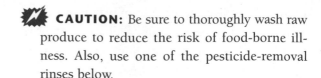 **CAUTION:** Be sure to thoroughly wash raw produce to reduce the risk of food-borne illness. Also, use one of the pesticide-removal rinses below.

## Moldy Food

Mold is not a good thing. While it probably won't kill you, it can make you sick. If you see mold on any kind of food, do not give it the "smell test" to see if it has gone bad. Just a whiff of the mold spores can trigger an allergic or respiratory reaction.

Get rid of any soft foods or drinks that have even a hint of mold. However, if certain hard foods, such as Swiss cheese, contain mold, you can chop off the moldy part (play it safe and discard an inch all around the moldy part) and salvage the rest.

## Herb and Spice Storage

▶ Store fresh or dried herbs and spices in a cool, dry area. The refrigerator is ideal. When exposed to heat, such as from the kitchen stove, many spices and herbs lose their potency…and their colors fade, too.

## Remove Pesticides from Fruits and Vegetables

Poisonous sprays and pesticides can be removed from raw produce using Jay "The Juiceman" Kordich's method.

▶ Fill the sink with cold water, then add 4 tablespoons of salt and the fresh juice from half a lemon. This will make a diluted form of hydrochloric acid.

Soak most fruits and vegetables for five to 10 minutes…soak leafy greens two to three minutes…soak strawberries, blueberries and all other berries one to two minutes. After soaking, rinse the produce thoroughly in plain cold water and enjoy.

▶ You can also soak produce in a sink or basin with ¼ cup of white vinegar. Then, with a vegetable brush, scrub the produce under cold water. Give it a final rinse, then it's ready to be eaten.

## Sweet and Salty Substitutes

▶ When substituting honey for sugar in a recipe, use ½ cup of honey for every cup of sugar. Honey has about 65 calories per teaspoon—sugar has 45 calories per teaspoon. Since honey is twice as sweet as sugar, you need to use only half as much honey as sugar. You end up saving calories by using honey.

**WARNING:** Diabetics and people who have honey allergies should not substitute with honey.

▶ If salt is a no-no, a spritz of lemon juice instead may help provide the kick that salt gives food.

## Working with Onions Tearlessly…Almost

In her search for a method of working with onions tearlessly, Joan has worn sunglasses, chewed white bread, let cold water run, frozen the onion first and cut off the root end of the onion last. *And then…*

▶ Joan heard *Wheel of Fortune* letter-turner Vanna White thank the TV game show's host, Pat Sajak, for this hint—put a match, unlit, sulfur-side out, between your lips as though it were a cigarette. Keep it there while you peel, grate or cut onions, and you won't have to worry about your mascara running.

This hint is, by far, the best, but a really strong onion will still bring a tear to Joan's eye.

## Unhand Those Garlic and Onion Odors

▶ This helpful hint works like magic. Take a piece of flatware (any metal spoon, knife or fork will do), pretend it's a bar of soap and wash your hands with it under cold water. The garlic or onion smell will vanish in seconds.

▶ Those pungent garlic and onion odors can also be removed by rubbing your hands with a slice of fresh tomato.

## Hold on to Your Pantyhose

▶ Onions and potatoes will keep better and longer if you store them in a piece of clean hosiery in a cool place. The hose allows the air to move around them.

## Natural Insect Repellents

▶ Ants steer clear of garlic. Rub a peeled clove of garlic on problem areas and they will be ant-free in no time. Also vampire-free.

▶ Make pomanders using oranges and cloves (*see* "Preparation Guide" on page 251). Put a pomander in each clothes closet and say bye-bye to moths.

▶ Flies are repelled by thyme tea. Fill a plant mister with a cup of thyme tea and spray around doors and windows to keep flies away.

▶ To keep insects out of bags of grain and flour, add a couple of bay leaves to the containers.

## Natural Air Cleaners

Your tax dollars have paid for research conducted by the National Aeronautics and Space Administration (NASA), and now you should—and can—benefit from it.

NASA's scientists in Washington, DC, discovered that several common houseplants can dramatically reduce toxic chemical levels in homes and offices.

If you don't think your home or office is polluted, think again. There's benzene (found in inks, oils, paints, plastics, rubber, detergents, dyes and gasoline)…formaldehyde (found in foam insulation, particle board, pressed-wood products, most cleaning agents and paper products treated with resins, including facial tissues and paper towels)…and trichloroethylene (TCE), which is found in dry-cleaning processes, printing inks, paints, lacquers, varnishes and adhesives. And that's just to name a few.

Here are low-cost, attractive solutions in the form of hardy, easy-to-find, easy-to-grow household plants…

◆ Spider plant (*Chlorophytum comosum "Vittatum"*)—very easy to grow in indirect or bright, diffused light. Be sure to provide good drainage.
◆ Peace lily (*Spathiphyllum species*)—very easy to grow in low-light location. But can be toxic to pets.
◆ Chinese evergreen (*Aglaonema "Silver Queen"*)—very easy to grow in low-light location. Remove overgrown shoots to

encourage new growth, and keep the plant bushy. Can be toxic to pets.
◆ Weeping fig (*Ficus benjamina*)—easy to grow, but requires a little special attention. Indirect or bright, diffused light is best.
◆ Golden Pothos or Devil's Claw (*Epipremnum aureum*)—very easy to grow in indirect or bright, diffused light. Can be toxic to pets.

Moderately moist soil is preferred for all of these plants.

NASA (*www.nasa.gov*) recommends placing 15 to 18 plants in an 1,800-sq. ft. home. In a small- to average-sized room, just one plant ought to be effective, especially if it's put where air circulates.

After the plants are in place, you, your colleagues and/or members of your household may notice that their sore throats, headaches, irritated eyes and stuffy noses have cleared up.

## Deodorizing Food Jars

▶ In order to reuse a jar, you may want to remove the odors left by its original contents.

For a medium-sized jar, put 1 teaspoon of dry mustard in the jar and fill it to the rim with water.

Leave it that way for four to six hours, then rinse with hot water.

## Salt Rub for Gas Odors

▶ To get the smell of gasoline off your hands, rub them with salt.

## Stuffed Toys on Ice

▶ Beanie Babies® and other beloved stuffed toys are home to dust mites. Those dust mites can trigger allergic reactions and asthma attacks. To kill those mighty mites, simply put the stuffed critter in a plastic bag and leave it in the freezer for 24 hours, once a week.

Explain to your child that the stuffed toy joined the cast of *Holiday on Ice,* and it is "showtime" every Sunday or whenever.

## Cradling Baby

▶ The Talmud (a book of ancient Hebrew writings) suggests that a woman who begins to nurse her child should start on the left side, as this is the source of all understanding.

The late Lee Salk, PhD, who was an expert in child and family psychology, found that 83% of right-handed and 78% of left-handed mothers held their babies on the left side.

Holding a baby on the left side frees up the baby's left ear to hear its mother's voice. Sounds that enter the left ear go to the right side of the brain, which processes tone, melody and emotion.

## Bathing Made Easy

For those of you who can't stand long enough to take a shower, or who find it very hard to get up out of a bathtub once you've gotten into it, make the bathing/showering process easier by placing an aluminum beach chair in the tub. Turn on the shower and sit in the chair.

Also, be sure to have those nonslip stick-ons on the floor of the tub. ■

# Sources

# Sources

## HERBAL PRODUCTS AND MORE

### Atlantic Spice Company
2 Shore Rd., Box 205
North Truro, MA 02652
Phone: 800-316-7965
Fax: 508-487-2550
*www.atlanticspice.com*

### Blessed Herbs
109 Barre Plains Rd.
Oakham, MA 01068
Phone: 800-489-4372
Fax: 508-882-3755
*www.blessedherbs.com*

### Flower Power Herbs and Roots, Inc.
406 East Ninth St.
New York, NY 10009
Phone: 212-982-6664
*www.flowerpower.net*

### Great American Natural Products
4121 16th St. North
St. Petersburg, FL 33703
Phone: 800-323-4372 or 727-521-4372
Fax: 727-522-6457
*www.greatamerican.biz*

### Herbs by Dial
60 N. Main St.
Manti, UT 84642
Phone: 800-288-4618 or 435-835-9476

### Indiana Botanic Gardens
3401 West 37th Ave.
Hobart, IN 46342
Phone: 800-644-8327 or 800-514-1068
Fax: 219-947-4148
*www.botanicchoice.com*

### Mountain Top Herbs, Inc.
Box 970004
Orem, UT 84097
Phone: 877-944-3727

### Nature's Apothecary/NOW Foods
395 South Glen Ellyn Rd.
Bloomingdale, IL 60108
Phone: 888-669-3663
*www.nowfoods.com*

### NewChapter, Inc.
90 Technology Dr.
Brattleboro, VT 05301
Phone: 800-543-7279
Fax: 800-470-0247
*www.new-chapter.com*

**Old Amish Herbal Remedies**
4121 16th St. North
St. Petersburg, FL 33703
Phone: 727-521-4372

**Penn Herb Co. Ltd.**
10601 Decatur Rd., Suite 2
Philadelphia, PA 19154
Phone: 800-523-9971 or 215-632-6100
Fax: 215-632-7945
*www.pennherb.com*

**San Francisco Herb Company**
250 14th St.
San Francisco, CA 94103
Phone: 800-227-4530 or 415-861-7174
Fax: 415-861-4440
*www.sfherb.com*

## GEMS, NEW-AGE PRODUCTS AND GIFTS

**Beyond the Rainbow**
Box 110
Ruby, NY 12475
Phone: 845-336-4609
*www.rainbowcrystal.com*

**Crystal Way**
2335 Market St.
San Francisco, CA 94114
Phone: 415-861-6511
Fax: 415-861-4229
*www.crystalway.com*

**Pacific Spirit**
1334 Pacific Ave.
Forest Grove, OR 97116
Phone: 800-634-9057
Fax: 503-357-1669
*www.mystictrader.com*

## VITAMINS, NUTRITIONAL SUPPLEMENTS AND MORE

**Bionatures**
16508 East Laser Dr., Suite 103
Fountain Hills, AZ 85268
Phone: 800-624-7114
Fax: 480-837-8420
*www.bionatures.com*

**Freeda Vitamins**
47-25 34th St., Third Floor
Long Island City, NY 11101
Phone: 800-777-3737 or 718-433-4337
Fax: 718-433-4373
*www.freedavitamins.com*

**NutriCology Inc.**
2300 North Loop Rd.
Alameda, CA 94502
Phone: 800-545-9960
Fax: 800-688-7426
*www.nutricology.com*

**Nutrition Coalition, Inc.**
Box 3001
Fargo, ND 58108
Phone: 800-447-4793 or 218-236-9783
Fax: 218-236-6753
*www.willardswater.com*

**Puritan's Pride/Vitamins.com**
1233 Montauk Hwy.
Box 9001
Oakdale, NY 11769
Phone: 800-645-1030
Fax: 800-719-5824
*www.puritan.com* or *www.vitamins.com*

**Superior Nutritionals Inc.**
8813 Dr. Martin Luther King, Jr., St. North
St. Petersburg, FL 33702
Phone: 800-717-RUNN (7866)
Fax: 727-577-3166

**TriMedica International, Inc.**
1895 South Los Feliz Dr.
Tempe, AZ 85281
Phone: 800-800-8849 or 480-998-1041
*www.trimedica.com*

**The Vitamin Shoppe**
2101 91st St.
North Bergen, NJ 07047
Tel: 888-223-1216
Fax: 800-852-7153
*www.vitaminshoppe.com*

## NATURAL FOODS AND MORE

**Barlean's Organic Oils LLC**
4936 Lake Terrell Rd.
Ferndale, WA 98248
Phone: 800-445-3529 or 360-384-0485
*www.barleans.com*

**Gold Mine Natural Food Co.**
7805 Arjons Dr.
San Diego, CA 92126
Phone: 800-475-FOOD (3663)
Fax: 858-695-0811
*www.goldminenaturalfood.com*

**Jaffe Bros. Natural Foods, Inc.**
28560 Lilac Rd.
Valley Center, CA 92082
Phone: 760-749-1133
Fax: 760-749-1282
*www.organicfruitsandnuts.com*

## BEE PRODUCTS AND MORE

**C.C. Pollen Co.**
3627 East Indian School Rd., Suite 209
Phoenix, AZ 85018
Phone: 800-875-0096 or 602-957-0096

Fax: 602-381-3130
*www.ccpollen.com*

**Montana Naturals**
19994 Highway 93 North
Arlee, MT 59821
Phone: 800-872-7218
Fax: 406-726-3287
*www.mtnaturals.com*

## PET FOOD AND PRODUCTS

**All the Best Pet Care**
8050 Lake City Way
Seattle, WA 98115
Phone: 206-524-0199
*www.allthebestpetcare.com*

**American Holistic Veterinary Medical Association**
218 Old Emmorton Rd.
Bel Air, MD 21015
Phone: 410-569-0795
*www.ahvma.org*

**Golden Tails**
6515 Transit Rd., Suite 2
Bowmansville, NY 14026
Phone: 877-693-6986 or 716-681-6986
*www.goldentails.com*

**Halo Purely for Pets**
3438 East Lake Rd., #14
Palm Harbor, FL 34685
Phone: 800-426-4256
Fax: 727-937-3955
*www.halopets.com*

**Harbingers of a New Age**
717 East Missoula Ave.
Troy, MT 59935
Phone: 406-295-4944
Fax: 406-295-7603
*www.vegepet.com*

## HEALTH-RELATED PRODUCTS

**Gaiam—A Lifestyle Company**
360 Interlocken Blvd.
Broomfield, CO 80021
Phone: 877-989-6321
*www.gaiam.com*

## HEALTH-RELATED TRAVEL PRODUCTS AND MORE

**Magellan's (Essentials for the Traveler)**
110 West Sola St.
Santa Barbara, CA 93101
Phone: 800-962-4943
Fax: 800-962-4940
*www.magellans.com*

## WHOLESALE/RETAIL HEALTH APPLIANCES

**Acme Equipment**
1024 Concert Ave.
Spring Hill, FL 34609
Phone: 352-688-0157

## AROMATHERAPY, FLOWER ESSENCES AND MORE

**Aromaland**
1326 Rufina Circle
Santa Fe, NM 87507
Phone: 800-933-5267
Fax: 505-438-7223
*www.aromaland.com*

**Aroma Vera**
5310 Beethoven St.
Los Angeles, CA 90066

Phone: 800-669-9514 or 310-574-6920
Fax: 310-306-5873
*www.aromavera.com*

**Flower Essence Services**
Box 1769
Nevada City, CA 95959
Phone: 800-548-0075
Fax: 530-265-6467
*www.floweressence.com*

## SERVICES

**World Research Foundation (WRF)**
For a nominal fee, cofounders LaVerne and Steve Ross will do a search (which includes 5,000 international medical journals) and provide the newest holistic and conventional treatments and diagnostic techniques on almost any condition. The Foundation's library of more than 10,000 books, periodicals and research reports is available to the public free of charge.
41 Bell Rock Plaza
Sedona, AZ 86351
Phone: 928-284-3300
Fax: 928-284-3530
*www.wrf.org*

**US Consumer Product Safety Commission**
This government agency, located near Washington, DC, has a toll-free, 24-hour hotline where consumers can obtain product safety and other agency information as well as report unsafe products.
4330 East-West Hwy.
Bethesda, MD 20814
Hotline: 800-638-2772
For hearing impaired: 800-638-8270
Fax: 301-504-0124 or 301-504-0025
*www.cpsc.gov*

**American Board of Medical Specialties**
The ABMS is an organization of 24 approved medical specialty boards. It offers a toll-free number

where you can confirm that a "specialist" is exactly that. Just provide the doctor's name, and the ABMS will verify whether the doctor is listed in a specialty and his/her year of certification.

> 1007 Church St., Suite 404
> Evanston, IL 60201
> Phone Verification:
> > 866-ASK-ABMS (275-2267)
> Phone: 847-491-9091
> Fax: 847-328-3596
> *www.abms.org*

## Consumer Information Catalog

The CIC lists more than 200 free and low-cost publications from Uncle Sam—on everything from saving money, staying healthy and getting federal benefits to buying a home and handling consumer complaints. *To get your free copy of the catalog...*

- ◆ Call toll-free: 888-8-PUEBLO (878-3256), weekdays 9 am to 8 pm EST.
- ◆ Send your name and address to:
  Consumer Information Catalog
  Pueblo, CO 81009
- ◆ Go to the Internet site *www.pueblo.gsa.gov* to order the catalog. You can also read, print out or download any CIC publication for free.

---

**DISCLAIMER:** Addresses, telephone numbers, Web sites and other contact information listed in this book are accurate at the time of publication. However, they are subject to frequent change. ■

# Health Resources

# Health Resources

**B**efore we begin www-ing through the pages, there is something you should know (but then, you probably already know this)—you can't always trust the information you get on the Internet.

Since we're talking about your health, it can be mighty dangerous to accept and use the wrong advice. We recommend you take whatever information you get online, and show it to and/or discuss it with your health professional.

And there's something else you may already know—and, if not, you should. There's an organization called the Health On the Net (HON) Foundation, which is associated with the University Hospital of Geneva in Switzerland. HON is like the Better Business Bureau for medical Web sites. Its prestigious governing body certifies sites that must abide by eight user-protecting principles. So, if HON gives a site its stamp of approval, you will see it on the site.

### Health On the Net Foundation (HON)
Medical Informatics Service
University Hospital of Geneva
    24, rue Micheli-du-Crest
    1211 Geneva 14

Switzerland
Phone: +41 22 372 62 50
Fax: +41 22 372 88 85
*www.hon.ch*

HON is not the only organization that certifies medical- and health-related Web sites. There's also the Internet Healthcare Coalition, which is committed to an eHealth Code of Ethics that enables consumers to use the Internet to its full advantage in order to improve their health.

### Internet Healthcare Coalition
    Box 286
    Newtown, PA 18940
    Phone: 215-504-4164
    Fax: 215-504-5739
    *www.ihealthcoalition.org*

At these Web sites, you'll find direct links to established (and certified, of course) medical and health resources. Although you may be able to trust the integrity of the information you find on the Web a bit more, it's still important to check out any and all advice with your health professional.

# Organizations, Associations and Journals

### Administration on Aging
Washington, DC 20201
Phone: 202-619-0724
*www.aoa.gov*

### Alzheimer's Association
225 North Michigan Ave., Floor 17
Chicago, IL 60601
Phone: 800-272-3900
312-335-8700
*www.alz.org*

### American Academy of Allergy, Asthma & Immunology
555 East Wells St.
Milwaukee, WI 53202
Phone: 800-822-2762
414-272-6071
*www.aaaai.org*

### American Academy of Dermatology
Box 4014
Schaumburg, IL 60618
Phone: 866-503-7546
*www.aad.org*

### American Academy of Medical Acupuncture
4929 Wilshire Blvd., Suite 428
Los Angeles, CA 90010
Phone: 323-937-5514
*www.medicalacupuncture.org*

### American Academy of Neurology
1080 Montreal Ave.
Saint Paul, MN 55116
Phone: 800-879-1960
651-695-2791
*www.aan.com*

### American Academy of Orthopaedic Surgeons
6300 North River Rd.
Rosemont, IL 60018
Phone: 800-346-AAOS (2267)
847-823-7186
Fax: 847-823-8125
*www.aaos.org*

### American Academy of Otolaryngology
One Prince St.
Alexandria, VA 22314
Phone: 703-836-4444
*www.entnet.org*

### American Association of Naturopathic Physicians
4435 Wisconsin Ave. NW
Suite 403
Washington, DC 20016
Phone: 866-538-2267
202-237-8150
Fax: 202-237-8152
*www.naturopathic.org*

### American Association of Poison Control Centers
3201 New Mexico Ave. NW
Suite 330
Washington, DC 20016
Phone: 202-362-7217
Emergency hotline: 800-222-1222
*www.aapcc.org*

### American Board of Medical Specialties
1007 Church St., Suite 404
Evanston, IL 60201-5913
Phone: 847-491-9091
Board Certification Verification:
866-ASK-ABMS (275-2267)
*www.abms.org*

### American Botanical Council
6200 Manor Rd.
Austin, TX 78723

Phone: 512-926-4900
Fax: 512-926-2345
*www.herbalgram.org*

**American Cancer Society**
1599 Clifton Rd. NE
Atlanta, GA 30329
Phone: 800-ACS-2345 (227-2345)
*www.cancer.org*

**American Chiropractic Association**
1701 Clarendon Blvd.
Arlington, VA 22209
Phone: 800-986-4636
*www.amerchiro.org*

**American Chronic Pain Association**
Box 850
Rocklin, CA 95677
Phone: 800-533-3231
*www.theacpa.org*

**American College of Obstetricians and Gynecologists**
409 12th St. SW
Box 96920
Washington, DC 20090
Phone: 800-673-8444
202-638-5577
*www.acog.org*

**American College of Rheumatology**
1800 Century Place
Suite 250
Atlanta, GA 30345
Phone: 404-633-3777
*www.rheumatology.org*

**American Council for Headache Education**
19 Mantua Rd.
Mt. Royal, NJ 08061
Phone: 856-423-0258
*www.achenet.org*

**American Council on Alcoholism**
1000 E. Indian School Rd.
Phoenix, AZ 85014
Phone: 602-264-7403
Alcoholism Treatment HelpLine:
800-527-5344
*www.aca-usa.org*

**American Council on Exercise**
4851 Paramount Dr.
San Diego, CA 92123
Phone: 800-825-3636
858-279-8227
*www.acefitness.org*

**American Dental Association**
211 E. Chicago Ave.
Chicago, IL 60611
Phone: 312-440-2500
*www.ada.org*

**American Diabetes Association**
National Call Center
1701 North Beauregard St.
Alexandria, VA 22311
Phone: 800-DIABETES (342-2383)
*www.diabetes.org*

**American Dietetic Association**
120 South Riverside Plaza
Suite 2000
Chicago, IL 60606
Phone: 800-877-1600
*www.eatright.org*

**American Foundation for Urologic Disease**
1000 Corporate Blvd., Suite 410
Linthicum, MD 21090
Phone: 866-746-4282
410-689-3700
*www.afud.org*

**American Gastroenterological Association**
4930 Del Ray Ave.
Bethesda, MD 20814

Phone: 301-654-2055
*www.gastro.org*

## American Geriatrics Society

350 Fifth Ave., Suite 801
New York, NY 10118
Phone: 212-308-1414
*www.americangeriatrics.org*

## American Heart Association

7272 Greenville Ave.
Dallas, TX 75231
Phone: 800-AHA-USA-1 (242-8721)
*www.americanheart.org*

## American Holistic Medical Association

Box 2016
Edmonds, WA 98020
Phone: 425-967-0737
*www.holisticmedicine.org*

## American Journal of Clinical Nutrition

9650 Rockville Pike
Bethesda, MD 20814
Phone: 301-634-7038
Fax: 301-634-7351
*www.ajcn.org*

## American Liver Foundation

75 Maiden Lane, Suite 603
New York, NY 10038
Phone: 800-GO-LIVER (465-4837)
212-668-1000
*www.liverfoundation.org*

## American Lung Association

61 Broadway, Sixth Floor
New York, NY 10006
Phone: 800-586-4872
212-315-8700
*www.lungusa.org*

## American Lyme Disease Foundation, Inc.

Box 466
Lyme, CT 06371
*www.aldf.com*

## American Macular Degeneration Foundation

Box 515
Northampton, MA 01061
Phone: 888-MACULAR (622-8527)
413-268-7660
*www.macular.org*

## American Pain Foundation

201 North Charles St.
Suite 710
Baltimore, MD 21201
Phone: 888-615-PAIN (7246)
*www.painfoundation.org*

## American Physical Therapy Association

1111 North Fairfax St.
Alexandria, VA 22314
Phone: 800-999-APTA (2782)
703-684-APTA (2782)
For hearing impaired: 703-683-6748
*www.apta.org*

## American Psychological Association

750 First St. NE
Washington, DC 20002
Phone: 800-374-2721
202-336-5500
*www.apa.org*

## American Red Cross

National Headquarters
2025 E St. NW
Washington, DC 20006
Phone: 202-303-4498
*www.redcross.org*

## American Running Association

4405 East-West Hwy., Suite 405
Bethesda, MD 20814
Phone: 800-776-2732
301-913-9517
*www.americanrunning.org*

**American Sleep Apnea Association**
1424 K St. NW, Suite 302
Washington, DC 20005
Phone: 202-293-3650
*www.sleepapnea.org*

**American Society for Nutrition**
9650 Rockville Pike
Bethesda, MD 20814
Phone: 301-634-7050
Fax: 301-634-7892
*www.nutrition.org*

**American Society of Hypertension**
148 Madison Ave., Fifth Floor
New York, NY 10016
Phone: 212-696-9099
*www.ash-us.org*

**American Society of Plastic Surgeons**
444 East Algonquin Rd.
Arlington Heights, IL 60005
Phone: 888-4-PLASTIC (475-2784)
*www.plasticsurgery.org*

**American Speech–Language–Hearing Association**
10801 Rockville Pike
Rockville, MD 20852
Phone: 800-638-8255
*www.asha.org*

**American Stroke Association**
7272 Greenville Ave.
Dallas, TX 75231
Phone: 888-4-STROKE (478-7653)
*www.strokeassociation.org*

**American Tinnitus Association**
Box 5
Portland, OR 97207
Phone: 800-634-8978
503-248-9985

Fax: 503-248-0024
*www.ata.org*

**Anxiety Disorders Association of America**
8730 Georgia Ave., Suite 600
Silver Spring, MD 20910
Phone: 240-485-1001
*www.adaa.org*

**Arthritis Foundation**
Box 7669
Atlanta, GA 30357
Phone: 800-568-4045
*www.arthritis.org*

**Asthma and Allergy Foundation of America**
1233 20th St. NW, Suite 402
Washington, DC 20036
Phone: 800-7-ASTHMA (727-8462)
202-466-7643
Fax: 202-466-8940
*www.aafa.org*

**Center for Science in the Public Interest**
1875 Connecticut Ave. NW
Suite 300
Washington, DC 20009
Phone: 202-332-9110
Fax: 202-265-4954
*www.cspinet.org*

**Children and Adults with Attention-Deficit/Hyperactivity Disorder**
8181 Professional Place, Suite 150
Landover, MD 20785
Phone: 800-233-4050
301-306-7070
Fax: 301-306-7090
*www.chadd.org*

**Colorectal Cancer Network (CCNetwork)**
Box 182
Kensington, MD 20895
Phone: 301-879-1500
*www.colorectal-cancer.net*

**Council for Responsible Nutrition**
1828 L St. NW, Suite 900
Washington, DC 20036
Phone: 202-776-7929
*www.crnusa.org*

**Crohn's & Colitis Foundation of America**
386 Park Ave. South
17th Floor
New York, NY 10016
Phone: 800-932-2423
*www.ccfa.org*

**Deafness Research Foundation**
2801 M St. NW
Washington, DC 20007
Phone: 866-454-3924
202-719-8008
For hearing impaired: 888-435-6104
*www.drf.org*

**Endocrine Society**
8401 Connecticut Ave.
Suite 900
Chevy Chase, MD 20815
Phone: 301-941-0200
*www.endo-society.org*

**Food and Nutrition Information Center**
National Agricultural Library
Room 105
10301 Baltimore Ave.
Beltsville, MD 20705
Phone: 301-504-5414
For hearing impaired: 301-504-6856
Fax: 301-504-6409
*www.nal.usda.gov/fnic/*

**Glaucoma Research Foundation**
251 Post St., Suite 600
San Francisco, CA 94108
Phone: 800-826-6693
415-986-3162
Fax: 415-986-3763
*www.glaucoma.org*

**Healthfinder**
National Health Information Center
Box 1133
Washington, DC 20013
*www.healthfinder.gov*

**Herb Research Foundation**
4140 15th St.
Boulder, CO 80304
Phone: 303-449-2265
*www.herbs.org*

**Hippocrates Health Institute**
1443 Palmdale Court
West Palm Beach, FL 33411
Phone: 800-842-2125
561-471-8876
Fax: 561-471-9464
*www.hippocratesinst.org*

**International Chiropractors Association**
1110 North Glebe Rd., Suite 1000
Arlington, VA 22201
Phone: 800-423-4690
703-528-5000
Fax: 703-528-5023
*www.chiropractic.org*

**International Food Information Council**
1100 Connecticut Ave. NW
Suite 430
Washington, DC 20036
Phone: 202-296-6540
Fax: 202-296-6547
*www.ific.org*

**Interstitial Cystitis Association**
110 North Washington St., Suite 340
Rockville, MD 20850
Phone: 800-HELP-ICA (435-7422)
301-610-5300
Fax: 301-610-5308
*www.ichelp.com*

**Journal of the American Medical Association**
515 North State St.
Chicago, IL 60610
Phone: 312-464-2403
Fax: 312-464-5831
*www.jama.ama-assn.org*

**Kushi Institute**
Box 7
Becket, MA 01223
Phone: 800-975-8744
413-623-5741, x101
Fax: 413-623-8827
*www.kushiinstitute.org*

**The Lancet**
Customer Services
Elsevier Ltd.
The Boulevard, Langford Lane
Kidlington, Oxford
OX5 1GB, United Kingdom
Phone: 800-462-6198
+1-407-345-4082
Toll-free Fax: 800-327-9021
*www.thelancet.com*

**Leukemia & Lymphoma Society**
1311 Mamaroneck Ave.
White Plains, NY 10605
Phone: 800-955-4572
914-949-5213
*www.leukemia-lymphoma.org*

**Melanoma International Foundation**
250 Mapleflower Rd.
Glenmoore, PA 19343
Phone: 866-INFO-NMF (463-6663)
610-942-3432
*www.melanomainternational.org*

**Merck Manual of Medical Information**
Merck & Co., Inc.
One Merck Drive
Box 100
Whitehouse Station, NJ 08889

Phone: 908-423-1000
*www.merck.com*

**National Cancer Institute**
6116 Executive Blvd.
Bethesda, MD 20892
Phone: 800-4-CANCER (422-6237)
For hearing impaired: 800-332-8615
*www.cancer.gov*

**National Capital Poison Center**
3201 New Mexico Ave. NW
Suite 310
Washington, DC 20016
Phone: 202-362-3867
Emergency line: 800-222-1222
*www.poison.org*

**National Center for Complementary and Alternative Medicine**
NCCAM Clearinghouse
Box 7923
Gaithersburg, MD 20898
Phone: 888-644-6226
301-519-3153
For hearing impaired: 866-464-3615
Fax: 866-464-3616
*www.nccam.nih.gov*

**National Center for Homeopathy**
801 North Fairfax St.
Suite 306
Alexandria, VA 22314
Phone: 703-548-7790
Fax: 703-548-7792
*www.homeopathic.org*

**National Eye Institute**
2020 Vision Place
Bethesda, MD 20892
Phone: 301-496-5248
*www.nei.nih.gov*

**National Headache Foundation**
820 North Orleans, Suite 217
Chicago, IL 60610

Phone: 888-NHF-5552 (643-5552)
*www.headaches.org*

## National Heart, Lung and Blood Institute

Building 31, Room 5A52
31 Center Dr., MSC 2486
Bethesda, MD 20892
Phone: 301-592-8573
For hearing impaired: 240-629-3255
Fax: 240-629-3246
*www.nhlbi.nih.gov*

## National Institute for Occupational Safety and Health

200 Independence Ave. SW
Room 715H
Washington, DC 20201
Phone: 800-35-NIOSH (356-4674)
513-533-8326
*www.cdc.gov/niosh/homepage.html*

## National Institute of Allergy and Infectious Diseases

6610 Rockledge Dr.
MSC 6612
Bethesda, MD 20892
Phone: 301-496-5717
*www3.niaid.nih.gov*

## National Institute of Arthritis and Musculoskeletal and Skin Diseases

One AMS Circle
Bethesda, MD 20892
Phone: 877-22-NIAMS (226-4267)
301-495-4484
For hearing impaired: 301-565-2966
*www.niams.nih.gov*

## National Institute of Dental and Craniofacial Research

National Institutes of Health
Bethesda, MD 20892-2190
Phone: 301-496-4261
*www.nidcr.nih.gov*

## National Institute of Diabetes and Digestive and Kidney Diseases

Building 31, Room 9A06
31 Center Dr., MSC 2560
Bethesda, MD 20892-2560
Phone: 301-496-3583
*www.niddk.nih.gov*

## National Institutes of Health

9000 Rockville Pike
Bethesda, MD 20892
Phone: 301-496-4000
*www.nih.gov*
(other toll-free NIH telephone numbers can be found at *www.nih. gov/health/infoline.htm*)

## National Institute of Mental Health

6001 Executive Blvd.
MSC 9663, Room 8184
Bethesda, MD 20892
Phone: 866-615-NIMH (6464)
301-443-4513
For hearing impaired: 301-443-8431
*www.nimh.nih.gov*

## National Institute of Neurological Disorders and Stroke

Box 5801
Bethesda, MD 20824
Phone: 800-352-9424
301-496-5751
For hearing impaired: 301-468-5981
*www.ninds.nih.gov*

## National Institute on Aging

Building 31, Room 5C27
31 Center Dr., MSC 2292
Bethesda, MD 20892
Phone: 301-496-1752
*www.nia.nih.gov*

## National Institute on Alcohol Abuse and Alcoholism

5635 Fishers Ln., MSC 9304
Bethesda, MD 20892

Phone: 301-443-0796
*www.niaaa.nih.gov*

**National Kidney Foundation**
30 East 33rd St.
New York, NY 10016
Phone: 800-622-9010
212-889-2210
*www.kidney.org*

**National Multiple Sclerosis Society**
733 Third Ave.
New York, NY 10017
Phone: 800-FIGHT-MS (344-4867)
*www.nmss.org*

**National Osteoporosis Foundation**
1232 22nd St. NW
Washington, DC 20037
Phone: 202-223-2226
*www.nof.org*

**National Prostate Cancer Coalition**
1154 15th St. NW
Washington, DC 20005
Phone: 888-245-9455
202-463-9455
*www.4npcc.org*

**National Psoriasis Foundation**
6600 SW 92nd Ave.
Suite 300
Portland, OR 97223
Phone: 800-723-9166
503-244-7404
*www.psoriasis.org*

**National Safety Council**
1121 Spring Lake Dr.
Itasca, IL 60143
Phone: 630-285-1121
*www.nsc.org*

**National Sleep Foundation**
1522 K St. NW, Suite 500
Washington, DC 20005

Phone: 202-347-3471
*www.sleepfoundation.org*

**National Spinal Cord Injury Association**
6701 Democracy Blvd.
Suite 300-9
Bethesda, MD 20817
Phone: 800-962-9629
*www.spinalcord.org*

**National Stroke Association**
9707 East Easter Ln.
Centennial, CO 80112
Phone: 800-STROKES (787-6537)
303-649-1328
*www.stroke.org*

**National Women's Health Information Center**
8550 Arlington Blvd.
Suite 300
Fairfax, VA 22031
Phone: 800-994-WOMAN (9662)
*www.4women.gov*

*New England Journal of Medicine*
10 Shattuck St.
Boston, MA 02115
Phone: 800-843-6356
617-734-9800
Fax: 617-739-9864
*http://content.nejm.org*

**Parkinson's Disease Foundation**
1359 Broadway, Suite 1509
New York, NY 10018
Phone: 800-457-6676
*www.pdf.org*

*Practical Gastroenterology*
c/o Shugar Publishing, Inc.
99B Main St.
Westhampton Beach, NY 11978
Phone: 631-288-4404
Fax: 631-288-4435
*www.practicalgastro.com*

**School of Natural Healing (and Christopher Publications)**

Box 412
Springville, UT 84663
Phone: 800-372-8255
801-489-4254
Fax: 801-489-8341
*http://schoolofnaturalhealing.com/ snh_cc.htm*

**SeekWellness.com**

26 South Main St.
PMB #162
Concord, NH 03301
Phone: 603-397-0103
*www.wellweb.com*

**Skin Cancer Foundation**

149 Madison Ave.
Suite 901
New York, NY 10016
Phone: 800-SKIN-490 (754-6490)
*www.skincancer.org*

**Susan G. Komen Breast Cancer Foundation**

5005 LBJ Freeway
Suite 250
Dallas, TX 75244
Phone: 972-855-1600
Toll-Free Breast Care Helpline:
800-IM-AWARE (462-9273)
*www.komen.org*

**US Centers for Disease Control and Prevention**

1600 Clifton Rd.
Atlanta, GA 30333
Phone: 404-639-3311
For hearing impaired: 404-639-3312
Public inquiries: 800-311-3435
*www.cdc.gov*

**US Department of Agriculture**

1400 Independence Ave. SW
Washington, DC 20250

Phone: 877-677-2369
202-720-5711
*www.usda.gov*

**US Department of Health and Human Services**

200 Independence Ave. SW
Washington, DC 20201
Phone: 877-696-6775
202-619-0257
*www.hhs.gov*

**US Food and Drug Administration**

5600 Fishers Ln.
Rockville, MD 20857
Phone: 888-INFO-FDA (463-6332)
*www.fda.gov*

**US National Library of Medicine**

8600 Rockville Pike
Bethesda, MD 20894
Phone: 888-FIND-NLM (346-3656)
301-594-5983
*www.nlm.nih.gov*

**US Soyfoods Directory**

c/o Stevens & Associates, Inc.
4816 North Pennsylvania St.
Indianapolis, IN 46205
Phone: 317-926-6272
*www.soyfoods.com*

**Weight-control Information Network (WIN)**

One WIN Way
Bethesda, MD 20892
Phone: 877-946-4627
Fax: 202-828-1028
*http://win.niddk.nih.gov/index.htm*

**Wunderlich Center for Nutritional Medicine**

8821 Dr. Martin Luther King, Jr.,
St. North
St. Petersburg, FL 33702
Phone: 727-822-3612
Fax: 727-578-1370
*www.wunderlichcenter.com*

# Online-Only Resources

### www.acupuncture.com
Information and resources on alternative medicine. It has a provider directory, provides answers to frequently asked questions, and allows you to call on its experts to answer more specific questions.

### www.altmedicine.com
Alternative Health News Online provides links to excellent sources of information on the Web about alternative health issues. Also provides a digest of new information.

### www.health-library.com/index.html
Links to a wide variety of health, fitness, nutrition and sexuality sites, with a section on alternative medicine.

### www.kidshealth.org
KidsHealth is the largest site on the Web providing doctor-approved health information about children from before birth through adolescence. The site was created by pediatric medical experts at the Nemours Foundation.

### www.mealsforyou.com
Thousands of recipes, meal plans and complete nutritional information. Look up recipes by name, ingredient or nutritional content.

### www.medlineplus.gov
Health information selected by the US National Library of Medicine and the National Institutes of Health (NIH) from a database of more than 4,000 medical journals.

### www.medweb.emory.edu
MedWeb is a directory of health-related Web sites, maintained by Emory University.

### www.mothernature.com
In addition to its main commerce area, this site provides a wealth of health information, an encyclopedia of natural health topics, expert advice and an archive of articles on a range of subjects.

### www.pain.com
This site offers comprehensive resources about pain studies, links to other pain-control sites and more.

### www.pitt.edu/~cbw/altm.html
The Alternative Medicine Homepage is a jumpstation for sources of information on unconventional, unorthodox, unproven or alternative, complementary, innovative and integrative therapies.

### www.webmd.com
This comprehensive site includes information on a variety of illnesses and diseases as well as herbs, alternative medicine and more. ■

# Recommended
# Reading List

# Recommended Reading List

## Body Power/Brain Power

*Body for Life,* by Bill Phillips with Michael D'Orso. HarperCollins.

*The Healing Power of the Mind,* by Rolf Alexander, MD. Healing Arts Press.

*Your Miracle Brain,* by Jean Carper. HarperCollins.

## Food, Healthful Eating and Weight Programs

*Flax for Life!,* by Jade Beutler, RRT, RCP. Apple Publishing.

*Food Enzymes—The Missing Link to Radiant Health,* by Humbert Santillo, MH, ND. Lotus Press.

*40-30-30 Fat-Burning Nutrition,* by Joyce and Gene Daoust. Wharton Publishing.

*Garlic—Nature's Super Healer,* by Joan Wilen and Lydia Wilen. Prentice Hall.

*Healthy Nuts,* by Gene Spiller, PhD. Avery Publishing Group.

*The Omega Diet,* by Artemis P. Simopoulos, MD, and Jo Robinson. HarperCollins.

*Seaweed—A Cook's Guide,* by Lesley Ellis. Fisher Books.

*7-Day Detox Miracle,* by Peter Bennett, ND, and Stephen Barrie, ND, with Sara Faye. Prima Lifestyles.

*Understanding Fats & Oils,* by Michael T. Murray, ND, and Jade Beutler, RRT, RCP. Apple Publishing.

## Herbs

*The Green Pharmacy,* by James A. Duke, PhD. St. Martin's Press.

*The Herbal Home Spa,* by Greta Breedlove. Storey Books.

*Herbal Remedy Gardens,* by Dorie Byers. Storey Books.

*Natural Healing with Herbs,* by Humbert Santillo, MH, ND. Hohm Press.

*10 Essential Herbs,* by Lalitha Thomas. Hohm Press.

## Just for Men

*The Viagra Alternative,* by Marc Bonnard, MD. Healing Arts Press.

## Just for Women

*The Estrogen Alternative,* by Raquel Martin with Judi Gerstung, DC. Inner Traditions International.

*Your Pregnancy—Every Woman's Guide,* by Glade B. Curtis, MD, OB/GYN. DaCapo Lifelong.

## Just for Pets

*Natural Pet Cures,* by John Heinerman, PhD. Prentice Hall.

## New-Age and Age-Old (Mostly Alternative) Therapies

*Alternative Medicine: The Definitive Guide,* compiled by The Burton Goldberg Group. Ten Speed Press.

*Ayurvedic Secrets to Longevity and Total Health,* by Peter Anselmo with James S. Brooks, MD. Prentice Hall.

*Common Scents,* by Lorrie Hargis. Woodland Publishing.

*Creative Healing,* by Michael Samuels, MD, and Mary Rockwood Lane, RN. John Wiley & Sons.

*The Healing Power of Color,* by Betty Wood. Destiny Books.

*Healing Visualizations,* by Gerald Epstein, MD. Bantam Books.

*Laffirmations—1,001 Ways to Add Humor to Your Life and Work,* by Joel Goodman. Health Communications, Inc.

*The Power of Touch,* by Phyllis K. Davis, PhD. Hay House, Inc.

*Prayer, Faith and Healing—Cure Your Body, Heal Your Mind and Restore Your Soul,* by Kenneth Winston Caine and Brian Paul Kaufman. Rodale Books.

*Qigong—Essence of the Healing Dance,* by Garri Garripoli and Friends. Health Communications, Inc.

*The Ultimate Healing System,* by Donald Lepore, ND. Woodland Publishing.

*Your Own Perfect Medicine,* by Martha M. Christy. Wishland Publishing.

## Specific Health Challenges

*An Alternative Medicine Definitive Guide to Cancer,* by W. John Diamond, MD, and W. Lee Cowden, MD, with Burton Goldberg. Alternativemedicine.com Books.

*Asthma-Free in 21 Days,* by Kathryn Shafer, PhD, with Fran Greenfield, MA. HarperCollins.

*Beyond Aspirin,* by Thomas Newmark and Paul Schulick. Hohm Press.

*Enhancing Fertility Naturally,* by Nicky Wesson. Healing Arts Press.

*Naturally Healthy Skin,* by Stephanie Tourles. Storey Books.

*The Pain Cure,* by Dharma Singh Khalsa, MD, with Cameron Stauth. Warner Books.

*The Prozac Alternative,* by Ran Knishinsky. Healing Arts Press.

*7 Weeks to Emotional Healing,* by Joan Mathews Larson, PhD. Ballantine Books.

## Vitamins and Other Supplements

*Dr. Heinerman's Encyclopedia of Nature's Vitamins and Minerals,* by John Heinerman, PhD. Prentice Hall.

*The Natural Pharmacist: Natural Health Bible,* edited by Steven Bratman, MD, and David Kroll, PhD. Crown Publishing. ■

# Recipe Index

**Breakfast Fare**
The Amazing Gin-Soaked Raisin
    Remedy, 13
Banana Bread Oatmeal, 22
Hazelnut Corn Bran Muffins, 278
Pancake Mix, 263
Three-Cherry Jam, 93
Waffle Mix, 263
Yogurt Cereal Bars, 283

**Beverages**
The Koch Family Guggle-Muggle, 41
Love Elixir, 148
Papaya Shake, 123

**Appetizers**
Apple Salsa with Cinnamon Tortilla
    Chips, 108
Cinnamon-Roasted Almonds, 132
New West Crab Cakes, 277
Sunrise Salsa, 34

**Salads**
Papaya Salad with String Beans, 11
Organic Garden Salad with Fresh
    Herbs, 26
Tropical Fruit Salad with Ginger and
    Peanuts, 280
Yogurt Fruit Salad with Sunflower
    Seeds, 75

**Soups**
Carrot Soup, 210
Chicken Soup with Okra, 48
Chilled Czech Blueberry Soup, 76
Dr. Ziment's Chicken Soup, 36
Garlic Soup, 269
Lentil Vegetable Soup, 231
Lillian Wilen's Essential Chicken
    Soup, 35

**Entrées**
Cashew Shrimp, 279
Champagne-Poached Salmon, 73
Curried Turkey, 282
40-Clove Garlic Chicken, 220
Four-Bean Bake, 261
Honey Lemon Basil Chicken, 260
Pasta with Zucchini and Roasted
    Garlic, 268
Pecan Four-Cheese Pizza, 278
Sautéed Tofu with Ginger Sauce, 273
Walnut Macaroni Casserole, 276

**Side Dishes**
Beets in Orange Sauce, 70
Broccoli Slaw, 90
Country Cole Slaw, 229
Cucumbers in Sour Cream, 120
Garlicky Greens, 141
Jade Green Broccoli, 39
Lemony-Parsley Carrots, 78

Mashed Sweet Potatoes with Garlic,
    268
Mexican Eggplant with Fennel Seeds,
    195
Peanut Slaw, 182
Roasted Garlic, 267
Sauerkraut, 253
Sexual-Stamina Eggplant, 221
Sweet Pickled Jerusalem Artichokes,
    18

**Dips/Sauces**
Eggplant–Yogurt Dip, 282
Emerald Sauce, 25
Ginger–Onion Vinaigrette, 272

**Desserts**
African Banana Fritters, 54
Apricot Snowballs, 168
Elderberry Pie, 163
Flax Cookies, 265
Ginger Cookies, 271
Make Your Own Yogurt, 284
Peanut Ice Cream, 280
Sweet and Spicy Pumpkin Seeds, 143

# Index

**A**

Acid burns, 30
Acne, 153–154
    in children, 207
    scars from, 155
Acorns for sexual problems, 159
Acupressure
    for appetite management,
        196
    for colds and flu, 38
    for constipation, 47
    for coughs, 50
    for depression, 55
    for diarrhea, 58
    for headaches, 105
    for hiccups, 117
    hoku point, 181
    for insomnia, 165
    for muscle cramps, 136
    for tension and anxiety, 175
    for toothache, 179
Acupuncture
    for colds and flu, 38
    eyes and, 79
Aduki beans for kidney problems,
    190
Aerobic exercise, hearing and, 68
Age spots, 28
Alcoholic beverages. *See* also
    Drinking
        calcium and, 229
        dehydration and, 129
        prostate problems and, 219
        weight control and, 201
Alcoholism, 59

Allergies. *See* also Asthma; Hayfever
    bee pollen for, 259
    to bee stings, 4
    hangovers and, 61
    to honey, 4, 49
    prevention of, 3
    honeycomb for, 4
    relief from, 3
Allicin, 37
Allspice for indigestion, 126
Almonds. *See* also Nuts
    allergy to, 4
    for dead skin, 155
    for headaches, 103–104
    for heartburn, 127
    for hemorrhoids, 113
    intoxication, preventing, with,
        63
    for memory problems, 132
Aloe vera
    for arthritis, 16
    for burns, 30
    for headaches, 105
    for shingles, 115
    for warts, 193
Alopecia, 94
Amber
    for nosebleeds, 140
    for sore throats, 43
Amethyst
    for memory problems, 132
    for preventing intoxication,
        63
Ammonia for insect stings, 7
Anemia, 5–6

Animals
    bee pollen for, 261
    bites, 6
Anise remedies
    for coughs, 209
    for halitosis, 184
    for indigestion, 122, 126
    for nightmares, 166
    for sore throats, 45
Anisette liqueur for flatulence, 125
Antibiotics, yogurt and, 281–282
Anticoagulants with garlic, 24
Anti-Jet Lag Diet, 129
Anxiety. *See* Tension and anxiety
Aphrodisiacs, 150–152, 272
Apple butter for burns, 30
Apple cider vinegar
    for aching feet, 84
    for arthritis, 13
    for colds and flu, 37–38
    for cold sores, 115
    for coughs, 48
    for fatigue, 82
    for hair problems, 96
    for headaches, 106
    for heartburn, 127
    for hiccups, 117
    for hoarseness/laryngitis, 44
    for indigestion, 123
    for kidney problems, 190
    for leg cramps, 135
    for memory problems, 132
    for pruritis, 143
    for rectal itching, 144
    for shingles, 116

in skin-awakener, 236
for sore throats, 42
for sprains, 171
for varicose veins, 88–89
for weight management, 196
Apples/apple juice remedies
cholesterol and, 20
for coffee breath, 184
for colds and flu, 39
for conjunctivitis, 71
for constipation, 46
for diarrhea, 58
for eye inflammation, 73
for high blood pressure, 119
for hoarseness/laryngitis, 44
for indigestion, 212
Apricot products
for anemia, 5
for asthma, 18
for constipation, 46
in stopping smoking, 169–170
Arginine
for herpes, 114
in nuts, 275
Arrhythmia, 110
Arrowroot for indigestion, 124
Arthritis
natural remedies for, 10–12
topical treatments for, 12–16
Artificial tears, 72
Ascorbic acid for hemorrhoids, 113
Asparagine for prostate enlargement, 218
Asparagus
as diuretic, 189
for kidney stones, 190
Aspirin
for hair problems, 98
for heart attacks, 109
Asthma, 16–19. *See also* Allergies;
Hayfever
wild cherry-bark tea for, 17
Atherosclerosis
cholesterol and, 20–22
natural remedies for, 19–20
Athletes, bee pollen for, 259
Athlete's foot, 87
Attention deficit/hyperactivity
disorder (ADHD), 208
Autohypnotic suggestions for
constipation, 47
Avocados
cholesterol and, 20–21

for dry elbows and knees, 158
for dry skin, 237
Ayurvedic medicine, 273

**B**
Back pain, 23–25
ginger for, 271
Baking soda
for animal bites or insect stings, 6
for corns and calluses, 85
for halitosis, 184
as hand cleanser, 101
for hives, 143
for pyorrhea, 181
for shingles, 116
Baldness, 94–95
Banana remedies
allergies and, 3
for bruises, 27
for cuts, 159
for depression, 53
for diarrhea, 58
for leg cramps, 134
for poison ivy, 147
for splinter removal, 159
in wrinkle prevention, 160
Bancha leaves for sties, 77
Bandage remover, pain-free, 240
Barley/barley water, 249
for coughs, 49
for diarrhea, 57–58, 210
for ulcers, 186
Basil
for indigestion, 124
menstruation, for bringing on, 227
in pain relief, 14
Bathing made easy, 293
Bay leaves
for colic, 212
for flatulence, 125
B-complex vitamins, when to take, 289
Beans. *See also* Black beans;
Garbanzo beans
for coughs, 50
in stabilizing blood sugars, 22
Beauty mask, making your own, 236
Bed rest, disadvantages of, 287
Bed-wetting, 188–189
in children, 208–209
Bee pollen, 258–262
for enlarged prostate, 217–218

for fatigue, 81–82
for menopause, 231
Bee stings, allergies to, 4
Beet remedies
for constipation, 46
for coughs, 49
for dandruff, 95
for low blood pressure, 121
Ben Wa Balls for sexual problems, 149
Bioflavonoids
for atherosclerosis, 20
for hay fever, 4
for nosebleed, 141
for spider bites, 9
Bites and stings, 6–9
Black beans
for back pain, 23–24
for hoarseness/laryngitis, 44
Blackberries for diarrhea, 58, 210
Black cohosh for menopause, 231–232
Black eyes, 28–29
Black radish for gallbladder
problems, 92
Blackstrap molasses
for bruises, 27
for canker sores, 185
for constipation, 48
in preventing tooth decay, 182–183
for warts, 193
Black thread as cough remedy, 209–210
Black widow spider bites, 9
Bladder control in women, 225
Bleeding disorders and garlic, 5
Bleeding gums, 180, 182
Blisters, fever, 115
Blood clots, rocking chair to prevent, 135
Blood pressure. *See* Hypertension;
Low blood pressure
Blood-related conditions
anemia, 5–6
Bloodshot eyes, 69
Blue
in attracting mosquitoes, 8
effect of, on suicide rate, 133
food consumption and, 199
Blueberries for night vision, 76
Body Mass Index (BMI), 202, 203
Body odor, 25–26

Boils, 156–158
Brain fog. *See* Jungle Punch
Bran
    for earaches, 65
    for indigestion, 125, 126
Brazil nuts, 275–276
Breast-feeding, 230–231
    colic and, 212–213
Brewer's yeast
    for acne, 154
    for cataracts, 70
    cholesterol and, 21–22
    for constipation, 47
    for corns and calluses, 86
    for eczema, 142
    for nursing mother, 230
    for wrinkles, 160
Broccoli remedies
    for colds and flu, 39
    for heart problems, 111
Bromelain for carpal tunnel
    syndrome, 34
Bronchial coughs, 51
Brown recluse spider bites, 9
Brown rice for acne, 154
Brown spots, 28
Bruises and skin discoloration,
    27–29
Burdock for carpal tunnel syndrome,
    34
Burning feet, 31
Burns, 29–31
Burnt throat, 31
Burnt tongue, 31
Bursitis, 10
Butcher's broom for phlebitis,
    142
Buttermilk. *See also* Dairy products
    for diarrhea, 58
    for enlarged pores, 155
    for freckles, 158
    for genital itching, 144
    in wrinkle prevention, 161
B vitamins, 6. *See* also specific
    vitamin
        for fingernail problems, 102
        for hangovers, 62

**C**
Cabbage remedies
    for alcohol consumption, 62
    for migraine headaches, 107
    for ulcers, 186–187

Caffeine. *See* also Coffee
    calcium and, 229
    depression and, 53
Calcium, 6, 281
    for leg cramps, 134, 135
    need for, 245
    nervous tics and, 55
    for premenstrual relief, 229
Calendula for hair problems, 97
Calluses, 85–86
Calories burned per hour, 199
Cancer therapy, bee pollen and, 260
Candida/yeast problems and carrot
    juice, 78
Canker sores, 185
Capsaicin for carpal tunnel syndrome,
    34
Caraway seed remedies
    for colic, 212
    for earaches, 65
    for indigestion, 122, 126
Carbonated drinks for nausea and
    vomiting, 137
Cardamom seeds for indigestion,
    122
Carob
    as caffeine substitute, 175
    for indigestion, 212
Carotenoids and stopping smoking,
    169
Carpal tunnel syndrome, 32–34
Carrots/carrot juice
    as blood fortifier, 6
    cholesterol and, 21
    for diarrhea, 210
    for dry skin, 238
    for eye problems, 78, 80
    for heartburn, 127
    for memory problems, 131
    for pruritis, 143
    in stopping smoking, 169
    for urinary problems, 188
    for vision, 76, 78
    for warts, 192
    for weeping sores, 156
Cashews, 275, 276, 277
Castor oil
    for canker sores, 185
    for corns and calluses, 85
    for earaches/ear infections, 65
    for freckles, 158
    for plantar warts, 193
    for rough hands, 101

    for tinnitus, 67–68
    for wrinkles, 160
Cataracts, 69–71
    sun blindness and, 77
Catnip for sprains, 172
Cavity prevention, 182–183
Cayenne pepper remedies
    for arthritis, 15–16
    for carpal tunnel syndrome, 34
    diarrhea and, 57
    for excessive menstrual flow, 228
    as fever reducer, 42
    for hangovers, 60
    for heart problems, 112
    for high blood pressure, 120
    for indigestion, 124
    for motion sickness, 138
    for nosebleeds, 140
    for sprains, 171
    for tension and anxiety, 175
    for toothache, 179
    for wounds, 156
Celery/celery juice
    for arthritis, 11
    for depression, 55
    as diuretic, 189
    for sciatica, 24
Cellulite, eliminating, 200
Chalk for warts, 193
Chamomile
    for carpal tunnel syndrome, 34
    for earaches, 65
    for eye problems, 71, 74, 76, 79
    for hair problems, 97, 99
    for heart palpitations, 110
    for indigestion, 123, 212
    for insomnia, 162, 164
    as mood lifter, 53–54
    for motion sickness, 138
    for nausea and vomiting, 137
    for oily skin, 237
    for picky eaters, 213
    for premenstrual relief, 229
    for sore throats, 43
    for toothache, 178
    for warts, 192
Champagne
    for exfoliation scrub, 239
Chapped hands, 101–102
Chapped lips, 239
Charcoal
    activated, for diarrhea, 57
    for flatulence, 125

Charley horse, 133
Chemical burns, 30
Chemicals as eye irritants, 72
Cherries/cherry juice
    for arthritis, 10–11
    for gout, 92
Cherry-bark tea for asthma, 17
Chia seeds
    as energy booster, 83
    for tension and anxiety, 176
Chicken pox
    in children, 209
    virus causing, and relation to
        shingles, 115
Chicken soup
    for colds, 35–37
    for hangovers, 62
Chickpeas for brown spots, 28
Chihuahuas, asthma and, 16
Children's health
    acne, 207
    attention deficit/hyperactivity
        disorder, 208
    bed-wetting, 208–209
    chicken pox, 209
    colds and flu, 209
    colic, 212–213
    coughs, 209–210
    croup, 210
    diarrhea, 210–211
    eye irritants, 209
    fever, 211
    foreign substance in the nose, 211
    head lice, 211–212
    indigestion, 212–213
    picky eaters, 213
    rashes, 213
    splinters, 213
    teething, 214
    tonsillitis, 214
Chinese balls for carpal tunnel
    syndrome, 33
Chives
    for hair problems, 96
    iron in, 5
Chocolate
    craving for, 175
    for firming facial treatment, 236
Cholesterol
    high, 20–22
    nuts to lower, 276
Choline for memory problems, 131
Chromium, cholesterol and, 21–22

Cinnamon remedies
    for bed-wetting, 208
    for diarrhea, 57, 210
    for excessive menstrual flow, 228
    for flu, 41
    for halitosis, 183
Citrus essential oils as mood lifter, 54
Clams for sexual problems, 150
Cleavers for weight control, 195
Clove remedies
    for halitosis, 184
    for memory problems, 131
    for nausea and vomiting, 137
    for paper cuts, 159
    in stopping smoking, 169
    for toothache, 180
Cobnuts, 277
Cob webs for wounds, 156
Coconut macaroons for diarrhea,
    58–59
Coconut milk, 249
    for enlarged prostate, 218
Coconut oil for type 2
    diabetes, 56
Cod-liver oil
    for arthritis, 12
    for boils, 157
Coenzyme Q-10 for pyorrhea, 181
Coffee. *See also* Caffeine
    for arthritis, 14–15
    elimination from diet, for prostate
        problems, 219
Coffee breath, 184
Cola syrup for nausea and vomiting,
    138
Cold feet, 86–87
Colds and flu, 35–45
    in children, 209
Cold showers in stimulating sexual
    desire, 221
Cold sores, 115
Colic in children, 212–213
Color as mood lifter, 55. *See also*
    Blue; Yellow
Combination skin, 242–243
Comfrey remedies
    for gout, 92–93
    for phlebitis, 89–90
    for sprains, 172
Computers, carpal tunnel syndrome
    and use of, 33
Confucius, 273
Conjunctivitis, 3, 71

Constipation, 46–48
    prunes for, 131
    during pregnancy, 230
Contact lens, removal of, before
    doing eyewash, 80
Copper, 5, 275
Coriander seeds for sexual problems,
    151
Corn for canker sores, 185
Cornmeal
    in dry shampoo, 97
    for stomach cramps, 128
Corn oil
    as source of polyunsaturated
        fats, 22
    for dandruff, 96
Corns and calluses, 85–86
Corn silk/corn silk tea
    for arthritis, 14
    for bed-wetting, 208
    for cystitis, 226
    as diuretic, 189
    for enlarged prostate, 218
    for urinary problems, 188
Cornstarch
    for bruises, 27
    in dry shampoo, 97
    for genital itching, 144
    for hives, 144
    for shaving rash, 145
Cortisone
    garlic therapy as substitute
        for, 17
    yucca as substitute for, 15
Coughs, 48–52
    in children, 209–210
Cox-2 inhibitors, 271
Crab for poison ivy, 147
Cracked heels, 88
Cramp bark for leg cramps, 135
Cranberries/cranberry juice
    for asthma, 19
    for cystitis, 226
    for hemorrhoids, 113
    for urinary problems, 188
Cream of tartar
    for hives, 144
    for sore throats, 42
Crohn's disease, 58–59
Croup in children, 210
Cucumber remedies
    for acne, 154
    for drinking problems, 60

for eye inflammation, 74
for high blood pressure, 119
for menopause, 232
Cuts and scrapes, 158–159
Cystitis, 225–226

**D**
Daikon
for bruises, 27
for indigestion, 122
Dairy products and asthma, 17
Damiana for impotence, 220
Dandelion remedies
for corns and calluses, 86
for freckles, 158
for warts, 192
Dandruff, 95–96
Dates for constipation, 47
Deep breathing, low blood pressure and, 121
Dental floss, bad breath and, 183
Dental work, preparing for, 180
Depression and stress, 53–55
Dermatitis, 3
Detoxification, 169
Devil's claw, 292
for carpal tunnel syndrome, 34
Diabetes, 56
coconut oil for, 56
infected sores and, 156
Diamonds for insomnia, 162
Diaper rash, 213
Diarrhea, 56–59
cherries as cause of, 11
in children, 210–211
yogurt for, 59, 282
Dill seeds for indigestion, 126
Diuretics, 188–189
potassium loss and, 134–135
Double-chin prevention, 239
Dried beans, soaking, in preventing gas, 126
Drinking, 59–63. *See* also Alcoholic beverages
Drug allergies, 3
Dry cough, 51
Dry eyes, 71–72
Dry shampoo, 97
Dry skin, 237–238
Dysentery, 59

**E**
Earaches, 64–65
Ear pressure, 66

Ears
infections in, 65–66
insects in, 66
wax build-up in, 67
Echinacea for colds and flu, 38–39
Eczema, 3, 142
Egg/egg white
for asthma, 17–18
for boils, 157
Eggplant
for impotence, 221
for oily skin, 237
Elbows, dry, 158
Elderberry
for insomnia, 162
for sciatica, 24
Emphysema, 69
Energy boosters, 82–84
Epsom salts
for aching feet, 84
for charley horse, 133
for depression, 55
for shingles, 116
for tooth extractions, 180–181
Escarole for constipation, 47
Essential fatty acids (EFAs), 262–266
Eucalyptus oil
for arthritis, 16
as mosquito repellent, 8
Exercise
for constipation, 47
hearing and, 68
Kegel, 149, 225
in preventing carpal tunnel syndrome, 32–33
weight management and, 199–200, 201, 202
Exfoliant, making your own, 239
Eyebright
for eye problems, 71, 76, 79
for memory problems, 132
Eyebrows, tweezing, 240
Eye irritants, 72–73
in children, 209
Eyelash nits, 211–212
Eyes
bloodshot eyes, 69
cataracts, 69–71
conjunctivitis, 71
dry eyes, 71–73
eye inflammation, 73–74
eye irritants, 72–73, 209
eyestrain, 74–75

eye strengtheners, 78–79
eye twitch, 75
glaucoma, 75–76
night vision, 76
puffiness, 74
sties, 76–77
sun blindness, 77
sunburn, 173
Eye wrinkles, 160

**F**
Face relaxer, tip for, 239
Facial masks, 236
for combination skin, 238
for dry skin, 238
for oily skin, 237
Fainting, 81
Fatigue, 81–84
Feet and legs. *See* Foot and leg problems
Fennel seed remedies
for colic, 212
for eye problems, 74, 76, 79
for milk production when breast feeding, 230
for sexual problems, 151
for weight control, 195
Fenugreek/fenugreek tea
for boils, 157
cholesterol and, 21
for hay fever, 4
for indigestion, 123
for sexual problems, 149–150
Fertility, bee pollen for, 259
Fever blisters, 115
Fevers, 288
in children, 211
relievers, 41–42
Fig remedies
for boils, 157
as energy booster, 83
for toothache, 180
for undereye circles, 28
for warts, 192
Filberts, 275, 277
Fingernail polish for cold sores, 115
Fingernails, 102–103
buffing, 94
manicure protection, 240
Finger sores, 103
Flatulence, 125–126
Flavonoids, 275

Flaxseed, 262–266
  blood-thinning medications and, 72
  cholesterol and, 21
  for constipation, 46
  for insomnia, 162–163
  for menopausal symptoms, 263
  for psoriasis, 142
Flu. *See* Colds and flu
Fluoride in preventing tooth decay, 182
Folic acid, 275
Food allergies, indigestion and, 122
Foot and leg problems, 84–90
Foreign substance in the nose in children, 211
Freckles, 158
Frostbite, 91
Frozen vegetables for black eye, 29

**G**

Gallbladder problems, 92
Garbanzo beans for brown spots, 28
Garlic, 266–270. *See* also Garlic remedies
  breath, 184–185
    odor on hands, 291
    supplements, 5, 269
Garlic remedies
  for acne, 154
  for arthritis, 12
  for asthma, 17
  for atherosclerosis, 19–20
  for athlete's foot, 87
  as blood fortifier, 5
  for boils, 157
  cholesterol and, 21
  for colds and flu, 37
  for cold sores, 115
  for constipation, 47
  for cystitis, 226
  for diarrhea, 58
  for flu, 40–41
  for gout, 93
  for hair problems, 95
  for headaches, 106
  for heart problems, 111
  for high blood pressure, 119
  for hoarseness/laryngitis, 44
  for impotence, 219
  for indigestion, 124
  as mosquito repellent, 8
  for plantar warts, 193
  for poison ivy, 147

for premenstrual relief, 230
for psoriasis, 142
for pyorrhea, 181
for ringworm, 145
for sciatica, 24
for sinus problems, 152
for tinnitus, 68
for toothache, 180
Gas, 125–126
Gem therapy
  amber, 43, 140
  amethyst, 63, 132
  diamonds for insomnia, 162
  jade for kidney problems, 190
  topaz for colds and flu, 40
  turquoise for sexual problems, 152
Genital herpes, 114–115
Genital itching, 144
Genital warts, 192
Geranium
  as mosquito repellent, 8
  for shingles, 116
  for wounds, 156
Gin for menstrual cramps, 228–229
Gin-soaked raisins, 13–14
Ginger, 270–274
  as anti-inflammatory, 271
Ginger remedies
  for arthritis, 16
  in bringing on menstruation, 228
  for carpal tunnel syndrome, 34
  for colds and flu, 39–40
  for coughs, 49
  for diarrhea, 57
  for earaches, 64
  for flatulence, 126
  for hair problems, 96
  for hangovers, 61
  for heart problems, 112
  for indigestion, 122
  for insomnia, 162
  for memory problems, 131
  for motion sickness, 138–139
  for muscle aches, 133
  for sprains, 171
Ginseng as aphrodisiac, 150
Glaucoma, 75–76
Glutamine for hangovers, 62
Goldenseal
  for colds and flu, 38–39
  for high blood pressure, 120
Gomasio
  for headache, 104

for heartburn, 127
for seasickness, 139
Gout, 10, 92–93
Grapefruit/grapefruit juice
  for dry elbows and knees, 158
  as energy booster, 83
  for insomnia, 162
  for muscle aches, 133
  reaction with medications, 47
  for swimmer's ear, 66
Grapes/grape juice
  for arthritis, 14
  as energy booster, 83
  as fever reducer, 42
  as source of iron, 5
Grooming, 239–240
Gum problems, 181–182
Gum remover, 100

**H**

Hair. *See* Hair problems
Hair dryer for migraine headaches, 107–108
Hair problems
  dandruff, 95–96
  dry hair, 96
  frizziness, 96
  gray hair, preventing, from yellowing, 100
  green tinge from chlorine, 98
  natural coloring, 99–100
  promoting growth, 94–95
  revitalizers for, 97–98
  setting lotions, 100
  stopping loss, 94–95
Hair spray remover, 100
Halitosis, 122, 183–185
Hand problems, 101–102. *See* also Fingernails
Hangovers, 60–62
Hawthorn
  for heart problems, 111
  for vein health, 90
Hay fever, 3–4. *See* also Allergies; Asthma
Hazelnuts, 276, 278
Headaches, 103–109
  lemon rind to relieve, 106
  sinus, 153
Head lice in children, 211–212
Hearing loss, 68
Heart, sex and, 222
Heart attack, 109

Heartburn, 127–128
Heart helpers, 110–112
Heart palpitations, 110
Heating pad, for tinnitus, 67
Heat rash, 145
Hemorrhoids, 112–114
Herbal bath, 250
Herbal tea, 250–251
Herbs, storage of, 290
Herpes, 114–116
Hiccups, 116–118
High blood pressure. *See* Hypertension
Hives, 143–144
Hoarseness, 44–45
Hobo spider, 9
Holidays, weight loss during, 201–202
Homeopathic eye drops, 71–72
Homeopathic theory, 60
Honey
    for acne, 155
    allergies to, 4, 49
    for arthritis, 13
    for asthma, 19
    for athlete's foot, 87
    bad breath and, 183–184
    in beauty mask, 236
    for boils, 157
    for burns, 30
    for cold sores, 115
    for colds and flu, 37–38
    for coughs, 49, 50
    for cuts, 158–159
    for diarrhea, 58
    for drinking problems, 60
    for dry mouth, 177–178
    for emphysema, 69
    in hair restoration, 95
    for hangovers, 61
    for headaches, 106, 107
    for heart problems, 110
    for heartburn, 127
    for hoarseness/laryngitis, 44
    for indigestion, 123
    for insect stings, 7
    for insomnia, 162
    for leg cramps, 135
    for low sex drive, 226
    for migraine headaches, 107
    as mood lifter, 54–55
    for rough hands, 101
    for sinus problems, 152–153
    for sore throats, 43
    for weeping sores, 156

    for wrinkles, 160
Honeycomb for managing allergies
    and hay fever, 4
Hop pillow
    for insomnia, 162
    for tension and anxiety, 175
Horehound for weight control, 196
Horse chestnut remedies
    for phlebitis, 90
    for varicose veins, 89
Horseradish remedies
    for acne, 153
    for arthritis, 12
    for asthma, 19
    for coughs, 49
    as diuretic, 189
    for insect stings, 6
    for sciatica, 24
    for sinus problems, 152
    for sore throats, 43
    for toothache, 179
Horsetail for eye inflammation, 74
Hot water compress for flatulence,
    125
Hypertension, 118–121
    licorice root and, 3
Hypnosis, auto-, for constipation, 47

**I**
Ice
    for earaches, 65
    for spider bites, 9
    for sprains, 171
    for tooth extractions, 181
Ice packs, 289
    for bruises, 27
    for fainting, 81
Immune system, confessions and, 244
Impotence, 219–222
Incontinence, 189–190
Indigestion, 122–125
    bad breath and, 183
    belching and, 126
    in children, 212
    gas/flatulence and, 125–126
    heartburn and, 127–128
    stomach cramps and, 128
Ingrown toenails, 87–88
Insect repellents, natural, 291–292
Insect stings, 6–8
Insomnia, 161–165
    onion chunks for, 162
Intoxication prevention, 62–63

Iron, 5
    barley as source of, 249
Iron-deficiency anemia, 5

**J**
Jade for kidney problems, 190
Jerusalem artichokes
    for asthma, 18
    in insulin production, 56
Jet lag, 129–130
Jogger's leg cramps, 136
Jungle Punch for brain fog, 131

**K**
Kegel exercises, 149, 225
Kelp in boosting metabolism, 200
Kidney problems, 190–191
    licorice root and, 3
Kidney stones, 190–191, 229
Kiwi, to lower cholesterol, 21
Knees, dry, 158
Kosher salt
    for arthritis, 13
    in body scrub, 239
    in dry shampoo, 97
    for sore throats, 42–43

**L**
Lactic acid in yogurt, 281
*Lactobacillus acidophilus,* 185, 281,
    282
Lactose in yogurt, digestibility of, 281
Lactucarium in lettuce, as sleep
    inducer, 163
Lanolin in sheep's wool, 102
Laryngitis, 44–45
Laughter for weight loss, 198
Lavender oil for weeping sores, 156
Laxatives. *See* Constipation
Lecithin, 264
    for acne, 154
    cholesterol, to lower, 21
    for colds and flu, 40
    for phlebitis, 90
    for prostate enlargement, 218
    for seborrhea, 146
    for ulcers, 187
    in weight management, 197
Leek remedies
    as diuretic, 189
    iron in, 5
    for sprains, 172
Leg cramps, 134–136
Legumes, 277

Lemon/honey/water fast, as blood fortifier, 5
Lemon remedies
    for aching feet, 84
    for bad breath, 184–185
    for blackheads, 155
    in body scrub, 239
    for boils, 157, 157–158
    for charley horse, 133
    for colds and flu, 37
    for constipation, 46
    for corns and calluses, 85
    for coughs, 49
    for cuts, 159
    for dandruff, 95
    for dry elbows and knees, 158
    for eye irritants, 73
    for finger sores, 103
    for freckles, 158
    for gallbladder problems, 92
    for hair coloring, 99
    for headaches, 106
    for heartburn, 127
    for hiccups, 118
    for insect stings, 7
    for itching, 143
    for kidney stones, 190–191
    for mosquito bites, 7
    for motion sickness, 138
    for paper cuts, 159
    for poison ivy, 147
    for rough hands, 101
    for sinus congestion, 152
    in skin toner, 236–237
    for stiff neck, 134
    for warts, 192
    for wounds, 156
Lentils for breast feeding, 230
Lesions, 156
Lettuce, 290
    for insomnia, 163
    for nightmares, 166
Lice in children, 211–212
Licorice
    as antiallergen, 3
    for asthma, 17
    for coughs, 50
    for lack of sexual interest, 226–227
    for low blood pressure, 121
    for menopause, 232
Lignans, 263, 264
Lip line, prevention of, 161

Lips, chapped, 239
Liver spots, 28
Low blood pressure, 121
Lysine for herpes, 114–115

**M**
Macaroons, coconut, for diarrhea, 58–59
Magnesium, 281
    for asthma, 18
    leg cramps and, 134
    nervous tics and, 55
Magnolia-bark tea in stopping smoking, 169
Makeup removers for different skin types, 237–238
Manicure, protecting, 240
Marjoram/marjoram tea
    for nervous stomach, 123
    for seasickness, 139
    in stopping smoking, 169
Massage
    in bringing on menstruation, 227–228
    for indigestion, 123
    for prostate enlargement, 217, 218, 219
Mayonnaise for hair problems, 96
Melanin in infants' skin, 172–173
Memory problems, 131–133
Men
    healing remedies for, 217–219
    sexual problems in, 219–222, 148–152
Menopause, 231–232
    flaxseed for, 263
Menstruation, 227–230
Metabolism, boosting, 200–201
Migraine headaches, 107–109
Milk. *See also* Buttermilk; Coconut milk
    and asthma, 17
    for boils, 157
    colic and, 212–213
    diarrhea and, 57
    for dry skin, 237–238
    for eye irritants, 73
    goat's, for insomnia, 163
    for oily skin, 237
    for poison ivy, 147
    for sunburns, 173
    and ulcers, 186

Mint
    for headaches, 104
    for impotence, 219
Mirror, shaving cream in cleaning, 240
Moisturizers
    for combination skin, 238–239
    for rough hands, 101–102
Mold, 290
Monounsaturated fatty acids, 20, 22, 47, 277
Mood lifters, 53–54
Morning sickness, 230
Mosquito bites, 7–8
Motion sickness, 138–139
Mouthwash, making own, 184, 185
Mud
    for insect stings, 6–7
    for poison ivy, 147
Muscle aches
    charley horse, 133
    leg cramps, 134–136
    neck tension, 133–134
    stiff neck, 134
    whiplash, 134
Mustard seed remedies
    for flatulence, 125
    for indigestion, 124
    for memory problems, 132
Myrrh
    for gum problems, 181
    for halitosis, 184

**N**
Napping, 244
Nausea and vomiting, 137–139
Neck tension, 133–134
Nervous cough, 52
Nervous stomach, 123
Nervous tics, 55
Neuralgia, 139–140
Niacin. *See* Vitamin B$_3$ (niacin)
Nicotine nails, 103
Night cream, enriched, 239
Nightmares, 165–166
Nightshade foods, 10, 12
Nighttime cough, 51–52
Night vision, 76
Nipples, cracked and/or sore, 230–231
Norepinephrine, 53
Nosebleeds, 140–141
Numb toes, 88

Nutmeg
    for acne scars, 155
    for insomnia, 161
    for neutralizing alcohol, 59
Nutrients, absorption of, 288–289
Nuts, 274–280

**O**

Oats/oatmeal
    for acne, 153–154
    cholesterol and, 22
    for coughs, 50
    as hand cleanser, 101
    for heartburn, 127
    for indigestion, 122, 125, 126
    for poison ivy, 147
    for pruritis, 143
    for sexual problems, 151–152
    for splinter removal, 159
    in wrinkle prevention, 160–161
Oily skin, 237
Okra, for constipation, 48
Olive oil
    for acne, 153
    for back pain, 24
    in body scrub, 239
    for burnt throat, 31
    for calluses, 85
    for cholesterol reduction, 22
    constipation and, 47
    for coughs, 48
    for earaches, 64
    for ear infections, 65
    for eye irritants, 73
    for frostbite, 91
    for hair problems, 94, 95, 97
    for hearing loss, 68
    for indigestion, 124
    for jellyfish stings, 7
    for rough hands, 101
    for scars, 159
    for sciatica, 24
    for sun-abused skin, 174
    for swimmer's ear, 66
    for teething, 214
    for ulcers, 186
    for warts, 192
    for weak fingernails, 102
    for wrinkles, 160
Omega-3 fatty acids
    artificial tears and, 72
    attention deficit/hyperactivity
        disorder and, 208

cholesterol and, 22
flaxseed and, 262–266
for heart problems, 111
hypertension and, 119
Omega-6 fatty acids, flaxseed and,
    264–265
Onion breath, 184–185
Onion remedies, 251
    for acne, 154
    for asthma, 19
    for athlete's foot, 87
    for brown spots, 27–28
    for bruises, 27
    for burns, 29
    for colds and flu, 40
    for corns and calluses, 85
    for coughs, 49
    for diarrhea, 57
    as diuretic, 187
    for dysentery, 59
    for earaches, 65
    for eye irritants, 73
    for fever, 41–42
    for flatulence, 125
    for hair loss, 95
    in hair restoration, 95
    for heart problems, 112
    for insect stings, 7
    for insomnia, 162, 165
    iron in, 5
    for itching, 143
    for laryngitis, 44
    for migraine headaches, 107
    as mood lifter, 53–54
    for nausea and vomiting, 137
    for nervousness, 175
    odor on hands, 291
    for pimples, 154
    for prostate enlargement, 218
    for pruritis, 143
    for sinus headaches, 153
    for splinter removal, 159
    for stomach cramps, 128
    for stress, 54–55
    for tension and anxiety, 175
    for toothache, 180
    for urinary problems, 187
    for warts, 192
    working with, tearlessly, 291
Optimism, 12–13, 287
Orange remedies
    for colds and flu, 39
    for indigestion, 124

for muscle aches, 133
    for sprains, 171
Orange-spice pomander, 251
Oregano
    depression and, 53
    for nervous stomach, 123
Osteoporosis, 281

**P**

Pain-free bandage remover, 240
Papaya remedies
    in beauty mask, 236
    for black eyes, 29
    for carpal tunnel syndrome, 34
    for combination skin, 238
    for corns and calluses, 86
    for dead skin, 155
    for heartburn, 127
    for hemorrhoids, 114
    for indigestion, 123–124
    for weeping sores, 156
Paper cuts, 159
Parsley/parsley water
    for arthritis, 11
    beta-carotene and vitamin C in,
        290
    for bruises, 27
    for colds and flu, 39
    as diuretic, 189
    for hair problems, 97
    for halitosis, 184
    as mosquito repellent, 8
    for prostate enlargement, 218
    for sciatica, 24
    for sinus problems, 152
    for sties, 76
    for stomach cramps, 128
    for urinary problems, 187
Passion fruit for sexual problems, 151
Peaches
    as blood fortifier, 5
    nausea and, 213
Peanut butter for preventing
    intoxication, 63
Peanut oil, 22
    for arthritis, 12
Peanuts, 277
    in preventing tooth decay, 182
Pearl barley, 249
Pecans, 275, 276
Peppermint tea
    for breast feeding, 230

for depression, 55
for flatulence, 125
for gallbladder problems, 92
for heart attack/palpitations, 109, 110
for hoarseness/laryngitis, 44
for indigestion, 123
for motion sickness, 138
for premenstrual relief, 229
Persimmon remedies
for constipation, 47
for hangovers, 61
Pesticides, removing, from produce, 198, 290–291
Petroleum jelly, for combination skin, 238–239
Phlebitis, 89–90
Phytochemicals, 276
Picky eaters, children as, 213
Pigeon toes, 88
Pills, secrets to taking, 288–289
Pineapple remedies
in beauty mask, 236
for black eyes, 29
for corns and calluses, 86
in preparing for dental work, 180
for sore throats, 42
Pinkeye, 71
Pistachios, 277
Plantar warts, 193
Plaque remover, 183
Plums for motion sickness, 139
Poison ivy, 146–147
Pollen, 3, 258–262
Pomanders, 251
Portuguese man-of-war bite, 7
Potassium, 198, 275, 281
leg cramps and, 134
Potato remedies, 251–252
for arthritis, 12
for black eyes, 29
for burning feet, 31
for burns, 30
for conjunctivitis, 71
for eczema, 142
for eyestrain, 75
for freckles, 158
for frostbite, 91
for headaches, 105
for heartburn, 127
for high blood pressure, 120
for indigestion, 122
for insect stings, 6

for sciatica, 24
for warts, 192
Poultices, 252
apple, 173
for black eyes, 29
blackstrap molasses, 193
for boils, 157
cabbage, 159
carrot, 44, 156
chamomile, 65
comfrey, 90, 172
for corns and calluses, 85–86
for earaches, 65
for eye inflammation, 74
garlic, 157
for headaches, 105, 107, 153
honey, 156
horseradish, 153, 179
for infections, 156, 157
kosher salt, 13, 42–43
onion, 107, 153, 175
for phlebitis, 90
potato, 29, 74, 105
sauerkraut, 30
for sores, 156
for sore throats, 44
for splinters, 159
for sprains and strains, 172
for sunburn, 173
for tension, 175
for toothache, 179
vinegar, 85–86
for warts, 193
yogurt, 71
Pregnancy, 230–231
Premature ejaculation, 221–222
Premenstrual relief, 229–230
Prescription reading, 288
Prostate cancer, zinc and, 26
Prostate enlargement, 217–219
Prune remedies
for constipation, 46, 48
for memory problems, 131
Pruritis, 143–144
Psoriasis, 142–143
Pumpkin
as blood fortifier, 5
for boils, 157
for burns, 30
for impotence, 221
for prostate enlargement, 217
for rectal itching, 144
for urinary problems, 188

Pyorrhea, 181

**Q**
Quinine for leg cramps, 135

**R**
Radish remedies
for hoarseness/laryngitis, 44
for indigestion, 123
iron in, 5
Raisins
gin-soaked for arthritis, 13–14
for hoarseness/laryngitis, 44
in managing anemia, 5
Rashes, 142–147
in children, 213
Raspberries/raspberry tea
for diarrhea, 57, 210–211
for labor and delivery, 230
for leg cramps, 135
for weight control, 195
Rectal itching, 144
Red clover, in stopping smoking, 169
Red eyes, 69, 79, 80
Red wine, for heart problems, 111
Reflexology, 61, 64, 98, 134
Retinal damage, sun blindness and, 77
Rheumatism, 10
Riboflavin. *See* Vitamin B$_2$
Rice
brown, for acne, 154
for diarrhea, 58
Ringworm, 145
Rocking chair, therapeutic value of, 135
Rope burns, 31
Rosemary
in cellulite elimination, 200
for eyestrain, 75
for hair problems, 97
for headaches, 104
in pain relief, 14
Rose petals
for arthritis, 12–13
as eye strengthener, 77–78
for the heart, 112
Rum for pruritis, 144
Runny ear infection, 65–66
Rutabaga for coughs, 49
Rutin
for atherosclerosis, 20

**S**
Saffron tea, as mood lifter, 54

Sage/sage tea
　　for body odor, 26
　　for depression, 55
　　for frostbite, 91
　　for hair problems, 97, 98
　　for insomnia, 162
　　for memory problems, 131
　　in pain relief, 14
　　for toothache, 179
Salad for weight loss, 197
Saliva, heartburn and, 127
Salt. *See also* Epsom salts; Kosher salt
　　for black eyes, 29
　　eye puffiness and, 74
　　for insect stings, 6
　　in managing snake bites, 9
Salt substitutes, 291
Sandalwood oil for sexual problems, 151
Sandbaths for arthritis, 15
Saponins, 50, 276
Sarsaparilla root
　　for menopause, 232
　　for psoriasis, 142–143
　　for sexual problems, 148–149
Sauerkraut, 252–253
　　for burns, 30
　　for canker sores, 185
　　for constipation, 46
　　for diarrhea, 58
　　for flu, 41
　　in fortifying blood, 5
　　for hangovers, 62
　　preparing own, 252–253
　　for sciatica, 24
Scars, 155, 159
　　honey and nutmeg for, 155
Sciatica, 24–25
Scotch barley, 249
Scrapes, 158–159
Sea salt for psoriasis, 142
Seasickness, 139
Seborrhea, 145–146
Selenium, 275
Serotonin in bananas, for depression, 53
Sesame remedies
　　for arthritis, 16
　　for hair problems, 95, 98–99
　　for menstrual irregularities, 229
　　for stretch marks, 159
Setting lotions, 100
Sexual problems, 148–152

Sexual vitality, bee pollen for, 259
Shaving cream for cleaning mirror, 240
Shaving rash, 145
Shingles, 115–116
Silva method for insomnia, 162
Sinus headaches, 153
Sinusitis, 152–153
Sitz bath for prostate pain, 218
Skin care, 235–239. *See also* Skin problems
　　bee pollen for, 259
　　paint remover for, 240
　　for sun-abused skin, 174
Skin discoloration, 27–29
Skin problems
　　acne, 154–155
　　blackheads, 155
　　boils, 156–158
　　cuts and scrapes as, 158–159
　　dead skin and enlarged pores, 155
　　dry elbow and knees, 158
　　freckles, 158
　　scars, 155, 159
　　splinters as, 159
　　stretch marks, 159
　　wounds and sores, 156
　　wrinkles, 160–161
Skin type, identifying, 235
Skunk spray, 9
Sleep apnea, 166–167
Sleeping
　　with carpal tunnel syndrome, 32
　　problems with, 161–167
Sleepwalking, 166
Slippery-elm for prostate enlargement, 218
Smell, use of, to lose weight, 202
Smoker's cough, 51
Smoking, 166–171. *See also* Tobacco
Snacks, healthy, 198–199
Snake bites, 8–9
Snoring, 166–167
Soda, appetite and, 201
Sores, 156
　　canker, 185
　　finger, 103
Sore throats, 42–44
Soup for weight loss, 197
Sour cream for sunburn, 173
Spices, storage of, 290
Spider bites, 9

Spinach
　　for anemia, 5
　　for constipation, 47
Spirulina for weight control, 196
Splinters, 159
　　in children, 213
Sprains and strains, 171–172
Squash as blood fortifier, 5
Stage fright, 177–178
Stained nails, 102
Steak for black eyes, 28
Sties, 76–77
Stings, insect, 6–7
St. John's wort for shingles, 115
Stomach cramps, 128
Stool softeners, 48
Strawberry remedies
　　for acne, 154
　　for cleaning teeth and gums, 182
　　for depression, 55
　　for gout, 93
　　for hangovers, 62
　　for headaches, 106
　　for kidney stones, 190
　　in skin toner, 236–237
Strep throat, 45
Stress. *See* Depression and stress
Stretch marks, 159
Sugar for hiccups, 117–118
Sun blindness, 77
Sunburn, 172–174
Sunchokes, 18, 56
Sunflower remedies
　　for asthma, 18
　　cholesterol, to lower, 21–22
　　for colds and flu, 38
　　for constipation, 46
　　for coughs, 50
　　for eyestrain, 74
　　as eye strengthener, 78
　　in inhibiting tooth decay, 182–183
　　for memory problems, 132
　　in stopping smoking, 170
Sunscreen, use of, on infants, 172–173
Superfoods
　　bee pollen, 257–262
　　flaxseed, 262–266
　　garlic, 266–270
　　ginger, 270–274
　　nuts, 274–280
　　yogurt, 280–284
Sweaty feet, 88
Sweet potatoes, 198

Sweet substitutes, 291
Swimmer's ear, 66
Systolic pressure, 119

**T**

Tangerine juice for belching, 126
Tartar remover, 183
Tea bags
    for corns and calluses, 86
    for eye inflammation, 74
    for sties, 77
    for sunburn, 173
    for tooth extractions, 180
Teas. *See* specific type of tea
Teething in children, 214
Teeth whitener, 183
Tennis elbow, 172
Tension and anxiety, 175–178
Tension headaches, 103–107
Testicles, touching, 148
Testosterone, 149
Thiamine. *See* Vitamin $B_1$
Thyme
    for excessive menstrual flow,
      228
    for nightmares, 166
    for pruritis, 143
Tick bites, 9
Tinnitus, 67–68
Tobacco. *See also* Smoking
    for hemorrhoids, 113
    for insect stings, 7
    for snake bites, 8
    for wounds, 156
Toenails, ingrown, 87–88
Tofu for poison ivy, 147
Tomatoes/tomato juice
    for skunk spray, 9
    for splinter removal, 159
Tongue
    burnt, 31
    scraping, 184
Tonsillitis, 45
    in children, 214
Tonsils, removal of, 45
Toothache, 178–180
Toothbrush
    cleaning, 183
    throwing away, 183
Tooth extractions, 180–181
Toothpaste for insect stings, 6
Tooth problems, 178–185
Tryptophan for insomnia, 165

Turmeric in preventing heartburn,
    128
Turnip greens and anticlotting drugs,
    111
Turnip remedies
    for aching feet, 85
    for body odor, 25
    for bruises, 27
    for coughs, 50
Tweezing, pain-free, 240
Tyramine for asthma, 17

**U**

Ulcers, 186–187
    and garlic, 5
Undereye circles, 28
Uric acid
    gout and, 92
    neutralizing, 11
Urinary problems, 187–191
Urticaria, 143
US Army, research on allergies, 4

**V**

Vaginitis, 227
Valerian root, 176
Valium, 176
Varicose veins, 88–90
    rocking chair to prevent, 135
Vegetable juices
    for arthritis, 16
    for asthma, 17
    depression and, 53
    for enlarged prostate, 218
Vinegar, white. *See also* Apple cider
    vinegar
    for athlete's foot, 87
    for brown spots, 28
    for corns and calluses,
      85–86
    for coughs, 49
    for headaches, 106
    for hives, 144
    for insect stings, 7
    for nosebleeds, 141
    for pimples, 154
    for poison ivy, 146
    prior to polishing nails, 240
    for sore throats, 43
    for swimmer's ear, 66
    for toothache, 179–180
Visualization, 245
    for asthma, 18
    for tension and anxiety, 177

Vitamin A, 6, 289
    kidney stones and, 191
Vitamin $B_1$ (thiamine), 6, 21, 275
    barley as source of, 249
    as mosquito repellent, 8
    for sciatica, 24
    for toothache, 180
Vitamin $B_2$ (riboflavin), 6, 21, 275,
    281
    in bloodshot eyes, 69
    deficiency in, as cause of
      cataracts, 70
    in glaucoma, 75–76
Vitamin $B_3$ (niacin), 21, 275
Vitamin $B_6$
    for carpal tunnel syndrome, 32
    for leg cramps, 135
    nervous tics and, 55
    for numb toes, 88
    in sauerkraut, 252
Vitamin $B_{12}$, 281
Vitamin C, 6, 289
    for atherosclerosis, 20
    for bleeding gums, 182
    to burn fat, 201
    cataracts, to prevent, 70
    cholesterol and, 21
    for headaches, 105
    for heat rash, 145
    for hemorrhoids, 113–114
    in night cream, 239
    in preventing nosebleed, 141
    for pruritis, 143
    rutin and, 20
    smoking and, 168
    for spider bites, 9
    for sunburned eyes, 173
Vitamin D, 289
Vitamin E, 275, 289
    for brown spots, 28
    for burns, 29
    for healthy heart, 111
    for leg cramps, 134
    in night cream, 239
    for shaving rash, 145
    for warts, 192
Vitamin K
    anticlotting medications and, 111
    in preventing nosebleed, 141
Vitamins, retention of, by
    microwaving, 290
Vomiting. *See* Nausea and vomiting

## W

Walking
    for heart problems, 110–111
    for hemorrhoids, 114
    for memory problems, 132
    varicose veins and, 89
    for weight loss, 201
Walnuts, 275, 276, 277
    for cold sores, 115
Warts, 193–194
Water
    for hiccups, 116–117
    for stomach cramps, 128
    weight control and, 201
Watercress remedies
    as antiallergen, 3
    as diuretic, 189
    iron in, 5
    for night vision, 76
    for sciatica, 24
Watermelon remedies
    as diuretic, 189
    for heat rash, 145
    for high blood pressure, 120
    for rashes in children, 213
Wax and pesticides, removing, from produce, 198
Weak ankles, 90
Weeping sores, 156
Weight control
    Body Mass Index (BMI), 202, 203
    calories burned per hour, 199
    cellulite, 200
    healthy snacks, 198–199
    herbs for, 194–196
    holiday challenges, 201
    hot-pepper sauce for, 200
    metabolism, raising, 200–201
    mustard for, 200
    slimming remedies, 196–198

smell, using, to lose weight, 202
    tips for, 194, 201–202
    vitamin C for, 201
    water or soda, 201
    yoga for, 199–200
Wheat germ/wheat germ oil
    for animal bites/stings, 6
    for dry, frizzy hair, 96
    for heart health, 111
    for rectal itching, 144
Wheat grass for body odor, 26
Whey, 282
Whiplash, 134
White wine for indigestion, 124
Whitlows, 103
Wild cherry-bark tea. *See* Cherry-bark tea for asthma
Willow bark for carpal tunnel syndrome, 33–34
Witch hazel remedies
    for black eyes, 29
    for hemorrhoids, 113
    for shingles, 116
    for varicose veins, 89
Women's health
    bladder control, 225
    carpal tunnel syndrome, 33
    cystitis, 225–226
    heart attack risk, 111
    intoxication, 63
    menopause, 231–232
    menstruation, 227–230
    pregnancy, 230–231
    vaginitis, 227
Wounds, 156. *See* also Bites and stings
    healing of, 245
Wrinkles, 160–161
    prevention of, 259

## Y

Yams, 198
Yarrow/yarrow tea
    for chicken pox, 209
    for excessive menstrual flow, 228
    for hair problems, 97
    for nausea and vomiting, 137
    for oily skin, 237
Yawning, 243
Yellow
    for indigestion, 123
    for memory problems, 133
    stress, contribution to, of, 175
Yellow sac spider, 9
Yerba maté. *See also* Jungle Punch
    for memory problems, 131
    for weight control, 195
Ylang-ylang oil for sexual problems, 151
Yoga
    alternate-nostril breathing in, 176
    for hemorrhoids, 114
    "lion" exercise in, 239
    to slow midlife weight gain, 199–200
Yogurt, 280–284
    for canker sores, 185
    for diarrhea, 58, 282
    frozen, 283
    goat milk, 71
    for oily skin, 237
    in skin toner, 236–237

## Z

Zinc, 281
    for body odor, 26
    for colds and flu, 38, 209
    prostate cancer and, 38
    for enlarged prostate, 217
Zinc sulfate for fingernail problems, 102
Zucchini for indigestion, 124